Staying Sharp

for
dummies®

A Wiley Brand

type who wants to check your figures against the tables, you can figure out your BMI in either pounds and inches or kilograms and meters:

» **Pounds and inches:** Calculate BMI by dividing weight in pounds (lbs) by height in inches (in) squared and multiplying by a conversion factor of 703.

- Weight (lbs) ÷ [height (in)]^2 × 703

- Example: Weight = 170 lbs, Height = 6' (72")

- Calculation: [170 ÷ (72)^2] × 703 = 23.05

» **Kilograms and meters:** You can calculate the BMI using the metric system by using weight in kilograms (kg) divided by height in meters (m) squared. Most often the height is measured in centimeters, so you have to convert the centimeters (cm) to meters by dividing the height by 100.

- Weight (kg) ÷ [height (m)]^2

- Example: Weight = 70 kg, Height = 183 cm (1.83 m)

- Calculation: 70 ÷ (1.83)^2 = 20.10

Recognizing unhealthy body mass

By BMI standards, people with a body mass index of less than 18.5 are underweight, and those with a BMI of 20 to 25 are within range of their ideal body weight. For the most part, the higher the BMI, the higher the associated health risks. If your BMI goes over 25, you're creeping into the dreaded "overweight" category. Following is a breakdown of the categories of BMIs that are outside the ideal range:

» **Underweight:** A person with a body mass index (BMI) of 18.5 or less is considered underweight. Remember, the BMI is just a tool. Having a low BMI may not mean you're unhealthy; underweight individuals are often perfectly healthy. If you experience any symptoms such as fatigue, thinning hair or nails, irregularity in periods (women), continuous weight loss, abdominal pains, or any other symptoms, see your doctor for further evaluation.

» **Overweight:** A person with a body mass index (BMI) of 25 to 29.9. Approximately 127 million adults (or 60.5 percent) in the United States are overweight. About 1 billion people in the world are overweight.

REMEMBER

Childhood obesity is already an epidemic in several countries and becoming one in many others. About 22 million children under the age of five are overweight, while obesity among children ages 6 to 11 has doubled since 1960.

>> **Obese:** A person with a BMI of 30 to 39.9. About 60 million adults (or 25 percent) in the United States are obese and 300 million obese adults exist worldwide. This number doesn't include children who are one of the fastest growing obesity groups.

>> **Morbidly obese:** A person 100 pounds over his normal weight or with a BMI of 40 or more. In the United States, 9 million adults (or 5 percent) are morbidly obese. This group has a definite increase in obesity-related illness and mortality. The good news is that people in this BMI category *can* lose the weight, just like the people in the other weight categories. Get motivated and consult your physician to get a weight-loss plan.

Weighing the Tolls of Extra Weight

Being just "a little bit overweight" doesn't mean that you can sit back and feel safe from the serious health concerns associated with being overweight. The most important fact to take away from this chapter is that if you're even a little overweight, you're just that — over your healthy weight — and you should try to get down to a healthy weight.

The majority of researchers feel that being overweight shares the same health risks as being obese. In today's overweight world, ignoring a little extra weight is easy, especially if you're the thinnest one in your family or your circle of friends. But this tendency can give you a false sense of comfort that can be dangerous to your health.

From a health-risk standpoint, there are only three categories: underweight, healthy weight, and overweight. You can have disease at any weight, and being underweight can be a serious health concern if associated with weight loss from bulimia or anorexia. The majority of weight-related disease is related to the overweight category, the fastest-growing weight sector.

Most people aren't aware of the range of medical conditions directly associated with being overweight or obese — from the mildly unpleasant heartburn to death from stroke or heart disease. Yes, it's *that* serious. According to the Journal of the American Medical Association, obesity is the second-leading cause of preventable death in the United States, right after smoking. The heavier a person is, the less mobile he becomes, which then leads to a more detrimental, sedentary lifestyle. Weight gain and poor nutrition precipitate lack of exercise and becoming sedentary, which then increases risk for illness and disease. It's a vicious cycle.

Staying Sharp
for **dummies®**
A Wiley Brand

**in conjunction with American Geriatrics
Society and Health in Aging Foundation**

for **dummies®**
A Wiley Brand

Staying Sharp **For Dummies**®

Published by: **John Wiley & Sons, Inc.,** 111 River Street, Hoboken, NJ 07030-5774, www.wiley.com

Copyright © 2016 by John Wiley & Sons, Inc., Hoboken, New Jersey

Published simultaneously in Canada

No part of this publication may be reproduced, stored in a retrieval system or transmitted in any form or by any means, electronic, mechanical, photocopying, recording, scanning or otherwise, except as permitted under Sections 107 or 108 of the 1976 United States Copyright Act, without the prior written permission of the Publisher. Requests to the Publisher for permission should be addressed to the Permissions Department, John Wiley & Sons, Inc., 111 River Street, Hoboken, NJ 07030, (201) 748-6011, fax (201) 748-6008, or online at http://www.wiley.com/go/permissions.

Trademarks: Wiley, For Dummies, the Dummies Man logo, Dummies.com, Making Everything Easier, and related trade dress are trademarks or registered trademarks of John Wiley & Sons, Inc., and may not be used without written permission. All other trademarks are the property of their respective owners. John Wiley & Sons, Inc., is not associated with any product or vendor mentioned in this book.

LIMIT OF LIABILITY/DISCLAIMER OF WARRANTY: WHILE THE PUBLISHER AND AUTHOR HAVE USED THEIR BEST EFFORTS IN PREPARING THIS BOOK, THEY MAKE NO REPRESENTATIONS OR WARRANTIES WITH RESPECT TO THE ACCURACY OR COMPLETENESS OF THE CONTENTS OF THIS BOOK AND SPECIFICALLY DISCLAIM ANY IMPLIED WARRANTIES OF MERCHANTABILITY OR FITNESS FOR A PARTICULAR PURPOSE. NO WARRANTY MAY BE CREATED OR EXTENDED BY SALES REPRESENTATIVES OR WRITTEN SALES MATERIALS. THE ADVICE AND STRATEGIES CONTAINED HEREIN MAY NOT BE SUITABLE FOR YOUR SITUATION. YOU SHOULD CONSULT WITH A PROFESSIONAL WHERE APPROPRIATE. NEITHER THE PUBLISHER NOR THE AUTHOR SHALL BE LIABLE FOR DAMAGES ARISING HEREFROM.

For general information on our other products and services, please contact our Customer Care Department within the U.S. at 877-762-2974, outside the U.S. at 317-572-3993, or fax 317-572-4002. For technical support, please visit www.wiley.com/techsupport.

Wiley publishes in a variety of print and electronic formats and by print-on-demand. Some material included with standard print versions of this book may not be included in e-books or in print-on-demand. If this book refers to media such as a CD or DVD that is not included in the version you purchased, you may download this material at http://booksupport.wiley.com. For more information about Wiley products, visit www.wiley.com.

Library of Congress Control Number: 2016934504

ISBN: 978-1-119-18779-0 (pbk); 978-1-119-18781-3 (ebk); 978-1-119-18780-6 (ebk)

Manufactured in the United States of America

10 9 8 7 6 5 4 3 2 1

Contents at a Glance

Table of Contents

Introduction

Welcome to *Staying Sharp For Dummies!*

Your brain plays a major role in almost everything you do, including thinking, feeling, communicating, breathing, remembering, working, playing, sleeping, and countless other activities. Maintaining and improving your brain's health is vital to your quality of life — a fact that becomes even truer as you get older. *Staying Sharp For Dummies* focuses on understanding how to maximize your brain power within the context of your overall health. The book aims to provide you with information, tools, resources, and tangible steps to keep a healthy, active mind. The good news is that you can do a lot to keep your brain sharp throughout your life.

About This Book

This book weaves together up-to-date information from a range of *For Dummies* titles into a fresh take on helping keep your body and your brain working better and longer. You'll find a wealth of tips and ideas not only for improving your memory and reasoning but also for practicing mindfulness, relaxing, eating right, exercising, and heading off common health problems as you get older.

Because this is a *For Dummies* book, the chapters are written and arranged so you can pick and choose whichever topics interest you most and dive right in. You don't need to read the chapters in sequential order, although you certainly can if you like — the topics are organized to provide a rich experience should you just plow through starting at Chapter 1.

Foolish Assumptions

This book makes some assumptions about you, the reader. Hopefully, one of the following descriptions fits you:

» You're young, bright, and healthy and want to stay that way as much as possible your whole life.

» You're entering middle age, and it's dawning on you that your past choices in lifestyle, habits, diet, and so on may be starting to affect your life in not entirely positive ways — and you want to turn things around.

» You're already experiencing health issues that seem to be affecting your brain function and quality of life, and you want to explore remedies and options for reversing some decline and/or staying as sharp as possible as you get older.

This book doesn't assume any particularly advanced knowledge of medicine or physiology (or any other *ology*, for that matter). All you need is a desire to investigate how your brain and body can work together as beneficially as possible. When followed properly, much of the advice herein could add years to your life — not to mention sparking interest, spurring action, strengthening, and even calming your soul. Not a bad deal.

Icons Used in This Book

Throughout the book, several icons designed to point out specific kinds of information. Keep an eye out for them:

TIP

A Tip points out especially helpful or practical information about a topic. It may be hard-won advice on the best way to do something or a useful insight that may not be obvious at first glance.

WARNING

A Warning highlights potential problems or trouble you may encounter and mistaken assumptions that can lead to difficulties.

TECHNICAL STUFF

Technical Stuff points out nonessential stuff that may be interesting if you're really curious about something. You can safely skip these bits if you're in a hurry or just looking for the basics.

Remember indicates stuff that you'll do well to stash somewhere in your memory for future benefit.

Beyond the Book

In addition to what you're reading right now, this product also comes with a free access-anywhere Cheat Sheet that provides tips on keeping your brain sharp through exercise, nutrition, reducing stress, and so on. To get this Cheat Sheet, simply go to www.dummies.com and search for "Staying Sharp For Dummies Cheat Sheet" in the Search box.

Where to Go From Here

You can approach this book from several different angles. You can start with Chapter 1 and read straight through to the end. But you may not have time for that, or maybe you feel like exploring, say, meditation or improving your diet or lowering your blood pressure. Try checking out the table of contents to see a map of what's covered in the book and then flip to any particular chapter that catches your eye. Or if you've got a specific issue or topic you're burning to know more about, try looking it up in the index.

When you're done with the book, you can further your adventures in staying sharp by checking out other titles written by the authors of the original books this material comes from. Check out the "About the Authors" page to see what else these experts have written on topics of interest to you.

Ultimately, the phrase *staying sharp* should imply long-term commitment to changing some of your habits and making different lifestyle choices. Science has learned a whole lot about how the body and brain work and what you can do to make them work better. This book is an attempt to provide a kind of synthesis of a lot of different areas of study, all converging on this integrated topic. You should aim to do that, too. Part of staying sharp, then, should include maintaining an interest in continuing to stay sharp. Never stop trying to challenge and improve yourself — just that by itself can do wonders. Good luck to you!

1

Getting Started with Staying Sharp

Chapter 1

Training Your Brain

You want your brain to work at its best, whether you want to stay sharp to keep up with your children or to excel at your work. The exciting thing is that science now provides evidence for what works and what doesn't. Training your brain no longer has to be a case of trial and error. *Staying Sharp For Dummies* covers some cutting-edge, scientific research and examines how this research can influence your life and change your brain for the better.

The brain weighs a mere three pounds, yet it's responsible for the smooth running of your whole body. With 100 billion cells, your brain is like the CEO of a giant corporation. How can something so small have so much responsibility? This chapter provides basic information on how your brain works. This understanding gives you the foundation for knowing how to best train your brain.

Getting Ready to Train

Brain training is a growing area of interest, both in research and in the public mind. Exciting emerging evidence indicates that you *can* train your brain and, as a result, change your circumstances. But what works and what doesn't? Can everyone benefit from brain training? The final section of this chapter looks at this issue in some detail.

People who use their brains more efficiently tend to have better jobs, better relationships, and more happy and fulfilling lives. Although you may have heard that you're stuck with the brain you have, scientific research has now found that this isn't true!

You're probably familiar with the left brain and the right brain. Well, it's true that the brain is made up of left and right hemispheres, which do have different functions. However, the idea that some people are only left-brainers and others are only right-brainers isn't entirely true. For example, language skills are located in the left hemisphere (see Chapter 2), and everyone uses this part of the brain! You don't need to hide behind the excuse that you're a right-brainer so you can't do math calculations. With the activities included in this book, you can get both halves of your brain working at their optimum levels.

REMEMBER

The different parts of the brain don't work in isolation; they work together as a team. When you train one part of the brain, the whole brain benefits. You can think of the brain like an orchestra or a sports team. The message is the same — one star player can't carry the rest of the team.

Developing a healthy brain

Mental health refers to your state of being. Are you happy? When do you find yourself frustrated? Do you feel stressed out? What makes you feel anxious? These questions are important in determining how well your brain functions, so make sure you pay attention to your mental health. Doing so can make the difference between living a fulfilled life or a frustrated one.

TIP

Don't take your passions and hobbies for granted. Discover how they can make your brain more creative. A more creative brain is a smarter brain. Whether you're a music lover, a budding writer, or a person with any of dozens of other interests, you can choose from a range of activities to help your brain.

REMEMBER

Getting swept into myriad things that demand your attention on a daily basis is easy. Yet, in this ever-demanding environment, finding time to quiet your brain and create a space for contemplation is increasingly important. Calm time brings tremendous benefits for your brain. You don't have to be a nun or a monk spending hours at a time to experience the benefits of contemplation. Scientific research has found that even ten minutes a day makes a big difference in improving how your brain functions.

TIP

One great way to train your brain is to keep it socially active. From picking up the phone to meeting for coffee to discussing the latest movie, growing research illustrates that friendships benefit the brain.

It's not just face-to-face interactions that make a positive impact. Virtual friendships and actively engaging with others via digital technology or interacting within virtual experiences can also boost your brain power. Note that this brain benefit requires active involvement on your part. You don't get that same cognitive benefit when you're passively watching a video on a TV or a computer screen.

Getting healthy for life

A healthy lifestyle leads to a more efficient brain — one that can respond better to stress, remember information, and be more attentive. What you eat and drink, what exercise you do, how much sleep you get — all these actions affect your brain. Understanding how your daily decisions in these areas can make a big dif- ference in your brain function is important. So before you take another bite of your sandwich or drink another glass of wine, find out what really is best for your brain.

Here are a few tips and strategies for tailoring your lifestyle to your brain's advantage:

>> **Eat for your brain.** Chocolate to boost your brain? Juice to help your mem- ory? Steak to maintain your attention? Eating the right brain food doesn't mean you end up eating only lettuce. On the contrary, many delicious and wonderful foods are packed with nutrients that are fantastic for your brain. See the chapters in Part 4 for more information on the best foods for your brain.

>> **Benefit from caffeine in moderation.** Caffeine is a double-edged sword. In some instances caffeine can help your brain work better. However, too much caffeine can impair other aspects of cognitive skills, such as the acquisition of new information, and increase your blood pressure. Best advice is to limit your caffeine intake.

>> **Skip cocktail hour.** Alcohol has a negative effect on the brain. When you drink beer, wine, or liquor, your blood absorbs alcohol, which then circulates into your brain. It affects the parts of your brain that control your judgment, memory, speech, vision, and movement. Some impairments (think of the typical signs of drunkenness) are detectable after only one or two drinks. Check out the later section "Does your brain shrink as you get older?" for more on how alcohol impacts your brain.

>> **Move it!** If you think Chapter 19, which is about exercise, is there to make you feel guilty for not getting a gym membership, don't worry. It isn't. Instead, you find out how the brain responds to physical activity, how you can keep depression and memory loss at bay, and even how to help your body heal more quickly.

>> **Manage stress!** Learning to relax and thereby giving your brain a break from its daily grind is essential to mental health. Check out Part 3 to find out about relaxation and the importance of managing stress to ensure that your brain is in great working shape.

Dispelling the myths of brain training

With the increase of brain training, people throw around many "facts." The following list covers some of the more common statements about brain training:

>> **You're stuck with what you have.** A long-held view is that you're born with the brain you have and you can't do anything about it. For example, if you have a poor memory, then you'd better carry a notebook to help you remember! But exciting developments in scientific research show that you can train your brain. Studies show that at any age, you can do something to make a difference.

>> **Your memory declines as you get older.** Here again, the general view is that memory gets worse as you get older. But recent evidence shows that this assumption isn't necessarily true. *Working memory* skills (short-term memory skills concerned with temporarily storing and manipulating information) continue developing in the 20s and peak in the 30s. And very little decline in working memory skills actually occurs after that. Working memory in people in their 60s looks like working memory for those in their 20s. So now you don't have an excuse for why you forgot to pick up milk on the way home.

>> **All brain training is the same.** Unfortunately, this generalization isn't the case. Many methods claim to train your brain, but not all methods work. Evaluate each method to decide whether evidence demonstrates that the method is effective. Check to make sure the method's scientific trials showed transfer effects, had a control group, and used randomized samples.

>> **Only one way to train your brain exists.** The brain has four main lobes, all of which are involved in making your brain work like a smooth-running machine. (Flip to the later section "Discovering How the Brain Works" for more on the parts of the brain.) This book is filled with different strategies for keeping your brain active, from what you eat to how you relax to how you exercise.

Using what works for your brain

Make sure the brain-training programs you use have these key features:

>> **Allow adaptive training.** *Adaptive training* means that the training changes to your needs and your ability. So you won't always work at the same level each time; if you're doing well, you're challenged with harder levels, and if you're struggling, then you move to an easier level. Adaptive training is important to continue to challenge your brain.

>> **Speed up.** Computer-based training often provides timed tests to help you improve your speed at solving problems. Studies have found that timed tasks make a difference by training your brain to work more quickly. Practicing timed tasks makes a difference to everyday activities as well. Try timing yourself when you solve a crossword or Sudoku. You'll notice yourself getting faster and even eliminating that tip-of-the-tongue phenomenon (see Chapter 2 for more strategies).

>> **Keep it regular.** Training regularly is important. If you only use a program once a week, don't expect to see results. Studies have found that you need to train at least three times a week to see maximum benefits for your brain. So get training!

TIP

The computer video game Tetris is an old favorite for many people. It requires you to rotate descending colored blocks so that they fit together without gaps rather than pile up. With each level, the blocks' speed increases to challenge you. Now fans of Tetris can play with impunity — scientific evidence is on your side! Research shows that spatial memory improves after you play Tetris. Some scientists have also observed that physical changes occur in the brain after subjects play Tetris for an extended period — and that these players worked more efficiently in certain tasks. Not a bad result for just rotating some colored blocks on the screen!

TIP

In a recent survey, people reported that they preferred to use computerized products than puzzle books. This tendency may explain why brain-training products have skyrocketed in recent years. However, don't give up on puzzles and board games. Strong evidence indicates that these activities keep your brain active. Even schoolchildren benefit more from playing board games like Scrabble than playing on a computer game. So don't stop playing word games, doing crosswords, or challenging your spouse to late-night Scrabble; it's great for your brain. (See Chapter 5 for a lot more about the science of brain games and Chapter 6 for plenty of actual games to try out.)

Discovering How the Brain Works

Understanding of the brain has come a long way since the notion of the four "humors" — black bile, yellow bile, phlegm, and blood. According to the ancient Greeks and Romans, an imbalance in one of these humors would result in illness and affect both mental and physical health. This dominant view remained firmly in place until the 19th century when modern medical research came on the scene.

Since then, scientists have made great strides in understanding how the brain works, and each day brings exciting new discoveries. In current understanding, the brain is divided into four parts.

The four-part brain

When Phineas Gage went to work on the morning of September 13, 1848, the 25-year-old probably had no idea that he was going to be immortalized in medical and psychology history for years to come.

Phineas was a railroad construction foreman who suffered severe head injuries as the result of a blast — a long iron rod was lodged in his head, entering the top of his skull and exiting through his cheek (see Figure 1-1). Remarkably, Phineas survived! He could walk, communicate, and seemed to be aware of his surroundings. However, his personality changed completely. He had great difficulty controlling his anger. After the accident, he transformed from a mild-mannered young man into a violent and hot-tempered individual. People who knew him before his accident said that he was no longer the same Phineas Gage they knew.

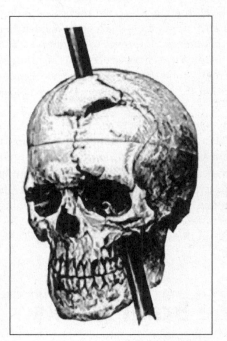

FIGURE 1-1: The skull of Phineas Gage impaled with the iron rod.

Phineas's injury provided the medical and psychological professions with great insight into how the brain works. By looking at the trajectory of the iron rod through his head, experts were able to begin to understand the link between different parts of the brain and everyday functioning.

Parts of the frontal lobe are linked to personality. Unfortunately for Phineas, this part of his brain sustained the most damage, resulting in his dramatic change in character. Other sections of the frontal lobe are associated with language and motor skills, which, thankfully for Phineas, remained intact.

Figure 1-2 shows the four major areas of the brain. Each of these lobes has a left and right side. The left and right sides of the brain are called the hemispheres of the brain.

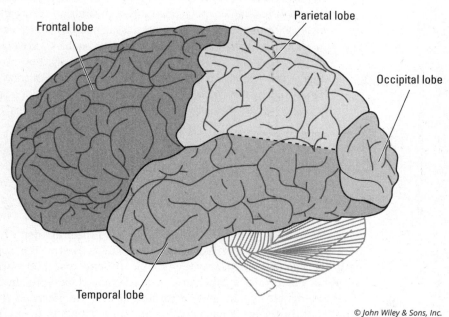

FIGURE 1-2:
The four major lobes of the brain.

© John Wiley & Sons, Inc.

>> **Frontal lobe:** As the name suggests, the *frontal lobe* is located in the front of the brain and makes up the largest part of the brain. A main function of the frontal lobe is to plan and organize incoming information. For example, if you have to plan a party, draw up the guest list, and organize the catering, your frontal lobe is critical in carrying out all these activities.

The frontal lobe is also instrumental in regulating behavior and emotions. This part of the brain, which is associated with a chemical known as *dopamine*, is sometimes called the brain's pleasure center because it's linked to attention, planning, motivation, reward, and enjoyment.

The frontal lobe doesn't fully develop until people reach their 20s, which may explain why it's so hard to convince a toddler to stop throwing a tantrum, or get a teenager to consider the long-term consequences of her decisions. Both of these scenarios involve the use of the frontal lobe to plan actions, consider consequences, and then alter actions as necessary.

- **» Parietal lobe:** The *parietal lobe* is crucial to integrating and processing information from a range of different sources, including our senses and our vision. Information such as taste, temperature, and touch are processed here. The parietal lobe enables a person to integrate visual information in order to perceive spatial relationships such as where the body is located in relationship to other objects. It also enables drawing, writing, and calculating ability.

- **» Temporal lobe:** The *temporal lobe* is the home of language processing. It's responsible for auditory perception such as hearing and processing the sensory information from the ears into meaningful units such as words and sounds in our environment. The temporal lobe enables you to speak and to comprehend speech you hear. The temporal lobe is also home to another key player — the hippocampus, which allows the conversion of short-term memory to long-term memory and enables spatial navigation. (See the upcoming section "Maintaining decision-making and memories" for more.)

- **» Occipital lobe:** The *occipital lobe* is the smallest of the four lobes and is located at the back of the brain. It's home to the visual cortex and is responsible for processing visual information, perceiving motion, and detecting color differences. The occipital lobe lets you make sense of incoming visual information.

As mentioned earlier in the chapter, the parts of the brain don't function in isolation; they work together like members of an orchestra. But sometimes all the parts don't contribute the way they should. In some cases, certain parts underperform, but other parts overperform. One example is exhibited by individuals with attention–deficit hyperactivity disorder (ADHD). Research on ADHD has established that these people have underactive components in the part of their frontal lobes responsible for planning and controlling behavior but overactive parts of the frontal lobe's motor cortex, which is necessary for managing motor functions. The combination of underperformance in one area and overperformance in another area results in the hyperactive and impulsive behavior that is characteristic of ADHD.

Maintaining decision-making and memories

The *prefrontal cortex*, located within the frontal lobe, is one of the most crucial parts of the brain. It's linked with *executive function* skills, which you use for everyday tasks like decision-making and planning.

For example, say you're driving down a busy road at rush hour and you're late for a meeting. You're alone in the car, but you see the carpool lane traffic is moving much more quickly. Should you switch to that lane so you can get to your meeting

A LESSON FROM THE PAST: LOBOTOMIZING THE PREFRONTAL CORTEX

Your knowledge of a lobotomy may be based on Jack Nicholson's excellent portrayal of a rebellious patient at a mental hospital in the film *One Flew Over the Cuckoo's Nest*. In this movie, a lobotomy effectively reduces someone to the same mental state as a shop window mannequin — expressionless and unemotional.

The lobotomy procedure consists of cutting the brain connections that go in and out of the prefrontal cortex. Mid-20th century doctors considered a lobotomy the final step for modifying extreme behavior when other treatments such as electrical shock therapy, failed. Doctors thought that a lobotomy calmed the patient, reduced aggressive behavior, and improved the patient's quality of life. However, they now know that this procedure is barbaric and certainly not helpful.

Perhaps one of the youngest known recipients of a lobotomy is Howard Dully, who was only 12 years old at the time. As a result of a diagnosis of childhood schizophrenia (that was unconfirmed by other medical professionals at the time), Dully underwent the lobotomy procedure. His mental illness manifested itself in some ways as a typical teenage personality: He was moody, insolent, and contrary. However, the truth behind his behavior was harder to decipher. What was Dully really like, and was his behavior so extreme that a lobotomy was the only option? These questions have spawned Dully's lifelong search for answers.

He took several decades to recover, drifting from a mental institute to prison and finally to the streets. He's since overcome his setbacks and recounted his story in a harrowing tale of survival and redemption from a brutal procedure once considered acceptable by doctors but, thankfully, no longer in practice today.

Dully's story is interesting because it reveals that our knowledge of the brain is evolving. His journey has also served to fuel many heated discussions about how the brain works and the impact of removing sections of the brain.

on time? You see a police car up ahead has pulled over a speeding car. You're weighing the choice of staying out of the carpool lane and being late for your meeting versus illegally entering the carpool lane in order to get to your meeting on time but having the chance of getting pulled over. Complex decisions like this one, where you have to plan your actions and weigh the resulting consequences, require your prefrontal cortex to perform executive function.

Here's another scenario: The phone rings, and it's someone giving you important information about an event you're attending. You're busy writing down all this information when you hear a beep from your computer alerting you that an email has just come in from a friend. You decide to open your email, but as you're skimming it you get distracted and miss some of the event information over the phone.

Both of these examples illustrate how you use your prefrontal cortex to make decisions daily. You have to keep a goal in mind (reaching your destination or writing down key information), juggle different scenarios (should you go in the carpool lane?) or tasks (should you check your email while on the phone?), and inhibit potentially distracting information to reach your goal (putting the thought of using the carpool lane out of your head; delaying the desire to read your email at that moment).

In addition to the prefrontal cortex, the hippocampus and amygdala are key players in keeping your brain active and alert.

Hippocampus

The name *hippocampus* comes from the Greek word for "seahorse," and it's called such because it looks very much like a seahorse. The hippocampus is located deep in the temporal lobe near the center of the brain.

The hippocampus has two main functions: long-term memory and spatial understanding. (See Chapter 10 for more information on long-term memory.) The brain stores two types of long-term memories in the hippocampus:

>> *Autobiographical memory* stores meaningful events — birthdays, weddings, graduations, and so on. Such memory is based on personal experiences with specific objects, people, and events you've experienced at particular times and places in your life.

>> *Declarative* or *semantic memory* is general knowledge and facts about the world.

The hippocampus also functions like a spatial map that helps with directions and navigation. So if you get lost often while you're driving, blame your hippocampus!

Damage to the hippocampus can result from Alzheimer's disease, oxygen deprivation, and epilepsy that affects the temporal lobe, where the hippocampus is located. People who sustain damage to the hippocampus experience difficulties in forming new memories, a condition known as *anterograde amnesia*. Hippocampus damage can also erode older memories (known as *retrograde amnesia*). However, if your hippocampus is damaged, you still retain *procedural memory* — that is, how to do things like walking, talking, or biking or other motor tasks. (See Chapter 12 for more on this topic.) The fact that long-term memories are stored in different parts of the brain can explain why an amnesic patient may not be able to remember important events from her life but may still remember how to play the guitar.

The hippocampus is also linked to mental health. Research into patients with depression has found that the hippocampus is usually smaller (by around 10 to 20 percent) compared with those not suffering from depression. The actual reduction of the hippocampus depends on the frequency of depressive episodes as well as the length of time the depression went untreated. This explains the cognitive deficits that are associated with major depression including *declarative memory*. Antidepressant medications work to treat the underlying neurochemical imbalances that occur in clinical depression that cause these symptoms.

TESTING YOUR PREFRONTAL CORTEX'S FUNCTION

Here's an example of a test to measure how well your prefrontal cortex works.

Say these words as fast as you can:

Cat Dog Dog Cat Dog Cat Cat Dog Cat Dog

Now say them when you see the pictures

Now here's the tricky part: Say the opposite word of what you see. If the word is *Cat*, say "Dog"; if the word is *Dog*, say "Cat."

Cat Dog Dog Cat Dog Cat Cat Dog Cat Dog

How did you do? Here's a final one: Say the opposite word of the picture.

It's a lot harder than it looks, isn't it? You had to suppress or inhibit your automatic response to say the word rather than its opposite. You may be familiar with a more common version (called the *Stroop test*) where you have to state the color that a word is printed in rather than the actual word itself — for example, the word *blue* written in green ink.

Amygdala

The name *amygdala* comes from the Greek word for "almond" due to its physical similarity to that nut. The amygdala is located next to the hippocampus in both sides of the brain. It's associated with emotional memories — those that make you laugh and those that make you cry or feel afraid. For instance if you ever were bitten by a vicious dog, the amygdala helps you process that event, making you more alert and fearful around dogs.

The amygdala also helps you store information over the long term. If you have an emotional connection to the information you're trying to learn, you're more likely to transfer this knowledge to your long-term memory. For example, if you're trying to learn a new language, you can associate the new words with an emotional memory to help you make those words stick.

The amygdala is linked with higher creative activity (see Chapter 3 for more on boosting your creative skills).

Separating Fact from Fiction

Some popular notions of certain "facts" about the brain persist. You've heard these so-called facts before, but, like urban legends, you must question whether they're really true. This section discusses three widespread notions about the brain.

Do you really use only 10 percent of your brain?

No evidence supports the statement that humans use only a tenth of their brains. Although this idea has been highly popular (see the nearby sidebar "Bending the truth"), no research whatsoever demonstrates that it's true.

Here are a few ways you can be sure that this statement is false.

>> **Look inside.** Brain imaging techniques clearly reveal that people use their entire brains. Although you may use only a small part of your brain for a simple activity, whenever you engage in a complex activity, you're using multiple parts of your brain simultaneously. A useful analogy is to think of your muscles. When you're eating, you may only be using muscles relevant for chewing and swallowing. But that doesn't mean that you only ever use 10 percent of your muscle group. In fact, it sounds ludicrous to suggest that! In the same way, you use all of your brain at one point or another every day.

BENDING THE TRUTH

The notion that people use only 10 percent of their brains was made especially popular in the 1990s by psychics who wanted to promote the idea that if you use only a small portion of your brain, you can develop the rest of the brain for psychic activities. You may have heard of a psychic named Uri Geller, whose claim to fame is his ability to bend spoons and make broken watches work again. How does he do it? In his writings, Geller attributed his fantastical "achievements" like spoon-bending and telepathic power to his ability to harness the unused 90 percent of his brain.

However, as is so often the case, the truth is much less sensational. The spoon-bending trick is thought to be the result of misdirecting the audience's attention to focus on something else and then revealing an existing bend. In fact, when Geller was asked to perform his signature trick on silverware that he didn't have access to previously, he failed. His famous clock-starting trick was thought to be the result of using magnets, as slow-motion television footage revealed.

» **Consider the widespread effects of localized brain damage.** The idea of using only 10 percent of the brain suggests that the brain has very specialized purposes — that you only need certain parts of the brain to function efficiently. This idea supposes that the other 90 percent of the brain is like your tonsils or your appendix — it's there, but you don't really need it for anything important. This assumption is *not* true. Even damage to a small area of the brain caused by a stroke, head injury, or certain disorders like Parkinson's disease has a devastating impact on the brain; it can leave people with difficulty speaking, remembering loved ones, and even forming new memories. All of your brain is necessary to function successfully.

» **Say baaa.** The average human brain weighs about 3 pounds (1,400 grams). Removing 90 percent of the brain would leave only about 0.3 pounds of brain tissue (140 grams) — the size of a sheep's brain. So the next time someone tells you that people use only 10 percent of the brain, say baaa!

Does your brain shrink as you get older?

The short answer is yes, but not as much as you think — and brain training can make a difference. As you get older, your brain does shrink around 2 percent every ten years. This shrinkage actually begins in early adulthood but is unlikely to be noticeable on brain imaging until you hit your 60s. A greater percentage of brain shrinkage is linked with dementia. In other words, a certain amount of brain shrinkage is normal, but too much is a telltale sign of problems like Alzheimer's and dementia.

TIP

To keep your brain functioning effectively as you get older despite any age-related brain shrinkage, pay attention to these tips:

>> **Pass on the alcohol.** Studies confirm that alcohol isn't great for your brain. In addition to all the negative health side effects, it makes your brain smaller. Alcohol dehydrates your tissues, and when this happens constantly, your most sensitive tissue — your brain — starts losing volume.

Multiple studies have found that the more a person drinks, the more his brain volume diminishes. However, even light drinkers (meaning those who consume one to seven alcoholic drinks per week) suffer these effects of alcohol on the brain. A study that looked at people in their 60s found that even light drinkers had a smaller brain volume compared with those who abstained from alcohol. Heavy drinkers — those who drank more than 14 drinks each week — suffered the most when it came to brain volume. However, research has shown that with abstinence, the brains of alcohol-dependent subjects return to nearly the same size as those of their non-drinking counterparts.

WARNING

Take special care if you're a woman — the brain volume of women is more affected by alcohol than men, meaning that the effects of light drinking can be more pronounced in women compared to men.

>> **Relax.** Stress can also impact your brain (see Part 3 for more on developing a positive mindset and learning to relax). Stress impact happens especially when you experience repeated stress, such as a prolonged illness or difficulty at work.

The prefrontal cortex, linked to decision-making and attention, and the hippocampus, linked to long-term memory, are most affected by stress (see the earlier section "Maintaining decision-making and memories"). Stress makes it harder for people to focus on the task at hand or take in new information. When people are overstressed, they lose their ability to be *mentally flexible*, meaning that they have trouble shifting a course of action according to the changing demands of a situation.

>> **Teach yourself.** Some brain shrinkage is normal, but this shrinkage doesn't have to impact the way your brain functions. In fact, studies have demonstrated that people in their 60s to 90s are able to "buffer" the effects of brain shrinkage. How? Simple: They kept their brains active by learning new things.

People who spend time discovering and learning something they didn't know give their brains more protection against dementia and memory loss. By keeping up your intellectual activity, you're mentally exercising your brain to keep it fit as you grow older.

Can you change your brain?

Yes! Yes! Yes!

The exciting news is that you can alter the impact of aging on your brain. Read on to find out more about how you can maintain (and further develop) your mental agility.

The brain has a certain *plasticity*, which means that you can change. In fact, most of this book is dedicated to providing you with tips on what you can do to make a difference to your brain.

TECHNICAL STUFF

Brain plasticity or *neuroplasticity* refers to the changes that occur in your brain pathways and brain cell connections due to changes in your behavior, environment, and emotions. Your experiences actually reorganize the neural pathways in your brain, so persisting functional changes occur in your brain when you learn new things and have new experiences.

Scientific evidence has shown that performing certain activities can change your brain. Here are a few examples:

» **Train it.** The idea of brain training is a new and exciting area of research, and growing evidence suggests that you can do something to change your brain. However, be aware that not all brain-training processes give you the same results.

» **Get moving.** Exercise isn't only good for your body — it's great for your brain too! For starters, exercise increases the blood flow to your muscles and to your brain, which helps them work better. Physical activity can also renew parts of the brain that are damaged and lead to new brain stem cells. This change means better memory and an improved ability to learn.

» **Make time for bingo.** If exercise sounds like too much work for you, you'll be happy to know that socializing is also great for your brain. Studies have found that when people spend time interacting, the brain releases a feel-good hormone — *oxytocin* — which can boost memory.

THE ACTIVE STUDY

In 2006, the National Institute of Aging and the National Institute of Nursing Research completed a study of cognitive training in older adults. This study, called Advanced Cognitive Training for Independent and Vital Elderly (ACTIVE), was the first randomized controlled trial to show long-lasting positive benefits of brief cognitive training in older adults.

The study subjects were 2,802 healthy seniors over age 65 that were living independently. Participants were randomly assigned to the four study groups. Three of these groups attended up to ten computer-based training sessions that emphasized a particular cognitive ability, including memory, reasoning, and processing speed (or how quickly subjects could respond to prompts on a computer screen). The fourth group served as a control group and didn't participate in any cognitive training. Eleven months later, 60 percent of those who completed the initial training also participated in 75-minute "booster" sessions designed to help maintain cognitive improvements gained from the earlier training.

Participants were given cognitive tests before the training, after both the initial and booster training sessions, and annually for the following five years. The researchers found that the cognitive improvements gained from the training basically counteracted the degree of decline in cognitive performance that would be expected over a 7-to-14-year period in seniors without dementia.

The study showed significant improvements in the skills taught after the initial training in the study groups, including 26 percent of the memory group, 74 percent of the reasoning group, and 87 percent of the processing-speed group. After five years, the participants in the study groups all performed better on tests in their respective areas of training than did people in the control group who received no training. The greatest improvement was seen in the reasoning and processing-speed groups who received the booster training.

The researchers also looked at the effects of the study on subjects' everyday lives. After five years, all three study groups who received cognitive training reported less difficulty than the control group in daily tasks such as preparing meals, managing money, and doing housework. However, these results were only statistically significant in the group with reasoning training.

The ACTIVE study showed that cognitive training is useful —that even a relatively brief intervention with targeted cognitive exercises can produce lasting improvements in the skills taught. Based on this study, you can see the benefit of brain-training to help you stay sharp as you age.

Chapter 2

Improving Your Language Skills

L anguage is one of the first skills you learn. From infancy, coos and aahs are early steps in communicating with those around you. These cute early sounds are known as *babbling* because they represent babies trying out new sounds that they've heard. Babies develop these skills and begin using one word coupled with actions to let others know their intentions. For example, an 18-month-old will point to a bottle of milk and say "Mi-mi" to express her desires. Language develops at an impressive rate, with children learning hundreds of new words in the first few years of their lives.

As you get older, your language skills get more sophisticated. You can speak freely to express your ideas, debate with friends on topics of interest, and share your feelings with loved ones. You can use the techniques in this chapter to help you stay sharp verbally as you age.

Finding the Right Word

Searching for the right word in the middle of a conversation can be frustrating. With normal aging, you may take longer to retrieve the word you want to use when engaged in a conversation. However, you don't need to find yourself in a situation where you're searching for the right word. You can do several things to avoid this problem as you get older.

Banishing the tip-of-the-tongue phenomenon

Everyone struggles with the *tip-of-the-tongue phenomenon* (TOT for short) — when you can describe a word in detail but you just can't remember what it is.

Here's how TOT works. You're thinking of a fruit; you ate it for breakfast, it's juicy, and you can see it in your head, but you just can't remember what it's called. Two hours later, the name pops into your head while you're in the middle of a meeting — it was a kiwi. This example is simple; more commonly, you search for words you say less frequently.

Communicating something that you can see in your mind but can't remember the name of is frustrating. Sometimes it's even harder to describe what you want to say because another word is "stuck" in your mind. In the previous example, maybe all you could think of at the time was a strawberry rather than a kiwi! You're searching for the word and you know that you know it, but you just can't find it when you want to say it. Why did you keep thinking of a strawberry, and why was it stopping you from thinking about a kiwi? Actually, thinking about a strawberry was your brain's way of helping you think of kiwi. Your brain tried to find related words, such as the names of other juicy fruits, to trigger the missing word.

Psychologists describe this situation as a temporary breakdown in your mental dictionary: You can think of the meaning of the word but not how to say it. You store information in different parts of your brain. You store images (a picture of a kiwi) in one part of your brain and the related meaning (the description of a kiwi, recipes using kiwis, and the taste of a kiwi) in another part of the brain. With TOT, it's as if the bridge connecting your images and understanding of the item and the word for that item is temporarily blocked.

It may be that you haven't used this particular connection very often and so it becomes rusty. The item you want to say may be one you infrequently use, so it may take longer to find and retrieve it in your memory banks. Some say it's like an overgrown bike path. Once it was smooth and clear, but because you haven't used it much, weeds and grass overgrow, and it becomes harder to bike on. The path is still there, but it takes longer to travel on.

People's names are also hard to remember because they're arbitrary. The name Tracy doesn't necessarily remind you of something specific, and so it's easy to forget the association between a name and a face if you don't attach a meaningful connection to the name, such as *Tracy, my childhood friend.*

REMEMBER

Everyone experiences TOT. Although it may be annoying and frustrating, it's not something you should panic about. Read on for techniques to minimize the occurrence of TOT.

Using a variety of words

Don't get stuck in a rut, using the same words and same ideas every day. In order to avoid TOT, keep your word-image-meaning connections active. The more often you use language and seek out opportunities to use language creatively, the less likely you are to experience TOT.

TIP

Here are some suggestions that can help:

>> **Play games with yourself.** Set yourself a target — for example, name as many animals as you can in 30 seconds. Try to name one animal per second. Now make it harder — name as many animals as you can that start with the letter *B* in 30 seconds. Try a different topic — maybe fruit or furniture. Try it for 15 seconds if you find it too easy, or pick less common letters of the alphabet. The goal of this game is to challenge your mind to create connections between items in a category. Also try to think of words you may not use very often. You may even find yourself making a mental store of animal names when you read the newspaper!

Doctors sometimes use these listing games when testing for dementia because patients with dementia lose the cognitive ability to make these lists. Often, they can only think of three or four animals in 30 seconds and sometimes repeat animal names they've already listed.

>> **Do crosswords.** Crosswords are a fun and fantastic way to keep those word-meaning connections alive. If you're not a big fan of crosswords, start with something easy on a topic you enjoy, such as gardening or travel. Crosswords are very effective in combating TOT because they give you a clue and you have to search for the word, which exercises your ability to retrieve information from your memory banks.

>> **Give yourself clues.** If you're a list-writer, here's a technique you can try. Instead of writing down what you need to do — for example, take out the chicken from the freezer, get rosemary from the garden, or buy carrots — why not write it out in clues? So here's what a list may look like: Take the *bird* out of the freezer; in the garden, get the *herb* that starts with the name of a flower; and buy a *vegetable* that's supposed to give you great eyesight. By doing so, you're giving yourself descriptions that force you to think of the word. (You may not want to do this if you're giving the list to someone else unless the other person has a sense of humor.)

>> **Keep a diary.** Writing in a diary is a proven way to keep your language skills intact. You can write just a little every day, but try to use words that you wouldn't usually use and be as descriptive as possible. Imagine yourself as the next Mark Twain and try to write about your day as if it's a detective story, romance, or whatever genre you prefer. The goal is to challenge your mind to think about your day and to use language in a creative way.

>> **Finish your thoughts.** And finally, always finish your thoughts. Sometimes it's easier to let someone guess what you want to say, so you start saying something but then trail off at the end. Try to avoid this tendency. Even if it takes you a little longer, finishing your thoughts is an important habit to establish. You need to be active in communicating your ideas if you want to keep the paths between images, descriptions, and words clear.

Remembering Your Shopping List and Other Important Things

How many times have you found yourself standing in the middle of an aisle full of food, scratching your head and trying to remember what you needed for dinner that night, or suddenly stopping while driving somewhere because you couldn't remember where you were going? These moments happen to everyone. People have busy lives, and sometimes some things like shopping lists or where you're supposed to go get pushed to the back of your mind.

Don't worry too much about this kind of thing. The problem arises when it happens all the time rather than just occasionally. If you're regularly forgetful in this way, this section includes some helpful tips.

Repeating, repeating, repeating

People sometimes forget that repetition can be a powerful tool to move something into their long-term memory (which is the permanent memory). But there's a knack to using repetition.

Here are a few guidelines:

>> **Repeat only for a short time.** You don't need to spend hours repeating something, such as a topic you want to remember. In fact, if you spend too long doing that, you'll overtire yourself. Instead, spend just a few minutes mentally going over what you want to remember.

>> **Repeat what you want to remember periodically.** You don't have to do this at a set time every day — in fact, it's better if you do it at different times. For example, while you're brushing your teeth, go over what you want to remember. The next day, do it while you're getting dressed. When you repeat information at varying times, you tell your brain that this information is important, and it creates a strong connection in your long-term brain stores so you'll remember it for a long time.

TIP

>> **When you repeat information, don't forget to say the list from the beginning.** Often you may only repeat things at the end of your list or even out of order. This approach isn't a good way to train your memory, and you'll end up forgetting things more often than not. Train yourself to consistently repeat things in the order you hear them and from the beginning of the list, and you'll notice a big difference.

Rhyming to remember, and other helpful strategies

Your brain stores information by using different clues. One clue uses *phonological information* — the way the word sounds. Your brain makes a connection between words that sound the same and remembers these words when you're trying to think of another word (see the earlier section "Banishing the tip-of-the-tongue phenomenon" for more). Phonological links can explain why when you're trying to say "pear," all you can think about is "bear," or why you think someone's name is Diane when it's actually Donna. The fact that your brain makes a connection between words that sound similar makes rhyming words such a great trigger for remembering things.

Another clue your brain uses is *semantic information* — factual information about the word, such as the category it belongs to and its purpose. Think of your long-term memory as a big library. Your filing system groups words into categories, such as names of fruit, furniture, or animals. Then it divides each category into more-specific categories, such as pets, wild animals, animals that fly, and animals that swim.

TIP

Many great tips can help you remember information when you don't have a paper and pencil in hand. One is to try to create an association and to link it with another word. Choosing rhyming words is a good technique because your brain remembers words that sound similar. If you put them to music, the words become even more memorable. For example, if you have a doctor's appointment, you can make up a rhyme like "See Dr. Brown when I go to town." The rhymes that you make up can even be silly or nonsensical; that just helps the words be more memorable (think of the works of Lewis Carroll).

Another tip is to remember words in categories. If you're trying to remember your shopping list, think of all the items you can find in the dairy aisle, the vegetables in the produce section, and the breads in the bakery. If you have a meeting and you need to remember several key points, organize them in categories. This helps you to remember more information than if you just kept a running tab of all your ideas for the meeting in your head.

REMEMBER

Don't forget to repeat the information to yourself. Just coming up with a rhyme or an organization style isn't enough to ensure that you remember. You need to repeat the information a few times to yourself to make sure the connection is strong. If you have something important that you need to remember in the morning, repeat it to yourself several times before you fall asleep. It will almost always be the first thing you think of when you wake up in the morning. Try it to see for yourself!

Measuring Your Language Skills with IQ Tests

Psychologists use many different types of tests to measure how the brain works, including IQ tests. *IQ* stands for "intelligence quotient." A person's IQ is defined by how that person performs on one of several standardized tests designed to assess human intelligence.

The benefit of IQ tests to measure language skills is that they're based on the responses of thousands of people from different backgrounds. Such IQ scores provide an excellent representation of standard language ability across different age brackets. For example, verbal IQ tests reveal the expected language ability for individuals in their 20s, 30s, 40s, 50s, 60s, 70s, 80s, and so on. So you don't have to guess how good your skills are — you can measure by comparing your scores to your age group on an objective test.

Looking at the verbal scores on IQ tests

The purpose of the verbal component of IQ tests is to measure your language skills. If you haven't already guessed, your mastery of language is important in everything you do.

These questions measure how well you use language to express your thoughts, understand ideas, and converse with other people. You can see examples of a variety of questions from different aspects of IQ tests in the next section.

IQ TESTS OF THE PAST

You may have had an IQ test while you were in school. These tests are sometimes used to identify gifted students so they can be accelerated or to identify students who are struggling so they can be offered support. In fact, IQ tests were first developed in the beginning of the 20th century to identify students with learning problems. At that time the questions were more entertaining: Students were asked to touch their noses or ears and draw a design from memory. Now IQ tests are more sophisticated.

IQ tests are also used for adults. An early use of IQ tests for adults was to select those with high scores for the armed forces. Today, medical examinations sometimes incorporate these tests to check whether a patient has good language skills. Employers may use such tests as part of a job interview. Although a good IQ score doesn't necessarily make someone a more productive employee, many employers still use the tests to select job applicants.

WARNING

You can find a range of tests on the Internet that claim to give you an accurate score for your IQ. You may find taking such tests to be a good mental exercise. However, remember not all online tests are accurate. To be accurate, an IQ test must have undergone the strict scientific rigor to make sure it measures your skills in a reliable and valid manner. Don't worry, though. If you're interested in finding out what your IQ is, many tests *are* scientifically valid and can provide insight into your abilities.

Measuring your brain's IQ

Would you like to test your IQ? Here are some examples of IQ test questions you can answer:

>> How are a dog and a cat the same?

>> How are an apple and an orange the same?

You may have guessed that this type of test measures how well you can compare things in the world around you. You may have said that a dog and a cat are both animals, which is a good response. But a better response would be that they're both domesticated animals or pets. What about an apple and an orange? Some people point out that they're both round and, of course, they're both fruits. The purpose of this test is to measure how well you can verbalize in detail how two different things (dog and cat) can be considered alike.

Try some different ones now:

>> Give a short definition for the word *fashion*.

>> Give a short definition for the word *democracy*.

The answers you give for these questions tend to reflect your own experiences. For example, you may define *fashion* as "useless" or "a waste of time." Although this description may accurately reflect your own views, you'll probably get a score of zero. A good answer would be "a prevailing style or custom." This answer would get a score of 2. An IQ test like this one measures not only how well you know the definition of a word but also how well you can define it.

Try one more pair of examples:

>> What would you do if you saw someone running off with a shopping bag and a woman crying "Help"?

>> What would you do if you saw someone struggling in the water?

These questions measure how well you can respond to social situations and apply your common sense. Here again, your experiences may direct your responses. For example, you may have just read in the news about a man who successfully chased away a burglar from his house and, inspired by this story, you respond that you'd pursue the person running off with the bag. Or perhaps you have a fear of water and wouldn't want to jump in to help a struggling person, but you may answer the second question by saying you'd throw her a rope so you could help pull her to safety.

TECHNICAL
STUFF

Psychologists and statisticians have carefully vetted the questions in an IQ test to make sure they provide an accurate measure of your language and other cognitive skills. After completing an IQ test, you get a score ranging between 50 and 150.

So what does your score mean? Most people score between 85 and 115. That's pretty good considering a score of 100 is the middle point. But some people (less than 3 percent of the population) score above average: 130 or higher. On the flip side, some people get a low score, perhaps close to 50. Here again, a small percentage of the population gets such a low score. But remember: Your IQ score doesn't define you. Making the most of your brain power and staying sharp mentally is the key, no matter what your IQ score.

IN THIS CHAPTER

Unleashing the creative side of your brain

Making music for your brain

Drawing to find creative solutions to problems

Chapter 3

Sparking Your Creativity

From music to drawing, you can get your creative brain working in many ways. The benefits to getting the creative side of your brain working include being able to think outside the box at work, to come up with unique solutions to problems, and even to enjoy certain activities more.

Find something you enjoy doing and make time to do the activity regularly. Your work life benefits from your creative activities as well. This chapter talks about how to get your creative juices flowing.

Boosting Your Brainpower with Creative Endeavors

Training your brain isn't only about hard work! *Creative thinking* — being able to come up with original solutions to problems — is a great way to encourage your brain to integrate information from different sources (see Chapter 1 for more on how the brain works). It means not giving up when a problem seems hard but rather finding a different perspective — something unusual or unique.

TIP

Not everyone can become the next Beethoven or da Vinci, but here are some things you can do to develop your creative side:

>> **Be prepared.** "Fortune favors the prepared mind." This quote from famous scientist Louis Pasteur sums up what scientists now know from studying brain patterns. Different parts of the brain show more activation just before a problem is presented. This means that the brain gets ready and gathers information from different parts in order to generate a solution.

When you're faced with a problem, the solution seldom comes from thin air. It's often the result of hours (sometimes years) of preparation. So the next time you have a problem to tackle, do your homework and prepare well. A creative solution will soon follow.

>> **Shh, no more talking.** Sometimes talking about a problem too much can ruin the creative process. Studies have found that the creative process works best if you're not constantly vocalizing your plans. In many ways the creative solution is an automatic process. Some even suggest that creativity has a subconscious element to it — you're creative without even thinking about being creative. So the next time you're trying to be creative, avoid talking about it and let your brain do the work.

>> **Look away.** Sometimes focusing on a problem for too long can reduce your creativity. Scientists have now found evidence that the brain produces an excessive amount of *gamma waves,* linked to excessive amounts of attention, when you focus on a problem for too long. This increase in gamma waves leads to a mental roadblock, which of course won't help you solve the problem.

So if you've lost your creative vibe, get up and walk away from the problem. Do something else for a bit — anything else, as long as the activity isn't related to the problem you're trying to solve. Let your mind rest for a time so when you come back your brain is recharged.

WARNING

Studies have found that people who use their creative skills for their work can end up struggling to balance their responsibilities at home and at work. Because the creative process isn't often confined to an office space, they often do work-related tasks outside of normal work hours. As a result, these people can experience more job pressure, which impacts social and family relationships.

If you're involved in a creative work environment, try to see the positive side of your job. Most creative people enjoy thinking about their work and coming up with creative solutions. Creative work isn't a stressful problem they have to solve so they can sleep at night. Instead, creative work gives people a sense of accomplishment and fulfillment, especially when they find a solution. Remember to focus on the satisfaction you get from using your creative skills rather the potential stress of solving a problem (see Part 3 for more on managing stress and anxiety).

Tapping out Tempo

"If music be the food of love, play on." Given the evidence of music's power for the brain, this famous quote from the opening of Shakespeare's *Twelfth Night* could be changed to "If music be the food of the brain, play on." From infants to seniors, music can make the brain think in more creative ways.

TIP

Here are some ways you can encourage your musical side:

>> **Sing along.** Infants respond to the pitch and rhythm of language. The term *motherese* refers to the high-pitched, cooing voice that mothers often use to speak to their babies. (Fathers use it, too, but the term *dadese* hasn't really caught on.) Studies demonstrate that babies pick up on these pitch patterns and coo back, following the same patterns. Early communication is characterized by mimicking the tempo and rhythm of language. When the mother coos in a certain way, the baby does, too.

>> **Play music to pay attention.** Music lessons help students learn to pick up on classroom instructions better. Research has found that playing an instrument is useful in helping youngsters filter out noisy distractions in the classroom and focus on the teacher's voice more accurately. Playing a musical instrument doesn't just teach the brain to turn up the volume of all sounds but also helps the brain distinguish the noise from the relevant information effectively.

When someone learns a musical instrument, she trains her brain to extract the relevant musical patterns, such as harmony and rhythm. The brain is then able to apply this same skill to filtering and picking up on language and other sounds, whether in the classroom or at the playground.

>> **Listen to the sound of music.** Listening to music activates different parts of the brain related to attention, memory, and processing of information and emotions. What's really powerful is that music can heal the adult brain as well. Studies reveal that just listening to music can result in faster cognitive recovery in stroke patients. The patients' verbal memory and attention improves more quickly than the memories of people who just listen to audio books. As a bonus, listening to music during stroke recovery also helps prevent negative moods such as depression.

>> **Improve your memory.** Studies have found that when words are put to music, the memory of people with early Alzheimer's disease improves significantly. Parts of the brain associated with memory (see Chapter 1) work at a slower pace in those with Alzheimer's disease. But putting words you need to remember to music creates a stronger memory link than just repeating the words on their own. So if you know someone with early Alzheimer's disease who's struggling to remember daily tasks, put the list of jobs to music and sing the list to the person.

Reaping the benefits of musical training on your brain

Scientific evidence demonstrates that musical training improves memory; musicians tend to remember more information compared to non-musicians, even when you take their education levels and their ages into account. In other words, playing a musical instrument activates part of the brain (the cerebral cortex), which in turn boosts recall of information.

Working memory — the ability to keep information in mind and manipulate it — is a crucial component of musical skills as well. For example, pianists use working memory when they read music. While they're fingering the piano keys, they're also looking ahead to read the notes that are coming next. Expert musicians need to have good working memory to make the correct sounds while simultaneously anticipating and preparing for the next action.

In addition to working memory, the brain also processes musical information with both the left and right hemispheres of the brain (see Chapter 1 for an inside look at the brain). This mental cooperation during musical instruction can also impact how children learn. (Check out the nearby sidebar "Getting an early start on music lessons" for info on how music instruction impacts learning.)

TECHNICAL STUFF

Which part of the brain is involved in processing music? The right hemisphere is more involved in processing pitch, melody, and harmony as well as structure and meaning in musical sequences (see Chapter 1 for more on brain hemispheres). Studies using brain imaging to measure brain activity of newborns (just a few days old) found that the infant brain already comes equipped with specific and

GETTING AN EARLY START ON MUSIC LESSONS

Music training is good for schoolwork. Children who are exposed to music lessons that involve complex rhythms and tones usually have better reading skills than children of the same age who don't have music lessons. But it's not just reading that improves. Psychologists have found that math skills and spatial reasoning are also better in students who receive music lessons.

But *when* you teach music is as important as *what* you teach. Studies have found that growth spurts in brain development occur up until the age of seven. So simply saying that music makes you smarter isn't accurate. If you're going to provide music lessons, introduce the lessons by seven years of age if you want to also see benefits in reading, math, and reasoning skills.

specialized functions for understanding music. The right hemisphere processes music that's *tonal* (with pitches arranged in a regular hierarchy). But the left hemisphere (the left inferior frontal cortex) processes music that's *dissonant* (or not harmonious or melodic).

TIP

If you're too embarrassed to sing karaoke with friends, you can use music in other ways to boost your brain. Here are some things you can try:

» **Clap your hands.** It sounds surprising, but children who sing songs that involve hand clapping have neater handwriting and fewer spelling mistakes. It may be that the motor skill component of hand clapping helps in the classroom. But clapping isn't just for kids' songs. Make an effort to clap along when you hear a song. Focus on the beat of the song and clap in tempo. Doing so trains your brain to follow the tempo.

» **Get a drum.** Rhythm links to working memory skills. For example, something as simple as being able to remember the sequence of taps relates to how well you can remember what someone's just told you. Most information involves a sequence. For example, you have to remember how to do things in the order that you were told. This progression of doing one thing first, followed by another and finally the last is very similar to how people remember a sequence of sounds. So the next time you listen to a song, pay attention to the beat to boost your memory for a sequence of tasks.

» **Write a song.** You don't have to be Beethoven or Beyoncé to come up with a song. Remember when you were a kid and loved to make up silly songs?

As an adult, you can keep your love of singing and making music alive. The easiest place to start is with a sentence that expresses your emotions. Write a few lines and then put a little tune to the lines. If you can't come up with a tune on your own, use one from a song you like. The goal of this activity is to integrate different parts of the brain during song writing — from writing words to thinking of the tempo to putting it all to music. Who knows; you may even get your family to start singing your songs.

TECHNICAL STUFF

If you're one of those people who think that their singing should never leave the shower because you can't carry a tune, you're not alone. Around 10 percent of the population is *tone deaf*, which means that they can't sing in tune. Tone-deaf people also can't consciously tell that their singing is off-key. New scientific research has identified a specific brain circuit that links sound perception with producing language that's missing in people who are tone deaf.

WARNING

Listening to music has many benefits, from improving language skills to recovering more quickly from a stroke. However, if you're trying to concentrate, listening to music (and singing along!) can distract you. Studies have found that when people do two things at the same time, they become less efficient and make more mistakes. And it doesn't make any difference whether you enjoy the music you're listening to — having music on can still cause you to make more mistakes. In one study, researchers asked people to remember a list of words and do some mental math tasks while listening to music they liked, listening to music they didn't like, or in a quiet environment. People did the best on the tasks when they did them in a quiet environment. So although music is great for your brain, it's not so good if you're listening to it while doing something that demands your attention. If you're a music lover, consider enjoying your music beforehand rather than playing tunes in the background.

Drawing Isn't Just for Picasso

If you've never thought of yourself as a creative person, it's time for a change of thinking. Each person has the potential to unlock an aspect of creativity. The following sections list a few suggestions to help you get going. They include tips on simple drawing activities to get you started — but if you feel that you still need more encouragement, why not simply begin by doodling?

Doodling to stay on task

TIP

Are you a doodler? Do you find your papers covered in scribbles and scrawls? Well, now scientific research supports your efforts to stave off boredom. A recent study compared the working memory of two groups of people: doodlers and non-doodlers. Both groups were asked to listen to a pre-recorded phone message about a birthday party and remember the names of the people coming. The doodling group remembered more names and places mentioned in the phone message compared to the non-doodlers. Doodling while listening can be beneficial because it helps you focus and maintain attention instead of tuning out altogether. Doodling isn't a demanding activity, and it acts like a buffer that prevents other activities like daydreaming from interfering with what you have to remember. Doodling also allows you to associate the new information with the visual creation of drawing. So if you're worried that you'll start zoning out during a meeting, grab a pencil!

Drawing to release your creative side

Drawing increases your imagination, which is critical in helping you find creative solutions to problems. So if doodling is natural to you, and you feel you're capable of drawing something a little more demanding than squiggles on the page, go ahead and dive right in.

TIP

Here are some ideas to get you drawing:

» **Make a maze.** Start with one thought. It doesn't have to be profound; it can even be an object if that's easier. Write down the thought on a regular sheet of paper. Now think of another thought. How can you connect the two ideas? Keep going until your paper looks like a maze of thoughts and ideas. The maze may not make sense in the beginning. But after a few tries, you'll find that this process becomes easier. And you'll notice that your brain starts making connections between different events more, which can start snowballing your creative process (see the section "Looking at the Difference a Creative Brain Makes" later in this chapter for more on how the brain of a creative person works).

» **Make a card or scrapbook.** The next time you have to buy a card for someone's birthday, why not make one? You have unlimited options for what you can do, from drawing a picture to painting something to using old photos to recreate a precious memory you shared together. Not only is making a card a more meaningful way to share your thoughts, but it also lets you be creative.

Or consider scrapbooking. You can finally do something with all those photos you have lying around, and it's a great way to capture your memories. If most of your photos are digital, note that many online sites let you do virtual scrapbooking and share your pages with family and friends.

ROME WAS BUILT IN A DAY

Well, maybe not, but it was at least drawn in just two days. After a single 30-minute helicopter ride above the city in 2005, Stephen Wiltshire recreated the city from memory in amazing detail. When Steven was a child, he was diagnosed with autism and was able to communicate only by drawing. He's now an architectural artist who draws and paints cityscapes from memory after just seeing them once.

For example, after flying over London briefly in a helicopter, he was able to draw a perfectly scaled aerial illustration of four square miles of the city from memory in just three hours. His drawing included more than 10 major landmarks and 200 buildings.

Stephen has drawn panoramic perspectives of cities all over the world; Sydney, Frankfurt, Madrid, Tokyo, Hong Kong, and New York have all been subjects of his unique skill and mastery. His artworks are internationally recognized and fetch handsome sums at auctions.

>> **Draw a cartoon.** Cartoons or even graphic novels are great ways to journal your thoughts. Instead of trying to find the right words to express how you felt today draw a picture. You may even surprise yourself! If you feel brave, post your cartoons online using a blog or social media and get your friends' feedback. You can also keep cartooning as something you do just for yourself. Whatever you choose, creating this type of diary is a fun way to express your thoughts and release a more creative you.

Looking at the Difference a Creative Brain Makes

"Is the brain of a creative person different from a methodical person?" To answer that question, researchers looked at the brain activity of those who solve problems creatively with that burst of "Aha!" compared to those who solve problems more systematically. They asked each participant to relax for a few minutes while they used an *electroencephalogram* (EEG) to record the electrical activity in participants' brains. Next, they gave the participants an anagram to solve. Try one for yourself: MPXAELE.

(Answer: EXAMPLE.)

The brain-activation patterns of the creative types and the methodical types were very different. The researchers found that the creative people used the right hemispheres of their brains when they were problem solving. Even when they weren't trying to solve a problem, creative people's EEGs showed the right hemispheres of their brains were active.

Creative people are very flexible in their thinking. Think of a maze that has multiple paths that lead to other paths that link to new ones, and so on. That's what the brain activity of the creative person is like. One idea will trigger another, which will spark yet another in a creative chain reaction. For example, a conversation may trigger a picture the person saw last month, which reminds her of a dream she had last week, which leads her to a new idea.

The brain of a methodical thinker is different. It's like a straight road that starts at one end with the problem and moves systematically along a single path until it finds a solution. Methodical or analytical thinkers don't allow their brains to get distracted by other ideas; they just focus exclusively on what they need to do and the steps they need to take to solve the problem at hand.

You can train your brain to be more creative by looking at problems in new ways and using different perspectives. To think outside the box, try to look at the box from new angles. Imagine the box in a different color or with different decorations. Think of new ways to use the box. Mentally transform the box. With practice, you can come up with new, creative ways to address problems you face in your daily life. After all, electric lights, cars, computers, and cellphones all started as creative ideas to solve problems in new ways.

IN THIS CHAPTER

Boosting your visual and spatial skills

Using easy tricks to keep your visual and spatial skills intact

Testing your visual-spatial memory

Chapter 4

Recognizing Faces and Remembering Directions

You're offered two apples. How do you choose between them? Chances are that you'll pick the bigger one. But you may have also used color or other visual features, such as whether one had a bruise, to choose between the two apples. You're using your visual-spatial memory skills to make that decision. You kept the image of one apple in mind while looking at the other. Even the simplest everyday tasks require you to use your visual-spatial memory skills. This chapter covers tips on how to develop your visual and spatial skills.

Understanding Visual-Spatial Memory Skills

Visual-spatial memory skills are how you learn about the world right from the beginning. As a baby, your visual-spatial skills are especially strong. Perhaps because babies haven't yet developed language skills, they're able to quickly take a snapshot of the world and remember certain visual features. Think for a moment about a baby's world. You give the baby a toy. How does he know whether this toy is a new one that he hasn't seen before or an old toy from his toy box? He has to bring up his mental images of his toys and decide whether this toy in front of him matches the images of the toys he's already played with or not. Psychologists suggest that babies remember the features of their toys: color, shape, and specific features such as button eyes, floppy ears, or soft fuzzy texture.

What do babies' perceptions of toys have to do with you as an adult? You perform the same mental comparisons when you meet someone new. You may even think, "He looks familiar. Have I met this person before?" Or you may notice specific features such as his hair and think, "He reminds me of Uncle Jack, who has hair like that."

Banishing the "You Look Familiar, But I Can't Remember You" Phenomenon

You know the feeling. You're at a social function, and two people greet you. One gestures to the other and says "You remember Joe." So you look at Joe and know that you should remember him — he does look familiar — but you just can't place him. Where do you know him from — work, the gym, the local café, or your kids' school or sports? If it makes you feel any better, the "You look familiar, but I can't remember your name" phenomenon happens to everyone.

What happens if your work or social obligations require that you remember people's names when you see their faces? Don't fret! You can train your brain to remember names for those faces.

Psychologists have recently discovered that your brain still stores info on the forgotten faces. You just need to know how to unlock the memories of those faces. Psychologists showed people pictures, waited a while, and then showed them the same pictures again and asked the people whether they'd seen the pictures before. When people could clearly remember what they saw, there was a strong brain

YOU NEVER FORGET A FAMOUS FACE

What's remarkable is that your memory for names of famous faces tends to be preserved. Psychologists have found that healthy older people (defined as age 60 to 91) have great memories for famous faces and remember information those people based on their faces. For example, when shown a photo of Frank Sinatra, these mature adults could identify that he was a singer and even name one or two of her songs.

wave pattern. When they were struggling to remember whether they'd seen the pictures previously, the same brain wave pattern existed, but it was weaker. This result means that your brain remembers when you've seen something before, even if you don't know it! Chapter 1 offers tips on how to train your brain to remember new information.

REMEMBER

Ordinary tasks like configuring the settings on a new computer tablet, TV, or DVD player require complex visual-spatial skills as well. You have to look at the manual, keep that information in mind, transfer your focus to your device, and input the information accurately to set it up to do what you want it to do. In contrast to language skills, you actually have a much smaller "space" to remember visual-spatial information. Psychologists suggest that, on average, people can only remember three or four visual images at the same time. So don't feel too bad if you have to look at the instructions multiple times to get the settings right on your device. You're not alone!

Reasoning and logic: The key to training your visual-spatial skills

The good news is that you can improve your visual-spatial skills. The first step is to test them. Try the following fun example.

Testing your logic and reasoning

Figure 4-1 shows a common task that instructors give to psychology students to test their logic and reasoning skills. You see four cards, with only one side showing.

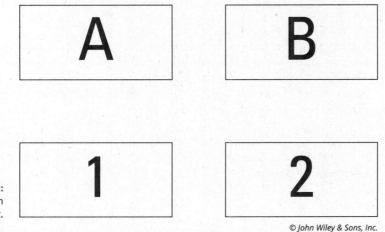

FIGURE 4-1:
A common
reasoning test.

Here's the rule: If one side of the card displays a vowel, then the other side of the card can only show an even number.

Which card do you turn over first to check this rule? Most people turn over the card with the letter *A*. That's correct. Now which card do you turn over next? You may be tempted to turn over the card with the number 2, but you should actually turn over the card with the number 1.

Why? Look at the rule again: If one side of the card displays a vowel, then the other side of the card can only show an even number.

You turned over the card with the letter *A* to confirm this rule because *A* is a vowel. You don't need to turn over the card with letter *B* because the rule said nothing about consonants. You may think you don't need to turn over the card with the number 1, but you do need to check whether it has a vowel on the other side. If it does have a vowel, then it's violated the rule. You don't need to turn over the card with the number 2 because the rule doesn't state what should happen if you have an even number on one side.

If you're still puzzling over this, don't worry. Most people find this test very difficult. Try this version.

Here's the rule: If you're under 21, you can't drink alcohol.

You're the bartender and you have to make sure that no one breaks this rule. Figure 4-2 shows what you see at one table.

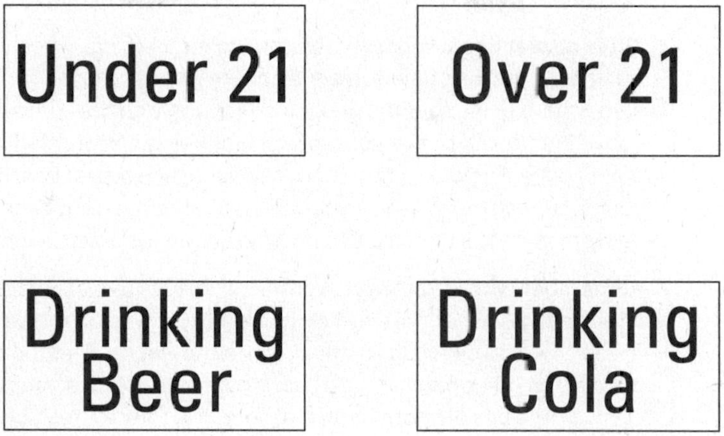

FIGURE 4-2: A reasoning test with a bartender.

Under 21

Over 21

Drinking Beer

Drinking Cola

Whose age will you check? You'll probably check the first person who looks under 21. And you'd also check the person drinking beer to make sure that he's 21 or over. You aren't worried about the person drinking cola because it doesn't matter whether he's older or younger than 21; cola isn't an alcoholic drink.

These kinds of tasks aren't meant to frustrate psychology students (though they may do that too!) but to illustrate how people use logic and reasoning in everyday situations. In the scenario with the drinks, you can save time by checking only certain people's ages rather than checking everyone's age.

Using your reasoning skills to the max

Life presents you with many opportunities to recognize patterns and use your reasoning skills to their full potential.

TIP

Here are some suggestions that can help you strengthen the patterns and associations you may need daily:

>> **Face facts.** Test your visual memory. Look at famous faces and see how quickly you can come up with the people's names. Too easy? Try to come up with one fact about each person. Remember, don't just use "celebrity" faces; try to include political and historical figures as well.

>> **Remember me.** Try the face facts game with familiar faces. Start with people you know well — family members and close friends. This time, try to state five things you know about each person. Now look at photos of people you may

not know as well — maybe colleagues from work or friends from school with whom you're no longer in contact. Try to remember the people's names and one thing about each of them. For work colleagues or school friends remember what department they work in or a funny incident that you shared in class.

>> **Filter distractions.** You're more prone to forget things when you're distracted. So the next time someone's giving you directions over the phone, go somewhere quiet, shut the door, and focus only on the conversation. When you're introduced to someone new at a buffet luncheon, stop refilling your empty plate and look at her, shake her hand, and repeat her name. Increase your focus by strengthening your ability to filter out distractions. Work on being present like this so it becomes an automatic practice for you.

>> **Remember where you were.** Your brain remembers odd little bits of information, such as the smell of the freshly cut grass in the park when your friend gave you directions to the party on the weekend, or the smell of the pizza at the office party as your boss introduced you to an important potential client. These bits of information that your brain stores may seem irrelevant, but they can serve as powerful clues to trigger your memory. When you're trying to remember something, think back to where you were when you first heard the information. Do you remember anything specific about the location? What was the person wearing? What were you doing? All these questions can help you reconstruct the moment, which in turn unlocks your memory.

>> **Make your own box.** It's no wonder that the saying "Think outside the box" has caught on. People who can think beyond what others normally do have an advantage. They're more creative and come up with ideas that the others haven't thought about before. If you can't find a solution right away, maybe you're approaching the problem in the wrong way. Try to ask different questions. Think outside the box. The solutions that come to you may be surprising.

Working Your Memory Muscle

You store information in different parts of your brain. The brain keeps visual information in one part and spatial information in another. However, your brain is very efficient in combining information from different parts to work together when you need to remember something.

TECHNICAL STUFF

The *hippocampus* is located in the temporal lobe of the brain and is responsible for storing spatial memory and helping you navigate your body in space. Individuals who suffer damage to their hippocampus also experience deficits of their spatial memory. Such individuals feel disoriented and forget where they are or where they're going.

TIP

To keep your visual-spatial skills sharp, here are some tips:

>> **Puzzle me this.** Jigsaw puzzles aren't just for kids. They're a great way to boost your visual-spatial memory skills and develop your ability to see patterns. You have to recognize patterns between the pieces and learn to predict what you think the piece represents. This means that you have to keep in mind what the complete puzzle picture looks like and try to match the place of a single piece. People tend not to use these skills very often in everyday activities, so doing a puzzle is a great way to target these skills.

>> **Spot the difference.** *Change blindness* is a term that psychologists use to describe people's inability to spot changes in scenes around them. In many experiments a man stops to ask for directions, and halfway through, a woman takes the man's place. Most people don't even notice! A lot of newspapers and magazines display pictures where you have to spot the difference between two pictures. Sometimes it's a weekly contest. If you used to ignore this puzzle, from now on take a moment to see how quickly you can do it. It's good practice for you to strengthen your visual-spatial skills.

FOR A BIGGER BRAIN, DRIVE A TAXI

A group of psychologists in London were interested in the brains of taxi drivers. In particular, they wanted to know whether cabbies' visual-spatial skills were better than other people's.

There are many reasons that may be true. For starters, directions are taxi drivers' lifeblood — they need to know their way inside and out of a city like London. They also have to take an extensive test called "the Knowledge," which requires drivers to know over 400 routes. The Knowledge is so demanding that 75 percent of people drop out of the course. Yet sticking with the course has its rewards, especially financial gain. Drivers stand to make significantly more money after passing the test.

However, the psychologists discovered a surprise bonus: Taxi drivers have bigger brains! Yes, it's true. The part of brain associated with directions (visual-spatial memory) is actually larger in experienced taxi drivers compared to the average individual. Their brains changed to accommodate the increasing amount of information on navigating and directions that are required for them to work as taxi drivers.

This is an exciting finding because it demonstrates that the brain has a certain amount of flexibility and can expand in response learning. But you don't have to be a taxi driver to expand your visual-spatial brainpower. Everyone can benefit from working memory muscles.

TIP

Use your visual-spatial skills to spot the differences in everyday situations. When you walk into your supermarket, try to pick out three things that are different from the last time you were there. Are the vegetables in the same place? Is a new display of sale items sitting at the end of aisle 10? Training your eyes to focus on things that are different not only makes you more observant, but also preserves these skills that you need to remember faces and directions.

Measuring Your Brain's Visual-Spatial IQ

Would you like to test your visual-spatial IQ? Here are some examples of questions you can answer that can help you do so.

TIP

Take a look at Figure 4-3. Can you figure out the next shape in the sequence? You may have correctly guessed that the next shape will be a circle. As you're probably aware, this type of test measures how well you can spot the pattern and follow the sequence of objects. Other tests require you to construct a shape out of different colored blocks. A key component in these tasks is that you gain extra points the more quickly you do these tasks.

FIGURE 4-3:
A visual-spatial
IQ test.

© John Wiley & Sons, Inc.

In timed tests, older people tend to lose points. However, when you remove the timed aspect, older people perform at the same level as younger people. As you get older you may take longer on these tasks because you may have adopted a more methodical approach to problem-solving.

Other tests measure your reasoning skills. Take a look at these statements:

Bird—Nest   _____?—Kennel

Hammer—Nail   _____?—Paint can

The purpose of these questions is to measure how well you can make associations between two things. First look at the word pair of Bird—Nest. Now look at the next word pair with the missing word: _____?—Kennel. Use the relationship between *bird* and *nest* to figure out the word that goes with *kennel*. Now look at the next word pair: Hammer—Nail. Try to work out what you think their association is and then figure out the correct word to pair with *paint can*. The correct answer to the former is *dog,* and for the latter the correct answer is *paintbrush.*

Chapter 5

Getting a Handle on Brain Games

As an isolated activity, working a logic puzzle or untangling a word scramble may not dramatically change anyone's cognitive ability. But combined with other lifestyle changes, working puzzles — or doing other types of mentally stimulating activities — may have profound long-term effects on memory and overall cognitive ability. This chapter talks about the benefits of working puzzles and what else you can do to try to stay sharp. Chapter 6 gives you actual puzzles to work on.

Some people adore puzzles that allow them to play with words: logic puzzles, riddles, word searches, word scrambles. They just seem to have the knack for solving them. Others don't have the knack, so they struggle with puzzles. If you want to be able to look a puzzle squarely in the face and say, "You're not keeping me awake tonight," what can you do (other than keep the answers handy)?

You may have started working puzzles in elementary school, when teachers had you fill in crossword puzzles or do word searches that reinforced your lessons. Chances are you're familiar with most of these puzzles and have had at least some experience working them.

But that doesn't necessarily mean you're comfortable with them. In fact, you may feel downright nervous when you sit down to work a crossword these days.

The benefits of working puzzles are potentially great. Plus, they're a lot of fun — after you get past the fear and frustration. This chapter gears you up for how best to work through puzzles.

Pumping Up Your Synapses

On the off chance that you aren't a neurologist, here are a couple of definitions: *Neurons* are cells that make up your central nervous system — your brain and spinal column, and the nerves connected to them. *Synapses* are tiny connections between the neurons in your brain. When synapses are working correctly, they allow your neurons to communicate with each other, which keeps your nervous system functioning the way it should. Your nervous system must function properly in order for you to learn new things, retain information, and use your powers of logic and reason.

You're feeling some love for your synapses now, aren't you?

You have about 100 billion neurons in your brain, but each neuron has multiple synapses connecting to multiple other neurons. As a result, you have literally trillions of synapses — possibly even a *quadrillion* (that's a 1 followed by 15 zeroes). It sure seems like you have plenty to spare, but as you age, your synapses deteriorate. And because your brain activity takes place courtesy of synapses, their deterioration equates to a decrease in your brain function, including memory.

The take-home point here is that if you want your mind to stay sharp to a ripe old age, you need to do more than just take care of your body (although that's crucial too, as explained later in this chapter). You need to keep your synapses in top condition. How do you do that? Keep reading!

Building a Cognitive Reserve

In the late 1980s, a study published in the *Annals of Neurology* raised questions about why some people develop symptoms of Alzheimer's disease and some don't. Autopsies were conducted on 137 former nursing-home patients. As expected, the brains of those who had demonstrated symptoms of Alzheimer's were filled with *plaques* (brain deposits made up of dead cells and proteins) and *tangles* (nerve cells that had become tangled together) — characteristic physical signs associated with the disease.

Here's the unexpected part: The brains of ten patients who *didn't* show any symptoms of Alzheimer's contained the same level of plaques and tangles. If the physical reasons for the disease were present in those people, why didn't they get the symptoms?

There was another twist as well: The ten patients in question had heavier brains and more neurons than they should have given their age.

What made these ten people different from their peers?

REMEMBER

As a result of this study, a new theory emerged: the *cognitive reserve* theory. It essentially says that people who have a larger reserve of neurons and stronger cognitive abilities can tolerate some brain deterioration without showing symptoms. In other words, the more you use your brain, the greater your chances of avoiding symptoms of Alzheimer's.

Strong stuff, huh?

Obviously, no one is offering guarantees here. There's no guarantee that anything suggested in this book will add X number of years to your life, and that those years will be free of any symptoms of memory loss or other mental decline. But study after study in the past few decades has shown that mental activity can — and often does — have a positive effect on your quality of life in the long run.

How do you build a cognitive reserve? The same way that you keep your synapses happy and healthy. Keep reading — the following section offers specific suggestions.

Taking a Whole-Body Approach to Brain Health

The great news about the steps you can take to improve your chances of long-term cognitive health is that many of them are the same steps you take to keep your body healthy. You need to add just a couple of items to a list that's probably already familiar. And the new items are fun.

Here's the familiar stuff:

>> **Reduce stress.** If you've heard this advice from your doctor in relation to a physical condition, you now have double the reason to heed it. Research shows that stress causes synapses to malfunction.

Long-term stress can cause a *neurotransmitter* (a chemical that carries messages between nerve cells) called *glutamate* to build up in your synapses. If enough of it accumulates, it can become toxic and interfere with your memory and your ability to learn.

» **Get aerobic exercise.** Aerobic exercise can help you manage and resist stress, which is enough reason to make it part of your daily routine. But among its many other benefits, studies suggest that it stimulates the creation of new neurons and strengthens the connections between them.

» **Eat a diet rich in antioxidant foods.** If your physical health alone hasn't inspired you to stock up on blueberries and spinach, do so for your mental health. Foods rich in antioxidants may help counteract effects of free radicals in your brain. (*Free radicals* are molecules that contain oxygen that attack cells throughout your body. They've been linked to cancer and heart disease as well as brain deterioration.)

» **Control high blood pressure and diabetes.** A study published in the journal *Neurology* in 2001 showed that the mental abilities of participants with high blood pressure or diabetes declined more rapidly than those of other participants. High blood pressure is a risk factor for a condition called *vascular dementia,* in which a series of tiny strokes can affect memory and other cognitive abilities.

REMEMBER

Early diagnosis and tight control of high blood pressure and diabetes may help prevent some of the ill effects on your cognitive health.

Ready for the steps that may be new on your to-do list?

» **Get lots of mental stimulation.** Ahhh, *this* is where the puzzles come in — finally!

You may be hard-pressed to find a scientist who would claim to know exactly how much mental stimulation the average adult of a certain age needs or what types of mental activities are best for a certain population. The science is fairly young, so you'll certainly hear a lot more about it in the years to come. But the general consensus is this: Mental stimulation of any kind can have positive effects on warding off memory problems and other declines in cognitive function, and lack of stimulation is a serious factor in mental decline.

How should you use your brain to get the maximum results? Only you can answer that question. That's because whatever you do, it has to be enjoyable enough to truly stimulate you and to keep you coming back for more, day after day. It's a mental marathon, not a sprint, so go ahead and read *War and Peace* or pull out your old calculus textbook (but only if that's what you really want.) Otherwise, look for other types of activities that will keep you interested in the long term. (Anyone for Sudoku?)

The bottom line: If there's a hobby you love that you haven't ma[de]
years, make time for it. If there's an activity you've been meanin[g to]
have put on the back burner because it seems less important th[an]
laundry, do it. If there's a subject you've been curious about for ages bu[t]
haven't had time to study, study it. And if anyone (including your conscience)
pesters you about how you're spending your time, memorize your new
mantra: *My brain needs me.*

>> **Stay curious.** This is an extension of the preceding point. If you've buried your
curiosity about the world around you because you haven't had time to explore
it since childhood, now's the time — no matter how old you are or what your
life circumstances are — to rediscover how curiosity feels.

REMEMBER

Whatever activities you choose to help keep your brain stimulated, you need to
enjoy them enough to do them regularly. You can't get your body fit by working
out three hours in a row and then ignoring your health altogether for two weeks
(because you're so sore from the marathon workout that you can't move for the
first five days!). You benefit much more from working out consistently for shorter
amounts of time — for example, every day for 30 minutes or four days a week for
45 minutes each time.

REMEMBER

The same seems to be true of mental exercise. Your goal should be to make time for
mental stimulation at least several days a week — ideally, every day. If you can't
devote time to working a crossword every day, no problem. But don't let a month
go by between mental workouts. You have to invest the time if you want the results.

Getting Logical

Logic puzzles can take a variety of forms. They can involve words, numbers, or
images, and — like all puzzles — they can be fairly easy or extremely difficult to
solve.

Preparing to solve logic puzzles isn't like preparing to solve a crossword or Sudoku
puzzle. You don't need to understand how the puzzle is constructed or what the
rules are. You don't have many specific strategies to consider. However, you
should keep the following in mind:

>> As with other puzzle types, each logic puzzle has a unique answer. The puzzle
constructor doesn't intend for you to be able to solve one puzzle in multiple ways.

>> In many cases, the person writing the puzzle is intentionally veiling the answer. The way the puzzle is written may be deceptive to some degree — the degree of deception partly determines the puzzle's level of difficulty.

Logic puzzles are a varied lot. You'll likely find that some answers spring to mind as soon as you've read the puzzle; your own logic will make them seem obvious to you. But others will be much more diabolical.

TIP

If you spend a good amount of time studying one puzzle and just can't seem to figure it out, walk away and come back later. A fresh look may be your best bet. If that fails, you may want to enlist help from a friend or family member.

Another thing to keep in mind is that the more puzzles you solve that are written by the same puzzle constructor, the better your chances of figuring out whether (and how) that person is trying to deceive you. For that reason, you should start with the easy logic puzzles in Chapter 6, even if you don't find them very challenging. They give you a sense of who the puzzle constructor is and how he writes logic puzzles. That information can help when you reach the toughest of the tough. By that point, you may have some insights regarding the constructor's use of language and his thought processes.

REMEMBER

Don't look at the answer pages (at the end of Chapter 6) until you've given each puzzle a good effort. You want the best workout your mind can get, and sometimes that means allowing some time for frustration as you try to find the solution.

Fiddling with Riddles

If logic puzzles appeal to you, you'll probably like riddles as well. These two types of puzzles are close cousins; however, riddles are often shorter than logic puzzles and involve plays on language. For example,

What becomes larger the more you take away from it and smaller the more you add to it?

The answer is *a hole*. The reason this riddle works is because it forces you to think in a new way — to realize that not everything gets larger when you add to it.

Here are some more:

>> What has one eye but can't see?

Answer: A needle.

>> What gets wetter and wetter the more it dries?

Answer: A towel

>> "That attorney is my brother," testified the doctor. But the attorney testified he didn't have a brother. Who was lying?

Answer: Neither; the doctor was the attorney's sister.

REMEMBER

As with logic puzzles and other puzzle types, each riddle should have just one unique answer. If you can think of two or more reasonable answers to the same riddle, chances are you've outwitted the puzzle constructor!

Riddles are a great way to introduce kids to the joy of playing with language. And for adults, they're a great way to keep the mental gears cranking even when you have only a short time each day to devote to puzzling.

Decoding Cryptograms

Cryptograms are more complicated than word searches and word scrambles, and they'll almost certainly require more of your time. But solving a cryptogram is really satisfying — it makes you feel like a master detective — so the extra time is well worth it.

A cryptogram is a sentence or phrase that's *encrypted* or *enciphered.* Each letter has been substituted with a different letter like a code. (In some cases, nonletter characters — such as numbers — are used as substitutions as well, but this book uses only letters.) So within the sentence or phrase, for example, every *A* may be replaced with an *N* and every *S* replaced with a *P.* In order to figure out what the sentence or phrase says, you have to figure out each substitution — not an easy task!

Even with the following strategies in mind, sometimes solving a cryptogram is tough. Your best bet is often just to make guesses and see what sticks. But the tips offered here should at least help you refine your guesses.

TIP

» **Use a pencil.** Because you're bound to be making guesses at least some of the time, you want the ability to erase and guess again if you discover you've made a mistake. And keep scrap paper close by.

» **Know that no letter substitutes as itself in a cryptogram.** The puzzle constructor won't try to trick you by using an *A* to represent an *A*, for example.

» **Remember that only one solution is possible for a cryptogram.** Part of the puzzle constructor's job is to make sure the sentence or phrase is long enough that the solution must be unique. In other words, you can't come up with two or more logical solutions to the same puzzle.

» **If a hint is provided, look at it first.** This book may offer hints that indicate, for example, how often a certain letter appears or where you may find a certain letter (at the start or end of a word).

Other puzzle constructors may give you a different type of hint. For example, a hint may be a phrase that's only partly encrypted, such as MICKEY PRTIN. When you figure out that PRTIN represents MOUSE, you then look for instances within the encrypted sentence or phrase where you can substitute *M* for *P*, *O* for *R*, and so on.

In other cases, the puzzle constructor may show you a few letters in the solution itself.

» **Look for one-letter words (if the puzzle has any), which have to be either *I* or *A*.** You could find an instance of a single-letter word being *O*, but that's pretty rare.

» **Two- and three-letter words should be your next targets.** Consider common two-letter words such as *an, as, at, by, in, is, it, no, of, on, or, so,* and *to*. Frequently used three-letter words are *and, but, for, the,* and *you*.

» **If you see an apostrophe in the encrypted text, you can guess that what follows it is an *S* or *T*.** *D* is also possible, but contractions such as *he'd, I'd, they'd,* and *we'd* aren't that common. If you see more than one instance of an apostrophe, and the letters before and after each apostrophe are the same, you can guess that you're looking at an *N* before each apostrophe and a *T* after it. (Think *can't, don't,* and *won't*.) If you don't see that repetition before and after multiple apostrophes, you're likely looking at possessives (ending in *S*).

>> **Double letters are also good places to focus.** For example, say you see RR in an encrypted word. You may not immediately know whether you're looking at an *LL,* an *EE,* an *SS,* or some other double-letter combination, but you can guess that *R* doesn't substitute for letters that aren't commonly doubled (such as *A, I, H, Q,* and *U*).

You can also consider how frequently each letter appears in the cryptogram. You can assume that if you see a letter only once, for example, it's probably not an *E,* a *T,* an *A,* an *O,* or an *N.*

WARNING

But going much deeper with *frequency analysis* (considering how often certain letters typically appear in the English language and comparing that with how often the encrypted letters appear) is pretty complex stuff and may suck the fun out of solving the puzzle. Hopefully, the tips in the bulleted list can help you solve a handful of letters, which in turn help you make educated guesses about a few of the words, which give you solutions to more encrypted letters and help you break the code.

REMEMBER

If you get stuck, make some guesses based on what you've figured out so far. And walk away if you need to — it's better to come back to the puzzle with fresh eyes later than to get frustrated!

Straightening Out Word Scrambles

You can play word scramble puzzles in various ways, including the following:

>> You look at a group of letters placed in random order and rearrange them into one word, using every letter. The words to be rearranged may be rather

short — between five and eight characters. For example, unscramble the capitalized word in quotations to solve this riddle:

Where a sauce may "THICKEN". _ _ _ _ _ _ _

Unscrambling words of this length isn't usually very difficult (although you could well get stuck). The answer to this riddle, by the way, is *kitchen.*

The difficulty increases along with the number of letters and words involved. For example, try to solve this one:

Where's a good place to see a "SCHOOLMASTER"? _ _ _ _ _ _ _ _ _ _ _ _

The answer is *the classroom.*

>> You solve a series of word scrambles similar to those described in the previous bullet, but various letters in those puzzles are circled. After you've solved the individual puzzles, you use only the circled letters to solve one more scramble: You rearrange them to create a word or phrase that answers a clue given by the puzzle constructor.

In this step, you're likely dealing with quite a few characters, and you're often creating more than one word. As with the examples shown in the previous bullet, the puzzle constructor usually provides blanks that show how many words are in the solution and how many characters are in each.

>> You look at a group of letters and try to create as many words as possible from them. You don't have to use every letter in every word you create. For example, if you're given eight letters, you can create words with three letters, four letters, and so on. The goal is to make as many words as possible, and the puzzle constructor may tell you how many words you're aiming for. The puzzle constructor may also set certain rules, such as "No two-letter words."

The strategies for approaching word scrambles are pretty straightforward:

>> If you're working on a series of jumbled words, look at each one in turn to see whether any words jump out at you. You'll be amazed by how quickly you can solve some scrambles; the human mind seems built for this type of task.

>> When an answer doesn't jump out at you, try writing the letters in a different order. Don't worry about creating a word right away — just putting them in a new order may trigger that "aha!" moment you're looking for.

>> If the "aha!" remains elusive, try grouping together letters in what seems to be a logical way. Consider how many vowels you have; if you have twice as many consonants as vowels, chances are the word begins with a consonant. Try putting together common groupings such as *ing, sh,* or *th.*

Keep rearranging letters as long as it takes to find what you're looking for. Eventually, you'll stumble onto a combination that makes sense.

SEEKING WORD SCRAMBLES

Test yourself with the word scrambles located in Chapter 6 as well as on these websites:

- www.word-game-world.com/free-word-scramble-games.html
- www.puzzles-to-print.com/word-scrambles/
- www.novelgames.com/en/scramble/

» If you're playing the type of scramble that asks you to generate smaller words from a larger one, be sure to look for words that can be pulled directly from within the words you've already created. For example, if you've written down *player,* be sure to also write down *play, lay,* and *layer.* You can also write down *pay, per, year, reap,* and so on, but the point is to notice the words that are already spelled out, in order, within the longer words you've created — they're your easiest finds.

Relaxing with Word Searches

As with crossword puzzles, you were probably introduced to word searches early in life. Most people work them in elementary school to reinforce their spelling and vocabulary lessons.

In case you've never seen one before, a word search is simply a grid of letters — in a square or rectangular shape — that contains hidden words. Your goal is to find and circle the words, which may appear horizontally, vertically, or diagonally within the grid. Some words may be written backward. Some word searches are constructed around a central theme, which means all the words you're finding are related to one topic.

How do you know what words to look for? The puzzle constructor usually provides a list — that's the case in this book. You may encounter word searches that don't provide a word list, in which case the puzzle constructor tells you how many words you're looking for (and whether they all relate to a certain theme). Those searches are more challenging, of course.

TIP

The puzzle constructor may let you know that the word search contains a hidden message (related to the theme, if the puzzle has one), which you discover only after circling all the words. To find the message, you identify, in order, all the letters you *haven't* circled. The letters form words that spell out the secret message.

Word searches are really low-stress. If a word list is provided, it's guaranteed that you can complete the search — no matter how large the grid or how many words you're looking for. How often in life do you get the satisfaction of knowing you're going to get the right answers? That fact makes working word searches fun. Plus, they're great for increasing your concentration and blocking out the world for a while.

Tackling the Crossword Grid

For space reasons, this book doesn't include actual crossword puzzles for you to work, but they're nearly ubiquitous — the nearest newspaper can get you started. Wherever you get your crossword puzzles, here are some suggestions for completing them:

>> **Use a pencil rather than a pen.** Some people disagree, insisting that working in pen is the only way to go. But until you get truly comfortable at working crosswords, don't give yourself a reason to stress about mistakes.

>> **Read through the clues one by one and answer those that seem obvious**. Even in the toughest puzzle, you're likely to find at least a handful of clues you can answer immediately.

>> **After you fill in the easy answers, go back and see whether any of the letters you've written down help you solve any of the other, less-obvious clues.**

REMEMBER

Take your time with this step, and don't get frustrated if answers don't jump to mind immediately. You're still getting familiar with the puzzle constructor's phrasing at this point. It's almost as if he has written clues in a dialect that's new to you; the more time you spend reading them, the better you'll be able to interpret what's being asked.

>> **If the crossword has a theme, try to determine whether every clue seems related to it.** If not, see whether you can identify the clues that relate directly to it, and work on those answers.

>> **If you're willing to use outside resources, identify clues that fall into the "Trivia" category.** They're often the easiest to solve by consulting a website or other resource.

>> **Look for clues written as plurals, and consider penciling in an *S* at the end of each grid entry.** You may end up erasing some of them (because plurals can be formed in other ways, of course — think *geese*), but that's why you're using a pencil!

TIP

If you find yourself feeling stuck, step away from the puzzle and go back to it with fresh eyes later. You may want to work multiple puzzles at the same time for this reason. When you're stumped on one, start a new one. By doing so, you expose yourself to various styles of clue phrasing, you start to notice that certain words — especially short ones — appear in lots of crossword puzzles (even though the clues differ from puzzle to puzzle), and you build your confidence.

And don't forget: It can be fun to bring your family members or friends into the mix. If you're truly stumped, give a tough clue to someone else to chew on for a while.

CLUEING IN TO CROSSWORD PUZZLES

Looking to test your crossword puzzle skills and further boost your brain? Check out these websites for some fun and challenging puzzles:

- http://games.aarp.org/games/crossword-easy.aspx
- http://puzzles.usatoday.com/
- http://games.aarp.org/games/crossword-expert/crossword-expert.aspx
- http://games.latimes.com/games/daily-crossword/

Chapter 6

Puzzles

Puzzles are labeled by type and difficulty level. Levels are Easy, Tricky, Tough, and Treacherous, "Easy" being (of course) the easiest puzzles, and "Treacherous" being the most difficult ones. When you finish solving all these puzzles, see the end of the chapter for the answers. Have fun!

Logic Puzzles

Put on your thinking cap to solve these logic puzzles! Each has just one answer. See Chapter 5 for tips on tackling logic puzzles.

Easy

 PUZZLE 1 How many times can a mathematician subtract ten from 100?

PUZZLE 2 Decipher this clue: YYYMEN

Tricky

PUZZLE 3 A woman gave birth to two boys on the same day, in the same year, within minutes of each other, yet they were not twins. How is this possible?

PUZZLE 4   Add one line, and one line only, to make the following statement correct: 5 + 5 + 5 = 550

PUZZLE 5   Alexander is a great magician, skilled in many things. He weighs exactly 199 pounds and is about to cross a bridge with a strict weight limit of 200 pounds. The problem is he is carrying three pieces of gold, each weighing 8 ounces each. The gold puts him 8 ounces over the strict weight limit. What does Alexander do to cross the bridge safely with all three pieces of gold?

Tough

PUZZLE 6   Two people stand on opposite corners of a handkerchief. They do not stretch or alter the handkerchief in any possible way. How can they both stand on the handkerchief simultaneously without having any possibility whatsoever of touching each other?

PUZZLE 7   Under what circumstance could a person walk along a railroad track, discover an oncoming train, and have to run *toward* the train to avoid being struck?

PUZZLE 8   Imagine this scenario. You have an extremely valuable item you need to send in the mail to an acquaintance. You have a special container that has the perfect amount of space for the item, but no extra space whatsoever. The container does, however, have a place for locks on the outside. You have locks and keys, but your acquaintance does not have keys to unlock any of your locks. How can you send the extremely valuable container using your lock and have your acquaintance eventually be able to open the package?

Treacherous

PUZZLE 9   In a remote country ruled by a brutal monarch, a man was sentenced to death. Feeling godly, the brutal monarch told the man he would allow one final statement. The monarch advised the man that if he lied in his final statement, he would be drowned, but if he told the truth in his final statement, he be shot by firing squad. The man thought, and made his final statement. Due to the statement, the monarch was forced to release the man unharmed. What could the man possibly have said?

PUZZLE 10 There is an English word that is nine letters long that can form a new word each time one letter is removed. In fact, it can change to a new word every time a letter is removed until only one letter remains. What is the word, and what is the sequence of words formed by removing one letter at a time?

Riddles

Each riddle here has just one answer. Think hard, and see Chapter 5 for information on good ways to approach riddles.

Easy

PUZZLE 11 What becomes larger the more you take away from it and smaller the more you add to it?

PUZZLE 12 What grows up at the same time it grows down?

PUZZLE 13 What gets larger as it eats but smaller as it drinks?

Tricky

PUZZLE 14 What has a foot on either side and another foot in the middle?

PUZZLE 15 Although it is always before you, what is it you can never see?

PUZZLE 16 What is constantly coming but never actually arrives?

PUZZLE 17 What goes up and down without actually moving?

Tough

PUZZLE 18 What is impossible to hold for more than several minutes although it is lighter than a feather?

PUZZLE 19 Girls have it, but boys do not. It's in your windows but not your walls. It's in everyone's life but not in anyone's death. What is it?

PUZZLE 20 There are two Ws in front of two other Ws. There are two Ws behind two other Ws. There are two Ws beside two other Ws. How many Ws are there in all?

PUZZLE 21 *Homonyms* are words that are spelled differently but sound exactly the same. One pair of homonyms is unique in that although they are true homonyms, the two words are also exact opposites of each other. What are the two words?

Treacherous

PUZZLE 22 You have a balance-type scale with two trays and nine seemingly identical coins, except that one of the coins is a fake. The weight of the fake coin is slightly less than the authentic coins. What is the easiest way to find the fake gold coin?

PUZZLE 23 What word can be read left to right, right to left, and can be written forward, backward, or upside down?

PUZZLE 24 What two English words have three consecutive repeated letters?

PUZZLE 25 It is more powerful than God. The poorest of the poor have it. The richest of the rich need it. If you eat it or drink it, you'll die. What is it?

Cryptograms

Here a phrase or sentence is *encrypted* — each letter is substituted with a different letter or character. To know what the sentence or phrase says, figure out each substitution. Hints are given for each puzzle. See Chapter 5 for more information on cryptograms, and keep scrap paper close by in case you need it.

Easy

PUZZLE 26 BJVAY JSN CYP FULBN BJVAYI FOCY QUV. ISULP JSN QUV IBPPK JBUSP.

Hint: *E* appears 5 times.

PUZZLE 27 UP YIGPBXW QB RQXG FNQXJNFD. FNPR ZIR UPYQZP AQGOD IF IVR ZQZPVF.

Hint: *E* appears 6 times.

PUZZLE 28 NOWY AJUSYSNN. AC AN COS ZWNC COLC LCCLFOSN ACNSUR CE COS GENC VZAUUALYC GSCLUN.

Hint: *H* appears 5 times.

PUZZLE 29 QD Q OLKG SLBG ND VZ SULBLSOGB, VZ BGIMOLOQNY XQWW OLKG SLBG ND QOPGWD.

Hint: *I* appears 5 times.

Tricky

PUZZLE 30 OA GOJ AFXZKRTFOAF OTF ZVNEFAYX KB YJTFA ZYL WJPPZYL FOJGF XOZX OTF VAZFJY TF GAZS

Hint: *H* appears 7 times.

PUZZLE 31 QCHPHKHN B ZHHV VBFH HMHNUBTBPY, B VBH RXQP OPWBV WCH ZHHVBPY LGTTHT.

Hint: The letter *B* is not used at all.

PUZZLE 32 FEIDF UVIE VSC JCDFJCAF. UVIE BJDFPXND BJKHF PD SNWW ON UVIE VSC JCDFNPR VG DVBNVCN NWDN'D.

Hint: *H* appears just one time.

PUZZLE 33 WAG MIER CGMCEG OAM ELTWGI WM QMWA TLHGT MP S PSKLER ZVSXXGE SXG WAG IGFW-HMMX IGLJAQMXT.

Hint: *X* appears one time.

PUZZLE 34 GSS LBO DOGTLYKTS HOALYUOALH YA LBO ZNFSX ZOYJB SOHH LBGA G HYAJSO SNPOSM GWLYNA.

Hint: *I* appears 6 times.

PUZZLE 35 VKMDM'Q SEVKYSF YS VKM HYTTGM EZ VKM DEPT ORV XMGGEA QVDYUMQ PST TMPT PDHPTYGGEQ.

Hint: *I* appears 5 times.

PUZZLE 36 VZO ROW YFKKXV LO MXGEAZOI UEVZXBV SCEYVEXK, KXC WFK MOCSOYVOI UEVZXBV VCEFGA.

Hint: *THE* appears only once.

Tough

PUZZLE 37 IYUYUSYI, XWYL MWY DYRJTJV ZMIAMZ WEZ ZMAQQ WY ZWTXZ WEZ SRJVZECY MT WRGQ MWY XTIGC.

Hint: One word ends with *O*.

PUZZLE 38 XHWZ QM KFXXCQKIG HUS SGFBI WHJOI RQGI MHFXJGIO DAHU XHWZ QM FUDIXXFLIUWI HUS HVFXFDT.

Hint: *F* appears 3 times.

PUZZLE 39 QWHYWBW YI VD KVI, VKPW MZVK U IYEW, UHH EWEQWDN VT IFW TUEYHX FUL QDWUJTUNI IVAWIFWD.

Hint: *THE* appears just one time.

PUZZLE 40 CQ HLI XCPP MYTRN ULVT FCUT MDSVYTRCRB FDT SJ, HLI'PP MYTRN PTMM FCUT ZDLYYCRB XLLN.

Hint: *G* appears 2 times.

PUZZLE 41 ZQA NXYOQTL DXOZ PKKALZPIUA ZX MXC KXDAO EYXD P ZQPVFESU PVC KQAAYESU QAPYZ.

Hint: *EE* appears one time.

PUZZLE 42 ZNO GHRF PV UBGL HRF NPROX NHD BZD FKHTSHJLD. XPA JHR QOZ LBJLOF SX H JPT HRF DZARQ SX H SOO.

Hint: *K* appears 4 times.

PUZZLE 43 YDGF L ZLF RGGR ODG DLFSYXQOOFE CF ODG YLNN, ODGXG QR MXCKLKNP L TDQNS QF ODG HLZQNP.

Hint: The letter *U* is not used at all.

Treacherous

PUZZLE 44 LSOQJDCIZFG PCD JLSD YJJOQ, MXF JDIG PACOCPFSO PCD NSSL FASE JLSD.

Hint: *K* appears just one time.

PUZZLE 45 NRL'W QRZRGGGRS SDCC IV IVQQVG QXEU EUH HVWQVGLEH HRO XEBV VBVG PURSU.

Hint: The letter *C* is not used at all.

PUZZLE 46 JSNI HLTEXV QS ESH ASUG MYAW; HLG VDSWGE RSIQ, HLG VLSH YIISR, HLG DYVH PTJG, YEQ HLG EGXPGAHGQ SDDSIHNETHZ.

Hint: *W* appears 2 times.

PUZZLE 47 C ZCQDNNF BQJV VUDA ECXACQHICXURX SDQ ZOJS AUR GRDXAX: ZCQDQYCDN VJOOCRX.

Hint: The letter *P* is not used at all.

PUZZLE 48 YD AGTTJDY TD HNNHEZCGMMS QDUT ZXH RJYK DN GMM JZT
ADBHQT DN GEZJYV GYK QHGTDYJYV GT NHGQ.

Hint: *B* appears just one time.

PUZZLE 49 ZNKQYNM OG UPY FKRKFOUM US RYNHSNC RNSRYNAM YQYD
BPYD GFKNYT PKAH US TYKUP.

Hint: *W* appears just one time.

PUZZLE 50 NHHNLBEQZBJ ZC OZCCAG WJ ONCB HANHMA WATXECA ZB ZC
GLACCAG ZQ NIALXMMC XQG MNNVC MZVA PNLV.

Hint: The letter *H* is not used at all.

Word Scrambles

Unscramble the capitalized word(s) in quotation marks to solve the riddles. See
Chapter 5 for more details on word scrambles.

Easy

PUZZLE 51 What some feel "ELVIS" does. _ _ _ _ _ _

PUZZLE 52 What some "ACTORS" hate to do. _ _ - _ _ _ _

PUZZLE 53 What mishandling "ROSES" can lead to. _ _ _ _ _ _

PUZZLE 54 How a "RESCUE" can make the saved person feel. _ _ _ _ _ _ _

Tricky

PUZZLE 55 Easy thing to do when one is "SILENT". _ _ _ _ _ _

PUZZLE 56 What "THE EYES" do. _ _ _ _ _ _ _ _

PUZZLE 57 What "THE IRS" thinks your money is. _ _ _ _ _ _ _

PUZZLE 58 What courtroom figures in "ROBES" are. _ _ _ _ _ _

PUZZLE 59 Simple thing to do with a "STIPEND". _ _ _ _ _ _ _ _

PUZZLE 60 What a student may be doing while a teacher is "TEACHING". _ _
_ _ _ _ _ _

PUZZLE 61 Where a sauce may "THICKEN". _ _ _ _ _ _ _ _

Tough

PUZZLE 62 Option for those with "BAD CREDIT". _ _ _ _ _ _ _ _ _ _

PUZZLE 63 This occurs when one is "PAST DUE". _ _ _ _ ' _ _ _

PUZZLE 64 Where's a good place to see a "SCHOOLMASTER"?
_ _ _ _ _ _ _ _ _ _ _ _

PUZZLE 65 What illegal auto "RACES CAN RUIN". _ _ _ _ _ _ _ _ _ _ _

PUZZLE 66 What "THE DETECTIVES" do. _ _ _ _ _ _ _ _ _ _ _ _ _

PUZZLE 67 What's "TWELVE PLUS ONE"? _ _ _ _ _ _ _ _ _ _ _ _

Treacherous

PUZZLE 68 What's "HOTTER IN DEGREES"? _ _ _ _ _ _ _ _ _ _ _ _ _ _ _

PUZZLE 69 PAYMENT RECEIVED! _ _ _ _ _ _ _ _ _ _ _ _ _ _ _

PUZZLE 70 What many people leave "SLOT MACHINES" with.
_ _ _ _ _ _ _ _ ' _ _

PUZZLE 71 Some people consider them to be "LIES. LET'S RECOUNT".
_ _ _ _ _ _ _ _ _ _ _ _ _ _ _ _ _ _ _

PUZZLE 72 What a "CURE FOR BALD MALES" may be.
_ _ _ _ _ _ _ _ _ _ _ _ _ _

PUZZLE 73 Some consider it "CRAP BUILT ON LIES".
_ _ _ _ _ _ _ _ _ _ _ _ _

PUZZLE 74 One in a group of "NOTIONS WE RARELY USE".
_ _ _ _ _ _ _ ' _ _ _ _ _ _ _ _

Word Searches

Try to find as many words as you can in each puzzle. Chapter 5 contains more information on word searches.

Easy

```
Y M C W J E Z Q K O O H T A E M Q O E U V
K E E T M A N A G E M E N T P F I P A L M
I C V U F O X T U P U A X Q V O H T J L X
P N J N D I D T N A D N E T T A V S T E C
E A X L O V L U F L D H G D Z V T S T T O
G D O F E C M Z J D A V E P H A O M S A M
R I X Y M J V B R S J L R Y F H Q J I I M
A U I E K L L I S O I L I F S G L A F C A
H G H W S B M I B V O C E U H N N X J O N
C I W R X Q S H E A W R P W O R K E R S D
A I E F K T O R C N E P M M J Q A X Y S T
Q V G T A L G I T H O M Q U W P Q T Z A H
T Y Y N D L E R C R E S L A B O R E R B Z
I G T E A K B J T U I U E V U X C G B X Q
L R R D I A O K G D W D J Y H O W X D O L
D N A H D B Y A E F G Z G E T K G W J A X
L Z X I E J E K D F N B L E N Y O L U W L
E Z C T I L I O X F G P Y H J T S N K M A
Q Q U E L C G V N F E B F V E D A R M O C
W Z K O K Y X K Q R D E R   H M O J D W B
C L C K S Y Q P F R E E Y O L P M E S Q K
```

PUZZLE 75

AIDE	EMPLOYEE	LIFT
ASSISTANT	FIST	MANAGEMENT
ASSOCIATE	GUIDANCE	MANUAL
ATTENDANT	HAND	MEAT HOOK
CHARGE	HANDYMAN	MITT
COLLEAGUE	HELPER	PALM
COMMAND	HIRED	SIDEKICK
COMRADE	HIRED HAND	STAFFER
CONVEY	JOBHOLDER	SUPPORT
DELIVER	LABORER	WORKER

```
Y Q Q K L Q E X S X J G S P S Q J S C Q R
N D P F E Q A R W N X W J I C Z U C C B D
X W B R G N K O P P Q Z G X O M S R Y G F
P Q O E Z J M M P O H N D P U Y I E Y W T
M J E D T V N A S U A K Y U O K O A Y S K
S A X W D U W L D L T E E R G T H M I P Q
R D C S E N L C M O C U O C A G G N L G B
B D L H Q L A A U S G A K K X T A Y Q U O
I R A T A L C P S S R A N N S O A H P X E
E E I R A N J O U G A I Z O H A L L O O T
U S M X D H D R M P W W C I K P R W P L K
D S E J P V S S S E M C X T J G Y G L Y A
I V I J B P N E H W A U S A V T R Q L S Q
X V S J V O U O N A N H J T Y S C T Q T X
T X O H N K C T D O K S R U S I T I E R T
T K O U U V F U Y T P E A L N N U E B U A
F I E E W U G O V E L I I A M G O G E C E
M T Y O V H R H Z L L C T S A O S A L O L
X E H C H I K S O H E L L O C U U M L U I
R D E H L I A H D J P Y S S X T B O O J M
W B T T G C X Q C D Z B X J H G Z H W X S
```

PUZZLE 76

ACCOST	HANDSHAKE	SHOUT
ADDRESS	HELLO	SIGNAL
ALOHA	HOLLER	SINGOUT
BELLOW	HOMAGE	SMILE AT
CLAMOR	JUMP UP AND DOWN	SOOEY
COOEE	MEET	TIP ONE'S HAT
CURTSY	OUTCRY	WELCOME
EXCLAIM	ROAR	WINK AT
GREET	SALUTATION	YELL
HAIL	SALUTE	
HALLOO	SCREAM	

```
B Q F X H A I M N T K T A G R E A T G J V
Y Y U B Q Z E P O R T L Y H E G C M Y F B
T Q T M S A J J H T Q Y T I S N E M M I Y
I R D C S G C L C O L O S S A L G B W W M
S D O U K W P W I C M X C S S J C N L E O
N Y R T T H D P D M L P L C T R A M K I N
E E V U U N Q U A N T I T Y Q Y K Q D G S
D C O R P N K M U Q T K S T X K L U B H T
H W Y E U R D Z C K U Z I U M J D B Z T R
Z A W K W A R D F H O I M T B T H I C K O
U I Q M V E V T N E T X E A E S M U G L U
D I M E N S I O N F S J Q S G O T F G H S
H H W T O V R E T T A M X Z G N H A M E S
R P R O D I G I O U S H X C P P I O N I T
S M Y M E X O B E S E G N F F B L T Z C J
Y S D F M I J Z F V C E F W M M N E U B E
S L A T U F E C N E L U P R O C B Y M D S
Q L G M L O N N I G G I J R J U E U D F E
S G A J O Y F S X R H Z D Q Q G E N Q K X
J S B T V I J H U A C R Z O V H L S O J C
M R P R G N E W K L D G C I N A T I T Q J
```

AWKWARD	IMMENSITY	PRODIGIOUS
BULK	LARGE	QUANTITY
COLOSSAL	MAGNITUDE	ROTUND
CORPULENCE	MAMMOTH	SIZE
DENSITY	MASS	STOUT
DIMENSION	MATTER	SUBSTANCE
EXTENT	MEASURE	THICK
GREAT	MONSTROUS	TITANIC
HEFT	OBESE	VOLUME
HUGE	PORTLY	WEIGHT

```
O C E S S A T I O N C R O S S O U T P K F
T Z W I P L L A C E R N G I C B F C R E F
E P H O T J C O W Z S U J M I T N E N K O
V X T D X A M B D N A M R E T N U O C V Y
N S G K L L K T C A R T E R O W L J G I W
E Z Q K L A D E P K C A B A I C L J L T V
T D E Z B L W G B R L S W T Y P A G Y I P
A J M H D E T A C A V F L O H Z N E F A M
D S H X K M W P A N C W F S H C D D I T E
I T S Z D A W H P N G K F U N A V I L E O
L Q I R O Z I K C U Q Y C P V N O R L K K
A K L E I Q M Q P L H B X E Q C I R U V R
V R B V X J C R P N O B Q R N E D E N O V
N E A E D E E J C M U R C J L V V P K E
I P T R A G L N P O Q Z Q E B P E O Z C R
N E S S M H A E C X K M Z D A D B W N O I
E A E E R U N G X G S P J E U K L U V N Q
G L S V L L D E V G D M N J O U O H W U X
A D I S C H A R G E D D Q S G N A F A H C
T T D L S G I O M U X N T J E D F S F V Q
E U N I T N O C S I D N A R O K H U N L P
```

PUZZLE 78

ANNUL	DISESTABLISH	REPEAL
BACKPEDAL	INVALIDATE	RETRACT
BREAK OFF	NEGATE	REVERSE
CANCEL	NULL AND VOID	STOP
CEASE	NULLIFY	SUPERCEDE
CESSATION	OVERRIDE	TAKE BACK
COUNTERMAND	QUASH	VACATE
CROSSOUT	RECALL	VETO
DISCHARGE	RENEGE	VITIATE
DISCONTINUE	RENOUNCE	VOID

```
L K W W T S L H J J E Y G I D L C I I Z Y
A Y V H S U T C E P S O R P A T A Q D P F
S H G C Z H O Z P E B M R J X F D E R E E
O J O E W N O I T P E C N O C X H O D F A
P X A M T Z Y I K M A L E D P X G F K H S
O L L E W A A N O I T A N I M R E T E D P
R B E H U G R D R N X I V M A F C I P E I
P U Q C F C D T K D X A T M J B R U C S R
C V J S L N R A S Z T K P S M E R C A I A
O G I J H O A M W C S K H R S P A E L R T
N D D O K I W B J Q A K E O O L R V C E I
T U P S T T U I H Q R J L S C J T I U E O
E E P Q H A P T D I S U E J E F E T L R N
M Z G Q R T A I S M T I L N N I I C A A T
P O E N K I P O B I M A J W I G P E T E B
L N G Y D G L N O O T L O F L U B J I G T
A Q F M G O A N X E B N P W T R K B O E U
T E J D F C N B R C E O E Z U I Q O N I Q
I G B P P Y D D E S I G N T O N Z G X K V
O W S I V E E T Q N I C L W N G S L X E O
N H E N N F P O T B U Q U G S I T L R I R
```

AMBITION	DETERMINATION	PLAN
ASPIRATION	DRAW UP A PLAN	POINT
CALCULATE	FIGURING	PROGRAM
CALCULATION	GOAL	PROJECT
COGITATION	HOPE	PROPOSAL
CONCEPTION	IDEA	PROSPECTUS
CONTEMPLATION	INTENT	PURPOSE
DEAL	MIND	RESOLUTION
DESIGN	OBJECTIVE	SCHEME
DESIRE	OUTLINE	STRATEGY

PUZZLE 80

```
W J P R P Q O E C J C T Y J L X T P R X E
Z T R D T U S K C I N B J Z F L D O L P Q
A Z S A M A E P Q T P T R G W I G H D N H
N R A E E H E V V N Y X A E Q S L S E A G
S M A R C S B G O E F I F A Z G T W D L U
Q S C P J W G N K M N G Y X L Z J E I N O
X N E S S R E I D P G O A H E A D L R E R
I Q L R G O F L A O E K H Q J D Z L T Y H
N R J O G P P A K L G E K L D J N I S B T
H O N C S O L C O E E A D J A V C H I B K
D T I N A E R S L V V G N I T N U O M N A
L R W S A T N P S E S I F K S E V I K Z E
A A U O N S C O I D V T K R B C L W T F R
K C V B R A C H G U Z A E W Q C O T L Z B
R P V I E G P E U R T M E P M U D V U A O
X X J M V S V X N P O U N H F Q O I E I L
P O E H F E A C E T S U X W I O R O S R C
J Y N R F U R T H E R A N C E I W G G P Y
L A H C N D J W T V D L T D S Q J A Z R U
H D H G R A D U A T I O N E V W G S R P A
T Z B I B C D U W U I N I O D Z J U W D Y
```

ADDITION	EXPANSION	PRODUCTION
ADVANCE	FURTHERANCE	PROGRESS
ASCENSION	GAIN	PROMOTION
ASCENT	GO AHEAD	REVIVAL
BREAKTHROUGH	GRADUATION	RISE
CATCH UP	GROWTH	SCALING
CLIMB	INCREASE	SPREAD
CONTINUE	INNOVATION	STEP FORWARD
CREATION	INVENTION	STRIDE
DEVELOPMENT	LOSE NO GROUND	SWELL
DISCOVERY	MOUNTING	
ELEVATION	MOVE UP	

Tricky

```
K W S U N T B I B X V L Z A A D P K C T L I S
Y L G Y Z D T N A T I S E H A N Z B O N U S E
F F O K A E R B S C G C T W M F D I N A N M M
L H C N H S P A B C I F P U W V E D S V N I M
U A A T E K U C U U L L N V O L I F I R A N A
F S G L P D S O A G A Y N N A C R G D E Y D L
H M U Q T L M W I V N I W D E E R O E S E F E
C T A O N Q K H E T T O E C V H O A R B V U R
T C R Z T H O E M K U P O V C S W X A O T L T
A E D B J I G E P X K A S S M A R T T W A R Y
W P E B O L C D M C P V C H K Q N B E E O J T
A S D D R U N I A E W D X E I Q O A H V V U H
H M U U A F I B L P B U T F Y M B U A I N D O
Y U D W H E N D T O V M P R U D E N T T H I U
C C A P P R E H E N S I V E Z O L E Q N G C G
Q R I Z H A E G R N W F E P I L O W C E I I H
E I Q H V C Q G K E R D I S C R E E T T Q O T
T C J B N W Y V A Z C E X L Z P I M I T Z U F
W C Y S A U E O V R S O C S K G Y L Y A B S U
N H T N R H U Z P L D V I N M V O E T Y W C L
D A V P Y Z S E L U M F X Y O P Y Q E A L E J
I R V J P Y K G K D J Q U B D C Y A P Z V A H
F Y A M U M F J Q K P V B L H Z R Y P X H H N
```

PUZZLE 81

ALERT	CONCERNED	ONGUARD
APPREHENSIVE	CONSIDERATE	POLITIC
ATTENTIVE	DISCREET	PRUDENT
AWAKE	GUARDED	REGARDFUL
AWARE	HALT	SOLICITOUS
CANNY	HEED	THOUGHTFUL
CAREFUL	HESITANT	VIGILANT
CAUTIOUS	JUDICIOUS	WARY
CHARY	MINDFUL	WATCHFUL
CIRCUMSPECT	OBSERVANT	WORRIED

```
M Y T E V O W E C P U O Q S F J K F U M X P L
R U Z Y U G E J O H X I S Y T H G I E X Z P R
F G Q S N Z X S D G U Y D W P E X T S S R N U
D O X I N B Y I E W D C H I J A C B T Z G H H
M G L W J F C T V F H A K L J V P R O J E C T
T S L H T H R K I E G P R R V E E E B U X J X
O B Z T B I M O H J W N G T F W T R U P S X V
S F H H D N E S R E T T A C S M S O H N S G X
C I G O Q R E O F C Z G X G S W L E P O R P P
P K F T O S S O U T W B C N T H O W F G I Y V
O A M R E T T A P S G F U I Y I O N S T K W A
C F N G M J P H Q S H M B L P C G O C L P V C
Z J S L U W C M B S U D D F B N A H T X R C V
S S G D Y N I M P E R K D M P E I S S D J D J
X W Q T U L P V R R M A G U C C X L T G A M V
P L T A H O C O I S B U J F B G O Z R E M O B
C O L L M C O T S P O I Z S Y U X B R L S W I
Q H U W K D N U J R G A P X G J H P S O S X V
J L P U R T S P G I C R R H H N S S F G A A H
S Y A Y N T H E L N F H M A Z U M L A J E R K
J J T H R O W Z K K I G M Q E Z I L W D N K H
Z M A N U D S F E L S T N Y P R H G A P I Q V
H O C Q J O J A G E H A T A T Y L F T E L K H
```

PUZZLE 82

CAST	HEAVE	SHOOT
CATAPULT	HURL	SLING
CHUCK	JERK	SLOUGH
DART	LAUNCH	SPATTER
DASH	LET FLY	SPREAD
EIGHTY-SIX	PITCH	SPRINKLE
EJECT	PROJECT	SPURT
FLING	PROPEL	STREW
FLIRT	SCATTER	THROW
GET RID OF	SEND	TOSS OUT

```
G Y L V U A C N Z Z D L U E F S H P X Y H M V
L G V X G M I Q M I H N M Y T I R A H C Y Z E
Y T I U T A R G S V S L N S Z A C V S P T P I
A V Z W K W S D Z E V K H D I Z N H S E I E N
P T A B G U E B L T R O V A F U Q O S N N C O
J L G E L N T F I G D V T T V P R F D O G N I
J B E P V A I H R O T S I Q A B V T S I I E T
Y O C H M S E V U E E K R C E O R C L T N C U
T N Q Q H Z T C I U L W L S E E S Z J A E I B
I U V O F K E S Q G D I T I F P M X W L B F I
N S A H Q U Q E E R T O E F B D Q O G B G I R
A W H F R G B X P P W T O F E E Y B M O R N T
M I M U X F A C A Y X V V T T P R X U A A U N
U D N I K L A U G P W A R L A K C A D I N M O
H Z Z I M D F T A F T A C D F Q I W L B T N C
E Y Q B O C R G N A E N G E N E R O S I T Y K
O X S L C O N L V H N B E O J J S L K S T L F
J L E E X Z N K G J P R O S C X A M F F N Y C
O D O V T U Z I F Q J D U U E D L I L T B C F
I X U V W R B R N B L E S S N R W L F A L L B
Z L W S E E U Q Z P P B H P H T P I R V R L C
I O D E P G F O F K N R C R I Z Y D L H Q O J
A K S U Z P C C C O J P R E Z V X E R L T W D
```

PUZZLE 83

AGAPE	CONTRIBUTION	HUMANITY
ALMS	COURTESY	KIND
GIVING	DOLE	LIBERALITY
ALTRUISM	DONATE	LOVE
BENIGNITY	DOUCEUR	MUNIFICENCE
BEQUEST	FAVOR	OBLATION
BESTOW	GENEROSITY	OFFER
BIGHEARTED	GIFT	PLUS
BLESS	GOODWILL	PRESENT
BONUS	GRANT	RELIEF
BOUNTY	GRATUITY	SERVICE
CHARITY	HELP	UNSELFISH

```
B D Q G K K O H A V C E V C C T E C K Z F U X
F O O Q O K G W B X F G Z I E Q J E L K Y Q M
Y M K K S U T T S B J Y T Y N X P A V R N K A
R R U F A T K C A S P S E H T I L B R X W L U
F N E L L R N M O M I R T H F U L E G H X U G
I I K E I Q I A V M E O T Y H P M U N A R D R
N Y N P H A Q Q I T C P W O N Y X J I P B J Z
B B Z G B C M T A R Q Z X L C U C S O P J S K
Y J N L O Q P L D E B O N A I R E F G Y U C D
Y L E W G O E K P O S I T I V E E U Y G F Q O
D S L P V Z D E I Z W L L V L U R N S O J U U
F F A O Z V Q S I X D B U O M Z F C A L S H L
N T C E J C Y U P R W E I J U E E O E U L A L
S J W E D Q Y H R I J A R W G Y R P K C U P A
U U R M S N Z A Y K R E X U L T A N T K F P I
O B N N A C A M R Y P I X I T M C H T Y E Y V
I I G N M X T E R I G S T B E A M L N Z E A I
R L U H Y O Y I E I J Z A S A I N Q A Z L S V
A A X B G I A I Q R H D R J N D Q D Y J G A N
L N O H G L V M N P F R I E N D L Y O Y M L O
I T T P R H W S L A I N E G V O B G U O N A C
H F J B G M D O A T R E J O I C E V B L G R S
L I G H T H E A R T E D Y Z E E R B D V K K G
```

PUZZLE 84

AIRY	EXULTANT	JOYFUL
AMIABLE	FREE AND EASY	JUBILANT
BEAM	FRIENDLY	LAUGH
BLITHE	GENIAL	LIGHTHEARTED
BREEZY	GLEEFUL	MERRY
BUOYANT	GOOD-NATURED	MIRTHFUL
CAREFREE	HAPPY AS A LARK	OPTIMISTIC
CHEERY	HAPPY-GO-LUCKY	POSITIVE
CONVIVIAL	HILARIOUS	REJOICE
DEBONAIR	IN GOOD SPIRITS	RIANT
EASYGOING	JOLLY	SUNNY
ELATE	JOVIAL	

```
F V F Z M F W T M P X U N Z T M N D I M Y T P
M I A L C O R P I H E Z H N V Z V U B F E I P
P C E D U E A P W U T V H Y E D U U S R S M S
N T Q E V T M B V Y R I W N J D S T C E R E P
J U G C P E T S U R F B R O L T S C K D E J R
A O D L W C R E H R G E D N R A G A U N P Q E
H E R A L D W T R B P R H E C D L L D A S W A
E V I R A E I Q I O N U W D L Q O I G E R F D
L I S E P D D S R S T M A I Z L S R O M E L S
X G P L V R F T P W E O P P I T N W S O T E C
U Y D H A P H L F E R R U T R T N C L R N N F
C I R C U L A T E B R M V I L C E X A D I W S
Q Q A V Z O I M C C K S B R J L Q V O S E O B
U L X J Q B E I Z W R U E J N V E U J A O N V
P E R Q A S W Z R E T T A C S L T G C X S K S
B J Y E Q M H S S E X Q J U E T L W J O B E P
U Y T Q W R M A C A H M P Z G C Z A H C C K F
L E E I T C A F Q L Q G R R F O N Q E F N A R
Y B L A Z O N X N J U E H S I L B U P A U M I
A L L X W T E Y F Y N O I S E A B R O A D A S
P R O M U L G A T E K N H V E S R B X N Q P S
G F P U B L I C I Z E W O U T F Z O T T N W U
X N M L T P A Y K V W P E V E M A N A T E A E
```

PUZZLE 85

ADVERTISE	GIVE OUT	REPORT
ANNOUNCE	HERALD	RUMOR
BESTREW	INTERSPERSE	SCATTER
BLAZON	ISSUE	SEND OUT
BROADCAST	MAKE KNOWN	SPREAD
BRUIT	MEANDER	STREW
CIRCULATE	NOISE ABROAD	TELL
DECLARE	PLACARD	TRAVEL
DISPERSE	PROCLAIM	UTTER
DISTRIBUTE	PROMULGATE	VENT
EMANATE	PUBLICIZE	
EMIT	PUBLISH	

```
R Z J T C W G O A C Z B A U N I T E K G I S F
U K X S O K N U T C O Y F F F J B F N P D Y W
O U L N U P K T Q B K M D Q Q Q A L L M Y N X
F B M E P G E B W E G M P H L Q K G E H N T V
W W M Z L U S N N E G N U O N T N T M N T H G
S C Q O E B E L B M A R C S S L I D K X D E B
C P Y Q C U M I H E T A G I V E L C M K O S B
C T A I P Y E U I P K Y E J P L V I T C X I E
V O C I X I W S J G Y T W F H Y O L L A Q Z N
Y X R K R S W V J L V F R I N B U T X Y N E O
I O B R J U C O M P O U N D I M D F G J R N I
C E S E E C P J S E Y T C K P G Q I H I X C S
C O K X F L L T F H Y Z P T N P G X S Y R O U
O B I I C N A W Q C K X O V N K H J J L S M F
N N V U P P O T M A N G E I R E K J G Z Y M O
S X U T C P G C E T E M U L L I N T E R M I X
O S R G R I A J U T G T A U G K W U M R X X A
L S M J E O G R H A U E D T R N B I H O R D P
I B P S S M Y E T G M E R G E F I O D O M J Q
D I S T K C R J N N C O N N E C T M Z I R C A
A N D W H I O F T N E F Q P S J V T X J E V E
T D E I J I L R Z E V R R G Z M T R M A T C H
E V O N N C Y Z C Y A L E K O Y H M G X Q R B
```

PUZZLE 86

ADMIX	CORRELATE	MERGE
ALLOY	COUPLE	MINGLE
ATTACH	FUSION	PAIR UP
BIND	INTERMIX	PARTNER
BLEND	JOIN	SCRAMBLE
COMBO	JUMBLE	SYNTHESIZE
COMMIX	LEVIGATE	TWIN
COMPOSE	LINK	UNITE
COMPOUND	LUMP TOGETHER	YOKE
CONNECT	MATCH	
CONSOLIDATE	MATE	

Tough

```
M D N A E Z B A L M O E P I U U T W B I Y
X R O O I K A N L J B C F X A E C Y L A T
E V L J Y N I E E C L W A E W Z A D G S Y
V E T I Q A J O T K I F C R J I X N P P X
O S R N M S L P X T G Z S O D R E I C T G
E N M C A P E B C N A L P C M O L O T P C
A K U C E R O U C T T E B T F H G J G N W
K T A Q B D R S K M E P R A F T P N H D K
P P N M H T I A E M Z M K J L U J E L W L
L Y H I S E J V W U L O F L S A T V R Y L
N T D N O A A L H S P C I U U Q H E L B E
E U I S L P S M L I O O U V M K D K I T E
G D M E E X P Y C F Z F N P M R D N A R F
R R E R F G B A Z G P S X E O Z B N I A D
A F G N O P U T C I L F N I N U G U C R N
H E B I R C S E R P M I O U F I Q L I I A
C G B R C F Z N L K J A J F S E V V J R M
F R Y G E V W A G U O K O E R E W U Y D E
E R U J D A C C O H R O D L E T A T C I D
A S S I G N K T L B N O U U F K A D W X E
U Y C T C E R I D H V G D N A M M O C S Z
```

PUZZLE 87

ADJURE	DIRECT	OBLIGATE
APPOINT	ENACT	ORDER
ASSIGN	ENJOIN	PRESCRIBE
AUTHORIZE	EXACT	REQUIRE
CHARGE	FORCE	RULE
COMMAND	GIVE ORDERS	SUBPOENA
COMPEL	IMPOSE UPON	SUMMON
DECREE	INFLICT UPON	TELL
DEMAND	INSTRUCT	WARRANT
DESIGNATE	LAY ON	
DICTATE	MAKE	

```
G N T G G E N I L T U O A D O N G G P M Z
K N O I N Q I B L U Z J M E N L L C A C U
G S I I N I G O U J H L Z X O N U V G I F
N R K C T N K S Y S T E M O T D A P U E I
I D R E H C D C G D E V M U Z D N T U N G
T P E H L J U S A L U P V V U H E Z U E U
N S H L W E G R X B P K T A O P A S P R R
U B C Y F M T L T A E I F U O N X A I Q E
O T Y H S G D O M S Y D S E S W H E A G M
M E J K E I G R N R N I U I T S Y B N Q N
O M Z T R M Q L W X N O U T S A B I P U S
L P D U U D E U Y G J I C F I S T E H I T
K E D Y O C M W E Y Q D C A U T A S S A R
B R Y I T F D D Y C R X B T E B T H C P U
Q A M G N P X Z N K E V D S M L O A C A C
T M O E O L B I Z Q D M W B A F O V D A T
P E T H C M O O D Z R C C O K B U I L D U
U N A X U Y S B D W O A R D E Y R D O C R
H T N W E L A Q Q Q B S T Y D G S U M Z E
F R A M E V L C B I O E Q G S T M N B T B
F O Y S D I C D I S P O S I T I O N F I P
```

PUZZLE 88

ANATOMY	DISPOSITION	PHYSIQUE
ATTITUDE	FIGURE	SCHEME
BACKING	FRAME	SETTING
BODY	HOUSING	SHAPE
BORDER	HULL	SKELETON
BUILD	MAKE	STATE
CASE	MOLD	STRUCTURE
CHASSIS	MOOD	SYSTEM
CONSTRUCTION	MOUNTING	TEMPERAMENT
CONTOUR	NATURE	
DESIGN	OUTLINE	

```
R T X M U D U W W H S U L B R K U S G B R
E B T W M I N N G B F S V R U O S H Y C C
K G D S P A R K L E G L E A M J L M E G V
C R E J O P J X V A Z R W N Z Q Y O L A U
I E T C Y U L E K G M V A R T R K I C J T
L D A I F E R V O R M P R L E H M H I O E
F L M S N F I R E W P M M T I M G P O C U
O O I J X G R O G O L S T U E A Y I N H N
K M N G N L L T K L G I H R X T N E R S O
H S A Y H B Y E F G L Z B S I D C C H B I
G K Q B W T A K P G X L H S J S R I E F T
G V Z L C S F N W V O I N G E Y M K J J A
I E V W L K G T O N E V B T M X J A A I
D E Z I U F L A M E T W U S E O T S U G D
K H J S V A O L W N F R C R B I Y U J H A
E M H D E I U I I Y L V B Q N Q B A K N R
I J R W K C D Q G Y F E K P U I W U P S W
C D W M L N F N K B X U Z E Q C Z J R W C
E S S E N H S E R F M D A A Y A K W N P
Y U J Y O W O O B S B P R S E G U A C A A
C L K H Y I Y H V X S R U G J T E Z C W T
```

PUZZLE 89

ANIMATED	FLUSH	RADIANCE
BLOOM	FRESHNESS	RADIATION
BLUSH	GLEAM	RUBESCENCE
BRIGHTNESS	GLIMMER	SHIMMER
BURN	GLITTER	SHINE
COLOR	GLOW	SMOLDER
FERVOR	GUSTO	SPARKLE
FEVER	HEAT	TINGLE
FIRE	INTENSITY	VIVIDNESS
FLAME	LAMP	WARMTH
FLICKER	LIGHT	

```
C B K N A Z H G B Y U T Y R T G U I D E L
N E C L V W U D F U D H B W E H P C M Y X
R I D N A M M O C T Y I O U H H L F O T T
E U T N A D N E T T A K R N I A S C V I D
T S L R K L V T N J E L A E C R O U N F D
T L T B W F C I J Y F U O M C U E C Q R Q
A T B G W U Y T S W K D A R N T V E E O E
P N J Q D T F O X O L P B S T F P H T L Y
N X Z N F W V S V Y R U E O Y N P M D S S
K B O G U D V J C N T L C H Z E O N E A D
D C Y H G U B C Y L O E B P H T A C L C H
R G P Q D A R L E R L C G S G H K T E C E
Q U Q O I L T R I P L E D O M G R O S O J
Z Z L O G J E E M A R S H A L T F L L M N
M G P E A G U A K T R O C S E E A I S P D
L O S J U I X D M E W A N L A A A P S A C
N C N L I E B Z N U E L P U M C Y D Z N C
C E A I R O T N E M F P C T P H O W E Y I
W T A M T G Q L C K Z N E T A E D Z Y R J
E S U I T O I A W D Y Z W R O R Z N M Y N
O K C F W Z R T I M B G A K H J K A L T G
```

PUZZLE 90

ACCOMPANY	ESCORT	PATTERN
ADVISOR	EXAMPLE	PILOT
ATTENDANT	GATEKEEPER	REGULATE
BUTLER	GUIDE	RULE
COMMAND	HANDLE	SHEPHERD
CONDUCT	LEADER	STEER
CONTROL	MARSHAL	TEACHER
CONVOY	MENTOR	USHER
COUNSELOR	MODEL	
DIRECT	MONITOR	

```
D A O L P Q D X F V Q B T B D W P M B J X
B P Y G G J J G P Y C E O L A I O F F U B
P Q R Y D B T F D V N L Y U Z A G L E A M
L U T V S S E N T H G I R B Z J L X G H R
E U M N E S V E K Y A D I X L K K E G S B
N D C I J V U C C P R E M I H S F K I R
E A Q E C S Z E R N A M C Z N K I X Q L I
G H H E N E U C Z T A R B M G N B O O O L
E E O N W T X N N V A H W J E J P R S P L
C V K C E G L A Z E P P N S T X M G U D I
U A M C T J I G J E F O S E C C R G X Y A
V H J C N D G E F N P E E R J A E Z V R N
I S S O A Y C L L E V Y Z Q H W S F E U C
L R O R L E X E N A C V I E Q K H T R R E
H B K R I S X I X U A Y B Q E C S H I E B
G C N E T P F R E T S U L S F J I T V R P
Z V K C U E S U P W R G L C S S N O N A N
C O H T R N W H L N E H W C C S R O Q L E
L F W P I Y Z V I N R K M B X P A M G G E
L D V T P L U S F N H F Q T M L V S X L H
A F M M X Y H J J V E U D I J F Z E Z B S
```

PUZZLE 91

AGLEAM	GLARE	POLISH
BRIGHTNESS	GLAZE	PUMICE
BRILLIANCE	GLEAM	RADIANT
BUFF	GLOSS	REFINE
BURNISH	GLOW	RUTILANT
CORRECT	IMPROVE	SHEEN
DAZZLING	IRRADIANT	SHIMMER
ELEGANCE	LUCENT	SHINE
ENHANCE	LUSTER	SMOOTH
FINESSE	PERFECT	VARNISH

```
G L T N F Z S M T P J Q V J L Z S C J Y D
F Z V K C W H G V F F F O W O H S P F E W
F Q S U O P M O P V X N Q N S G A J X T A
M C A X G C E U A M I A J U J R J V A G P
W G H D D T E I R R T I C W A B F W I Q X
J C Z L A Y N T T D E T B D S V L B F W T
I N O L Q G R R R N E G E R M C K M F E V
J N F N L Z E U H E A H G E D L M Y T M Y
G N V O C Z F M K R T G T A A F T I C T B
I T R I D E J P U U X S O T W U K F H Y X
Z Y I J B S I E R H F G U R A S D G F K O
H Y K C O C U T S S Q A M L R E U U W Y D
S M V M J G S R E T S I O R B A B R E Y A
B B F K L C K L K M O L T E H R U V G O V
K P U D E F F U P V A U N T A H W P V T A
G H C R B P B S Z O F D S G J O G T H R R
R H V U R E M B L A Z O N A W T P G F T B
D F L A U N T F L S H A U P O A Y R S J R
R Q I W S A O I T J O N E X U I E A O F K
A S F O H C U M E K A M H G E R O M Y U W
E D H T D Y N M B E A R Z W L B K E M B D
```

PUZZLE 92

ARROGANT	HAUGHTY	SHOW OFF
BEAT THE DRUM	HOT AIR	SKITE
BLUSTER	INFLATE	STRUT
BOAST	MAKE MUCH OF	SWAGGER
BRAG	PARADE	TALK BIG
BRAVADO	POMPOUS	TRUMPET
COCKY	PROUD	VAINGLORY
CONCEIT	PUFFED UP	VAUNT
EMBLAZON	ROISTER	
FLAUNT	SELF-PRAISE	

Treacherous

```
Y D Z S G O E Z T W U W T Z G C C U T H P R Q
Y F I T A R L O L E G A L I Z E A D N V W V S
F U I D A O B D E L E G A T E P Y Z A A M B Z
T I F T U O A E T A T I C A P A C F R L M R E
F E H D R L N B M S X K I R H Q D N R I M B T
V L F E V E E O E W O M O M L O O R A D Q Q U
D T L P E H C V C C C V T N F R H C W A C M T
W J W U N X N G O P E U F O T R G L E T I X I
O B P T T I J M E Y S A X J L I Z N H E C M T
Q K F E R A M B Z T N E M U C O D S T L R D S
E J V R U I Y F I L A U Q I W O I J S N F M N
S C Z D S R L I C E N S E E W L U A E M V H O
I U O S T K W S W X R U Z T B A N Z M N B Y C
H I I N X Y G I M R N Y R A D C W P E E D P T
C O L G F C G C E T M K T T T R V Y Z Z E U I
N G U B I I R T E S P S I I I W Z P I I L I E
A G D W Z Z R Z N Q E B O L G I E Q L R T O E
R V S U Q A T M W O U N W I J R A A A O I F W
F T T R H S D R Z U I I P C Q U S E M H T G Y
X C A C C R E D I T V Q P A X S C L R T N H R
N K B Y S T R I S K C F X F I Q S H O U E E O
E E Y S F U I Z Y W Z N V S T O F P F A H W I
O Y A Q Q P O Q F S N A T F V X O I N M S D Z
```

PUZZLE 93

ACCREDIT	DEPUTE	FRANCHISE
APPROVE	DOCUMENT	INVEST
ASSIST	ENABLE	LEGALIZE
AUTHORIZE	ENDOW	LICENSE
CAPACITATE	ENDUE	OUTFIT
CERTIFY	ENTITLE	QUALIFY
CHARTER	ENTRUST	RATIFY
COMMISSION	EQUIP	SANCTION
CONFIRM	ESTABLISH	VALIDATE
CONSTITUTE	FACILITATE	WARRANT
DELEGATE	FORMALIZE	

```
K X T Q E L E I R U Y O D I C Y S I N A X H Y
B O Z R V C Y G U L P R B I Y G O C A S G X E
P P U Y J O U U E B J I L Q N W G V I R I P E
C P U Z J H K I H L X E Y I Y S X H D A V Z C
K T Y B L I R D X I G A E F G I G T R P Y Z N
S L G T Z B I A U N H B A K S J V Q A H Y D B
G M O F A V E N A I Q V F B A O O B U A I I Y
W N L G I T Z C N O V G S Q N I C G G E F E E
Z I O N I S N E C C J R Z Z G H Q P Y L O H Y
P E E M I C H A E L M A S N E B C C J R B B B
Z V H R Q J W P I B Q T F R L H X G X N S Y U
M E T S E Z A F G D D L U A O I Q N H P L H W
I I H B Z D X Z V Y A B E I L I G H T N A K Y
H L K Y K Y R T M G I R R O O O S I E M R M B
P E A A U P H O G M E S T F G O S V W E F A E
A B Y R M Z L L D H T Y C D Y A A I Y S S X A
R B U N C R F X T N I Q V N L E N D Z S K M U
E J M Z Y H R E D R O T S E H G I H F E A S T
S J Y Q T D A M B B M C O Z E B W E F N L D I
K A M N T P M N F E R M E D B L T A O G G W F
L H J O Q N X H G D K W O S Q A W R S E Q O U
I H Y Q E Y H X V E Z U F H J Z E Y O R P T L
E V O L X V K E U R L I Z C E L E S T I A L R
```

PUZZLE 94

ANGELIC	ETHEREAL	MICHAELMAS
ANGELOLOGY	FEAST	PURE
ARCHANGEL	GABRIEL	RADIANT
BEAUTIFUL	GUARDIAN	RAPHAEL
BEINGS	GUIDANCE	SECOND ORDER
BELIEVE IN	HEAVENLY	SERAPHIM
CELESTIAL	HIGHEST ORDER	THEOLOGY
CHERUBIM	LIGHT	URIEL
CHOIRS	LOVE	WINGED
DIVINE	MESSENGER	

```
D P H A T N E U L F F A Y F I H D T C C U O R
N B J L K A T V T A T J S M V K E Z E R R E G
M M C Q A E K T A Q C M M D N I T H C A X S C
M F D E K C O T S L L E W I H C E B H C S T T
H E S P I I H U E Q A X Y E M B A W E E N M C
P X L H N Y C C J S M H F J P T D S L L W C J
J T T P N G R C U X T W H G T W S M A N L Z C
E R U A Q E I R R M V D G L L I O R Q I O S O
L A M W L C A T A I S O E W V T E X H M U C M
B V B N T B O N V E C F X E T B Q M Y O Z K P
I A U D L N H V L L W H U O I S D T E K P R E
T G M E F S J B O U T S B L P K N T M S L R T
S A P N M U D X N U U B Y I L A N P B S E Y I
U N E B R P P A G O I H L L D U W T T G N Y T
A T R W K J L Q R K T L U N G J X M A R T A I
H X D Q B I N E G L I R U B X S S G O E Y V O
X C B U R F M N A N A B Z V L C I O C I R E N
E V N U C U A E G N A L W Y J V K R E D D G G
N U I N N R W O F M M S G Y C M B Z O P E R I
I I L B Z R V D U E P H S X H Z C S F H Q A F
W O B T M E K C T Y L O Z H U T I Y Q F O L I
N P L X R Z K P K F E Y S O G M S O Q K W Q C
X D G C O N F L I C T G B D E C D X U W C R T
```

PUZZLE 95

ABOUNDING	GREAT	PACKED
ABUNDANT	HUGE	PLENTEOUS
AFFLUENT	IMMEASURABLE	PLENTIFUL
AMPLE	INEXHAUSTIBLE	PLENTY
BOTTOMLESS	LARGE	RICH
BOUNTEOUS	LIBERAL	SPILLING OVER
BOUNTIFUL	MANY	THICK
BUMPER	MUCH	UNMEASURED
EXCESSIVE	NUMEROUS	WEALTHY
EXTRAVAGANT	OVERABUNDANT	WELL-STOCKED
FULL	OVERFLOWING	

```
E V T V E C L M X H T B R Y E E A P F S J S S
Z H N J N X O C Z X J K T L T L E B Z L Z X B
O P E Y R P U O R G M Z V G E D H L U K M E Y
U X K N T T W R V S S K A E K W Y P D X P G U
B V S I X W C D A M E K V L C P O U C N M S A
O L C N U U W K Z E K Y O M I T E T I T U R D
U N L A H E R D N Z Y Z U F H B U N C H L B K
Q S L M X Y Z K C L P N O I T C E L L O C I G
U B X A P R J G E Y D M I O V R F E W K E N B
E K V E K N O T W F E T M H Y F J A Z Z I V J
T P E O B A N D J L S V Y H K B S V A R A J A
F Q K U Y T F A C O W S N I O H Q W E Z S S B
Q T Q D U I Z X W C G B U O P N S H P C R D P
O F R C F G Y X A K Q W R R C I T O H J X G G
F L G B U F S Q Y A O Q P U T A T O A U Y D A
D T E I D D O A A L I O G G G F O O U P G E B
Z B Z U W I P B M L B T P X T L X Y Q R V A E
Q E A B O D Y R P G H M Z R N B G P S O T S V
N L J T R Q A F X R A G E P J C G H R X I O Y
P I C B C W E I O E V I H S O L E D I J K R Z
U P A R S H I N G R O V E Y S A V G U R W S J
H L G T D C G R R I L C O M P A N Y W P A C K
E Z N U M B E R R E T S U L C J D J Y O I T L
```

PUZZLE 96

ASSEMBLY	COLLECTION	HIVE
BALE	COMPANY	KNOT
BAND	CONVEY	NUMBER
BATCH	CROWD	PACK
BEVY	DROVE	PILE
BODY	FLOCK	POSY
BOUQUET	GATHERING	SCHOOL
BUNCH	GROUP	SWARM
BUNDLE	GROVE	THICKET
CLUMP	HEAP	THRONG
CLUSTER	HERD	TRUSS

```
Y G X L W N P Z G C M F D J G X W V H O D Q K
S Y I H P D M N Y O N E I D F U X G K R T Y M
K M E O H O L G O G S B P Z D H R V I K D S E
S A J L I P S N B P G I P N F V I Z J G Y E G
M E I S V Y L A I D T O B I O F Z C L F N D B
F T T J L E H L O N H F F A R L K M L S P Q D
X S F U S S C J U C G Y X T Y K Z S D Q V P V
S D T S N E F R G C N U E W B B Z O V K T J Z
M I E R U C S B O A U M R L K Z I M Y G W D K
O V O Q N H L E L S D Q O N O Z W B Z C R W V
F D X Y E C M E G P E G R D I A G E A E G T W
H M Q M D L X R A T M M M X D U Y R A P V P A
U Y Y F A O O B N R L R I Z Y V O R O A B K B
G T L D E U Q W X T C A D S G I Y D S D U A F
X O E H L D S P E P A H R X T O A P D G D N S
R U B C L Y S Y Y R L U A I R Y X A X S Y Q Y
U R I Q C C W Z W W I C V A P O R O U S Y G Q
Z W S O Y O A C U N G N P U P K X Y L M G R D
J O M K D H G A B T I D G M E Y V N O U H R W
T C R A K U F T K K N C A N L A H O M U I D H
Y U H T S A C R E V O D E S E R L M M P P X L
M S D J Y J S X R S U D F H B G J I P Z U C E
P V T L X G P F P X S S W I L U D Y Y F P J E
```

PUZZLE 97

CALIGINOUS	GRAY	MURKY
CLOUDY	HAZY	OBSCURE
DAMP	HEAVY	OVERCAST
DARKENED	HUMID	SHADOWY
DREARY	LEADEN	SOMBER
DRIPPY	LOWERING	STARLESS
DRIZZLY	MISTY	STEAMY
ECLIPSED	MOIST	SUNLESS
FOGGY	MOONLESS	UNCLEAR
GLOOMY	MUGGY	VAPOROUS

```
R Q M X T J N F W E R E S H I A B S F V R F J
F K W T L N W M I H K C A T C H N P K W G F K
P J E M Z Z S U W A U T M P W A T B C O H Z R
Q U N O P U N E T S A F T T G L Z D L I H E U
I G D K A P P R E H E N S I O N P L C S N V C
K R M N G K L F M A Q S P J C E G V K S G U D
O M C A R E T A A H I C C P N Z Y M N O R G N
O F O D L O H Y A L G Y T J C P N A M A K D Y
H C R V D W A N A V M Y S A Q U R E M S N H G
J L O X H J G S S J X C Y L I E Y R K Z U S X
I U F F F O S M F G C R E T J J C S G I S R E
R T E P N M S F T D E R Y H M G T P C D A S I
S C P T E D F J V V D D M T N R S Z A N V S S
N H O P R Q B Y M C E S C H F A I P S A L C W
A F R I U O G T M C I O Z L E S Q Z T T E E K
T I G L T R R K A Z O G B P I P R I P L U F P
C O J C P E A R C H F G O L K N I E E P S D C
H S N K A A B D V X H U B Y K V G R M Y J C L
J P E Q C M W Z G K N H B E A A T A G F L R I
E E P I E V T H N C C L F D Z M L F G E W P N
Z A K D Z O H G E N E L U M S C U W N A A E C
R S E E P E Q O D U X O M U P L D C D Y L W H
D B E K X F N V M R P P C J J S H R B S C O K
```

PUZZLE 98

APPREHENSION	CLIP	HANG ON TO
CAPTURE	CLUTCH	HOOK
CARE	EMBRACE	LAY HOLD OF
CATCH	ENSNARE	MAKE A GRAB AT
CLAMP	FASTEN UPON	POUNCE ON
CLASP	GRAB	SEIZE
CLAW	GRASP	SNAG
CLENCH	GRIP	SNATCH
CLINCH	GRIPE	TAKE
CLING	GROPE FOR	

Answers

Please do not read these answers until you've worked on the puzzles earlier in the chapter!

PUZZLE 1 Once. After that, the mathematician would be subtracting ten from 90, then 80, then 70 . . .

PUZZLE 2 Three wise men

PUZZLE 3 They were part of a set of triplets, the third child being a daughter

PUZZLE 4 5 + 5 4 5 = 550 (add one diagonal line to the second "+" to make it a "4")

PUZZLE 5 Alexander juggled the gold as he crossed the bridge, keeping at least one piece in the air at all times.

PUZZLE 6 One person stands on one corner of the handkerchief and closes a door. The second person stands on the corner of the handkerchief protruding under the door. With the door between them, they cannot possibly touch.

PUZZLE 7 The person is on tracks in a railroad tunnel walking toward the train and is close to the end when the oncoming train is discovered. The person must then run forward to clear the tunnel before the train enters.

PUZZLE 8 You send the container with one of your locks securing the container. Your acquaintance receives the container, and without trying to open it, attaches his lock next to your lock. He then sends the container back to you. You use your key to unlock your lock, remove it, and send the container back to your acquaintance with only his lock on the container. He can then open the container using his own key to his own lock.

PUZZLE 9 The man said, "I will be drowned."

PUZZLE 10 The word is STARTLING and the word sequence is: STARTING STARING STRING STING SING SIN IN I

PUZZLE 11 A hole in the ground

PUZZLE 12 A goose

PUZZLE 13 A fire

PUZZLE 14 A yardstick

PUZZLE 15 The future

PUZZLE 16 Tomorrow

PUZZLE 17 Stairs

PUZZLE 18 Your breath

PUZZLE 19 The letter *i*

PUZZLE 20 4, positioned like this: WW   WW

PUZZLE 21 Raise and raze

PUZZLE 22 Taking any eight of the nine coins, load the scale with four coins on either side. Whenever two sides are equal, the remaining coin is the fake.

PUZZLE 23 NOON

PUZZLE 24 Bookkeeper (oo-kk-ee) and sweet-toothed (ee-tt-oo)

PUZZLE 25 Answer: Nothing

PUZZLE 26 LAUGH AND THE WORLD LAUGHS WITH YOU. SNORE AND YOU SLEEP ALONE.

PUZZLE 27 BE CAREFUL OF YOUR THOUGHTS. THEY MAY BECOME WORDS AT ANY MOMENT.

PUZZLE 28 SHUN IDLENESS. IT IS THE RUST THAT ATTACHES ITSELF TO THE MOST BRILLIANT METALS.

PUZZLE 29 IF I TAKE CARE OF MY CHARACTER, MY REPUTATION WILL TAKE CARE OF ITSELF.

PUZZLE 30 HE WHO ESTABLISHES HIS ARGUMENT BY NOISE AND COMMAND SHOWS THAT HIS REASON IS WEAK.

PUZZLE 31 WHENEVER I FEEL LIKE EXERCISING, I LIE DOWN UNTIL THE FEELING PASSES.

PUZZLE 32 TRUST YOUR OWN INSTINCT. YOUR MISTAKES MIGHT AS WELL BE YOUR OWN INSTEAD OF SOMEONE ELSE'S.

PUZZLE 33 THE ONLY PEOPLE WHO LISTEN TO BOTH SIDES OF A FAMILY QUARREL ARE THE NEXT-DOOR NEIGHBORS.

PUZZLE 34 ALL THE BEAUTIFUL SENTIMENTS IN THE WORLD WEIGH LESS THAN A SINGLE LOVELY ACTION.

PUZZLE 35 THERE'S NOTHING IN THE MIDDLE OF THE ROAD BUT YELLOW STRIPES AND DEAD ARMADILLOS.

PUZZLE 36 THE GEM CANNOT BE POLISHED WITHOUT FRICTION, NOR MAN PERFECTED WITHOUT TRIALS.

PUZZLE 37 REMEMBER, WHEN THE PEACOCK STRUTS HIS STUFF HE SHOWS HIS BACKSIDE TO HALF THE WORLD.

PUZZLE 38 LACK OF WILLPOWER AND DRIVE CAUSE MORE FAILURES THAN LACK OF INTELLIGENCE AND ABILITY.

PUZZLE 39 BELIEVE IT OR NOT, ONCE UPON A TIME, ALL MEMBERS OF THE FAMILY HAD BREAKFAST TOGETHER.

PUZZLE 40 IF YOU WILL SPEND MORE TIME SHARPENING THE AX, YOU'LL SPEND LESS TIME CHOPPING WOOD.

PUZZLE 41 THE WORSHIP MOST ACCEPTABLE TO GOD COMES FROM A THANKFUL AND CHEERFUL HEART.

PUZZLE 42 THE LAND OF MILK AND HONEY HAS ITS DRAWBACKS. YOU CAN GET KICKED BY A COW AND STUNG BY A BEE.

PUZZLE 43 WHEN A MAN SEES THE HANDWRITING ON THE WALL, THERE IS PROBABLY A CHILD IN THE FAMILY.

PUZZLE 44 PERSONALITY CAN OPEN DOORS, BUT ONLY CHARACTER CAN KEEP THEM OPEN.

PUZZLE 45 GOD'S TOMORROW WILL BE BETTER THAN ANY YESTERDAY YOU HAVE EVER KNOWN.

PUZZLE 46 FOUR THINGS DO NOT COME BACK; THE SPOKEN WORD, THE SHOT ARROW, THE PAST LIFE, AND THE NEGLECTED OPPORTUNITY.

PUZZLE 47 I FINALLY KNOW WHAT DISTINGUISHES MAN FROM THE BEASTS: FINANCIAL WORRIES.

PUZZLE 48 NO PASSION SO EFFECTUALLY ROBS THE MIND OF ALL ITS POWERS OF ACTING AND REASONING AS FEAR.

PUZZLE 49 BRAVERY IS THE CAPACITY TO PERFORM PROPERLY EVEN WHEN SCARED HALF TO DEATH.

PUZZLE 50 OPPORTUNITY IS MISSED BY MOST PEOPLE BECAUSE IT IS DRESSED IN OVERALLS AND LOOKS LIKE WORK.

PUZZLE 51 LIVES

PUZZLE 52 CO-STAR

PUZZLE 53 SORES

PUZZLE 54 SECURE

PUZZLE 55 LISTEN

PUZZLE 56 THEY SEE

PUZZLE 57 THEIRS

PUZZLE 58 SOBER

PUZZLE 59 SPEND IT

PUZZLE 60 CHEATING

PUZZLE 61 KITCHEN

PUZZLE 62 DEBIT CARD

PUZZLE 63 DATE'S UP

PUZZLE 64 THE CLASSROOM

PUZZLE 65 CAR INSURANCE

PUZZLE 66 DETECT THIEVES

PUZZLE 67 ELEVEN PLUS TWO

PUZZLE 68 THE DESERT REGION

PUZZLE 69 PAID ME EVERY CENT

PUZZLE 70 CASH LOST IN 'EM

PUZZLE 71 ELECTION RESULTS

PUZZLE 72 DREAM FOR CUE BALLS

PUZZLE 73 PUBLIC RELATIONS

PUZZLE 74 NEW YEAR'S RESOLUTION

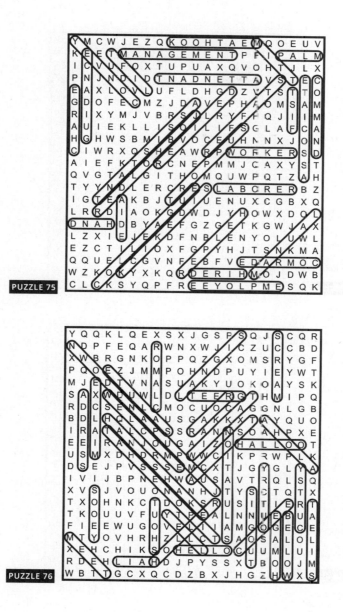

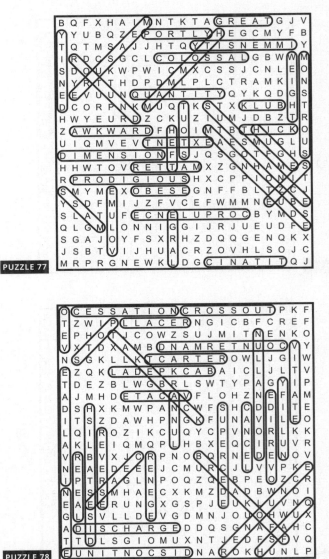

PUZZLE 77

PUZZLE 78

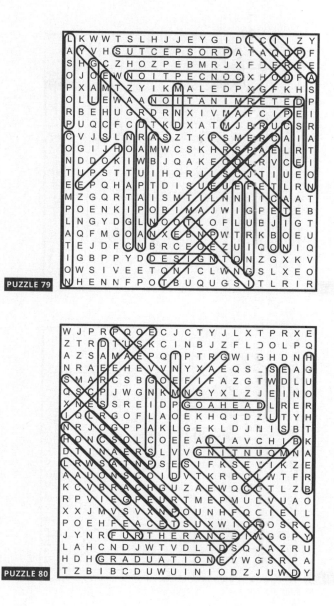

PUZZLE 79

PUZZLE 80

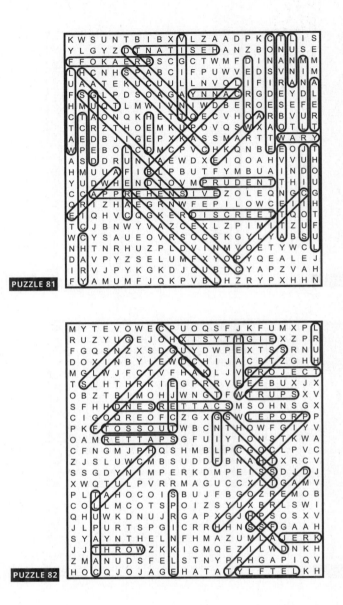

PUZZLE 81

PUZZLE 82

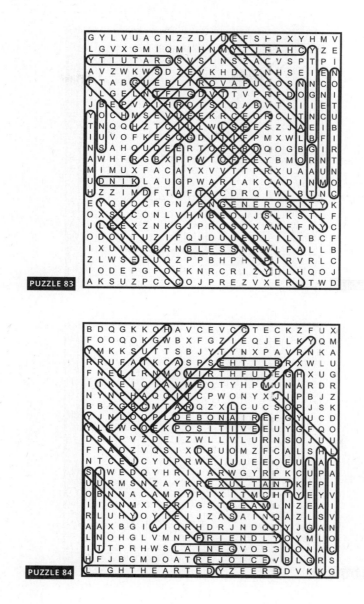

PUZZLE 83

PUZZLE 84

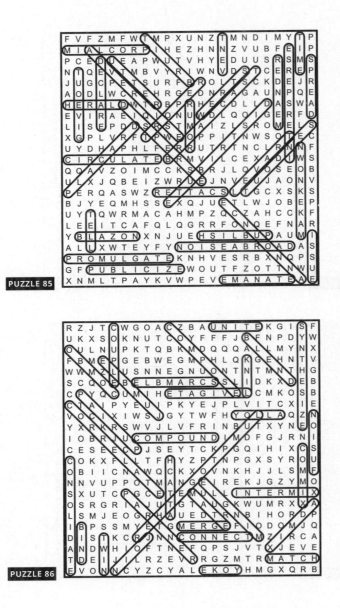

PUZZLE 85

PUZZLE 86

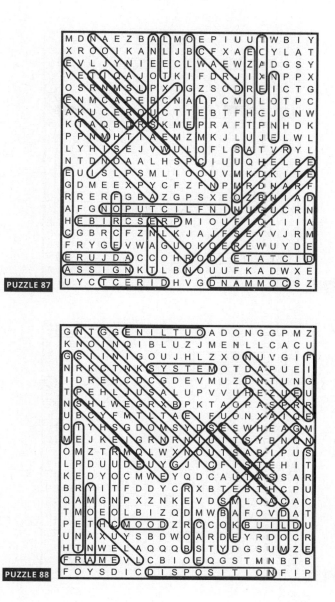

PUZZLE 87

PUZZLE 88

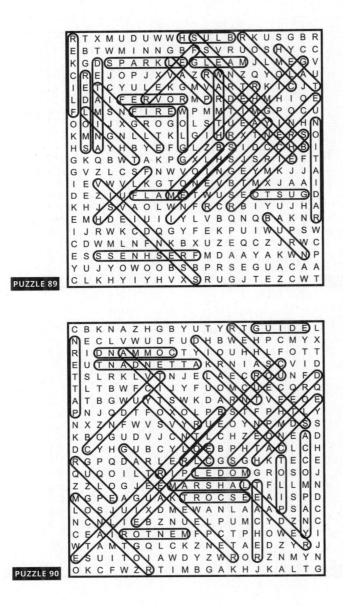

PUZZLE 89

PUZZLE 90

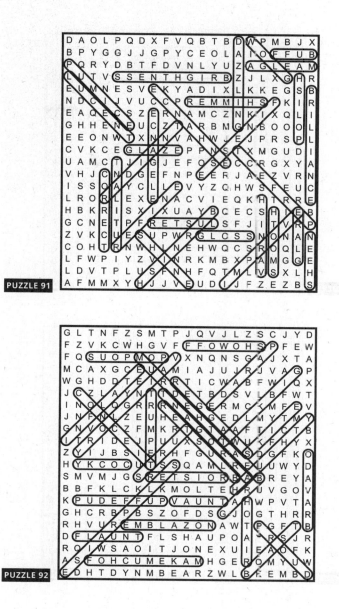

PUZZLE 91

PUZZLE 92

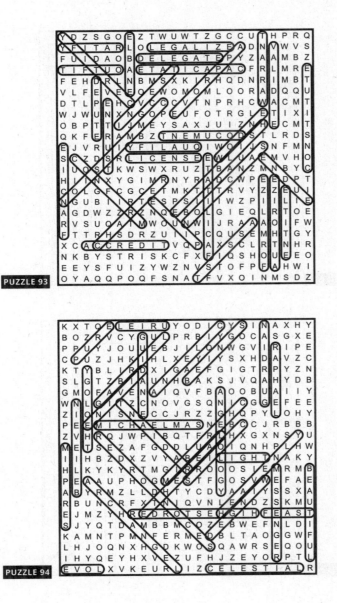

PUZZLE 93

PUZZLE 94

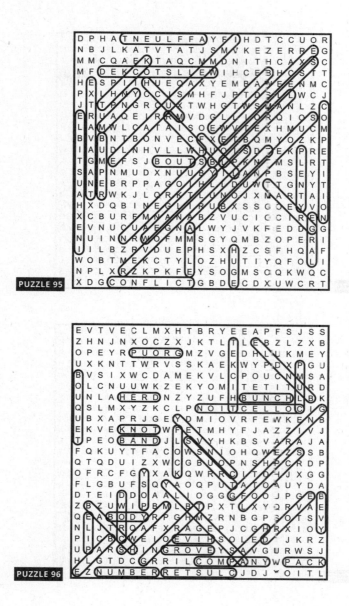

PUZZLE 95

PUZZLE 96

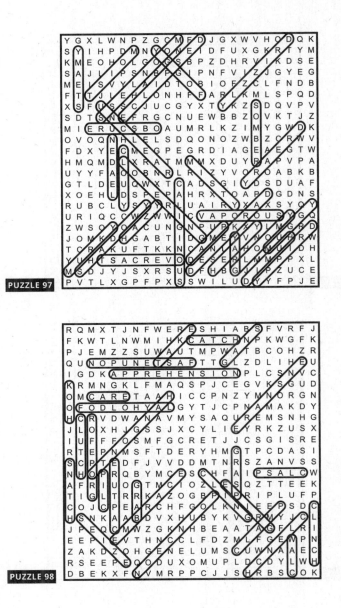

PUZZLE 97

PUZZLE 98

2

Boosting Your Memory

Chapter 7

Cultivating Your Memory Skills

N ine out of ten people say that they want to improve their memories. Are you one of them? Are you also one of the six out of ten people who tell pollsters that they've had the awkward experience of walking into a room — and forgetting why?

These numbers seem to suggest that planet Earth is experiencing an epidemic of declining memories, but that's not the case. Nearly everyone wonders from time to time whether he or she is losing memory power.

By reading this chapter, you're demonstrating that you want to have the best memory possible. Therefore, the job of this chapter is to show you how to improve your memory and how to avoid losing it. Find out what to feed your brain and what not to feed your brain to help you stay sharp and uncover a little more about how your brain works. You also discover your memory systems and how to expand their ability.

Wondering about Skips in Your Memory

Nobody's memory is perfect all the time. Everyone is forgetful and absentminded on occasion. Forgetting your keys and forgetting names are quite common. But frequent and more severe memory glitches are another thing entirely.

Types of memory loss that are cause for alarm include repeatedly getting lost on a familiar route home; having difficulty finding words to express yourself; having trouble identifying common objects; not knowing where you are; not knowing the time of the day; and asking the same question over and over again when you aren't hoping to get a different answer than you got previously.

WARNING

If you've noticed an abrupt and severe loss of memory, you should consult your doctor right away. This sudden and severe loss may be a symptom of a major health problem that needs immediate attention. You may be suffering from any of a wide variety of major medical problems, or you may be taking medications that have side effects that affect your memory. Don't wait before consulting with your doctor. This book isn't meant to be an alternative to first-line medical help.

Being present rather than absentminded

No doubt, you're like most people who've locked themselves out of the house or forgotten what they were going to buy after they arrived at the store. If you can't immediately locate your lost keys just by thinking, you retrace your steps and try to make associations when you enter each room. You may remember opening the refrigerator door to pull out a container of orange juice and putting the keys down on the counter so you could open the cabinet door to grab a glass.

Absentmindedness means what it says: Your mind is absent from where you are in the present. Don't expect to remember what you were doing if your mind was elsewhere.

Before going to bed each night, some people find themselves checking to see that the doors are locked — sometimes twice. They may waste this time not because they have obsessive-compulsive disorder (OCD) but because they were thinking or talking about something else while they checked the locks previously. Their minds were absent from what they were doing, so they didn't remember doing it.

TIP

If you don't need the exercise of checking the doors two times every night, make the check only one time with your mind in gear. Make it part of a routine, like brushing your teeth. Find yourself noticing the differences in the locks, like their firmness or loose hardware. Be mindful of the process of checking (see Chapter 14).

WARNING

Everyone makes mistakes when not focused on what he or she is doing. That's why distracted driving is so concerning. With all the smartphones, GPS systems, radios, and other technology in cars, you can easily shift your attention away from the road and cause an accident.

On the tip of your tongue

You're probably familiar with this experience: You're in the middle of a conversation, and even though you know the word you want to utter, you just can't think of it. Perhaps you know that the word starts with two letters, *T* and *I*, and you begin to start your search. Tianna? No. You know you're trying to remember a northern city in the country of Mali. You know where the city is located, you know how the name is often used as the epitome of remoteness . . . "Oh yeah, Timbuktu."

In fact, people in Timbuktu (or any other place in the world) have had this problem. In Korean, the term for the *tip-of-the-tongue* (TOT) phenomenon is called *hyeu kkedu-te-man-dol-da.* In Afrikaans, it's *op die punt van tong;* in Italian, *sulla punta della lingua;* and in Estonian, *kee le otsa peal.* (See if you can remember those expressions!)

The TOT phenomenon provides clues about the complexity of memory. When you feel that you know a word but can't seem to recall what it is, you're still recalling something. You know that a word applies succinctly to what you're trying to say.

These TOT experiences are common and may increase as you age. They have been described as being on the verge of a sneeze.

Your memory ability isn't set in stone. It's a skill that can be improved. There's a difference between whether you remember something in specific detail and whether you remember it at all. Like the TOT problem, you remember that you have that memory somewhere in your mind, but you just can't recall the details. That's what you need to retrieve!

TIP

If you want to recall a word that's eluding you, think around it. Look for associations — connections between that word and other ideas and concepts. (See Chapter 9 for more on association.) In the Timbuktu example, instead of focusing on the sound of the word (Tim . . . Tutt . . . Tot), think of the meaning of the word. With Timbuktu, you may want to focus on the metaphoric meaning of the word. Next, think about how the name has a unique sound that in many ways reflects its remoteness. By thinking around the actual word, the association helps you to narrow in to the word itself, hopefully sooner than later.

Unblocking the block

Chances are, you've forgotten your PIN or password. Most people have had the experience of feeling as if they know something but something else is "blocking" their memory. Some people even say, "I'm blocking on that." This blockage is similar to the tip-of-the tongue problem in the preceding section, but it doesn't involve trying to remember one thing like a name or password. Instead, it involves a more complex memory, such as the story Carol told yesterday at work.

The more you "try" to remember, the more you feel the block. Forcing your memory compounds the problem, as if you have your foot on the gas pedal and the brake at the same time.

THE ANCIENT MEMORY TRADITION

Before Gutenberg developed the printing press, which made the written word widely available, many great thinkers in history praised memory as a window to the divine. Being able to remember was a means of absorbing wisdom and disseminating information.

Pre-Socratic poet Simonides regarded memory as the means through which the arts and wisdom interact. He was the originator of mnemonic techniques to aid memory. Roughly a century later, Plato believed that knowledge is latent in our memories. (We already know, so all we have to do is remember.) He proposed that memory is what makes higher processes of thought possible.

The Romans, so dependent on Greek thought, cultivated memory techniques as part of their rhetoric (the art of using words). Cicero and Quintilian wrote books focusing on the techniques of memory that were used through the Middle Ages. The Roman philosopher and a teacher of rhetoric, Seneca, was said to be able to repeat 2,000 names in the order given to him. Several centuries later, St. Augustine boasted that his friend could recite Virgil backwards. And at the end of the Middle Ages, St. Thomas Aquinas was famed for having a phenomenal memory.

Throughout the ages, personal memory skills were revered as a means of absorbing and then sharing information. "External memory" became available only after the advent of the printing press and the subsequent proliferation of books. With books, people no longer had to memorize something to remember it. They could rely on written words to help them remember.

TIP

A good way to allow the block to ease up is to take your foot off the gas for a moment. In other words, stop trying. Take a brief break and a few deep breaths. Go do something else. If you're with other people, say, "It'll come to me in a minute." Talk about something else for a while. Allow your mind to wander. Before long, you'll likely pick up an association that triggers the full spectrum of memories you were trying so hard to dig up.

Clearing the Air of Random Noise and Ridiculous Ideas

Society inundates people with stimuli that demand attention. Email, faxes, cellphones, and the constant bombardment of commercials litter our minds and clutter our memories. Life was simpler in years past. Today's world puts more demands on your memory skills.

How many things can you pay attention to at the same time? Some people keep the television on all the time, thinking it's "only in the background." They mistakenly think that the distraction is "no bother unless I look at it." Some teenagers do their homework with loud rock-and-roll music blasting their ears. If you have a teenager at home, you've probably asked him to turn down the music, thinking it's interfering with his ability to remember what he's studying — and you're right.

Although he may think that he's taking in what he needs to remember, he is limited in how much he can actually absorb. Think of your brain as capable of multitasking, but at a cost. When you multitask, you spread yourself thin, diluting your attention. If your attention is compromised, so is your ability to remember.

If you want to remember the important stuff, you need to know where to focus your attention. If you say, "I need to pay attention to everything," you're being unrealistic. You need a way to sift the wheat from the chaff. That is, you need to develop the ability to pay attention to what's important and allow yourself to forget what's not important.

Before you can improve your memory, you need to be realistic about your potential memory capabilities. You can improve your memory, but you don't want to set impossible goals, such as the following:

>> Being able to pay attention to several things at once and remember them all with great accuracy

>> Expecting to improve your memory without effort

>> Assuming that you'll remember everything you've ever experienced

Sorting fact from fiction

You've probably read sensational claims saying that you can "boost your brain-power" by following some supposedly foolproof method. Some hucksters claim that you're using only 10 percent of your brain, which is false. The more precise way to address this issue isn't by how much (quantity) of your brain you're using but how well (quality) you're using it. If you improve the way you use your brain's thinking ability, your memory can improve greatly.

Some so-called experts offer a single method to improve memory. They claim that with their single tool, you can master any memory task and impress your friends. Of course, the idea that a single tool can improve your memory is ridiculous because your mind is far too complex.

Some claim to offer "the secret" to a good memory. But just as there's no single tool to improve your memory, there's no one secret to explain memory. In fact, what psychologists know about memory isn't a secret at all. You just haven't discovered it yet.

Some claim that your mind can become a gigantic sponge that takes everything in and won't forget anything. This notion is not only impossible but also absurd and impractical. Would you really want to remember everything? Imagine the debris of memories you'd have to wade through when trying to retrieve one important memory. You'd have to search through lots of rocks before you found the diamond you were looking for. The reality is that you must forget some things so you can remember others. You need to get rid of the unimportant chaff in order to retain the important wheat. Otherwise you'd drown in a sea of extraneous and trivial information.

Your working memory must be short for you to maintain an ongoing presence in the world. Because your working memory rapidly cleans its slate, it becomes available for the next things you need to experience, learn, and remember. Then, with crucial information now stored away in long-term memory, you can move on to the next moment.

Imagine how cluttered your mind would be if you remembered each and every detail of your life all at once. Instead, your mind transfers important information into long-term memory for later use, making it ready to collect new information as you experience it.

The good-news/bad-news reality

The good news about your memory is that a wide variety of techniques *can* improve your memory skills. The bad news is that no single trick, pill, or secret magically moves your memory into high gear. More bad news: Laziness makes your memory skills dull. However, if you apply yourself, you have tremendous opportunity to improve your memory. Such effort doesn't have to be torture. It can be fun, stimulating, and invigorating.

REMEMBER

The old adage "use it or lose it" applies to your memory. Using it is fun and rewarding. So why just sit there not using it and end up losing it?

Modern psychologists have shown that your IQ score isn't a limit but rather a starting point for intellectual growth. You can permanently raise your IQ score by continuously pushing yourself to learn new things, which exercises your brain and expands neural networks. Your memory skills form the foundation for most of your thinking abilities. Therefore, by improving your memory skills, you become better able to reach your thinking potential in many ways with the added benefit of increasing your IQ.

Improving Your Memory

Never fear! Improving your memory isn't difficult if you do the following:

>> Understand how your memory works (see Chapter 8).

>> Keep your mind sharp with intellectual challenges (see Chapter 6).

>> Pick up memory techniques, such as mnemonics (see Chapter 9).

>> Apply your memory skills regularly throughout your day (see Chapter 14).

Discovering what your memory skills are

To improve your memory, you need to know what memory is and isn't. You need to understand the facts about your memory and discard the myths.

Some of the following facts may surprise you:

>> **Your memories are constantly reshaping throughout your life.** They aren't snapshots of information, frozen in time. Throughout your life, you go through all sorts of changes: You mature, learn from previous mistakes, and even get tainted by unfortunate experiences. Your perspective changes over

time, and the lens you use to look back at your memories colors those memories. Your brain is complex and always changing, which affects the way you look at your memories. Those memories are subject to modification by everything new you experience and learn.

>> **Memory is a skill that you can cultivate and improve upon, no matter what your age, intelligence level, or socioeconomic class.** Memory isn't something that you have or don't have. It can't be lost or found like a flash drive. However, it's dependent on your brain structure and especially the connections between different parts of your brain. If you experience brain damage, your memory can be affected (depending on what parts of your brain were injured).

>> **Your entire brain works together as one system.** Each memory has input from a wide variety of different parts of your brain. Memories aren't stored in one place in your brain. Your brain codes memories as a system of different units. Some areas of your brain have unique talents in coding memories in special relationships. Whereas others areas code in words. These brain areas work together, so when you're trying to remember a 1969 Volkswagen Beetle, you remember the shape with one area (the right hemisphere) and the words *Volkswagen Beetle* with another area (the left hemisphere). See Chapter 8 for more details.

The more dimensions and parts of your brain you can involve in a memory, the more easily you can remember it later. Remembering a 1969 Volkswagen Beetle is easier than remembering a 1969 Plymouth Valiant because of the shape of the Beetle and the word *Beetle* give you a visual context (see Chapters 8 and 9).

>> **Your brain possesses several key parts that play a major role in forming the foundation of your memory.** The *hippocampus* is the key part of your brain that moves short-term memories into long-term storage. (You can find more details about the parts of a brain and how they relate to memory in Chapters 1 and 8.)

The short-term memories you move into long-term memory depend largely on three factors:

- **Your attention:** Generally, a measure of short-term memory

- **The meaningfulness of the information:** The more meaningful or relevant the information, the greater your chances of remembering it

- **How well the memory fits into what you already know:** A foundation of prior memories helps with new learning

>> **Your memory depends on your attention.** Your memory simply doesn't work unless you're paying attention. But when you're paying attention, your brain is capable of extraordinary mental gymnastics. So paying attention helps you stay sharp.

YOUR PHENOMENOLOGICAL LOOP

At the interface between short-term memory and long-term memory, a *phenomenological loop* acts as a gateway for new words. You use this loop when building your vocabulary, either by learning specific new words or when earning a new language. The phenomenological loop is centered in the left hemisphere of your brain. If your left prefrontal cortex is damaged, you have trouble expressing words (output). If the back part of your left temporal lobe is damaged, you have trouble understanding what's being said to you (input).

Maintaining your brain properly

Your ability to remember depends on a number of factors, the first of which is maintaining a healthy brain through adequate nourishment, exercise, and rest. To ensure that your brain works at an optimum level, follow these guidelines:

>> **Eat a balanced diet.** What you eat affects your brain's chemistry. Eating the right foods gives your body the building blocks to manufacture brain chemicals called *neurotransmitters.* Neurotransmitters affect not only your mood and ability to think clearly but also your ability to remember.

   A simple, balanced meal consists of a carbohydrate, a protein, and a fruit or vegetable. Eating a balanced meal regularly can provide you with a sound foundation for your brain and its memory. (See the chapters in Part 4 for more on nutrition.) There is growing evidence that excessive carbohydrates may contribute to cognitive deficits.

>> **Get regular exercise.** Exercise enhances your memory because it helps your brain receive the nutrients it needs. Every time you exercise, you increase your respiratory rate, your metabolism, and your energy level. Regular walking for exercise can actually increase your memory and your brain volume over years of sticking to it! (For more details on exercise and the brain, see Chapters 19 and 20.)

>> **Get enough sleep.** You need a certain amount of sleep at night to function properly. But did you know that regular restful sleep actually improves your memory? While you sleep, your brain is busy reorganizing your memories. By going through all the stages of sleep, including REM (rapid eye movement) sleep, your brain builds relationships between your new and old memories. Studies have shown that being deprived of sleep for 24 hours decreases memory and concentration. So be sure to let your brain get the sleep it needs for proper thinking and memory building! See the section "Sleeping well to remember" later in this chapter for more detail.

>> **Rest well.** The amount of sleep you get is only part of the equation; the quality of your rest also counts. To promote restful sleep (and avoid insomnia), cut down on sugar and caffeine intake (especially at night), avoid alcohol, maximize bright light in the daytime and minimize it in the evening (including light from electronics), and exercise three to six hours before going to bed.

Avoiding food, drink, and drugs that depress memory

Foods, drinks, and chemicals that your brain is exposed to have major effects on your memory. If you eat junk food loaded with sugar, you set yourself up to crash, finding yourself full of anxiety and short of short-term memory. Similarly, if you drink too much caffeine, the liquid anxiety scatters your thoughts and shatters your memory ability. Keep these two guidelines in mind:

>> Avoid sugary foods (like candy, cookies, pastry, cakes/icing, and regular soda pop). Remember that regular soft drinks contain 39 grams of sugar in one 12-ounce can.

>> Minimize caffeine.

If you treat your brain badly, your long-term memory can erode, and your brain will struggle to remember. You can avoid devastating your memory by staying away from the following substances:

>> **Alcohol:** It kills not only your brain cells but also what they produce — a good memory. Alcohol affects memory of all types: short-term, long-term, and working memory. Chapter 16 has more on this topic.

>> **Drugs:** Marijuana can cloud your memory and cause you to lose the ability to focus. The chemical found in marijuana, called *tetrahydrocannabinol* (THC), causes brain cell loss in the hippocampus, resulting in memory loss. Other illegal drugs — heroin, LSD, methamphetamines — all have serious harmful effects on brain health and memory.

>> **Neurotoxins:** These poisons include petrochemicals, solvents, pesticides, and herbicides. They kill brain cells when you're exposed to them.

Working your memory systems

Whatever your age or background, you can improve your memory skills using numerous memory techniques, such as *mnemonics* (cues that you can use to remind yourself of information). Some mnemonic techniques include peg, loci, and the story and link systems. Chapter 9 defines these terms and provides other details.

TIP

Mnemonics can remind you by associating a letter or number to information. For example, if you're trying to remember the names of the Great Lakes, use the first letter as a cue. By using the word *homes*, you can remember each of the lakes: Huron, Ontario, Michigan, Erie, and Superior.

Priming: To retrieve "lost" information

A process known as *priming* can also help you remember. When you're priming memories, you remember some related things in hopes of remembering the "lost" information. For example, if you forget where you've put your keys, you retrace your steps. You try to remember where you were and what you were doing, priming out the memory of where you left your keys.

You can structure information all sorts of ways to help you remember it. If you organize the information by serializing, chunking, or even rhyming it, you can remember it.

TIP

When you chunk information, you break it up into bite-size segments that are easier to remember. For example, when you learned to remember your social security number, you didn't memorize it as one long chain of nine numbers; you broke it up in three chunks: the first three numbers, the middle two, and the final four.

Associating: When you can't remember the person's name

If you're like most people, you've felt embarrassed because you've blocked on a person's name. You've probably seen a few people at the supermarket and found that, though they look familiar, you can't remember their names. Chapter 4 talks a lot more about remembering faces and names.

You can help your ability to remember a person's name by associating it with one or more of the following:

>> Her occupation

>> A physical characteristic, such as height or weight

>> A unique facial feature, such as a sharp chin or red hair color

>> The way she moves

DRIVING IN THE FAST LANE

Because stress can be a drain on your memory skills, job stress can bog down your memory while you're at work.

Have you ever felt like you're juggling several tasks at once while trying to do your job? It's one thing to be under pressure because of the workload but quite another if the pressure you feel is self-imposed.

In today's fast-paced society, where people talk on cellphones while they drive through fast-food restaurants before going home to simultaneously check email and voice mail, you're at risk of feeling stressed and scattered. Your memory skills are also stressed and scattered. If you import this scattered lifestyle into your work and constantly try to juggle four or five tasks at once, you needlessly deplete your short-term memory.

You may say, "Yeah, but it's hard to maintain a slower pace than everyone else. The go-go mentality is contagious!" But if you don't resist, your memory at work can't reach its potential.

The bottom line is that each of the tasks you juggle gets only a portion of your attention. None of the tasks can be completed in a thorough and comprehensive way. You find yourself forgetting what you were doing on each task. They begin to blur together.

Take a few steps back from the frenzied social climate and resist the temptation to juggle. Follow each task through to its completion before going on to the next task.

Putting your memory skills to the test

You can use memory techniques at school, at work, in social situations, and during exams. Waiting until the last minute to study and trying to "cram" the information into your memory in the last hour before you need it is one of the worst ways. On the other hand, if you organize and spread out your studying time, you'll do much better.

TIP

Some of the same tips students use to effectively study for exams can help you improve your memory outside the classroom:

>> Stretch out your learning instead of waiting until the last minute to cram.

>> Organize your studying by starting with the outline and main subject areas and then homing in to the specific.

>> Cover the main points and the "*main* main" points by using underlining and highlighting.

>> Get feedback early and adjust accordingly.

>> Use mnemonics, symbols, and visual images.

Keeping your mind sharp

By maintaining a mind free of distractions, you increase your readiness to remember. Anxiety, depression, and sleep deprivation can put a damper on your memory skills (see the chapters in Part 3 for a lot more on this).

Learn to relax and stay alert enough to form memories. Relaxation techniques include progressive relaxation, meditation and/or prayer, self-hypnosis, imagery, and exercise. See Chapters 16 and 17 for more on stress reduction and meditation.

Your memory skills depend on your ability to pay attention. If you're not mentally present because you're distracted, you wish you were somewhere else, or you're anxious, then you can't code into memory or retrieve memories to your fullest ability.

TIP

Try *mindfulness* (discussed in Chapter 14) to be fully present. Not only does this approach improve your memory because of your attentiveness and clarity of mind, but it also improves the quality of your life. Mindfulness involves being fully attentive to the moment, feeling and savoring every sensation, and slowing down to live in the present or the "now."

So get going. Cultivate your presence in the now. Clear your mind of distractions and benefit your memory.

Chapter 8

Discovering How Your Brain Remembers

You possess the most complex organ on the planet. Your brain is more powerful than any computer — it can leap beyond any PC in one single memory. Your brain remembers with feeling, with the rich context of experience. No computer can do that.

In this chapter, you find out how your brain forms memories, how your brain remembers, the stages that each memory goes through, and how the pathways through which your memories are coded illustrate the dynamic and ever-evolving nature of your memory skills.

Navigating Through Your Hemispheres and Lobes

Your brain has two large hemispheres: the left cerebral hemisphere and the right cerebral hemisphere. As Figure 8-1 illustrates, each hemisphere consists of four lobes: the frontal, temporal, parietal, and occipital. These lobes provide a great deal of area to store memories. Each of the four lobes offers a unique talent and way of coding memories, as explained later in this chapter.

The right hemisphere controls the left side of your body, and the left hemisphere controls your right side. The crossover of nerve fibers from the right side of your brain to the left side, and vice versa, takes place deep within your brainstem in a structure called the *medulla oblongata.*

The right hemisphere is adept at storing visual and spatial memories. Spatial memory involves anything that occupies physical space — remembering the shape of this book, for example. The left hemisphere is more adept at storing verbal memories. The two hemispheres work together in everything you do.

Introducing your right hemisphere, the emotional side

Your *right hemisphere* has more extensive connections than does your left hemisphere with certain other parts of your brain, especially the limbic system. In other words, the right hemisphere can pick up the emotional climate of conversations better than the left hemisphere. (For more on the limbic system, see the section "T is for temporal: Remembering what you hear" later in this chapter.)

The band of fibers that bind your two hemispheres together is called the *corpus collosum.* This band serves to connect neurons from each hemisphere, enabling them to work together to add dimension and depth to everything you do and think.

Interestingly, the corpus collosum is denser in women than in men, which means the two hemispheres work more evenly together in women. Perhaps the denser corpus collosum is one reason women seem to be more intuitive by accurately sensing the emotional climate of a conversation or situation.

In spite of some hard-wired gender differences, people can become more balanced in the way they lead their lives. You may be familiar with the caricature of a "typical" man — someone who isn't in touch with his feelings, not wanting to be bothered by the nuisance of emotions. Yet, in the 21st century, men are becoming more sensitive and women are becoming more assertive. The sexes are beginning to achieve more balance through changes in culture and in the way people think.

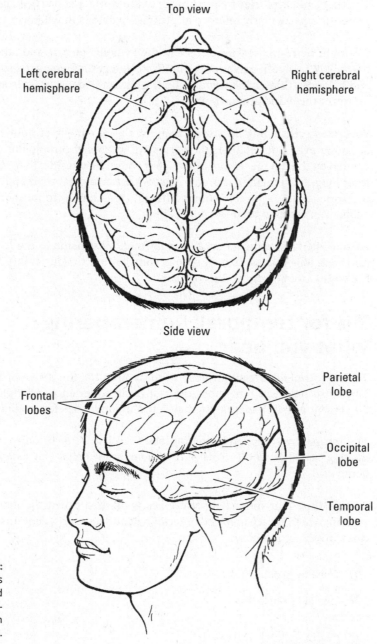

Top view

Left cerebral hemisphere

Right cerebral hemisphere

Side view

Frontal lobes

Parietal lobe

Occipital lobe

Temporal lobe

FIGURE 8-1: The brain consists of the left and right hemispheres, each with four lobes.

Illustration by Kathryn Born, MA

Meeting your left hemisphere, the orderly side

The *left hemisphere* tries to bring order to the world and has been called the interpreter. It's particularly talented at picking up details in whatever you learn.

The right hemisphere tries to take in the "whole" picture and takes information literally. When both halves of the brain work together, you get a system of checks and balances that enables you to be flexible and adaptive. This system lets you interpret the world around you.

Your memories don't lie stored away in the basement of your brain, lost and decaying over time. Rather, memories are dispersed throughout your brain and colored by the unique talents of the lobes where they reside. In fact, as people age, their long-term memories aren't what wither away; it's their ability to store new memories that may become more difficult. (See Chapter 10 for more on how older people can sharpen their memory skills.)

Each of the two hemispheres adds a different dimension to the lobes it contains. And each lobe makes its own unique contribution to your ability to think, sense the world around you, and remember.

T is for temporal: Remembering what you hear

Your *temporal lobes* contain your primary area for the sense of hearing. These lobes also help you remember the gist of an experience. All right-handers and 80 percent of left-handers use their left temporal lobes for language.

The top part of your left temporal lobe is called *Wernicke's area*, which involves making sense of words. This part of your brain helps you comprehend what's being said.

Deep within your inner temporal lobes is an area called the *limbic system*. This system, which is very involved in recalling your emotions, contains two key structures involving memory:

>> The amygdala

>> The hippocampus

CARL WERNICKE'S DISCOVERY

In 1881, physician Carl Wernicke found a man who suffered from damage to the upper-left temporal lobe with what later became known as *Wernicke's aphasia*. The term *aphasia* refers to the loss of the ability to understand or express speech (caused by brain damage). This patient had *receptive aphasia* (also called *sensory or fluent aphasia*); he couldn't understand what he was being told or what he read, but he could speak fluently. The only problem was that the words he spoke made no sense. Because he didn't understand the meaning of spoken or written language, he was unable to create understandable speech.

The almond-shaped *amygdala* plays a big role in recording the emotional context of your memories. When you experience an event, your amygdala records your emotional reaction to it and provides a memory of what you felt at that time.

A person with a damaged amygdala has trouble remembering the emotional context of an event and may underreact or overreact to it. For example, if she again meets a person who was emotionally abusive to her in the past, she may react to him with indifference — as if she has totally forgotten about the incident despite her memory of abuse. People with normal amygdalae would more likely show fear and anxiety at such a meeting.

The amygdala evaluates the personal significance of new experiences, adding emotional feelings to a memory. If fear is appropriate, the amygdala kicks activating hormones into gear to help you be alert to danger and records the emotional reaction to that trauma. People with post-traumatic stress disorder (PTSD) have persistent, difficult, emotion-based memories of their traumatic events.

Another part of your limbic system that's centrally involved in memory is your *hippocampus*, shown in Figure 8-2. The hippocampus is the key structure that moves short-term memory into long-term memory. If an experience is important enough, your hippocampus codes the memory and stores it away so that you can recall it later.

If your hippocampus receives personally significant information, it marks that information and puts it in your long-term memory. Regardless of whether an experience is positive or negative, having that experience repeatedly will cause your hippocampus to transfer it to long-term memory.

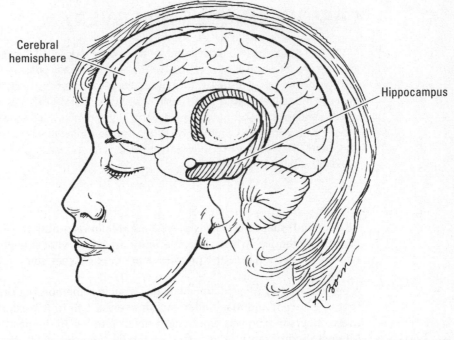

Cerebral
hemisphere

Hippocampus

FIGURE 8-2:
The hippocampus
moves short-term
memory into
long-term
memory.

Illustration by Kathryn Born, MA

Here's an example of this principle at work: The folks who produce television commercials may or may not know specifically the role of your hippocampus, but they do know that repetition equals retention. When you repeatedly see or hear a particular commercial — especially when laced with a catchy tune or silly joke — you have trouble forgetting it (even if you try). Then, two days later as you walk down the supermarket aisle, you may find yourself humming the tune for bath soap and end up with six bars of it in your grocery basket.

Your hippocampus is tucked away deep within your temporal lobes. If it's damaged in any way, you'll have trouble moving short-term memories into long-term memories. (See the related sidebar "H.M.'s new day.")

F is for frontal, as in "frontal assault"

Your *frontal lobes* contain your primary area for initiating movement. These lobes are more complex than that of any other species on the planet and involve far more than movement. The frontal lobes represent what's most human about you: This part of your brain helps you form a sense of identity. Although all mammals have frontal lobes, your far frontal area represents the biggest evolutionary leap.

This area is your executive control center, which is the last to mature as you grow up. That's why teenagers often struggle with questions such as "Who am I? How do I find my place in the world?"

The back parts of your frontal lobes direct your movements and mature before other parts do. Your first movements came from major muscle groups, such as your limbs, and then came fine motor control in your fingers. You could grab toys before you could put toys together.

The lower parts of your left frontal lobes help you elaborate memories before they're encoded in your long-term memory. This area doesn't work well when you get distracted. Absentmindedness occurs when this area isn't working to its fullest potential, such as when you're trying to pay attention to too many things at once.

H. M.'S NEW DAY

One of the most famous neurosurgery patients of the 20th century was someone referred to by his initials, H. M. This patient suffered from severe epilepsy until a neurosurgeon removed most of his temporal lobes and all of his hippocampus and amygdala.

The surgery was a success with respect to curing H. M.'s epilepsy; he no longer experienced seizures. Unfortunately, a severe side effect occurred: H. M. lost his ability to create new memories. Though his long-term memory was intact for events that took place in his life before the surgery, H. M. was put into a perpetual state of "now." He couldn't transfer new information from his short-term memory to his long-term memory. He couldn't form new memories from his life following the surgery. When distracted, he would lose all his short-term memory.

If you were to meet H. M., you'd probably enjoy a good conversation with him. However, if you walked out of the room for a few minutes, he'd forget who you were when you came back and greet you as if you were someone completely new to him. He was in a state of perpetual novelty — everything was new to him. H. M. could watch the same movie repeatedly, as if he had never seen it each time.

Despite having both his right and left hippocampus removed, along with the inner parts of both temporal lobes, H. M. was able to deal well with his immediate world. He was intellectually capable; he scored as well on intelligence tests after the surgery as he had done before.

Going up on the outside of your left frontal lobe, you come to an area that helps you find the words you need when you're speaking. The name for this area is *Broca's area.* People with damage to Broca's area have *expressive aphasia,* also known as *non-fluent aphasia,* which is the loss of the ability to express themselves with spoken or written language. People with expressive aphasia can comprehend what is said to them, but they can't formulate words from their thoughts to speak to others. (Don't worry; just because you periodically get stuck recalling a name doesn't mean you have expressive aphasia.)

Your left frontal lobe is quite involved in reflecting on your memories and trying to make sense of them. In depressed patients, the left frontal lobe is underactive. Depressed people tend to focus on negative memories that cloud their perception of the future. In general, every effort you make to initiate or inhibit a behavior involves your frontal lobes. Damage to this area can make you either listless or terribly impulsive.

Believe it or not, back in the 1930s one of the treatments for severe mental illness was a *frontal lobotomy.* In this procedure, doctors would sever the frontal lobes from the other parts of the cerebrum. Patients who had this procedure tended to became listless and unmotivated.

P is for parietal — sensory stuff

The primary area of the *parietal lobe* deals with sensory feelings and spatial relationships. Your parietal lobes help you know where on your body you've been touched and where you are in space. This *sensory area* lies at the very forward part of your parietal lobes, bordering your *motor strip* (the area of your far back frontal lobes that controls your movements). Together, they're called the *sensory motor strip.*

The back parts of your parietal lobes help you sense yourself in space. Your right parietal lobe is especially adept at remembering shapes and forms. Damage to this area causes difficulty remembering spatial forms. When asked to draw something he saw ten minutes before, this person's right parietal lobe will falter, while his left parietal lobe won't. As a result, his drawing may show many details of what he saw (left parietal lobe) but none of its form (right).

O is for occipital — visual stuff

Your *occipital lobes* allow you to see. If your occipital lobes are damaged, you can become blind even if you have functional eyes. The occipital lobes in some animal species are much larger than that in humans. For example, gorillas have much larger occipital lobes so that they can visually detect details humans would miss in the dense forest.

The occipital lobes don't have a monopoly on your visual memories, however. Even your memory of a specific object — for example, the chair at your friend's house — is dispersed throughout your brain. You remember the elegant shape of the chair (right parietal lobe). You remember how firm it felt as you squirmed in it during your friend's long-winded monologue (the sensory motor strip). You remember looking back at the chair as you were leaving the room and noticing its deep cinnamon color (the occipital lobe).

Brain Cells: Zooming in for a Closer Look

Your brain is an electrochemical organ that functions partly via electrical firing and partly via chemistry. The word *electrical* doesn't mean your brain has electricity running through it. Rather, it highlights the fact that your brain cells (*neurons*) fire impulses on and off like an electrical current. But to communicate between neurons, your brain relies on chemistry. Your neurons communicate with one another by chemical messengers called *neurotransmitters.*

Understanding your chemical messengers

You have more than 50 types of neurotransmitters operating in your brain enabling you to think, feel, and remember. Your neurons specialize in particular neurotransmitters.

Some neurotransmitters, such as *dopamine,* activate you, keeping you alert; others, such as *GABA,* make you mellow and calm. Still others, such as *serotonin,* help keep you from becoming depressed. The activating neurotransmitter *norepinephrine* both elevates your mood and helps you code memories.

The neurotransmitter *acetylcholine* plays a critical role in learning and memory. When acetylcholine becomes blocked in some way, your memories suffer. On the other hand, when acetylcholine is present and accounted for, your ability to remember improves. Acetylcholine is lacking in brains of Alzheimer's disease patients. The drugs to treat this condition work by increasing acetylcholine in the brain to help with memory.

All these neurotransmitters work by traveling across a gap between your neurons called a *synapse.* Every time you remember a new piece of information or learn a new fact, changes occur at the synaptic level. Those connections between neurons adjust to accommodate the new memories. The more times you repeat the experience or recall the memory, the stronger those connections become.

TECHNICAL STUFF

On one side of the synapse, a neuron's presynaptic membrane contains little sacs filled with specific neurotransmitters that release if the neuron fires. When a neurotransmitter is released, it floats around in the synapse until another neuron picks it up or until the one that released it reabsorbs it.

Sometimes, these connections provide memories you'd probably rather forget. The neurotransmitter norepinephrine helps record into memory particularly emotionally laced events. If you suffer from post-traumatic stress syndrome, you get a big boost of norepinephrine each time the memory occurs. As a result, you experience intense and intrusive replays of the memories of that traumatic event.

Your brain is a charged, constantly evolving, electrochemical organ; it modifies itself as you live your life. Two other ways your brain changes over time as you experience and remember are through the processes of myelination and dendritic branching. The next two sections cover these processes.

Coating your axons

Myelination and dendritic branching involve parts of the neuron, shown in Figure 8-3. At the heart of your neuron lies its nucleus. Other parts of a neuron consist of the axon, which sends out information, and dendrites, which pick up information. (For details on dendrites, see the section "Branching out for new thoughts and memories" later in this chapter.)

SYNAPSES HELP FORM MEMORIES

Your neurotransmitters operate in your synapses to form memories. Here's how the process works: Neurons release neurotransmitters, which other neurons pick up by finding binding sites that are receptive to the neurotransmitters. The neurotransmitter has to have the right chemical structure (like a key) to get into the receptor (the lock) of the post-synaptic membrane. If the chemical structure is correct, the neurotransmitter unlocks and opens a channel in the new neuron, making that neuron fire. The firing neuron sends its own neurotransmitter out into another synapse, and the entire process goes on and on.

Another way to look at the way neurotransmitters work is to visualize differently shaped pegs all trying to get through a pegboard with assorted shapes cut out. Only the round peg can get through the round hole on the board, the square peg through the square hole, and so on. When the right peg gets through the right hole, it sets off a reaction. (In the case of a neurotransmitter that enters a neuron, the reaction is that the neuron fires.)

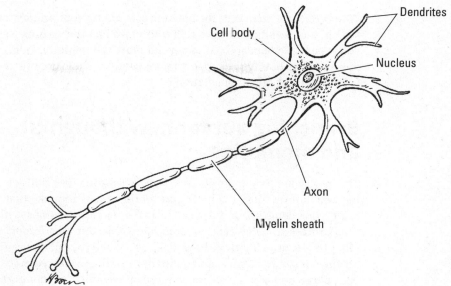

Cell body

Dendrites

Nucleus

Axon

Myelin sheath

FIGURE 8-3:
A neuron has a nucleus, axons, dendrites, and myelin sheaths.

Illustration by Kathryn Born, MA

TECHNICAL STUFF

As you grow and mature, your axons become *myelinated.* In this process, axons develop a coating of a fatty substance. These coats, or myelin sheaths, help your axons have better conduction to send information more efficiently and quickly.

Think of ripping off the wall paneling in an old house to reveal the electrical wiring. You can see that many of the wires are exposed because their insulating coating is frayed. These wires probably short out constantly, and chances are good that an electrical fire may develop.

In another wall, you find newly installed wiring that has plastic sheaths as insulation. No shorting out or fire to worry about here. You then realize that this wall feeds the plug that services the TV, which never seems to fail. The bad wall wiring services the plug in the kitchen where you plugged in your toaster, which always seems to go on the blink. Now you know why taking the toaster in for repair last week didn't fix the problem. Just like wiring in the house, your nerve cell's axon needs insulation so it can have good conduction. Otherwise, the signals that axon sends will falter.

Under healthy conditions, as you gain life skills and mature, the myelination of your neurons' axons simultaneously increases. This myelination process makes the neurons supporting those skills communicate more effectively and efficiently.

When you were an infant, the neurons controlling your primary senses of hearing, seeing, and feeling and your ability to move had their axons well myelinated. As you expanded your capabilities beyond those rudimentary abilities, the neurons in areas of your brain that support more-complex skills became myelinated. That's how important myelin insulation is!

Branching out for new thoughts and memories

The more you think in novel ways, such as learning new skills or curiously exploring new information, the more your brain adjusts to make that happen. Specifically, your dendrites branch out to make new connections with other neurons. This process is called *dendritic branching* or *dendric arborization*. Picture a tomato plant that is growing three long stalks. To make your plant branch out, you pinch off the ends of the stalks, and out of each stalk grow three more. Keep arborizing your plant, and you'll have much more opportunity for tomatoes to grow.

TIP

When you face having to relearn a skill, do just as you did with the plant. Pinch off or resist doing the task the same old way, and your dendrites will branch out in search of other neurons for input for new solutions. The more you think in novel ways, the more your brain will dendritically branch out.

Albert Einstein didn't have more neurons than you do. He had more connections between his neurons because he was always using his brain to branch out in novel thoughts. Although the chances of you coming up with a major modification of his theory of relativity are pretty slim, you can branch out in new thoughts of your own. By doing so, you cause your dendrites to branch out, making new connections with other brain cells. By being curious and keeping your mind active, you increase dendritic arborization, and your memory ability expands because your neurons have more connections to help them encode and recall memories and perform other thinking functions.

Staging Your Memories: Long Term, Short Term

More than 125 years ago, German philosopher Herman Ebbinghaus performed a series of memory experiments on himself. Ebbinghaus tested his own ability to remember thousands of strings of letters. He found that after a short period, he forgot much of what he tried to remember.

These days, psychologists refer to two different memory processes: short-term and long-term memory. Each type corresponds to a length of time:

>> A *short-term memory* (or *working memory*) generally lasts for no more than 30 seconds.

>> A *long-term memory* can last a lifetime.

Short-term memory is a gateway to long-term memory. A short-term memory must be made before it can be transferred to a long-term memory. Recently, psychologists have begun to use the term *working memory* to refer to short-term memory. The phrase derives from the fact that you're always working with immediate memories in your current experiences.

Working memory has a lot to do with your attention span. One way that psychologists measure working memory is to ask you to repeat a string of numbers, draw a design, or identify an image that you saw just seconds before. The more you remember, the better your attention and working memory.

Never fear; you can't clutter your mind with too many memories. Your brain has an extraordinary ability to remember vast quantities of information in long-term memory. As for your working memories, you shed almost all of them seconds after you pick them up. When someone gives you another string of numbers, you'll most likely forget the set they gave you before. Only the important stuff goes into long-term memory. So how do you decide what's important?

Imagine that you're simultaneously talking to your boss on the phone, checking your email, and listening to music when your favorite song starts to play. Do you focus on the email that says your electric bill is past due (even though you sent in the check last week)? Do you listen to the song or to your boss? What you pay attention to is the key to what you remember because attention is the gateway into short-term memory. If you want to keep your job, you focus your attention to the instructions your boss is giving you and purge the song and the email out of your working memory (for now). The importance you place on what you do listen to dictates what you store in your long-term memory.

Within your long-term memory, one memory can trigger another memory like a chain reaction. For example, if you begin to describe an event from earlier in your life, you may be surprised that you're reminded of other circumstances surrounding the event. You unleash a whole chain of associations and rekindle a much wider spectrum of memories.

TIP

Try this: Think back to an event in your childhood. Reflect on where that event took place and who was there at the time. Chances are good that a wider picture of what occurred on that day will form in your mind.

Short-term memory and long-term memory differ in many ways. Time is a main distinguishing factor, but so is storage capacity. Although a limit exists on how much you can store in working memory, your long-term memory has no such constraints.

RIDING YOUR BIKE DOWN MEMORY LANE

You may have noticed you can do many things over and over without even having to try to remember how to do them. Riding a bicycle is a great example. When you first learned to ride, you had to try to remember each step. You probably said to yourself at one point, "Okay, I need to stop this thing! Where's the brake? Oh yeah — I remember — there it is!" Later, these steps became so ingrained that you didn't have to try to remember. You were on automatic pilot.

Psychologists differentiate between these two types of memory. *Explicit memory* requires that you intentionally and consciously recollect in order to recall something. This type of memory operates when you're trying to remember specifically where the brake is on that bike when you're just learning to ride. Through the process of applying the brake for the first time when you are learning to ride, you develop explicit memory of where the brake is located and how to operate it. The second time you ride a bike, you call on your explicit memory and have to consciously recall where the brake is and how to use it. However, after you have ridden a bike for a few days, you're relying on *implicit memory* to know where the brake is and how to use it. Implicit memory uses previous experiences to aid the performance of a task *without* conscious awareness of those previous experiences. That is, you didn't have to think about all the times you previously rode your bike; you just sat on the seat and started to pedal automatically and knew how to brake without paying it another thought.

Though implicit memory is well ingrained in your long-term memory, explicit memory goes through three steps before getting there:

1. **Acquiring a memory:** Sometimes, this phase is called *encoding* or *coding* a memory. This process occurs as you learn the basic information needed to ride a bike for the first time.

2. **Storing or recording a memory:** At this stage, you file the memory into storage for later use as you work at learning to ride.

3. **Retrieving a memory:** This is when you recall the memory into consciousness. In short, you have to consciously remember the basic process of riding the second time you hop on the bike.

Disruptions to your working memory can occur in a number of ways. Because attention and concentration enable short-term memory, any distraction can hamper your memory. You may be reading this page and the phone rings. After the call, you return to the page and have to reread to see where you left off when the phone rang. Because you were distracted, you forgot what you were holding in working memory. This principle doesn't apply to long-term memory because that kind of memory is relatively permanent. Drug abuse, alcohol abuse, and traumatic brain damage can wreak havoc on your short-term memory; long-term memory remains generally intact, but your ability to retrieve those memories may erode.

Assuming the ideal circumstances, you can count on the following as being the key demands of a good memory:

>> **Attention:** This is the key to your short-term memory.

>> **The degree of importance that information holds for you:** This drives the strength of the memory into long-term storage.

Sorting and Recovering Your Memories Down Pathways

You retrieve your long-term memories via multiple pathways. The pathway you use to retrieve a memory has a lot to do with how you learned the information in the first place. You may be a visual learner, so you learn by seeing and remember by visualizing the images that you saw. Or you may be an auditory learner, meaning you learn by hearing sounds and retrieve memories by recalling the associated sounds.

Common mechanisms of learning memory retrieval pathways include the following:

>> Emotions (feelings)

>> Smells (olfactory)

>> Sounds (auditory)

>> Sights (visual)

>> Movement or three-dimensional perspective (spatial)

>> Touch/sensation (tactile)

Feeling memories

One of the ways that your brain codes memories relates to your emotions at the time the memory was created. How you felt emotionally during the event is tied to your memory of the event. This combination of memory and emotion is often called *state-based*. The emotional state you were in at the time of the event carries your memory. Perhaps you're feeling sad and you suddenly think about your favorite late uncle, Fred. Your emotional state of sadness triggered the parts of your brain associated with the memory of that emotion, and you remember how sad you felt when Uncle Fred died.

Smelling memories

Have you ever smelled a particular aroma and found yourself overwhelmed by a memory of an event long since past? You may smell fresh bread baking and remember the homemade loaves your mother made when you were a child. Or the whiff of a certain perfume in a crowded elevator conjures up memories of your grandma.

Why does this sudden memory happen? Is it some kind of magic? In a way, it is — it's the magic of evolution. As a mammal, you're the product of millions of years of evolution. Your olfactory bulbs, which record the sense of smell, lie almost on top of your hippocampus. They are like two elongated petals that act like sensory shortcuts for memory.

Experiencing memories

As a mammal, you have emotionally based experiences via your limbic system. Yet you also have a large cerebral cortex sitting right on top of this limbic system that tempers and controls those emotions. Maybe you were bitten by a big dog as a child, so when you encounter a big dog as an adult, you experience fear. This reaction happens because your prior experience of being hurt by a big dog made you feel afraid. But because of your mammalian heritage, you can adapt your emotions and override prior state-based memories. If your spouse became blind and required a large seeing-eye dog, you could overcome your previous dog-fear association through new positive interactions with the new big working dog.

TIP

You remember an event far more easily if it has emotional meaning for you. The more important the information is to you, the more prominent it will be in your memory. Similarly, the more motivated you are to remember an event or information, the better chance you'll have remembering it.

Hearing memories

Your memories for what you hear are found largely in your temporal lobes (discussed earlier in the chapter). Sounds of all types carry with them memories colored by when and how you've heard them.

The sound of a firecracker elicits different memories for different people. One person may happily remember the beauty of Fourth of July fireworks. However, a war veteran with post-traumatic stress disorder wounded by a bomb during combat may feel a surge of panic and fear upon hearing the same sound.

You may have experienced driving down the road and hearing a piece of music on the radio that lifted you to memories that you hadn't tried to recall. You may remember the first time you heard it or a time you spent with someone you loved. Memories of that person pepper the highway in front of you.

TYPES OF MEMORY

Psychologists identify a number of types of memory. *Procedural memory* is a type of implicit or unconscious memory of skills and how to do things. With enough practice, you should be able to look at the screen rather than the keyboard as you type because you remember the procedure of typing from years of practice.

Semantic memory involves the recording of facts, knowledge, and information you've learned, as well as the meaning of words. When you memorize facts like the state capitals or the alphabet, you use semantic memory. Your left hemisphere is involved in semantic memory, allowing you to express and understand language.

There are two main types of *prospective memory,* which involves remembering to do a planned action at a future time and when to do it. *Event-based prospective memory* comes into play when you're trying to remember to do something later. When the outrageous electricity bill comes, you remember you have to pay the bill before the due date. *Time-based prospective memory* is remembering to do something at a specific time, such as when you need to remember to go to your 2 p.m. doctor's appointment tomorrow.

Episodic memory is your unique memory of events you've experienced; it differs from another person's memory of the same events. It involves remembering not only the event but also where and when it occurred. An example would be your memory of sharing New Year's Day with your aunt June in Florida last year.

This is only an overview of the types of memory; for more detailed information, check out www.human-memory.net/types.html.

You have your own associations to different types and pieces of music, especially if you've heard the music on many occasions in more than one setting. The mood of the music can change your mood. Music therapists utilize this knowledge and play upbeat music for emotionally troubled people to help them perk up.

Seeing memories

The phrase *a picture is worth a thousand words* may be trite, but it's true. You use visual imagery to code a vast number of your memories. Each visual image carries with it numerous thoughts, and trying to remember all of those thoughts is much more difficult than remembering the image itself.

REMEMBER

Thoughts that evoke visual images are far clearer later on than those that don't evoke visual imagery. This dual coding creates a stronger memory: You code not only the thoughts or experiences but also the visual image associated with it.

The power of visual images can resonate with you for years. Take a moment to prove this point to yourself: Look at some object in the room, like a chair. Now close your eyes. For a few seconds, you'll notice an afterimage. However, that image fades away as you go on to note new sensations and thoughts. Now go back to reading and don't look back at the chair. Notice that many of the details of the chair have faded. The image probably isn't as sharp as it was before.

That image is affected by your mood and what you've been thinking about since originally seeing it. Now when you try to visualize that chair's image, it's no longer an objective representation of the image but one colored by your mood and your most recent thoughts.

TIP

You don't need a photographic memory, however, to use visual images as memory enhancers. A simple visual image can carry with it an association to an abstract concept, whereas a simple word may not.

Here are some other examples of how using visual images can help you remember:

>> You want to remember the abstract idea of *location*. The location includes a lake, and that's much easier to remember. With the word *lake,* you have an opportunity to visualize an image of a lake. You may even embellish that image with the sun gently reflecting on the still waters of the lake. The word *lake* can even carry a personal association. Perhaps you vacation each summer on a lake or are a hearty ice fisher who braves below-freezing temperatures as you sit above a hole cut into the ice. Now think of the word *location.* Which location? Perhaps a lake?

>> Suppose you want to try to remember the *decadence* of the late Roman emperors such as Caligula and Nero. Try to imagine a banquet with toga-clad people gorging themselves and throwing grapes at one another. That scene will help you remember better than you would if someone just told you to remember the words *Caligula, Nero,* and *decadence.*

>> You're trying to remember to ship documents to your sister across the country. You need to try to remember the words *ship* and *package.* Imagine a large package floating in the sea with two large masts with sails being blown across the water.

As a practical memory aid, choose images that represent the information you want to remember and put them into an exaggerated scene. This technique really works!

Verbal memories

Obviously, visual images aren't as useful if you're blind. In that case, other senses and memory triggers such as smell, touch, sound, and words become much more important. (Of course, they're also important if you can see!)

The degree to which words are useful as memory cues depends on how adept you are at using words. If you're very skilled using words, the subtle nuances of words can carry complex memories. Poets have a high linguistic intelligence and are masters of this talent.

The combination of visual imagery (or other sense experiences) and words as cues for memory is the most powerful of all. Any time you have an opportunity to try to remember something by using multiple channels, your memory will be stronger and your recall will be easier.

Compared with adolescents or adults, young children are more adept at visual imagery than at verbal memories. This conclusion comes as no surprise because young children are just beginning to learn language. A child's vocabulary jumps astronomically between the ages of 1 and 5 and continues to expand into adulthood. The rate of vocabulary growth slows down as people get older because they've learned most of what they need to know to talk. However, you can continue to expand your vocabulary. Learn new words by taking classes, reading, or doing crossword puzzles. Doing so increases your capacity to remember based on verbal cues.

Chapter 9

Memory Tricks and Tips

Your memory skills are as strong as the memory techniques you use. If you don't use any techniques, chances are that your memory isn't what it could be.

This chapter gives you several effective techniques to enhance your memory skills. You see how to use specific words to lock in memories. These words, called *pegs*, do just that — they peg a memory. Using the loci system, you can use a location in a room to remind you of memories. You can also wrap up memories in a story so that when you tell the story later, your memories unfold.

Introducing Mnemonics, Your Memory Sidekick

You've probably heard of mnemonics (nee-mon-iks). *Mnemonics* are memory devices, such as a pattern of letters, ideas, or associations that help you retain information in ways that you can more easily remember. These devices are cues or links to other information — almost like the hyperlinks you click when surfing the Internet. Click a link, and another page pops up on your screen.

For example, in the spring and fall, people in certain time zones change their clocks by one hour due to the beginning or end of daylight saving time. The simple mnemonic "spring forward, fall back" helps people remember to set their clocks an hour forward in the spring and back in the fall. Because the verb *spring* implies upward or forward movement and the verb *fall* implies backward movement, this catchy phrase is an excellent mnemonic. (Of course, nowadays many clocks automatically adjust for daylight saving time, but the mnemonic still helps you to know what's happening.)

To use a mnemonic, all you have to do is

» Decide what you want to remember.

» Match what you want to remember with an image or word cue.

» Refer to the cue to recall your memory.

Think of mnemonics as a way for you to organize information so you can later recall it more easily. The word *mnemonic* means "aiding memory." You can structure or package your memories so they're easily available to you. A mnemonic is like the beginning strand of a ball of yarn. When you pull it, a whole string of memories unfolds.

Mnemonics allow you to translate information into a form that's easier for you to remember. They're successful memory aids because your brain prefers to remember personal, silly, and logical things you can relate to rather than dry factual information and data. By associating the new factual information you need to remember with relatable personal things you already know, you're able to remember them more effectively and in context. Mnemonics let you associate new information with a more familiar framework to enable you remember.

Hanging Memories on Pegs

Word pegs are so named because you do just that — you peg a word to another word or number that's easier to remember. Pegs are "hooks" that you can use to hold the word you're trying to remember, just like a coat rack peg holds your jacket. By thinking of the peg word, you think of the word you want to remember.

To put the peg system into action, try the following brain workout. The goal is to remember a list of ten words, in order. Sound hard? Don't worry, here's a hint: The pegs for remembering the words are the numbers one through ten.

The words you need to recall appear in the following list. Slowly read through the list just one time, and, as you do, attach a number to each word, beginning with one:

Sun

Due

Sea

Door

Hive

Stick

Heaven

Gate

Tine

Hen

Now, quick — cover up the list! Can you repeat the words in order? (No peeking!) Sure you can. The pegged word ties to the number. All you have to do is run through the numbers one to ten to remember the words. Each number is pegged to a rhyming word that you remember by association.

TECHNICAL STUFF

This example uses *phonetic* or *rhyming mnemonics*. The rhyming words (*one sun, two due*) enable you to remember the list in order of the increasing numbers by looking at their sounds (phonetics) and rhyming with the numbers.

This is a simple example, but you get the point: Peg words attach easily to the words you want to remember. Making the peg word rhyme with the target word makes this technique easy to use. For example, in "eight gate," the sound of the word *gate* gives you the clue you need.

You can also use alphabet pegs to tie letters to words. The letter of the alphabet can be either a rhyme or just contain the letter within it. For example:

A-acorn   B-bee

C-sea   D-dog

E-eel   F-frog

G-goat	H-hut
I-eye	J-jay
K-cake	L-elf
M-mate	N-nut
O-oh	P-pea
Q-cue	R-ray
S-star	T-tea
U-umbrella	V-volt
W-wheel	X-axe
Y-why	Z-zebra

You can use letter pegs by just tying your memory to the first letter of a word. A first–letter memory clue is quite economical because it narrows your search down to a letter. All you have to do is associate the first letter of a word with what you're trying to remember, such as using the acronym ROY G. BIV to remember the colors of the rainbow. Using the first letter of each color, you spell out this name, which makes remembering red, orange, yellow, green, blue, indigo, and violet. You're pegging each color to a letter.

Putting Memories into Familiar Places

Realtors are fond of saying that the three most important factors to remember when buying property are *location, location, location.* Location is also the most important element in the mnemonic technique called *loci* (*lo*–sigh). (See the related sidebar "Old, but not forgotten.")

The loci system has two main steps:

1. **Commit to memory several locations of a familiar place (for example, the rooms in your house) in the order you want to remember them.**

2. **Associate the things you want to remember with the various locations.**

By taking these two simple steps, you can recall what you're trying to remember by looking at the location (the living room, for example) or simply picturing it in your mind.

Skeptical? Give it a try. Suppose you want to memorize a poem, a speech, or your lines in a play. When rehearsing, walk around your living room as you speak and make specific associations to the various objects or locations. At your coffee table, remember the first part of the speech. Then go to the lamp, couch, and TV, assigning a new part of the speech for each location. As you rehearse, walk around the room and time your presentation to match the locations with each part. Next, stand in one spot and look at each location as you go through the presentation again, matching each part with each location. Finally, leave the room physically but reenter it mentally, going through your presentation and again making the same matches as you picture your living room in your mind.

This loci method really helps you remember what you need to say in the proper order. By the time you need to present your speech, you can skip your crib notes. You can just go into the room in your imagination and make the presentation by seeing each location in order and remembering the lines you associated with it.

OLD, BUT NOT FORGOTTEN

Twenty-six hundred years ago, Mnemosyne, the Greek goddess of memory, was said to know everything — the past, present, and future. Old storytellers, sometimes called bards, learned how to remember long poems and epic tales by relying on Mnemosyne. The truth is, they used a mnemonic technique later to be called loci.

Loci is plural for *locus,* which is Latin for place or location. Sometimes, the loci system is referred to as the topical system. *Topo* (as in topography) is Greek for location. It's also called the *journey system* because it's based on memorized associations and spatial relationships through a journey of specific, mentally visualized locations.

Like many aspects of Roman culture, the loci technique originated in Greece. Building on the Greek use of location, orators and performers memorized locations to help them remember their lines without having to rely on notes. The speakers would walk past or look at specific locations, and the line that was associated with that location would come to mind.

Unbeknownst to the audience, the storyteller or orator purposefully walked around the room in a dramatic fashion not so much for the effect but rather to jog his own memory. The audience found these movements stirring, not distracting, and had no idea that the speaker was using an ingenious technique to remember.

Imagine the ancient Roman orator Cicero rousing the audience with his eloquence and provocative phrases. The audience had no idea he was using the loci method to remember his lines.

Telling Yourself a Story to Link Memories

Everyone loves a good story. People gather around storytellers, read good novels, and enjoy movies. Stories are a part of the fabric of culture. You use stories as a way to learn, teach, and pass the time. Well, as it turns out, you can also use stories to link information you want to remember.

The link system: Remembering a list without paper and pencil

The *link system* is a mnemonic technique that helps you link memories of serial-type information, such as lists of words. As the name implies, this system helps you link a chain of information to help you remember it. This system is sometimes called the *chain method* because your task is to chain together the items on the list like links on a chain.

Suppose you have to run to the grocery store to buy food for dinner. You frantically open the glove box for a pad and pencil because halfway to the store, you realize you forgot your list. Alas, you find only a torn map, a crumpled candy wrapper, and the sunglasses you broke last week. For a moment, you forget what you decided to make for dinner. Then it comes to you as your stomach growls: You had decided to make fettuccini with clam sauce. Now you remember that you have to buy olive oil, fettuccini, parsley, garlic, clams, and Parmesan cheese. You decide to chain together the items into some kind of image that you're able to remember when you get to the store. A picture comes to mind of Uncle Fred (for "freduccini") sitting under an olive tree (olive oil) with parsley growing as high as grass. Uncle Fred is chopping garlic, grating Parmesan, and storing those ingredients in clamshells. As you walk into the market, that picture draws you into the entire chain, which links together the items on your shopping list. (Now all you have to do is remember how to cook it.)

The story system: Weaving a story to recall a list

The *story system* of mnemonics is similar to the link system in the preceding section but a little more elaborate. This technique requires more time than the link system. To use it, you develop a story about what you have to memorize by associating each item in the list with logical elements that form a story. Your story should weave together the list items in the order you want to remember them. Those items should connect with one another in a meaningful way as the story unfolds. That way, when you remember the story, you remember your list.

EVEN TWAIN USED MNEMONICS

Mark Twain, never lacking for words, relied on mnemonics to get through speeches. Twain wrote that he would often rely on pictures that he had drawn to help him link together elements of his speech. For example, he once drew a haystack with a squiggly line to remind him that he was to talk next about the West. He gazed down again at his sheet of paper and saw two jagged lines to remind him of lightning. In this case, he was trying to remind himself about talking about the weather in San Francisco, its lack of lightning, and its frequent fog in the summer. He went on to quip about San Francisco weather, "The coldest winter I ever spent was a summer in San Francisco."

TIP

The more ridiculous the story you create, the more memorable it is.

The story system works best when the list contains abstract words that are harder to visualize. However, it's less effective than the link system for longer lists because it's more difficult to arrange a long list of items into a meaningful story than to link them together with basic associations.

REMEMBER

With the link system, you use primarily visual images, whereas you may not need them with the story system. But if you're able to develop visual imagery within your story, it's easier to remember. Visualization strengthens both these mnemonic techniques.

Imagine that you've been awakened by a furious storm. When you go downstairs to make breakfast, you notice that the ceiling just above one of the window frames is leaking. You surmise that the storm, with its near-sideways pounding rain, tore up some flashing on the roof, allowing some rainwater to seep down into the wall. The water dripped all over the windowsill and onto the carpet. You check the garage for something you can use to plug the spot but find nothing suitable.

You hop into the car to go to the hardware store and drive faster than you should through the flooded streets. As you drive, you think up a list of items to buy, but you have no pencil and paper. You come up with the following story to take with you into the hardware store:

> Mr. Moosely found that he was out of denture adhesive (caulking), so he used one of his finest steak knives (putty knife) to mince up dinner. But he worried that mashing up the minced food with his gums would result in food dribbling out of his mouth and onto his new shirt. Therefore, he took out a plastic bib (plastic sheet) that was left in his apartment the last time his young grandson was visiting. He realized that the bib was far too small, and he could hardly tie it around his neck. Mr. Moosely knew that if he used this small bib, food would fall onto the table or floor. He managed to find a rectangular container (drip pan) from the cabinet. It was only then that he was able to enjoy his minced meal.

Choosing the Right Mnemonic at the Right Time

Not all mnemonic systems are equally effective for everyone. People are unique, and so are their needs and preferences. What you find useful as a mnemonic may be totally useless to your neighbor, and vice versa.

Picking a mnemonic that works for you

TIP

Choose the mnemonic that fits best with your experience. Doing so can increase your chances of remembering your memory-aid in the future.

To use mnemonic aids effectively, make sure the mnemonic follows these basic principles:

>> It gets your attention.

>> It contains an easy association.

>> It's organized in such a way that it's easy for you to remember.

>> It's meaningful to you.

Use mnemonic techniques that suit you personally. Each person's life experience is different, so people respond to images in their own ways. Consider the image of an onion dome on a Russian Orthodox church. The shape of that dome may symbolize a burning candle flame for a member of that faith and be associated with a candle lit in prayer for a family member. A person of another faith can look on the same dome and simply see an onion due to different life experiences.

TIP

Mnemonics that grab your attention and make remembering fun are always more effective. If your mnemonic is stale and boring, you tend to forget it. Make the mnemonic stand out by making it silly, funny, absurd, or even titillating.

Matching the mnemonic to what you want to remember

If your mnemonic has little to do with what you're trying to remember, you'll probably forget it. For example, say that you're trying to remember that the Galapagos Islands off the coast of Ecuador have one of the widest ranges of unique animal species, including aquatic dragon lizards. The overall concept to remember is that the Galapagos Islands are a geographical location so remote that living species have evolved differently from others on the mainland.

You may think of mnemonics like these:

>> **A knight fighting off a dragon just outside a medieval castle.** You're trying to associate the dragon lizards on the Galapagos Islands with the image of castles and knights. Hmm — sounds like a tangent. Remember, you're trying to recall the Galapagos Islands, not the British Isles.

>> **A huge number of gallon containers with dragon lizards crawling out.** With the word *gallon*, you have a link to the word *Galapagos Islands*, and you've added the lizards. Maybe you want to organize your imagery in such a way to carry a broader point — namely, that a wide range of other animals also live on the Galapagos Islands. To remember this, you may want to envision the gallon containers brimming over with a wide variety of creatures, not just the dragon lizards.

>> **Darwin's boat, the Beagle, anchored in the bay, and hundreds of gallons of containers on shore, brimming over with life.** Make sure that there's personal meaning to the image you're trying to remember. If you're a history buff, an actual image from history (Darwin's boat) may work.

Selecting a mnemonic that fits the situation

Although the visual mnemonic route (the link system) can potentially carry much more than just one image, occasionally utilizing an image may be impractical in some situations. Visual mnemonics take much more time for you to develop than do peg, link, or story mnemonics. When you don't have a lot of time and need to develop a quick way to remember something important, using a peg may be wiser. For example, if you're listening to a lecture and don't have a notepad, you'll end up in the dust when the lecturer moves on to another subject while you're still trying to conjure up a visual image to help you remember the information later.

One of the advantages the peg system has is that you can select individual items from a list, whereas the link system relies on a sequence of associations. However, the pegs depend on prememorized word connections. The loci system also requires some upfront work to memorize location-connected links.

The more complex or abstract the noun, the more difficult it may be to associate with other words or ideas. The nouns are most useful in these mnemonic techniques if they're concrete nouns you can visualize.

Whatever mnemonic system you use, make sure it's flexible and meets the demands of what you're trying to remember. Practice using mnemonics so you're be versatile. Mnemonics have a long history and have been used successfully all over the world for many years. Make them work for you.

Chapter 10

Keeping Your Memory Sharp as You Grow Older

When you find yourself forgetting what you were going to say, you may think, "I'm having a senior moment." This common saying really overplays the reality of aging; aging doesn't cause you to lose your memory as dramatically as it implies. Normal aging brings subtle changes in memory, but the general global decline that society associates with getting older is far from correct.

Many people do note some memory problems as they age, but not everyone experiences memory loss at the same rate or the same degree. In this chapter, you find out why, how aging can affect your memory skills, and what to do about it. Watch out for ageist stereotypes! Utilize the tips in this chapter to keep your mind active, alert, learning, and remembering as the years go by.

Mentally Noting How Memory Changes with Age

The American Psychology Association (www.apa.org) has summarized the consistent memory change patterns that researchers identify in normal older adults compared to younger counterparts in the following categories:

>> Episodic (what did I eat for supper last night?)

>> Source (who told me that I should see that new movie?)

>> Flashbulb (where were you when President Kennedy was shot?)

>> Semantic (fact information)

>> Procedural ("after you learn to ride a bike, you never forget")

Episodic, source, and flashbulb memory decline the most with age, and semantic and procedural the least. Although these patterns have emerged through studies of healthy seniors, researchers emphasize that these changes show very different rates of decline and vary greatly among individual people. So what may be noticeable in Fred may not be an issue at all for George. Remember, everyone is unique, and aging changes in memory are no exception.

As people age, their storage room for memories doesn't fill up as though they have only so much capacity available. Instead, memory changes seem to center in how people encode memories for storage and then retrieve the memories they've stored. Distraction from a memory task, such as because of a phone call, impacts encoding ability more. Slower retrieval processing may make it harder to remember names or dates. Despite these subtle changes, most older people are still able to competently take in new information, encode it, store it in long-term memory, and retrieve it when needed.

REMEMBER

Middle-aged folks may start to notice memory changes, but their sensitivity about such changes is worsened by society's constant comparison of everyone to the young as the pinnacle for mental ability. Researchers suggest that when identifying what is normal for a certain age, comparing yourself to healthy, age-matched peers is much more realistic and meaningful than comparing yourself to someone many years younger.

Making Full Use of a Vintage Brain

You don't *know* less in your old age; you know more due to your years of life experience. However, during your advanced years, your information-processing speed slows down a bit. But don't worry; your long-term memory remains intact, and your understanding of what you already know is broader, more thoughtful, and wiser than during your early adulthood.

Here's more good news: You were probably taught in school that you have all the brain cells you'll ever have at the moment you're born, right? From then on (the lesson continued), you lose about 10,000 brain cells every day — and even more if you drink alcohol.

Well, it turns out that this old wisdom isn't true. You *do* have an opportunity for dendrite growth. *Dendrites* are the part of your neurons that branch out to pick up information from other neurons (see Chapter 1 for an introduction to the parts of your brain). What you do with your brain determines what happens to it.

Now, for the not-so-good news: Your brain's levels of neurotransmitters (see Chapter 8 for a bit more on neurotransmitters) — and various hormones, such as melatonin, testosterone, and estrogen — do decline. Your arteries and capillaries grow less flexible and, in some cases, become clogged, hindering the flow of vital oxygen and nutrients to your brain. Uncontrolled stress and high blood pressure make matters only worse.

Reducing stress, keeping the blood flowing

As you age, you want to retain your power to learn and recall — and maybe even get better at those things if you can. If that's your agenda, here are three things to start doing today:

>> Reduce your stress level.

>> Control your blood pressure.

>> Improve your blood circulation.

Stress kills memory. High levels of stress hormones, such as cortisol, are destructive to your brain and decrease its ability to adjust to new learning and memory. The chapters in Part 3 talk in much more detail about managing stress and the importance of relaxation.

As you age, the blood flow to your brain reduces, especially if your diet is high in saturated fats or if you drink alcohol or smoke. This reduction means that your neurons get less life-sustaining nutritional support. Your blood brings not only the glucose, which acts as fuel to your brain, but also the amino acids that are synthesized into neurotransmitters.

The reduction in blood flow to your brain doesn't necessarily happen at the same pace in your neighbor down the street who's the same age. Despite normal aging changes, you do have some control over it. One of the best things you can do to keep your blood flowing is to exercise on a regular basis. You not only do your heart a big favor but also help clear out cholesterol from your arteries and increase the longevity of the elasticity of your arteries and capillaries.

To minimize stress and keep the blood flowing, consider these tips:

>> **Exercise.** Take regular walks, swim, bike, or work out in the gym — whatever fits your style.

>> **Join a yoga or meditation class.**

>> **Eat a balanced diet.** Keep the saturated-fat level low.

>> **Minimize consumption of alcohol.**

>> **Moderate your caffeine intake.**

>> **Don't smoke.**

>> **Avoid high-stress activities.**

>> **Learn and use relaxation techniques on a regular basis.** See Part 3 for more on ways to relax.

Free radicals also begin to take their toll as you age. Free radicals break down tissue and kill cells. The main targets of free radicals in your brain are the *myelin sheaths,* the oily substance that covers your axons to improve conduction. *Axons* are the part of your neurons that send information. They help your neurons fire at maximum velocity. When free radicals eat away the myelin, your axons lose their conductivity. This lack of conductivity means your brain doesn't process information as quickly. Memories are both harder to form and harder to recall. Chronic stress increases hormones that then increase inflammation and worsen this free radical damage to your nerve cells. (See Chapter 15 for more on stress.)

The other big targets of free radicals are your dendrites. Dendrites (like tree branches) are the part of your neurons that receive information from other neurons. Free radicals cause your dendrites to thin out (have fewer branches and therefore fewer connections), leaving your brain less able to process information in the ways it had before. You may find yourself forgetting jokes that you were once able to tell with great punch.

TIP

One way to combat free radicals is to consume foods that are rich in antioxidants. See Chapter 22 for more on free radicals and antioxidants.

Compensating for your graying senses

Although vision and hearing issues often emerge as you get older, these changes don't have to be a burden like they did in years past. With the advent of wonders like eyeglasses, cataract surgery, large-print books, and hearing aids, folks today are much better off than their ancestors were when it comes to the eyes and ears.

Of course, picking up important information is more difficult if your vision or hearing isn't in top working order. If you don't get all the information others get, you may remember less.

BRAIN WAVE SLOWDOWN

Your reaction time slows down with age. This slowdown is partly due to a decline in your ability to process information at the same rate as when you were younger and contributes to being less able to do several things at once. Unfortunately, multitasking has become a way of life in today's society. People talk on smartphones while shopping online and exchanging email. Older people have more difficulty shifting between tasks because their brains have a harder time breaking away from one task and refocusing on the other, making it difficult to engage in both activities simultaneously.

In early adulthood, certain brain waves (known as alpha waves) occur at the rate of 11 cycles per second. By the time you reach age 65, they fade to nine cycles per second. By age 80, alpha waves fade to eight cycles per second.

This reduction in alpha waves occurs at the same time that your sleep cycle changes. As you age, the amount of time you spend in deep sleep decreases. Deep sleep is the most restorative stage of sleep. It's where your immune system is bolstered and you truly achieve relaxation from sleep. The lack of restorative sleep can be a drag on you during the day when you're trying to maintain attention and form memories.

All these problems make it more difficult for you to pay attention at the level you could when you were younger. Resist this decline by staying mentally active. Challenge yourself by taking classes, reading, and going to lectures.

ACCESSING BRAIN BENEFITS FROM A TECHNOLOGY-DRIVEN WORLD

These days, you have a multitude of options to keep you mentally active and sharp, especially online. Here are a few ideas:

- **Classes:** You can find a variety of classes online. For example, more than 1,000 schools (kindergarten through college) and cultural institutions offer free classes through the Open University on iTunes U (www.open.edu/itunes). You can search for classes on any subject; access complete courses with videos, lectures, books, and more; and experience them on computer, tablet, or cellphone.

- **TED talks (www.ted.com):** TED is a nonprofit organization devoted to spreading ideas, usually in the form of a short, powerful talk (18 minutes or less). It covers almost all topics imaginable in over 100 languages. It's a great place to keep your mind active and sharp.

- **E-books:** These are available all over the Internet, maybe even from your local library, on whatever topic you desire. Read in whatever subject or genre tickles your fancy.

- **Audiobooks:** Read by listening as you take a walk, do the dishes, or drive the car on long trips. You can check them out from your local library, buy them online, or download them from your local or state digital library collection.

Other people may misread your visual or hearing deficits as a decline in your overall intelligence. Do everything you can to keep your eyesight strong and your hearing acute so people don't get the wrong idea! Maximize your sensory ability by compensating for any problems you may develop:

» If hearing is the issue, see an audiologist and get a hearing aid if needed. Then *use it*.

» If your eyesight is the issue, see an optometrist to find out whether you need to wear glasses. The optometrist also screens your eyes and may refer you to an ophthalmologist (medical eye doctor) for treatment if you're developing cataracts, have increased eye pressure (signaling glaucoma), or if you have macular degeneration that needs medical attention.

Mental Gymnastics: Inflating a Shrinking Brain

Starting at age 50, your 3-pound brain gradually loses its volume in weight, so that, by age 75, it weighs roughly 2.6 pounds. A lot of the shrinkage in your brain is from a loss of water.

TECHNICAL STUFF

Different parts of your brain lose their volume at different rates. Your *frontal lobes* — which serve as your executive control center, giving you your sense of judgment and allowing you to avoid blurting out rude and inappropriate comments — show the greatest amount of shrinkage compared to any other part of your cortex (see Chapter 1 for more on the cortex and other parts of the brain). The frontal lobes can shrink up to 30 percent between the ages of 50 and 90. Looked at another way, your frontal lobes lose 0.55 percent of their volume every year after age 50. As the frontal lobes shrink, you may lose some of your capacity to be in control — that is, you may be less inhibited about what you say or do. (Perhaps now you won't be as surprised by some of the rude comments that come out of your grandfather's mouth.)

Your frontal lobes also play a big role in your ability to pay attention long enough to form short-term memories. If your frontal lobes do an inadequate job, they can make you prone to absentmindedness. As you age, you may become more apt to forget where you placed your keys or why you walked into a room. The frontal lobes are also responsible for *verbal fluency* (which is the ability to find the words you want when you want them) and executive function, which may also require more mental effort as the years go by.

The second-most affected area is your *parietal lobes.* Because they control construction ability, coordination, and spatial orientation, these skills can also be affected, contributing to the increase in falls seen in older people. Your *temporal lobes,* which help you remember the gist of an experience, shrink up to 20 percent as you age. This means that your ability to remember what you hear and say falter as you get older. Your temporal lobes also have to try to interpret inadequate information coming in if your hearing is failing.

To combat this shrinkage of your temporal lobes, you need to push them to be more active. To keep those lobes sharp, do the following:

>> Engage in debate — participate in a political campaign or join a community group.

>> Listen to lectures and audiobooks and discuss them afterward (see the nearby sidebar "Accessing brain benefits from a technology-driven world"). A local book club is a great forum to keep your mind actively engaged and get social enjoyment simultaneously.

>> Engage in discussion with your spouse, partner, and lifelong friends about memories you collectively hold. Call up your college friend and talk about old times.

Intellectual activity like that has the same beneficial effect on the temporal lobes as pumping iron has on the biceps. (But don't worry — your head won't bulge out like a weightlifter's arms.)

As you age, your *hippocampus* also shrinks. Between the ages of 50 and 90, it loses up to 20 percent of its volume. The levels of the neurotransmitter *acetylcholine* — critical for memory and active in your hippocampus — fall as you age and as your hippocampus shrinks. Your hippocampus is centrally involved in moving your short-term memories into long-term memories.

TIP

The loss in volume of your hippocampus means that acquiring new memories may be a little more difficult compared to earlier in your life. However, the situation is far from hopeless. Your brain is highly affected by changes in your nutrition, so your job is to make sure that you have the best nutrition possible. Eat three balanced meals a day. (See the chapters in Part 4 for details on nutrition.)

Your *occipital lobes* — commonly referred to as the *visual cortex* — lose mass, too. The occipital lobes' ability to process visual information falters, but like your temporal lobes, they have to deal with inadequate information coming in. This lack of information to process is largely due to the deterioration of your optic nerve and retina.

TIP

To keep your occipital lobes functioning well, do the following:

>> Attend art and photo exhibits.

>> Go on sightseeing trips.

>> Share your pictures with friends and relatives.

>> Use eyeglasses if you have them and update your prescription at least every other year with the help of your optician. Keep up with eye health through regular check-ups with your eye doctor.

Because the occipital lobes are responsible for interpreting visual information, doing things that demand visual memory provides a good workout for the lobes.

Keeping your neurons from shrinking

The shrinking in your brain isn't due only to the loss of water. Your dendrites shrink, too, and have fewer branches and therefore fewer connections. Your dendrites form the part of your neurons that reach out to other neurons and draw in information. Fewer dendrites and dendrite branches mean less opportunity to think and for connections form memories from multiple channels.

REMEMBER

The more you challenge yourself intellectually, the more your brain develops new dendritic connections with other neurons. Your brain can make new dendritic connections throughout your life despite your age. One great way to fight the trend of memory loss is to learn new information, challenge yourself to branch out, and think in ways you haven't before. If you have more dendritic connections to start with, you experience less of an impact on your brain when you start to lose some over time.

Becoming an Old Dog Who Remembers New Tricks

The adage that you can't teach old dogs new tricks doesn't have to apply to you. Old dogs become old dogs by only relying on *old* tricks and not being open to learning new ones.

Some older people depend on doing things the same way they've always done them. They may say to themselves, "This is the way I've always done it, and I'm not about to change now" or "It's worked for me all my life, and you want me to change now?"

REMEMBER

If you learn new tricks as you age, you don't become that old dog who is stuck in the rut of routine. Stay young by not retiring from life. Instead, engage in learning daily. Don't think of yourself as over the hill. Don't use phrases like, "Back in my day. . . ." Reminiscence is fine, but don't live in the past. *Today* is still your day if you want it to be.

Branching out of routine

Memory problems often involve experiences that fall outside your routine. You probably rarely forget to brush your teeth or take a shower. You do those things every day, so they become habits. You don't have to think about them or make plans to do them. Slips in your memory are more likely to occur when you have to remember to do something that's not part of your routine.

WARNING

If you're older, you must get out of the mindset of thinking that you're too old to use your mind in a new way. You have your routines perfected down to the exact time each day. However, you may have memory problems when you have to do something outside of your routine. Breaking out of routine and trying something new keeps you alert and activated mentally. Otherwise, you're flying on automatic pilot, which doesn't work in the changing conditions of modern life.

FOLLOWING PEOPLE AS THEY AGE

Psychologists have found that the elderly possess a rich and varied knowledge base and can either match or outperform their younger counterparts in many skills.

Since 1958, researchers from Johns Hopkins University Medical Center have closely followed normal, healthy adults as they've aged. These adults were evaluated every two years in a variety of ways, including medical and psychological tests. Despite popular belief, people didn't lose their mental abilities. Their vocabularies continued to expand, and their reasoning skills were enhanced. The only ways that they did apparently decline were in reaction time, attention span, and specific aspects of short-term memory. Long-term memory remained intact.

THE EDUCATION EDGE

Studies have shown that 70-year-olds with college and graduate degrees outscore younger high-school dropouts on many measures of cognitive ability and sometimes outscore middle-aged people who graduated from high school.

Study after study has shown that people who stay active intellectually in their later years build up resistance to cognitive decline. Think of it this way: If you start to suffer from one of the tragic brain-wasting diseases, such as Alzheimer's disease, you'll have far more reserve intellectual ability to lose than someone whose intellectual activity is composed of watching television all day or stewing over what went wrong at the store yesterday. To put it simply: The more intellectual abilities you've developed by keeping your mind active, the more you have in reserve to compensate for any future loss.

For this reason, when using psychological tests, psychologists have greater difficulty detecting signs of cognitive decline among those who were very bright previously. If a person would've scored in the superior range previously and he now scores in the high average range, that's a decline. But what if the psychologist doesn't know that he scored so highly before? The psychologist may misinterpret his current high score as a sign that he's still doing well. This problem is why psychologists always have to know the previous level of functioning.

Numerous studies have shown that people who have the greatest degree of education experience the least memory decline. This result works on the principle that the more you expand your mind, the better you able you are to use it — even during declines.

You're never too old to become more educated. In fact, you're actually becoming more educated right now by reading this book. Don't stop now! Keep reading book after book!

As you age, you may have the tendency not to scrutinize your memories. You may jump to conclusions and actually "remember" something that, in fact, didn't occur. You're especially at risk of remembering incorrectly if the activity or occurrence was outside of your routine.

For instance, suppose you waved to a friend as you drove into the supermarket parking lot while she was driving out. Later that day, another friend mentions that she saw Betty at the supermarket. You know that you often see Betty shopping there, too. You say, "Oh yes, I saw her, too." The fact was, you saw a friend at the supermarket, but it wasn't Betty. That friend was actually Marjorie, but that fact slips your mind.

The point here isn't that routines are bad; they're useful and help you get things done. But to stay sharp, you need to engage in behaviors that go beyond routine. Doing so is good for your brain and your memory.

To stay alert to the world around you, try to do the following:

>> Vary your activities.

>> Choose different routines.

>> Take daily walks, but vary the route.

>> Take classes or go to programs to learn new things (online, at your local library, or at community college).

>> Interact with younger people and learn from their perspectives.

Educating your memory skills

The more educated you are, the less susceptible you are to memory loss. Experts generally believe that a greater degree of education allows you to use your brain in a variety of ways.

But educating yourself doesn't always mean formal education. Become your local library's best patron. Stimulate your brain by reading books, magazines, and newspapers. Participate in community classes. Learn a new craft or instrument. The more you think in novel ways and keep learning, the greater the

HANG OUT WITH YOUNG PEOPLE

Experts know that people who lead full and varied lives into their later years suffer less from degenerative brain diseases. They stay sharp longer. You can, too.

One of the 20th century's most famous psychological theorists, Eric Erickson, became an elder statesman at the San Francisco Psychoanalytic Institute because of his contribution to the understanding of how people develop psychologically as they age.

In the last few years of his life, Erickson and his wife chose to live in a house with young people. He pointed out that he wanted to keep his mind young and challenged. He dreaded taking up a life of routine and mental retirement. By living and constantly interacting with young people, he made sure that he'd be challenged, be on his mental toes, and stay sharp.

number of connections between your neurons. Although you may not have any more neurons than someone less educated, you provide yourself with many more connections between your neurons.

These connections are the key; they provide you with many more ways to code and recall memories. As you age, the more connections you've developed, the more your brain can resist potential decline in memory and cognitive ability.

Getting artsy

Many people begin to cultivate an aesthetic sense and become more interested in the arts as they get older. You can be one of them. You can take art classes, start playing an instrument, go to concerts, garden, or do whatever pleases your sense of aesthetics.

Many colleges and universities are finding that mature adults in general and retired people specifically are some of the best students. They're taking classes because they want to take classes. They attend to learn for the sake of learning, whereas some of their younger fellow students are obligated to go to school in order to get a good job later.

Several colleges and universities throughout the United States have tuition-reduction programs, and some even spend money on providing seniors with special housing. Take advantage of these opportunities; give your memory the education edge. The advantages include the following:

>> You think about things from more angles.

>> Your perspective enlarges; you see the bigger picture.

>> Your memories have more dimensions — more associations.

TIP

Start a new to-do list with these items:

>> Take classes.

>> Go see live music and theater.

>> Travel.

>> Turn off the television.

>> Read and learn!

Chapter 11

Schooling Memory

You don't have to be a traditional student attending school to benefit from knowing how to study and how to remember what you studied. Such skills are applicable to learning anything whether at school, work, or just for fun. Besides, everyone is a student of life with a lot to learn.

When it comes to schooling, *how* you study is very different from *how much* you study. This difference is the same as the difference between quantity and quality. Simply studying "hard" or "a lot" can be like spinning your wheels if you don't do it correctly. You want to improve the quality of your studying rather than maximize the quantity of your studying.

Instead of spinning, you want your wheels to get some traction. The traction here is your memory of what you've studied. How you study determines whether you spin your wheels or make traction. Choosing the right techniques can improve the quality of your studying and make sure you don't spin your wheels and waste time.

In this chapter, you discover how to make the most of your time and increase the likelihood that you'll remember what you learn.

Organizing Your Recall

Organizing your studies isn't something you do only if you're obsessive-compulsive. It's something that all good students do. Organized learners remember more, and that's what learning is all about.

TIP

Your recall of important information depends more on *how* you organize information in your mind than on *how much* material you've memorized.

Think of loading files on your computer. If you simply save the material on your hard drive with no organization to where you put it, you may have a lot of trouble trying to access that information later. Without organizing the input not only have you wasted time accumulating random information, but you also can't locate it when you need it.

Think how much easier it would be to retrieve the information you need (when you need it) if you had placed it in clearly marked files organized with related material.

REMEMBER

When preparing to remember important information, ask yourself the following questions:

>> How is this information organized? What format is it? (For example, is the information a poem, a mathematical equation, or a speech?)

>> How will I be required to recall the information? (For example, will I have to stand in front of a class and recite it or answer a question on a multiple-choice exam?)

These questions have a bearing on which method you use to learn the information. The way you learn the information prepares you for the way you recall it. For example, if you want to remember a series of events that are described in your history book, you'd be wise to understand the context in which the events took place.

Suppose you're trying to remember the creation of the Works Projects Administration (WPA). If you understand the context in which it was created — massive unemployment and poor shape of public works in the United States in the 1930s — it may hang in your memory longer. When you think about the full context of the Great Depression years, the WPA makes more sense because you understand why it was created: to employ Americans and improve public infrastructure.

You may even want to use mnemonic devices to remember names and dates. The initials themselves (*W* and *P*) help code the memory, and you can remember that people were **w**orking on **p**rojects. (Turn to Chapter 9 for more on mnemonic devices.)

RECOGNITION: THE POLICE LINEUP OF MEMORY

You remember in many ways. Sometimes you don't have to search your mind to recall a memory. Instead, you identify the item you're trying to remember because it's right in front of you, allowing you to recognize it.

Recognition is much easier than recalling a memory. If you can't remember through free recall, recognition allows you another way to remember.

A multiple-choice exam is a type of recognition method. For example, pretend you're asked the following:

What is the most demanding way to remember information?

a. Free recall

b. Recognition

c. Standing on your head

d. True or false question

You'll recognize that the right answer is *a) Free recall.*

Another form of recognition is the police lineup. Often, six or seven individuals are lined up, and a witness is asked which one of those people he saw at the crime scene. The idea is that the simple presence of the prime suspect is meant to jog the witness's memory into recognizing him.

Yet this form of recognition is now controversial in criminal justice because it's a *forced-choice* question. In an exam at school, the student knows for sure that the right answer is present among the four possibilities offered. The person guilty of the crime may not even be in the police lineup, but the witness is asked who he thinks is the criminal among those in the line. Some witnesses feel obligated to select an individual from the police lineup, which is forced recognition.

Stretching out your learning

Procrastination and laziness are two reasons why you may wait until the night before the exam to start studying. You may think that studying at the last minute keeps the information fresh in your mind. This method of studying is called *cramming*. Cramming is a way to forget, not remember.

Cramming may be marginally useful if you're going to be tested right after the cramming session. However, its usefulness also depends on the complexity and amount of the material you cram into your brain. The information you cram in needs to be relatively superficial and limited, such as recognizing a short list of names. If the information you need to learn is more complex or there's lots of it, you'll remember very little by cramming.

REMEMBER

Another frequent mistake many students make is to stay up late burning the midnight oil the night before the exam. Not only does this late-night cramming contribute to poor memory, but the sleep deprivation also makes your mind less able to concentrate enough to recall the crammed information (see Chapter 19 for more on the importance of sleep). Make sure you get enough sleep the night before an exam. Even superficial knowledge can be accessed more easily if you're well rested.

Because cramming is such an ineffective learning method, it's just a waste of your time. Sure, you may remember a little for the next morning, but your memory of crammed information is limited, so next time, start earlier and take the time to actually learn the material!

TIP

Economize your time. If you've been told that you need 20 hours of studying on a particular subject, don't spend all those hours in a concentrated period. Spread those hours out over days and even weeks. You remember the material better.

Think of the information you're studying as seeds needing fertile ground to grow in. You won't harvest much of a crop unless the seeds are properly cared for with water, sunlight, and fertilizer. You want to be picking up the fruit and vegetables from that garden for years to come, so carefully tending the seeds makes sense.

As you spread out your studying of a subject, do a quick review of what you learned the previous session — not only to tune yourself up to take in more information but also to be able to build on top of what you've already learned. Most subject areas are cumulative. That is, today's lesson builds on yesterday's lesson.

TIP

Follow these steps:

1. **Study at first study session (sow the seeds).**

2. **Review (let the rain fall on the crops).**

3. **Study again (fertilize).**

4. **Review (let the sun shine on the crop).**

When organizing your required time to study, don't skimp on the time you devote to each lesson. You don't want each session to be so brief that you barely allow yourself to get a whiff of the material before closing the book.

Using the 20-hour allotment mentioned earlier in this section, the best way to divide your time would be to spread your 20 hours over the next 10 weeks, 2 hours per week. If you study daily for ten weeks, you'll study ten minutes per day. That's not enough! You need to allow yourself time to absorb the information. And take breaks. Taking a break not only allows your mind time to rest up but also allows you to integrate and absorb the information.

WARNING

At the other extreme, if you concentrate your studying time to four five-hour blocks, you should anticipate becoming tired and needing a break. If you don't take a break, you may waste time daydreaming or thinking about something completely irrelevant to the subject that you're trying to concentrate on.

Sectioning learning

What do you do if you have many subjects to study in one night?

TIP

If you go from one subject to another without a break between studying each subject, you run the risk of not allowing yourself the transition. That transition is critical because you want to be ready to absorb new information. You can separate your study time for various subjects by taking a break or even going to a different room. Here, you're controlling the context in which you're learning the information. You may even want to use a different pen for each subject or write notes for one subject and type on the computer for another.

If possible, segregate the times you spend on each subject, such as before and after dinner.

Learning deeply

Not only do you need to make sure that the information you're committing to memory is well organized and learned over time, but you also need to put it in context. Ask yourself how the new information relates to other information that you already know and remember. You're building a body of information that can grow over time. For example, when learning a foreign language, you need to be able to conjugate verbs, use vocabulary, string together a sentence, and respond conversationally to someone in the context in which you're meeting them.

If you sputter out a crude "You were okay?" in a foreign language rather than "How are you?", the person you're meeting may be pleased you're making an effort to speak her language, but she's probably not going to go beyond saying, "Fine. And you?" She's noticed your poor sentence construction and inappropriate verb usage. Speaking a new language requires more than learning a few words. You need to learn the many facets of the language. If you try to take in a brief tape before a trip to France, you'll remember much less than if you were to take an immersion course or live in France, or read a copy of *French For Dummies*!

In this way, the body of information you learn forms the basis for more learning. Without forming this body, you wouldn't allow yourself the opportunity to inter-link new information and probably would forget it.

Relearning

TIP

Another way to make sure that you remember is to *relearn* the subject matter. By the second and third time, you really learn the information; the previous memories are freshened up. Relearning, or freshening up, memories deepens your knowledge of the subject. A good example of relearning is taking a course in a language all over again. Each time you take the class, you get a little better, and understanding and speaking becomes a bit easier. Learning a language requires practice.

Putting relearning and direct recall together

Relearning by taking the same course a second or third time is a luxurious way to improve your memory. You may not have that option. You have to take the shorter, harder route of *direct recall.* The big problem with direct recall is that it's open-ended, kind of like the memory equivalent of staring into space and hoping to spot a shooting star.

You can make direct recall work better if you box it in with some relearning techniques. Suppose you're asked to name the capitals of all the states on the East Coast of the United States, recalling a lesson from the past. When you begin thinking, you may decide to use the *cued recall* approach, using the state name to remind you of the capital city name, like this:

    Maine: _____

    New Hampshire: _____

    Massachusetts: _____

Rhode Island: _____

Connecticut: _____

New York: _____

New Jersey: _____

Maryland: _____

Delaware: _____

Virginia: _____

North Carolina: _____

South Carolina: _____

Georgia: _____

Florida: _____

If your teacher sees you sweating bullets and is tenderhearted, she may offer an additional cue to help you make an association — the first letter of each capital city:

Maine: A_____

New Hampshire: C_____

Massachusetts: B_____

Rhode Island: P_____

Connecticut: H_____

New York: A_____

New Jersey: T_____

Maryland: A_____

Delaware: D_____

Virginia: R_____

North Carolina: R_____

South Carolina: C_____

Georgia: A_____

Florida: T_____

Because you've probably encountered this information before, when you went over the list, you probably challenged yourself to remember the capitals again. You relearned the material.

What if you were to relearn the list of the presidents of the United States? If asked to list them in order, you'd be performing a *serial recall task*. Now suppose you were asked to list the first 12 presidents and given only the first letter of each of their last names:

W_____

A_____

J_____

M_____

M_____

A_____

J_____

V_____

H_____

T_____

P_____

T_____

In this case, you were relearning information by using a *peg first-letter cue* in a serial arrangement. As you can see, the peg technique cues your recall by using the first letters of the presidents' surnames in historical order (see Chapter 9 for more on pegs and other mnemonic devices). By requiring yourself to use a peg cue to recall information you learned previously (such as the previous example), you'll probably remember it well into the future.

Striving for Meaning Rather Than Rote

Rote learning is the regurgitation of unattached and meaningless facts. These facts are prone to be forgotten because you haven't incorporated them into a body of knowledge. You have no context in which to remember them.

Unfortunately, too much of what's taught in school is still based on rote learning. Your job is to deepen the meaning of what you learn and put it in context so that you can remember it later.

To *have knowledge* means that you understand the meaning of facts, how they're organized, and how they fit into what you already know about a particular subject area. Because the meaningfulness of information determines how well you remember it, rote memorization isn't exactly the best method of learning. (Maybe schools will someday realize this truth, too.) An example of rote learning would be to try to memorize the list of presidents in the preceding section without any association or memory cues.

When you try to remember the list by factoring in meaning, you may consider, for example, that George Washington was the principal general who helped the colonies gain independence from England. In addition, the three presidents to follow were major contributors to the Declaration of Independence and the Constitution.

How well the information that you're trying to remember is organized has a lot to do with the degree of its meaningfulness. So, the more meaningful the information is, the more likely you are to remember it.

Having some interest in the subject matter that you're trying to commit to memory is helpful. This interest forms part of the meaning that you can attach to the information to help you remember it.

For example, many people complain that they have little interest in mathematics, yet they're required to learn it nevertheless. You may say, "I'm no good at math." Your lack of interest or your self-paralyzing fear of math creates a self-fulfilling prophecy — you don't retain what you learn.

TIP

If you're trying to remember something, you can always *think around it*. For example, suppose you're trying to remember who was the second president of the United States after Abraham Lincoln; Johnson succeeded him, but who came next? If you *think around* the question, perhaps you'll touch on Reconstruction and then move back to Lincoln. Perhaps you'll move back to the Civil War and then to the surrender at Appomattox. You begin to wonder which two generals were present. Robert E. Lee for the South, of course, and Ulysses S. Grant for the North. Hey, wasn't Grant later elected president?

This chain of associations is like a series of links that you click as you surf the Internet. As you read about the Civil War on one page, you click on the blue hypertext word *Appomattox*. Then at that page, you click on word *generals*. These links are associations. They each focus on one topic, but they link and relate to similar topics and give you a broader knowledge base.

Taking Notes and Remembering What You've Heard

You're often going to be slightly familiar with some of the information presented during a lecture. For example, you know a little about the Middle East, but not much. Your task is to link up and modify what you already know with the new information that you're not familiar with, making associations and links.

WARNING

Some people take notes during a lecture and never read them over again. Don't be one of those people! Although you'll probably remember *some* main points without reviewing your notes, think of all the information you're throwing away. Your notes provide a condensed outline of what the lecture was about from your perspective, which can be very useful for learning the material in a meaningful way to ensure that you'll remember it well.

TIP

Try to go over your notes soon after the lecture while everything is still fresh in your mind. Doing so can help you code the information more thoroughly, which allows you to move it into long-term memory.

As you go over your notes, you can highlight, scratch out, or add to what you've written down. You'll have a better picture of the subject matter and of how all the elements of information are integrated into a whole body of knowledge.

TIP

Highlighting is a great way to bring out the major points. Some people underline; others use a colored highlighter. Either way, you're making your next glance at your notes more productive because those highlighted points will stand out and form the essentials of what you need to remember. From this perspective, you can look back at your notes and make better links between points and what you already knew about the information.

TIP

Use diagrams and visual props in your notes whenever possible. Visual images can help anchor concepts into memory and serve to boil down or connect subjects. For example, if you write words like *short-term, long-term, recall, recognition,* and so on and draw arrows to the word *memory,* you'll know that they're all related to or part of memory.

When going over the notes, you also want to look for gaps. Ask a peer who was with you at the lecture if he "got what the lecturer said about. . . ." You allow yourself to fill in the gaps of information you missed (which is typical because lecturers often go over material faster than most people can integrate it).

TIP

An even better way to fill the gaps in your notes is to go up to the lecturer after the talk and ask her to fill in the parts you didn't quite get. She'll most likely elaborate and provide you with additional useful information that helps you to integrate the subject into your long-term memory.

In a classroom setting, you can also go early to the next class and ask for clarification on the areas you're still hazy on. You may be better able to formulate a good question after you've gone over your notes and done the assigned reading. She'll respond by not only answering your questions but maybe also even beginning the next lecture in such a way that she integrates what she said previously. She'll also realize that other students need more clarification as well.

Don't be afraid to approach the lecturer in these ways. She won't take your questions as a sign that you're dumb. Rather, she'll take them as a sign that you're attentive, motivated, interested, and really want to understand the material.

REMEMBER

One of the most important prerequisites for memory is attention. If you attend a lecture and only your body is in attendance, you probably won't remember anything. Make sure your mind's there, too — no matter how boring the lecture may be.

TIP

Challenge yourself to see beyond the lecturer's inadequacies and the social scene. Think of the content of the lecture as a destination you must travel to despite being blasted by a dust storm. Try to forge ahead with your goggles on and your head tucked into your scarf. You can usually see where the lecturer is pointing you to go even if the directions are fuzzy. Go there and meet the information, even if it's badly presented.

Remembering What You Read

If you're like most people, you've had the experience of reading an entire page and then realizing that you weren't paying attention. Your mind was off daydreaming about what you planned to do on the weekend or what you should've said to that rude store clerk.

Reading retention is a big issue in educational circles. Having the ability to read a sentence, pronounce all the words fluently, and have a vocabulary wide enough that doesn't necessitate referring to a dictionary is one thing. But having the ability to remember what you read is something else entirely. If you can't remember what you read, why read at all?

If you want to make sure you retain what you read, try to use one or part of the various study systems developed by educators. Along with psychologists, they've been studying how people retain what they read for a long time. Learn from their experience!

TIP

One of the oldest such systems is called *SQ3R*. (Many of these systems have names that make them appear more complicated than they really are.) The SQ3R system works like this:

S = **S**urvey the book.

Q = **Q**uestion. Generate questions based on your survey.

R = **R**ead the book.

R = **R**ecite the material.

R = **R**eview.

To begin with, consider what you do when you open a nonfiction book you hope to be able to remember after you've completed it. If you simply barrel into reading it without looking it over, you may find yourself wondering what's coming up or not understanding how this body of knowledge is organized.

Survey the book

The first step in remembering what you read is to *survey* the material. Scan the book cover to cover. Read the dust jacket (if it has one) and the preface. Then read the acknowledgments section to get an idea of what the author went through to write the book, who the author was influenced by, and who made significant contributions.

Scan the table of contents to see how the book is organized and how the chapters present the information. Read the chapter summaries and look at the graphs, pictures, and diagrams. This way, you learn a great deal about the subject before you actually read the book. In many ways, you've begun to glimpse the big picture that the book offers. This overview gives you a framework on which to hang the new information you gather as you read the book.

Develop questions

Generate *questions* based on what you saw in your scan of the book. These questions can provoke other thoughts about what you expect when reading further.

Later, during the actual reading (remember, you haven't even begun reading yet), your questions may be answered as you begin to master the subject matter. If not, you can always find more books on the subject and read further to get more answers.

Read the book

The third step in the SQ3R system is to read everything. Don't skim. You can highlight or underline the important bits, such as the passages that answer the questions you formulated, as you go along.

WARNING

Don't underline or highlight too much. Not everything you read is intended to be a kernel of truth or the heart of the subject matter. When you go over the material later, you don't want to sift through page after page of over-underlined sentences, wondering why you went crazy with your pen. Remember that a highlighter should light up the high points.

TIP

In addition to underlining, use vertical lines to the right or left of the text to indicate particular sections that are important. These sections elaborate upon the sections that you underline above or below the vertical lines. Use a double line to indicate that the section is particularly important.

Many people do their underlining on the second reading to ensure that they don't underline points that don't end up being that important. If you don't have time for two readings, you can underline as you do your one read through the material. (Just don't let your highlighter get carried away and underline every word as you read it!)

Recite the material

After you finish reading the entire book, you can now move to the next step of the SQ3R system: reciting. Reciting the material can help you integrate, understand at a deeper level, and pull everything together. If you can explain the material to another person, you really do understand it.

One advantage of teaching is that by speaking so much out loud, the teacher is forced to really know the material. In this way, teaching is learning.

Spend as much time as possible on the material that you aren't quite sure about. As you do, you bring it into focus with the material you already understand and deepen your memory of it.

Review main points and notes

Your job isn't completely done yet. The next task is to review. Here's your chance to go over it all again. Make use of your underlined passages and highlight as review your notes. In fact, incorporating review into your reading process is always a good idea. After you read each section (even the first time through), review the main points in that section.

Because most forgetting occurs soon after information is read, the reviewing step allows you the opportunity to really lay down those memories in a comprehensive way, inputting them into long-term storage.

IN THIS CHAPTER

Getting happiness from childhood memories

Creating connections for new information

Developing skills for a lifetime

Chapter 12

Honing Your Long-Term Memory

Long-term memory is when you retain information for a long period of time. You remember some events like your special sweet 16 birthday for years and years, yet other, less memorable events don't last more than a week.

Think of long-term memory like a library full of books. Some books get read more than others, so it's easier to remember which shelf you left them on. With long-term memory, some experiences are better remembered than others because you think about those memories more.

Chapter 13 discusses short-term memory, which is like browsing a library's shelves. You may remember the titles in front of you for a brief time but you wouldn't be able to recite them the next week. Short-term memory is just that: short.

Remembering Your Past: Autobiographical Memory

Your childhood memories play an important role in keeping your brain alert. For starters, remembering past experiences is important because they serve as a template for how to solve present and future problems. These types of memories act as a guide for both brain and behavior in responding and reacting successfully when presented with a challenging situation. Past experiences, such as your childhood memories, act like a bridge to connect new information with stored knowledge.

Discovering the importance of childhood memories

It's often hard to remember memories before the age of 3 because language skills aren't well developed. If you can't speak, how can you talk about what you did that day? And if you can't articulate what you did, how can you add it to the library shelf of your long-term memory?

I KNOW THAT YOU DID IT!

False memories can appear in adulthood. You may remember an incident with a friend that never actually occurred or a trip that you never took. Although most of these memories are usually quite harmless, sometimes they can cause a problem. Eyewitness testimony is one such example. People are actually very bad at remembering important details and are easily misled by the questions people ask. Psychologists tested this theory with a group of adults by showing video footage of a car accident. The psychologists asked one group to estimate the speed of the car when it *hit* another car. They asked the other group the same question, but using the phrase *smashed* the other car. People in the second group "remembered" broken glass in the video footage, even though no broken glass was present at all. It seems that when you ask people a misleading question, their memory of the event is wrong.

Other studies have found that when faced with something is shocking in an event, like a man holding a gun, people only focus on the gun and can't remember what the man looks like. Imagine what happens when an observer sees a crime. So much is going on — people are yelling, cars are honking, everything is chaotic. Can you really expect that memory of the criminal's face to be reliable? What if the man was wearing a hat or covering his face? How can witnesses be sure of what they saw?

It's actually quite difficult to recognize someone's face. One tip is to immediately focus on something distinctive, like facial hair or piercings. This can make it a little easier to identify someone at the crime scene. You can also write down what you saw right away. Chapter 4 provides more suggestions on how to improve your memory for faces, whether for business, pleasure, or as a critical eyewitness to a crime.

Another reason memories from a very young age are hard to remember is because the brain isn't fully developed then. Chapter 4 talks about the hippocampus. This part of the brain plays an important role in consolidating memories, and it's not fully developed before two years of age. This makes it hard for very young children to form connections between their experiences and transfer that into their long-term memory library.

TIP

To remind yourself of your happy childhood memories, take a walk down memory lane. Flick through your photo albums to trigger happy holidays, and read through old birthday cards and letters that you've exchanged with loved ones. Sometimes you can forget how many happy moments you've had, and reminding yourself is important. Don't store your photo albums in a hard-to-reach place like an attic. Instead, keep them in a prominent place like a bookshelf so you can reach for them regularly.

WARNING

Not all memories are reliable. A *false memory*, as the name suggests, is a memory of an event that never happened or an embellishment of an event that did happen. This occurrence is most common with childhood memories. You may remember an event that never occurred, such as owning a rabbit when you were little. You can also have a memory that elaborates on an event that did actually occur. If, for example, you had a dog as a pet, you may remember that you and your dog used to chase rabbits in the nearby field. However, your parents may point out that you lived in a busy city with no fields nearby.

Harnessing the power of happy memories

Emotions play a big role in how much you remember as well. You may remember something from your childhood because you did it all the time, but some memories last because they create a vivid snapshot of an experience. This can be a happy and unexpected event, but it can also be something shocking.

TECHNICAL
STUFF

Do you remember where you were when you first heard of President Kennedy's or Princess Diana's death? What were you doing when the news of the 9/11 attacks broke? Most people remember these events in vivid detail even though they were just doing something ordinary. Why is that? *Flashbulb* memories are memories that contain strong emotion and therefore become significant. As a result, mundane events suddenly become more meaningful, and you remember trivial details. But just because you remember the events doesn't mean that all the details you remember are correct. One man described how he was woken up at 6 a.m. by an earthquake. However, reports show that the earthquake took place at noon, not 6 a.m.

Here are some suggestions on how you can focus on your happy memories:

>> **The past is the past**. If you have a difficult memory, don't sit around and feel sorry for yourself. You can't change that memory, only how you feel about it.

Be more positive. Think of ways that event made you a stronger and better person. You may also think of reasons why people did what they did. For example, now that you're older (and wiser), you may realize what a difficult life your school bully had. This knowledge doesn't make the memory go away, but you can understand it better in retrospect. Putting this more positive twist on your experience can drive change in your life.

>> **Scrapbooking is no scrappy task.** Forgetting what a great holiday you had is easy, especially as time moves on and you get more entrenched in the daily grind. But stopping to remember what a wonderful time you had is important. Scrapbooking is a fun and great way to preserve precious memories. Many different websites give you guidelines and templates to get you started. Some people save tickets stubs to events they went to, brochures or postcards of places they visited, or even a leaf or flower from a hike in a park that they loved. You can add all these mementos to your scrapbook. You can even buy special books and materials for scrapbooking if you want a little help displaying your photos and mementos creatively.

TIP

Many scrapbooking groups exist, so why not join one? Sharing your happy memories strengthens them in your mind and brings pleasant details to mind.

>> **Have a snack.** Think back on those lazy, sunny summer days when you didn't have to go to school and could spend all day at the park. Food can serve as a fantastic trigger for happy childhood memories because the taste and smell can remind you of a specific event. If you're missing your family and childhood friends, even thinking about the foods you used to enjoy together can boost your mood.

TECHNICAL STUFF

If you were to sit down and list your top 20 memories, you might find that most of them are from your 20s and 30s. That's not unusual. Most people try big things for the first time during this period and so tend to remember them more clearly. This may include first mature relationships, books that sparked late-night debates, special trips, and first mortgages. This period is known as the *reminiscence bump* because a "bump" or peak in the number of memories that you can easily recall from this time exists.

Using Your Everyday Knowledge: Semantic Memory

Semantic memory refers to your library of knowledge — bits of information that you've collected over the years. Consider the useless facts about the animal kingdom, treasured details about football statistics, and even capital cities of countries you've visited. Think of semantic memory as your personal encyclopedia or Wikipedia in your head.

Look at this list of words and say out loud the first thing that comes to your mind.

Bread — ?

Dog — ?

Tea — ?

You may have said the following pairs:

Bread — butter

Dog — cat

Tea — coffee

What words you came up with isn't really significant because most people have a huge knowledge store to match the words in this example. If asked to name three things about a bird, you'd use information from your semantic memory to answer.

Knowing the Eiffel Tower from the Leaning Tower

Learning facts about the world is something you never stop doing. Just because you're no longer at school doesn't mean you stop gaining knowledge. Learning something new is a three-stage process:

>> *Encoding* refers to how you represent the information in your memory.

>> *Storage* is how you keep the information in your head.

>> *Retrieval* is how you access the information when you need it.

Here are some tips to help you encode information better:

>> **Picture this.** If you have to remember a list of new words, create a visual image in your mind instead of just repeating the words in your head. If you're at a party, don't just say someone's name to remind yourself. Think of what the person's wearing and where she was standing when you met her. All these visual cues help trigger your memory when you have to remember the

person's name at a later date. Chapter 4 lists more strategies to help you remember names and faces.

>> **Make it deep.** It's easier just to remember something new that you read by looking at it superficially, such as what the words looks like or sound like. But this method doesn't help much at all to create a long-term memory. Instead, think of what those words mean; make a mental picture of what those words convey. As a result, you think about the information in a more meaningful way, which makes the information stick in your head much more thoroughly.

>> **Organize, organize, organize.** Has anyone ever said to you, "I already told you that so many times; why can't you remember?" Everyone knows the feeling — you can hear something over and over again and yet never remember it. But you can change that. Create a framework to help you organize new information. When you read something, think of your framework and attach what you're reading to your framework. It helps you remember the contents of what you read much better.

>> **Create a connection.** Link new information to something you already know. Don't just list the new information that you're learning, but think carefully about how you can connect it to something you know well. If you're learning a new history fact, think of an event with which you're familiar and create a link between the new and familiar historical facts. This process — called *semantic linking* — can help you retrieve the information later on.

TIP

Just repeating something is unlikely to help you remember. You need to make the information meaningful if you want to remember it. That's why late-night cramming before exams doesn't work very well. Instead, when you elaborate on what you're learning using the strategies listed in the preceding bulleted list, you're more successful at encoding the information for recall later.

The following section lists additional ways for better storage.

Making associations that last

Why do you forget things? First of all, realize that forgetting is simply the natural course of information. Items in your memory decay over time, just like food grows stale in the pantry. Another reason you forget is that when you learn something new, you can confuse it with something old. If the information is similar, it's easier to get confused. A third possibility for why you forget is because you can't remember "where" you stored the information.

DOMINIC O'BRIEN'S AMAZING MEMORY

Dominic O'Brien, eight-time winner of the World Memory Championships, holds many titles in the *Guinness Book of World Records*. One amazing feat he performs is memorizing 54 decks of playing cards in just a few hours.

Dominic uses a great illustration to create a bridge between new information and long-term knowledge (semantic memory). He usually uses a list of 10 to 15 words, but 5 can be used to describe the process: *bomb, helium, light, beryl, coal*. Most people struggle to remember all the words, and if they read them in the morning, by lunchtime only a handful of folks can still recite even three words from the list.

Dominic tells the following story:

You're asleep in your bed one night when you hear a loud explosion. It sounds like a **bomb**! Before you can do anything, you spot a **helium** balloon in the sky shining a bright **light** on the ground. You think that they're looking for the perpetrator. The light seems to be moving toward your room but instead it stops and shines on your neighbor **Beryl's** house. You start to worry that more bombs are going to start going off so you make your way out of the house and into the garden. Someone has left a large bag of **coal** in the middle of the walkway, and you trip over it in the dark.

The story goes on, and as you can imagine that most people are drawn into it. To their amazement, they find that by the end of the day, they're able to remember the five words in the correct order and can even recite the list backward! The story has given them a framework to remember the words in context. The words in the list provide a clue to the first few elements in the periodic table: bomb (hydrogen), helium (helium), light (lithium), beryl (beryllium) and coal (carbon). Now you too can easily remember these words simply by thinking about the story.

Use the following tips to help you remember where you were when you learned that information that keeps escaping your memory:

>> **Contextualize.** The context in which you hear information is a powerful trigger to unlock your memory. If you're struggling to remember something, go back to the place where you first heard or read the information. At work, go back to the room where you stood and recreate the scenario to trigger your memory. If a friend gave you some important information to remember, go back to the café or restaurant where you had that conversation. If you forgot why you went into the living room, retrace your steps, and the reason may come back to you. (For a detailed example, see the nearby sidebar "Where you are matters.")

>> **Remember your state.** The mood you were in when you learned the information also can act as a trigger to help you remember. If you were in a good mood when you first heard the instructions for your next work project but now can't remember them, try to think about that same emotion. Remembering how you felt at the time of learning can help you recall what you learned.

TECHNICAL STUFF

Proactive interference is when old information you know makes it harder to remember new information. An example of proactive interference is when you finally get a new PIN for your credit card but keep trying to use the old number instead. *Retroactive interference* is when something new makes you forget something you were previously thinking about. An example is when you forget where you're going because you had to stop to look for your car keys.

TIP

Still struggling? Use cues to trigger your memory. Imagine that you're learning the Spanish words for *shoes, hat, belt, shirt, trousers, chair, table, desk,* and *lamp.* First, group the items that belong together and then think of category headings to help you retrieve this information. Studies have found that when you use category cues, like *clothes* and *furniture* for this example, you're twice as likely to remember all the words associated with the category. You can try this with any group of items, like colors or eating utensils (such as *fork, spoon,* and *knife*).

WHERE YOU ARE MATTERS

A diving instructor was puzzled because his divers kept forgetting objects that they'd observed underwater, even when he asked the divers about the objects they'd seen shortly after they were back on dry land. To find out why this was the case, some psychologists conducted an experiment testing divers' memories.

The psychologists gave one group of underwater divers a list of words to learn underwater and gave another group a list to learn on land. They then tested the divers' memories of the word list both on land and underwater.

The group that learned the list underwater remembered the list much better when they were back in the water but struggled to remember it on land. They remembered better in the environment in which they'd learned. The reverse occurred with the group who originally learned the list on land; they had better memory of the list when on land than when they were underwater.

This story is a great example of how remembering where you were when you learned the information can boost your memory.

50 FIRST DATES

You may remember a quirky movie called *50 First Dates* about a woman, played by Drew Barrymore, who's lost her ability to form long-term memories. Although this storyline may seem far-fetched, some people do suffer memory loss like this as the result of a brain injury. Consider the story of 47-year-old Michele. As a result of two car accidents, all her memories before 1994 have been "erased." Her long-suffering husband has to show her their wedding photos daily to remind her of what they share.

To complicate things for Michelle, she's unable to convert daily experiences in her short-term memory to long-term memory. This means that it's not unusual for her to leave the house only to forget where she's going. She relies on technology like GPS guidance to get her to places just half a mile from her house. Michelle describes each day as a new day with no memory of what she experienced the day before. Although she loves certain TV programs, she can't remember the characters and can't follow the plotlines. She's upbeat, though, and says that at least she feels that she's never seen the same show twice.

Did you ever get the feeling that you know what something is but you just can't get the right words to say it? Chapter 2 discusses the *tip-of-the-tongue phenomenon*.

Long-term Skills: Procedural Memory

Can you describe how you tie your shoelace? You may struggle, though you'd probably have no difficulty if you actually had a shoe in your hand and had to get ready to go out. Why is it so difficult to give a step-by-step breakdown for simple tasks that some people do every day, like tying a shoelace, driving a car, or even writing your name?

Procedural memory refers to the skills you have that are automatic — things you no longer have to spend much time thinking about, like writing your address or tying a tie. Your brain remembers what to do without actually keeping track of each step. That's why it's often hard to break down the process. How do you learn something so well that it becomes procedural memory and you no longer have to think about it? For example, you may be trying to learn a new language. Initially, you have to translate each word you want to say from English. But over time (with practice) you learn to speak fluently without the translation step.

The following sections offer tips to transfer that new information into a long-lasting memory.

Practicing for perfection

Practice makes permanent. This statement holds much truth. When you do something over and over again, you're training both your brain and your muscles to remember it. Athletes refer to this as *muscle memory* (see Chapter 4), where you do an action automatically because your muscles "remember how to do it," such as riding a bicycle or skating. If you don't learn something correctly the first time, your body has to unlearn the incorrect way first before it can learn a new and better way of doing something.

Think of how you hold a pencil. Maybe your teacher was very strict with all her students, and you could only hold the pencil one way or you'd get in trouble. That pencil-holding technique was likely ingrained, and you'd find it uncomfortable to hold a pencil any other way. Or maybe you like skiing and decide to take some lessons — despite having skied already for a number of years. You may be surprised to discover that your posture and form aren't good. Your instructor will have to work harder to get you to change your form than if she was teaching a person who never skied before. That's because your muscles have learned a certain way of skiing that you now have to unlearn in order to pick up the correct form. So the next time you're learning something new, make sure you do it the correct way the first time around. That way you don't have to learn it twice.

The *law of effect* illustrates the power of reward in learning and remembering what you learned. This law is very simple: If you receive something enjoyable as a result of learning something new, you're more likely to repeat the behavior that caused you to learn. As a child, these rewards may be gold stickers or a good grade on an exam. As an adult, they may be praise from a loved one or even a promotion at work. But there's another side to the law of effect: If you receive something negative, such as criticism or disappointment, as a result of learning something new, you're less likely to repeat that behavior.

TIP

Reward yourself! Gold stars and colorful stickers aren't just for the classroom. Set up a reward system when you're trying to learn something new. Break down the information into smaller chunks. Each time you're successful at learning a chunk, give yourself a "sticker." After you've successfully completed the task, treat yourself to the reward you set — a new dress, a short holiday, a trip to the movies. The treat doesn't have to cost money; it can also be a special day with friends. The goal is to create incentives for your brain to absorb the information and associate positive emotions with the learning process. This method not only makes learning more pleasurable but also helps you remember the information for much longer.

As a bonus, when you think back on your reward or look at photos of the event, it serves as a trigger to help you remember the information that you learned.

Many famous athletes have a little superstitious routine that they do before a game. Maybe they tie their laces a certain way or sleep in their uniform the night before a big game. One major league hockey player stuck his hockey stick in the toilet before each game! Although these routines do very little to help create connections in memory that last, some people think that repeating familiar routines can help to reduce anxiety before an important performance or activity.

You may have your own superstitions about doing something before you go on a date or give a presentation. But it's far more productive to think of positive actions that are directly related to the event rather than something unrelated. For example, before a date, think of questions that you want to ask the person (not in an interrogative way); and before a presentation, think of the key points that you want to get across.

Training in your sleep

Sleep is a great booster for learning. Having a rest after learning something strengthens the information you learned. Think of your school days. Remember those multiple-choice exams? They looked so easy, yet they could be so confusing because when more than one choice seemed like the right answer. Many situations in daily life can be confusing. For example, you may forget whether you turned off the oven when you left the house.

Not only does sleep improve memory, but when you're rested you also make fewer errors in working on a task. When you sleep, your brain uses this time to recharge and separate real events and factual information from information that's not correct. As a result, you're more refreshed and less likely to get confused and forget whether you left the oven on. Chapter 19 talks more about the power of sleep in recharging your brain.

Thinking like a musician

When musicians try to memorize a piece of music, they don't just play a song over and over again. They also get their brain involved and *think* about what they're doing. The reason is simple. If all musicians do is play a song over and over again, their muscles learn the movement, but if they get distracted partway through the song, it's hard for them to pick up and carry on playing where they left off. In fact, some people have to start all over from the beginning because they can't just pick up playing from a random point in the song.

TIP

You don't have to be a virtuoso musician to benefit from musicians' techniques. When you're learning something new or have to do something that makes you nervous, such as giving a presentation at work, get your brain involved. Focusing carefully on what you need to do. First, get rid of distractions. Next, instead of just giving your presentation over and over again out loud, you can also give it in your head. Go over different questions that your colleagues may ask you. Finally, stop and think about your answers to these questions when you're halfway through the presentation. And then pick up from where you stopped and continue your presentation.

Chapter 13

Improving Your Short-Term Memory

You're meeting some friends after work and one of them introduces you to a new person. After exchanging names and spending the evening sharing similar interests, you make plans to keep in touch. The man gives you his phone number, but you realize you can't easily get to your cellphone to add him to your contacts. "Never mind," you say. "I can remember it." After repeating the phone number a few times to yourself, you head home. Sensibly, you decide to jot down the number as soon as you walk in the door. Too late! You can't remember the last four digits.

Short-term memory is the space that you have to hold information for a brief time. You can think of short-term memory like a holding zone: You don't keep information in your short-term memory for long — just long enough until you can transfer the information to a piece of paper, your computer, or even your long-term memory store.

This chapter looks at how you can train three types of short-term memory: verbal, visual, and spatial. Although you may sometimes use these types of memory together, you usually tend to focus on one at a time.

Speaking Your Brain's Language: Verbal Memory

Verbal short-term memory refers to language and information that you hear.

Ask someone to read out the following letters while you try to remember them:

NBCUSAATM

How did you do? Were you able to remember all nine letters in the correct order? You may have figured out that you can break up these letters to look like this:

NBC — USA — ATM

You can see that each unit represents a very common acronym. This probably made it a lot easier for you to remember the letters.

Now try this one, already broken into smaller sections for you:

CRM — BRD — UAL

You probably found this example more difficult. Even breaking the letters down into smaller sections didn't help. You may have already guessed why: The acronyms were unfamiliar. This is what they mean:

CRM: Customer Relationship Management

BRD: Biological Resource Division

UAL: United Airlines

Did knowing what the acronyms mean help you remember the letters? It may not have because here again the meanings may have been unfamiliar.

Most people can remember only seven pieces of information at a single time. A *piece* of information can refer to one number or one word, or even one instruction. When you group information together into three-letter sets, such as in the example with the letters (NBC — USA — ATM), each group counts as one piece of information, not three, so you only have to remember three pieces of information total rather than nine separate letters. This process of *chunking* or grouping information together is the reason you may be able to recall a seven-digit local phone number better than a ten-digit mobile number.

REMEMBER

A common expression when discussing the limits of short-term memory is *seven plus or minus two*. This idea means that a few people can remember up to nine pieces of information, and some as little as five, but most remember seven.

So how can you boost your verbal short-term memory? The following sections give you strategies and tips to do just that.

Giving your brain the best chance to remember

The human brain is a marvel, but you can give yours a further leg up by keeping these tried-and-tested short-term memory tips in mind:

>> **Time matters.** When you hear information affects how well you remember it. For example, you remember words at the beginning of a list better than words presented in the middle of a list because you're able to rehearse them more. This is known as the primacy effect. Also, you best remember items at the end of a list, even more than those words at the beginning, because you've just heard them and don't need to remember them for as long. This is known as the recency effect. So if someone gives you a long list of things to do, break it down into smaller lists to avoid the "slump" in the middle of the list.

>> **Turn down the distractions.** An unrelated thought springing to mind, a telephone ringing, a child crying, or any other distraction is often sufficient to erase the contents of your verbal short-term memory. That's because unless you continue to pay full attention to the contents of short-term memory, they decay very rapidly and are soon lost for good. Placing yourself in situations that minimize distractions is very important if you're going to make effective use of working memory. Background noise also plays a role in how much material you can remember. Silence is much more conducive to good verbal short-term memory. If you're trying to remember important information, you may find that turning off the music helps.

>> **Focus on one thing.** Activities that require you to switch your attention from one thing to another can speed up how fast you forget something. The act of switching or multitasking can overload you and result in your forgetting even simple things. You may find yourself standing at top of your stairs thinking, "What did I come up here for?" Doing too many things at the same time means you're unable to do each thing well, including remembering. So cut back — do one task at a time. You'll find yourself doing each task better and with greater memory of what you're doing.

SPEED IT UP!

Psychologists have found that talking quickly can make a difference in retaining information. Look at these lists of words:

> Four — six — four — seven
> Pedwar — chwech — pedwar — saith

The first list takes a lot less time to say than the second list. Does this affect verbal short-term memory?

Psychologists found that English-speaking children could remember the first list of numbers much better than the second list. They gave the second list of numbers (in Welsh) to students in Wales. Their scores were much lower despite their understanding the words.

This result was very puzzling until the psychologists realized that speed does matter! It took the Welsh students much longer to say the numbers in Welsh, which affected their scores. After they took the speed of saying the numbers out of the equation, no difference between the two groups of children existed.

WARNING

>> **Know your limits.** Although breaking longer lists into smaller parts can be helpful (see the first bullet in this list), avoid overloading your memory by giving yourself bite-sized chunks of information to remember. Remembering the key chunks of information is more important than trying to prove yourself as the next memory champion by keeping a long string of information in your head.

Talking fast to remember more

You may think of a fast talker as a smooth operator or someone who's trying to scam you by selling you something you really don't need. Actually, talking fast can do wonders for your verbal short-term memory.

REMEMBER

Saying information that you need to remember over and over again can help you remember what you need. But keep two things in mind:

>> **Length counts.** The length of a word makes a big difference in how well you can remember it. Look at these words: *refrigerator, hippopotamus, Mississippi, aluminum.* You're more likely to forget them compared to words that you can repeat more easily, such as *bus, clock, spoon,* and *fish.* The *word length effect* is

the idea that longer it takes to repeat or rehearse something, the harder it is to remember; that is, longer words are harder to remember. To boost your memory of longer words, be sure to look at a ist in addition to just listening to it. The visual image will enhance your verbal remembrance.

>> **Sounds matter.** A list of words that have distinct sounds (such as *bus, clock, spoon, fish,* and *mouse*) is much easier to remember than a list of words that sound very similar (such as *man, cat, map, mat can,* and *cap*). When things sound similar, you're more likely to get confused and forget.

Seeing Your Brain's Perspective: Visual Memory

Visual short-term memory deals with images, such as photos and pictures — information that's not in verbal form. You use visual short-term memory to recognize places you've been, photos you've seen, and other images you need to store mentally.

Try your visual short-term memory on the test shown in Figure 13-1. Look at the image and then cover it up and look at the empty grid in Figure 13-2.

In Figure 13-2, point to where the dots were on the grid in the correct order that they were shown in Figure 13-1. How many dots can you remember? Most adults can remember about three or four dots in the correct order.

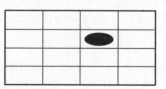

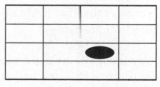

FIGURE 13-1:
An example of a visual short-term memory test — part one.

© John Wiley & Sons, Inc.

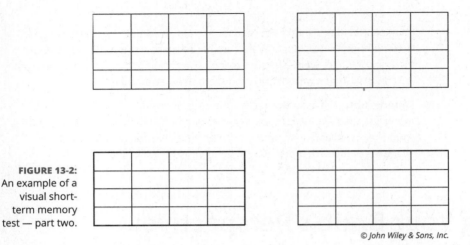

FIGURE 13-2:
An example of a
visual short-
term memory
test — part two.

Visual short-term memory doesn't last very long. Yet it's quite resistant to distraction. When you were looking at Figure 13-1, you probably blinked several times, looked away to check something else out, and maybe even let your mind drift to another thought. But you did quite well at remembering the locations on the grid in Figure 13-2 because your eyes take a "snapshot" of what they see, and your brain stores that image. Your brain doesn't save the image for long, though, which explains why you find it easier to recognize someone you just met on that same day than a few days later.

TECHNICAL
STUFF

Visual short-term memory skills are usually slightly weaker than verbal short-term memory ones. Most people find it easier to remember words, numbers, and verbal information than to remember images. One explanation for this is that memory is used much more for language than for images.

Chapter 4 discusses how visual memory is at a high level before you learn to talk. However, as you learn language, your brain uses visual memory less (and verbal memory more), so visual memory ability becomes rusty. That chapter mentions ways you can keep your visual memory sharp whatever your age.

Harnessing the power of visualization

Visualization is a powerful tool. Don't underestimate its effectiveness. Numerous studies show that the brain responds to visualization in the same way as it does to physical practice.

Psychologists divided basketball players into three groups. They asked one group to practice shooting baskets daily; another group to only visualize shooting baskets but not actually practice; and a final group to do nothing at all. After a month, the psychologists tested the basketball skills of all three groups. As you may guess, the people who'd been practicing diligently for the last month improved their skills by 24 percent. Most surprising was that the people who'd just visualized shooting baskets *also* improved their skills to almost the same level as those who were actually practicing! And as expected, the people who'd done nothing did really poorly and seemed to have lost some of their skills.

Not convinced yet? A Harvard study found that people who visualized playing the piano activated the same part of the brain as those who actually practiced the piano.

Here are some pointers for how to harness the power of visualization in your own life:

>> **Close your eyes.** Sometimes this tactic can help you block out distractions around you and focus just on what you want to remember. Is it someone's face? A map? Close your eyes and imagine the image in your head.

>> **Draw it out.** If you're a list writer, here's a twist. Instead of writing down what you need to do — for example, if you've invited friends over for a Sunday roast and you need to remind yourself to thaw the meat and buy potatoes — why not draw it? Another way to visualize things is to make a graph or a diagram. You outline everything you need to do to prepare for your Sunday dinner — take out the meat to thaw, season it, put it in the pan with the potatoes, and slide the pan into the oven — as a diagram.

>> **Write it out.** Keep in mind that visualizing doesn't just use pictures or images. If you're the type of person who needs to see things written out, don't change that. Keep writing down what you need to remember. Just keep the information accessible and visible so you don't waste mental energy trying to remember where you left your list.

TIP

Some people find it useful to leave their list near their task. For example, you can place a shopping list on the fridge door, directions to a party near your car keys, and a list of errands for the day in your coat pocket. Put your list in a meaningful location right away. Chances are you'll forget where you left your list if you wait until later.

>> **Be an imaginary teacher.** If you're trying to remember some particularly difficult information, perhaps when studying for a course or a presentation at work, imagine yourself teaching the information to an imaginary audience. Visualizing yourself giving your presentation ahead of time can have the same impact as practicing it over and over again. This technique is particularly useful if you don't have a lot of time to prepare. Visualize yourself in front of your colleagues, going over each aspect of your presentation and answering anticipated questions. Visualization helps make the whole process more automatic and therefore easier.

TIP

When you're trying to remember faces, create a visual association. Think of an association (perhaps a prominent feature like big eyes or a small nose) to help you to remember a new colleague's name. Now picture it in a location — maybe Jim's nose in a taco shell if you were eating a taco when you were introduced to him. By creating a connection between a visual feature (the nose in a taco shell) and verbal information (Jim's name), you're increasing your chances of remembering that information.

Photographing your memory

You may have heard of people who have a photographic memory — they look at something once and they can remember it. Less than 10 percent of people have this skill, and for those who do, it's most evident in childhood, when visual memory is functioning at a high level. However, even most of these people tend to lose much of their ability to create "snapshots" of what they see as their language skills develop. As a result, so-called photographic memory is quite rare in adults.

TECHNICAL STUFF

Iconic memory is the fleeting memory of a visual image that your eyes take in. It's how your brain remembers what you just saw. Your eyes store images in less than a second. That visual image that remains in "your mind's eye" is your iconic memory of that object.

TIP

Here's a quick way to train your photographic memory. If you enjoy reading blogs, you may have noticed that some of them have *tag clouds* — visual descriptions of different topics included on that blog. Figure 13-3 shows you an example of a tag cloud. Some words are larger to illustrate which topics the blogger discusses more often. If you read that blog regularly, train yourself to recognize changes in the size of the text in the tag clouds. Look at the text for a couple of seconds only, then close your eyes and try to decide which text has "grown" since you last read the blog. (See Chapters 5 and 6 for more on games and memory.)

FIGURE 13-3:
A tag cloud.

© John Wiley & Sons, Inc.

TIP

If you have to remember to do something, bring up a photograph in your mind. For example, you need to bring a cake to the Christmas party. Think of a photo with a cake in it from last year's party. It's much more memorable than repeating your to-do list over and over to yourself.

Moving at Your Brain's Pace: Spatial Memory

Spatial short-term memory relates to how well you can recall locations and directions.

Tap out a square with your right hand on the table in front of you. Do this a few times. Now do it without looking at your hand and go as fast as you can without making any mistakes. So far, so good? Now use your left hand to draw circles in the air while still tapping a square with your right. How is your right hand doing? Any mistakes? You may have already given up by now. You may be wondering why you found this simple activity quite difficult.

The answer: You use the same part of your brain to plan and control your movements for both actions. When you attempt these two different activities at the same time, you have to process two different movements simultaneously.

REMEMBER

You use different parts of your brain to remember verbal and spatial information. So if you're trying to remember directions, why not draw it out instead of writing it? This way if you're distracted by someone talking, you're less likely to forget what you're doing. Chapter 4 provides strategies to help you remember directions.

Getting a bird's eye perspective

Spatial memory works best when you can look from above, like a bird, rather than look around you. Check out these tips on how to achieve a bird's eye perspective to keep your spatial memory sharp:

>> **Change shoes.** Imagine you give a friend who was new in town directions to a café. When she still hasn't shown up an hour later, you begin to worry. Then you find out she walked in the opposite direction from your instructions, despite your giving her many landmarks. Different spatial perspectives can get you lost. People often give directions from their viewpoint, not realizing that they need to take the other person's perspective into account.

SEE MY WORLD

Researchers often use computer games to understand how spatial memory works. One great way to examine this is to ask people to experience different types of virtual environments. Some people see objects moving toward them and others see themselves moving through the virtual environment. The first perspective is known as an *object-moving perspective,* where you're stationary and watch objects come toward you — for example, while waiting at a bus stop, you see the bus move toward you. Think of a third-person adventure game, where you move relative to the objects around you. The second is known as the *ego-moving perspective,* where you're moving and passing by objects — for example, walking down a street past shops, houses, and parked cars. Think of a first-person car-racing game, where you're driving the car and moving past the scenery around you; you (ego) appear to be traveling past the objects around you as you change your position. This difference in perspective impacts how you remember spatial relationships. Like everything else, how you look at something is what determines how you perceive, understand, and remember it.

Language is flexible and doesn't always make sense. Many words are ambiguous, especially directional words like *left, right, front, back, up,* and *down.* Your spatial perspective makes a big difference in how you interpret what people are saying when they use such words. Field studies show that travelers' spatial perspective changes during their journey. People who are about to begin a journey are more likely to have an ego-moving perspective. The same is true for those who've just completed a trip. But *during* their journey, the travelers tend to view the world from an object-moving perspective.

This tendency can result in a lot of frustration when you try to follow directions from someone else. Next time, put yourself in the other person's shoes — see it from her perspective — and give directions accordingly.

>> **Walk the walk.** The next time someone gives you directions to his house, adopt an ego-moving perspective while he's talking. Imagine yourself walking through that route in your head. Make that right turn, stop at the traffic light, turn down that second street, and mentally scan for his house. Then, when you actually make that journey, you've already done it once in your head. Now you have no excuse for getting lost. Chapter 4 has more tips for remembering directions.

>> **Look down.** It helps to view locations and directions in a grid-like way. Try to create an aerial view of where you are and where you need to go. People who do this have a much better sense of direction. Imagine you're a bird and flying over the next few streets that you walk down. How would the streets look?

Where would you turn? This strategy of creating an aerial perspective can also help you find your way back from your destination to your original starting point. Even if you haven't been to the area you're in before, creating an aerial view from what you do know about the area (such as a street or a landmark) helps you to navigate better.

TIP

Video games tend to polarize thinking: Some argue that they're a waste of time, but others insist that they're a worthy hobby. Now the pro-video gamers can take comfort in the knowledge that gamers tend to have significantly better visual-spatial skills than nongamers. They're much faster not only in playing the game they love but also in other unrelated tasks that involve problem-solving. Skeptics used to think that a trade-off existed: With increased speed, you lose accuracy. However, research now shows that this isn't the case. Gamers are faster but also more accurate because they have better developed visual-spatial skills due to their multidimensional experiences in video games. So if you want to improve your visual-spatial skills, maybe it's time to hit the video game shop or look online for a virtual experience to develop those skills.

Move through space

If you've ever had the pleasure of talking to an animated and excited young child, you probably noticed how often he moved about while he spoke. One thing that children frequently do is mirror the actions of one hand with the other. Ask a child to count using his fingers. A young child often raises his fingers on both hands. You can see this action in children, known as *mirror movements*, not just with hands but also with toes and feet. This section discusses how different movements can help your spatial memory.

TECHNICAL STUFF

It's much less common for adults to show such *mirror movements*. Those who do so find that they can't move one side of the body without moving the other. Scientists have now discovered that a crossover exists. When the brain sends a message to the limbs to move, it sends it to both sides rather than just one. Although very few adults have this problem, this crossover effect gives an important clue for how the brain works to move the body.

TIP

Here are some tips on how to use actions to help your memory:

>> **Mirror, mirror.** Look at Figure 13-4. Can you guess whether the object on the right is a mirror image of the one on the left? Your skills at mentally rotating an object are linked to spatial memory.

FIGURE 13-4:
Rotating objects.

>> **Move your marbles!** Marbles can get you to think back on happy, carefree days as a child and make you feel good as an adult. Psychologists found that a simple thing like moving marbles up into a higher box is more likely to make you think of positive memories. However, when you move marbles down into a lower box, you remember more negative or sad experiences. Why is this? The language people use to describe emotions is closely linked with spatial movements: "I'm on top of the world" or "I feel down today." When you move marbles up, that action triggers words that describe forward positive motion, which in turn triggers good feelings. So the next time you're feeling down, start lifting marbles and your mood.

REMEMBER

To boost your spatial memory, don't just think of the route to get to a place. Find out what landmarks are present along your journey and create a mental map of the path you take using those landmarks. The combination of a mental map of the route matched with visual landmarks boosts your spatial memory. Visualizing both the route and the scenery will give more depth to your memory of the directions.

Chapter 14

Keeping Your Memory Intact in a High-Speed World

M odern society is saturated with tweets, likes, shares, apps, blogs, emails, wikis, forums, and instant messages via computer, smartphone, tablet, or whatever device you happen to have on hand. People entertain themselves by vicariously experiencing movies and television shows and play video games based in virtual reality.

In this modern social climate, your memory skills can't help but be strained as you go about everyday business. When so much is vying for your attention, how do you know what to pay attention to and what to remember? In this chapter, you discover ways to allow your memory skills to weather the media and tech blizzard.

Staying Organized at the Center of the Cyclone

Contemporary society is charged with a whirlwind of activities that people somehow feel compelled to participate in. If you feel such an obligation, you may sacrifice some of your memory skills along the way.

Want proof? Tag along with a soccer mom as she zooms her child from the playing field to the music lesson to the dentist appointment and somehow gets home in time for dinner and, hopefully, homework. With such a complex schedule, chances are she forgot a few things along the way.

WARNING

A harried existence makes you less capable of memory. You need to take control of three major factors if you expect to remember anything at the center of the cyclone:

>> **Pace:** Think of it this way: As you race from one event to another, the quality of your involvement in each event diminishes. You're like a rock skipping the water. To be able to retain a memory of what you did, slow down and see where you are before moving on to the next event or task.

>> **Depth:** Depth means prioritizing your activities and eliminating the items that are low on the list, thus freeing more time and permitting more depth for the top priorities. The more time you spend with an activity, the more vivid and accurate your memory of that activity becomes. Otherwise you're like that rock skimming only the surface of the water.

>> **Organization:** You know a lot about organization already. Understanding how to make a clean break between one activity and the next helps to keep your memories clear and distinct.

Doing all these things may sound like a very tall order. You may feel that you have no choice but to satisfy all those demands on you. But you have to ask yourself how willing you are to sacrifice your memory skills by engaging in a whirlwind of activities. The cost to your memory is as great as the speed in which you dash from one event to another. In this case, speed kills — memory, that is.

Setting priorities

Overextending yourself can have memory-costing consequences. You essentially dilute your memory of each of the projects or engagements that you're racing between.

REMEMBER

By imposing a sense of organization and simultaneously slowing your pace, you allow yourself the opportunity to remember what you did. To accomplish this goal, don't forget to do the following:

>> Prioritize your activities.

>> Eliminate those activities that are low on your priority list.

>> Increase the time you're involved in the activites that you chose to stay with.

>> Cultivate greater depth in that activity.

>> Impose a coherent sense of organization to your activities.

For example, suppose you're the secretary of the local PTA, a member of the Rotary Club, a full-time employee, a spouse, and a parent of two children ages 7 and 10. Obviously, you're a busy person. But chances are, you're also a person who may be at risk of forgetting a lot as you dart from one activity to the next.

By prioritizing your involvements, you can give each of your commitments the attention they need. Here's how you rank your priorities:

>> Family

>> Job

>> PTA

>> Rotary Club

As you increase the time you spend with your priorities, you realize immediately that something has to give. You have to cut out something. You decide that, because the Rotary Club is the lowest priority, it has to go. You also realize that your tenure as the PTA secretary may have to go at the end of your term. You can still stay with the PTA, but now you'll be an attendee rather than an officeholder. These cuts leave you with more time and energy to increase the time you devote to your family and your job. You maintain your family as your highest priority, followed by your job, so now you have the ability to devote much more quality time with each commitment.

Organizing your memory of priorities

Everything you do has a *context* — a surrounding set of circumstances — that gives the activity meaning and relevance. For example, when you recall the assignment your boss gave you yesterday, the context includes the project you're already working on, the goals and time commitment of the new project, the people involved, the new project's impact on the rest of the company, and so on.

If you begin work on one project but then shift to another project, you must rekindle your memory of the appropriate context when you shift back to the first project. For example, you're completing your income tax forms when you answer the phone. When you turn your attention back to the tax forms, it takes you a few minutes to get back into your calculations.

TIP

Applying your memory skills when you alternate between projects can work best if you do the following:

>> Fully disengage from one context before moving on to another.

>> *Think around* the new project by reflecting on all the issues that are related to it and the people involved.

>> Talk to someone involved in the project to help you remember details.

You need a boundary and transition between one project and another to be able to make full use of your context-specific memories. Your memories related to one project probably don't apply to the next project. This brief gap in time between projects allows you to regroup and focus on the new task. Go to the bathroom or get a drink of water to give your mind a break. Then, when you get back to your desk, you're ready to tackle the next project.

Talking to another person involved in the same project helps jog your memory and puts you back in the frame of mind appropriate to recall memories. In fact, this person is part of the context of the memories for the project.

By keeping your life organized and setting your own pace, you increase the depth of your involvement in those activities you find to be of high priority. As the quality of your involvement increases, so does your memory regarding each activity.

Dodging the Hazards of Multitasking

You may be one of the millions of people juggling several tasks at once:

>> Talking on the phone while emailing

>> Checking social media while standing in line at the grocery store

>> Reading an e-book while watching television

>> Writing a memo during a meeting about something completely different

>> Phone conferencing while driving

This kind of complicated juggling is referred to as *multitasking* because you're doing more than one thing at a time. Multitasking has become a normal way of functioning in today's world.

WARNING

If you're proud of being able to multitask, you should be concerned about what it's doing to your memory. Recent research has made clear that divided attention dampens memory. Though you may be able to glide through the day, touching bases with colleagues and dealing with busy work, the depth to which you remember any of it is reduced as you engage in multiple activities simultaneously that really require more concentration.

Being mindful of the pitfalls of multitasking

Imagine yourself sitting at a meeting at work and feeling pressed for time with too many people wanting your attention. Twice, you get up to answer a text. After you sit back down in the meeting, you decide that you'd better get that memo to the staff written. In one ear, you hear the director of the company talk about new budget restrictions. In the other ear, you listen to two of your fellow supervisors gossiping about how the director is dating his assistant, Debbie.

You decide that you'd better get this memo written before the end of the meeting because you have a teleconferencing meeting in an hour and you still have to return some emails while returning some phone calls. So you write the memo on your laptop. After the meeting, you send it to your secretary and ask her to print it out and deliver it to everyone's mailbox.

After you go to the teleconference, you get an urgent call from the director. He summons you to his office. You arrive to see him glaring at you. He hands you a copy of your memo. It reads, "Debbie and the director want you to . . ."

Having that memo fly back in your face in this way would be enough to make you reconsider whether you should continue multitasking. However, don't wait to change your ways until you experience such a dramatic humiliation. Most likely, the memory mistakes you make while multitasking are far more subtle. Perhaps they're so subtle that you don't even notice them because you're so busy multitasking. But multitasking eventually takes its toll.

Multitasking decreases your memory ability. Each task that you're engaged in drains part of your mental energy. This is why multitasking breeds absentmindedness. You can say that your mind is absent because your complete mind isn't present when you're constantly shifting from one task to another and back again.

Knowing when to choose multitasking

The plain truth is that you don't have unlimited ability to pay attention to several things at once. With each new task you toss in to the juggling act, you dilute your investment in each task. Consequently, even if you do complete one of the juggled tasks, you may not remember how you did it.

You may ask, "Is the solution to avoid multitasking?" The simple answer to this question is yes. Although you may think you don't have a choice at times, you may have a bigger choice than you think. True, you may have to do some juggling sometimes, but these times are probably fewer than you think. Your challenge is to know the difference between the times you absolutely *do* have to multitask and the times you don't.

For example, you may have to wash the dishes while you call your mother because they'll otherwise stack up in the sink and be sitting there the next morning. That multitasking works because you can give each activity an appropriate amount of focus. You can do the dishes without thinking about it, which allows you to focus on talking to your mom. But you definitely shouldn't text while you're driving a car because both of these activities require your full attention. Trying to multitask in this instance is a recipe for disaster.

Even if you're compelled to multitask, you still may be able to retain some memory of what you did on one task before you shift to another. You can make this shift successfully if you shift your pace. Yet just slowing down isn't enough because you still need to break the pace up with islands of sanity. You need to come up for air periodically.

Consider the break in pace to be an opportunity to remember what you just completed. It's a time for you to integrate that task with all the other tasks you completed in the same project. As you fit in the latest tasks with the other ones, you can see how they all relate to the bigger picture.

WARNING

If you don't take breaks, you may be spinning your wheels by either repeating the same task because you forgot that you did it before or doing work you don't need to be doing anyway.

Use this *stop-and-focus technique* to break the pace and remember what you did:

>> Walk outside for a break.

>> Go get a refreshment from the cafeteria or kitchen.

>> Take notes on what you just did.

>> Tell a peer, supervisor, or friend what you've just accomplished.

By doing any or all of those simple things, you're shifting your attention to the next task you need to focus on. You allow yourself a brief moment to breathe and subsequently to remember what you just did.

TIP

You can even take mini breaks, just a few seconds long, while you're in the process of completing several tasks in succession. Try any one or all of the following to establish boundaries between tasks you're juggling:

>> If you've been sitting, stand up and stretch.

>> Take a few deep breaths to slow down your heart rate.

>> Clear your mind for a few moments of all the tasks you've been working on as well as the one's you've yet to accomplish.

Breaking Away from a Media-Crazed World

The movies and television programs that you're exposed to are increasingly sensationalistic because producers assume that you're too numb to pay attention. The average movie now is packed with car crashes, exploding bombs, and people being murdered.

Amidst this fast-paced, media-blitzed world, you may have a hard time knowing where to focus your attention. Your ability to home in on information and events in your life may be numbed by the blitz of overstimulation, which hinders your ability to remember. You're not absorbing information; you're just being bombarded by it.

TIP

You have to recognize you're being overstimulated to shake off this numbness. You have to be more discriminating about where you focus your attention. For example, don't get caught up in feeling the need to keep every high-tech gadget on and in use throughout the day, especially when you're supposedly trying to concentrate on something else. Be selective in what stimulation you expose yourself to and how you participate in this media-crazed world. Don't isolate yourself, but try to utilize current gadgets and conveniences to benefit you rather than wear you down. If you watch television, be selective about the shows you watch. Don't watch it or even have it on all the time. If you use a smartphone or tablet, use it selectively.

Remembering yourself

Forgetting your goals, tastes, interests, and even self-awareness is often too easy in this blizzard of overblown commercialism in today's society.

You can't watch the Olympic Games on television without being bombarded by more commercials than actual games. What's more, the programming itself is hard to separate from the commercials because the "up close and personal" spots on athletes "with gold in their eyes" are increasingly blurring the line between coverage and ad. As you're bombarded by all the slippery commercial hype, you run the risk of being worn down and forgetting memories of your own tastes and interests.

To regain a memory of yourself and your true interests, you have to create islands of individuality that allow you an opportunity to reconnect with yourself. Creating these islands is actually quite simple.

TIP

To disconnect from all the media and even from other people vying for your attention, try the following:

>> Take long walks in places where you won't meet anyone you know or, preferably, anyone at all.

>> Go to a local park and just sit and feel the sun on your back.

>> Go into your backyard and just sit without thinking of all the things you need to do and all the people you need to talk to.

>> Get away from the rest of your family for a few hours to take a long bath and relax.

The point of taking these mini-vacations is to regroup and regain your perspective. Focusing on goals is fine as long as they're long-range goals that you're working toward and not immediate short-term goals of endless busywork. You need to take these breaks to provide yourself with an opportunity to reflect on what's really important in your life rather than what you've been persuaded to believe is important.

Essentially, breaks allow you to go off automatic pilot. When you're on automatic pilot, who controls where you're going? You need to get back into the driver's seat to ensure that you don't forget who you are and where you're going.

Focusing on the here and now

Attention plays an important role in your memory skills. Simply put, if you're not paying full attention to what you want to remember, you won't remember most of it.

Nowadays, people are assumed to be incapable of paying attention for longer than a few minutes at a time. Scripts for movies and television are developed with fewer and shorter lines. That's because producers are worried that you'll lose interest and walk out of the movie theater or change to one of the other few hundred channels on your flat-screen TV.

You may be asking, "How on earth can I fight this deluge of fast-paced onscreen action to pay attention?" Perhaps you're one of the few people who gets angry when intense, meaningful dialogue in a movie is disrupted by flashes of sensationalism like a murder that can make it difficult to follow the underlying story line.

You have to disconnect from the feverish frenzy at least periodically. Otherwise, you can't consolidate the important memories of the details of what and who you've been involved with during the day.

TIP

You also can benefit from *monotasking.* This frame of mind is the opposite of multitasking. It involves being completely present and focused on the process of performing the task at hand with heightened attention. Your mind may wander at first, but with practice, you can learn to focus more easily and not worry about other tasks that await your attention.

TIP

You may also want to try a practice called *mindfulness,* which can be useful to help you focus. Mindfulness is actually a meditative technique taught to people wanting to learn to relax, to people suffering from chronic pain, and even to people wanting to improve the quality of their lives. This practice helps you increase your presence and attention. The chapters in Part 3 go into a lot more detail about relaxing your mind and body.

A great side-effect of mindfulness is improved memory. Because you're more deeply involved in what you're doing — being mindful of the task — your memory of the details of the task greatly improves.

Mindfulness involves completely absorbing yourself in whatever you're doing. That total absorption that concentrates your attention turns the task into a rich and pleasurable experience. Because you're completely invested in the task at hand, you can remember more about it.

Think of how easily your mind wanders as you engage in any task. Everyone's mind has the tendency to wander, some more than others. You can rein in your wandering mind by being mindful of the task you're doing at that moment.

As people age, they can become creatures of routine. Routine isn't necessarily a bad thing as long as you leave room for novel experiences and remain mindful of each task you do.

Think of the life of a monk. Each routine in his life can be a meditative experience because he's mindful of each experience; his mind isn't distracted." As a result, his memories are vivid. Each experience resonates in the here and now, and as a result he remembers it later with clarity.

If you do practice this level of concentration and mindfulness, you can have a better quality of experience and remember more about it. Here's a simple example of how you can practice this technique while washing your car:

As you rinse the car before scrubbing, notice the power of the hose shooting out the nozzle. Listen to the water pounding on the surface of the car. Notice what parts of the car the dirt clings to despite the power of the spraying water. Then, as you scrub the car with a soapy sponge, notice the different textures. The areas where the dirt still clings become smoother as you scrub off the dirt. Later, when your spouse asks you, "Did you clean those spots in the corner of the windshield?", you can respond by saying, "Oh yes, I remember those spots. Yes, I did get them clean."

Had you not engaged in the cleaning job mindfully, your mind probably would've been elsewhere. When asked if you cleaned those windshield spots, you'd realize you hadn't even noticed the spots. However, you do remember because you were mindfully involved in a task that otherwise may have seemed laborious and boring.

The point isn't that letting your mind wander is bad. A wandering mind is perfectly natural. If you want to remember the journey, being mindful can help. But if you don't, that's fine, too.

Flowing with memory

The more you can flow with whatever you're doing at the moment, the better you can remember it later. "Okay," you say. "But exactly how do I flow?" The answer may sound ridiculously impossible, but here it is: Achieve a state of ecstasy.

In *Flow: The Psychology of Optimal Experience*, psychologist Mihaly Csikszentmihalyi described how people are happiest when they're in a state of *flow* —complete concentration and absorption in the activity they're doing. Flow results from your ecstatic experience of being "at one" with your actions. Time flies. You forget about everything else; you're in the zone. You become so at one with what you're doing that all other distractions fade away.

Think of this flow experience as a highly motivated mindfulness. Motivation is a key ingredient of flow. Think of it as the drive and energy that keeps you focused when you're interested and invested in what you're doing at the moment. To achieve flow, you must reach a balance between the challenge of the task and your skill level. If a task is too easy and you're highly skilled, you get bored. If a task is too hard and you aren't sufficiently skilled, you get frustrated.

Optimism helps, too. Psychologist Dr. Daniel Goldman points out that several "emotional" factors make up what he calls *emotional intelligence,* and optimism is one of them.

Ambition is also good. Ambition and optimism complement each other and help your memory. (Ambition in this sense has nothing to do with getting ahead of anyone else. It has to do with maximizing your potential and striving for personal goals.)

Put them all together (motivation, optimism, and ambition), and you're in the flow — prepared to remember all the details of a significant experience, even in the middle of a frenetic world.

Aiding Your Memory with External Cues

Even if your goal is to improve your memory, there's nothing wrong with getting a little help from external reminders. Using a calendar to track your schedule or making a shopping list is the mark of an organized person. It doesn't mean you have a defective memory. In fact, the world is so cluttered with trivial information that even someone with a super memory can make good use of memory clues.

Sometimes you may find that you don't have time to use a mnemonic technique (such as the ones in Chapter 9). You need to rely on an external cue. Consider the following as potentially useful external cues:

>> To-do lists

>> Notes to yourself

>> Sticky notes

>> An outline for a speech with bullets

>> Notecards

>> Date books and daily organizers

>> Alerts you set on your phone

>> Electronic calendars or good old-fashioned wall calendars

Many of these external cues, such as to-do lists and shopping lists, have a time factor built into them. When you're at the store, you know to pull out your shopping list so you buy all the groceries you need.

One now famous incident occurred when former President Clinton was giving his State of the Union speech and the teleprompter broke. As his aides scrambled to fix it, Clinton felt that he couldn't wait any longer. To almost everyone's amazement, he completed his speech without a glitch, as if the teleprompter had been on. Moral of the story: Don't rely solely on external cues!

Date books and calendars are excellent ways to offload memories of important dates. With consistent updates, you can be confident that you at least have the dates down. But you need to refer to your calendar on a regular basis for it to help you.

TIP

If you use to-do lists or apps, try not to keep multiple lists. If you do have more than one list, always keep and constantly update one master list.

THE BOOK-BY-THE-DOOR MEMORY AIDE

You've surely had the experience of remembering something you need to do the next day just as you're trying to fall asleep. You may get up and write it down so you won't keep yourself up worrying that you'll forget it.

But sometimes you're just too tired to get up and write it down — but not too tired to roll out of bed and prop a book against the door. The book is an external cue to help you remember the next morning. In the morning, you'll go to the door and wonder, "Why is that book there?" Then it will dawn on you that you left the book there to remind you about something. At that point, you may say, "Oh yeah! I've got to remember to talk to Jean about that flight to Vancouver."

3

Managing Stress: Relaxing Mind and Body

Chapter 15

Understanding Stress

You've heard the word *stress* a million times. But if you're pressed to explain the concept, you may find yourself a little stuck. Intuitively, you know what stress is, but explaining it isn't easy. This chapter helps you answer the question, "What exactly is stress?"

On any long trip, you want to have a pretty good idea of where you're going and make sure you have the right equipment to get you there. The same wisdom holds true as you begin your journey on the road to becoming your own stress manager. You want to begin with the proper gear: an accurate road map, a good compass, and the right attitude (and maybe a light lunch).

This chapter gives you the important tools you need to become aware of the stresses in your life and where they come from. It helps you identify your stress triggers and shows you how to create a stress journal to help you pinpoint specifically when and where you feel stressed. These insights become important as you add tools and strategies to your repertoire to help you manage, reduce, and even eliminate much of your stress, allowing you to keep your focus sharp and giving you the ability to take control over everyday happenings.

Most people feel that their lives are too stressful. These stresses may come from your job or lack thereof, your money worries, your personal life, or simply not having enough time to do everything you have to do — or want to do. You can use some help. Thankfully, you can eliminate or at least minimize much of the stress in your life and better manage the stress that remains. This chapter helps you get started.

So What Exactly Is Stress Anyhow?

Defining stress isn't easy. Professionals who've spent most of their lives studying stress still have trouble defining the term. As one stress researcher quipped, "Defining stress is like nailing Jell-O to a tree. It's hard to do!" Despite efforts during the last half century to assign a specific meaning to the term, no satisfactory definition exists. Defining stress is much like defining happiness. Everyone knows what it is, but no one can agree on a single definition.

TECHNICAL STUFF

An Austrian-born endocrinologist named Hans Selye actually came up with the word *stress* to describe a physiological and emotional response. In the 1930s, Selye came upon the stress response while working with animals in his laboratory at McGill University in Montreal. Selye went on to publish widely in the area of stress and is today considered the "father of stress." The word comes from the Latin *stringere,* "to draw tight." Before Selye coined the term, stress didn't have any of the meanings associated with it today. Selye later admitted that he may have misnamed what he was studying. He borrowed the term from the fields of physics and engineering, where the concepts of stress and strain were in common use. English wasn't his mother tongue, and he later realized that the word *strain* would've been more appropriate. Too late. The term had stuck.

Sorry, but I really need a definition

Perhaps you always began your high-school English essays with a dictionary definition ("Webster defines tragedy as . . ."), and you still have to start with a definition. Okay, here's the scientific definition:

> *Stress* describes a condition where an environmental demand exceeds the natural regulatory capacity of an organism.

Put in simpler terms, stress is what you experience when you believe you can't cope effectively with a threatening situation. If you see an event or situation as only mildly challenging, you probably feel only a little stress; however, if you perceive a situation or event as threatening or overwhelming, you probably feel a lot of stress. So having to wait for a bus when you have all the time in the world triggers little stress. Waiting for that same bus when you're late for a plane that will take off without you triggers much more stress.

This difference between the demands of the situation and your perception of how well you can cope with that situation is what determines how much stress you feel.

Stress causes stress?

Part of the problem with defining stress is the confusing way the word is used. People use the word *stress* to refer to the thing or circumstance that stresses them (stress = the bus that never comes, the deadline, the traffic, the difficult boss, and so on). They then use the same word to describe the physical and emotional discomfort they feel about that situation (stress = anxious, headachy, irritated, and so on). So they end up feeling stress about stress, which can be confusing. *Stressor* or *stress trigger* are alternatives that refer to a potentially stressful situation or event, leaving *stress* for your emotional and physical responses.

Understanding Where All This Stress Is Coming From

Just glance at any magazine stand, and you'll find numerous cover stories all about stress. Most larger bookstores devote an entire section to books on stress. TV and radio talk shows regularly feature stories documenting the negative effects of stress. Why all the fuss? Hasn't stress been around forever? Wasn't it stress that Adam felt when he was caught red-handed with little bits of apple stuck between his teeth? Is all of this just media hype, or are people really experiencing more stress today?

One good way of finding out how much stress people are experiencing is to ask them. Here are some findings from recent polls and surveys that did just that:

>> A 2010 study published by the American Psychological Association found that 44 percent of Americans said that their stress levels had increased over the past five years.

>> That same study reported that one in five American adults (22 percent) believe themselves to be in fair or poor health, and this group reports higher levels of stress than those in better health.

>> A Harris Interactive survey of more than 1,550 Americans found that 46 percent reported that their stress levels are higher than they were five years ago. Eighty percent said they experienced medium or high stress levels at work. Sixty percent said they experienced these same levels at home.

LESS LEISURE TIME?

In her insightful 1993 book *The Overworked American: The Unexpected Decline of Leisure* (Basic Books), economist Juliet B. Schor points out that, in spite of all the new innovations and contraptions that make life easier, what has to be done at home requires about the same amount of time to do. In the 1910s, a full-time housewife spent about 52 hours a week on housework. Sixty years later, in the 1970s, the figure was about the same. Yes, some activities did become less time consuming. Food preparation fell by almost ten hours a week, but this drop was offset by an increase in the time spent shopping and taking care of the home and kids. Contrary to everyone's predicted expectations, we have *less* leisure time now than we did 50 years ago.

In his prophetic book *Future Shock* (originally published by Bantam in 1984), Alvin Toffler observed that people experience more stress whenever they're subjected to a lot of change in a short span of time. If anything characterizes life these days, it's an excess of change. People are in a continual state of flux. They have less control over their lives, live with more uncertainty, and often feel threatened and, at times, overwhelmed. The following sections explain some of the more common sources of modern stress.

Struggling in a struggling economy

A 2010 study published by the American Psychological Association shows an America still recovering from the recession. Americans reported that money (76 percent) and the economy (65 percent) were their most common sources of stress. A difficult and uncertain economy has become *the* major source of stress in Americans' lives. The recession and its aftermath have resulted in prolonged financial and emotional distress for too many.

Money may or may not be the root of all evil, but worrying about it certainly is a major source of stress. Balancing your checkbook at the end of the month (if you bother) reminds you that living is expensive. You remember that your parents bought their house for a pittance and now realize that today you couldn't afford to buy that same house if you wanted to. The mortgage, college tuition, braces for the kids' teeth, camp, travel, taxes, savings for retirement — it all adds up. And so does the stress.

Getting frazzled at work

Having a job lets you avoid the stress that comes with unemployment, but it certainly doesn't guarantee a stress-free existence. For many people, jobs and careers are the biggest source of stress. Concerns about job security, killer hours, long commutes, unrealistic deadlines, bosses from hell, office politics, toxic coworkers, and testy clients are just a few of the many job-related stresses people experience. Workloads are heavier today than they were in the past, leaving less and less time for family and the rest of your life.

A new lexicon of work-related stresses also exists: outsourcing, downsizing, organizational redeployment, forced early retirement. Whatever the word, the effects are the same: insecurity, uncertainty, and fear. People are experiencing more stress at work than ever before, as these findings illustrate:

>> A 2012 workplace survey carried out by Harris Interactive for the American Psychological Association found that two in five employed adults (41 percent) typically feel stressed out during the workday.

>> In that same study, fewer than six in ten (58 percent) reported that they had the resources to manage stress effectively.

>> About two-thirds (62 percent) of Americans cite work as one of their main sources of stress.

>> The overall cost of job stress at work is estimated at $300 billion.

>> One in four workers has taken a "mental health" day off from work to relieve stress.

>> About a quarter (26 percent) of workers say they're "often" or "very often" burned out by their work.

Feeling frazzled at home

After you leave work, you may start to realize that the rest of your life isn't exactly stress-free. These days, life at home, your relationships, and the pressure of juggling everything else that has to be done only add to your stress level.

Life at home has become more pressured and demanding. True, microwaves, robotic vacuums, and take-out menus make some things more convenient, but the effort and stress involved seem to be growing rather than lessening. Meals have to be prepared, the house tidied, the clothing cleaned, the bills paid, the chores completed, the shopping done, the lawn and garden tended, the car maintained and repaired, the phone calls and emails returned, the homework supervised, and the kids chauffeured. And that's for starters.

GENDER ROLES AND STRESS

Women face added pressures and limitations in the workplace. Women are paid less and promoted less frequently than their male counterparts, even though they may be more qualified. If a woman has children, her career may be shunted onto the "mommy track," a glass ceiling that limits career advancement.

More subtle pressures come from the prevailing notions of the different roles and behaviors expected from men and women. Men and women can act in similar ways that may advance their careers — competitive, aggressive, and assertive — but a double standard is common. When such behavior comes from a woman, people often view the behavior negatively as unfeminine and inappropriate. But when that same behavior comes from a man, people see him as strong and in control.

Sexual harassment for women on the job is no small source of stress. A woman may find herself in the no-win situation of either openly complaining or silently enduring the abuse. Both options can be highly stressful. Women who belong to a racial or ethnic minority may experience even more stress. Hiring and promotional practices may act in subtle and not-so-subtle discriminatory ways. Even where affirmative action policies are in place, women may experience the stress of feeling that others see their hiring or advancement as unfairly legislated rather than legitimately deserved.

I need two more hours in the day!

This plea is a commonly heard lament. The stress of not having enough time to do everything that has to be done is enormous. People overwork at home and at their jobs. The result? They just don't have enough time.

Ozzie and Harriet who?

Some of this stress comes from the ways in which families have changed over the years. In two-parent families, it's now common for both parents to work. One-parent families have even more stressors. These days, more women are the main earners in the home (almost 40 percent) or are bringing in essential income needed to maintain the family. Nearly half of all marriages end in divorce. The number of single-parent households is multiplying. Families tend to be more fragmented, with relatives often living great distances away. Although in certain cases this situation can be stress-reducing (your annoying Aunt Agnes is moving to Dubuque!), more often it promotes a greater sense of disconnectedness and alienation.

A woman's work is never done

Forty years ago, one-third of all workers were women; now nearly half are. Add on the additional stress of being a mother with a family to manage at home, and you compound a woman's level of stress. Women may find themselves in the not-so-unusual position of having to cope with the problems of aging and ailing parents in addition to the problems of their own children. Caught in this generational divide, this "stress sandwich" can be incredibly draining, both physically and emotionally. Although men give lip service to helping with the kids and the elderly (and they do, in fact, help more than their fathers or grandfathers did), women are still the ones who most often take primary responsibility for these care-giving roles.

A 2009 study reported in *Time* magazine found that 55 percent of women strongly agree that in households where both partners have jobs, women take on more responsibilities for the home and family than their male partners do. The men in the study saw it differently: Only 28 percent agreed. Sixty-nine percent of women say that they're primarily responsible for taking care of their children; only 13 percent of men say this of themselves. As an old adage reminds us, "Father works from sun to sun, but Mother's work is never done." However, with continued recognition that providing care for children or elderly parents isn't solely a woman's job, more men are stepping up to the plate. Lots more fathers today know how to change a diaper than their fathers did.

Piling on new stresses with technology

People's lives have become stressful in ways they never would've imagined even a decade ago. Whoever said there was nothing new under the sun probably never scoured the web for the name of a restaurant or texted a friend. Changes in technology have brought new pressures and new demands — in short, new sources of stress. For example, one study of more than 1,300 people found that those who regularly used their cellphones or portable devices for communication experienced an increase in psychological distress and a decrease in family satisfaction, compared with those who used these devices less often. Imagine this implausible scenario:

You've been in a coma for the last 15 years or so. One day, out of the blue, you wake up and take the bus home from the hospital. You quickly notice that life has changed. Technology rules. On the bus you notice that everyone is pushing buttons on small plastic devices. You ask the person next to you what's going on, and he looks at you strangely and explains what a smartphone is, what downloading means, and what email does. You reach your home and discover that your old television and computer have become relics. Everything is digital. Everything is portable. People are magically "downloading" movies and television shows on their telephones. Your cassette player is a joke (although your record player is now cool again). Just as quickly, you realize that you have no idea how to operate any of these digital tools. You have no idea what the words *Skype, Netflix, Kindle, Facebook,* and *podcast* even mean. All this technology is driving you a bit crazy. Your next-door neighbor, who was never in a coma, is just as stressed as you. He's also trying to keep up with all this technological change and finding the task overwhelming.

Dealing with daily hassles (the little things add up)

When you think of stress, you usually think of the major stresses you may face: death, divorce, financial ruin, or a serious illness. And then of course there are those so-called moderate stresses: losing your wallet, denting your car, or catching a cold. Finally, you face the even smaller stresses: the mini-stresses and micro-stresses. These stresses are what are known as hassles.

Here is just a sample of the kinds of hassles you face every day (a complete list would be endless):

>> Noisy traffic jams

>> Loud neighbors

>> Rude salesclerks

>> Crowds

>> Long waits for telephone customer-service representatives

>> Deliveries promised "sometime between 9 and 5"

>> Computers that crash

>> Robo calls and telemarketers

>> Airport delays

>> Cellphones that go off in theaters and restaurants

The small things can add up. You can deal with one, maybe two, or even three of these at once. But when the number begins to rise, so does your stress level. When you reach a high enough level of stress, you may overreact to the next hassle that comes along. And that results in even *more* stress. Alas, life is loaded with hassle. The funny part is that people usually deal fairly well with the bigger problems. Life's major stresses — the deaths, illnesses, divorces, and financial setbacks — somehow trigger hidden internal resources within them. They rise to each demand, summoning up some unrecognized inner strength, and somehow manage to cope. What gets to them are the little things, which add up. It's the small stuff — the persistent little annoyances, petty frustrations, and minor irritations — that ultimately lead to a continuing sense of stress.

Looking at the Signs and Symptoms of Stress

The signs and symptoms of stress range from the benign to the dramatic — from simply feeling tired at the end of the day to having a heart attack. The more serious stress-related problems come with intense and prolonged periods of stress. These disorders and diseases are saved for later in this chapter. Here are some of the more benign, commonly experienced stress signs and symptoms. Many are probably all too familiar to you.

>> Physical signs of stress

- Tiredness, fatigue, and lethargy
- Heart palpitations; racing pulse
- Rapid, shallow breathing
- Muscle tension and aches
- Shakiness, tremors, tics, and twitches
- Heartburn, indigestion, diarrhea, and constipation
- Nervousness
- Dry mouth and throat
- Excessive sweating, clammy hands, and cold hands and/or feet
- Rashes, hives, and itching
- Nail-biting, fidgeting, hair-twirling, and hair-pulling
- Frequent urination
- Lowered libido
- Overeating or loss of appetite
- Sleep difficulties and insomnia
- Increased use of alcohol and/or drugs and medications

>> Psychological signs of stress

- Irritability, impatience, anger, and hostility
- Worry, anxiety, and panic
- Moodiness, sadness, feelings of upset, and depression
- Intrusive and/or racing thoughts

- Memory lapses, difficulties in concentrating, and indecision
- Frequent absences from work and lowered productivity
- Feeling overwhelmed
- Loss of sense of humor

That's just for starters. Prolonged and/or intense stress can have more serious effects: It can make you sick (see the following section).

Breaking Down How Stress Can Make You Sick

Researchers estimate that 75 to 90 percent of all visits to primary care physicians are for complaints and conditions that are, in some way, stress-related. About 50 percent of those surveyed said that stress was affecting their health. Every week, 112 million people take some form of medication for stress-related symptoms. This statistic isn't surprising given the wide-ranging physiological changes that accompany a stress response. Just about every bodily system and body part is affected by stress. Stress can exacerbate the symptoms of a wide variety of other disorders and illnesses as well. Stress is linked to the five leading causes of death: heart disease, cancer, lung disease, accidents, and suicide. The following sections illustrate some of the more important ways stress can negatively affect your health and well-being.

REMEMBER

All the symptoms, illnesses, and conditions mentioned in this section can result from a number of medical conditions, not just stress. For many of them, stress may make the condition worse even though it isn't the direct cause. If you're concerned about one or more of these symptoms, be sure to consult your physician. He or she is the best person to give you advice and guidance.

Feeling like stress is a pain in the neck (and other places)

Your muscles are a prime target for stress. When you're under stress, your muscles contract and become tense. This muscle tension can affect your nerves, blood vessels, organs, skin, and bones. Chronically tense muscles can result in a variety of conditions and disorders, including muscle spasms, cramping, facial or jaw pain, teeth-grinding, tremors, and shakiness. Many forms of headache, chest pain, and back pain are among the more common conditions that result from stress-induced muscle tension.

Taking stress to heart

Stress can play a role in circulatory diseases such as coronary heart disease, sudden cardiac death, and strokes. This fact isn't surprising because stress can increase your blood pressure, constrict your blood vessels, raise your cholesterol level, trigger arrhythmias, and speed up the rate at which your blood clots. Science is showing that stress, inflammation, and heart disease are all linked. Psychosocial stress induces a physiological inflammatory response in blood vessels. When vessel walls are damaged, (such as from chronic high blood pressure), inflammatory cells come into the vessel walls. Among other things, these cells release chemicals that may cause further damage. If the stress is chronic, the result is chronic inflammation. A growing number of studies show that individuals with higher amounts of psychosocial stress and depression display elevated C-reactive protein and IL-6 levels, both markers of inflammation.

REMEMBER

Stress is now considered a major risk factor in heart disease, right up there with smoking, being overweight, and not exercising. All this becomes very important when you consider that heart disease kills more men over the age of 50 and more women over the age of 65 than any other disease.

Hitting below the belt

Ever notice how your stress seems to finds its way to your stomach? Your gastrointestinal system can be a ready target for much of the stress in your life. Stress can affect the secretion of acid in your stomach and can speed up or slow down the process of peristalsis (the rhythmic contraction of the muscles in your intestines). Constipation, diarrhea, gas, bloating, and weight loss all can be stress-related. Stress can contribute to gastroesophageal reflux disease and can also play a role in exacerbating irritable bowel syndrome, colitis, and Crohn's disease.

WHAT ABOUT STRESS AND ULCERS?

Once considered the poster disease for stress, ulcers have lost much of their stress-related status in recent years. Although stress can contribute to the development of ulcers, there are many more causes. It now appears that a bacteria called *Helicobacter pylori* (*H. pylori* for short) is often the culprit. But a majority of those who do carry the *H. pylori* bacteria don't develop ulcers, and many who don't carry it still develop ulcers. Medications, such as NSAIDS (including over-the-counter ibuprofen, naprosyn, and aspirin), are also frequent causes of ulcers, especially bleeding ulcers.

But despite these other causes, stress can affect secretions in the stomach that contribute to ulcer development. The bombing of London during World War II and the earthquake in Kobe, Japan, both precipitated outbreaks of ulcer disease.

Speaking of your belt, it's important to recognize that people under stress usually experience changes in their weight. Stress can affect you in two very different ways. When you're highly stressed, you may find yourself eating less. You may even find yourself losing weight. This "stress diet" isn't the best way to lose weight, and if the stress is prolonged it can result in lower overall health. For many others, though, stress, especially moderate stress, can result in overeating. In effect, you're "feeding your emotions." The intent, often unconscious, is to feel better — to distract yourself from the emotional distress. The trouble is that "good feeling" lasts for just a few seconds before you need another fix. And that means putting another notch on your belt. But it's not just your caloric intake that contributes to weight gain. When you're stressed, your body releases a hormone called cortisol, which causes fat to accumulate around your abdomen. Cortisol also enlarges individual fat cells, leading to what researchers term "diseased" fat. Chapter 19 has more on combating stress-eating.

Compromising your immune system

In the last decade or so, growing evidence has supported the theory that stress affects your immune system. In fact, researchers have even coined a name for this new field of study: psychoneuroimmunology. Quite a mouthful! Scientists in this field study the relationships between moods, emotional states, hormonal levels, and changes in the nervous system and immune system. Without drowning you in detail, stress — particularly chronic stress — can compromise your immune system, rendering it less effective in resisting bacteria and viruses. Research has shown that stress likely plays a role in exacerbating a variety of immune system disorders such as HIV, AIDS, herpes, cancer, viral infection, rheumatoid arthritis, and certain allergies, as well as other autoimmune conditions.

The cold facts: Connecting stress and the sniffles

In that wonderful musical comedy *Guys and Dolls*, a lovelorn Adelaide laments that when your life is filled with stress, "a person can develop a cold." It looks like she just may be right. Research conducted by Dr. Sheldon Cohen, a psychologist at Carnegie Mellon University, has concluded that stress really does lower your resistance to colds. Cohen and his associates found that the higher a person's stress score, the more likely he was to come down with a cold when exposed to a cold virus.

Chronic stress, lasting a month or more, was the most likely to result in catching a cold. Experiencing severe stress for more than a month but less than six months doubled a person's risk of coming down with a cold, compared with those who were experiencing only shorter-term stress. Stress lasting more than two years nearly quadrupled the risk. The study also found that being unemployed or under-employed or having interpersonal difficulties with family or friends had the greatest effect. The exact mechanism whereby stress weakens immune functioning is still unclear. Tissues, anyone?

Not tonight, dear. I have a (stress) headache.

A headache is just one of the many ways stress can interfere with your sex life. For both men and women, stress can reduce and even eliminate the pleasure of physical intimacy. Stress can affect sexual performance and rob you of your libido. When you're under stress, feeling sexy may not be at the top of your to-do list. Disturbed sexual performance for men may appear in the form of erectile dysfunction, premature ejaculation, or delayed ejaculation. For women the most common effects of stress are a lowered level of sexual interest and difficulty in achieving orgasm. The irony is that sex can be a way of relieving stress. However, for some people, sexual activity makes them feel more stressed.

Stressing Out Your Family and Friends

Being stressed is a little like having a cold. Others can catch it. When you're stressed, your moods change, your behavior changes, and you trigger a downward spiral of negative interactions. You may find yourself more upset, angry, and worried. You're not the same you.

STRESS AND INFERTILITY

If you're trying to have children, stress can make it harder for you to become pregnant. Stress may account for up to 30 percent of all infertility problems. Stress changes your body's neurochemistry, which can affect the maturation and release of the human egg. Stress can also cause the fallopian tubes and uterus to spasm, which can impair implantation. In men, stress can alter the sperm count and cause erectile dysfunction.

In a recent survey, 21 percent of those responding said that stress was negatively affecting their friendships. Nineteen percent said that stress was hurting their marriages. When you're distressed, your happiness level tanks. Your fuse gets shorter, and you become more irritable. People under stress tend to withdraw emotionally and communicate less. Friends and family may not understand what's going on and in turn become stressed. The cycle can escalate, leading to even more distress.

Most parents don't think their stress affects their children. They're wrong. Just ask the kids. Ninety-one percent of children say they know when their parents are stressed. They can see them worrying, yelling, complaining, and arguing. Children who see their parents stressing out tend to become stressed themselves.

A large survey completed in 2010 found that only 14 percent of children say that their parents' stress doesn't bother them. When children see their parents stressed or worried, they also feel sad, worried, and frustrated. And it's not just their emotional state that is affected. That same study found that nearly one-third of the children reported physical health symptoms that tend to be stress-related. Thirty-eight percent reported trouble falling asleep at night. One-third experienced headaches, and almost one-third reported having an upset stomach in the past month. Chronic stress can also impair children's developmental growth by lowering the production of growth hormone from the pituitary gland. Traumatic, stressful experiences in childhood can cause damage to developing bodies and brains that lasts into adulthood.

Can Stress Be Good?

Not all stress is bad. As Hans Selye, the pioneer researcher in the field of stress, said, "Stress is the spice of life." He termed the good kind of stress *eustress*, as opposed to *distress*, or the nasty kind of stress. (The "eu" part of eustress comes from the Greek meaning "good.") Stress can be a positive force in your life. Watching a close playoff game, taking a ride at an amusement park, solving an interesting problem, falling in love — all can be stressful. Yet these are the kinds of stresses that add to the enjoyment and satisfaction of your life. You want more of this kind of stress, not less.

And even many of the less pleasant uncertainties and surprises of life can be a source of challenge and even excitement and interest. That nervousness you're experiencing about that presentation you're making tomorrow can actually improve your performance. The right amount of stress can motivate you, focus you, and get you to perform at your peak. Change and the pressures of modern life don't necessarily create the bad kind of stress. Rather, how you view the potential stresses in your life and how you cope with them make all the difference.

A surprising number of people claim to thrive on stress. They like to be challenged, to have their abilities stretched and tested. For them this is a good kind of stress that can be satisfying and rewarding. Many people who claim to thrive on stress are workaholics. They get stressed when they have nothing to do. Lying on a beach, sitting in the park — now that's stressful for them!

Interestingly enough, some research suggests that part of the addictive quality that some people feel about stress may be more than just psychological. It may be that people can become hooked on the adrenaline secretions that occur during a stress response. Like other addictions, this adrenaline boost may be experienced by some people as pleasurable. This could explain that feeling of being "truly alive" that some people feel when they're super-stressed. Most of the rest of the population, however, could live quite nicely without this boost, thank you very much.

REMEMBER

Realize that change itself causes stress, even if it's change for the good. Being promoted to a new job, starting college, getting married, and having a baby are all wonderful life events. However, the change each of these events brings to your daily life requires many adjustments, including schedule, time management, responsibility, and daily patterns.

How This Whole Stress Thing Got Started

Believe it or not, you have stress in your life for a good reason. To understand why stress can be a useful, adaptive response, you need to take a trip back in time.

Imagining you're a cave person

Picture this: You've gone back in time to a period thousands of years ago when people lived in caves. You're roaming the jungle dressed in a loincloth and carrying a club. Your day, so far, has been routine. Nothing more than the usual cave politics and the ongoing problems with the in-laws. Nothing you can't handle.

Suddenly, as you stroll along, you spot a tiger. This isn't your ordinary tiger; it's a saber-toothed tiger. You experience something called the *fight-or-flight* response. This response is aptly named because, just then, you have to make a choice: You can stay and do battle (fight), or you can run like the wind (flight — probably the smarter option here). Your body, armed with this automatic stress response, prepares you to do either. You're ready for anything. You're wired.

Surviving the modern jungle

You've probably noticed that you don't live in a cave. And your chances of running into a saber-toothed tiger are slim, especially because they're extinct. Yet this incredibly important, life-preserving stress reaction is still hard-wired into your system. And once in a while, it can still be highly adaptive. If you're picnicking on a railroad track and see a train barreling toward you, an aggressive stress response is nice to have. You want to get out of there quickly.

In today's society, you're required to deal with very few life-threatening stressors — at least on a normal day. Unfortunately, your body's fight-or-flight response is activated by a whole range of stressful events and situations that aren't going to do you in. The caveman's physical dangers have been replaced by social and psychological stress triggers, which aren't worthy of a full fight-or-flight stress response. But your body doesn't know this, and it reacts the way it did when your ancestors were facing real danger.

Imagine the following modern-day scenario: You're standing in an auditorium in front of several hundred seated people. You're about to give a presentation that is important to your career. You suddenly realize that you've left several pages of your prepared material at home on your nightstand. As it dawns on you that this isn't just a bad dream that you'll laugh about later, you start to notice some physical and emotional changes. Your hands are becoming cold and clammy. Your heart is beating faster, and you're breathing harder. Your throat is dry. Your muscles are tensing, and you notice a slight tremor as you hopelessly look for the missing pages. Your stomach feels a little queasy, and you notice an emotion that you'd definitely label as anxiety. You recognize that you're experiencing a stress reaction — the same fight-or-flight response that your caveman ancestors experienced. The difference is that you probably won't die up there at that podium, even though it feels like you will.

In the modern jungle, giving that presentation, being stuck in traffic, confronting a disgruntled client, facing an angry spouse, or trying to meet some unrealistic deadline is what stresses you. Despite not threatening your existence, these stressors trigger that same intense stress response. It's overkill. Your body isn't just reacting; it's overreacting. And that's definitely not good.

Knowing the Signs of Stress

An important part of managing your stress is knowing your response to stress. Your stress responses can take different forms: bodily changes, emotional changes, and behavioral changes. This section gives you a clearer picture of what these changes look like. Although they look very different, they're all possible responses you may have when confronted with a stressful situation.

Your body reacts

When you're in fight-or-flight mode, your physiological system goes into high gear. Often your body tells you first that you're experiencing stress. You may notice that you're breathing more quickly than you normally do and that your hands feel cool and more than a little moist. But that's just for starters.

But inside your body additional changes are happening. Your *autonomic nervous system* regulates your body's unconscious actions. It's comprised of two main divisions: the *sympathetic nervous system* and the *parasympathetic nervous system.* Your sympathetic nervous system controls your fight or flight response to stressors and is constantly active in controlling most of your body's internal organs. Your parasympathetic nervous system works to support your body at rest rather than when it's stressed. Your *hypothalamus*, a small portion of your brain located above the brain stem, is responsible for many autonomic nervous system functions. When you're under stress, your hypothalamus instructs the pituitary gland to release *adrenocorticotropic hormone* (ACTH) into the bloodstream, which transports it through your blood to your adrenal glands (which sit on top of your kidneys) and causes them to secrete stress hormones into your bloodstream. These hormones — cortisol, *adrenalin* (epinephrine), and noradrenaline (norepinephrine) — then distribute through your bloodstream and affect all your other body systems, causing the physical fight-or-flight stress response.

Figure 15-1 shows a diagram to help you see the biochemical domino effect you experience when you sense a stressor.

More specifically, here are some highlights of what ultimately happens to your body when you face a stressor:

>> Your heart rate speeds up, and your blood pressure rises, causing more blood to pump to your muscles and lungs and preparing you to fight or flee.

>> You breathe more rapidly, and your nostrils flare, causing an increased supply of air to your lungs.

>> Your digestion slows. (Who's got time to eat?)

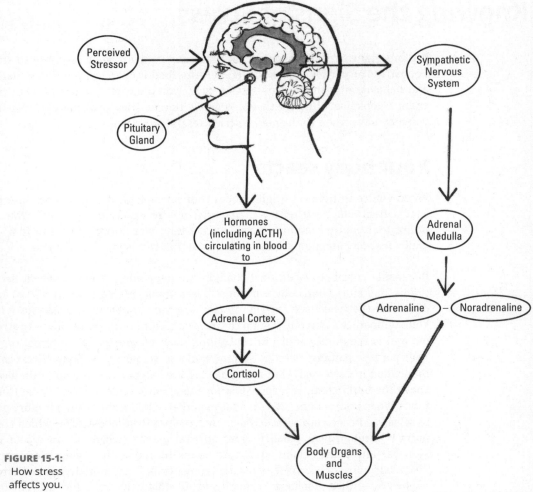

FIGURE 15-1:
How stress
affects you.

Illustration by Pam Tanzey

>> Your blood is directed away from your skin and internal organs and shunted to your brain and skeletal muscles. Your muscles tense. You feel stronger. You're ready for action.

>> Your blood clots more quickly, ready to repair any damage to your arteries if they're damaged in a fight.

>> Your pupils dilate, so you see better.

>> Your liver converts glycogen into glucose, which teams up with free fatty acids to supply you with fuel for quick energy. (You'll probably need it.)

In short, when you're experiencing stress, your entire body undergoes a dramatic series of physiological changes that readies you to effectively respond to a life-threatening emergency. Clearly, this stress response has adaptive survival potential. Way back when, it was nature's way of keeping you alive.

Your feelings and behavior change

Your physical body isn't the only thing that responds to a stressor. You also react to a stressor with feelings and emotions. A partial list of emotional responses to stress includes feeling anxious, upset, angry, sad, guilty, frustrated, hopeless, afraid, or overwhelmed. Your emotional reactions may be minor ("I'm a wee bit annoyed" or "I'm a bit concerned") or major ("I'm furious!" or "I'm very anxious!").

Your body's responses and emotional reactions occur simultaneously to activate changes in your behavior when you're stressed. These changes help you fight or flee. Fight-or-flight may not be an appropriate response to a non-life-threatening situation such as misplacing your keys or failing your driving test. The right amount of anxiety can motivate adaptive behavior, such as doing your best and working toward important goals. However, too much anxiety or anger can cause you to overreact or underreact. Annoyance can escalate to anger, and concern can turn into anxiety. Excessive emotion can result in inappropriate responses. You may act too angrily, quarrel, and later regret what you said or did. If you're feeling anxious or fearful, you may go in the other direction. You may withdraw, avoid, and give up too quickly.

REMEMBER

What makes stress such a problem — both physiologically and emotionally — is that it's often continuous and ongoing. Modern life demands a lot, and keeping up with these demands causes lots of stress. A stressor here and there, now and then — that you can handle. If you're stressed out only once in a while, then stress isn't really a concern. Your body and mind react, but you soon recover and return to a more relaxed state. But when the stream of stressors is nearly continuous, you don't get enough time to recover. Figure 15-2 helps you understand what this looks like.

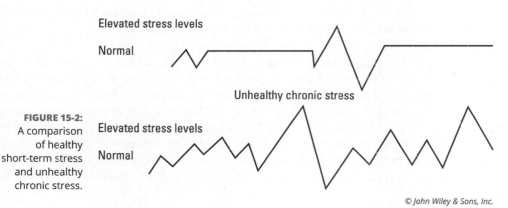

FIGURE 15-2:
A comparison of healthy short-term stress and unhealthy chronic stress.

© John Wiley & Sons, Inc.

Understanding Stress Is As Simple As ABC

One of the best ways to understand stress is to look at a model of emotional distress elaborated by psychologist Albert Ellis. He calls his model the ABC model, and it's as simple as it sounds:

A → B → C, where

>> A is the activating event or triggering situation. It's the stressor.

>> B is your beliefs, thoughts, or perceptions about A.

>> C is the emotional, physical, and behavioral consequence or stress that results from holding these beliefs.

In other words,

A potentially stressful situation → your perceptions → your stress (or lack of stress)

Real-life examples make this model more understandable. Following are two situations that may seem familiar.

Consider one of the more common sources of stress in many people's lives: the fear of being late. You're in a taxi headed for the airport, where you'll board a plane for Philadelphia to interview for a job. You didn't expect traffic to be so heavy. Your taxi is barely moving forward. Your palms become sweaty, and your breathing becomes rapid and shallow. You're feeling increasingly anxious and start to panic. You're stressed out!

Using the ABC model of stress, the sequence looks something like this:

A → B → C

Late for the plane → "I'm never going to make it, and I won't get this job!" → Anxiety and panic with sweaty palms and rapid, shallow breathing

Or consider this scenario: You're trying to get your two kids off to school in the morning. Your husband, who is normally terrific at helping, is on his way to Philadelphia for a job interview. He normally drops off the older child at school while you take your younger daughter to day care. You have a job, too, and today you're expected to show up for an important 9 o'clock meeting. The plan was for the three of you to leave earlier than usual so you'd have time to drop them both off. But this morning your daughter woke up crying and feeling sick. You're caught off guard. You don't have a plan B and certainly not a plan C. You have to scramble to figure out whom to call for help and what to do. You feel anxious and panicky. You become upset and feel your heart rate rise. You're feeling very stressed.

With the ABC model, your stress looks something like this:

Important meeting this morning and daughter isn't feeling well → "OMG! What do I do? I can't skip this meeting!" → Anxiety and panic

Managing Stress: A Three-Pronged Approach

This three-pronged model of dealing with stress provides you with a useful tool to help you understand the many ways you can manage and control your stress. You have three major choices, outlined in the following sections. (*Note:* This section deals with the ABC method of describing stress, explained in the preceding section.)

Handling your stressors

The events that trigger your stress can range from the trivial to the dramatic. They can be very minor (a hassle such as a broken shoelace, a crowded subway, or the world's slowest check-out line) or more important (losing your wallet, hearing sharp words from your boss, or getting a bad haircut a week before your wedding). More serious stressors can be even more dramatic — a divorce, a serious illness, the loss of a job, or the loss of a loved one. The number of potential stressors is endless.

Changing your A means altering, minimizing, or eliminating your potential stressors. Following are some examples of what this may look like:

Potential Stressor	Modified Stressor
A crowded commute	Leaving home earlier or later
Constant lateness	Learning time-management skills
Conflict with relatives	Spending less time with them
Anger about your golf game	Taking some golf lessons
A cluttered home	Becoming better organized
Dissatisfaction with your job	Looking for another job

(continued)

Potential Stressor	Modified Stressor
High credit-card bills	Spending less
Missed deadlines	Starting projects sooner
Angst about the subway	Taking the bus

Often you can't change the world or even what goes on in your own house. You want to change what other people think or do? Good luck! But you *can* sometimes minimize or even eliminate a potential stressor. Your ability to modify your stressors is strengthened if you have the relevant skills. Changing your world isn't always possible, but when it's, it's often the fastest route to stress relief.

Changing your thoughts

Even if you can't significantly change the situations and events that are triggering your stress, you *can* change the way you perceive them. What happens at B — your beliefs, thoughts, perceptions, and interpretations — is critical in determining how much stress you feel. Whenever you perceive a situation or event as over-whelming or beyond your control, or whenever you think you can't cope, you experience stress. You may find that much, if not most, of your stress is self-induced, and you can learn to see things differently. So if you're waiting in a long line, perhaps you're thinking, "I just can't stand this! I have so much else to do! What a waste of my time! I hate waiting! Why can't they figure out a better way of doing this? I hate lines!" Chances are, you're creating more than a little stress for yourself. On the other hand, if you're thinking, "Perfect! Now I have time to read these fascinating articles on alien babies and celebrity cellulite in the *National Tattler*," you're feeling much less stress. Your thinking plays a larger role than you may believe in creating your stress.

Directing your stress responses

Even if you can't eliminate a potential stressor and can't change the way you view that situation, you can still master skills to better control how you respond to stress. You can learn how to relax your body and quiet your mind. Chapter 16 offers ways to reverse the stress response — how to turn off that fight-or-flight cascade and recover a sense of calm.

Stress is part of life. No one makes it through life totally stress-free. You wouldn't want to. You certainly want the good stress, and you even want some of the stress that comes with dealing with life's challenges and disappointments. But too much (or prolonged) stress can become a negative force, which can rob you of much of life's joy. Too little stress means you're missing out, taking too few risks, and playing it too safe. Finding the right amount of stress is like finding the right tension in a guitar string. Too much tension and the string can break; too little tension and there is no music.

You want to hear the music without breaking the strings.

How Stressed Are You? Finding Ways to Measure Your Stress Level

Certainly, one of the first steps in mastering your stress is knowing just how stressed you're feeling. But measuring stress is a trickier business than you may think. Part of the difficulty stems from the multifaceted nature of stress. That is, stress is both a stimulus and a response; it's what's on your plate and how you react to what's on your plate. Unfortunately, your doctor can't just hook you up to a machine and measure your stress level like she does your blood pressure or heart rate. Even though stress can manifest itself as various biochemical and physiological changes in your body, such changes can occur for non-stress reasons. So how exactly do you measure your stress level? The following sections show you some relatively easy ways to identify and quantify just how stressed you're feeling.

Starting with a simple gut check

Oddly enough, one of the best ways to measure your stress is asking yourself this simple question:

"How much stress am I currently feeling?"

In an age of high-tech, computer-driven, digitally monitored gadgets and gear, this lowest-of-low tech gauge may seem like a joke. Yet it really is an incredibly useful way of assessing your stress level. This subjective measure of your stress level has some advantages. One, it measures the severity of your personal feelings of being stressed, such as anxiety, anger, or fatigue. Two, it's sensitive to the ways in which your stress level can change from day to day and even from moment to moment.

TIP

If you don't trust your own judgment, ask someone who knows you well to tell you how stressed you seem. Your spouse, sibling, and best friend may have a better handle on your distress level than you think. They see sides of you that you may miss (or choose to ignore).

Using a stress gauge

To help you put a number on your stress level (and to give this approach the appearance of technological sophistication), use this simple ten-point scale (shown in Figure 15-3) to calibrate your level of stress in a more quantitative way.

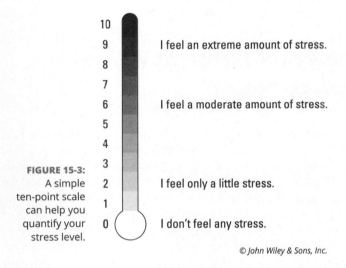

FIGURE 15-3: A simple ten-point scale can help you quantify your stress level.

So right now, you may say to yourself, "I'm feeling a little five-ish." This morning when you were stuck in major traffic, you probably would've described your stress level as a seven.

You can get the hang of using this scale quickly. It's a handy tool for you to have as you master some of the stress-management tools presented here.

Measuring your stress in other ways

In order to get a more complete picture of your overall stress experience, a more objective measure of your stress level may be useful. Sometimes you experience stress but aren't aware of it. That's where the questionnaires in the following sections can help. The stress-symptom questionnaire asks you to rate the frequency of each of the symptoms listed. The stressor-identification questionnaire asks you to rate the severity of the stress you're experiencing in each situation listed. These two measures provide you with valid and reliable measures of your stress level.

REMEMBER

If you aren't in a test-taking mood right now, you can skip this section and come back to it later. But don't skip it entirely. These measures are useful in helping you better understand your present experience of stress. If you retake these scales from time to time, you can track your progress. Your scores can tell you how well you're doing in controlling your responses to stressful situations as you master stress-management techniques over time.

The stress-symptom scale

This index gives you a measure of your stress level by looking at the number and the severity of your stress-related symptoms and behaviors. To use this measure, simply rate the frequency with which you've experienced each of the listed items during the last two weeks. Use this helpful rating scale:

» 0 = Never

» 1 = Sometimes

» 2 = Often

» 3 = Very often

Fatigue or tiredness	____
Pounding heart	____
Rapid pulse	____
Increased perspiration	____
Rapid breathing	____
Aching neck or shoulders	____
Low back pain	____
Gritted teeth or clenched jaw	____
Hives or skin rash	____
Headaches	____
Cold hands or feet	____
Tightness in chest	____
Nausea	____
Diarrhea or constipation	____
Stomach discomfort	____
Nail biting	____
Twitches or tics	____
Difficulty swallowing or dry mouth	____

(continued)

(continued)

Colds or flu	____
Lack of energy	____
Overeating	____
Feelings of helplessness or hopelessness	____
Excessive drinking	____
Excessive smoking	____
Excessive spending	____
Excessive drug or medication use	____
Upset feeling	____
Feelings of nervousness or anxiety	____
Increased irritability	____
Worrisome thoughts	____
Impatience	____
Feelings of depression	____
Loss of sexual interest	____
Feelings of anger	____
Sleep difficulties	____
Forgetfulness	____
Racing or intrusive thoughts	____
Restless feelings	____
Difficulty concentrating	____
Periods of crying	____
Frequent absences from work	____
Your total stress-symptom score	____

Now compare your scores on this stress-symptom survey with the scores of others. No, you don't have to flag down passersby and make them take the test so you have scores to compare; you can use the handy chart in Table 15-1 instead. The higher your score, the more stress symptoms you're reporting. A higher frequency and/or intensity of stress-related symptoms and behaviors is generally associated with higher levels of stress.

TABLE 15-1 **Determining Your Stress Rating**

Your Score	Your Comparative Rating
0–19	Lower than average
20–39	Average
40–49	Moderately higher than average
50 and above	Much higher than average

WARNING

Many of the symptoms and behaviors in this list can result from factors other than stress. Many medical conditions and disorders can have the same symptoms as those seen as responses to stress. If any of your symptoms persist and/or are worrisome, be sure to speak with a medical professional. Your doctor or other healthcare provider is in the best position to help you identify what your symptoms mean and what you should do about them.

The stressor-identification scale

This scale helps you not only assess the amount of stress you're experiencing now but also identify where that stress is coming from. Items in the scale include major life changes, important issues, and worries and concerns that you may be experiencing now. Use this simple scale to help you quantify how much stress the listed categories give you:

>> N = No stress

>> S = Some stress

>> M = Moderate stress

>> G = Great stress

Conflicts or concerns about your marriage or relationship	____
Concerns or worries about your children	____
Concerns or worries about your parents	____
Pressures from other family members/in-laws	____
Death of a loved one	____
Health problems or worries	____
Financial worries	____

(continued)

(continued)

Concerns related to work/career	____
Long or difficult commute to work	____
Change in where you're living or will live	____
Concerns with current residence or neighborhood	____
Household responsibilities	____
Home improvements or repairs	____
Balancing demands of work and family	____
Relationships with friends	____
Limited personal time	____
Concerns with social life	____
Concerns with your appearance	____
Issues with your personal traits or habits	____
Boredom	____
Feelings of loneliness	____
Feelings about growing old	____

Note that this scale isn't designed to provide you with a quantitative measure of your overall stress level. Rather, it's a qualitative tool that helps you pinpoint specific stresses in your life and assess the impact of each at the present time. It's an index of what's on your plate.

Monitoring Your Stress with a Stress Journal

Hopefully, using the measurement tools in the preceding sections gives you a better picture of just how much stress you're currently experiencing. Another tool you need is one that both shows you what's triggering stress for you right now and measures your ongoing stress level: a *stress journal.*

A stress journal or stress log is one of the more useful items you can carry in your tool belt. To effectively manage your stress, you need to become aware of when you're feeling stressed and be able to identify the sources of that stress. A stress journal can help you do just that by very specifically showing you when you experience stress and pinpointing the situations or circumstances that trigger those stresses. By recording your experiences and responses, you figure out what sets off your fight-or-flight response and can recognize and respond to those situations differently. By keeping a longer-term record of your daily stressors, you're in the best position to formulate a comprehensive stress-management program that integrates the stress-reducing strategies and tactics that work best for you.

Maintain a stress journal to help you become more self-aware of stresses in your life. Even after you get better at stress-management, you should still monitor your stress on an ongoing (but perhaps less frequent) basis to help you stay tuned in to your needs.

TIP

Make your journal small and compact enough that you can carry it with you. A small notebook can work well. Your journal's form and format are less important than the fact that you use it on a regular basis. If you're a high-tech kind of person, you can work your stress journal into your laptop, smartphone, or tablet. You can find apps that make your record-keeping easier.

Knowing how to record your stress

Here's what someone's stress log may look like on a Wednesday morning:

DAY: WEDNESDAY, NOVEMBER 9, 2016

Time	My Stress Trigger (Importance Level)	My Stress (Stress Level)
7:45 a.m.	Couldn't find my keys (2)	Annoyed, upset (4)
9:30 a.m.	Subway stalled for ten minutes (1)	Annoyed (3)
11:30 a.m.	Mail came; big credit-card bill (6)	Upset, worried (8)
12:30 p.m.	Given a deadline for project (4)	Worried, anxious (8)

The following sections walk you through the four steps you need to make your journal as useful as possible, with each day on a separate page.

Step 1: Write down what's stressing you

In the "My Stress Trigger" column, write down exactly what is triggering your stress. It may be an event, a situation, an encounter, or a problem. Be sure to also note the (approximate) time in the "Time" column.

TIP

Be brief in your trigger descriptions. You don't need to relive the event; you just want to record that it happened. For example:

> "I was so annoyed because I thought I had left my keys on the hall table. They weren't there, and I had no idea where they were! What a pain! This is the third time this month this has happened. I need a brain transplant!"

becomes

> "Couldn't find my keys!"

Or consider this potentially stressful trigger:

> "I was so upset when I got that flat tire on my way to the bowling alley. This was our big night. We were in contention. We could win the team title. That is, if Mable shows up. She's the real star."

becomes

> "Flat tire on way to bowling!"

Step 2: Rate the relative importance of the stressor

Next to your stressor description, rate the relative importance of that stressor on a ten-point scale like the one in Figure 15-4.

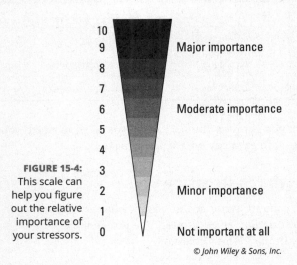

FIGURE 15-4: This scale can help you figure out the relative importance of your stressors.

10
9   Major importance
8
7
6   Moderate importance
5
4
3
2   Minor importance
1
0   Not important at all

© *John Wiley & Sons, Inc.*

To help you get the feel of the scale, think of major difficult life stressors that could happen or have happened to you — the death of a loved one, a major financial loss, a life-threatening illness, the loss of your job, or chronic pain. Remember, good changes can also be major stressors — starting college, relocating to a better job, getting married, or having a baby. These major, life-altering events will likely be your eights, nines, and tens.

More moderate stressors may include breaking your leg, losing your wallet, or having your car break down on the highway. Big deals, but not catastrophes. These are your fours, fives, sixes, and sevens.

Your ones, twos, and threes are the everyday hassles: being late for a movie, getting caught in the rain with no umbrella, encountering a rude clerk, and so on.

REMEMBER

Be careful here. You aren't rating how stressed you were about these events and situations; you're just rating their objective importance as a life stressor. So even if you go absolutely ballistic and sulk for days when your favorite team loses a game, the trigger "losing a game" is still only a one or two in life. (Okay, if it's a playoff game, maybe a three.)

Step 3: Write down your response to the stressor and rate your distress level

In the "My Stress" column, describe your stress response. Look at your emotional responses — worried, anxious, upset, fearful, angry, and so on.

Now rate the level of your distress caused by the stress trigger. Use a ten-point scale like the one in Figure 15-5.

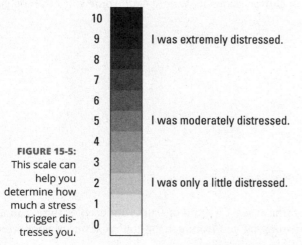

FIGURE 15-5:
This scale can help you determine how much a stress trigger distresses you.

© John Wiley & Sons, Inc.

Knowing when to record your stress

When you have the stress journal format down (see the preceding sections), you need to use it.

REMEMBER

Make keeping your journal easy so that you're more likely to keep it up. Bear in mind that you don't have to record every single stressor in your day. A few of the more important and/or recurring ones will do.

Note when you're feeling stressed by becoming aware of negative emotional changes. Anxiety, worry, shame, upset, fear, and anger are usually a tip-off that you're feeling stressed.

You don't have to record your stressors at the exact time they occur. However, the sooner you make the entry, the more likely you are to recall what occurred and how stressed you were about that occurrence. Making the entry later in your day is still better than not making an entry at all.

Facing Roadblocks

If you recall your last attempt at losing a few pounds or getting rid of all the clutter in your house, you may recognize that good intentions don't always guarantee success. Almost always, you encounter at least one or two roadblocks. But being aware of potential obstacles in your path and figuring out ways to avoid them makes reaching your goal more likely.

Here are some of the more commonly experienced roadblocks (whether your goal is managing stress, cutting clutter, or losing weight) and some ways to help you avoid them:

>> I don't have time.

>> I'm too busy.

>> I have too much stuff to learn.

>> It's too much work.

>> It's not my cup of tea.

>> I tried it once and it didn't work.

Each of these excuses contains at least a grain of truth. But each of them can act as a roadblock, slowing or stopping you from getting the most out of your stress management efforts. The following sections give you some ideas and suggestions to help you get around these potential obstacles.

Take it a step at a time

Learning any new skill takes time. The trick isn't to tackle everything at once but rather to spread your learning out over time. Start slowly; don't overwhelm yourself. Set aside 15 or 20 minutes in your day and practice one of the stress management methods in this book. It may be on your way to work in the morning, during a coffee break, on your lunch hour, or after work when you come home.

Give it a try

Some approaches may feel a tad foreign and not immediately comfortable. Yet, with a little getting used to, these techniques may be the very ones you routinely use down the road. For example, you may not think that breathing exercises are your thing, but you may be pleasantly surprised to find them wonderfully calming and relaxing. Keep an open mind. Give everything at least one good try.

Accept your different strokes

Although being open-minded about stress management and relaxation techniques is important, you ultimately need to put together a package of tools that reflects your personal needs and lifestyle. No two people are exactly alike. One size rarely fits all. For one person, the picture of ideal relaxation may be lying on a beach in the Caribbean with a page-turner in one hand and a piña colada in the other. For someone else, this scenario may trigger some an eye-rolling "Do I have to?" His or her idea of a relaxing vacation may be visiting every museum in a 50 mile radius. As a general rule, if you aren't comfortable with a technique or strategy, you're less likely to make it a part of your life. If meditation doesn't do anything for you, that's fine; move on to something that does.

Practice to make perfect

Most of the methods and techniques presented here require some practice before you can master them. Even though you can pick them up pretty quickly at an intellectual level, you need to spend some time repeating them to truly reap their benefits. Don't give up too easily. Learning to ride a bike, drive a car, and play tennis all take time. Why should discovering how to manage the stress in your life be worth less time and effort? Here again, practice makes perfect.

Find a quiet place

You need a place to do all this practicing. Hopefully, you can find one that's relatively quiet and relaxing, at least for a short period of time each day. Given the realities of your life, your quiet place may have to be a setting that is far from ideal. Your office — when the door is shut — may work for you. You can also try your bedroom or bathroom (sometimes the only private place!) at home, or your car when you're stopped in traffic or commuting to work.

Link up

Listening to audio instructions can be a marvelous way to learn and practice many of the relaxation and stress-reducing exercises presented in this book.

TIP

Go to www.dummies.com/extras/stressmanagement to access a free guided relaxation exercise that you can download to your computer or mobile device.

Get a stress buddy

Doing something by yourself can be hard. Losing weight, going to the gym, and stopping smoking are all easier when you do them with a friend. The same holds true for stress management. See if you can interest a friend in joining you. Your stress buddy can gently prod you to practice and put your new skills into daily use.

Don't expect overnight results

You've spent years creating your stress-producing styles and patterns. Fortunately, you can change these patterns, but it takes some time. You can't expect miraculous stress-relief overnight. You need to change your behaviors and thinking, not to mention modify your lifestyle and work style. You get there step by step. Look at your daily encounters and experiences as opportunities for growth and improvement. Day by day, you'll change. Remember, practice makes perfect.

IN THIS CHAPTER

Understanding the effects of tension

Recognizing your tension

Breathing properly

Using suggestion to relax

Stretching and massaging

Chapter 16

Relaxing Your Body

When people hear the word relaxation, they tend to think of activities that take their minds off the stresses in their lives: watching some TV, curling up with a good book, playing a round of golf, taking a nap — anything that can take them out of their world of worry, fear, and concern. In this chapter, though, *relaxing* means something different. It means acquiring specific relaxation skills that can help you reduce bodily tension in a direct and systematic way. Instead of simply distracting you or providing you with some temporary pleasure, these approaches focus more directly on releasing muscle tension and allowing you to keep your mind in sharp focus.

This chapter describes strategies and techniques that can help you let go of tension and relax your body — an important stress-management skill.

Stress Can Be a Pain in the Neck (and That's Just for Starters)

The following is a short — and only partial — list of some of the effects tension has on your body. Unfortunately, many of these symptoms are all too familiar.

>> Neck pain/stiffness

>> Headaches

>> Stomach cramps

>> Nausea/diarrhea

>> Heartburn

>> Back pain

>> Fast heartbeat

>> Clenched, painful jaw

>> Teeth grinding

>> Sore shoulders

>> Muscle spasms

>> Tremors or twitches

>> Sweating and sweaty palms

Inside your body, additional tension-related changes are happening. Here is a sampling of what else is quietly going on in your body when you feel tense:

>> Your blood pressure goes up.

>> Your stomach secretes more acid.

>> Your cholesterol goes up.

>> Your blood clots more quickly.

All in all, knowing how to prevent and eliminate bodily tension is a pretty healthy idea.

Funny, I don't feel tense

The fact is you may not know when your body is tense. You get so used to being tense that you may not notice that you feel tense. Muscle tension creeps up on you over time. Slowly and often imperceptibly, your muscles tighten and, voila, the tension sets in. You don't feel the tension until it reaches the headache or tight-neck-and-shoulder-muscles stage. At that point, alleviating your symptoms takes longer. The trick is to become aware of bodily tension before it builds up and makes you feel bad. Tuning in to your body takes a bit of practice. The next section gives you a simple awareness technique that helps you recognize your body is tense before it becomes a bigger problem.

Invasion of the body scan

One of the best ways to recognize bodily tension is to use this simple one-minute scanning exercise. Find a place where you can sit or lie down comfortably and be undisturbed for a moment or two (see Figure 16-1). Scan your body for any muscle tension. Start with the top of your head and work your way down to your toes. Ask yourself:

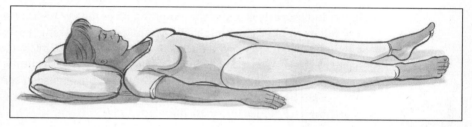

FIGURE 16-1: A good position for body scanning.

Illustration by Pam Tanzey

>> Am I furrowing my brow?

>> Am I knitting my eyebrows?

>> Am I clenching my jaw?

>> Am I pursing my lips?

>> Am I hunching my shoulders?

>> Am I tight/stiff/sore in my neck or back?

>> Am I feeling tension in my arms?

>> Am I feeling tightness in my thigh and calf muscles?

>> Am I curling my toes?

>> Do I notice any discomfort anywhere else in my body?

With a little practice, you can scan your body in less than a minute, quickly finding where you feel tension. When you have the hang of it, try the body scan while sitting at a desk or standing up. See whether you can do a body scan three or four times a day. It's a great way of becoming aware that you're stressed and therefore tense.

When you find your sites of tension, of course, you want to do something about them. The following sections give you some options to alleviate your stress symptoms.

Breathing Away Your Tension

Breathing properly is one of the simplest and best ways to drain away your tension and relieve your stress. Simply by changing your breathing patterns, you can rapidly induce a state of greater relaxation. If you control the way you breathe, you have a powerful means of reducing bodily tension. Just as important, you have a tool that can help prevent your body from becoming tense in the first place. This section shows you what you can do to incorporate a variety of stress-relieving breathing techniques into your life.

LOOKING UNDER THE HOOD

Breathing provides your body with oxygen and removes waste products — primarily carbon dioxide — from your blood. Your lungs carry out this gas exchange. Lungs, however, don't have their own muscles for breathing. Your diaphragm is the major muscle necessary for proper breathing. The diaphragm is a dome-shaped muscle that separates your chest cavity from your abdominal cavity and acts as a flexible floor for your lungs.

When you inhale, your diaphragm contracts by flattening downward, creating more space in the chest cavity and permitting the lungs to fill with oxygen. You can see your stomach rising as you take a deep breath. When you exhale, your diaphragm relaxes and returns to its dome shape, pushing the used air (carbon dioxide waste products) out of your lungs. *Diaphragmatic breathing,* also called *abdominal breathing,* provides the most efficient way of exchanging oxygen and carbon dioxide.

Your diaphragm is controlled by your brainstem and therefore works automatically without your having to think about it. But you can override this process. When you're under stress, you tend to breathe more quickly, take shallower breaths, and even hold your breath without realizing it. And that's where problems can arise. Too often when you're tense, you neglect to use your diaphragm effectively when you breathe. This shallow breathing interferes with the proper exchange of gases in your system, resulting in greater tension, more fatigue, and more stress.

No mints required: Tackling bad breathing

Your breath is fine; it's your breathing that's bad. *Bad breathing* can take a number of forms. You may be a chest and shoulder breather, bringing air into your lungs by expanding your chest cavity and raising your shoulders. This description certainly fits if you have more than a touch of vanity and opt for never sticking out your tummy when you breathe. You also may be a breath holder, stopping your breathing entirely when you're distracted or lost in thought. Both are inefficient, stress-producing forms of breathing. And when you're under stress, your breathing patterns deteriorate even more. To make things worse, when your breathing goes awry, you feel even more stressed. Quite a nasty cycle.

You probably take your breathing for granted. And why not? You've been breathing for most of your life; you'd think by now you'd have figured out how to do it right. No such luck. When you're feeling stressed, your breathing becomes faster and shallower. When you breathe this way, your body reacts as follows:

>> Less oxygen reaches your bloodstream.

>> Your blood vessels constrict, increasing your blood pressure.

>> Less oxygen reaches your brain.

>> Your heart rate increases.

>> You feel light-headed, shaky, and more tense.

Our primitive ancestors knew how to breathe. They didn't have to deal with the IRS, stacks of unpaid bills, or the Boss from Hell. These days only opera singers, stage actors, musicians who play wind instruments, and a couple of dozen moonlighting yoga instructors actually breathe effectively. The rest of us don't know how.

However, for a period of your life, you did get the whole breathing thing right. As a baby lying in your crib, you breathed serenely. Your little belly rose and fell in the most relaxed way. But then you grew up and, poof!, you started having to deal with life's stresses and your correct breathing blew by the wayside. Thankfully, all is not lost. You can reteach yourself to breathe properly.

You probably think of breathing as just a way of getting air into your lungs. However, in times past, breathing was elevated to a more important status. Many religious groups and sects believed that a calming breath replenished the soul as well as soothed the body. In fact, the word *ruach* in Hebrew and the word *pneuma* in Greek have double meanings, connoting both breath and spirit. Calming breaths bring you to a state of peace and relaxation, although for the most benefit, you need to breathe deeply, smoothly, and easily.

Evaluating your breathing

You may be one of the few people who actually breathe properly. But before you skip this section, read a little further. To find out whether the way you breathe is stress-reducing, take this simple test.

1. **Lie on your back.**

2. **Put your right hand on your belly and your left hand on your chest, as shown in Figure 16-2.**

   Try to become aware of the way you breathe. Check to see whether your breathing is smooth, slow, and regular. If you're breathing properly, the hand on your belly rises and falls rhythmically as you inhale and exhale. The hand on your chest should move very little, and if that hand does rise, it should follow the rise in your belly.

FIGURE 16-2: Evaluating your breathing.

Illustration by Pam Tanzey

Cutting yourself some slack

REMEMBER

Many people who want to adopt new patterns of breathing have a fervent desire to get it perfectly right. They frequently get so lost in lung mechanics that they wind up more stressed out than they were before they started. Don't let this happen to you. There's no one exactly right way to breathe all the time. Give yourself lots of room to experiment with your breathing. And don't overdo it. If you've been breathing inefficiently for all these years, changing gears may take some time. Above all, you're not taking a test. Don't grade yourself on how deeply you can breathe or how flat you can make your diaphragm. Remember, the goal is to reduce your stress, not add to it.

Changing the way you breathe, changing the way you feel

Sometimes, all it takes to make you feel better is one simple change. Changing the way you breathe can make all the difference in how you feel. The following exercises present various ways to alter your breathing. Try them and discover whether all you need is one simple change.

Breathing 101: Breathing for starters

Here is one of the best and simplest ways of introducing yourself to stress-effective breathing.

1. **Either lying or sitting comfortably, put one hand on your belly and the other hand on your chest.**

2. **Inhale through your nose, making sure that the hand on your belly rises and the hand on your chest moves hardly at all.**

3. **As you inhale slowly, count silently to three.**

4. **As you exhale through your parted lips slowly count silently to four, feeling the hand on your belly falling gently.**

   Pause slightly before your next breath. Continue to breathe like this until you feel completely relaxed.

Something more advanced: Taking a complete breath

Taking complete breaths (or doing diaphragmatic or "Zen" breathing, as it's often called) helps you breathe more deeply and more efficiently and helps you maximize your lung capacity.

1. **Lie comfortably on a bed, in a reclining chair, or on a rug.**

   Keep your knees slightly apart and slightly bent. Close your eyes if you like. You may feel more comfortable placing a pillow under the small of your back to help relieve the pressure.

2. **Put one hand on your abdomen near your belly button and the other hand on your chest so that you follow the motion of your breathing.**

   Try to relax. Let go of any tension you may feel in your body.

3. **Begin by slowly inhaling through your nose, first filling the lower part of your lungs, the middle part of your chest, and finally the upper part of your chest.**

   As you inhale, feel your diaphragm pushing down, gently extending your abdomen, making room for the newly inhaled air. Notice the hand on your abdomen rise slightly. The hand on your chest should move very little, and when it does, it should follow your abdomen. Don't use your shoulders to help you breathe.

4. **Exhale slowly through your parted lips, emptying your lungs from top to bottom.**

   Make a whooshing sound as the air passes through your lips, and notice the hand on your abdomen fall.

5. **Pause slightly and take in another breath, repeating this cycle.**

   Continue breathing this way for ten minutes or so — certainly until you feel more relaxed and peaceful. Practice this technique daily if you can. Try this exercise while sitting and then while standing.

With a little practice, this form of breathing comes more naturally and automatically. With time and practice, you can begin to breathe this way much more of the time. Stick with it.

Trying some belly-button balloon breathing

A simpler way of breathing more deeply and more evenly is to work with a visual image — in this case a balloon. Here's what you do:

1. **Imagine that a small balloon — about the size of a grapefruit — is replacing your stomach, just under your belly button, as shown in Figure 16-3.**

2. **As you inhale through your nose, imagine that you're actually inhaling through your belly button, inflating this once-empty balloon.**

   This balloon is small, so don't overinflate it. As the balloon gets larger, notice how your belly rises.

3. **Exhale slowly through your nose or mouth, again imagining that the air is leaving through your belly button.**

   Your balloon is now slowly and easily returning to its deflated state.

4. **Pause slightly before the next breath in and then repeat, gently and smoothly inflating your balloon to a comfortable size.**

   Repeat this exercise as often as you can, whenever you can.

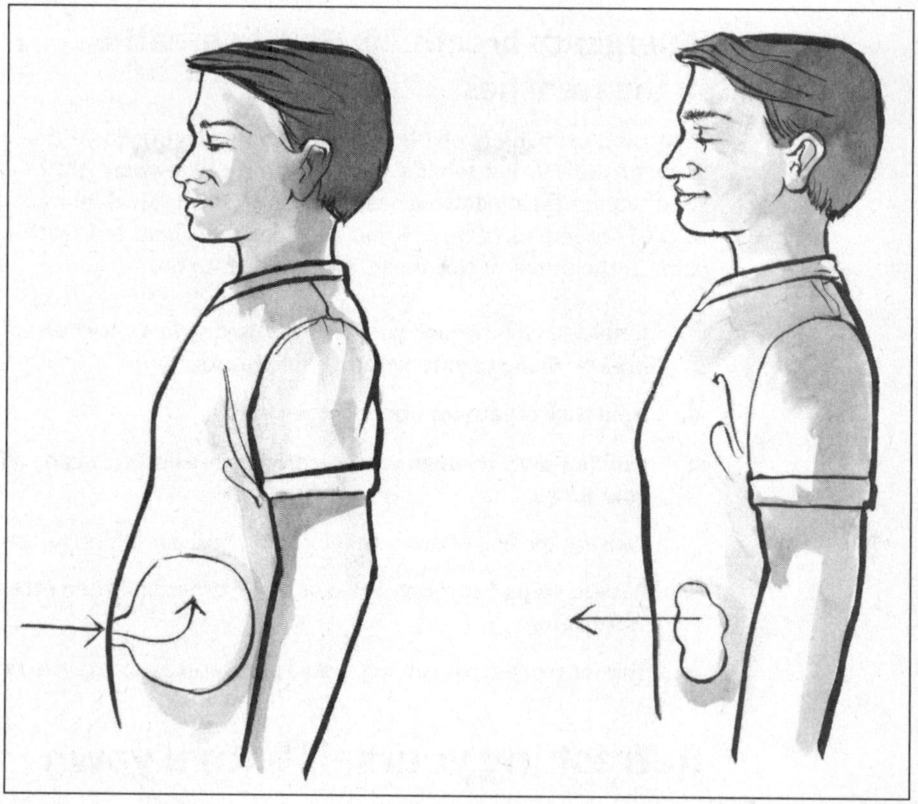

FIGURE 16-3: Balloon breathing.

Illustration by Pam Tanzey

STANDING UP STRAIGHT

Your mother was right! When you're under stress, you have a tendency to hunch over, making your posture lousy and impairing your breathing. When you hunch over, you breathe less deeply because your lungs have less room to expand in your chest cavity, which denies your body of the proper supply of oxygen. As a result, your muscles get tense. When you stand or sit up straight, you reverse this process, giving your lungs more room to expand and bringing in more oxygen. You needn't stand like a West Point cadet to correct bad posture. Overdoing it probably produces as much tension as you felt before. Just keep your shoulders from slouching forward. If you're unsure about what your posture looks like, stand naturally in front of a mirror or ask a loved one.

Emergency breathing: How to breathe in the trenches

Breathing properly is no big deal when you're lying on your bed or vegging out in front of the TV. But what's your breathing like when you're caught in gridlock, when you're facing down a deadline, or when the stock market drops? You're now in crisis mode. Chances are you need another form of breathing to help you feel calm in the midst of the storm. Here's what to do:

1. **Inhale slowly through your nostrils, taking in a very deep diaphragmatic breath, filling your lungs and your cheeks.**

2. **Hold that breath for about six seconds.**

3. **Exhale slowly through your slightly parted lips, releasing all the air in your lungs.**

   Pause at the end of this exhalation. Now take a few "normal" breaths.

4. **Repeat Steps 1 through 3 two or three times and then return to what you were doing.**

   This form of deep breathing should put you in a more relaxed state.

Refreshing yourself with a yawn

Yawning is usually associated with being tired or bored. Business meetings you think will run well into the next millennium or endless talking-head commentary on the latest news event or political debate may trigger more than a few yawning gasps. However, when you yawn, your body is trying to give you an important message.

Yawning is another way Mother Nature tells you that your body is under stress. In fact, yawning helps relieve stress. When you yawn, more air — and therefore more oxygen — enters your lungs, revitalizing your bloodstream. Releasing that plaintive sound that comes with yawning is also tension reducing. Unfortunately, people have become a little oversocialized, stifling their yawns to be polite. But such wimpy yawns don't help your body. You need to recapture the lost art of proper deep yawning.

The next time you feel a yawn coming on, go with it. Open your mouth widely and inhale more fully than you normally would. Take that breath all the way down to your belly. Exhale fully through your mouth, completely emptying your lungs. What a feeling! Enjoy it. So what if your friends don't call you anymore? At least your body will be getting better oxygen supply!

Tensing Your Way to Relaxation

After you master the art of breathing (see the exercises in the preceding sections), you're ready to discover another way of relaxing your body. One of the better relaxation techniques derives from a method called *progressive relaxation* or *deep-muscle relaxation*. This method is based on the notion that you're not aware of what your muscles feel like when they're tensed. By purposely tensing your muscles, you're able to recognize what tension feels like and identify which muscles are creating that tension. This technique is highly effective and is a valuable tool for quickly reducing muscle tension and promoting relaxation.

Exploring how progressive relaxation works

You begin progressive relaxation by tensing a specific muscle or group of muscles (your arms, legs, shoulders, and so on). You notice the way the tension feels. You hold that tension for about ten seconds and then let it go, replacing that tension with something much more pleasant — relaxation. By the time you tense and relax most of your major muscle groups, you feel relaxed, at peace, and much less stressed. The following general guidelines set the stage for muscle-group-specific relaxation techniques later in this chapter.

1. **Lie down or sit, as comfortably as you can, and close your eyes.**

   Find a quiet, dimly lit place that gives you some privacy, at least for a while.

2. **Tense the muscles of a particular body part.**

   To practice, start by tensing your right hand and arm. Begin by simply making a fist. As you clench your fist, notice the tension and strain in your hand and forearm. Without releasing that tension, bend your right arm and flex your bicep, making a muscle the way you would to impress the kids in the schoolyard.

   REMEMBER

   Don't strain yourself in any of these muscle-tensing maneuvers; don't overdo it. When you tense a muscle group, don't tense as hard as you can. Tense to about 75 percent of what you can do. If you feel pain or soreness, ease up on the tension, and if you still hurt, put off your practice till another time.

3. **Hold the tension in the body part for about seven seconds.**

4. **Let go of the tension quickly, letting the muscles go limp.**

   Notice the difference in the way your hand and arm feel. Notice the difference between the sensations of tension and those of relaxation. Let these feelings of relaxation deepen for about 30 seconds.

5. Repeat Steps 1 through 4, using the same muscle group.

6. Move to another muscle group.

Simply repeat Steps 1 through 5, substituting a different muscle group each time. Continue with your left hand and arm and then work your way through the major muscle groups listed in the following sections.

After you finish the sequence in the following sections, let your body sink into an even deeper state of relaxation. Let go more and more. Mentally go over the sensations you're feeling in your arms, face, neck, shoulders, back, stomach, and legs. Feel your body becoming looser and more relaxed. Savor the feeling.

TIP

You don't have to remember all the various instructions and muscle groups. Head to www.dummies.com/extras/stressmanagement and listen to a guided progressive muscle relaxation.

Relaxing your face and head

Wrinkle your forehead (creating all those lines that everybody hates) by raising your eyebrows as high as you can. Hold this tension for about five seconds and then let go, releasing all the tension in your forehead. Just let your forehead muscles become smooth. Notice the difference between the feelings of tension you felt and the more pleasant feelings of relaxation.

Now clench your jaw by biting down on your back teeth. At the same time, force a smile. Hold this uncomfortable position for about five seconds and then relax your jaw, letting your mouth fall slightly ajar.

Finally, purse your lips, pushing them together firmly. Hold that tension for a bit and then relax, letting your lips open slightly. Notice how relaxed your face and head feel. Enjoy this sensation and let this feeling deepen by letting go of any remaining sources of tension around your mouth and lips.

Relaxing your neck and shoulders

Bend your head forward as though you're going to touch your chest with your chin (you probably will). Feel the tension in the muscles of your neck. Hold that tension. Now tilt your head slightly, first to one side and then to another. Notice the tension at the side of your neck as you do so. Tilt your head back as if you're trying to touch your upper back. But don't force it or overdo it, stopping if you notice any pain and discomfort. Now relax, letting your head return to a more comfortable, natural position. Enjoy the relaxation for a moment or so.

Now scrunch up your shoulders as though you're trying to reach your ears. Hold it, feel the tension (again for about five seconds), and let your shoulders fall to a comfortable, relaxed position. Notice the feelings of relaxation that are spreading through your shoulders and neck.

Relaxing your back

Arch your back, being careful not to overdo it. Hold that tension for several seconds and then let your back and shoulders return to a more comfortable, relaxed position.

Relaxing your legs and feet

Either sitting or lying down, raise your right foot so that you feel some tension in your thigh and buttock. At the same time, push your heel out and point your toes toward your head, as shown in Figure 16-4. Hold this tension, notice what it feels like, and then let go, letting your leg fall to the bed or floor and releasing any remaining tension. Let that relaxation deepen for a while. Repeat this sequence with your other leg and foot.

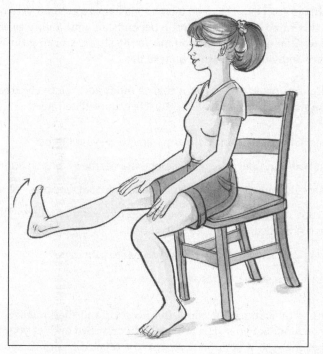

FIGURE 16-4:
Relaxing your feet and legs.

Illustration by Pam Tanzey

Relaxing your buttocks

Tense the muscles of your buttocks, noticing what that feels like. Hold that tension for several seconds. Slowly release that muscle tension, letting go and letting the muscles in your buttocks gently release. Notice those feelings of relaxation and let them deepen even further.

Relaxing your stomach

Take in a deep breath and hold that breath, tensing the muscles in your stomach. Imagine that you're preparing yourself for a punch in the stomach. Hold that tension and then relax, letting go of the tension.

Scrunching up like a pretzel

When pressed for time, you can do a quickie version of the progressive relaxation exercise mentioned in the preceding sections. Simply, this technique compresses all the muscle-tensing and relaxing sequences into one. Think of it as one gigantic scrunch.

To do this pretzel exercise, you have to master the gradual version first. The success of this rapid form of relaxation depends on your ability to create and release muscle tension quickly, skills you master by slowly working through all the muscle groups individually. Here's what to do:

Sit or lie comfortably in a room that is quiet and relatively free of distractions. Now simultaneously tense all the muscle groups listed here:

>> Clench both fists, bend both arms, and tense your biceps.

>> Lift both legs until you notice a moderate degree of tension and discomfort.

>> Tense the muscles in your buttocks and hold that tension.

>> Scrunch up your face, closing your eyes, furrowing your brow, clenching your jaws, and pursing your lips.

>> Bring your shoulders as close as you can to your ears.

>> Tense your stomach muscles.

Hold this total scrunch for about five seconds and then release, letting go of any and all tension. Let your legs fall to the floor or bed and let your arms fall to your sides. Let the rest of your body return to a relaxed position. Repeat this sequence at various points throughout your day.

Mind over Body: Using the Power of Suggestion

Another important approach to bodily relaxation is called *autogenic training*, or AT for short. The word *autogenic* means "self-generation" or "self-regulation." This method attempts to regulate your *autonomic nervous functions* and more specifically your *parasympathetic nervous system* (your heart rate, blood pressure, and breathing, among others) instead of relaxing your muscles. With autogenic training, you use your mind to regulate your body's internal stress levels.

AT relies on the power of suggestion to induce physiological changes. These suggestions are mental images that your subconscious picks up and transmits to your body. Just thinking about certain changes in your body produces those kinds of changes. As a result, you experience deep feelings of relaxation. AT may sound mysterious, but it isn't. After you master this technique, AT is a highly effective way of putting yourself in a more relaxed state. The method described here is a more abbreviated form than the one originally devised. However, it's better suited to a busy lifestyle. Here's what you do:

1. **Get comfy.**

   Find a suitably quiet, not-too-hot, and not-too-cold place. You can sit or lie down, but make sure your body is well supported and as comfortable as possible. Try to breathe slowly and smoothly.

2. **Concentrate passively.**

   For this approach to be effective, you need to adopt a receptive, casual attitude of passive concentration. You want to be alert — not falling asleep, but not asking your mind to work too hard. You can't force yourself to relax. Just let it happen. Be aware of your body and your mind, but don't actively analyze everything or worry about how you're doing. If a distracting thought comes your way, notice it and then let it go. If the relaxation doesn't come at first, don't worry. It comes with more practice.

3. **Allow various body parts to begin feeling warm and heavy.**

   Although autogenic training utilizes many suggestions and images, the two most effective images are warmth and heaviness. Start by focusing on your right arm. Now slowly and softly say to yourself:

   I am calm . . . I am at peace . . . My right arm is warm . . . and heavy . . . My right arm is warm . . . and heavy . . . My right arm is warm . . . and heavy . . . I can feel the warmth and heaviness flowing into my right arm . . . I can feel my right arm becoming warmer . . . and heavier . . . I can feel my right arm becoming warmer . . . and heavier . . . I can feel my right arm becoming warmer . . . and heavier . . . I am at peace . . . I am calm . . . I am at peace . . . I am calm.

Take the time to become aware of the feelings in your arm and hand. Notice that your arm is becoming warmer and heavier. Don't rush this process. Enjoy the changes your body is now beginning to experience.

4. **After you complete the phrases, remain silent and calm for about 30 seconds, letting the relaxation deepen; then focus on your left arm.**

Repeat the same phrases again, this time substituting "left arm" for "right arm." (Hopefully by now you've memorized these phrases and can close your eyes and not worry about a script.)

5. **Move to other parts of your body.**

Focus on other areas, repeating the same phrases but substituting other parts of your body. Here is the complete sequence: right arm, left arm, both arms, right leg, left leg, both legs, neck and shoulders, chest and abdomen, and finally your entire body.

Completing the entire sequence shouldn't take you more than a half hour or so. If you can fit in two or three autogenic sessions a day, all the better. You may need some time to master this technique, but the results are well worth the effort.

TIP

USE YOUR IMAGINATION? YOU'RE GETTING WARMER!

With autogenic training, you may find that using the "warm and heavy" suggestions and images isn't effective for you. You may need a different image to release the tension in your body. Here are alternate suggestive images that can induce feelings of warmth and heaviness.

- **Heat me up:** Imagine that the body part in question (arm, leg, and so on) is wrapped in a heating pad. Slowly but surely the heat permeates your body, relaxing your muscles more and more.

- **Get in hot water:** Imagine that you're immersing your arm or leg in soothing warm water.

- **Sunny-side up:** Mentally direct a sun lamp to a particular part of your anatomy.

- **Heavy metal:** Visualize weights attached to your arm, leg, and so on.

- **Get the lead in:** Imagine that your limb is filled with lead.

Stretching Away Your Stress

Stretching is one of the ways your body naturally discharges excess bodily tension. You may notice that you automatically feel the need to stretch after waking up in the morning, just before retiring at night, or after a long car ride. But a good stretch can drain away much of your body's tension at other times, too. You may be desk-bound or otherwise required to sit for long periods of time during the day, causing your muscles to tense and tighten. Consider adopting one or more basic stretches and taking a stretch break at various points throughout the day. Cats do, dogs do; why not you?

Following are two tension-relieving stretches that are wonderful ways of draining off a lot of excess tension. They're simple and shouldn't evoke much comment or ridicule from friends or coworkers.

>> **The twist:** This stretch is great for your upper body. Sitting or standing, put both your hands behind the back of your head, locking your fingers together. Move your elbows toward each other until you feel some moderate tension. Now twist your body slightly, first to the right for a few seconds and then slowly to the left. When you finish, let your arms fall to your sides.

>> **The leg-lift:** This stretch is good for your lower body. Sitting in your chair, raise both your legs until you feel a comfortable level of tightness in them. Maintaining that tension, flex and point your toes toward your head. Hold that tension for about ten seconds and then let your legs fall to the floor. If doing both legs together is a wee bit uncomfortable, try it one leg at a time.

REMEMBER

Stretch slowly and don't overdo it. You're trying to relax your muscles, not punish them.

ALL THIS RELAXING IS MAKING ME TENSE!

Believe it or not, you may find that practicing relaxation can be stressful, at least at first.

Changing your breathing patterns, tensing and relaxing muscles, and exploring autogenic exercises can have some side effects. You may notice some tingling or a feeling of restlessness and, paradoxically, an increase in tension. This result isn't unusual; although it's distracting, don't take it as a sign that you're doing something wrong. Give it time and practice. As you become more familiar with how your body feels when it's in a highly relaxed state, these sensations disappear.

Massage? Ah, There's the Rub!

Massage and other touch and pressure therapies are among the most popular ways of relieving muscle tension. These days you can get a massage almost as easily as you can get your hair cut. In the past, the idea of a massage usually conjured up an image of a liniment rubdown in a sweaty gym or pampered caresses in a swanky health spa. No more. Massage and related treatments have come of age.

The range and popularity of touch and pressure disciplines and therapies have grown enormously in recent years. A partial list of available methods and techniques include the following:

>> Swedish massage

>> Reflexology

>> Shiatsu massage

>> Chiropractic manipulation

>> Acupressure

All these methods have their origins in early medicine and healing. Many claim spiritual as well as physical changes. Rather than go into each of these disciplines separately, the following sections discuss several of the simpler stress-relieving approaches from the preceding list that are particularly useful and easy to grasp.

You have several choices when it comes to massage. You can spend some bucks and get a professional to give you a massage (or can find someone who will give you a massage for free). You can also give yourself a massage. This last option is often the cheapest and doesn't require friends. (If you're really into massage, you may want to grab a copy of *Massage For Dummies* by Steve Capellini and Michel Van Welden [Wiley].)

Massaging yourself

You can go two ways: high-tech or low-tech. The high-tech route usually requires a wall socket or lots of batteries. Many specialty stores stock massage paraphernalia. A high-end choice is a mega-buck relaxation chair that transports you to relaxation heaven with the flick of a switch. On the less expensive side, a handheld vibrating massage tool loosens those tight and tired muscles, leaving you much more relaxed. Alternately, you can forgo the batteries and save the cash by letting your fingers do the work. Fingers are cheaper, easier to control, and readily available. Following are three simple ways to rub away your stress.

For your hands

Hold your left palm in front of you, fingers together. The fleshy spot between your thumb and index finger is a key acupressure point that should spread a sensation of relaxation when massaged. Using your right thumb, massage this spot in a circular motion for a slow count of 15. Switch hands and repeat.

For stress-related fatigue, pinch just below the first joint of your pinkie with the thumb and index finger of the opposite hand. (Pressure should be firm but not painful.) Increase the pressure slightly. Make small circular movements in a counterclockwise direction while maintaining pressure. Continue for 20 seconds. Release. Wait for ten seconds and repeat up to five times.

For your feet

Try this sole-soothing exercise. Take off your socks and shoes and sit comfortably with one leg crossed over the other. (The sole of your foot should be almost facing you.) With both hands, grasp the arches of your foot and apply pressure, especially with your thumbs. Now knead every part of your foot with your fingers and thumbs, working your way from your heel right up to your toes. Give each of your toes a squeeze. Now massage the other foot in a similar way.

TIP

If crossing your legs is more stressful than it used to be, go to the kitchen and get your rolling pin. Sit in a chair and position the rolling pin next to your foot. Gently roll your bare foot back and forth slowly for two minutes or so. Then try it with the other foot. Now wash the pin. If you don't own a rolling pin, work with a tennis ball or a can of soup. Put it under the arch of your bare foot, put some pressure on that foot, and move the item backward and forward. Keep this rhythm going for about two minutes, and then switch to your other foot.

For your neck and shoulders

Stress most often finds its way to your neck and shoulders. To dissipate that tension, take your left hand and firmly massage your right shoulder and the right side of your neck. Start with some gentle circular motions, rubbing the muscle with your index and pointer fingers. Then finish with a firmer massage, squeezing the shoulder and neck muscles between your thumb and other fingers. Now switch to the other side.

For your face

Start by placing both of your hands on your face with the tips of your fingers resting on your forehead and the heels of your palms resting just under your cheeks. Gently pull down the skin on your forehead with the tips of your fingers while pushing up the area under your palms. Rhythmically repeat this movement, contracting and releasing your fingers and palms.

You can also try pulling on your ears in different directions.

Becoming the massage-er or massage-ee

Having someone else give you a massage certainly has its advantages. When someone else does all the work, you can completely let go: Sit or lie back and totally relax. And another person can reach places on your body that you could never reach. You can visit a licensed massage therapist or you ask a friend to give you a massage. Of course, you may have to reciprocate, but even giving someone else a massage can relieve some of your tension. Here are some general hints and guidelines to get you started:

>> **Use some massage oil or body lotion to add a relaxing aroma and smooth the massage process.** Warm the oil to room temperature so as not to shock your or your partner's system.

>> **Lower the lights to provide a soothing, relaxing atmosphere.** Calming music also adds a nice touch (try some Enya or other new age tunes).

>> **Focus your massage on the lower back, neck, and shoulders — places stress tends to reside and cause the most discomfort.**

>> **Start by applying pressure lightly until the massage-ee is relaxed.** Then increase the pressure, using your palms to knead the muscles.

>> **Finish up with a lighter massage, and let your partner linger for a while after the massage to extend the sense of relaxation.**

>> **Don't overdo it.** A good massage shouldn't have the massage-ee writhing in pain. A bad (too rough) massage can cause more stress than it attempts to relieve.

Taking a Three-Minute Energy Burst

Any concentrated expenditure of energy produces more stress by tensing your muscles, speeding your heart rate, and quickening your breathing. However, after you stop expending energy, you find that your muscles relax and your heart rate and breathing slow down to a level that is lower than when you started. This energy boost can come from walking briskly, running for a short distance, doing jumping jacks, jumping rope, doing sit-ups or push-ups, running up steps — anything that gets your body going.

>> **Become a shaker.** Shaking off tension is fun. You can do this exercise either sitting or standing. Begin by holding your arms loosely in front of you and shaking your hands at the wrists. Now let your arms and shoulders join in the fun. Continue for a short while and taper off slowly, letting your arms fall comfortably to your sides. Now lift one leg and start shaking it. Then shift to the other leg. (If you're sitting, you can do both legs at the same time.) When you finish, notice the tingling sensations in your body and, more importantly, the feelings of relaxation. Admittedly, it looks a little strange, but it works.

>> **Soak up your stress.** Think of your bathroom as a mini health spa and your bathtub as a pool of relaxation. Besides, not only do you emerge relaxed and destressed, but you're also clean. Here's the recipe for that relaxing soak:

- A spare half hour

- A tub of hot, soapy water

- Soothing scents, such as lavender Epsom salts or scented bubble bath

- Soft lighting

- Relaxing music

- A phone that is turned off or at least silenced

Minding More Ways to Relax

A few relaxation techniques from off the beaten path:

>> **Throw in the towel.** Barbers used to give their customers shaves along with haircuts. In those days, you felt marvelous as your barber carefully placed moist, hot towels on your face. These days, stylists often only cut hair. And unless you fly first class to Europe or dine in an upscale Japanese restaurant, you're unlikely to experience the joy of a hot towel on your face — unless, of course, you put it there yourself. Simply take one or two washcloths and immerse them in hot water. Squeeze out the excess water, lie back, close your eyes, and put the towels on your face. Ah, nirvana

And what if you don't have a towel or hot water? Use your hands. Rub them together till they feel warm. Place each hand on a side of your face. No, the feeling isn't quite as good as a moist, hot towel, but it can still help you relax.

>> **Jump into a hot tub.** If you have a hot tub, great, but keep in mind that many bathtubs have the same benefits. Check out this promo from one hot-tub manufacturer: "When you slip into the hot massaging waters, your muscles will relax, and your mind will clear." Maybe so.

» **Go East; try some yoga.** Why reinvent the wheel when some marvelous relaxation approaches have been around for many years? Yoga has been practiced for 5,000 years. Yoga looks at health and well-being from a broad, holistic perspective that sees the mind and body as dynamically intercon-nected. This ancient Eastern tradition combines physical and postural exercises with meditation practices, breathing techniques, and mindfulness that can help you relax your body and calm your mind. Most people who have tried yoga swear by it. Find a good teacher and give it a try. (Ask friends about yoga classes in your community.)

TIP

You may want to take a look at the latest edition of *Yoga For Dummies* by Georg Feuerstein and Larry Payne (Wiley). While you're at it, consider other Eastern practices such as T'ai Chi (check out *T'ai Chi For Dummies* by Therese Iknoian with Manny Fuentes, published by Wiley).

» **Relax in the bedroom.** Sex can be a marvelous way of unwinding and letting go of physical tension. Including some form of mutual massage in your lovemaking can increase the relaxation benefits.

HAVE A DRINK?

Should you use an alcoholic beverage as an agent of relaxation? Yes and no.

For some time now, research literature has supported the value of moderate drinking. Moderate intake of alcohol (especially red wine) has been found to raise levels of HDL (the good cholesterol) and lessen the risk of heart disease. However, the risks from excessive drinking far outweigh these benefits, so to benefit you have to stick to the appropriate daily allotment. For many, drinking can be a slippery slope and lead to alco-hol abuse. For more detailed information, check out the National Institute on Alcohol Abuse and Alcoholism website: `www.niaaa.nih.gov/alcohol-health`.

The bottom line: Don't put alcohol at the top of your stress-reduction list. If you've suc-cessfully integrated a daily drink into your life, fine. But always remember, you can reduce your stress in better ways.

Chapter 17

Stress-Reducing Organizational Skills

I f you've ever felt like tearing out your hair when you can't find your keys or that paper napkin where you wrote that phone number, you know that disorganization can trigger a whole lot of stress. Now, having a messy desk isn't as stressful as having a serious illness, getting fired, or losing everything in a house fire. Yet being disorganized can fuel a long list of frustrations, delays, lost time, and missed opportunities — all accompanied by varying levels of anger and irritation.

Who needs it? Your stress level is already high enough. This chapter shows you how to get organized. It gives you tools to overcome the disarray, chaos, and confusion in your life.

Figuring Out Why Your Life Is So Disorganized

Okay, so your life isn't a model of order and organization. Don't be embarrassed; lots of people have too much to do and too little time to do it. Their possessions threaten to swallow them in clutter. This section helps you get to the bottom of your organizational challenges so you can take action.

Are you organizationally challenged?

Your first step in coming up with effective organizational strategies is recognizing how disorganized you've become. Take this unofficial test and see whether better organization may help you.

Read the following statements and rate to what extent each statement describes you. Use the following ratings to help you better gauge your level of disorganization.

3 = Very much like me

2 = Somewhat like me

1 = A little like me

0 = Not at all like me

>> Your home is filled with far too much stuff.

>> Your closets, drawers, and cabinets are disorganized.

>> You're frequently late for your appointments.

>> You're a big procrastinator.

>> You find that you spend lots of time looking for things you've misplaced.

>> You're often late paying your bills.

>> Your friends and family tell you that you have a problem with clutter.

>> You feel stressed out by all the stuff in your home.

>> Your computer files are generally disorganized.

>> You rarely use lists to help you get organized.

>> You buy duplicates of things you already own because you can't find the originals.

>> Your desk or workspace is disorganized.

>> You feel you don't have enough time to get organized.

Most people answer a two or three for at least several of these items, which means poor organization is creating excessive stress in their lives. Identifying your specific areas and patterns of disorganization is critical. The following section can help you do just that.

Identifying your personal disorganization

Getting better organized means being aware of the areas in which you can use some help. Disorganization can be broken down to more discrete sub-groups. See which ones best describe your own forms of disorganization.

>> **You don't manage your time well.** If your time-management skills are wobbly, you find that you often run late, miss deadlines, work inefficiently, procrastinate, plan poorly, and feel overwhelmed by not having enough time. Too many things don't get done.

>> **You're surrounded by clutter.** You own far too many things, and those things are way out of control. Your flat surfaces are invitations to put stuff on, preferably in piles. You have great difficulty getting rid of your stuff, whether it's clothes, books, papers, out-of-date electronics, or broken just-about-anything. You feel like you're drowning in things, and you're not terribly optimistic that the situation is going to change.

>> **Your home is in constant disarray.** Your storage spaces are cluttered. Cabinets and closets are a mishmash of organization. Finding anything is a hit-and-miss affair. You make poor use of containers, storage bags, shelves, and drawers. You rarely use labels.

>> **You lack a good system for keeping track of bills and other important information.** Your personal records, bills, passport, mortgage paperwork, and important files are somewhere, but you aren't sure just where. You have no filing system. You don't use your computer, tablet, or smartphone to help you organize your life.

If you struggle with any or all of these areas, the following sections provide specific guidance for getting your life (and your stuff) in order.

Clearing Away the Clutter

If you lived in a place with infinite space, had a live-in maid, and were independently wealthy, you could consider your clutter a charming quirk or amusing oversight. But more likely your clutter has become a painful and constant source of stress. De-cluttering can seem overwhelming. It's only a matter of time before you feel like you're lost in the piles of stuff. You need help. You're ready to start. But where do you begin? The following sections walk you through the de-cluttering process.

Bust those clutter excuses

If you're going to war against clutter, you need to understand the enemy. The following are ten reasons why people hang onto stuff. At times, giving up your prized possessions is harder than pulling teeth. When pressed, you may vigorously defend your decision to hold onto some small thing. All the following excuses contain at least a sliver of truth. And all guarantee that after your funeral, your relatives will hold the world's biggest garage sale. See whether you can recognize some of your favorite clutter excuses:

>> **Someday I'll need it.** This clutter excuse can be compelling. After all, you *may* need it someday. This is where your what-iffing comes into play. The odds of your actually needing this thing are probably very small. That unread article or outdated computer cord will most likely never be reused. Do a cost-benefit analysis and ask yourself, "Am I not better off just getting rid of this stuff rather than keeping it on the very unlikely chance that I *may* use it?"

>> **It was a present for my ninth birthday.** This stuff is your sentimental clutter. Anything that reminds you of your past or a pleasant memory or has sentimental value can be tough to let go. This category of clutter may include every piece of artwork you or your child ever brought home from school, the playbill from every play you've ever seen, and large boxes of family photos (or even slides!). Create a scrapbook of selected items, letting the rest go. Better yet, scan all the items you want to save into your computer and keep only a select few original items. If you don't have a scanner, take pictures. Who says you can't have your cake and eat it too?

>> **Somebody will want to buy this.** Good luck with this one! Go ahead and list the item on eBay or Craigslist or have a garage sale. But make the decision: "I'll put this up for sale now, give it away, or chuck it."

>> **I'm sure I'll find the matching one.** Usually, this excuse is for orphaned socks or gloves. If you haven't found the matching item in three months, let it go. Besides, everybody knows that washing machines eat socks.

>> **Yes, it's broken, but it can be fixed.** Fix it, give it away, or throw it out. These days fixing something electronic probably costs you more than replacing it, but if you feel it can be reasonably repaired, commit to locating a repair service this week.

>> **If I just lose 10 pounds, I'll fit into this.** For many people, losing weight is a difficult task, but storing multiple sizes of clothing (including those skinny jeans) can be a real closet-clogger. Why not keep a few items of this clothing that you absolutely love to motivate you and donate all the rest? After you've shed those pounds, you can reward yourself with some serious shopping for smart new togs.

>> **My kids will want to give it to their kids.** You may be shocked to learn that kids rarely relish getting old stuff from relatives. Ask them whether they want these objects. If they say yes, ask them to take possession of them now. If your kids are very young, don't hold your breath. Remember that just because something is important to you doesn't mean its important to anyone else. This concept is really tough to accept.

>> **I got it on sale.** This stuff is your bargain clutter. It's hard to resist a good deal. Half-price sale? No problem! Buy one get one free? Let's do it! Shopping at the big-box stores can be a trap. When you see something on sale, it becomes hard to resist. And if you buy it, it's hard to get rid of because it was a bargain. What you want to avoid is *impulse* buying. If you're seduced by a "bargain," whether you see it online, in print, or in a store, stop and ask yourself some pertinent questions:

- Do I really need this?

- Will I use it enough to justify buying it?

- Would I ever buy this if it weren't on sale?

- Do I have a place to put this?

If possible, give yourself time to reflect on whether you really think this item is a smart purchase. Most sales give you some wiggle room to think before you buy. If the idea still seems right the next day, and you're still determined to buy it, go ahead. If you're in a store and it's now or never, do your other shopping first and then ask yourself the questions. If the answer to any of them is "no," take a pass. Even if you regret not making the purchase later on, you'll almost always have a second chance to buy it at a bargain price. And if you're still paralyzed with indecision, get another opinion from someone who knows you well.

>> **It will be a collector's item one day.** If you've ever watched the TV show *Antiques Roadshow,* you know that one person's garbage can be another person's treasure. But more often it just becomes another person's clutter. Get an objective appraisal from a trusted, neutral source. If the item is worth something, sell it now. Searching the Internet often lets you get an idea of what the item is worth by seeing what it's selling for online.

>> **I plan on reading this.** This excuse keeps you from ever throwing out a book you haven't read or that newspaper, magazine, or article you hope to read one day but probably never will. If you haven't read it by a reasonable time, you probably won't. Give your books to the school or library used book sale. Your shelves will thank you. If an article is important to you, scan it and put it in an organized digital file.

Get yourself motivated

Sometimes good intentions alone just don't cut it. You may find that you need a kick in the pants or some other form of external motivation to get you to clean up. Here are some field-tested ideas that can keep you on track:

>> **Schedule it.** When you schedule things, you have a better chance of getting them done. People generally show up for dentist and doctor appointments, business meetings, and other engagements that they purposefully schedule. The same tactic can work when it comes to getting things done around the house. Commit to a definite time and write down the appointment in your calendar, daily planner, or whatever you use to keep track of your life.

>> **Work with shame.** Your home is probably at its neatest about three minutes before invited guests ring your doorbell. You're motivated and determined to make sure that others don't see how disorganized your place can be. Use that motivation! Set a date and invite over some new friends whose approval you desperately want or need. Take this time to make some real organizational changes and maintain them.

>> **Find your clutter threshold.** Some people actually don't mind a little clutter in their lives. For some, those minimalist, absolutely-nothing-out-of-place living spaces are scary. These people require a touch of clutter to make them

feel emotionally comfortable. But more than just a little bit of clutter begins to stress them out. Other folks are totally clutter-adverse. For them, any clutter is too much. You have to find your own clutter threshold, below which you get twitchy and above which you feel stressed. Then work hard to keep your clutter level under that threshold.

Draw yourself a clutter road map

TIP

Instead of seeing all the clutter in your life-space as one massive pile, see it as a succession of tasks that you can chip away at little by little. One way to decide where to start, and where to go after you start, is to create a clutter road map. Begin by choosing a number of areas of your life-space that desperately need organizing. These areas may be geographical (a specific room in your home, the yard, or the garage) or topical (your clothing, magazines, or toys). Then come up with a sequence of areas that you want to work on over time. After you deal with one bit of clutter on your list, move on to the second and then on to the next, and so on. Think of your map as a kind of sequential to-do list. It takes you where you want to go.

A clutter road map allows you to know where you're going and gives you a pretty good idea of how far you've moved toward your final goal. For many people faced with overwhelming clutter, having this game plan creates a feeling of being in control, which can reduce the anxiety often associated with de-cluttering. Be sure to make each piece on your map relatively small and doable. Start by choosing areas of your life-space that will give you a great deal of personal satisfaction after they're organized.

Get your feet wet

One famous bit of self-help advice is the Nike slogan "Just do it!" However, "just doing it" for most people is probably not going to do it. A more realistic version may be "Just get started!" Deep down, you realize that you'll be better off if you get rid of much of that unneeded stuff. So jump in.

Have you ever noticed that after you start something, the momentum of doing that thing keeps you going? This is especially true when you're de-cluttering. After you get yourself in de-cluttering mode, go with it. Don't stop just because you finish a small section. Keep going. Build on your success. You may be surprised at how much you can get done when you're into it.

Stop kidding yourself

It's easy to fool yourself. Some small part of you really does believe that you'll clean out the basement, box up those old clothes, give them to a thrift shop, and throw out those magazines that you've been hanging onto forever.

The reality is that unless you are serious about removing your clutter, it will continue to spread. If you're going to successfully de-clutter, you need to convince yourself that the quality of your life will improve measurably after you unload many, if not most, of the objects you've collected. You'll feel so good when you find your long-lost birth certificate and the mates to those single socks lying in your bedroom drawer.

TIP

You can share the things you no longer need with people that can put them to good use. You benefit by debulking your stuff, and others benefit from your sharing. Focus on charitable giving. Be generous. This approach can open your heart and help you part with more.

Simplifying your life-space takes grit. Your attitude as you approach the task should be "I'm sick and tired of this, and I'm not going to take it anymore!" You may find this approach a bit too merciless, but be firm in your decision to clean out: You're a powerful force when you're truly bitten by the de-clutter bug. Ask yourself the following questions to help increase your de-cluttering grit:

>> Do I really want to spend the next 20 years living with this item?

>> If my place were on fire and I could save only half of what I own, would I save this particular item?

>> Would the quality of my life be seriously diminished if I didn't have this item?

>> Can someone else use this item more than I can?

In 90 percent of the cases, the answers to these four questions are no, no, no, and yes.

Avoid discouragement

A mistake that many people make when de-cluttering is thinking that they can finish it in one short Saturday afternoon. They get discouraged when they realize just how much stuff they have and how much de-cluttering they still have to do. Then they feel overwhelmed by the mountain of a task before them and just give up.

ARE YOU A HOARDER?

You've probably heard the term *hoarder* from reality TV shows and talk shows. The most iconic hoarders were the Collyer brothers, Homer and Langley, who lived in New York. Both were eventually found dead in the Harlem brownstone where they had lived, surrounded by more than 140 tons of items they had amassed over several decades. You're not a hoarder just because you like to collect things, have too many possessions, and/or have trouble getting rid of your stuff. *Hoarding* refers to a more severe, pathologic form of cluttering. For some people, the degree of clutter escalates to become dysfunctional and life-limiting. Their clutter grows so excessive that it becomes a central disabling force in their lives. Here are some warning signs that you're crossing the line from a basic pack rat to a true hoarder:

- The amount of clutter is so excessive that your living space is severely compromised. You can't use your living space in the way it was intended or the way you want to.

- Your clutter causes you significant stress and upset, overwhelms you, and affects your relationships.

- Your clutter makes it difficult for you to navigate your living space.

- The degree of clutter in your home threatens your health and well-being.

- You've been told by others (who weren't kidding) that you could use professional help.

If several of these criteria describe you, you may want to seek additional help. Professional groups and organizations can provide assistance and direction. Counselors with expertise in hoarding, anxiety, depression, obsessive-compulsive disorders, addictions, and phobias are a good place to start to find help.

Remember that de-cluttering your home is an important long-term project that's truly worthwhile. It's not going to happen overnight. It took you years to amass all your wonderful possessions, so recognize that reversing the process will take time. However, when you figure out how much time you can save by not having to look for misplaced items, you quickly realize that you'll be way ahead of the game after you finish. Accomplishing most anything in life that's worthwhile takes effort and persistence. Mastering golf or tennis, learning to ski, or figuring out how to get the most out of your computer doesn't happen overnight. Stick with it. You'll be glad you did!

Get down to the nitty-gritty

Okay, you've psyched yourself up for some serious de-cluttering. When you get into the trenches, try using the following clutter-busting techniques:

» **Pick any number from one to two.** When considering what to do with an item of clutter, remember that you have two basic options: Keep it or lose it. If you decide to keep it, you must figure out what to do with it. If you choose to lose it, you can chuck it or give it away. Clearly, the biggest obstacle to getting rid of anything is having to make this choice.

» **Take a second look.** You can always get rid of some of the stuff you decide to keep. Go back over your keeper pile and take another look. Organizing even a small pile of things you decide to keep takes a lot of time and effort. Finding sufficient storage plays an important role in managing all the possessions that clutter your life, but simply getting rid of stuff often makes more sense.

» **Use the triage method of clutter control.** Create three categories: Definitely Keep, Definitely Get Rid Of, and I'm Not Sure. Throw out or give away everything in the last two categories. The upside of unloading much more of your clutter far outweighs the downside of making a mistake. Don't look back.

» **Get a clutter buddy.** Ask your mate or a friend to help you de-clutter. Listen to that person and do what he or she tells you. Remember, it's for your own good.

» **Get some emotional support.** De-cluttering can be a lonely and emotionally taxing job. You may need someone more emotionally supportive than your clutter buddy. This should be someone you feel comfortable talking with — a family member, a good friend, a colleague you trust, or perhaps a counselor. This support can keep you going when the going gets tough and you start to feel discouraged.

» **Play the dating game.** If you can't bring yourself to throw something out, put it in a box and put a date on the box that's exactly a year away. Don't list what's in the box — just the date. If the future date comes and goes without your needing anything in the box, take a quick look inside. If nothing critically important catches your eye, chuck it or donate it without a second look. Don't look back. If you *do* need an item from the box, find a better place to keep it.

» **Use the three-month rule.** Ancient periodicals can easily accumulate and gather dust. Take a look at the dates on your magazines. If they're older than three months for monthly publications or three weeks for weekly ones, chuck 'em.

» **Find a clutter recipient.** Getting rid of stuff is much easier when you know that it won't end up in the trash but rather in the hands of somebody who wants it, needs it, and can use it. In fact, your rejects may be someone else's cup of tea. Clothing, sports equipment, books, and furniture are often welcomed by others.

Give your relatives and friends first crack at your treasures (but give them a definite time limit to come, look, and take). The Salvation Army, Goodwill Industries, thrift shops, and charity drives will be delighted (usually) to take the stuff in reasonable condition that your family and friends turn down. You can even get a tax deduction for donating to charitable organizations. Donating your stuff to those in need is a win-win situation!

» **Consider consignment.** Sometimes it's hard to give an object away because you really do believe it's worth something. You may be right. Putting it up for *consignment,* where you let a business sell the item for you and take a cut of the proceeds, may just do the trick.

» **If it doesn't work, toss it.** Look around your home for any broken small appliance (blender, clock, or whatever) that hasn't worked for a long while and ask yourself whether you truly need it. If you decide to fix it, fix it. If not, replace or discard it. Replacing the item may actually be cheaper than having it repaired. However, chances are good that if you haven't needed to use it in the last year, you probably don't need it at all.

» **Whatever you do, don't leave the broken item in your home.** Throw it out or, better yet, give it to a charitable organization that will repair it and give it to someone who will use it. Or attach a "Free" sign to the item (and explain what's wrong with it) outside your building or at the end of your driveway. Go check later; odds are, it'll be gone.

» **Handle things only once.** You may be in the habit of putting some things aside and saying you'll figure out later what to do with them. This strategy just adds to the problem. Deal with each item right in the moment. File it, pay it, delete it, or chuck it, but address it only once! Otherwise, it will just keep stacking.

» **Invest in doors and drawers.** If you absolutely must keep something, hide it. Unless the object in question is something you're very fond of or somehow adds to the visual aesthetic of your decor, keep it out of sight. Store things in cabinets, closets, bureau drawers, or file cabinets — anyplace that contributes to a sense of visual order. But remember that the space things occupy behind doors is still space that you could use for something else.

REMEMBER

Whole stores are now dedicated exclusively to storage furniture and containers. Don't make added storage a new part of your clutter.

» **Take an art sample.** It's easy to save that big painting your son made for you in the third grade (15 years ago), but those grade-school masterpieces pile up quickly. Get a large folder and take a sampler of your children's artwork that you're especially fond of. Store this art folder in a back closet. Scan the smaller masterpieces and mementos and electronically file them. This way you can save the images you enjoy without saving every art project your child has brought home from school. (And when your children become famous artistes, you can cash in.)

>> **Take a picture.** Often, items in your I'm Not Sure pile have sentimental value but are too big to keep around. You want the memories but not necessarily the object. Take its picture. Pictures (especially the digital variety) take up far less space and still can bring a warm smile to your face. You may also want to include someone in the picture. Looking at your daughter squeezing Cuddles is a lot more satisfying than just looking at Cuddles alone. You can then start a scrapbook or start a digital file to save the memories.

Organizing Your Space

Being organized is about more than just being neat and tidy. It also means having items and information in places where you can reliably find them, use them, and then put them back where they belong. Part of your problem may be that you don't know how to organize and store your things. Here are some guidelines and suggestions:

>> **Start big.** Rather than organize your stuff item by item, start with a more ambitious agenda. First, pick an area you want to organize, such as your medicine cabinet. Take out everything and put it on the bathroom counter. Have a trash can handy. Give the cabinet a wipe and you're ready to go. Now group the cold medicines together and put them on a shelf. If you come across items that you never use or that are out of date, throw them in the trash can. Move on to another category. Put the stuff you use most in the most convenient accessible locations. Label the items that are hard to spot or aren't clearly marked. When you've finished with the medicine cabinet, you can move on to your refrigerator, clothes closet, shoes. Remember, not everything has to be saved.

>> **Use containers.** First, figure out which containers you need to store what you want to store. Jars, hooks, file cabinets, plastic boxes, plastic bags, and even baskets can find their places in your reorganization planning. Food containers should most often be clear with lids so you can easily see their contents. Objects like crayons, small toys, and blocks all do well in see-through containers as well. To save space, go with square containers rather than round ones. Stackability is a plus because it takes advantage of vertical space. Containers make cleaning up a lot easier by giving you definite places to return the things you use when you've finished using them.

>> **Label it.** Whatever container you use, labeling the contents helps. For opaque containers and boxes, labeling becomes a must. Write on blank adhesive address labels and stick them on containers. On plastic bags, a permanent marker does the trick. An inexpensive labeler may prove useful when you can't write on a container.

>> **Categorize.** Although sticking all your books into a bookcase looks orderly, it may not be the best organizational strategy. Grouping can help you navigate. Come up with some basic categories without overdoing it. Start with fiction/nonfiction and add one or two more subcategories. In the kitchen, you can use a simple alphabetical (A-F, G-N, and so on) system instead of throwing all your spices together. Labeled spice racks could do the trick as well. Just keep them where you can see them and use them effectively.

Categories work on a larger scale, too. Instead of having your electronic gadgets all over the house, create a drawer or shelf just for these alone. Have a container for the small stuff that may otherwise get lost. Put all your sports equipment into a bin labeled for each particular sport. Smaller sports items (such as balls, pucks, and tees) can go in a box or container within the bin. In your medicine cabinet, group your medicines, soaps, and razors in separate sections or on different shelves.

>> **Prioritize usage.** Some things you use frequently; others, much less often. In your refrigerator, keep the most-used items near the front and on the most accessible shelf. In your closet, socks, underwear, and favorite shirts and pants should be where you can easily reach them. Put the once-in-a-blue-moon stuff in the back. Better yet, if you haven't used it in years, give it away.

>> **Put it back!** If you use it, put it back where you found it. Don't let all that organizational effort go to waste. You want to be able to find the things you need the next time you need them!

Organizing Information

Organizing the "stuff" in your life is only part of the problem. You may not know whether you have paprika in the back of that kitchen cabinet, but that's less important than knowing where your birth certificate, mortgage or lease paperwork, and college transcripts are. To make things even more complicated, more and more information now comes to you electronically. You can be swamped by your emails, tweets, attachments, downloads, and more. Here are some suggestions to help you manage this information overload.

Losing the paper trail

When computers first began appearing, there was grand talk of living in a paperless world. We're not there quite yet. In fact, the use of paper has doubled in the last ten years. Those who have made the study of clutter their life's work say that paper is the real enemy. Your paper clutter can include everything from a toaster warranty to your last electric bill; an endless stream of circulars, catalogs, junk mail, instruction manuals, and other paper items passes through your hands every day. Here's how to start organizing that proliferation of paper.

To merge or to purge? That is the question.

The two secrets to managing the paper in your life are fairly simple. In fact, they're amazingly similar to the two options you have when considering what to do with your non-paper clutter. You can either throw out the paper if you don't need it or find an effective way to organize it if you do need it.

REMEMBER

This approach to paper sounds pretty easy, but the problem lies in actually doing the throwing out and organizing. Sorting through all that paper takes time and effort, and you have to find the fortitude to throw out that coupon for a ten-gallon jar of spaghetti sauce or read that article on skiing in the Himalayas.

Your snail mail: Cut 'em off at the pass

Finding a birthday card or letter from a friend in your mailbox is fun. Finding bills and junk mail? Not so much. Your mailbox can be an insidious force, feeding you an unstoppable river of solicitations, announcements, catalogs, flyers, and bills. You can slowly drown in this incoming sea of paper. The trick is to catch it early, before it has a chance to collect. Here are some tips for keeping your mail from becoming a huge problem:

>> **Junk junk mail.** Keep a recycling bin near your front door. Throw out junk mail immediately. Don't open it. Don't be intrigued. Realize that no matter how much mail you receive telling you that you may have won a million dollars, the chances of it actually happening are infinitesimally small.

>> **Get yourself off mailing lists.** Being on one list quickly puts you on many others. Get yourself taken off mailing lists. The Internet can make this task relatively easy. The World Privacy Forum research group offers a how-to list on the top opt-outs (www.worldprivacyforum.org/2015/08/consumer-tips-top-ten-opt-outs/) that gives you a number of suggestions for cutting down on unwanted mail.

>> **Curb your catalog habit.** Leafing through a catalog and mentally shopping can be fun. And if you have an absolute favorite, keep it. But cancel the others. Virtually every catalog you receive in the mail can be viewed online. Peruse the Web and save the paper. Catalogchoice.org, a service of TrustedID, and

dmachoice.org, created by the Direct Marketing Association, allow you to opt out of a particular company's catalogs. Both are free.

>> **Go electronic.** Ask that bills, credit-card statements, bank statements, investment information, catalogs, and magazines — just about anything, really — be sent to you electronically. Then you can access them on your computer, tablet, or smartphone. If possible, create a separate and secure email address for your important documents so they don't get lost in your email shuffle. Remember, you can pay many of your bills online without using a single sheet of paper. (You'll save money on stamps and also save trees!)

Organizing the papers you do need to keep

The notion of having a method of organizing the paper in your life probably doesn't come as an earth-shatteringly new idea. Yet many people still don't have one, and those who do often use theirs inefficiently.

Coming up with a system of organization takes thought and planning, and using it requires time and effort. In the short run, letting papers pile up is a lot easier. But in the long run, doing so can turn into a major headache. Taking the time and effort to develop a systematic way of organizing your papers can result in a lot less stress and hassle. Try the tips in the following sections as you create your filing system.

Start simple

Come up with a filing system that's relatively easy to use. You don't want your filing system to be more stressful than the stress it's supposed to alleviate. You may not need a formal filing cabinet at home, but if you have the room, and if you have a lot of paper to file, it may not be a bad idea. Alternatively, you can work with desk drawers that hold files, or even plastic or cardboard filing boxes.

Be colorful with your files and folders

Files and folders or tabs and labels of different colors can not only turn your filing system into a work of art but also make finding different subjects and interests easier by grouping them together. Make your files easy to recognize so you can identify the contents. Put those files you need most often in a place that's easy to access.

Keep important papers where you know how to access them

Keep your original documents in a safe place, but make sure you can easily get hold of them when you need them. And back them up! Keep a digital copy that's easily findable. Lest you forget, here are some of the more important documents to keep track of:

- Automobile registration, title, and insurance documents
- Bank account numbers/ information
- Birth certificates
- Citizenship papers
- Credit-card numbers
- Deeds, leases, and contracts
- Mortgage documents
- Important receipts
- Instruction manuals
- Insurance policies
- Loan agreements
- Marriage licenses
- Divorce decrees
- Estate-planning documents and wills
- Adoption papers

- Medical records
- Passports
- Powers of attorney
- Health proxies
- IDs and passwords
- PINs
- School transcripts
- Service contracts
- Social security cards (originals)
- Tax returns
- Warranties
- Backups of important computer files
- Photographs, letters, and other personal papers
- Anything else you don't want to lose

Some of these categories warrant their own separate files. Some, like your important account numbers and PINs, you can combine. For the more important documents, you may want to keep the originals in a fireproof safe or safe-deposit box and keep copies in your files. Storing copies on your computer is certainly a good backup option. Storing them in *the cloud* (where the info is stored on a third-party data center rather than your personal device) makes it easier to access this information from any computer.

REMEMBER

If you choose to store information virtually, you must consider the possible risk that others may obtain access to your files and documents. Be aware of the security level of the sites you choose to use for virtual cloud storage.

Safeguarding your digital documents

It's more likely that someone will steal files and information from your computer than from your bottom dresser drawer. Although you may not care much if someone hacks into your computer and steals Aunt Agnes's prized recipe for brisket, you probably will be much more distressed if someone steals your social security number, passport information, or personal IDs and passwords. Here are some steps to help you store your digital information more safely:

» **Use a password manager.** *A password manager* is software that takes over the creation and storage of passwords in your life. A good one generates random, hard-to-crack passwords for you, and you don't have to remember them. There are even good free password managers, such as KeePass (http://keepass.info/), LastPass (www.lastpass.com), and PasswordBox (www.passwordbox.com).

» **Go to the cloud.** Find a cloud storage company that's well regarded and has a solid reputation and clear security policies. This may take some research on your part, but the result is well worth the effort.

» **Get encrypted.** Find out whether your data and documents will be encrypted when stored in the cloud. With no encryption, anyone may be able to get access to your files. You want to ensure that the files you don't want others to read are protected and accessible only by you.

» **Pick a strong password.** Whether your personal documents are stored on your computer and/or in cloud storage, a password that protects you is vital. In general, the longer the password, the better. The best passwords use seven or eight characters, with at least two being numeric. Also try to include punctuation characters and mix in upper- and lowercase letters.

WARNING

Don't use personal information, such as the names family members or pets, as passwords. Don't use your telephone number, anybody's birth date, any part of your social security number, your driver's license number, or any of these written backward. These are easy targets for hackers

» **Have more than one password.** Don't have just a single password for everything. If someone cracks that password, he or she has easy access to everything you've got.

» **Store your passwords.** After you come up with these hack-resistant passwords, you need a place to put them. These days, password-management systems store your passwords and other login info either on your computer or in the cloud. You can create a setup in which your multiple passwords can be accessed only with a master password. This master password must be a lengthy, brilliantly conceived winner. (Some apps will do this for you.)

A GOOD WAY OF CREATING A GOOD PASSWORD

Come up with a phrase or expression that's easy to recall. It can be a favorite song lyric, a line from a poem, or a catchy slogan — anything you can easily recall. For example: "Do you know the way to San Jose?" Create the password by linking together the first letter of each word — Dyktwtsj? — and replace the "to" with 2, ending up with Dyktw2sj?. You can be even more creative. Just don't be so creative that you can't remember how you came up with your masterpiece.

>> **Have a magic number**. As an added safeguard, create a PIN, a personal number (three or four digits) that's never written down, stays stored only in your head, and is memorable (but not a piece of personal data). Your new password is a combination of what you've written down or stored on your computer or in the cloud *plus* your PIN. That way, even if your written-down passwords are discovered, you have another layer of protection.

Never put all your papers in one basket

Organizational expert Stephanie Culp suggests that you have four baskets for your paper (in addition to the extremely important shredding/recycling basket):

>> **A To-Do basket:** The wire see-through kind works best.

>> **A To-Pay basket:** Again, wire works best here.

>> **A To-File basket:** Use a larger wicker basket.

>> **A To-Read basket:** Try an even larger wicker basket with handles.

Culp recommends that you stack your To-Do basket on top of your To-Pay basket on your desk. Keep the To-File basket under your desk, out of the way of your more immediate paper needs. You can keep the To-Read basket in a different part of your home — such as your bedroom or study (or bathroom!) — so you can catch up on your reading whenever the opportunity arises.

Make filing a habit

Find a time during the week to empty your To-File basket and file those needed papers away. This task really shouldn't take long; 15 or 20 minutes should do it.

Fine-tune later

At a later date, take a look at what's in your files. Usually, you find that a file is either underused or bulging. If you find that you have only one or two things in a file folder, find or create a file that's broader in scope to consolidate. Alternatively, if you find that a folder is overflowing with contributions, create subcategories, either by topic or by date.

Organizing electronically

When it comes to getting organized, your computer can be your best friend. It may not help you store your shirts or sports equipment, but it can be invaluable with records, papers, pictures, and other forms of information. An organized electronic filing system is the key to effective electronic organization, storage, and retrieval! Without it, you can find yourself spending lots of time trying to locate a document, article, or file you know you have — somewhere. If this sounds very much like finding your misplaced phone charger, you're absolutely right. The good news is that filing electronically uses the same principles as manual filing.

Decide what you want to keep electronically

Your first step is asking yourself what you want to store on your computer. Some of the more common choices include photos, recipes, music and video files, personal documents, movies, tax information, letters of recommendation, college transcripts, books, contacts, restaurant information, contracts, children's art, and report cards. The list of potential categories is endless. Pick the ones that make sense for you. Remember that anything that can be scanned into your computer can be saved there.

Create folders

Your computer already has wonderful organizational tools built into it. It already outlines the more common organizational folders or categories. You can create additional folders that are relevant to your needs. "My recipes" or "my taxes" are good examples. Create these categories or folders as concisely as you can, but make it clear what's in each folder.

Think hierarchically

Create subfolders that fine-tune the information you have in the primary folder. For example, a folder for recipes can have subfolders for desserts, soups, entrees, and so on. Similarly, a "travel" folder may have subfolders for specific destinations. Your "tax" folder may include individual years.

WARNING

Watch out for too many levels. Going deeper than a few subfolders may cause confusion down the road. Come up with a digital organizing system that's relatively easy to use. You don't want your filing system to be more stressful than the stress it's supposed to alleviate.

Scan, scan, scan

A scanner is an important tool in helping you become better organized. By scanning all your important papers, correspondence, articles, documents, receipts, children's artwork, report cards, business cards, and recipes into your computer, you can organize and share them with others without taking up any physical space. Just be sure to keep important necessary originals in a safe place.

Back it up!

You may think your computer will never let you down, but it can and, at some point, will. You've heard this many times before: Always back up your important files on discs, flash drives, or external hard drives. Better safe than sorry. Back up your files on a regular basis to keep new, current files protected. Pick a time — weekly, biweekly, or monthly — to back up your computer and stick to doing it religiously. If you prefer (or are perpetually forgetful), connect with an online back-up service that automatically creates back-up files for you on a regular basis.

Managing your email

Your email can be a source of delight or major stress depending on how many messages you get, whom they come from, and what the senders want from you. Not only do you have to read most email, but sometimes you even need to respond. You can easily feel overwhelmed. The following are some simple strategies to help you manage your inbox.

Check your email, but don't overdo it

Most people fall into one of two groups: They either undercheck or overcheck their email. Checking your email too infrequently can get you into trouble. When people send you an email, they expect that you'll respond in a reasonable time frame. Delaying responses to personal emails can trigger the ire of family and friends. The damage of tardy responses in work-related situations can be even more serious. But you can also go too far in the other direction. Constantly looking at your email can become somewhat compulsive. It can disrupt the flow of your day and create an unwelcome source of constant distraction.

Find some set times when it's convenient for you to check your email throughout the day. It may be in the morning with your coffee, before lunch, and toward the end of the day. This approach ensures that your inbox doesn't overflow and that you respond to important emails in a timely manner. A good time to check your email is after you've completed some other chore or piece of work. You're ready for a break, and looking at your email gives you breathing space.

Be efficient

Reading your email can become a black hole that sucks up your time and attention. Minutes can turn into hours, especially if you follow all the interesting hyperlinks your friends share with you. Unless you have that free time or you just really enjoy digging into email correspondence, keep your time per email short and to the point. Remember that bit of sage advice: "Only handle your mail once." The same principle holds for email as well as snail mail. If you read it, answer it right away and as briefly as possible.

Have more than one email address

One effective way of organizing your email is to have a second email address. Doing so ensures that email regarding specific parts of your life can be separated.

Keeping Your Life Organized

Say you've managed to reverse eons of disarray and disorganization and now, having applied much grit and determination, you have a clean slate. You've cleared your space and given your mind breathing room to focus on what's necessary. Instead of waiting for the disorganization to return, you can do a number of things now to maintain the order and harmony that you've achieved.

Being proactive

Following is a list of tips to help you keep your life organized:

>> **Do it now.** Rather than postpone clearing up clutter, do it as soon as you create it.

>> **Do it every day.** Try to spend 15 to 30 minutes at the end of the day putting things away so that you can start tomorrow in a (relatively) organized place.

>> **Become aware.** Every time you come across an item or piece of paper, ask yourself two questions:

- How long have I had this?
- Do I really need this?

  If your answers are "too long" and "no", pitch it!

>> **Build it in.** Create patterns. Clean up the yard every spring. Do the shopping on Saturdays. Clean the house on Wednesdays. Create a routine that frees you from having to make decisions. They you'll do it automatically. You'll do it because your calendar says so.

>> **Delegate or team up.** You may not have to do all of this alone. Don't be bashful about getting others (your partner, your kids, your guests) to pitch in with the program. Sharing the cleanup can be very rewarding because more than one person gets the satisfaction of a job well done.

Buying less

One of the reasons your life becomes more stressful is that you probably have too many things. Fewer possessions mean a less complicated life. You can really live happily without many of the things you buy. So before you pull out your wallet at the cash register or click your mouse to order something, ask yourself the following questions:

>> Do I really need this item?

>> Would the quality of my life be seriously compromised if I passed this up?

>> How many of these do I already have?

If you're like most people, your answers to these questions are "no," "no," and "enough."

Here are some other buying suggestions you may want to consider:

>> Don't buy stuff just because it's on sale. It's not a good deal if you don't need or won't use it.

>> Don't buy in bulk unless you're sure you'll use all of it or can share the extra.

>> Don't buy anything without considering where you're going to put it.

Chapter 18

Meditation 101

The great thing about meditation is that it's actually quite simple. Just sit down, be quiet, turn your attention inward, and focus your awareness. That's all there is to it really (see the sidebar "Meditation: It's easier than you think"). Then why, you may be wondering, do people write so many books and articles (and, uh, chapters) about meditation? Why not just offer a few brief instructions and forget about all the verbiage?

Say you're planning to take a long trip by car to some picturesque location. You can just jot down the directions and follow them one by one. After a few days, you'll get to where you want to go. But you'll enjoy the trip more if you have a travel guide to point out the sights along the way. And you may feel more secure if you carry a troubleshooting manual to tell you what to do when you have problems with your car. Perhaps you want to take some side trips to scenic spots or even change your itinerary entirely and get there by a different route or a different vehicle.

MEDITATION: IT'S EASIER THAN YOU THINK

Meditation is simply the practice of focusing your attention on a particular object — generally something simple, like a word or phrase, a candle flame or geometrical figure, or the coming and going of your breath. In everyday life, your mind is constantly processing a barrage of sensations, visual impressions, emotions, and thoughts. In general, when you meditate, you narrow your focus, limit the stimuli bombarding your nervous system — and calm your mind in the process.

For a quick taste of meditation, follow these instructions.

1. **Find a quiet place and sit comfortably with your back relatively straight.**

   If you tend to disappear when you sink into your favorite chair, find something a bit more supportive.

2. **Take a few deep breaths, close your eyes, and relax your body as much as you can.**

   If you don't know how to relax, you may want to check out Chapter 16.

3. **Choose a word or phrase that has special personal or spiritual meaning for you.**

   Here are some examples: "There's only love," "Don't worry, be happy," "Trust in God."

4. **Begin to breathe through your nose, and as you breathe, repeat the word or phrase quietly to yourself.**

   You can whisper the word or phrase, *subvocalize* it (that is, move your tongue as though you're saying it, but don't say it aloud), or just repeat it in your mind. If you get distracted, come back to the repetition of the word or phrase. (If you have difficulty breathing through your nose, by all means breathe through your mouth instead.)

   As an alternative, you can rest your attention on your breath as it comes and goes through your nostrils, returning to your breathing when you get distracted.

5. **Keep the meditation going for five minutes or more and then slowly get up and go about your day.**

How did you feel during meditation? Did it seem weird to say the same thing or follow your breath over and over? Did you find it difficult to stay focused? Did you keep changing the phrase? If so, don't worry. With regular practice, you gradually get the knack of it.

Of course, you could easily spend many fruitful and enjoyable years mastering the subtleties and complexities of meditation. But the good news is that, the basic practice is actually quite simple. You don't have to be an expert to meditate and therefore enjoy its extraordinary benefits.

In the same way, you can consider the practice of meditation to be a journey of sorts. This chapter provides an overview of your trip, offers some alternative routes to your destination, explains the basic skills you need to know to get you there, and points to some detours that may advertise the same benefits but don't really deliver.

This chapter also explores some of the problems that meditation can help resolve. You know the old expression "If it ain't broke, don't fix it"? Well, the reality is that many people find that their lives are "broke" in some pretty significant ways.

Getting an Overview of How the Journey Unfolds

If you're like most people, you're searching for something more in life — more peace of mind, more energy, more well-being, more focus, more meaning, more happiness, and more joy. You've heard about meditation and you wonder what it has to offer.

Think of meditation as a climb up a mountain. You've seen snapshots of the summit, but you can barely glimpse it through the clouds from the bottom of the mountain. The only way to get to the top is to climb up one step at a time.

Different paths up the same mountain

Imagine you're getting ready to climb a mountain. How are you going to get to the top? You could take climbing lessons, buy the right gear, and inch your way up one of the rocky faces. Or you could leisurely hike up one of the many trails that meander up the mountain. (Of course, you could always cheat and drive your car to the top, but that would ruin the metaphor.)

Although they all end up at the same place, every approach has its unique characteristics. One may take you on a gradual ascent through forests and meadows, whereas another may head steeply uphill over dry, rocky terrain. From one, you may have vistas of lush valleys filled with flowers; from another, you may see farmland or desert. You may want to charge up the summit directly or, depending on your energy and your motivation, you may choose to stop at a picnic spot in route and while away a few hours (or days) enjoying the peace and quiet. You may enjoy that one spot so much that you decide not to climb any higher. Perhaps you'd rather climb one of the smaller peaks along the way instead of going the distance to the top.

REMEMBER

Well, the journey of meditation has a great deal in common with climbing a mountain. You can aim for the top, or you can just set your sights on some grassy knoll or lesser peak halfway up the slope. Whatever your destination, you can have fun and reap the benefits of just breathing deeply and exercising muscles you didn't even know you had.

People have been climbing the mountain of meditation for thousands of years in different parts of the world. As a result, topographic maps and guidebooks abound. Each one provides its own unique version of how to make your way up the mountain and its own recommendations for the trip.

Traditionally, these guidebooks describe a spiritual path involving a set of beliefs and practices. A long time ago, these secrets were passed down verbally from one generation to the next (see the sidebar "Meditation's spiritual roots"). More recently, Western researchers and teachers have distilled meditation from its spiritual origins and now offer it as a remedy for a variety of 21st-century issues.

The maps and books may describe the summit differently; some emphasize the vast open spaces, others pay more attention to the peace or exhilaration you feel when you get there, and some even claim that there's more than one peak. But consider the ancient sage who said, "Meditation techniques are just different paths up the same mountain."

Here are a few of the many techniques that have been developed over the centuries:

>> Repetition of a meaningful word or phrase, known as a *mantra*

>> Mindful awareness of the present moment

>> Following or counting your breath

>> Paying attention to the flow of sensations in your body

>> Cultivation of love, kindness, compassion, forgiveness, and other healing emotions

>> Concentration on a geometric shape or other simple visual object

>> Visualization of a peaceful place or a healing energy or entity

>> Reading and reflecting on inspirational or sacred writings

>> Gazing at a picture of a holy being or saint

>> Contemplation of nature

>> Chanting praises to the Divine

The view from the summit — and from other peaks along the way

When you reach the summit of the meditation mountain, what do you see? If you can trust the reports of the meditators and mystics who have climbed the mountain before you, you can declare with some confidence that the top of the mountain harbors the source of all love, wisdom, happiness, and joy. Some people call it spirit or soul, true nature or true self, the ultimate truth, or the ground of *being* (or just *being* itself). Others call it God or the Divine or the Holy Mystery, or simply the One. There are nearly as many names for it as there are people who experience it. And some spiritual traditions consider it so sacred and powerful that they hesitate to give it a name at all.

As for the *experience* of reaching the summit, seasoned meditators use words like *enlightenment* (from ignorance), *awakening* (from a dream), *liberation* (from bondage), *freedom* (from limitation), and *union* (with God or being).

An old saying likens all these words and names to fingers pointing at the moon. If you pay too much attention to the finger, you risk missing the beautiful moon, which is the reason for pointing the finger in the first place. Ultimately, you need to experience the moon — or in this case, the summit — for yourself.

Of course, you may have no interest in lofty states and experiences like enlightenment or union. Perhaps you're reading this chapter simply because you want to reduce stress and stay sharp. You may be saying, "Forget about the Holy Mystery; I just want a little more clarity and peace of mind, thank you very much!" But a primary way to stay sharp mentally is to apply meditation to your daily life.

Here are some specific benefits meditation can provide:

>> Stronger focus and concentration

>> Reduced tension, anxiety, and stress

>> Clearer thinking and less emotional turmoil

>> Lower blood pressure and cholesterol

>> Support in kicking addictions and other self-defeating behaviors

>> Greater creativity and enhanced performance in work and play

>> Increased self-understanding and self-acceptance

>> More joy, love, and spontaneity

>> Greater intimacy with friends and family members

>> Enhanced feelings of happiness, contentment, and subjective well-being

>> Deeper sense of meaning and purpose

>> Glimpses of a spiritual dimension of being

REMEMBER

As you can see, these way stations are actually major destinations in their own right, and they're all well worth reaching. You may be quite content to stop halfway up the mountain after you've reduced your stress, improved your health, and experienced greater overall well-being. Or you may feel inspired to push on for the higher altitudes that the great meditators describe.

The taste of pure mountain water

To elaborate on this mountain metaphor further, imagine a spring at the summit gushes forth the pure *water of being* and never runs dry. (Depending on your orientation, you may prefer to call it the *water of grace* or *spirit* or *unconditional love.*)

MEDITATION'S SPIRITUAL ROOTS

Although many ordinary folks are meditating these days (including, quite possibly, people you know), the practice wasn't always so readily available. For centuries, monks, nuns, mystics, and wandering ascetics preserved it in secret, using it to enter higher states of consciousness and ultimately to achieve the pinnacle of their particular spiritual paths.

Highly motivated laypeople with time on their hands could always learn a few techniques. But the rigorous practice of meditation remained a sacred pursuit limited to an elite few who were willing to renounce the world and devote their lives to it.

How times have changed! From the influx of Indian yogis and swamis in the 1960s to the more recent fascination with mindfulness, meditation has become mainstream. Its practical benefits are applauded in every medium, both actual and virtual.

Meditation has been studied extensively in psychology labs and reduced to formulas like the Relaxation Response (a simple technique for diminishing stress). Yet it has never entirely lost its spiritual roots. In fact, the reason meditation works so effectively is that it connects you with a spiritual dimension, which different commentators give different names but you can call simply *being*.

Those who make it to the summit get to dive into the pool that surrounds the spring and immerse themselves completely in the water. In fact, some even merge with the water and become identical with *being* itself. (Don't worry. You won't merge if you don't want to.)

But you don't have to climb all the way to the top to enjoy the pure taste of *being*. The water flows down the mountain in streams and rivulets and nourishes the fields and towns below. In other words, you can taste *being* everywhere, in everything, because *being* is the essence that keeps life going at every level. Until you start meditating and access this pure water, you may not know what *being* tastes like.

DISCOVERING THE TREASURE IN YOUR OWN HOUSE

The Jewish tradition tells a story that has a counterpart in all the world's great meditative teachings. Simon, a simple tailor, fantasizes night and day about the great treasure he will one day find when he leaves his family home in his little village and ventures forth into the world. Late one night, with a few belongings on his back, he sets off on his travels.

For years, Simon wanders from one great city to another, making his living mending clothes, searching for the treasure he knows belongs to him. But all the people he asks about the treasure have problems of their own and are unable to help him on his search.

One day he comes upon a psychic known far and wide for her extraordinary abilities. "Yes," she says, "there is indeed a vast treasure that belongs to you and you alone." Hearing this, Simon's eyes light up with excitement. "I will tell you how to find it," she continues, giving Simon complex directions that he meticulously records.

When she comes to the end of her instructions and describes the very street and house where this treasure is allegedly buried, Simon can't believe his ears. For this is the very home he had left years before when setting out on his quest.

Quickly he thanks the psychic, stuffs the directions in his pocket, and hurries back in the direction from which he came. And lo and behold, much to his surprise, he does indeed find a vast and unfathomable treasure buried beneath the hearth in his own house.

The point of this story is obvious: Though you may wander in search of inner peace and experiment with all kinds of meditative practices, the peace and love and wisdom you seek are inevitably here all along, hidden within your own heart.

REMEMBER

When you meditate, you travel closer to the summit spring that is the source of the water and therefore get a more pure taste of this water of *being* and learn how to recognize its taste. (Depending on their personalities and where they are on the mountain, people use different terms to describe the water's taste, such as *calm, peace, well-being, wholeness, clarity,* and *compassion.*) It doesn't matter where you stop on your way up the mountain; you still get to dip your hands into the water of *being* and taste it for yourself. When you know the flavor, you can begin to find the taste of *being* wherever you go.

There's no place like home — and you've already arrived!

The preceding sections use metaphor of the mountain, and yes, the journey of meditation requires steady effort and application like a climb up a mountain. But that metaphor hides some important paradoxes:

>> **The summit doesn't exist in some faraway place outside you; it exists in the depths of your being — some traditions say in the heart — and awaits your discovery.** See the nearby sidebar "Discovering the treasure in your own house."

>> **You can approach the summit in an instant; it doesn't necessarily take years of practice.** While meditating, for example, when your mind settles down and you experience a deep peace or tranquility, sense your interconnectedness with all beings, or feel an upsurge of peace or love, you're tasting the sweet water of *being* right from the source inside you. And these moments inform and nourish you in ways you can't possibly measure.

>> **The mountain metaphor suggests a progressive, goal-oriented journey, whereas the point of meditation is actually to set aside all goals and just** ***be.*** As the title of the bestseller by stress-reduction expert Jon Kabat-Zinn puts it, "Wherever you go, there you are." Or as Dorothy says in *The Wizard of Oz,* "There's no place like home." And the truth is that, like Dorothy, you're always already there.

Of course, you're not going to give up all your doing and striving instantaneously and just automatically sense *being,* even when you meditate. You have to slowly work up to letting it all go by practicing your meditation. By gradually focusing and simplifying until you're doing less and less while you meditate, you find you're just *being* more and more. The following are a few of the stages you may pass through on the path to just *being:*

BECOMING AWARE OF YOUR AWARENESS

Most of the time, you probably don't pay much attention to your awareness. Yet the truth is that it's crucial to everything you do. When you watch TV, study for an exam, cook a meal, drive your car, listen to music, or talk with a friend, you're being aware, or paying attention. Before you begin to meditate in a formal way, you may find it helpful to explore your own awareness.

First, notice what it's like to be aware. Are there times in your life when you're not aware of anything? Complete this thought: "I am aware of. . . ." Do this again and again and notice where your awareness is centered.

Do you tend to be more aware of internal or external sensations? Do you pay more attention to thoughts and fantasies than to your moment-to-moment sensory experiences? Notice whether a preoccupation with mental activity diminishes your awareness of what's happening right here and now.

Next, pay attention to whether your awareness tends to focus on a particular object or sensation or tends to be more expansive and inclusive. You may find that your awareness resembles a spotlight that flows from object to object. Notice how your awareness flows without trying to change it.

Does your awareness shift quickly from one thing to another, or does it move more slowly, making contact with each object before moving on? Experiment with speeding up and slowing down this flow of awareness, and notice how that feels.

You may discover that your awareness is drawn again and again to certain kinds of objects and events but not to others. Where does your awareness repeatedly wander? Which experience does it seem to selectively avoid?

Now experiment with gently directing your awareness from one focus to another. When you pay attention to sounds, you may notice that you momentarily forget about your hands or the discomfort in your back or knees. Try to focus on one object of attention for as long as you can. How long can you remain undistracted before your mind skips to the next thing?

>> Getting used to sitting still

>> Developing the ability to turn your attention inward

>> Struggling to focus your attention

- » Being distracted again and again
- » Becoming more focused
- » Feeling more relaxed as you meditate
- » Noticing fleeting moments when your mind settles down
- » Experiencing brief glimpses of stillness and peace

And here's perhaps the greatest paradox of all: If you practice meditation diligently, you may eventually come to realize that you've never left home, even for an instant. You find that you've traveled deep within yourself.

Developing and Directing Awareness: The Key to Meditation

If, as the old saying goes, a journey of a thousand miles begins with a single step, then the journey of meditation begins with the cultivation of *awareness* or *attention*. In fact, awareness is the mental muscle that carries you along and sustains you on your journey, not only at the start but also every step of the way. No matter which path or technique you choose, the secret of meditation lies in developing, focusing, and directing your awareness. (Incidentally, attention is just slightly focused awareness. See the sidebar "Becoming aware of your awareness.")

To get a better sense of how awareness operates, consider a natural metaphor: light. You may take light for granted, but unless you've developed the special skills and heightened sensitivity of the blind, you can barely function without it. (Have you ever tried to find something in a pitch-dark room?) The same is true for awareness: You may not be aware that you're aware, but you need awareness to perform even the simplest tasks, just like you need light to see.

You can use light in a number of ways. You can create ambient lighting that illuminates a room softly and diffusely. You can focus light into a flashlight beam to help you find things when the room is dark. Or you can take the very same light and concentrate it into a laser beam so powerful that it can cut through steel or send messages to the stars.

TIP

Likewise, in meditation, you can use awareness in different ways. You can increase your powers of awareness by developing concentration on a particular focus, whether it's a word, image, object, symbol, or spiritual concept. (For a brief list of meditation techniques, see the section "Different paths up the same mountain" earlier in this chapter.)

Then, when you've stabilized your concentration, you can, through the practice of receptive awareness, expand your awareness — like ambient light — to illuminate the full range of your experience. Next, you can concentrate even further to cultivate positive emotions and mind-states. Or you can use awareness to investigate your inner experience and contemplate the nature of existence itself.

These four practices — *concentration, receptive awareness, cultivation,* and *contemplation* — constitute the major uses of awareness throughout the world's great meditative traditions. The following sections discuss each of these practices further.

Building concentration

To do just about anything well, you need to focus your awareness. The most creative and productive people in every profession — for example, great athletes, performers, businessmen, scientists, artists, and writers — have the ability to block out distractions and completely immerse themselves in their work. If you've ever watched Rafael Nadal hit a forehand shot or Meryl Streep transform herself into the character she's portraying, you've witnessed the fruits of total *concentration.*

REMEMBER

Some people have an innate ability to concentrate, but most people need practice to develop it. Buddhists like to compare the mind to a monkey — constantly chattering and hopping about from branch to branch, topic to topic. Did you ever notice that most of the time, you have scant control over the whims and vacillations of your monkey mind, which may space out one moment and obsess the next? When you meditate, you calm your monkey mind by making it *one-pointed* rather than scattered and distracted.

Many spiritual traditions teach their students concentration as the primary meditation practice. They advise to just keep focusing your mind on the mantra, symbol or visualization. Eventually you attain what is called *absorption,* or *samadhi.*

In absorption, the sense of being a separate "me" disappears, and only the object of your attention remains. Followed to its natural conclusion, the practice of concentration can lead to an experience of union with the object of your meditation. If you're a sports enthusiast, this object could be your tennis racket or your golf club; if you're an aspiring mystic, the object could be God or *being* or the absolute.

Even though you may not yet know how to meditate, you've no doubt had moments of total absorption, when the sense of separation disappears: gazing at a sunset, listening to music, creating a work of art, looking into the eyes of your beloved. When you're so completely involved in an activity that time stops and self-consciousness drops away, you enter into what psychologist Mihaly Csikszentmihalyi calls *flow*. In fact, Csikszentmihalyi claims that activities that promote flow epitomize what most people mean by *enjoyment*. Flow can be extraordinarily refreshing, enlivening, and even deeply meaningful — and it's the inevitable result of unbroken concentration.

Opening to receptive awareness

The great sages of China say that all things comprise the constant interplay of *yin* and *yang* — the feminine and masculine forces of the universe. Well, if concentration is the yang of meditation (focused, powerful, penetrating), then *receptive awareness* is the yin (open, expansive, welcoming).

Where concentration disciplines, stabilizes, and grounds the mind, receptive awareness loosens and extends the mind's boundaries and creates more interior space, which enables you to familiarize yourself with your mind's contents. Where concentration blocks extra stimuli as distractions to the focus at hand, receptive awareness embraces and assimilates every experience that presents itself.

Most meditations involve the interplay of concentration and receptive awareness, although some more-advanced techniques teach the practice of receptive awareness alone. Just be open and aware and welcome whatever arises, these techniques encourage, and ultimately you'll be "taken by truth." Followed to its conclusion, receptive awareness guides you in shifting your identity from your thoughts, emotions, and the stories your mind tells you to your true identity, which is *being* itself.

Of course, if you don't know how to work with attention, these instructions are impossible to follow. That's why most traditions prescribe practicing concentration first. By quieting and grounding the mind just enough so it can open without being swept away by a deluge of irrelevant feelings and thoughts, concentration provides a solid foundation on which the practice of meditation can flourish.

Using contemplation for greater insight

REMEMBER

Although concentration and receptive awareness provide enormous benefits, ultimately it's insight and understanding — of how the mind works, how you perpetuate your own suffering, how attached you are to the outcome of events, and how uncontrollable and fleeting these events are — that offer freedom from suffering. And in your everyday life, it's creative thinking — free from the usual limited, repetitive patterns of thought — that offers solutions to problems. So *contemplation* is the third key component that transforms meditation from a calming, relaxing exercise to a vehicle for freedom and creative expression.

After you've developed your concentration and expanded your awareness, you eventually find that you have access to a more penetrating insight into the nature of your experience. You can use this faculty to explore your inner terrain and gradually understand and undermine your mind's tendency to cause you suffering and stress. If you're a spiritual seeker, you can use this faculty to inquire into the nature of the self or to reflect on the mystery of God and creation. And if you're a person with more practical concerns, you may ponder the next step in your career or relationship or contemplate some seemingly irresolvable problem in your life.

Cultivating positive, healing states of mind

Some meditations aim to open the heart and develop certain life-affirming qualities like compassion, love, kindness, equanimity, joy, or forgiveness. On a more practical level, you can use meditation to cultivate a proactive, healthy immune system or to develop poise and precision in a particular sport. For example, you can visualize killer T cells attacking your cancer or imagine yourself executing a dive without a single mistake. These kinds of meditations are called *cultivation*.

Where contemplation aims to investigate, inquire, and ultimately see deeply into the nature of things, cultivation can help you transform your inner life. By directing your concentration, cultivation strengthens positive, healthy mind-states and withdraws energy from more reactive and self-defeating thoughts.

Making Meditation Your Own

Developing and directing your awareness may be the foundation of effective meditation, but like any good foundation, it's only the beginning. The next step is to build your house brick by brick, meditation session by meditation session. By discovering what works for you and what doesn't, your meditation practice becomes stable and grounded. Or, to conjure up the journey metaphor, awareness is the muscle that propels you up the mountain. But you need to choose your route, find your pace, and navigate the obstacles that get in your way. In other words, you need to fashion and maintain your own practice and troubleshoot whatever difficulties arise.

Designing your own practice

When you begin to develop and direct your awareness in meditation, you're faced with the challenge of putting all the pieces together into an integrated practice that's uniquely suited to your needs. For example, consider the following possibilities:

>> You may find yourself drawn to forms of meditation that emphasize focused concentration and have only minimal interest in the more open, allowing quality of receptive awareness.

>> You may cherish the peace and relaxation you experience when you simply sit quietly without any effort or focus, not even the effort to be aware.

>> You may have a specific purpose for meditating, such as healing an illness or resolving a disturbing psychological issue, and feel drawn only to approaches that help you meet your goals.

The key is to experiment with different forms of meditation and trust your intuition to tell you which ones are best suited for you at this particular point on your journey up the mountain. Inevitably, yin and yang tend to balance each other out. That is, you may start out with intense concentration and end up with more relaxed, receptive awareness. Or you may begin in a more receptive mode and gradually discover the virtues of focus. The journey of meditation has its own lessons to teach, and no matter what your intentions may be, you generally end up encountering those lessons that you were destined to learn.

Of course, if you intend to maintain your practice from week to week and month to month, the only way to reap the benefits of meditation is to practice meditating. You need to draw on some of those time-honored qualities that every sustained enterprise requires: motivation, discipline, and commitment. These qualities are relatively rare in Western culture, where people generally expect to have their needs met right now, if not sooner, but they aren't difficult to cultivate. In fact, they arise naturally when you're engaged in and passionate about what you're doing.

Troubleshooting the challenges

As your meditation practice deepens and evolves, you may find yourself encountering unexpected challenges that you don't quite know how to handle. Here again, the mountain metaphor comes in handy. Say you're halfway up the trail when you hit a patch of icy terrain, or boulders block your path, or a thunderstorm sends you scurrying for cover. What do you do? Do you pull out your special equipment and consult preestablished guidelines for dealing with the difficulties? Or do you just have to improvise as best you can?

MINDFULNESS: MEDITATION AS A WAY OF LIFE

What the Buddhists call *mindfulness* is the ongoing attention to whatever arises moment to moment. Mindfulness, which blends concentration and receptive awareness, is one of the simplest techniques for beginners to learn and also one of the most readily adaptable to the busy schedules most people face. After all, if you're like most people, you're primarily concerned with living a more harmonious, loving, stress-free life — not lifting off into some disembodied spiritual realm divorced from the people and places you love.

In fact, the beauty, belonging, and love you seek are available right here and now! You only need to clear your mind and open your eyes, which is precisely what the practice of mindfulness teaches. When you pay attention to your present experience from moment to moment, you keep waking up from the daydreams and worries your mind fabricates and returning to the clarity, precision, and simplicity of the present, where life actually takes place.

The great thing about mindfulness is that you don't have to limit your practice to certain places and times — you can practice waking up and paying attention wherever you happen to be, at any time of the day or night.

EATING A PIECE OF FRUIT

For this in-the-moment exercise, imagine that you've just arrived from another planet and have never encountered an orange before. Now take a few minutes to experience a piece of fruit in a fresh new way:

1. **Place an orange on a plate and close your eyes.**

2. **Set aside all thoughts and preconceptions, open your eyes, and see the fruit as though for the first time.**

   Notice the shape, the size, the color, and the texture.

3. **As you begin to peel the orange, notice how it feels in your fingers.**

   Notice the contrast between the flesh and the peel and observe the weight of the fruit in your hand.

(continued)

(continued)

4. **Slowly raise a piece of the orange to your lips and pause a moment before eating.**

   Notice how it smells before you begin.

5. **Open your mouth, bite down, and feel the texture of its soft flesh and the first rush of juice into your mouth.**

6. **Continue to bite and chew the orange, remaining aware of the play of sensations from moment to moment.**

   Imagining that this may be the first and last orange you'll ever eat, let each moment be fresh and new and complete in itself. Notice how this experience of eating an orange differs from your usual way of eating a piece of fruit.

The good news is that people have been climbing this mountain for thousands of years. They've crafted tools and fashioned maps for traversing the terrain as smoothly and painlessly as possible. For example, if powerful emotions like anger, fear, sadness, or grief sweep through your meditation and make it difficult for you to stay present, you can draw on techniques for loosening their grip. Or if you encounter some of the common obstacles and roadside distractions on the path of meditation, such as sleepiness, restlessness, rapture, or doubt, you can count on time-honored methods for moving beyond them so you can continue on your way.

How Life Drives You to Meditate

Although you may be reluctant to admit it, at least publicly, life doesn't always live up to your expectations. As a result, you suffer — from stress, disappointment, fear, anger, outrage, hurt, or any of a number of other unpleasant emotions. Meditation teaches you how to deal with difficult circumstances and the tensions and emotions they evoke with balance, equanimity, and compassion. But before this chapter ventures into the positive solutions that meditation has to offer — and rest assured, there are plenty — you get a whirlwind tour of the problems they're intended to solve.

The myth of the perfect life

Many people suffer because they compare their lives to some idealized image of how life is supposed to be. Cobbled together from childhood conditioning, media messages, and personal desires, this image lurks in the shadows and becomes the standard to which every success or failure, every circumstance or turn of events, is compared and judged. Take a moment to check out your idealized image.

Perhaps you've spent your life struggling to build the American dream: two kids, house in the suburbs, brilliant career — what Zorba the Greek called the "full catastrophe." After all, that's what your parents had (or didn't have), and you decided that you owed it to them and to yourself to succeed in attaining that dream. Only now you're juggling two jobs to save the money for a down payment, your marriage is falling apart, and you feel guilty because you don't have enough time to spend with the kids.

Or maybe you believe that ultimate happiness would come your way if you could only achieve the perfect figure (or physique). The problem is, diets haven't worked, you can't make yourself adhere to exercise regimens, and every time you look in the mirror, you feel like passing out. Or perhaps your idea of earthly nirvana is the perfect relationship. Unfortunately, as you're watching the years pass by, you still haven't met Mr. or Ms. Right. You scour the personals while secretly fearing that you must have some horrible social disease.

REMEMBER

Whatever your version of the perfect life — a perfect home, perfect vacations, perfect sex, perfect health, even perfect peace of mind or total freedom from all tension and stress — you pay a high price for holding such high expectations. When life fails to live up to those expectations, as it inevitably does, you end up suffering and blaming yourself. If only you had made more money, spent more time at home, been a better lover, gone back to school, lost those extra pounds . . . the list is endless. No matter how you slice it, you just don't measure up.

Or perhaps you're among the elite few who manage to get everything you want. The problem is, you eventually find yourself becoming bored and wanting more — or you spend every spare moment struggling to protect or control what you have.

The great meditative traditions have a more humane message to impart. They teach that the ideal earthly life is a myth. As an old Christian saying puts it, "Man proposes; God disposes." Or, in the words of a popular joke, "If you want to make God laugh, tell him your plans." These traditions remind you that far more powerful forces are at work in the universe than yourself. You can envision and intend and strive and attempt to control all you want — and ultimately even achieve some modicum of success. But the truth is, in the long run, you have only the most limited control over the circumstances of our lives. Life is what happens when you have other things planned.

When things keep falling apart

Because it runs counter to everything you've ever been taught, you may have a difficult time accepting the basic spiritual truth that humans have only limited control over the events in their lives. After all, isn't the point of life to go out and "just do it," as the old Nike ads urged? Well, yes, you need to follow your dreams and live your truth; that's a crucial part of the equation.

But when life turns around and slaps you in the face, as it sometimes does, how do you respond? (Look at the Olympic skiers who spend years in training only to have their hopes for a medal wiped out in an instant by bad weather or a patch of ice.) Or when life tears you down and deprives you of everything you've gained, including your confidence and your hard-won self-esteem, where do you go for support? How do you deal with the pain and confusion? What inner resources do you draw upon to guide you through this frightening and unknown terrain? Consider the following story.

One day a woman came to see the Buddha with her dead child in her arms. Grief-stricken, she had wandered from place to place, asking people for medicine to restore him to life. As a last resort, she asked the Buddha if he could help her. "Yes," he said, "but you must first bring me some mustard seed from a house in which there has never been a death."

Filled with hope, the woman went from door to door inquiring, but no one could help her. Every house she entered had witnessed its share of deaths. By the time she reached the end of the village, she had awakened to the realization that sickness and death are inevitable. After burying her son, she returned to the Buddha for spiritual instruction. "Only one law in the universe never changes: that all things change and all things are impermanent," he explained. Hearing this, the woman became a disciple and eventually, it's said, attained enlightenment.

APPRECIATING IMPERMANENCE

In his book *Thoughts without a Thinker,* psychiatrist Mark Epstein recounts this teaching by the Thai meditation master Achaan Chah. "You see this goblet?" Achaan Chah asks. "For me this glass is already broken. I enjoy it; I drink out of it. It holds my water admirably, sometimes even reflecting the sun in beautiful patterns. If I should tap it, it has a lovely ring to it. But when I put this glass on the shelf, and the wind knocks it over or my elbow brushes it off the table and it falls to the ground and shatters, I say, 'Of course.' When I understand that this glass is already broken, every moment with it is precious." When you recognize the impermanence of life, you can better appreciate and enjoy the present moment.

The fact is that life is a rich and perplexing interplay of light and dark, success and failure, youth and age, pleasure and pain — and, yes, life and death. Circumstances change constantly, apparently falling apart one moment, only to come together the next. As the contemporary Zen teacher Shunryu Suzuki puts it, everything is constantly "losing its balance against a background of perfect balance." In reality, the only constant in life is change itself!

TIP

The key to your peace of mind lies not in your circumstances, but in how you respond to them. As the Buddhists say, suffering is wanting what you don't have and not wanting what you do have, while happiness is precisely the opposite: enjoying what you have and not hungering for what you don't have. This concept doesn't mean that you must give up your values, dreams, and aspirations — only that you need to balance them with the ability to accept things as they are. Meditation gives you an opportunity to cultivate acceptance by teaching you to reserve judgment and to open to each experience without trying to change or get rid of it. Then, when the going gets rough, you can make use of this quality to ease your ruffled feathers and maintain your peace of mind.

Dealing with the postmodern predicament

Of course, it's news to no one that circumstances change constantly — certainly pundits and sages have purveyed this truth for ages. But perhaps at no time in history has change been as pervasive and relentless — or affected lives so deeply — as during the past few decades. Watching the evening news or reading a paper, you're flooded with statistics and images of violence, famine, natural disaster, global climate change, and economic instability, all depicting a world that seems to be coming increasingly unstitched.

On a more personal level, you may have lost your job because of corporate downsizing, ended a relationship because your lover was relocated to another state, been a victim of a violent crime, or lost a bundle in a volatile market. Perhaps you spend your spare time figuring out how to stay one step ahead in a competitive work environment. Or you may simply lie awake each night worrying about when the tidal wave of change will finally reach you and sweep you away. Does any of this sound familiar?

Sociologists call this period the *postmodern era,* when constant change is becoming a way of life and time-honored values and truths are being rapidly dismantled. How do you navigate your way through life when you no longer know what's true and you're not even sure how to find out? Do you search for it on the web or somehow glean it from the latest pronouncements of media soothsayers and corporate CEOs?

Despite the unarguable advantages of all the electronic devices that have become indispensable since the 1990s, you may have noticed that the faster you communicate, the less you really connect with others in a rich and meaningful way. Sure, you're constantly being stimulated and distracted by social media updates, text messages, and emails — but do they really provide you with the intimacy and fulfillment you crave?

REMEMBER

Such relentless change exacts a steep emotional and spiritual price, which people tend to deny in their collective attempt to accentuate the positive and deny the negative. Here are a few of the negative side effects of life in the postmodern age:

>> **Anxiety and stress:** When the ground starts shifting beneath your feet, your first reaction may be anxiety or fear as you attempt to regain your stability. This gut-level response has been programmed into our genes by millions of years of living on the edge. These days, unfortunately, the tremors never stop, and small fears accumulate and congeal into ongoing tension and stress. Your body may feel perpetually braced against the next onslaught of difficulties and responsibilities — which makes it virtually impossible to relax and enjoy life fully. By relaxing your body and reducing stress, meditation can provide a much-needed antidote.

>> **Fragmentation:** Most Americans once lived, shopped, worked, raised their kids, and spent their leisure time in the same community. They encountered the same faces every day, worked the same job for a lifetime, stayed married to the same person, and watched their children raise their own children just down the block. Now they often shuttle the kids off to school or daycare and commute long distances to work while checking messages on their cellphones. On the way home, they grab some fast food and then spend their evenings aimlessly surfing the web. They change jobs and partners more frequently than ever, and when the children grow up, they often move to another state — or another country. Although you may not be able to stem the tide of fragmentation, you can use meditation to connect with a deeper wholeness that external circumstances can't disturb.

>> **Alienation:** When your life appears to be made up of disconnected puzzle pieces that don't fit together, it's no wonder you wind up feeling completely stressed out. With so much downsizing and outsourcing, many people are forced to work at marginal jobs that pay the bills but fail to connect them to a deeper sense of value or purpose. According to an article in *American Demographics* magazine, more people are flocking to small towns in an attempt to recapture a sense of community, and fewer and fewer are voting in each election, apparently because they believe that they have little power to change things. Never before, it seems, have human beings felt so alienated, not only from their work and their government but also from others, themselves, and their own essential being — and most people don't have the skills

or the know-how to reconnect! By bridging the chasm that separates you from yourself, meditation can help heal your alienation from others and the world at large.

>> **Loneliness and isolation:** With people moving from place to place more frequently and families fragmenting and scattering across the globe, you're less and less likely to have regular contact with the people you know and love — and even if you do, you may be too busy to relate in a mutually fulfilling way. Instead of sharing family dinners, mom, dad, and the kids call or text each other on the fly while hurrying from one activity or job to the next, rarely ending up in the same place at the same time. Of course, you may not be able to overcome the forces that keep people apart. But you can use your meditation to turn every moment with your loved ones into quality time.

>> **Depression:** Feeling lonely, alienated, stressed out, and disconnected from a deeper source of meaning and purpose often lead some people to end up feeling depressed. In a nation where *antidepressant* is a household word, millions of people take mood-altering chemicals each day to keep from feeling the pain of postmodern life. Meditation can connect you with your own inner source of contentment and joy that naturally dispels the clouds of depression.

ACCEPTING THINGS THE WAY THEY ARE

The Zen tradition tells the story of a poor farmer who lost his only horse. His friends and neighbors bemoaned his plight, but he seemed unperturbed. "We'll see," he said with an enigmatic smile.

Several days later, his horse returned with a pack of five wild stallions that had joined it along the way. His neighbors rejoiced in his good fortune, but he didn't appear to be excited. "We'll see," he said again.

The following week, while attempting to ride and tame one of the stallions, his beloved only son fell and broke his leg. The ever-solicitous neighbors were beside themselves with grief, but the farmer, though he comforted and cared for the boy, didn't seem to be concerned about the future. "We'll see," he mused.

At the end of the month, the local warlord arrived in the farmer's village to conscript all the healthy young men to fight in the latest campaign. But the farmer's son . . . well, you can imagine the rest of the story.

In case you hadn't noticed, life's a roller-coaster ride. You can't control the ups and downs. If you want to hold on to your lunch — and your sanity — you need to learn how to maintain your peace of mind.

>> **Stress-related illness:** From tension headaches and acid indigestion to heart disease and cancer, the steady rise in stress-related illness reflects a collective inability to cope with the instability and fragmentation of today's times. This situation fuels a billion-dollar healthcare industry that often only masks the deeper problems of fear, stress, and disorientation. As numerous scientific studies have shown, the regular practice of meditation can actually reverse the onslaught of many stress-related ailments. (See the section "How to Survive the 21st Century with Meditation" later in this chapter.)

Four popular "solutions" that don't really work

Here's a quick look at a few popular approaches to handling stress and uncertainty that create more problems than they solve:

>> **Addiction:** By distracting people from their pain, encouraging them to set aside their usual concerns and preoccupations, and altering brain chemistry, addictions mimic some of the benefits of meditation. Unfortunately, addictions also tend to fixate the mind on an addictive substance or activity — drugs, alcohol, sex, gambling, and so on — making it even more difficult for people to be open to the wonders of the moment or to connect with a deeper dimension of *being*. Besides, most addictions involve a self-destructive lifestyle that ultimately intensifies the problems the addict was attempting to escape.

>> **Fundamentalism:** By advocating simple, one-dimensional answers to complex problems, offering a sense of meaning and belonging, and repudiating many of the apparent evils of postmodern life, fundamentalism — be it religious or political — provides a refuge from ambiguity and alienation. Alas, fundamentalists divide the world into black and white, good and bad, us and them, which only fuels the fires of alienation, conflict, and stress in the world at large.

>> **Entertainment:** When you feel lonely or alienated, just turn on the tube, download a movie to your computer or smartphone, or head to your local multiplex. That will calm your anxiety or soothe your pain — or will it? In addition to providing entertainment, the media seemingly create community by connecting you with other people and the events around you. But you can't have a heart-to-heart conversation with a TV celebrity or hug your favorite movie star. Besides, the media (intentionally or not) manipulates your emotions, fills your mind with the ideas and images of the popular culture,

and focuses your attention outside yourself instead of giving you the opportunity to find out what *you* really think, feel, and know.

>> **Consumerism:** This bogus solution to life's ills teaches that wanting and having more is the answer — more food, more possessions, more vacations, more of every perk that plastic can buy. As you may have noticed, however, the thrill fades fast, and you're quickly planning your next purchase — or struggling to figure out how to pay the credit-card bill that arrives like clockwork at the end of the month.

How to Survive the 21st Century with Meditation

Now for the good news! As mentioned earlier in the chapter, meditation offers a time-honored antidote to fragmentation, alienation, isolation, stress — even stress-related illnesses and depression. Although it doesn't solve the external problems of your life, it does help you develop inner resilience, balance, and strength to roll with the punches and come up with creative solutions.

TIP

To get a sense of how meditation works, imagine for a moment that your body and mind are a complex computer. Instead of being programmed to experience inner peace, harmony, equanimity, and joy, you've been wired to respond to life's inevitable ups and downs with stress, anxiety, and dissatisfaction. But you have the power to change your programming. By putting aside all other activities, sitting quietly, and attuning yourself to the present moment for a minimum of 10 or 15 minutes each day, you're developing a whole new set of habitual responses and setting yourself up to experience more positive emotions and mind-states.

Of course, if you find it distasteful to think of yourself as a computer, you can picture life as an ocean, with the constant ups and downs you experience as the waves churn the water's surface. When you meditate, you dive beneath the surface to a quiet place where the water is calmer and more consistent.

Whatever your favorite metaphor, the point is that meditation provides a way of transforming stress and suffering into equanimity and ease. In this section, you get to see how meditators have been reaping the remarkable benefits of meditation for millennia — and how you can, too.

Advanced technology for the mind and heart

REMEMBER

Traditionally, the Western world has emphasized external achievement, and the East has valued inner development. The great scientific and technological advances of the past 500 years originated in the West, while yogis and roshis in the monasteries and ashrams of Asia were cultivating the inner arts of meditation. Now the currents of East and West and North and South have joined and are intermingling to form an emerging global culture and economy. As a result, you can apply the inner "technology" perfected in the East to balance the excesses of the rapid technological innovations perfected in the West.

Like master computer programmers, the great meditation masters throughout history developed the capacity to program their bodies, minds, and hearts to experience highly refined states of being. While the West was charting the heavens and initiating the Industrial Revolution, they were chalking up some pretty remarkable accomplishments of their own:

>> Penetrating insights into the nature of the mind and the process by which it creates and perpetuates suffering and stress

>> Deep states of ecstatic absorption in which the meditator is completely immersed in union with the Divine

>> The wisdom to discriminate between relative reality and the sacred dimension of *being*

>> Unshakable inner peace that external circumstances can't disturb

>> The cultivation of positive, beneficial, life-affirming mind-states, such as patience, love, kindness, equanimity, joy, and — especially — compassion for the suffering of others

>> The ability to control bodily functions that are usually considered involuntary, such as heart rate, body temperature, and metabolism

>> The capacity to mobilize and move vital energy through the different centers and channels of the body for the sake of healing and personal transformation

>> Special psychic powers, such as *clairvoyance* (the ability to perceive matters beyond the range of ordinary perception) and *telekinesis* (the ability to move objects at a distance without touching them)

Of course, the great meditators of the past used these qualities to seek liberation from suffering, either by withdrawing from the world into a more exalted reality or by achieving penetrating insights into the nature of existence. Yet the meditation technology they developed — which has become widely available in the West in the past few decades — can be used by the rest of us in ordinary, everyday ways to yield some extraordinary benefits.

The mind-body benefits of meditation

Although the earliest scientific studies of meditation date back to the 1930s and 1940s, research into the psychophysiological effects of meditation took off in the 1970s, fueled by a burgeoning interest in Transcendental Meditation, Zen, and other Eastern meditation techniques. Since then, thousands of studies have been published, with an exponential increase in research in the past 10 to 15 years as brain-imaging technology has become increasingly sophisticated. Here is a brief synopsis of the most significant benefits of meditation:

Physiological benefits:

» Decreased heart rate

» Lower blood pressure

» Quicker recovery from stress

» Decrease in *beta* (brainwaves associated with thinking) and increase in *alpha*, *delta*, and *gamma* (brainwaves associated with deep relaxation and higher mental activity)

» Enhanced *synchronization* (that is, simultaneous operation) of the right and left hemispheres of the brain (which positively correlates with creativity)

» Fewer heart attacks and strokes

» Increased longevity

» Reduced cholesterol levels

» Decreased consumption of energy and need for oxygen

» Deeper, slower breathing

» Muscle relaxation

» Reduction in the intensity of pain

Psychological benefits:

» More happiness and peace of mind

» Greater enjoyment of the present moment

» Less emotional reactivity; fewer intense negative emotions and dramatic mood swings

>> More loving, harmonious relationships

>> Increased empathy

>> Enhanced creativity and self-actualization

>> Heightened perceptual clarity and sensitivity

>> Reductions in both acute and chronic anxiety

>> Complement to psychotherapy and other approaches in the treatment of addiction

TUNING IN TO YOUR BODY

Like Mr. Duffy in James Joyce's novel *Ulysses,* most people "live a short distance" from their bodies. The following meditation, which has counterparts in yoga and Buddhism, helps reestablish contact with the body by drawing attention gently from one part to another. Because it cultivates awareness and also relaxes the muscles and internal organs, it makes a great preamble to more formal meditation practice. Allow at least 20 minutes to complete.

1. **Lie on your back on a comfortable surface — but not too comfortable, unless you plan to fall asleep.**

2. **Take a few moments to feel your body as a whole, including the places where it contacts the surface of the bed or floor.**

3. **Bring your attention to your toes.**

   Allow yourself to feel any and all sensations in this area. If you don't feel anything, just feel "not feeling anything." As you breathe, imagine that you're breathing into and out of your toes. (If this feels weird or uncomfortable, just breathe in your usual way.)

4. **When you're done with your toes, move on to your soles, heels, the tops of your feet, and your ankles in turn, feeling each part in the same way that you felt your toes.**

   Take your time. The point of this exercise isn't to achieve anything, not even relaxation, but to be as fully present as possible wherever you are.

5. **Gradually move up your body, staying at least three or four breaths with each part.**

   Follow this approximate order: lower legs, knees, thighs, hips, pelvis, lower abdomen, lower back, solar plexus, upper back, chest, shoulders. Now focus on the fingers, hands, and arms on both sides; and then on the neck and throat, chin, jaws, face, back of the head, and top of the head.

By the time you reach the top of your head, you may feel as though the boundaries between you and the rest of the world have become more fluid or have melted away entirely. At the same time, you may feel silent and still — free of your usual restlessness or agitation.

6. **Rest there for a few moments; then gradually bring your attention back to your body as a whole.**

7. **Wiggle your toes, move your fingers, open your eyes, rock from side to side, and gently sit up.**

8. **Take a few moments to stretch and reacquaint yourself with the world around you before standing up and going about your day.**

A Dozen More Great Reasons to Meditate

You don't have to join some cult or get baptized or bar mitzvahed to enjoy the benefits of meditation. And you don't have to check out of your everyday life and run off to a monastery in the Himalayas. You simply need to practice your meditation regularly without trying to get anywhere or achieve anything. Like interest in a money-market account, the benefits just accrue by themselves.

Awakening to the present moment

When you rush breathlessly from one moment to the next, anticipating another problem or hungering for another pleasure, you miss the beauty and immediacy of the present, which is constantly unfolding before your eyes.

Meditation teaches you to slow down and take each moment as it comes — the sounds of traffic, the smell of new clothes, the laughter of children, the worried look on an old woman's face, the coming and going of your breath. In fact, as the meditative traditions indicate, only the present moment exists anyway — the past is just a memory and the future a fantasy, projected on the movie screen of the mind right now.

Making friends with yourself

When you're constantly struggling to live up to images and expectations (your own or someone else's) or racing to reinvent yourself to survive in a competitive environment, you rarely have the opportunity or the motivation to get to know yourself just the way you are. Self-doubt and self-hatred may appear to fuel the fires of self-improvement, but they're painful — and besides, they contribute to other negative mind-states, such as fear, anger, depression, and alienation, and prevent you from living up to your full potential.

When you meditate, you learn to welcome every experience and facet of your being without judgment or denial. Through the process, you begin to treat yourself as you would a close friend, accepting (and even loving) the whole package.

Connecting more deeply with others

As you awaken to the present moment and open your heart and mind to your own experience, you naturally extend this quality of awareness and presence to your relationships with family and friends. If you're like most people, you tend to project your own desires and expectations onto the people close to you, which acts as a barrier to real communication. But when you start to accept others the way they are — a skill you can cultivate through the practice of meditation — you open up the channels for a deeper love and intimacy to flow between you and those around you.

Relaxing the body and calming the mind

As contemporary health researchers have discovered — and traditional texts agree — mind and body are inseparable, and an agitated mind inevitably produces a stressed-out body. As the mind settles, relaxes, and opens during meditation, so does the body — and the longer you meditate (measured both in minutes logged each day and in days and weeks of regular practice), the more this peace and relaxation ripples out to every area of your life, including your health.

Lightening up!

Perhaps you've noticed that nonstop thinking and worrying generate a kind of inner claustrophobia — fears feed on one another, problems get magnified exponentially, and the next thing you know, you're feeling overwhelmed and panicked. Meditation encourages an inner mental spaciousness in which difficulties and concerns no longer seem so threatening, and constructive solutions can naturally arise, along with a certain detachment that allows for greater objectivity, perspective, and, yes, humor. That mysterious word *enlightenment* actually refers to the supreme "lightening up"!

Enjoying more happiness

Research reveals that the daily practice of meditation over just a few months actually makes people happier, as measured not only by their subjective reports but also by brain-mapping technology. In fact, meditation is apparently one of the only things that can permanently change your *emotional set point* — your basic level of relative happiness that scientists say stays the same throughout your life, no matter what you experience.

If you want lasting happiness, leading-edge science and spiritual wisdom have the same advice to offer: Forget about winning the lottery or landing the perfect job and begin meditating instead!

Experiencing focus and flow

When you're so fully involved in an activity that all sense of self-consciousness, separation, and distraction dissolves, you've entered what psychologist Mihaly Csikszentmihalyi calls a state of *flow* (discussed earlier in this chapter). For human beings, this total immersion constitutes the ultimate enjoyment and provides the ultimate antidote to the fragmentation and alienation of postmodern life. No doubt you've experienced moments like these — writing a report, creating a work of art, playing a sport, working in the garden, making love, singing a song. Athletes call it *the zone.* Through meditation, you can discover how to give the same focused attention to — and derive the same enjoyment from — every activity.

Feeling more centered, grounded, and balanced

To counter the escalating insecurity of life in rapidly changing times, meditation offers an inner groundedness and balance that external circumstances can't destroy. When you practice coming home again and again — to your body, your breath, your sensations, your feelings — you eventually grow to realize that you're always home, no matter where you go. And when you make friends with yourself — embracing the dark and the light, the weak and the strong — you get thrown off-center less and less frequently by the slings and arrows of life.

Enhancing your performance at work and at play

Studies have shown that basic meditation practice alone can enhance perceptual clarity, creativity, self-actualization, and many of the other factors that contribute to superior performance. In addition, specific meditations have been devised to enhance performance in a variety of activities, from sports to schoolwork.

Increasing appreciation, gratitude, and love

As you begin to open to your experience without judgment or aversion, your heart gradually opens as well — to yourself and others. You can practice specific meditations for cultivating appreciation, gratitude, and love. Or you may find, as so many meditators have before you have, that these qualities arise naturally when you gaze at the world with fresh eyes, free from the usual projections and expectations.

Aligning with a deeper sense of purpose

When you practice making the shift from doing and thinking to *being*, you discover how to align yourself with a deeper current of meaning and belonging. You may get in touch with personal feelings and aspirations that have long remained hidden from your conscious awareness. Or you may connect with a more universal source of purpose and direction — what some people call the *higher self* or *inner guidance*.

Awakening to a spiritual dimension of being

As your meditation gradually opens you to the subtlety and richness of each fleeting but irreplaceable moment, you may naturally begin to see through the veil of appearances to the sacred reality at the heart of things. You eventually may come to realize (and this one could take lifetimes) that the very same sacred reality is actually who you are in your own heart of hearts. This deep insight — what the sages and masters call "waking up from the illusion of separation" — cuts through and ultimately eliminates loneliness and alienation and opens you to the beauty of the human condition.

GETTING INTO THE HABIT

Take a habit that you wish you could break but can't. Maybe it's smoking, drinking coffee, or eating junk food. The next time you do it, instead of spacing out or daydreaming, turn it into a meditation. Pay close attention as you draw the smoke into your lungs, for example, or chew the French fries. Notice how your body feels. Whenever your mind drifts off, notice where it goes — you may have favorite fantasies that accompany this habit — and then gently bring it back to your experience.

Don't try to stop or change the habit; just do it as usual, except this time you're doing it with full awareness. The next time you indulge the habit, notice how you feel. Has your attitude changed in any way? What are you aware of this time that you weren't aware of before?

4
Improving Your Lifestyle: Nutrition and Exercise

Chapter 19

Eating, Exercising, and Getting Your Zzzs

Remember when you were a young child and you got cranky when you were hungry or tired? Those weren't your finest moments. Your ability to cope with frustration and disappointment was all but nonexistent.

Now that you've grown up, your stresses may be different, but your physical state still plays a major role in determining how stressed you feel. What you eat, when you eat, your level of overall fitness, and the quality of your sleep all affect your ability to cope with stress and stay sharp.

This chapter shows you how you can develop a more stress-effective lifestyle — through diet, exercise, and sleep — which can in turn strengthen your body's ability to cope with potential stress and help you resist its negative effects. Simply put: Your body is a temple. Treat it nicely. A healthy body leads to a healthy mind.

Surveying Stress-Effective Eating

If you're like most people, your dietary habits are less than perfect. Your eating is probably a hit-and-miss affair — inconsistent, rushed, and tailored to meet your busy schedule. Your life is already stressed enough without having to worry about what goes into your mouth. However, what you eat — and how you eat it — can contribute significantly to your ability to cope with stress. Eating the wrong things or eating at the wrong times can add to your stress level. Not to worry. Help is here.

Feeding your brain

In recent years, a lot of attention has been paid to the relationship between food and mood — what you eat and how you feel. Researchers now have a better idea of how different foods affect your psychological states and how food can increase or decrease the stress in your life.

Serotonin is a naturally occurring neurotransmitter in your brain that affects your experience of stress. When you're clinically depressed, your serotonin levels fall, and you become more stressed. Antidepressant medications such as Prozac, Paxil, and Zoloft increase the amount of serotonin in your brain, which then alters your mood and affects how you cope with a potential stress.

The foods you eat can also change the serotonin levels in your brain. Your diet is an important way of regulating serotonin. Putting the right stuff on your plate means you have a better chance of giving your brain what it needs.

Choosing low-stress foods

The following are some specific food guidelines that can help you choose foods to lower your stress and help your body cope with stress:

>> **Include some complex carbohydrates in every meal.** Complex carbohydrates, such as pasta, whole-grain cereals, potatoes, and brown rice, can enhance your performance when under stress. Foods rich in carbohydrates can increase the levels of serotonin in the brain, making you feel better. Too many complex carbohydrates, however, aren't the best thing for you. Remember: Moderation.

>> **Reduce your intake of simple carbohydrates.** Sweetened, sugary foods — simple carbohydrates like soda and candy — can make you feel better in the moment but worse in the long run.

>> **Eat adequate amounts of protein.** Foods high in protein enhance mental functioning and supply essential amino acids that can help repair damage to your body's cells. Eat more fish, chicken, and other lean meats. If your dietary preferences take a vegetarian direction, look to beans, nuts, and seeds (garbanzo beans, pinto beans, soybeans, tofu, and lentils), dairy (yogurt and cottage cheese), eggs, and fruits and vegetables (avocados, broccoli, and spinach) to meet this goal. If you're vegan, you can follow the same guidelines minus the dairy and eggs.

>> **Eat your vegetables.** Beans, peppers, carrots, squash, and dark-green leafy veggies, whether cooked or raw, provide your body with the vitamins and nutrients it needs to resist the negative effects of stress.

>> **Don't forget fruit.** Fruit can be a good source of vitamins and minerals that can help your body combat stress. Vitamins A, C, and E are antioxidants that have been shown to relieve stress. The B vitamins, thiamin (B1), riboflavin (B2), niacin (B3), pantothenic acid (B5), pyridoxine (B6), and biotin (B7), help your our body obtain energy from the food you eat.

>> **Get plenty of potassium.** Milk (especially the low-fat variety), whole grains, wheat germ, and nuts all can provide your body with potassium, a mineral that can help your muscles relax. Bananas are also a good source of potassium.

TEN STRESS-RELIEVING FOODS

Here's a more specific list of ten foods that not only are good for you but also can help lower your stress level:

- **Nuts:** Almonds, which have lots of magnesium, B2 (riboflavin), zinc, and vitamin E, are an especially good choice. Almonds can help regulate cortisol levels. But don't overdo it. Nuts can be caloric, but they're great as a snack in small amounts.

- **Broccoli:** Your mother was right. Eat your broccoli. It contains lots of B vitamins and folic acid, and it's great as a side dish with fish or chicken.

- **Fish:** Most varieties of fish contain the important B vitamins, B6 and B12. These can play a role in synthesizing serotonin, which can affect your moods. Tuna and salmon are loaded with omega-3 fatty acids that can play a role in regulating adrenaline.

- **Milk:** Score another one for mom. Milk contains vitamins B2 and B12, along with antioxidants that are often associated with reducing stress. It also contains tryptophan, which can increase the production of serotonin. Milk also has calcium, magnesium, and potassium, which are important stress-regulating elements. You don't have to drink your milk straight; pour it on some cereal instead. Go for the skim variety.

- **Bananas:** They're full of potassium. They're also a great snack when you need some fuel in your system, and they're a great addition to fortified cereal.

(continued)

(continued)

- **Blueberries:** These are filled with antioxidants and vitamin C, which help fight stress. Grab a handful when you need a healthy treat or sprinkle some on your cereal.

- **Oranges:** Stress can reduce your levels of vitamin C, but oranges can replenish that vitamin, which boosts your immune system. Oranges also make a great snack.

- **Sweet potatoes:** Actually, they're not really potatoes — they're roots. They're also a great source of fiber, vitamin B6, vitamin A, and antioxidants such as beta-carotene.

- **Brown rice:** This is much better for you than the white variety. Brown rice has much more manganese and phosphorus than does white rice. It contains more iron and greater amounts of vitamins B3, B1, and B6, all known to have stress-reducing properties. Brown rice is richer in fiber, selenium, and antioxidants. It also has a great "nutty" flavor.

- **Avocados:** These are loaded with potassium and vitamin A. The taste and texture can be highly satisfying.

Stopping the stress-eating cycle

Are you an emotional eater? If so, you may eat whenever you're anxious, upset, nervous, or depressed. Although emotional eaters can still put it away when they're happy, delighted, non-anxious, and non-depressed (and yes, during those rare times when they're actually hungry), most emotional eaters eat when they feel they need to feed their stress.

When you feed your stress, a destructive cycle begins. You feel stressed, so your food choices aren't always the best. For some reason of cruel fate, foods that tend to make you feel good are usually the foods that aren't so good for your body. Research studies have shown that stressed emotional eaters eat sweeter, higher-fat foods and more energy-dense meals than unstressed and non-emotional eaters. Chocolate, ice cream, pizza, cake, donuts, and cookies may make you feel terrific — but, unfortunately, only for about 17 seconds. Then, of course, your stress returns (plus a ton of guilt), and you feel the need for another bout of eating. The cycle repeats itself.

The first step in breaking the cycle is becoming aware of exactly when you're distressed and identifying your feelings. When you feel the urge to open the refrigerator door, you need to realize that you're experiencing some form of discomfort. It may be hunger, but more likely it's stress.

TIP

Before you put any food in your mouth, stop and take stock of your emotional state. Ask yourself, "Am I really hungry or am I feeling emotionally distressed?" If it's truly hunger, eat. Otherwise, label your feelings (for example, "I'm upset," "I'm nervous," or "I'm a wreck!"). One way of determining whether you're truly hungry or merely having an emotional desire to eat is to ask yourself another question: "Would healthy foods (a salad, low-fat yogurt, a banana, or an apple) appease my desire to eat?" If not (and you're thinking about fast food, chocolate, pizza, cake, or ice cream), your eating is probably not about satisfying basic hunger. It's about eating in response to stress. Simply breaking the stress-eating connection for even a moment can give you a different perspective and an increased level of motivation that can sustain you until you find something a little more redeeming than filling your mouth.

The following sections have some other tips that you can use to improve your relationship with food when you're stressed.

Distract yourself

One of the best things you can do is involve yourself in some activity you enjoy that can take your mind off eating. Do something. Anything. Some eating substitutes that keep you away from the kitchen include the following:

>> **Get out of the house.** Often, simply changing your environment can rid you of the old eating cues. Go for a walk. Do an errand. Visit a friend.

>> **Get some exercise.** Hit the stationary bike or treadmill, or simply do some floor exercises like sit-ups or even just stretching.

>> **Read a good book.**

>> **Accomplish a task, such as cleaning a closet or working on a craft.**

Another option: Cook something. This idea may seem like asking for trouble, but often the process of cooking can serve as a substitute for eating. A hint: Don't make cookies or cakes. Try something like a soup or a casserole: something that is filling, takes time to prepare and cook, and isn't immediately ready to eat.

Substitute relaxation for food

Whenever you're about to open the refrigerator to calm your frayed nerves, consider substituting a relaxation break. Simple deep breathing, relaxation, or meditation (see Chapter 18) can induce a feeling of emotional calm that can reduce your desire to eat. That's all you may need to ease you past a difficult moment.

Work with a stress cue

Sometimes a little reminding goes a long way. Create a stress-eating reminder that you can put on the fridge or cabinet where you keep delicious snacks.

Try taping the question "Are you really hungry?" to your kitchen door. Even more private and innocuous is a simple little colored circle of paper you can affix at strategic places in your kitchen. It reminds you that you shouldn't open the door unless you're hungry. Only you know what it represents and why it's there.

Eat your breakfast

Research shows that eating a nutritious breakfast gets you more alert, more focused, and in a much better mood than if you have a high-fat, high-carbohydrate breakfast or have no breakfast at all.

Skipping breakfast can lower your body's ability to cope with the stress that lies in wait for you later in the day. Starting the day on the right nutritional foot is important. When you wake up in the morning, as many as 11 or 12 hours have passed since you last ate. You need to refuel.

And don't forget lunch

Lunchtime tends to be one of the busier times of your day. With a lot to do, eating lunch may be low on your list of priorities, but don't skip it. Your body functions best when it gets fed regularly. Missing lunch can leave you feeling tense and edgy.

When you do have lunch, don't overdo it. A big lunch can leave you lethargic and dreaming of a mid-afternoon nap.

Eat like a cow, not like a pig

Eating a big meal can result in your feeling lethargic soon after eating. To digest that heavy meal, your body needs a greater supply of blood. This blood has to come from other places in your body, like your brain, depriving it of some of the oxygen it needs to keep you alert. The solution? Don't scarf down your food like a pig. Graze like a cow.

Spread out your eating fairly evenly throughout the day. Avoid those huge meals that load you down with calories and leave you feeling ready for a nap. Instead, consider smaller, lighter meals at your regular mealtimes. Supplement meals with healthy snacks if needed. Have breakfast, a mid-morning snack, and then a light lunch, another snack later in the afternoon (a piece of fruit is good), and a moderate dinner. An evening snack (try some air-popped popcorn) should avert any hunger pangs. Eating by grazing evens out your blood sugar and avoids the big spikes of less frequent but heavier meals.

Drink like a camel

Most people don't get enough liquids because they get busy and forget to drink. Every day you lose water through your breath, perspiration, urine, and bowel movements. For your body to function properly, you need to replace this water loss by drinking beverages and eating foods that contain water. So how much should you drink? The *8 by 8 rule* (eight 8-ounce glasses of water a day) is popular because it's easy to remember. The Institute of Medicine's estimate agrees with this determination (1.9 liters per day). Really, you can replace "water" with "fluid" because all fluids count toward the daily total. Bottom line: Stay hydrated!

REMEMBER

For many, the notion of drinking this amount of liquid seems like a joke. If you're like most people, you usually wait until you're thirsty before heading for the kitchen. Unfortunately, by then it's a little late. Your body needs the liquid before you feel that thirst. You may need to modify your liquid intake depending on your level of activity, the climate you live in, your health status, and whether you're pregnant or breast-feeding.

Load up earlier in the day

The simplest way to lose weight is to eat more in the first half of the day than in the last half. Then you have time to burn off many of those earlier calories. Recall that old bit of nutritional wisdom, "Eat like a king in the morning, a prince at noon, and a pauper at night."

Eating mindfully

Mindful eating can help you not only become more aware of what you eat but also control what and how much you eat. Shamash Alidina, in his useful *Mindfulness For Dummies* (Wiley), suggests the following steps to help you master mindful eating.

1. **Remove distractions.**

    Turn off the TV. Get away from your computer. No book, newspaper, nothing. Sit down, just you and your meal.

2. **Do three minutes of mindful breathing.**

    Simply notice and focus on your breathing (see Chapter 16 for more).

3. Become aware of what you're eating.

Notice the colors and shapes of the food on your plate. Notice how it smells.

4. Notice what your body is doing.

Salivating? Notice what your hunger feels like. Pay attention to your thinking. See your thoughts as thoughts rather than facts. Let any extraneous thoughts go.

5. Slowly put a morsel of food into your mouth. Be mindful of the taste, texture, and smell of the food. Chew slowly, noticing how the texture of the food changes.

6. When you're ready, repeat with another mouthful.

Continue to eat mindfully, becoming aware of how your stomach feels. Are you feeling more full?

7. Stop eating when you feel that you're full and don't need to eat more.

You may find that you're full a lot sooner than you may have felt previously. Eat more slowly to give your stomach time to recognize it's full.

8. Do some additional mindful breathing.

If you still feel like eating more, remember that your desire to eat may reflect a thought ("I have to eat!") rather than genuine hunger. You don't have to react to every urge. Let the urge slip by. Don't trust your emotional impulses to eat.

Try this approach daily for a week or so and see whether it changes the way you look at food and eating.

Mastering the art of anti-stress snacking

Feeling anxious, nervous, stressed out? Need a quick food fix? Snacking, when done right, is an art. Anyone can down a candy bar or a bag of chips and a soda. The real skill is coming up with a snack that not only doesn't add to your stress level but also helps you reduce the stress you already have. Here are some guidelines:

>> **Avoid highly sugared treats.** They give you a boost in the short run but let you down in the long run. You'll crash.

>> **Stick with snacks that have high-energy proteins and are high in complex carbohydrates.** They give you a longer-lasting, sustained pick-me-up.

Here are some specific suggestions of quick bites and snacks that can boost your mood and help alleviate some of your stress:

>> A piece of fruit — an orange, peach, apple, or banana. Any fruit is fine.

>> A handful of mixed nuts.

>> A bowl of whole-grain cereal with a sliced banana.

>> A spinach salad.

>> A bowl of fruit salad.

>> A soft pretzel.

>> A handful of blueberries.

>> Air-popped popcorn.

>> An English muffin. (Go easy on the butter or margarine. A little jelly is fine.)

>> A bowl of high-protein Greek yogurt.

>> A piece of dark chocolate (but just a piece).

>> A serving of sorbet.

Eating out

These days it seems as though more people are eating out or bringing in already prepared foods. To be fair, more fast-food places have modified their menus to include healthier fare. Still, temptations can run high, and you're more than a little likely to fall into a nutritional pothole. Here are some fast-food guidelines:

>> Go with turkey, chicken breast, or lean roast beef rather than salami, ham, and cheese.

>> Avoid the chef's salad. It sounds healthy, but it isn't. The eggs, bacon, cheese, and dressing turn it into a nutritionally bad idea.

>> Tuna is great. But add a lot of mayo and it becomes a mistake.

>> Have a hamburger rather than a cheeseburger.

>> Never order a large-sized anything.

>> Eat only half your French fries or split a regular order of fries with someone. No super-sizing!

>> Have a slice of pizza without any meat toppings.

>> Take the skin off your roasted chicken.

>> Eat half of your meal and wrap up the rest to take home.

Curing "menu weakness"

Menu weakness is a condition you may encounter when you sit down in a restaurant and the server hands you a menu. All you can see are the alluring descriptions of food possibilities that all sound tasty. Any healthful habit or nutritional resolve vanishes. You wind up ordering things you later regret. Usually, the creamy, cheesy entrees or that pie a la mode look good. But the high fat, salt, and sugar content will get you. To cure this affliction, you need a strategy. The best thing you can do is be prepared. Before you enter a restaurant, decide what you'll order. By now, you probably have a pretty good idea what types of dishes are available on most menus. Or you can look up the menu online ahead of time. When the server comes, tell him or her what you want without glancing at the menu. Ask to have the gravy or dressing on the side so you can control the amount you use. Yes, in the short run it's less satisfying, but you'll have fewer regrets later on.

Becoming salad bar savvy

When salad bars first became popular, they really were "salad" bars. They contained mostly foods that were green, healthy, and nutritious. That was the first week. Then the good-tasting stuff started showing up, and there has been no going back. However, with some control over your tong hand, you can once again make the salad bar your body's friend.

Here's the secret to healthy salad-bar visits: Never eat anything in a heated bin. The hot items are the most toxic. True, tuna salad loaded with mayo won't win any nutritional awards, but compared to the food farther down the line, it can be considered a health food. By steering clear of anything reheated, you can avoid such nutritional disasters as breaded chicken, creamy soups, macaroni and cheese, and the rest of the tasty warm foods that beckon you from their aluminum trays.

Embracing moderation

At this point, you may feel that much of the joy and pleasure of eating has been taken away from you. To some extent, yes. However, a good philosophy about food has always been "Everything in moderation — *including moderation.*" You really don't have to give up anything entirely. You can still have a steak, pizza, ice cream, or anything else that captures your fancy *but not all the time.* Just eat less of it.

Examining Stress-Reducing Exercise and Activity

You already know how beneficial exercise can be as a way of keeping your weight down, your body buff, and your heart ticking for many more years.

What you may not know is that exercise is one of the better ways of helping you cope with stress and keep a clear head. Exercise and sustained activity — in whatever form — can decrease your blood pressure, lower your heart rate, and slow your breathing — all signs of reduced arousal and stress. Exercise is a natural and effective way of slowing and even reversing your body's fight-or-flight response. This section shows you how you can make exercise and activity your allies in winning the battle against stress.

Calming your brain naturally

When you exercise, you feel different; your mood changes for the better. This difference isn't just a psychological response to the fact that you're doing something good for your body. It's physiological as well.

When you exercise, you produce *endorphins* (literally, natural morphine from within your body), which can produce feelings of well-being and calming relaxation. These positive feelings help you cope more effectively with stress and its effects.

Thinking activity, not exercise

Exercise has never been a favorite word for most people. It connotes too much work with too little fun, like taking out the garbage or making the bed. Exercise is something you endure and complete as quickly as possible. The word *exercise* is associated with sweating, stretching, straining, pulling, lifting, more sweating, and taking a long shower. At least the last part is fun.

TIP

You may think of exercise as something outside the range of your normal day-to-day activities. However, a better way of approaching the goal of staying fit is to replace the word *exercise* with the term *activity*.

The word exchange is more than semantic. Any increase in your level of bodily activity — aerobically or non-aerobically — and any muscle-toning or stretching contributes positively to your state of physical well-being. And who ever said activity has to be in a gym, on a court, or with a dumbbell? Many people mistakenly believe that to exercise you must engage in rigorous sports, go to a health club, or find some other specialized facility. Not so.

After a hard day of work, the chances of your putting on a sweat suit and lifting weights or completing a 5K run are slim. The good news is, you don't have to. The trick is to find naturally existing outlets for activity that are readily available and easily integrated into your lifestyle and work style.

Exercise, cleverly camouflaged as daily physical activity, is all around you. The hard part is knowing it when you see it.

REMEMBER

Never jump abruptly into a new program of physical exercise. Your head may be ready for the change, but your body needs more time to get used to the idea. This strategy becomes all the more important if you've led a rather sedentary life in the past. Check with your doctor first for an official okay, and then begin slowly, gradually adding more time and effort to your workout.

The following are some simple ways you can introduce small bits of activity into your day:

>> Park your car a little farther from your office and walk the rest of the way.

>> Use your TV time effectively. While you're watching TV, do some sit-ups, jumping jacks, push-ups, or stretches; ride an exercise bike, or walk on a treadmill.

>> Walk away from your stress. As an exercise, walking has always had wimp status. But if done consistently and for a sustained period of time, it's a terrific way of staying in shape. The nice thing about walking is that it can be pleasantly camouflaged as strolling or sight-seeing — both painless activities. And if you crank up the pace and distance a bit, you have a wonderfully simple form of aerobic exercise that can enhance your feeling of well-being, mentally and physically. Walking is a great way to clear your head and calm your mind.

REMEMBER

Take a mini walk or two during your day. Your walks can be as short as down the block to the corner store or a lap around your office or house.

>> **Do something you like.** If you don't like the exercise or activity you're doing, the chances of sustaining it are small. Find something you really enjoy, like one of the following:

- **A favorite sport.** Golf, tennis, bowling, baseball, basketball, racquetball — whatever.

- **A favorite activity.** Horseback riding, dancing, trampolining, swimming, ice-skating, or rope-jumping — anything that gets your body moving.

- **Gardening.** Yes, if done for a sustained period, gardening can be considered a form of exercise.

- **Bicycling.** Find a place where you can bike safely and enjoyably. If you don't know where those places are, contact your local parks and recreation office. Or ask friends or people you see on bikes what they suggest. Of course, you can also use a stationary bike at home. **Remember:** Be sure to wear a helmet and other protective gear when you're on your bike — even on short rides in your neighborhood. Accidents can happen anywhere.

- **Dancing.** Many classes are available for all types and skill levels.

- **In-line skating.** In-line skating is here to stay because it's great exercise and one of the more painless ways of getting a physical workout. After you've figured out how to stop, no one will be able to hold you back. And be sure to wear the safety gear (a helmet, elbow pads, wrist pads, and knee pads). The stress of finding yourself in an ER shouldn't be included in your already stressful day.

» **Become a player**. One of the better ways of staying in shape is playing at something you like. Every big city has just about every conceivable kind of sports team, from softball leagues to pick-up games in the park. You don't even have to be especially proficient at a sport to get on board. Check with your local YMCA or community center for teams that are forming, and ask at work whether teams already exist. Go online to find a meet-up site that brings together like-minded weekend players for just about any activity.

» **Climb your way out of stress.** Research done at Johns Hopkins University shows that by climbing stairs for a mere six minutes a day, you can add up to two years to your life. Even better, if you live in a big city, you encounter lots and lots of stairs every day. With land at a premium, most cities are designed with height rather than width in mind. Although some cities are more vertical than others, all have more than their share of opportunities to climb stairs.

If you don't live in a big city, you can find climbing opportunities in other places. Ask at your local high school to see whether you can climb the football stadium bleachers. Does your shopping mall have stairs? If so, become a mall walker! Avoid elevators and consider it a challenge to find stairs wherever you live.

Doing the gym thing

Maybe it's a case of misery loving company. Or maybe it's just more fun to do something with others around. Whatever the case, consider joining a gym or health club. After you enter the door of a health club or gym, you rarely leave without some kind of workout.

TIP

The biggest obstacle to joining a health club is the cost. Like the airlines, each gym charges a different price to do exactly the same thing. You have to shop around for the best deal. Generally, a YMCA or community center, though less trendy, offers better bargains. Also, if you can arrange your schedule so that you can go at off-peak times, many gyms give you a cheaper rate. Almost all health clubs offer some corporate discount, especially if your corporation is in the neighborhood. Some companies even subsidize your membership. There may even be a senior discount.

Try out a club before you join. Ask for a guest pass or two. Many clubs offer short-term trial memberships that allow you to try them out before signing on for a longer period of time.

Finding those "hidden" health clubs

These days more places are available to work out than you may expect. More and more health clubs and gyms are scattered around in hotels, office buildings, and apartment buildings. No signs advertise their existence, but they're there. The equipment at a "hidden" health club may not be elaborate, but you probably don't need elaborate to get the job done.

To find these hidden treasures, you need to do a little detective work. Start with the newer apartment buildings and the bigger hotels in your area. Some of these places offer memberships to nonresidents and guests at a reasonable cost. Ask at your place of employment whether another company in the building where you work or in a neighboring building has any health facilities. You may be surprised by the number of companies that have installed workout equipment on their premises.

Sweating at home

Of course, you don't need to lay out money for a gym or health club if you purchase a piece or two of exercise equipment that you can use right in your own home. Alas, many pieces of home exercise equipment go badly underused. They become places to hang your clothes or serve as dust collectors.

However, don't let this deter you from converting an extra bedroom or study into a home fitness center. To make sure that your killer ab machine doesn't just collect dust, schedule time with yourself when you commit to working out. And stick to it. Turn on the TV when you exercise to help ease any discomfort.

GO ELECTRONIC WITH YOUR WORKOUTS

These days your DVD player, computer, tablet, smartphone, and gaming system can be valuable sources of workout material. The menu ranges from aerobics to Zumba. These videos and games can inject a fun and exciting quality into what normally would be a repetitive, uninspiring workout. Many are interactive, with motion-based sensors that literally put you in the picture. Some are incredibly intense, guaranteed to work up a sweat. Your options can include yoga, T'ai Chi, volleyball, football, table tennis, salsa, and just about every classic form of exercise.

Keeping yourself motivated

Often, remaining motivated is no small matter. You start with the best of intentions but somehow run out of motivational steam fairly quickly. The following tips and suggestions should help you stay the course.

Get a workout buddy

A workout buddy or partner provides you with added incentive to make sure you get there. Working out can also be more fun if you go with someone whose company you enjoy. The time on the treadmill just whizzes by when you're lost in talk with the person next to you. As a bonus, many health clubs offer a membership discount if you bring in a friend.

Get your day off to a good (and active) start

Some exercise, especially aerobic exercise just after you get up in the morning, is a great way to get your juices going and get you prepared for any stress that may come your way later in the day. Aerobic activity introduces more oxygen into your body and makes you more alert and focused. If you make that activity a little more vigorous, your system releases those endorphins, which can produce a calming feeling of relaxation.

Remember that every little bit counts

You may have a mistaken idea that if you do something for only a small bit of time, it really isn't worth much. The reality is that if you do it consistently, it adds up. A recent research study found that if you walk briskly for only ten minutes a day, three times a day, you get the same fitness and weight loss benefits as you would if you walked briskly for 30 minutes, once a day. So fit in a few minutes of activity wherever possible in your day

Do it; don't overdo it

REMEMBER

Yes, you really can have too much of a good thing — even exercise. Anecdotal reports show that elite athletes complain of being more susceptible to colds and other maladies when they overtrain or merely train intensely. Recent studies further suggest that your immune system can be weakened by excessive exhaustive exercise. So take a pass on that triathlon if you haven't run more than 20 feet in the last 10 years. Be realistic!

Getting a Good Night's Sleep

The first thing you notice when you work with people under a lot of stress is how often they say, "I'm tired." For some, the stress of the day is what wears them out. But for most people, it's a matter of not getting enough sleep. And they're hardly alone. Unfortunately, rest certainly takes a back seat in everyone's busy life.

The fact is, most people don't get enough quality sleep. When you're tired, your emotional threshold is lowered. You're more vulnerable to all the stresses around you. Stress breeds even more stress. Breaking the cycle and getting a good night's sleep becomes very important.

The secret to getting a good night's sleep is figuring out your sleep needs and what strategies work best for you. You need to experiment. Something that works for one person may not work for you. What follows are a number of techniques, ideas, and strategies that have been shown to be effective in helping people get a better night of sleep. Consider them all and put together your own personal sleep program.

Knowing your sleep needs

Your first step is knowing just how much sleep you need. Most Americans get between 60 and 90 minutes less a night than they should for optimal health and performance. Though most people need about seven or eight hours of sleep a night, 20 percent of Americans get less than six hours of sleep, and 50 percent get less than eight hours. And it doesn't look like the situation is going to improve anytime soon.

No fixed rule can tell you how much sleep you need. So take the following simple sleep quiz to see whether you're getting enough sleep at night. Answer true or false, depending on whether the following statements apply to you.

>> I notice a major dip in my energy level early in the afternoon. ___

>> I need an alarm clock to wake up in the morning. ___

>> On the weekends, when I don't have to get up, I end up sleeping much later. ___

>> I fall asleep very quickly at night (in less than 15 minutes). ___

>> On most days, I feel tired and feel as though I need a nap. ___

Answering "that's me" to any of these suggests that you may want to reevaluate how much sleep you're getting and how much sleep you truly need. Try experimenting by getting a bit more sleep at night and see whether you notice any changes in your stress level.

Hitting the sheets earlier

For many, getting to bed earlier is easy to suggest but much harder to do. Night-time is when you do the things you need to do (laundry, cleaning, paying bills). Or, if you're lucky, late nights are when you do the things you want to do, whether that's vegging out in front of the TV or turning the pages of the latest bestseller. You may try to burn the candle at both ends — stay up late and get up early. Often, this strategy just doesn't work, and you're tired the next day. To get the sleep you need, realize that you have to get to bed earlier. It's as simple as that.

TIP

If you determine that you are, in fact, not getting enough sleep at night, try getting to bed 20 minutes earlier and see if the quality of your day improves. To get to bed just a few minutes earlier, turn off the TV or computer at a more reasonable hour. If you must watch that *Seinfeld* rerun or catch *The Daily Show*, record it and watch it the next day.

Developing a sleep routine

The best sleep comes from having a regular sleep pattern. Your body's internal clock becomes stabilized with routine. This means getting to bed at the same time and getting up at the same time.

The following sections provide tips for putting together a successful sleep routine.

Getting a comfortable mattress

All mattresses aren't created equal. You may be ready for an upgrade. Ask yourself when you last bought a mattress. Is it really comfortable? You may need a partner or friend to give you another opinion. You shouldn't wake up with a sore back, sore neck, or sore anything. Try out different mattress surfaces and firmnesses at a showroom to see what you may be missing.

Using the bed for sleep (and sex) only

Ideally, you want to establish a set of reminders and habits that promote an effective sleep routine. The relationship in your mind should be that lying down in bed means you're going to sleep, which means you need another place to read, watch TV, or do whatever nonsleeping activities you normally do in bed. (Sex is an exception.)

That's the ideal. However, if you live in a small house or apartment, you may not have the luxury of keeping a whole room dedicated to just one or two activities. You may be one of the many who use the bedroom for just about everything. In this case, try to at least reserve the bed itself.

EXERCISE HELPS YOU SLEEP

Studies have shown that exercise during your day can improve your sleep at night. It not only makes your body more tired but also generally increases your body temperature as you exercise. This rise is followed by a drop in body temperature a few hours later, which can make it easier for you to fall asleep and stay asleep. A study at Stanford University found that subjects who exercised regularly with moderately intense aerobic exercises for 30 to 40 minutes four times per week slept almost an hour longer than those who didn't exercise. These subjects were also able to cut the time it took to fall asleep by half. But although exercising is great, exercising too close to your bedtime can rev you up and keep you awake.

Creating a sleep ritual

If you can't make your bedroom a room devoted only to sleeping, you may find that creating a bedtime ritual is more realistic. At a certain hour, make the bedroom a place where you wind down and relax. This means no upsetting discussions, no work from the office, no bill-paying, no arguments with the kids, no unpleasant phone calls, and no anything else that may trigger worry, anxiety, or upset. In this case, you can read, watch a relaxing TV show or movie, or whatever else it is that calms your body and quiets your mind. But skip your local news. Today's robbery, fire, or general mayhem isn't the last thing you want to hear about before your head hits the pillow.

Avoiding late heavy meals

A big dinner late at night may make you drowsy, but it may also interfere with your sleep. Avoid fatty and rich foods late at night. Otherwise, your digestive system functions on overdrive, and the quality of your sleep may be disrupted. Who wants to be searching for antacids at 2 a.m.?

Watching how much you drink

Too much liquid in your system may result in too many nighttime awakenings to go to the bathroom. Try to restrict your late-night liquid intake. Remember, caffeinated drinks can not only keep you awake but also act as diuretics (in other words, more trips to the bathroom). If you enjoy a sip before bed, try a cup of the many wonderful decaffeinated herbal teas available.

Turning the noise down

You may have trouble sleeping soundly because of noise. This is especially the case if you live in a place where wailing car alarms or party-loving neighbors interrupt even the pleasantest of dreams. Worse yet, you may be a very light sleeper and vulnerable to a host of far less dramatic noises. Here are some suggestions:

>> **Sound-proof it.** Even with the windows shut, a lot of sound still comes through. Consider installing double-pane windows. Heavy drapes or shutters can add to the sound-proofing. Carpets, rugs, wall hangings, pictures, bookcases, and bookshelves all help absorb excess noise.

>> **Mask it.** The secret of masking is finding a more tolerable noise and making it the one you hear. Most people first experience masking in the summer, when the soothing hum of the air conditioner or whir of the fan drowns out just about everything else. A sound generator can also mask less pleasant sounds and calm you down. Inexpensive models (available at most discount and department stores) can reproduce a variety of soothing sounds: white noise, a waterfall, a rain forest, or the chirping of crickets in a meadow. Inexpensive smartphone apps can also provide a variety of soothing sounds. You can also download white-noise files onto your smartphone, MP3 player, or laptop and create a repeating audio loop.

>> **Block it.** That Metallica groupie upstairs or a deafening sanitation truck outside may call for stronger measures. Sometimes earplugs are in order.

Turning the heat down

If your bedroom is too warm, it may affect your ability to get to sleep. Most people sleep better when the temperature is slightly cool (around 65 degrees). Also make sure that your bedroom gets enough ventilation.

Turning off the light

Sleep masks can rescue you from the sleepless consequences of an overly lit bedroom. Perhaps your source of unwanted light comes from your partner, who chooses to read in bed long after you close your eyes. It may come from streetlights outside your window or the (oh so early) onset of daylight. Not all sleep masks are created equal. Get one that's very comfortable and doesn't feel like someone has wrapped a tight elastic band around your head.

Watching the booze and avoiding the pills

The quality of your sleep is as important as the number of hours you sleep. A small single nightcap does little harm, but greater amounts of alcohol (even though they may help you fall asleep) disturb the quality of your sleep and leave you waking up feeling tired or even hungover. Routine use of medication, such as sleeping pills, to promote sleep can quickly become psychologically addictive and actually impair sleep. Such pills increase risk for falls and injuries during nighttime trips to the bathroom.

Looking out for hidden stimulants

Besides that cup of coffee or caffeinated soda that will probably keep you up until the middle of next week (regular coffee contains anywhere from 95 to 150 milligrams in an eight-ounce cup), other less-obvious sources of caffeine creep into your diet. Tea contains caffeine, but generally in much smaller amounts than coffee (about 15 to 40 milligrams in an eight-ounce cup). Chocolate contains caffeine, but only in small amounts (unless you eat a lot of chocolate). The amount varies according to the type of chocolate, but it's generally in the range of 5 to 10 milligrams per ounce of chocolate. Generally, the darker the chocolate, the more the caffeine.

Napping carefully

Naps can be a wonderful tool. A short nap (try to keep it in the 15 to 20 minute range) can reinvigorate you and give you the energy to enjoy the rest of your day. Research has shown that short naps may help you feel less stressed. Taking longer naps may leave you feeling somewhat groggy. Blocking out light, perhaps with a sleep mask, can help you fall asleep faster. Naps are best taken between 1 and 3 p.m. Napping too late in your day can make it hard to fall asleep later that night.

However, if you aren't sleeping well at night, avoid any daytime naps. Four out of five people with insomnia find that they do better during the night if they don't nap during the day. Also watch out for after-dinner drowsiness which may result in your dozing in your favorite chair in front of the TV. This unplanned nap can interfere with your nighttime sleep pattern. To combat early evening drowsiness, get up and do something — call a friend, surf the web, clean your closet, or make a casserole for tomorrow.

SLEEPING LESS CAN MAKE YOU FAT?

In a recent study, Harvard University researchers followed about 68,000 middle-aged women for more than 16 years and found that women who slept five hours or less per night weighed an average of 5.4 pounds more — and were 15 percent more likely to become obese — than women who got at least seven hours of sleep a night. Maybe being awake longer means more opportunities to eat. Such weight gain may also result from changes in the hormones ghrelin and leptin, which regulate appetite. Studies at the University of Chicago found that when volunteers had their sleep restricted to five and a half hours per night, they ate an average of 221 more calories from snacks when compared with non-sleep-restricted controls. In just two weeks, that extra nighttime snacking can add a full pound of body weight.

Checking for medical problems

Your sleep problems may be due to a physical condition. A variety of medical problems, including the following, can result in sleep disturbances and chronic insomnia:

» **Heartburn:** Heartburn is a common source of sleep distress. Certain foods — such as heavy meals, spicy foods, rich foods, fatty foods, alcohol, and coffee — ingested later in the evening can cause or exacerbate heartburn.

» **Sleep apnea:** *Sleep apnea* is a sleep disorder that occurs when a person's breathing is interrupted during sleep. People with untreated sleep apnea stop breathing repeatedly during their sleep, sometimes hundreds of times. This stoppage results in frequent awakenings and poor-quality sleep.

» **Diabetes:** Symptoms of this common, chronic condition can include night sweats, a frequent need to urinate, and possibly nerve damage in the legs and feet that may produce involuntary movement or pain.

» **Arthritis:** Pain from arthritis can make it difficult for people to fall asleep. The need to change position can also interfere with sleep.

» **Muscle conditions:** Conditions such as fibromyalgia may result in abnormal sleep patterns and poor quality of sleep. Leg cramps and restless leg syndrome can also disrupt sleep.

» **Breathing problems:** Conditions such as asthma can interfere with breathing and awaken the sleeper. Emphysema and bronchitis may make it more difficult to get to sleep because of coughing, shortness of breath, or excessive phlegm.

DO YOU HAVE DELAYED SLEEP-PHASE DISORDER?

Individuals with *delayed sleep-phase disorder* generally fall asleep a few hours after midnight and find it hard to wake up in the more usual morning hours. This condition differs from true insomnia because the *timing* of sleep is altered. Affected individuals are on a different cycle. A typical sleep schedule may be falling asleep around 4 a.m., sleeping soundly, and awakening well rested at noon (although this sounds suspiciously like the sleep habits of college students). One way of determining whether you have delayed sleep-phase disorder or insomnia is to track your sleep on a longish vacation. Notice what time you go to bed and when you wake up on your own. If you sleep a full six to nine hours, you may have delayed sleep-phase disorder and not insomnia. If you suspect you have this condition, consult your doctor.

Falling asleep

You have the right mattress, your bedroom is the right temperature, the noise level is low, the room is dark, you've eaten lighter meals before going to bed, you've skipped naps, and you've avoided alcohol and caffeine. You're convinced that nothing medical is going on. Still, you find yourself hitting the sheets and staring at the ceiling wide awake. Or you actually fall asleep pretty quickly but wake up in the middle of the night, unable to fall *back* asleep. In both cases you need some additional help.

Relax your body, quiet your mind

When your body is relaxed, your mind slows. When your mind is calm, your body relaxes. Learning to relax physically and mentally is an important key to falling asleep. Chapter 16 shares some pretty good ideas for how to relax. Put together your own personal relaxation package as follows.

>> **Relaxed breathing:** This technique works on two levels. By focusing on your breathing, you can distract yourself from your mental stressors. The breathing itself induces a deeper state of physical relaxation that can get you closer to sleep. Simply focus on your breathing, noticing the air entering and leaving your nose and mouth. The breathing itself doesn't have to be complicated. Simply try to breathe more slowly and more deeply. Silently say the word "calm" to yourself each time you exhale. Don't force your breathing; let it find its own rhythm.

>> **Progressive muscle relaxation:** Working your way up your body from your toes to your head, tense and then relax each muscle group. After you've gone through one tense-relax cycle, focus on deepening the relaxation without the tensing phase.

>> **Relaxation imagery:** Visualize a place, situation, or experience that you find calming and peaceful. It can be a vacation, a room at home, the beach — anything you find relaxing. Get into that image, noticing the sights, sounds, and even smells. Let the image transport you.

Turn off your mind

Being tired means you're more likely to fall asleep. Alas, it doesn't ensure that you will. You may find that your mind is racing a mile a minute. You hope you'll fall asleep at least before next Friday. The problem is the level of mental arousal. This mental mayhem may take the form of mental distress. You may be worried, upset, angry, or otherwise distressed, guaranteeing that you'll be revved up and awake. But it may have nothing to do with distress. You may be happy or excited, replaying some event or success that genuinely delights you. Or you may be happily anticipating or planning some future positive event or experience. The result is the same. You can't fall asleep.

Don't try to fall asleep

This advice may sound curious given the goal of getting you to fall asleep. Yet one of the biggest obstacles in getting to sleep is the self-induced pressure that you have to get to sleep. Have you ever noticed that you fall asleep most quickly when you don't intend to go to sleep — in front of the TV, in the back of the classroom, or on a plane? When you're lying in bed thinking, "I just have to get to sleep! I'll be dead tired all day tomorrow! I'll never get past this sleeping problem!" you almost guarantee that falling asleep will elude you. This performance anxiety creates even more mental arousal and makes it harder for you to fall asleep.

REMEMBER

Your first step toward easier sleep is accepting that it may take longer than you want to figure out what to do, and that sometimes you won't get enough sleep. Your catastrophizing and awfulizing only make things worse. If you can, replace that "I have to get to sleep — right now!" with "I'd like to be asleep, but if I'm not, I'm not." Therapists often use the technique of paradoxical intention to help people get to sleep by telling them to try not to fall asleep. The pressure lessens, and the chances of falling asleep increase. This idea may be too much of a stretch for you, but the principle still holds. Lower the pressure to be asleep.

Don't look at the time

Looking at your clock or watch in the middle of the night isn't going to help you fall asleep. You've probably noticed how quickly time flies when you can't fall asleep. You look at your clock, and it's 2 a.m. And what seems like only ten minutes later, you notice the clock says 3:15 a.m. The pressure to get to sleep increases, which doesn't help you. You may want to cover the clock so you can't look at it at night.

Aim for relaxation

Your goal should be to get into the right "pre-sleep" mode. You can control this aspect even though you can't control falling into sleep. That happens on its own. Start by relaxing your body and slowing down your mind. Your new goal, remember, isn't being asleep, but rather being in a relaxed state that allows your body to fall asleep on its own.

DOES COUNTING SHEEP HELP?

The notion of counting those wooly critters as they jump over that fence as a sleep-inducing remedy has been around forever. It probably has something to do with the counting system devised by shepherds in ancient Britain. But does it work? Researchers at Oxford University put it to a test. They split insomniacs into groups and looked at how effectively different techniques for falling asleep worked. They found that the group instructed to count sheep took slightly longer to fall asleep than subjects who were given no instructions at all. When members of the sheep-counting group were instructed to imagine a relaxing scene, they fell asleep an average of 20 minutes sooner than they did on the sheep-counting nights. The scientists concluded that counting sheep can be too boring and can fail to hold your attention, letting those worries creep back in. Not to mention that your anxiety level is likely to rise sharply as you hit the 1,000th sheep, guaranteeing a long (sleepless) night.

Refocus your mind

Shift your focus away from any worrying, planning, ruminating — anything that increases your level of cognitive or physiological arousal. Put more simply, you want your thoughts focused on more relaxing stuff. Shift your attention to pleasant or emotionally neutral content that takes the place of any negative, unwanted, or stimulating thinking. You may start with some image or memory that you find pleasing — maybe a favorite past vacation, on a warm beach, with a piña colada in your hand. The choice is a personal one, so come up with your own content. You may have to experiment a bit. If you're pulled away from these pleasant images by intrusive worries, gently bring yourself back to more positive content.

Deal with specific, persistent worries

Sometimes a specific worry or set of concerns is so strong that it dominates your thinking. You may need other strategies. Try these:

>> **Jot it down.** Keep a small pad and pencil near your bed. Write down the worrisome problem or thought on a piece of paper and decide that you'll work on the problem the next day. This strategy gives you some closure and allows you to leave that little bit of business alone.

>> **Just stop it!** Whenever you catch yourself obsessing or worrying about something, visualize a stop sign. At the same time, silently yell the word *stop* to yourself. This approach temporarily interrupts your worrying. Then replace the worry with a welcome and pleasant thought or image. Keep repeating this process until you've sufficiently broken the worry cycle or fallen asleep. This technique takes a bit of practice, but it really works.

Chapter 20

Maintaining a Healthy Weight and Fitness Level

t's a sad story, but the vast majority of folks nowadays are on the fast track to fat like a runaway train in a summer blockbuster movie. The saddest part isn't so much the daily discomfort and inconvenience as it is the cumulative effects of lugging around those extra lipids. That added weight can actually take years off your life and possibly plague your days with illness and disease.

So what's a person to do? The good news is that obesity-related diseases and illnesses are preventable for the vast majority of people if they just lose the excess pounds and maintain a healthy body weight. This is also an excellent way to add healthy years to your life. And contrary to popular assumption, very few people actually have a genetic predisposition to weight gain because of variations in hormones and metabolism. This means that you have hope, although the sooner you act, the better. The solution is simple, but it isn't always easy.

Please don't sigh and flip to the next chapter. This chapter arms you with a lot of information so you can understand how your weight affects your overall health and life expectancy. It takes you through the process of reaching your fitness goals even when they seem overwhelming (minus all the fad diets and overhyped weight-loss strategies, of course). So read on. You'll find this chapter well worth your effort.

Understanding Healthy Body Weight

Determining your "perfect" weight from a table can be difficult for the simple reason that everybody is different. Some people have bigger bone structures, more muscle mass, and/or carry weight in different areas of the body. These variations in people's frames make using any tool that categorizes someone as overweight or obese difficult.

Your ideal body weight is the eventual weight that your body adjusts to when you have a consistently healthy approach to eating and exercise. Your body wants to naturally maintain this weight based on your physiologic makeup. It may take some time to determine this number if you have weight to lose or if you're underweight now.

REMEMBER

The most common method for determining your ideal weight is the *body mass index* (BMI), a mathematical calculation of a person's ideal mass (weight) based on his or her height and weight.

The BMI doesn't discriminate between muscle, fat, or bone. People who know that they're at their ideal weight based on their nutrition and other fat measurements can and should ignore the BMI; if you have a greater amount of muscle than most people, this generalized calculation isn't going to apply to you.

In general, however, a person's BMI score is a relatively good tool for people over the age of 18. It isn't accurate for pregnant women, weightlifters, competitive athletes (their extra muscle adds extra weight even though they aren't overweight), or people with various chronic illnesses (they can suffer from muscle wasting and malnutrition).

Calculating body mass

Figuring out your body mass index sounds like an exercise in quantum physics, but don't despair. Plenty of online tables exist to do the work of calculating your BMI for you, given your height and weight. However, if you're the mathematical

Approximately 30 illnesses and diseases are linked to being overweight. The following represent only a handful of these medical conditions:

>> **Arthritis:** Pain, stiffness, and loss of mobility of the hands, hips, back, and especially the knees are worse in people with a BMI of 25 or greater. The joints are put under a greater load of pressure that makes osteoarthritis (OA) more prevalent in obese people. Recent research has shown that a one pound weight loss unloads four pounds of stress from the knee joint when you're standing. No wonder losing just 10 to 15 pounds is likely to relieve arthritis symptoms. Less pressure on the joints means less pain.

>> **Cardiovascular disease:** Obesity increases a person's risk for heart disease due to its effect on blood lipid levels. The American Heart Association recognizes obesity as a major risk factor for heart attack. Weight loss helps blood lipid levels by lowering triglycerides and LDL (lousy) cholesterol and increasing HDL (healthy) cholesterol.

>> **Diabetes (type 2, adult onset, non-insulin-dependent diabetes):** The number of type 2 diabetics keeps increasing annually. As many as 90 percent of individuals with type 2 diabetes are reported to be overweight or obese. If you're overweight, losing as little as 5 percent of your body weight can reduce your high blood sugar and lessen your risk.

>> **High blood pressure:** More than 75 percent of high blood pressure cases are reported to be directly attributed to being overweight.

>> **Sleep apnea:** Between 60 and 70 percent of people who have *sleep apnea* (they temporarily stop breathing while they sleep) are obese. Obesity is the largest risk factor for developing this condition.

>> **Strokes:** People with a BMI over 25 increase their risk of *ischemic* stroke (from fatty deposits that obstruct blood vessels to the brain). Being overweight or obese is associated with high cholesterol, which leads to *atherosclerosis* (narrowing of the arteries) — a direct risk factor for strokes.

In addition to those direct links, consider the following facts:

>> National Cancer Institute experts concluded that obesity is associated with cancers of the colon, breast (postmenopausal), endometrium (the lining of the uterus), kidney, and esophagus.

>> Forty-two percent of those diagnosed with breast and colon cancers are obese.

>> Of all gallbladder surgery, 30 percent is related to obesity.

The good news is that being over your ideal weight isn't a disease with no cure but rather a condition with multiple cures. Achieving a healthy weight is something that's very attainable.

WARNING

The government started recording life expectancy in 1900. The current obesity epidemic may well lead to the first downward turn in those numbers in the future. The *New England Journal of Medicine* already projects that obesity will decrease life expectancy by close to a year; other researchers see life expectancy numbers dropping by as much as five years in the near future.

Assessing Your Current Level of Health

No one ever said losing weight was easy. Okay, maybe some people say that, but they're usually people who have never had any weight to lose. Listing what you have to do to lose weight is easy; finding the right combination of what works for you can end up being a lifelong pursuit. It's an all-out tug of war, with your body fighting to hang on to every pound.

So where do you begin? You may be mentally ready to take on the battle, but how do you know whether you're physically ready and able to begin a serious weight-loss and exercise program? This section tells you how to get ready for the battle of the bulge — check in with your physician before checking in at the gym. It also looks at what you need to know about your own health before you can tailor your workouts to be safe and beneficial. Finally, it covers different ways to look at body composition to help you know where you stand and measure changes as you improve.

Evaluating your fitness level

Before beginning an exercise routine, ask yourself, "What's my baseline fitness level?" Translation: How active are you? Are you overweight? Do you exercise now? How many minutes a week do you exercise? Do you lift weights or do aerobic exercise? These questions give you, your doctor, and/or your personal trainer an idea of what your basic fitness level is.

The best personal fitness assessment comes from a personal trainer. Some gyms include the cost of an assessment as part of your membership, although others don't. You may also want to contact a local personal trainer specifically for this service.

Here are some elements the test may include:

>> **Exercise history:** What type of exercise have you done in the last year? Walked to the mailbox at the end of the street? Ran a half-marathon?

Someone who's starting a fitness program for the first time is very different from someone who's just taken a six-month hiatus after a long history of routine exercise.

>> **Height and weight:** The quick and easy way to assess your body weight is the BMI. See the section "Calculating body mass" earlier in this chapter to calculate your BMI.

>> **Body composition:** This element is much more pertinent to the experienced exerciser than the beginner. Some people can use a more detailed breakdown of their body, but, for the majority, a basic BMI (see the previous bullet) works fine initially.

>> **Resting heart rate:** This number is important to know when figuring out your target heart rate during exercise.

>> **Resting blood pressure:** Everyone starting an exercise program needs to check his blood pressure. Exercise can help lower blood pressure if elevated, but you need to have a medical doctor evaluate and manage any elevations prior to beginning an exercise routine. If your blood pressure is normal, you can monitor it yourself. Many personal trainers will also monitor your blood pressure.

>> **Flexibility test:** You don't want to hurt yourself and end up in worse health than when you started. Look at your range of motion and evaluate muscle weakness and tightness to avoid injury.

>> **Strength and endurance testing:** This one tests muscle strength and the amount of time it takes to reach muscle fatigue. Having areas of the body that are weaker may cause problems with balance and posture.

>> **Post-test consultation and goal setting:** Understanding your overall fitness level and areas of concern or concentration helps you observe your progress (or lack thereof). Setting goals keeps you on track and allows you to monitor incremental improvements as they occur.

The post–test consultation determines the following issues:

>> The level of weights you should begin using

>> How many days a week you should train

>> How long you should train each workout day

>> Which muscle groups require the most work

Getting the green light from your primary physician

Checking with a doctor before starting an exercise routine or weight-loss program is much more than just a legal disclaimer, so don't let this advice go in one ear and out the other. Some conditions and symptoms may require medical attention prior to jumping into exercise, just to make sure that your new exercise plan is right for you. This is a safety precaution; always err on the side of caution and see your doctor if you have any concerns. This section takes a look at some important questions that help you decide whether your first step should be on a treadmill or into a doctor's office.

If you're starting an exercise routine that consists of walking or light weights and you have no medical conditions or complaints, you probably don't need medical clearance. If you're not sure whether you need to see a doctor before starting a new or restarting an old exercise program, go through this health questionnaire. A "yes" answer to any of these questions means that you should consult a medical doctor first:

>> Are you over the age of 40?

>> Are you overweight?

>> Do you smoke?

>> Have you been sedentary for a long time?

>> Are you starting an exercise program that involves more than walking or light weights?

>> Has a doctor told you that you have a heart murmur?

>> Has anyone in your family died of heart disease prior to the age of 55?

>> Do you have a high risk of coronary heart disease or stroke?

>> Do you have any medical conditions, such as high cholesterol, diabetes, high blood pressure, or kidney disease?

>> Do your ankles swell?

>> Have you experienced severe pain in your leg muscles while walking?

>> Do you get short of breath more than usual when you're performing routine tasks?

>> Have you fainted or do you have dizziness?

>> Have you experienced any abnormal heartbeats or chest pain either at rest or when exerting yourself?

You may have noticed that the first question in the list asks about your age. If you're over 40, you may be thinking, "Hey, I'm in the best shape of my life! Why are they singling me out?" Being over 40 doesn't mean that you're old. You're on this list because some experts believe that people over 40, regardless of whether they're at risk for heart disease or other medical conditions, should have a complete physical examination before starting or intensifying an exercise program. This exam identifies elevated blood pressure and other physical issues that may need treatment before you begin.

REMEMBER

Relax; there aren't many situations where your doctor tells you that you can't exercise in some fashion. People with heart disease used to be discouraged from exercising, but studies show that, in many cases, exercise under medical supervision is helpful for patients with stable heart disease. In one study, patients with heart disease who were as old as 91 increased oxygen consumption significantly after six months of supervised treadmill and stationary bicycle exercises. Remember, though, that it's often difficult for a doctor to predict health problems that may arise as the result of an exercise program. So if you're at risk for any health problems, be aware of related symptoms you have while you exercise and report these to your doctor.

After getting the green light to exercise, it's time to put your plan into action (before you change your mind).

Crunching your body composition numbers

The BMI determines body mass, not fat percentage. For the percentages, you need a *body composition analysis,* which splits your body weight into individual components: most commonly, lean mass and fat mass.

When people ask you what your lean body mass (lean muscle mass) is, you likely think that it's an indication of strength and muscle. *Lean body mass* is actually the weight of your tissues other than fat; muscles, bones, organs and fluids of your body, of which 50 to 60 percent is water. *Body fat mass* is the percent of the body that is fat and is an important number that sets the mark for the rest of the body analysis. To figure your body composition, you measure the percent of fat mass, and then subtract that number from 100 to get the percentage of lean mass.

The ideal fat percentages for men and women differ. Men have a normal range of 8 to 25 percent body fat while women should be in the range of 18 to 32 percent body fat. All the testing measures in the following sections are inexpensive options to discover more about your body makeup.

Measuring waist circumference: Accounting for the most dangerous form of fat

Just to make it more confusing, all fat isn't created equal — one type of fat has more potential health concerns than the other. People with central obesity (think beer bellies), or fat that is predominantly found in the abdomen (*visceral fat*, which is fat packed around the organs in the abdomen) tend to have more health-related illnesses than those with mostly *subcutaneous fat*, which is the type of fat just under the skin and is largely located in the thighs and buttocks. (See Figure 20-1 for an illustration.) Think apples versus pears.

The difference in danger between the two locales of fat lies in two causes:

» Visceral fat, also known as "organ fat," is nearer to the body's most vital organs than subcutaneous fat, so this fat is the kind that leads to the bulging belly better known as a beer belly.

» Visceral fat contains properties that increase the risk of insulin resistance, which causes diabetes.

The ideal waist measurement for women is less than 35 inches. For men, an ideal waist is less than 40 inches. Go over 35 inches for women or 40 for men, and you

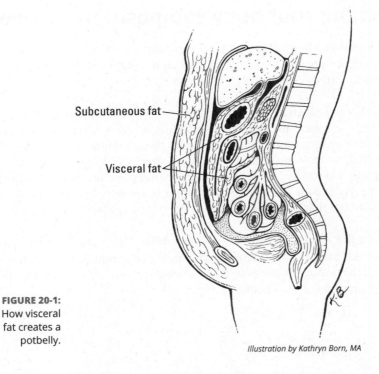

Subcutaneous fat

Visceral fat

FIGURE 20-1:
How visceral fat creates a potbelly.

Illustration by Kathryn Born, MA

increase your risks for health problems — regardless of height. If your BMI is in the normal range but your waist measurement isn't, go with your gut, literally — your waistline overrules your BMI on this one.

Liposuction is often sought after as a cosmetic procedure, but the fat it removes is just that — cosmetic. A study done by the *New England Journal of Medicine* found that because liposuction removes only subcutaneous fat, it doesn't have much effect on weight-related health risks.

Assessing overall fat and muscle percentages

A body composition analysis uses specific tools that calculate the percentage of body fat and muscle mass to determine a person's ideal weight. By far the most common tool is the simple *skinfold caliper,* a quick, cheap, and noninvasive device that most trained health or fitness professionals can use. It usually requires taking three measurements at different sites of the body (triceps, abdomen, and upper thigh) by pinching and measuring subcutaneous body fat at several points and then plugging these numbers into a formula that calculates body fat. Because the tool is manual, it may have a 3 to 5 percent error in measurement — the measurement can be affected by the skill level of the professional using the tool, and the measurement isn't accurate for very obese patients. (See Figure 20-2 for an illustration of how the skinfold caliper is used.)

FIGURE 20-2:
A skinfold caliper is a simple method for calculating your body fat percentage.

Illustration by Kathryn Born, MA

Other, less-common methods for measuring body composition include the following:

>> **Bioelectrical impedance:** This is a fairly inexpensive scale or handheld device that sends an electrical impulse through your body (don't worry; you can't feel it). It measures body fat by recording how easily the impulse is transmitted, because an electrical impulse travels through tissues with more water content (muscle) more easily than those with lower (fat). It gives a good sense of your body fat changes over time but may not be highly accurate. Readings can be easily affected by hydration status (the amount of fluids consumed, especially water), and muscle mass. Muscular athletes typically get higher-than-actual results.

>> **Underwater (hydrostatic) weighing:** This technique requires specialized equipment that includes a water tank with a mounted scale and chair and highly trained technicians to perform the test. While you're completely submerged in a tank of water, you breathe out all air from your lungs to decrease your tendency to float. The test measures body density, which is compared to your weight on land. When performed correctly, this assessment has less than a 3-percent error rate.

>> **Dual X-ray absorptiometry (DEXA):** This device is quick, easy, and very accurate, but it requires expensive equipment typically found only in hospitals and research centers. The DEXA is an X-ray of the body that shows fat, muscle, and bone mass based on differing densities.

>> **Bod pod:** You sit in the *bod pod,* an enclosed egg-shaped pod, for about five minutes while computers generate data from the sensors that determine the amount of air displaced by your body. These devices are available in most cities and are often used at local health fairs. Studies show that it's comparable to underwater weighing and DEXA, but more accurate. The major advantages are that the equipment is fairly inexpensive, it requires little training to operate, it's quick and easy, and it's comfortable for people of all shapes and sizes.

Custom-Designing Your Plan with Balance in Mind

With so many opportunities to supersize and so many unhealthy food choices prominently displayed in grocery stores, making healthy food choices and sticking to them in the long run is harder than ever. It's easy to yo-yo between starving yourself and stuffing yourself instead of settling comfortably in the middle (which is where you really need to be). After all, whether you spend your life worrying about your weight or neglecting it entirely, you're not living healthfully.

REMEMBER

The simple math is this: The cause of weight gain is eating more calories than you burn. Your body gains one pound for every 3,500 calories it doesn't use. People who exercise daily throughout their lives maintain their ideal body weight more easily than those who don't. It's that basic.

Counting calories for weight loss

Eating right is the best thing you can do for weight loss. Exercise is always important, but what you eat and how much is much more important in maintaining a healthy weight. If you exercise heavily for one hour every day of the week, but don't change your diet, you may not lose any weight. Everyone has a coworker, neighbor, or fellow gym attendee who exercises religiously for months but just doesn't seem to lose any weight, usually due to lack of dietary modifications.

You can find a lot of dieting options out there. Most options instruct that you drop your calories to between 1,200 and 1,800 calories based on exercise intensity and body size. The goal is to decrease your calorie intake by 500 calories below the minimum calories that you utilize in a day in order to lose one pound per week. This reduction in calories results in weight loss. A healthy weight-loss rate is one to two pounds a week.

Creating a safe and effective exercise program

The popular saying "What your mind can conceive, your body can achieve" is a great motto to live by. Everyone can live healthier and can improve in some areas.

After a doctor clears you to exercise, and you have some physical assessments done, you should be able to compile a personalized exercise program to follow. If you don't have the help of a personal trainer, set up a program based on your level of experience. This section guides the way.

Covering the bases: The components of a complete routine

A common misconception for people who are just starting a routine is to focus only on cardiovascular (*cardio*) or *aerobic* exercise. With aerobic exercise, your body burns energy stored in your muscles first and then burns fat. In *strength training* (anaerobic exercise), your body builds muscle. A true body transformation occurs most efficiently when you simultaneously gain muscle through strength training and lose fat through aerobic exercise and diet. It's like a tricycle — all three wheels have to turn at the same time to make it work effectively.

Keep these facts in mind as you build your personalized program:

>> **Aerobic training:** Activities like walking, jogging, swimming, rowing, and biking stimulate and strengthen the lungs and heart and use large muscle groups in your body (arms and/or legs). Any physical activity that makes you sweat, makes you breathe harder, and gets your heart pumping faster than it does at rest will do.

>> **Strength training:** Also called *resistance training*, activities like lifting weights or doing bench presses use resistance to make your muscles contract. It makes these muscle groups work harder, increasing their size and metabolism such that they use up more calories when they function. Strength training also helps maintain bone density.

Your body needs energy to sustain muscle mass because muscle cells are *metabolically demanding* (high-maintenance); for every pound of muscle you add, your body burns 30 to 50 more calories a day even at rest. How's that for a great bargain? (And those burned calories are more likely to come from fat reserves, which is really the whole point if your goal is to lose body fat.)

If you're just beginning a strength training routine, train for 20 to 30 minutes two to three days a week. If you're an old pro, you're most likely strength training 30 to 60 minutes four to five days a week, so keep it up. Don't forget to incorporate five to ten minutes of flexibility training to stretch your muscle groups before and after your strength training.

TIP

People over 60 who want to reduce their risk of falls and injury should start by strengthening legs, arms, and core muscles with two to three days of weight training a week for three to four weeks before walking long distances or engaging in aerobic exercise.

>> **Flexibility training:** To maintain good muscle health and reduce injury, incorporate flexibility training through stretching, yoga, and Pilates. These activities not only feel good but also increase the range of motion of your joints.

TIP

Aerobic exercise with weight training using lighter weights and more repetitions is better than weight training alone using heavy, bulking-type weights and exercises.

In order for your routine to work and be effective, it has to be something you want to do regularly. So while you decide what kind of workout you want (weight training and aerobics), where you're going to get it (at the gym or on the bike trail), and which days of the week to devote to which activity (Monday: gym, Wednesday: walk in the park, Thursday: swimming), personalize and work with your routine until it's comfortable. One trick to help you stay on track is to put your weekly plan on your personal calendar (or in your smartphone) on a Sunday night before you start your week. That way, you're more likely to stick to it.

Then, of course, you start working out. Many people are wonderful at putting plans together — and terrible at implementing them. The best exercise plan in the world won't do a thing for you unless you actually *do* it.

REMEMBER

People who have been sedentary for long periods (at least 6 to 12 months) may be at a higher risk for injury because muscle tone is weak, flexibility is limited, and balance is shaky. *Note:* Although most people consider walking the first step in becoming active, starting with strength training may be safer and more beneficial for people with limitations in their mobility (joint disease) or aerobic capacities (advanced heart or lung disease).

If you haven't had much experience in the gym, start with some basic training. Many fitness centers offer circuit training, which consists of multiple machines with instructions and displays of the muscle groups that they target. You cycle through the machines, targeting all the muscle groups. You can increase the intensity over time and concentrate on specific weak areas as you see fit. Aerobic activity can be worked into the schedule or you can alternate days between aerobic and strength training.

Factoring in your personality and lifestyle

When starting an exercise routine, you need to first evaluate your personality and lifestyle. If you create a routine that you don't enjoy, can't afford, or can't squeeze into your schedule, chances are good that you won't stick with it. Ask yourself the following questions:

» **What motivates me?** Motivation (or the lack of it) has the power to start and stop a routine as fast as lightening. A lot of people just won't do aerobic activities like running or biking but can play basketball or soccer for hours. Sports are a great source of exercise, and joining a league locks you into a schedule. Paying for a membership gets some people to commit to the gym because they want to get their money's worth. Make a bet or a deal with a colleague, friend, or partner that involves exercise or weight-loss goals. You can get motivated, but sometimes you have to be creative.

>> **Can I stick to my guns all on my own, or do I need the support of a group class, support group, planned weight-loss program, workout partner, or personal trainer?** Some people wake up one morning, make a decision to stop living life in an overweight or simply sedentary body, and change their habits instantly. Others have a bit more trouble following through. Maybe they need to socialize and engage with others who have the same goals to continue toward successfully achieving those goals. Do whatever works for you.

>> **What type of programs meet my health needs and interest me?** Carefully consider what keeps you coming back for more. For some people, various classes at the gym are helpful; for others, the commitment to an upcoming 5K or a mini-triathlon piques their interest. Some people train for the next Iron Man competition, and others with limiting health conditions may set a goal to maintain their current health.

>> **What resources are available to me, and how much money am I willing to spend?** You can find an exercise program for any budget. Remember that allocating funds for your health is an investment that can reduce medical visits, medications, and sick days. It could be the best money you spend!

>> **What time of day is best for me to work out?** There's really no perfect time of day that maximizes your workouts. Some researchers have tried to designate a particular workout time based on hormones and body rhythms, but no solid data is available. The best time of the day to workout is the time that's consistently available to you with the least interruptions (which makes you less likely to skip it).

Many people say that they don't have the time to exercise. That's ridiculous. If you can find the time for lunch, your morning coffee, a glass of wine before bed, or television, you can certainly find time to exercise. It's all a matter of setting priorities. *Everybody* can find two and a half to three hours per week to exercise. Maybe an exercise buddy can help you stay committed to regular exercise. You may have to set that alarm clock earlier or work out during lunch a few days out of the week while fitting in a quick meal before or after.

TIP

People who work away from the home statistically cancel workouts more often if they go home before heading to the gym or bike path. After you hit the couch, forget about it. You need to plan to do your exercising before you go home. If you don't, expect every excuse in the book to enter your mind after you walk through your front door.

FINDING A WEIGHT-LOSS PROGRAM THAT WORKS YOUR BODY, NOT JUST YOUR WALLET

If losing weight has been a losing battle for you, finding the best weight-loss program for you may be a bit like finding the proverbial needle in a haystack. People try programs and lose weight, only to gain it back again — and then some. Statistics consistently show that 90 percent of dieters fail, mostly after spending large sums of money for programs and supplements. *Maintaining* is the key in the weight-loss world, but maintenance in most programs is whispered about or promised with little success. Do your research to reduce the chance of becoming one of the failed-dieter statistics.

Before signing up for any weight-loss program, identify the factors that are most important to ensuring your success by considering the following questions:

- What does the menu plan look like? Are substitutions allowed? How many calories a day will you be eating? (Don't starve yourself; it isn't healthy. You should always be eating at least 1,000 calories a day.)

- Does the program promote drinking 80 to 100 ounces of water a day? (If not, move on to another program.)

- Does the program encourage exercising a minimum of one half hour a day, five days each week at some point?

- Does the program recommend checking with your doctor before starting weight-loss or exercise, or is it medically supervised?

- Does the program provide education on food and nutrition?

- Does the program use prescription appetite suppressants? Are they addicting? How long do you have to take them? Is there strict doctor supervision? Often use of appetite suppressants leads to regaining the weight you lost after the medicine is stopped.

- How much does the program cost? What does the cost include? Can you find client testimonials? Can you speak with any of those clients?

If you have a hard time staying motivated and dedicated to a plan, ask about the support throughout the program. Choose one that addresses your needs based on these questions:

- Will you have a personal weight-loss counselor or coach to help you reach your goals and answer your questions? If so, what is that person's availability (weekly appointments, phone, email, and so on)?

(continued)

(continued)

- Does the program include group support?

- Does the program offer a maintenance plan? If so, what's the format and length? What are the statistics on success rates?

Look into some of these healthy weight-loss programs:

- Jenny Craig (www.jennycraig.com)

- Nutrisystem (www.nutrisystem.com)

- The Trim Diet (www.trimlifestyle.com)

- Weight Watchers (www.weightwatchers.com)

- SparkPeople (www.sparkpeople.com)

Remember, no program magically causes permanent weight loss. Maintaining your weight loss takes persistence, dietary changes, and increased exercise after you get to your desired weight.

Getting the goods

You don't need to purchase expensive gym equipment to get a good workout. Sporting goods stores as well as major discount department stores have all sorts of products for use at home or in exercise classes. Many manufacturers feature products that run the gamut from the basics to complete home gym systems with all the bells and whistles. Of course, you do the workout, but what could be easier? Here's a list of some simple equipment to get you started:

TIP

>> **Handheld weights:** Hand weights (also known as *dumbbells*) are a must-have for any do-it-yourselfer. The most popular variety is vinyl-coated for comfort and easy grip and color-coded by weight. They range in increments from 1 to 10 pounds, and then go up to 12 and 15 pounds. If you don't want to buy weights, use cans of soup or 12-ounce plastic soda bottles filled with sand or water.

If you're adding hand weights to your daily walk, go light because there's a risk of joint inflammation and injury, especially if you use heavier weights and don't do adequate warm-up. If you're doing bicep curls, try a few reps in the store before you purchase. When your muscles fatigue at 15 repetitions, you've found a good starting weight.

>> **Resistance bands:** These bands are easy to use at any age or fitness level and offer your muscles a full range-of-motion workout. Resistance bands are long tubes that look like rubber jump ropes with handles. (Shorter versions come

without handles, but go for the longer ones — the most popular and versatile variety — because you can always shorten them up for working out your arms.) Resistance bands are color-coded to indicate their strength (thickness).

>> **Exercise stability balls:** Who would've thought that sitting on a big, round ball would be a workout? Seems like mere child's play until you try to balance yourself and realize that your body is using micro muscles you forgot you had. These balls offer numerous exercises that activate and strengthen those hard-to-reach core muscles often overlooked during normal training. The balls come in a variety of sizes according to your height. The most common are 55 cm (for people who are 5'1" to 5'7") and 65 cm (for people who are 5'8" to 6'1"), although they come as small as 30 cm and as large as 85 cm.

>> **Floor mat:** A *closed-cell* (moisture resistant) foam mat that's at least 5/8 inch thick is great to avoid slipping and provide comfort and support.

>> **Workout DVD:** You can find an endless variety of workouts for every age, lifestyle, and fitness level. Try one from your public library before you buy it or find a website with free videos for your use.

>> **Good quality shoes:** A comfortable and supportive pair of sneakers is essential. You don't have to spend a fortune on the latest in technology trainers either. Make sure your shoes have rubber soles and good arch support. More than anything, they should be comfortable. You may want to break them in before you wear them for your workout to avoid blisters. Good shoes are also important if you want to avoid knee pain. Many shoe manufacturers make cross trainers and other shoes for particular types of exercise. They need to be comfortably snug and have proper arch support and cushion to absorb the shocks of training. The wrong shoes can mean blisters, knee and back pain, and inflammation in the feet.

From trial to style: Making a (good) habit of it

Whatever the reason for starting an exercise routine, you need to have even better ones for keeping the fire burning. Too often, the smallest hurdle (a broken fingernail, a mild headache, or a friend saying, "Aw, do you have to work out today?") can put out that fire.

REMEMBER

Unfortunately, the people newest to the exercise scene seem to get sidetracked the most easily and have the hardest time getting back. Why? Most likely because exercise hasn't become an established way of life or a habit, like brushing their teeth and tying their shoes. If you're a newbie, the longer you delay returning to the schedule, the more you drag your feet going back to it.

So having the right expectation from the get-go is critical. In general, you need to follow a routine for 21 days in order for it to become habit. And to achieve a healthy body weight and maintain it, you must truly believe in making your exercise routine a regular habit.

To help avoid this pitfall, keep these suggestions in mind:

>> **Make exercise a priority.** Just like sleeping, eating, working, and spending time with your family — set a time in your schedule for exercise and stick to it.

>> **Practice saying "no."** You can do this in a kind but firm way. When friends and family try to interfere with your workout plans, say no.

Keep in mind, though, that your routine affects the people closest to you; it takes them time to adjust as well. When you're consistent in your regimen, it gets easier for everyone.

>> **Implement a system of checks and balances.** Every decision you make requires some sacrifice to keep things in balance. (No one can have it all, do it all, or eat it all and reach their goals.) Balance is the key to life, and weight loss is no different. Trying to lose weight requires sacrifices every day — but those sacrifices are balanced by the rewards. You have to get yourself ready by recognizing the difficult situations that make it hard to make those sacrifices. For instance, don't have candy in the house if you love candy. Environmental control promotes success. Out of sight, (hopefully) out of mind.

REMEMBER

Sacrifice is important, but torture is unnecessary. Make sure you have balanced alternatives in place to increase your chances of success. If you like coffee in the morning, have the coffee, but also drink more water. If you like to have a beer in the evening, switch to a light beer. If you want to have dessert on occasion, work out three days a week to balance out those calories. To succeed in the fitness world, finding balance is essential. When you establish balance, it becomes habit and a new lifestyle.

Evaluating the success of your efforts (and rewarding yourself along the way)

Sometimes, despite your best effort, you encounter the slump of discouragement and frustration, especially when you've tried to lose weight more than once only to gain it back. To bounce back from those self-defeating thoughts and feelings, refocus with the following methods:

>> Focus on the process rather than the end result.

>> Focus on what went well today (or this week) and your successes.

>> Use visualization and imagery techniques to focus on yourself (at your goal weight) participating in an enjoyable activity.

>> Focus on physical activity as an opportunity to do something enjoyable.

>> Put away the scale for a while and focus on making lasting lifestyle changes. As a result, the weight will come off.

Finding rewards at the end of your rainbow of sacrifices is easy. Every time you reach one of your goals, reward yourself. Every positive action deserves a pat on the back. Go shopping for some new (smaller) clothes. Take a mini-trip with a friend. Just make sure the goals you set are reasonable. Then you're more likely to attain them and feel successful, which motivates you to continue to improve.

When Weight Just Won't Come Off: Considering Weight-Loss Surgery

If you can't lose weight despite consistent dietary changes and physical activity, don't panic. Some people — although few — really do have medical reasons for weight gain and an inability to lose weight. Hormone imbalances, medications, and some genetic mutations can make weight loss difficult for some folks. Figuring out how to treat weight gain in these situations is now a major focus for many medical centers. If you've worked hard at weight loss and haven't seen significant results (meaning that you haven't moved out of the morbid obesity category after consistently following the kind of advice found in this chapter for six months and working with a physician to monitor your diet and exercise), you may want to consult a doctor who specializes in weight control.

The National Institutes of Health recommends that people with a BMI of 40 or greater (about 100 pounds overweight) and people with a BMI of 35 *plus* two or more significant obesity-related problems (like diabetes or high blood pressure) are appropriate candidates for weight-loss surgery.

If you're having a difficult time with your weight and have some other underlying medical conditions that raise the importance of weight loss, your doctor may decide that surgical treatment is the best option in your situation. But surgery should be the last resort for at least three reasons:

>> **Although it usually provides successful weight loss (at least in the short-term), no surgery is without risk.**

>> **Surgery isn't a miracle cure or quick fix for obesity.** Sure, it helps, but if you resume your bad habits after adjusting to life post-surgery, you can

actually undo the benefits of the surgery by stretching out a stomach that's been made smaller.

>> **The financial costs are high.** Sometimes insurance companies cover weight-loss surgeries, but with surgeries averaging $10,000 to $30,000, each person's provider must evaluate whether the benefits outweigh the medical risk and financial burden.

REMEMBER

People considering weight-loss surgery should exhaust *all* other options first. A dedicated lifestyle of nutritious eating on a reduced-calorie diet with vigorous exercise should always be the first course of action.

If your doctor and you do decide to go the surgery route, your options include the following:

>> **Stomach stapling:** This operation works on the premise that a smaller stomach pouch helps people lose weight because they feel fuller with less food. The size prevents people from overeating, and if they do eat too much, they feel ill.

>> **Lap-band:** Like stomach stapling, lap-band surgeries are less drastic and, therefore, more popular than bypass operations. A small adjustable band is placed around the upper part of the stomach, creating a smaller pouch, which limits the amount of food that you can eat at one time. However, patients can cheat more easily than they can with gastric bypass and stomach stapling because the anatomy of the stomach isn't as strictly reduced. As a result, weight reduction tends to be more limited.

>> **Gastric bypass:** This method involves altering stomach by creating a small pouch that restricts the amount of food that can be ingested and then attaching that pouch directly to the small intestine. About 10 to 20 percent of patients undergoing gastric bypass require follow-up operations to correct complications; the most common complaints are abdominal hernias. More than one-third of patients who have gastric bypass surgery develop gallstones. Gastric bypass is a major surgery reserved for severely obese individuals. Risks and benefits must be considered and evaluated very carefully.

Succeeding at the Hardest Part: Maintaining Your Healthy Weight!

Healthy eating is the biggest component of weight loss. Exercise definitely helps and is most important for burning off extra calories from those situations when you stray from your normal dietary habits such as vacations, parties, or just dessert after a good meal out. Weight maintenance, on the other hand, is the result of successfully incorporating good nutrition and routine daily exercise into your lifestyle. Many people can lose weight, but they gain the weight back quickly. Such yo-yo dieting by losing weight and gaining it back just to have to try to lose it again turns into a vicious, unhealthy cycle that you want to avoid.

Weight maintenance comes down to a few things:

>> Making consistently smart food choices

>> Staying committed to an exercise routine that's enjoyable and rewarding

>> Maintaining balance in your life and patience with yourself

>> Weighing yourself weekly; what you don't know *can* hurt you

>> Refusing to let "just a few little pounds" creep back up on you without taking immediate action

>> Setting goals that work for you, not for someone else

Moderation in life is apt to lead to more positive and long-lasting results than extreme approaches are. People who are able to successfully keep their weight down are the ones who have figured out how to make balanced choices. This isn't to say that you'll never eat another double fudge chocolate sundae — only that you've figured out how to make it part of your balanced choices. If you eat a sundae, sacrifice equivalent calories elsewhere or increase your exercise to burn the extra calories you took in. In the long run, maintaining a healthy weight is worth your effort.

Chapter 21

Considering a Plant-Based Diet

he goal of a plant-based diet is to eat more plants. Sounds simple enough — or maybe it doesn't. Eating nothing but plant-based foods is intimidating for a lot of people. Most people are comfortable with their current way of eating and are unsure about what to do with plants: Which ones should you eat and when? Can you get full on plants alone? Can you get all the protein you need from only eating plants? This chapter addresses these and other common questions.

It gives you an overview of how eating a plant-based diet can benefit so many aspects of your life — mainly your health. At the end of the day, it's all about feeling better, looking better, and just being better, and this way of eating can do just that.

But the plant-based diet isn't just about food; it's a framework for your well-being. Think of it as preventive healthcare. The money and time you invest now to better yourself through your diet pays off in leaps and bounds both sooner and later. How? So glad you asked. This chapter outlines the benefits of taking up a plant-based diet, from positive effects on sleep to weight-management and disease-fighting benefits. When you opt to transition to a plant-based diet, you make not only a positive lifestyle choice but also a smart health choice.

What Does "Plant-Based" Mean?

Eating a plant-based diet simply means eating more plants. No matter where you are or what you eat right now, you can eat more plants (everyone can). Of course, the goal of this chapter is to get you to eat predominantly (and, ideally, exclusively) plant-based all the time, but you'll likely have a transitional phase, and it starts with just eating *more* of the stuff that the Earth has so deliciously and naturally provided.

A few terms that are floating around represent a similar style of eating, yet they're all distinct. That doesn't mean you have to label yourself and stick with only that way of eating; these terms describe different ways of eating and help you understand what kinds of food choices fall within a certain category. Also, this breakdown can help you understand how a plant-based diet fits into the bigger picture.

>> **Plant-based:** This way of eating is based on fruits, vegetables, grains, legumes, nuts, and seeds with few or no animal products. Ideally, the plant-based diet is a vegan diet with a bit of flexibility in the transitional phases, with the goal of becoming 100 percent plant-based over time.

>> **Vegan:** This describes someone who doesn't eat anything that comes from an animal, be it fish, fowl, mammal, or insect. Vegans refrain not only from animal meats but also from any foods made by animals (such as dairy milk and honey). They often also abstain from purchasing, wearing, or using animal products of any kind (for example, leather).

>> **Fruitarian:** This describes a vegan diet that consists mainly of fruit.

>> **Raw vegan:** This is a vegan diet that is uncooked and often includes dehydrated foods.

>> **Vegetarian:** This plant-based diet sometimes includes dairy and eggs.

>> **Flexitarian:** This plant-based diet includes the occasional consumption of meat or fish.

Getting to the Root of a Plant-Based Diet

A core of foods make up a plant-based diet. Making sure that you really understand them is key for a strong foundational knowledge that you can continuously build on. You'll find so many wonderful foods to explore and try, but for now here are the basics on what foods to include and what foods to avoid.

What's included

The big question is, "If I'm not eating anything from an animal, what is there to eat?" There is a wonderful world of plants that you should get to know quite well on this journey. You'll find all sorts of diverse foods to enjoy (if you're new to this, prepare to be pleasantly surprised by what you find).

Valuable vegetables

You'll discover a whole array of veggies that you'll likely get to know quite well while eating plant-based. If you're new to this approach, you'll probably stick to tried-and-true, familiar veggies in the beginning because they'll feel safe — and that's okay. But over time, expand into new areas and pick up that funny-looking squash over there or try that wild, leafy bunch of something over here. Here's a starter kit:

>> Beets

>> Carrots

>> Kale

>> Parsley, basil, and other herbs

>> Spinach

>> Squash

>> Sweet potatoes

Fantastic fruits

Ahhh, the sweet juiciness of fresh fruit. If you don't love it, you need to get on this train because fruits are delicious; sweet; full of fiber, color, and wonderful vitamins; and so, *so* good for you. Here are some top picks to start with:

>> Apples

>> Avocados

>> Bananas

>> Blueberries

>> Coconut

>> Mangos

>> Pears

>> Pineapples

>> Raspberries

>> Strawberries

Wonderful whole grains

Consuming good-quality whole grains is a healthy part of a plant-based diet. Don't worry; you can still have your breads and pastas, but "whole" is the key word here. You don't want refined or processed — you want the real thing. When you buy these items, make sure the grain itself is the only ingredient. Although it's possible to buy proper whole grains off the shelf in packaging, make sure you double-check the label to confirm that it is, indeed, a whole grain (and only a whole grain). Here are some good ones:

>> Brown rice

>> Brown-rice pasta

>> Quinoa

>> Rolled oats

>> Sprouted-grain spelt bread

Lovable legumes

Learning to love beans on a plant-based diet is key because they're a great source of sustenance, protein, and fuel. It may take you and your body a little while to get used to them, but soon enough they'll be your friends — especially when you discover how great they are in soups, salads, burgers, and other creative mediums. Here are some of the best to start with:

>> Black beans

>> Chickpeas (garbanzo beans)

>> Kidney beans

>> Lentils

>> Split peas

Notable nuts and seeds

Most people love a good handful of nuts! But the thing about eating them on a plant-based diet is making sure that they're unsalted, un-oiled, and raw. As long as you enjoy them in their natural state, you can feel free to eat them in moderation alongside your other wonderful plant-based foods. Here are the best ones to start with:

>> Almonds

>> Cashews

>> Chia seeds

>> Flaxseeds

>> Hempseeds

>> Pumpkin seeds

>> Sunflower seeds

>> Walnuts

TIP

Try munching on a few nuts or seeds straight up or adding them to salads or other recipes. And if you can't decide which one you have a taste for, toss them all in a trail mix.

The extras

This category of foods isn't really a category, per se, but these foods are still part of the plant-based diet. This includes such things as exotic superfoods, sea vegetables, condiments, and natural sweeteners. Here are some specific examples:

>> **Cacao:** The pure form of chocolate

>> **Coconut oil:** Raw, virgin unprocessed oil (and the perfect butter substitute)

>> **Honey:** The raw stuff, not the kind in bear-shaped plastic bottles

>> **Maple syrup:** Again, the real stuff — no corn syrup here

>> **Nori:** A delicious and nutritious sea vegetable

>> **Tamari:** A versatile fermented soy sauce

What's off limits

As mentioned earlier in the chapter, you may need or want a transitional period during which you wean yourself off animal-based foods one at a time until you can avoid all things from the animal world — including meat, poultry, fish, eggs, milk, and other dairy products. In addition, because this is a clean way of living, you want to cut out most processed and fried foods that don't serve your body and your health on a nutritional level.

REMEMBER

Of course, this is the ideal — you have to find your own place on the spectrum of plant-based eating and do what works for you. Often, making something off limits just makes you want it more, so you have to strike the balance between being tough on yourself and being practical. It's one thing to eat animal product food once or twice a week, but it's another thing if you eat it daily. Figure out what level of plant-based eating makes you most comfortable. Just realize that it doesn't have to be all or none.

It's Not a Diet, It's a Lifestyle

The plant-based diet isn't the new fad or the latest thing that makes you lose a certain amount of weight in a certain amount of time. It's about changing your habits to the core. It's more than just a decision to change your food choices; it's a decision to change everything that comes with it.

How are you eating, when are you eating, and what else are you doing that can enhance, help, and sustain this lifestyle? Who else is on board with you? Do you have support? When you make a commitment to eat well, that commitment has to extend into all areas of your life. Eating is one of the main daily concerns we have as human beings. We need to tend to our diet in order to survive. Without food, we don't live. But without food there is no pleasure of taste and ultimately no health. A plant-based diet ensures that you get all of those needs met.

Any decision you make can positively impact you for the rest of your life. That is what the field of lifestyle medicine is all about (see the nearby sidebar). The truth is that when you embrace a healthy lifestyle, you get results. You sleep better, have more energy, notice better hair and skin, and improve your vitality. Heck, you may even lose that extra weight along the way.

The following sections explain some of the benefits and general principles that may become part of your new lifestyle, from eating more greens to coping with your body's reaction to the additional fiber you'll consume.

Appreciating the power of greens

The earth isn't half green for no reason. We were *meant* to eat greens. In fact, half of your plate at mealtime and at least half of what you eat daily from the plant world should be green.

Greens are the life force of the vegetable kingdom. Green leafy vegetables like kale, collards, Swiss chard, and spinach carry with them all the nutrients you need to thrive. They have everything from protein to trace minerals to calcium, and so much more — and guess what? They're low in calories! You can eat as many of them as you want, and they only help you get healthier. How is that for a deal? And there are lots of ways to make them taste good, too. You can get these guys into your body in myriad ways, from juices and smoothies to soups, sandwiches, salads, and more.

These powerful vegetables are the key to health. They help enliven and enrich your cells from the inside out. As long as they're kept in their prime and not over-cooked (meaning, staying green and not cooked to grey or brown), they can give you all the goodness they have.

Here are the best greens to start with, from sweetest to most bitter:

>> Lettuce

>> Spinach

>> Broccoli

>> Kale

>> Swiss chard

>> Bok choy

>> Collards

>> Arugula

>> Dandelion greens

>> Mustard greens

And here are some ideas of where you can add greens:

>> **Green juices:** Go to a store where they make fresh juices and test the waters. If you have a juicer at home, give it a go — soon, you'll be adding greens to every juice.

>> **Smoothies:** Add a handful of spinach or kale to your next fruit smoothie. You don't taste them, but you still get all the beneficial nutrients.

>> **Salads:** You don't have to use just lettuce. Try chopping kale and chard into bite-size pieces and adding them to your next salad. A salad allows you to get all the enzymes and nutrients greens have to offer in their raw state.

>> **Sandwiches:** Dress a sandwich with any green you want to add a little crunch.

>> **Soups and stews:** You can chop up greens and add them to your soup to give it a little texture. For those picky eaters, puree the leafy greens into a soup — they'll never know!

>> **Stir-fries:** Slice greens really thin and sauté them with olive oil and garlic, and then drop them into different recipes or serve them alongside other dishes.

>> **Pastas:** Add fresh greens at the end of the cook time for your pasta or sauce. Warm them up a bit to wilt them so they combine more easily with the pasta. (And the greens add a fun dose of color as well as nutrients.)

TIP

Try one new green a week. It's important to rotate your greens because each provides a slightly different array of nutrients to your diet.

Focusing on quality, not quantity

It's not about how much you eat; it's about *what* you eat. In fact, the amount you eat on a plant-based diet is irrelevant. That may shock you, given that most diets are so focused on portion size, calories, and grams of carbs and fats. Restricting food and calories is *not* the key to health. It's about what's in the food, what it's made up of, and what's in that recipe or box that counts. You should be so connected to your food that you become obsessed with ingredients and what's in your meals as opposed to how much your plate weighs. You may actually start to feel lighter just knowing you can let go of that concept here and now.

TIP

Try focusing on eating foods in their whole forms, not out of a package. Try to introduce at least one new whole food a week as you transition, while at the same time eliminating processed foods. Eat plants as grown.

It's all in the genes: Understanding and working with your code for health

People love to make the excuse that it's in their genes to eat a certain way or to give in to being overweight because their parents are. That's bananas. Yes, your genes do play a significant role and help to make up who you are. But they're not the be-all and end-all; you can work with them and around them. You can use your genes as a template, but don't let them lock you in. Let them help you understand who you are and how you can overcome them.

You may be prone to thyroid disease, cancer, diabetes, or osteoporosis (everyone is, to some extent). Instead of focusing on that, focus on how you can prevent or reverse the disease. If you have a family history of an illness or malady, diet can become an important part of your effort to avoid it. You don't have to be the next victim. You can do something about it.

Forging ahead with fiber

You can never see enough commercials telling you to eat more fiber; we are a society that lacks fiber because of not only the processed food but also the meat and dairy that the average North American eats, all of which have no fiber. It's a pretty sad state of affairs, actually. Luckily, the plant-based diet is full of fiber; in fact, you can't get away from it. Here is why fiber is so fabulous:

>> **Keeps you regular:** Fiber is the roughage from fruits and veggies. When it's in your body, your digestive system has no choice but to push the fiber and other things along and out, which makes for healthy daily deposits in your toilet bowl.

   Note: It's ideal to have a bowel movement at least once a day, but some people may not be so lucky. The goal is consistency, quantity, and ease of elimination.

WARNING

   Of course, it can work against you, too. If you're prone to constipation, your body may take a little longer to get used to the fiber from whole foods, so take it slow when introducing them into your diet.

>> **Keeps you fuller longer:** Fiber means bulk, which means you're fuller and therefore more satisfied. Fibrous foods send signals to your brain telling you that you're full much sooner than foods with no fiber. Therefore, you may find that you eat less than you're used to when you eat fiber-rich foods. Also, fibrous foods require more chewing because of the roughage, so it may take you longer to chew, swallow, and digest.

TIP

   Eating high-fiber foods — which take longer to eat — can mean that you ultimately eat less because your brain has more time to process the "I'm full" signal.

>> **Adds more texture to your foods:** The diversity of texture that fiber offers to your plate is exceptional. Each fruit, vegetable, and whole grain has its own complexity of fiber, which adds to the diversity in your meals.

WARNING

In the beginning, fiber may not seem like your friend. When you first introduce all the roughage, skins, seeds, and other textures of plants, your gut may have a not-so-fun time getting used to it all. Stick it out. Just eat it for a bit. You may feel gassy, bloated, and just "full" all the time, but your gut needs to get used to this and figure out how to pass these new foods along. When it starts working properly, you'll find that you depend on natural fiber from whole foods, not store-bought powders, to keep you going every day.

Because fiber draws water out of your body, drink lots of water when you eat fibrous foods to help it move along.

Answering Common Questions about a Plant-Based Diet

As with anything new, considering a plant-based diet can bring up all sorts of questions and concerns. Here are five of the most common questions about taking up a plant-based diet.

Can I get full eating only plants?

Absolutely! The wonderful thing about eating plants is that you're eating lots of fiber, and fiber makes you full. Also, the more wholesome the plants are (in other words, not processed), the more nutrients you're eating, which helps make you feel more satisfied. As the nutrients load your cells with vitamins and minerals, you feel pleasantly full but not stuffed.

Also, the diversity of texture can help with this. Because so many plant foods require you to chew more, you actually spend more time getting through the meal. So a big bowl of salad with lots of stuff in it may not seem that heavy, but it can fill you up quite fast.

How do I get protein?

This is always the big question. There's a big answer: from so many different places. A plant-based diet has so much protein, you may not even believe it. Although it may not seem like the grams of protein add up to the amount of protein you find in meat, what you soon realize is that it's not about the quantity but rather the quality. The standard American diet provides too *much* protein, and this can cause many chronic illnesses. Plant-based protein sources like legumes, nuts, seeds, quinoa, tempeh, avocado, and green leafy veggies all have their own breakdown of amino acids, which build up inside your body to make a complete protein. The best part is that they absorb into your body much better than animal-based protein. You don't feel that same heaviness eating plant-based protein as you do eating meat.

What about calcium?

What about calcium, you ask? Well, did you know that plant-based foods like sesame seeds, hempseeds, bok choy, carob, and figs are extremely rich in calcium? Almost more so than a glass of dairy milk. It may be hard to get your head around, but in most cultures, the less dairy is consumed, the more calcium is absorbed by the body.

So fret not — just because you have "grown-ups" thinking you need a glass of milk to get your daily dose of calcium, that doesn't mean these so-called experts are right. Turns out, you can eat almonds, seeds, and greens and get the same amount of calcium in your body. You don't feel bloated, either, as these sources of calcium are loaded with vitamins and minerals, making the nutrients much easier to absorb.

How do I get iron? Won't I become anemic?

Iron is definitely an area of concern for anyone not eating meat, so you need to be a bit more cautious to make sure you're consuming enough of plant-based sources such as these:

>> Dark leafy greens

>> Seaweeds

>> Nuts

>> Seeds

>> Legumes

>> Dried fruit

REMEMBER

Many people — even athletes and the like — survive and even *thrive* without meat.

Does eating plant-based help people lose weight?

People should never choose to eat a specific way for weight loss. This approach never proves to have beneficial long-term results and always backfires on people if their weight-loss plans aren't aligned for true health reasons. Focusing solely on weight loss or calorie counting can be extremely detrimental and can take up a lot of brain power and energy.

The good news is that by following a plant-based and healthy lifestyle, you start to feel great and lose weight naturally. When you focus on eating well-balanced and nutrient-dense meals, your body isn't deprived, and it starts to function efficiently. Deprivation isn't an option.

A Quick Guide to Making Plant-Based Eating Part of Your Everyday Life

You can start with simple ways to add plant-based foods to your existing diet. Here are a few suggestions to help you get started today:

>> **Replace one to three meals a week with plant-based ones.**

>> **Include healthy meat alternatives,** such as beans, legumes, nuts, and fermented soy, in place of meat in your meals.

>> **Choose healthy alternatives to dairy,** such as rice milk, almond milk, and hempseed milk, or try avocado and cashews in place of cheese.

>> **Explore new vegetables.** Go beyond your usual choices and experiment with new colors and different green leafy vegetables.

>> **Have a smoothie for breakfast.** Swap out bacon and eggs for a nutritious blended fruit smoothie to get you going in the morning.

>> **Swap out butter for coconut oil.** You can spread it on toast, use it in baking, and substitute it anywhere else you'd use butter or margarine.

>> **Pack power snacks.** Don't lurk around the vending machines, which are filled with non-plant-based ingredients in processed candy and chips. Bring trail mix (nuts, seeds, and dried fruit) to work or keep a small container of it handy at all times.

>> **Make a simple veggie dinner at least one night a week.** If you're just getting started, change up at least one of your meat-centered meals to something plant-based yet familiar, like a vegetable stir-fry, hearty soup, or pasta.

Eating According to a Plant-Based Food Guide

You've probably seen some version of a food guide — a graphic representation of food categories divided into segments. The more space a food group takes up, the more you're supposed to eat of it to maintain a healthy diet. Many traditional food guides include meat or protein, fruit, vegetable, grain, and dairy categories. Vegetarian food guides are also available to help guide your dietary choices.

This way of grouping foods to provide a one-size-fits-all way of eating isn't necessarily ideal for or relevant to everyone. Take all food guides in stride. How much you eat and what you choose to eat need to apply directly to you and your lifestyle, activity level, and health concerns.

The plan can be adjusted in cases of disease or food sensitivities, but for the most part this is an excellent foundation for superior health. Here's how this breakdown looks on a daily basis:

REMEMBER

» Fruits and vegetables

- These should make up a majority of your overall food intake, approximately 40 percent to 60 percent, with an emphasis on leafy green veggies.

- Include at least four servings of vegetables, three of which are raw, and make sure at least one serving is green vegetables and one or more servings are starchy and colorful, such as beets, carrots, or sweet potatoes.

- Use fresh vegetables whenever possible. If not, use frozen vegetables over canned vegetables, which usually contain large amounts of salt.

  Not all frozen veggies are the same. Many frozen vegetables are even more nutritious than fresh vegetables because they're frozen at their peak ripeness, which means they maintain their nutrients. Be sure to look for organic and non-genetically modified frozen (and fresh) vegetables.

- Include sea vegetables, such as arame, nori, and dulse.

- Have one to two (or more) servings of fresh fruit, preferably in season and organic.

» Whole grains

- Eat two to five servings.

- Focus on gluten-free whole grains, such as brown rice, quinoa, millet, and buckwheat.

- Choose alternatives to whole wheat as often as you can (kamut, spelt, rye, barley, and oats).

- Choose sprouted-grain products as often as you can.

» Proteins

- Have at least two servings, one of which is ½ cup of legumes, beans, tempeh, or tofu.

- If you're using plant-based protein supplements (such as hemp, pea, or brown-rice powders), use one scoop per day.

Protein supplements aren't usually necessary to obtain adequate protein on a plant-based diet because plant protein is abundant in many sources, such as nuts, seeds, fruits, vegetables, and whole grains. Therefore, be careful not to consume excessive amounts of protein. Focus on quality protein and not quantity.

>> Fats and oils

- Eat one serving (approximately ¼ cup) of nuts or seeds.

- Have one tablespoon of nut or seed butters.

- Use one tablespoon of oil for cooking or in salads. Grapeseed, coconut, and olive oils are good for cooking; reserve flax, hemp, and chia oil for foods that don't require heating.

- Enjoy one or more servings of whole fatty fruits, such as avocados, coconuts, and olives. This can be in the form of one quarter of an avocado, four olives, or ¼ cup fresh coconut meat.

Stick to these serving sizes of nuts, seeds, nut butters, and oils to get the nutritional benefits without packing on the pounds.

These are just general guidelines and suggestions to help get you started with your new plant-based lifestyle. As you become accustomed to these guidelines, adapt them accordingly to what works best for you.

Don't get too caught up in exact amounts or measurements of food or servings. As long as you're eating a well-rounded and balanced diet, your body gets what it needs. It's important to follow some general guidelines to get started, but in time you'll start to trust yourself because your body knows best.

Feeling Good with Food

Although it sounds simple, feeling good is really important. When you don't feel good, all other aspects of your life get out of balance — you can't be your optimal self, either personally or professionally. Luckily, you have an ace up your sleeve: proper nutrition. You have control over your diet every day, and you can choose what goes into your mouth. Choosing a plant-based diet can be extremely powerful in your quest to stay healthy. You may find that after you make the switch to this diet, you start to feel better, lose weight, have more energy, and sleep better. The following sections detail these benefits of a plant-based diet.

Weight management

Changing over from animal foods to plant foods means you consume far less saturated fat and fewer dense calories that can lead to weight gain. The calories and nutrients that come from plant-based foods do so much more for you, in terms of helping with metabolism and many functions in the body. By eating more fiber and nutrient-dense foods, you generally don't eat as much in one sitting. This may encourage you to eat more frequent meals, which is incredible for weight loss. Meat and dairy products are heavy and filled with saturated fat, and they pack on the calories. A plant-based diet is lean and efficient, preventing you from taking in food that just turns into fat.

People sometimes get hung up on the fact that following a plant-based diet means consuming more carbohydrates. That may be true, but it doesn't necessarily mean you'll gain weight. The key is to choose carbs that are high in fiber and contain lots of other nutrients. Your body digests them well and uses them for energy. You gain weight from carbs when you eat beyond your needs or you eat carbohydrates made from refined grains like spongy white bread.

TIP

When eating a plant-based diet, be sure to choose complex carbs (such as quinoa, sweet potatoes, apples, and rolled oats) that are rich in vitamins, minerals, and protein, and enjoy them in moderation. Stay away from simple carbs (such as sugars, breads, and pastas made with refined grains). If you follow those general guidelines, you can still reach your weight goals.

Energy and vitality

Within days of consuming more green, leafy veggies and fruits, you feel more energized. This is a result of the water content of these foods, which hydrates your body, providing your cells with more oxygen (as compared to meat), and it's also because of the life force running through these foods. They're filled with vitamins and minerals that infuse directly into your blood system, helping your body detoxify and rejuvenate itself. Heavy animal-based foods, such as meat and dairy, can weigh you down, decrease your energy, and make you tired. Plant-based foods are lighter and easier to digest.

Better sleep quality

When you eat better, you sleep better. When you nourish your body during the day with regular plant-based meals, you may find, in time, that the quality of your sleep is better. Many plant foods, such as green, leafy vegetables that are rich in magnesium and calcium, can help the body relax for a peaceful sleep. Other plant-based foods, such as whole grains, help the body produce serotonin, which has a calming effect on the body. Eating a plant-based diet doesn't necessarily mean you get more sleep — just better sleep. In fact, you may find that you need less sleep.

TIP

If you have problems sleeping, try having a banana, some oatmeal, or some almond butter on toast. These foods tend to help the body and the nervous system relax at night by causing the body to release the hormones required for a restful sleep. You can also try drinking herbal tea, such as chamomile, because it has a calming effect on the body and can aid in falling asleep.

Becoming a Wellness Warrior

By committing to a plant-based diet, you become a warrior of your own wellness — a soldier defending your health. A plant-based diet can go a very long way in this fight — specifically in helping to prevent many diseases. Common diseases like cancer, diabetes, heart disease, and osteoporosis have all been known to be lessened or even reversed with a high-quality plant-based diet that is rich in fiber, phytonutrients, and protein.

The following sections explain how to prevent, minimize, or eliminate certain health conditions by following a plant-based diet. However, please be sure to talk to your doctor or healthcare practitioner before making any significant dietary changes.

Cancer

Plant-based diets are effective against cancer because they're jam-packed with *phytonutrients* — the chemicals in plants that help prevent disease and infection. The more of them you eat, the better you feel, and the more you help yourself beat the odds of cancer.

If you want to prevent or fight cancer, focus on a diet that is rich in

>> **Colorful fruits and vegetables,** such as blueberries, mangos, grapes, squash, tomatoes, and cucumbers

>> **Green leafy vegetables,** such as kale, bok choy, collards, and Swiss chard

>> **Whole grains,** such as quinoa, brown rice, millet, and amaranth

>> **Legumes,** such as lentils, split peas, and mung beans

>> **A variety of healthy nuts and seeds,** such as almonds, pumpkin seeds, and sunflower seeds

Diabetes

Diabetes is becoming one of the leading diseases and causes of death in North America. With fast food, sugary snacks, and soda pop at everyone's fingertips, it's no wonder that this blood-sugar disorder has become so prevalent. Before you need to go on medication or inject yourself with insulin, understand that a plant-based diet has been known to dramatically shift and even reverse type 2 diabetes. For the most part, people living with type 2 diabetes can greatly control their disorder through their food choices.

REMEMBER

Those living with type 1 diabetes will never eliminate their need for insulin because their bodies don't make it naturally. However, by adopting a plant-based lifestyle, they may be able to keep their insulin doses to a minimum and reduce the risk of complications.

Type 2 diabetes occurs when your pancreas doesn't produce enough insulin or your body doesn't properly use the insulin it makes. As a result, glucose (sugar) builds up in your blood instead of being used for energy.

Here is a quick rundown of plant-based foods that have special properties for maintaining a healthy blood-sugar level:

>> **Avocado** contains a sugar that depresses insulin production, which makes it an excellent choice for people with *hypoglycemia* (low blood sugar). Try adding some slices of avocado to a piece of toast, blend it into a smoothie, or toss it in a salad. Guacamole is delicious too. Ideally, you should eat a quarter of an avocado several times per week.

>> **Soybeans and other legumes,** such as kidney beans, lentils, black-eyed peas, chickpeas, and lima beans, slow the rate of absorption of carbohydrates into the bloodstream because of their high protein and fiber content. Ultimately, this slower absorption can reduce spikes in blood sugar. Try making a dip with different kinds of beans or tossing them into a salad. They even make great veggie burgers. Eat at least ½ to one cup of legumes a day.

>> **Onions and garlic** normalize blood-sugar regulation by decreasing the rate of insulin elimination by the liver. Onions and garlic are the base of most soups and stir-fries, so consider sautéing them for your next meal. Try to consume half a clove of garlic twice a day and one onion per day.

>> **Other blood-sugar-controlling foods** include berries (especially blueberries); celery; cucumbers; green, leafy vegetables; sprouts; string beans; parsley; psyllium; ground flaxseed; chia seeds; lemons; oat bran; radishes; sauerkraut;

sunflower seeds; squash; and watercress. Many of these items can be combined into smoothies, breakfast cereal, or a colorful salad or grain dish.

Beyond knowing what foods are good to eat, knowing how and when to eat them can be vital in keeping diabetes in check. Here are some additional tips for naturally regulating your blood-sugar levels with plants:

>> **Eat a balanced plant-based breakfast every day.** Doing so helps kick your metabolism into gear, which is needed for proper sugar and insulin processing.

>> **Eat several small meals/snacks throughout the day rather than three large meals.** Even eating a small snack before bed may help. Eating more frequently helps keep blood-sugar levels in balance. You don't want to consume large, heavy meals because they can be hard for the body to digest. Additionally, excess food means excess calories, which can increase blood-sugar levels in the body and cause weight gain.

>> **Eat a diet high in fiber.** Fiber doesn't raise blood-sugar levels; instead, it helps with sugar digestion and elimination. Choose whole grains and legumes and include large amounts of vegetables (especially dark, leafy greens; squash; green beans; sweet potatoes; tofu; and whole fresh fruits).

>> **Use natural, low-glycemic sweeteners, such as brown-rice syrup, coconut sugar, and stevia — but only infrequently and in very small amounts.** These sweeteners have a low impact on blood-sugar levels and don't cause them to spike as much as white or brown sugar, which you should avoid completely.

>> **Stay away from highly fatty and fried foods because they typically contain excess processed oils, which can affect blood-sugar levels and increase caloric intake.** Instead, choose healthy fats, oils (avocado, coconut, olive, or other cold-pressed natural oils), raw nuts, and seeds.

>> **Remove alcohol, processed foods, sulfured dried fruits, table salt, white sugar, saturated fats, soft drinks, and white flour from your diet.** Also avoid food with artificial colors and preservatives. These foods are extremely refined and have little to no nutritional value. They can contribute not only to an increase in sugar intake (of the worst kind) but also to weight gain because they're all forms of empty calories. People with diabetes should focus on foods that are rich in vitamins, minerals, and nutrients and are beneficial to their blood-sugar levels and overall well-being.

Heart disease and hypertension

When it comes to heart health, a plant-based diet is really the only way to go. Because animal-based foods are loaded with fat and cholesterol that build up in your arteries, causing high blood pressure and worse, you need to avoid them completely if you're at risk for or have heart disease. Luckily, plenty of plant-based foods can provide your heart with maximum nutrition. These foods are all from whole sources. A diet rich in these foods not only helps your heart but also promotes an overall state of optimal health and well-being. Tables 21-1, 21-2, and 21-3 outline foods that are especially beneficial for your heart.

TABLE 21-1   ## Heart-Friendly Proteins, Grains, Nuts, and Seeds

Food	Vitamins and minerals	Ways to enjoy
Black or kidney beans	B-complex vitamins, niacin, folate, magnesium, omega-3 fatty acids, calcium, and soluble fiber	Stir some beans into your next soup or salad.
Tofu and tempeh	Niacin, folate, calcium, magnesium, and potassium	Thinly slice firm tofu or tempeh and marinate for several hours before baking, grilling, or stir-frying.
Brown rice and quinoa	B-complex vitamins, fiber, niacin, and magnesium	Cook up a pot and make pilafs or soups, or top it with a colorful vegetable stir-fry.
Oats	Omega-3 fatty acids, magnesium, potassium, folate, niacin, calcium, and soluble fiber	Top hot oatmeal with fresh berries for a heart-healthy breakfast. Oatmeal and raisin cookies also make a "hearty" treat.
Almonds	Omega-3 fatty acids, vitamin E, magnesium, fiber, heart-favorable mono- and polyunsaturated fats, and phytosterols	Mix a few raw organic almonds into coconut milk yogurt, trail mix, or fruit salads.
Flaxseed (ground)	Omega-3 fatty acids, fiber, and phytoestrogens	Hide ground flaxseed in all sorts of foods — coconut yogurt parfaits, morning cereal, homemade muffins, or cookies.
Pumpkin seeds	Protein, omega-3 fatty acids, iron, zinc, phosphorus, vitamin A, calcium, and B-complex vitamins	Eat them raw in trail mixes, salads, and granola, or toast them lightly for an extra boost of flavor.
Walnuts	Omega-3 fatty acids, vitamin E, magnesium, folate, fiber, heart-favorable mono- and polyunsaturated fats, and phytosterols	Walnuts add heart power with a flavorful crunch to salads, pastas, cookies, muffins, and pancakes.

TABLE 21-2   **Heart-Friendly Vegetables**

Food	Vitamins and minerals	Ways to enjoy
Acorn squash	Beta-carotene and lutein (carotenoids), B-complex and C vitamins, folate, calcium, magnesium, potassium, and fiber	Serve with sautéed spinach, pine nuts, or raisins.
Asparagus	Beta-carotene and lutein (carotenoids), B-complex vitamins, folate, and fiber	Grill or steam slightly, then dress with lemon.
Beets	Calcium; iron; magnesium; phosphorous; and vitamins A, B-complex, and C	Shred some raw into salad or steam and cut into slices (or hearts).
Broccoli	Beta-carotene (a carotenoid), vitamins C and E, potassium, folate, calcium, and fiber	Chop fresh broccoli and add it to store-bought soup or dip into hummus.
Carrots	Alpha-carotene (a carotenoid) and fiber	Cut into snack-sized pieces to munch on. Use in recipes such as stir-fries, salads, and soups, or sneak shredded carrots into spaghetti sauce or muffin batter.
Red bell peppers	Beta-carotene and lutein, B-complex vitamins, folate, potassium, and fiber	Grill or over-roast until tender. Delicious in wraps, salads, and sandwiches.
Spinach	Lutein, B-complex vitamins, folate, magnesium, potassium, calcium, and fiber	Choose spinach over lettuce for nutrient-packed salads and sandwiches. Tastes great when steamed and added to cooked dishes.
Sweet potato or butternut squash	Beta-carotene; vitamins A, C, and E; and fiber	Steam in steamer basket, bake, roast in oven, or boil in a pot of soup.
Tomatoes	Beta- and alpha-carotene, lycopene, and lutein (carotenoids); vitamin C; potassium; folate; and fiber	Try fresh tomatoes on sandwiches, salads, pastas, and pizzas.

TIP

One heart–friendly food that doesn't make the tables: dark chocolate. Good quality dark chocolate contains resveratrol and cocoa phenols (flavonoids). A square of dark cocoa is great for blood pressure, but choose varieties that have 70 percent or higher cocoa content.

TABLE 21-3   **Heart-Friendly Fruits**

Food	Vitamins and minerals	Ways to enjoy
Blueberries and blackberries	Beta-carotene and lutein (carotenoids), anthocyanin (a flavonoid), ellagic acid (a polyphenol), vitamin C, folate, calcium, magnesium, potassium, and fiber	Cranberries, strawberries, and raspberries are potent, too, and do well in trail mixes, muffins, and salads.
Cantaloupe	Alpha- and beta-carotene and lutein (carotenoids), B-complex and C vitamins, folate, potassium, and fiber	A fragrant, ripe cantaloupe is perfect for breakfast, lunch, or potluck dinners. Simply cut and enjoy.
Oranges	Beta-cryptoxanthin, beta- and alpha-carotene, lutein, flavones, vitamin C, potassium, folate, and fiber	Make your own orange juice with freshly squeezed organic oranges. Use the zest in marinades, chutneys, and salad dressing. You can even use it in baking.
Papaya	Beta-carotene, beta-cryptoxanthin, and lutein (carotenoids); vitamins C and E; folate; calcium; magnesium; and potassium	Mix papaya, pineapple, scallions, garlic, fresh lime juice, salt, and black pepper.

TOP NUTRIENTS FOR YOUR HEART

You may know which nutrients are good for your cardiovascular health, but you may not know why they're good. Here's a quick rundown of the most commonly mentioned heart-healthy nutrients and what good they do.

- **Folate or folic acid** helps reduce and prevent hardening of arterial walls.

- **Omega-3 fatty acids** help strengthen heart tissue.

- **B vitamins** help reduce plaque buildup on the heart.

- **Magnesium and calcium** help regulate electrical impulses of the heart, lowering cholesterol and blood pressure.

- **Potassium** helps the heart pump and move blood through the body by pushing sodium out of the system and relaxing blood-vessel walls, thereby lowering blood pressure.

- **Vitamins A, C, and E** are antioxidants that help with overall cardiovascular health.

- **L-arginine** is an amino acid that helps rid the body of ammonia and helps release insulin. It's also used to make nitric oxide, which is a compound that helps relax blood vessels.

Osteoporosis

Osteoporosis is the deterioration of bone mass in the body — that is, thinning of the bones — making them more prone to break. Osteoporosis can occur as a result of aging, lifestyle, and diet. Many people have grown up thinking that milk prevents osteoporosis. Although the dairy industry wants you to believe that, actually, the less dairy you consume, the better your bone health is. Many studies show that bone health is actually improved with a high percentage of plant-based foods (specifically dark, leafy greens and seeds) in your diet.

WARNING

Dairy foods are rather acidic and can leach calcium from your bones, causing bones to break down instead of building up. Plant foods, on the other hand, are rich in calcium and magnesium and directly nourish the bones, giving them the minerals they need to thrive and help prevent breakdown.

Plant-based foods provide your body with calcium while tasting delicious. There is no need to worry about exact measurements of calcium when you're getting it from whole-food sources. Just be sure to get a variety of items in your diet on a daily basis, and you'll be loaded with the right kind of calcium that your body will love.

Top bone-building foods include the following:

>> Beet greens

>> Collards

>> Kale

>> Bok choy

>> Carob

>> Beans and legumes (peas and lentils)

>> Sesame seeds

>> Hempseeds

Understanding that your calcium intake doesn't have to come from dairy may be difficult to digest because most people believe that dairy is the only source of calcium. However, the foods you need to focus on are ones that are loaded with calcium naturally. These foods give your body its calcium requirements, are easy to digest, and allow your body to soak up many other beneficial minerals and nutrients.

Gastrointestinal illnesses

Plant–based eating can help with a wide variety of gastrointestinal conditions. A diet high in fiber, vitamins, and minerals can help prevent the onset and progression of these common diseases:

» **Acid reflux:** In this condition, some of the acid content of the stomach flows up into the esophagus. Eating more plants eases acid levels by decreasing or eliminating animal protein (which is more difficult to digest) from the diet. A plant-based diet also improves elimination of wastes from the body by increasing fiber intake and removing foods that may cause an increase in acid levels in the stomach. The more veggies in your diet, the less inflammation of the upper digestive tract you get because plants (especially green ones) neutralize acid levels.

» **Irritable bowel syndrome (IBS) and inflammatory bowel disease (IBD):** IBS is characterized by chronic abdominal pain, discomfort, bloating, and alteration of bowel habits. IBD is a group of inflammatory conditions of the colon and small intestine.

Plant-based eating can be healing to the bowels. It can help stabilize blood sugar, thus promoting stable insulin levels and lowering inflammation. It allows for a more balanced intake of essential fatty acids (more omega-3s and omega-9s than omega-6s), which decrease inflammation in the body. Increased fiber in a plant-based diet improves elimination of wastes from the body, which promotes the flushing of harmful toxins. Plant-based eating is often alkalinizing (versus conventional meat, grains, dairy, and sugar, which are acid-forming), which also helps lower inflammation and creates an environment in which harmful bacteria starve and beneficial bacteria thrive.

» **Celiac disease:** Celiac disease is an autoimmune disorder of the small intestine that occurs in genetically predisposed people of any age. It's associated with pain and discomfort in the digestive tract. Consuming plants and gluten-free grains can help someone with celiac disease prevent flare-ups, discomfort, and bloating. When you eliminate gluten from your diet, it's essential to find substitutes and alternative grains that are healing. Eliminating milk products and meat — which are inflammatory — is also critical for intestinal healing. Plant foods are also rich in enzymes that aid digestion — an extra bonus for people with celiac disease.

Other conditions that benefit from a plant-based diet

The nutrients available in plant–based foods can drastically improve your health, no matter which disease you're suffering from or trying to prevent. Plants are nature's medicine! In case you need more convincing, here are some other chronic conditions that benefit from a plant-based diet.

Autoimmune diseases

An *autoimmune* disease is a condition in which a person's immune system attacks itself. This class of diseases includes many different disorders, including celiac disease (see the preceding section) that bring on a variety of symptoms. Some common autoimmune diseases include these:

>> **Graves' disease:** A hyperthyroid condition that causes the thyroid to enlarge to twice its size

>> **Rheumatoid arthritis:** An inflammatory disorder that affects tissues, organs, and joints

>> **Vitiligo:** A condition that causes skin depigmentation

>> **Multiple sclerosis:** An inflammatory disease where the insulating covers of nerve cells in the brain and spinal cord are damaged

For people with autoimmune diseases, plant-based foods can help minimize symptoms, boost energy, prevent the development of other diseases, and stop the disease from progressing any further. Meat and dairy have been known to have negative effects on people living with autoimmune diseases because they can aggravate the condition, so simply removing such foods from your diet and converting to plant foods can be very helpful.

Gout

Gout is characterized by sudden, severe attacks of pain, redness, and tenderness in joints — often the joint at the base of the big toe — but can occur in any joint. Obesity, unstable blood sugar, and, yes, a meat-based diet can increase the risk of developing gout. To combat it, eat fresh veggies, whole grains, nuts, seeds, and healthy fats. Plant-based eating aids blood-sugar management, helping you keep gout at bay. Because you fill up on whole foods, you have fewer cravings for and less dependence on refined grains and sugars and processed foods.

WARNING

When treating gout, limit your consumption of dried beans and lentils. These items are high in purines, which can increase the levels of uric acid in the body. This is a big problem because gout results from a buildup of uric acid, which crystallizes in a joint and can cause severe pain.

Alzheimer's disease

Glial cells, which provide support and protection for neurons in your brain and parasympathetic nervous system, are believed to help remove debris and toxins from the brain that can contribute to Alzheimer's disease. Many plant-based foods, especially those that are rich in antioxidants (such as green tea and dark berries), may help protect glial cells from damage. When glial cells are damaged, they lose their ability to function properly, which can affect brain function. Additionally, the increased fiber intake in a plant-based diet helps rid the body of toxins via elimination of wastes. Increased consumption of heavy-metal *chelators* (foods that help remove toxins from the body, such as cilantro, parsley, and chlorella) also helps remove toxins from the body.

PLANTS BENEFIT THE PLANET, TOO

Because the Earth is made up mostly of plants and the elements, the choice to eat a plant-based diet has a direct positive impact on the environment.

The resources used in the meat and dairy industries negatively affect the quality of soil and water, the welfare of animals, and, of course, human health. A 2006 United Nations report revealed that the livestock sector accounts for the creation of 18 percent of all greenhouse gases, more than the entire transportation sector combined.

The cost of meat isn't entirely reflected by the price you pay at the checkout stand; the real price goes all the way back to how animals are handled on the land — and how the land itself is handled, including the water resources used for industrial livestock farming and in processing facilities. Then add transportation costs, packaging, and advertising, and the cost really starts adding up.

By making the choice to eat less meat and more plant-based foods, you're helping the land, the animals, and your health.

Chapter 22

The Skinny on Superfoods

The superfoods all have super health benefits; however, they'll have a bigger impact if you improve the rest of your diet as well. This chapter introduces you to superfoods and fits them into overall good nutrition. It helps you figure out how many calories you need every day and has examples of how superfoods fit into a well-balanced diet.

People today typically eat for pleasure rather than for good nutrition. Unfortunately, there just aren't many health benefits in most of the foods they eat for pleasure. If eating a candy bar could decrease your blood pressure or reduce your risk for cancer, that'd make for one heck of a healthy population — but this just isn't the case.

One of the reasons people don't choose healthier food is because they haven't been educated on the health benefits of eating the good stuff. But read on to find out how the foods you and your family eat can affect — and even improve — your health, perhaps resulting in fewer visits to the doctor. If reducing your number of doctor visits each year simply by eating more healthfully is possible, why not?

Understanding the Difference between Foods and Superfoods

Your body requires food for essential nutrients and energy. But some foods are better than others. Some foods are bad for your health, and eating them can raise your risk of certain diseases. In contrast, other foods are good for you because they provide nutrients that give you energy. But at the top of the heap are superfoods, which are rich in nutrients and natural substances that have been shown by research studies to improve your health and reduce your risk for disease.

Disease is an impairment of health by a condition of the body or mind that causes dysfunction. Health is a condition of well-being free from disease. Eating foods that have poor nutritional value leads to malnutrition, which can cause dysfunction of the body and therefore is a form of disease. You need to eat foods rich in the correct nutrients to help keep yourself in good health.

Superfoods have been shown to be especially good for you because they're rich in vitamins and minerals, plus they have extra compounds that have a positive impact on your health. These compounds may include good fats like omega-3 fatty acids and monounsaturated fats, a variety of phytochemicals (natural chemicals found in plants), and dietary fiber. All the recommended superfoods in this chapter have been involved in scientific studies that back up the health claims.

REMEMBER

Adding a few superfoods to your diet can improve your health by keeping your heart healthy, boosting your immune system, helping you lose weight, fending off diabetes, and preventing some cancers. Eating a superfoods-rich diet promotes healthy aging.

Boning Up on Basic Nutrition

The foods you eat supply your body with the energy you need to get through the day, along with the raw materials to keep all your organ systems running smoothly. Eating a diet with the right amounts of nutrients accomplishes just that, and superfoods do it in spades.

When you eat a diet with too many calories from unhealthy foods, you gain weight and are at great risk of becoming obese. Not only do bad foods fail to give you all the nutrients you need, but they also damage your body. Although the occasional candy bar or bacon cheeseburger with fries probably won't hurt you, making a daily habit of eating these kinds of foods will. Superfoods contain lots of nutrients, so eating superfoods makes it easy to get the nutrients you need without unwanted calories and unhealthy ingredients.

Picking out foods is easier when you understand what nutrients are and what they do for your body. Nutrients are the substances in food that your body uses for energy and to build tissues. There are big nutrients, small nutrients, and special nutrients called phytochemicals. The following sections tell you what you need to know about each type.

Introducing the big nutrients you need: Carbs, proteins, and fats

Macronutrient is the technical term for the big nutrients: carbohydrates, protein, and fats. You need to eat foods that contain all three of the macronutrients in a healthful balance every day. Eating superfoods helps you maintain this balance because superfoods contain healthy ratios of these macronutrients and high amounts of the healthiest nutrients.

Coping with carbohydrates

Carbohydrates include simple sugars and complex carbohydrates (starches), and fiber goes in this category, too. Dietary carbohydrates are found in foods that come from plant sources. Your body uses carbohydrates as fuel, so a large part of your diet should be made up of carbohydrates. In fact, about half of your daily calories should come from carbohydrates — but some are better than others.

LOW FAT VERSUS LOW CARB: WHICH IS BEST?

Low-fat diets became popular in the 1980s. They emphasized cutting back on unhealthy, high-calorie, fatty foods, thereby helping people lose weight. Unfortunately, food manufacturers began making low-fat and non-fat foods that were still high in calories mostly from carbohydrates. Of course, these products became very popular but didn't actually help people lose weight.

In the 1990s, low-carb diets became all the rage, and, again, people lost weight when they cut high-calorie sugary foods out of their diets. Then low-carb, sugar-free foods arrived, but they, too, were high in calories, so Americans continued to gain weight.

So which is best? Somewhere in the middle, with a balanced diet and the right amount of calories. That means reducing the amount of bad fats (like the low-fat diets) but keeping the good fats. It also means dumping the sugar (like the low-carb diets) but keeping whole grains and healthful fruits and vegetables.

All carbohydrates are made up of some combination of three simple sugars officially known as monosaccharides (single sugar units). These three sugars are galactose (milk sugar), fructose (fruit sugar), and glucose (the type of sugar your body uses as fuel).

Sucrose (table sugar) and lactose (milk sugar) are other types of simple sugars called disaccharides (two-sugar units). Lactose is made up of glucose and galactose and is formed in the mammary glands in breast tissue. Sucrose is made up of glucose and fructose. It doesn't matter whether the sugar is white, brown, or raw (turbinado) — chemically they're all the same. Sucrose molecules are broken down and digested very quickly. Your body either uses the resultant fructose and glucose molecules as energy or converts them to fat and stores them on your body, usually on your belly, butt, or thighs.

Starch (a complex carbohydrate) is made up of long chains of glucose molecules. Starch isn't broken down as quickly as sucrose, but it's still metabolized efficiently. And, just like simple sugars, extra starch is converted to fat.

Fiber is plant material that you can't digest, but it's very important for good health. Insoluble fiber doesn't dissolve in water; instead, it absorbs it. Insoluble fiber remains in solid form, adding bulk to your stool, which helps the muscles of the colon move stool through the digestive system. Soluble fiber dissolves in water, forming a protective gel that also adds bulk (and works as a natural stool-softener) and has other important health benefits such as lowering cholesterol.

So which carbohydrates are good and which ones are bad? The refined carbohydrates that are accompanied by no (or only very little) fiber are usually bad, with table sugar and high fructose corn syrup (HFCS) being the worst. They're highly refined, so they add a lot of sweetness but don't provide any nutrition other than calories. Diets high in sucrose and HFCS lead to obesity, heart disease, and diabetes.

Refined flour is just a step or two above refined sugar. Refined flour has had most of the fibrous parts of the grain (along with a good bit of the nutrition) removed. Most flour is enriched, however, which means that several vitamins have been added back in. Foods like regular pasta, white bread, and saltine crackers are made from refined flour. Choose whole-grain (unrefined) products whenever possible to increase the amount of fiber in your diet. Unlike refined grains, whole grains retain the parts of the plant that contain the healthy fiber content.

REMEMBER

Good carbohydrates are usually accompanied by a good dose of fiber. Besides whole grains, good carbohydrates are found in fruits, vegetables, legumes, nuts, and seeds, many of which have attained superfood status. Fiber slows down the digestion and absorption of carbohydrates, which helps regulate your blood sugar level (which is good for energy and for preventing diabetes) and keeps you feeling full. The best part is that fiber has zero calories.

TIP

Fruit juices are high in natural sugars and low in fiber (unless you leave in the pulp), but they're also rich in vitamins and minerals. One bit of caution if you're watching your weight: The natural sugars in fruit juice are absorbed quickly and can be high in calories. Choose whole fresh fruits over juice whenever you can.

The best carbohydrates are found in most superfoods. They're unrefined carbohydrates accompanied by nutrients and phytochemicals (see the upcoming section "Zeroing in on superfoods nutrients: Phytochemicals"), and/or are high in fiber.

Pondering proteins

Proteins are chains of little chemical building blocks called amino acids. After you eat protein, the chains are broken down into individual amino acids, which are absorbed into your blood. Your body takes the amino acids, builds new proteins out of them, and uses them as the raw material to maintain and repair almost every part of your body.

All animal products contain protein, including meats, fish, poultry, eggs, and dairy products. The proteins in animal products are called complete proteins because they contain all the essential amino acids (amino acids that must be in your diet because your body can't make them on its own). Plant foods contain proteins, too — especially nuts, seeds, and legumes — but most plants are missing one or more of the essential amino acids and thus are called incomplete proteins. This distinction is important for vegetarians and vegans to know so they can find the right combination of foods to get all the amino acids. Fortunately, some food plants, like soy, are complete proteins. If you eat a variety of plant foods — grains, nuts, seeds, and veggies — every day, you can get all the amino acids you need without animal products.

Apart from being complete or incomplete, there isn't much difference in the proteins you eat. What makes proteins good or bad is the type of fat that accompanies them. For example, red meat containing lots of saturated fat isn't a good source of protein and should be limited. Lean meats are better, and fish that are rich in healthy fats are the best. Plant proteins are always a healthful choice because they're accompanied by good fats and fiber.

REMEMBER

Cooking methods make a difference, too. A piece of baked fish is good for you, but deep-fried fish isn't.

You don't need large amounts of protein. In fact, only about 15 to 20 percent of your calories should come from protein. Superfood proteins include whole grains, nuts, seeds, and legumes (beans, peas, and lentils).

What's the fuss about fats?

The fats and oils in the foods you eat are made up of individual molecules called fatty acids. Your body needs some fats; in fact, they should comprise about 20 to 30 percent of the calories you take in daily. Fats are important for lubrication of body surfaces, formation of hormones, energy storage, and insulation from cold. Limited amounts of fat help protect internal organs. Fats also carry the fat–soluble vitamins that are necessary components of the membranes that surround all the cells in your body.

But not all fats are created equal. Some are very good for you, whereas others are bad for your health:

>> **Saturated fats:** These fats are found mostly in animal products like red fatty meats, eggs, and dairy products. They're solid at room temperature. Coconut, palm, and other tropical oils also contain large amounts of saturated fat. Eating saturated fats causes your level of cholesterol (a type of blood fat) to go up and promotes inflammation. Diets rich in saturated fats are associated with both an increased risk of heart disease, strokes, and some cancers. Superfoods are all low in saturated fats.

   Avoid eating high-fat red meats. If you include animal protein in your diet, choose more fish and lean poultry. Don't forget legumes, nuts, and seeds.

>> **Trans-fats:** Most trans-fats are created by forcing hydrogen into vegetable oils to make them more solid. Some stick margarines, for example, undergo this process, called partial hydrogenation, which alters the structure of the fatty acids to look more like saturated fats. Unfortunately, trans-fats are worse for your health than saturated fats, and you should avoid them whenever possible. Trans-fats are most commonly found in processed snack foods, oils used for deep frying, and pastries, as well as some brands of margarine. (Dairy products have a natural trans-fat, but it doesn't seem to be as harmful as the artificial kind.) The superfoods don't have any trans-fats.

   Read the labels on packaged foods to be sure they don't contain any trans-fats.

TIP

>> **Monounsaturated fats:** These fatty acids are found in abundance in some plants. Olive oil is the best-known example, but canola oil, peanuts, and avocados also contain monounsaturated fatty acids. Monounsaturated fats are liquid at room temperature and are good for you. Substituting monoun-saturated fats for saturated fats has been shown to reduce the risk of heart disease. Monounsaturated fats lower your cholesterol, reduce inflammation, keep your blood vessels healthy, and may reduce your risk of some cancers. Many of the superfoods contain large amounts of monounsaturated fats.

Choose monounsaturated fats often — every day if possible. Use olive oil for cooking and as a salad dressing.

>> **Polyunsaturated fats:** These fats are liquid at room temperature and are abundant in plant oils and fish. There are two types of polyunsaturated fats: omega-3 fatty acids (found in fish, flaxseeds, and chia seeds) and omega-6 fatty acids (found in most vegetable and seed oils). Both of these fatty acids are important for good health. They're called essential fatty acids because you have to get them from your diet — your body can't manufacture them from other fats.

There's one problem with polyunsaturated fats, though. Most people get plenty of the omega-6 fatty acids in their diet; in fact, most people get too many because vegetable oils are common in many processed foods. The opposite is true for the omega-3 fatty acids: Most people are deficient. Eating too many of the omega-6s and too few of the omega-3s leads to an imbalance that promotes inflammation in the body. Eating the right amount — about a 4 to 1 ratio of omega-6s to omega-3s — helps reduce inflammation and improve your health. The typical ratio in the Western diet is 15 or 16 to 1.

Many superfoods are rich in omega-3 fatty acids, especially fish, flax and pumpkin seeds, and chia seeds.

Getting to know the little nutrients you need: Vitamins and minerals

Micronutrients (the little nutrients) include vitamins and minerals. You don't need large amounts of these nutrients compared to the macronutrients, but you do need small amounts on a regular basis to keep your body working at its best. Most of the superfoods are rich in some of the micronutrients, but none is rich in all of them — that's why you need a balanced diet.

When you eat a variety of fruits, vegetables, whole grains, nuts, seeds, legumes, fish, lean meats, and low-fat dairy products, you get the vitamins you need every day. (If you want to limit or remove animal products from you diet, check out Chapter 21 for information on maintaining a healthy balance from plants alone.) When you make sure some of those foods are superfoods, you get even more nutrition, plus all the powerful fats, fiber, and phytochemicals that keep you feeling young and healthy.

Becoming versed in water-soluble vitamins

Water-soluble vitamins dissolve in water and aren't as easily stored by the body as fat-soluble vitamins. If you consume more water-soluble vitamins than your body needs, the excess is excreted in your urine. The foods you eat must supply the eight B-complex vitamins and vitamin C every day because your body consistently eliminates them (except for vitamin B12). Water-soluble vitamins also are more fragile and can be destroyed during cooking. By eating a healthful superfoods-rich diet, you're able to get plenty of these vitamins.

The B-complex vitamins include thiamine (B1), riboflavin (B2), niacin (B3), pantothenic acid, pyridoxine (B6), folate, cobalamin (B12), and biotin. The B vitamins are found in a wide variety of foods (except for B12, which is only found in animal products). B vitamins help you convert the macronutrients from the foods you eat into energy, plus they're necessary for many other normal body functions.

Vitamin C is found in fruits and vegetables, especially citrus fruits, strawberries, and peppers. Your body needs vitamin C for normal immune system function, speedy wound healing, and strong connective tissue.

TIP

If you're following a vegan diet (one without any animal products), check with your doctor about taking a vitamin B12 supplement to make sure you have a regular source of this essential vitamin.

Finding the fat-soluble vitamins

Fat-soluble vitamins are stored in fatty tissues and your liver, so you don't become deficient in these vitamins as quickly as with the water-soluble vitamins. Vitamin A is needed for normal vision and cell growth and is found in both plant-based foods and animal products. Vitamin E is found in nuts and seeds and works as an antioxidant to protect the cells in your body from free-radical damage. Vitamin K is found in leafy green vegetables and is essential for normal blood clotting.

A healthful, balanced diet provides just the right amounts of these vitamins, except for vitamin D, which is made by your body after your skin is exposed to sunlight. You need about 5 to 20 minutes of sun exposure to your face, arms, or legs twice each week to form a sufficient amount of vitamin D. Some foods (like milk) are fortified with extra vitamin D, or you can always get vitamin D through supplements. The American Academy of Dermatology recommends utilizing fortified foods and supplements as your source for vitamin D rather than sun exposure because of the risk of skin cancer.

Minding the major minerals

Major minerals include calcium, magnesium, phosphorus, chlorine, potassium, sodium, and sulfur. They're called major because you need to replenish them with amounts greater than 0.01 percent of your body weight every day. Major minerals are found in a variety of foods. A healthful diet contains all the minerals you need, although calcium is commonly taken as a dietary supplement.

Calcium is important for many processes in your body and is especially important for strong bones, muscle function, and normal blood clotting. Magnesium and phosphorus are also important for bone health, and magnesium is present in your muscles, too. Potassium, chloride, and sodium are called electrolytes. They work to keep your body fluids in balance, which affects your blood pressure. Sulfur is used in making some proteins.

REMEMBER

Many of the superfoods are rich in calcium, magnesium, and potassium, while remaining low in sodium. Although sodium is necessary for good health, most people consume way too much of it, which can lead to high blood pressure.

Tackling the trace minerals

Trace minerals include iron, iodine, cobalt, copper, fluoride, manganese, molybdenum, selenium, vanadium, and zinc. You don't need quite as much of the trace minerals as you do the major minerals; however, they're just as important for maintaining a healthy body.

Iron, copper, and cobalt are necessary for normal red blood cell production; iodine helps your thyroid; fluoride is good for your teeth; molybdenum, vanadium, and zinc are included in many of your body's chemical reactions; and selenium is an antioxidant.

REMEMBER

Superfoods provide varying amounts of the trace minerals, especially iron, selenium, manganese, and zinc.

Zeroing in on superfoods nutrients: Phytochemicals

Phytochemicals are plant chemicals that offer a variety of health benefits, and all plant-based superfoods are rich in phytochemicals. There are several different types of phytochemicals. Here's a basic rundown:

>> Polyphenols are a family of related phytochemicals that includes bioflavonoids, tannins, and lignans.

>> Bioflavonoids are produced in plants and include some of the pigments found in red, blue, purple, and black fruits, vegetables, and legumes. Bioflavonoids like quercetin, anthrocyanadins, and catechins help to reduce inflammation, protect your heart, and reduce your risk of some cancers.

>> Tannins are found in tea and red wine. Tannins may help to keep your digestive system healthy.

» Lignans are found in the cell walls of plants and have hormone-like properties. Flax and soy are particularly rich in lignans and may help to reduce the risk of cardiovascular disease.

» Carotenoids are related to vitamin A and are found in red, yellow, and orange pigments. Examples include beta carotene, lycopene, and lutein. The carotenoids may help to keep your vision healthy, bolster your immune system, and reduce your risk of cardiovascular disease and some cancers.

» Phytosterols are the plant equivalent of cholesterol. However, unlike the cholesterol found in animal products, phytosterols are good for you. Some phytosterols, such as beta-sitosterol, help reduce the symptoms of an enlarged prostate and are effective for keeping your cholesterol levels in check.

REMEMBER

Not every superfood fruit or veggie contains all the phytochemicals you need. A good rule to remember is eat a rainbow of plant-based food daily. Because each color of fruit or vegetable provides different phytochemicals, eating a variety of colors helps you get what you need.

Creating a Healthy, Balanced Superfoods Diet

Creating a healthy diet requires a little planning, so start by determining how many calories you (and your family members) need. Knowing how many calories you need helps you determine how much and which kinds of foods you should eat. Superfoods have excellent nutrient-to-calorie ratios when compared to other foods.

If you need to lose some weight, cut back on calories by choosing more foods that are high in fiber and low in fat and sugar, which describes many superfoods. If you want to gain weight, add more energy-dense foods like olive oil, nuts, and seeds to your diet so you can gain weight without losing out on valuable nutrients.

TIP

You can find books and websites that list the calorie counts for many foods. The United States Department of Agriculture (USDA) has a very large database of nutrition information for just about every food you can think of at its Food-A-Pedia site: www.supertracker.usda.gov/foodapedia.aspx. In 2005, the old USDA food pyramid was replaced by MyPlate (www.choosemyplate.gov), which helps guide your dietary choices. If counting every calorie seems tedious, you may want to keep track of the number of servings you have of each of the food groups instead.

FORGOING FAD DIETS

Fad diets come and go quickly, mostly because, in the end, they're not particularly successful. The typical fad diet requires you to restrict specific foods (sometimes most or all of certain food groups) while claiming that you don't need to watch calories, exercise, or do anything else — except maybe buy expensive diet pills. Don't fall for these diet claims; they don't work in the long run. Fad diets may help with quick weight loss, but to lose weight and keep it off, you need to eat less, eat right, and exercise more. There aren't any exceptions.

How do you fit all those servings into your day? Planning your meals and your daily menus makes eating a healthful diet much easier. Plus, it makes grocery shopping less of a chore. By planning your meals for a week, you can make a shopping list and buy all the foods and ingredients you'll need at one time, possible saving a lot of tips to the store. You can also prepare a lot of your meals ahead of time to make eating healthfully easier if you have a hectic schedule.

Determining how many calories you need

Calories (sometimes called kilocalories) measure the amount of energy available in the foods you eat. The number of calories you need every day depends on how old you are, how big you are, whether you're male or female, how active you are, and whether you're pregnant or nursing. When you get the right number of calories every day, you maintain a healthful weight. If you don't eat enough calories, you become underweight; if you get too many, you become overweight and ultimately obese. Being overweight or obese increases your risk of cardiovascular disease, diabetes, and some cancers.

TIP

You can go online and find calculators to help you estimate how many calories you need every day to maintain, gain, or lose weight. Check out www.bmi-calculator. net or http://nutritiondata.self.com for easy-to-use calculators. You can try one of the many dozens of food-tracking apps available for Android and iOS devices, such as Wholesome, MyPlate, Fooducate, MyFitnessPal, Lose it!, or SparkPeople.

Or you can calculate your calorie needs with two formulas. The first one calculates how many calories you need just to be awake and breathing. The second formula factors in your activity level:

Basal Metabolic Rate (BMR) Formula

Women: BMR = 655 + (4.35 × weight in pounds) + (4.7 × height in inches) – (4.7 × age in years)

Men: BMR = 66 + (6.23 × weight in pounds) + (12.7 × height in inches) – (6.8 × age in years)

Harris Benedict Formula

If you're sedentary (little or no exercise): Calorie Calculation = BMR × 1.2

If you're lightly active (light exercise/sports 1–3 days/week): Calorie Calculation = BMR × 1.375

If you're moderately active (moderate exercise/sports 3–5 days/week): Calorie Calculation = BMR × 1.55

If you're very active (hard exercise/sports 6–7 days a week): Calorie Calculation = BMR × 1.725

If you're extra active (very hard exercise/sports and physical job or double training): Calorie Calculation = BMR × 1.9

For example, a 35-year-old, moderately active woman who is 5 feet 5 inches tall and weighs 125 pounds has a BMR of 655 + (4.35 × 125) + (4.7 × 65) – (4.7 × 35), or 1,340 calories. Because she's moderately active, she multiplies 1,340 × 1.55 for a grand total of 2,077, which is the number of calories she needs every day to maintain her weight.

Most superfoods are low in calories, and the ones that are more energy dense (higher in calories) are also very rich in nutrients, so you only need to eat a little bit to reap their rewards.

Planning superfood meals and menus

The first step in planning healthful meals is to go for a balance of carbohydrates, proteins, and good fats while reducing sugar, excess sodium, and bad fats. The second step is to find places to fit the superfoods into your menu. Superfood vegetables make great side dishes or salads. The fruits and nuts are perfect for snacks or dessert. The superfood fish and legumes fit nicely into any dinner. Oats are great for breakfast, and there's even room for a small glass of red wine with dinner or a piece of dark chocolate later on.

So what does a superfood menu look like? Start out by focusing on a healthful, balanced diet that includes two superfoods each day. Your day could look something like this:

» **Breakfast:** Oatmeal with low-fat milk, raisins, and honey; one slice of toast with a small amount of peanut butter; and coffee. Oatmeal counts as your first superfood of the day.

>> **Mid-morning snack:** Celery sticks with veggie dip.

>> **Lunch:** Chicken sandwich with one slice of cheese and lettuce on whole-grain bread and a small green salad with no more than 2 tablespoons of salad dressing. (Watch out for salad dressings because they can be full of fat and calories.)

>> **Mid-afternoon snack:** Six crackers with thin slices of cheese and one sliced pear.

>> **Dinner:** Roast beef, a baked potato with light sour cream, and a side of steamed broccoli with a dab of butter or non-trans-fat margarine. Broccoli is your second superfood for the day.

>> **Evening snack:** One cup of flavored yogurt.

As you can see, a daily menu like this has plenty of food and flavor without sacrificing good nutrition. And it's easy to add even more superfoods. Remember to drink water throughout the day. The following meal plan incorporates five:

>> **Breakfast:** Oatmeal with low-fat milk, blueberries, and honey; one slice of toast with peanut butter; and coffee. Oatmeal is your first superfood, and blueberries are your second.

>> **Mid-morning snack:** One apple with one slice of cheddar cheese. The apple is your third superfood.

>> **Lunch:** Bowl of low-sodium chicken noodle soup, one whole-grain roll, and a green salad with no more than 2 tablespoons salad dressing.

>> **Mid-afternoon snack:** A single-serving bag of almonds. Almonds are your fourth superfood.

>> **Dinner:** Baked salmon with mashed potatoes and green beans. Salmon is your fifth superfood for the day.

>> **Evening snack:** One cup of your favorite flavor of Greek yogurt.

These are just two examples of superfoods menus. As you can see, enjoying a superfoods diet is easy and delicious.

REMEMBER

Eating foods as grown is a good rule to follow. For example, you get more from eating the actual fruit picked off the tree than you do from drinking fruit juice.

Taking the First Steps toward a Healthier You with Superfoods

When you're armed with nutrition information and you know how to plan your meals, it's time to get started on your superfoods diet. Here's your game plan:

>> **Start with two superfoods each day and increase the number as you feel comfortable.**

>> **Reduce the amount of foods you eat that are bad for your health.** That includes the fatty red meats, deep-fried foods, sugary foods, greasy snack foods, and foods that are heavily processed. Replace those bad foods with good foods like fresh fruits and vegetables, whole grains, lean meats, nuts, seeds, legumes, and low-fat dairy products.

>> **Keep a food diary to help you keep track of your superfoods diet.** Writing down what you eat and drink every day improves your chances of turning your new dietary changes into a permanent lifestyle. You really don't need anything fancy; a small notebook will do. At the end of every day, you can see whether your food choices were good or bad and how many superfoods you ate.

>> **Exercise.** The American Heart Association recommends a minimum of 30 minutes of exercise five days a week. Exercise works along with superfoods to help you manage your weight and promote a healthy heart.

>> **Get your family and friends involved.** It's much easier to accomplish diet and exercise goals when you do it with a partner. Lead by example and rope some friends or family members into a healthy lifestyle. Fitness tracker apps allow you to follow friends (and them to follow you) for motivating encouragement and support as well as healthy competition.

If at first you don't succeed . . . don't give up! Rome wasn't built in a day, and you don't have to change your diet overnight. It's okay if you slip up — just start again and continue to make healthier food choices and add more superfoods. Ultimately, your superfoods diet will last a lifetime (and a long one at that).

Boosting Your Immune System

As you may expect, superfoods are good immune-system boosters, helping your body fight and prevent various diseases. Research on the abilities of certain foods to strengthen immune function, fight against heart disease, prevent cancer, and lower the risk of other inflammatory diseases has been consistently increasing.

Of course, cancer is much less common than colds and minor infections (thank goodness). Fortunately, superfoods can help with these everyday ailments, too. Here are two good examples:

>> **Resveratrol**, a compound found in red wine, has been shown to be quite beneficial. It has antiviral properties and can help prevent common cold viruses from taking hold in your body. It's also being studied extensively in anti-aging medicine, and early results are pointing at a breakthrough in this area.

>> **Garlic** has been used as a natural antibiotic for more than a century. Louis Pasteur studied the use of garlic as an antibiotic and found that it killed bacteria in the lab.

If you're on any medications, see your doctor before you add high doses of garlic to your regimen. Garlic can interfere with certain medication functions.

WARNING

WARNING

Superfoods have some great properties to help the body's immune system. However, if you're thinking of taking any superfood supplements, talk to your doctor first. Supplements, even those with superfood properties, can interact negatively with certain medications, so it's vital to discuss diet and supplements with your physician.

Helping Your Heart

Your heart pumps about 2,000 gallons of blood throughout your whole body every day, but most people don't appreciate that workload. You don't have to consciously think about your heartbeat, so it's easy to take your heart for granted. Unfortunately, sometimes it takes a serious medical condition like a heart attack to become aware of your heart — by which time you already have heart disease.

Heart disease is still the leading cause of death in both men and women, so reducing risks should be a priority for both genders. Superfoods can help by tackling cholesterol and triglycerides, believed to be major risk factors for cardiovascular disease. (Not sure what cholesterol and triglycerides are? Check out the nearby sidebar.)

TIP

The American Heart Association recommends that everyone 20 years of age and older have a fasting cholesterol profile test every five years. This test measures your total cholesterol and triglyceride levels to keep an eye on your risk for cardiovascular disease. If you have any underlying health conditions, such as hypothyroidism, diabetes, liver disease, or other cardiovascular risks, or are taking cholesterol lowering medications, your doctor may want to run this profile more frequently. After patients hit 40, most doctors check their cholesterol yearly.

CHOLESTEROL AND TRIGLYCERIDES

Cholesterol is a fat-like substance that's essential for normal body function. It plays a role in producing cell membranes and hormones. Triglycerides are a type of fat that makes up one portion of the cholesterol.

Cholesterol is found in different forms in your body. One form is "good" cholesterol, called high density lipoprotein (HDL), and the other is "bad" cholesterol, called low density lipoprotein (LDL). These lipoproteins are actually protein molecules that carry cholesterol through your bloodstream. LDL, the bad form, carries cholesterol from the liver, where it's made, to the rest of your body. HDL, the good form, carries cholesterol back to the liver, where it's removed from your body.

You need to know your ratio of HDL to LDL to determine just what harm cholesterol may be doing to your heart (your doctor can draw your blood and perform a fasting cholesterol profile test to determine your ratio). You want to have higher levels of HDL and lower levels of LDL because that means your body is getting rid of extra cholesterol. When your blood has too much LDL and too little HDL, the cholesterol may combine with other substances to form plaques on the walls of your arteries. Plaques make your arteries narrow and less flexible, which leads to a condition called atherosclerosis. Atherosclerosis reduces blood flow, often leading to strokes and heart attacks.

About two-thirds of the cholesterol in your body is produced in your liver, and the rest comes from the foods you eat. Your body needs cholesterol for certain functions; in most cases, the liver produces what the body will use and doesn't need extra. The balance between good cholesterol and bad is often determined by the food choices you make. Foods high in dietary cholesterol and saturated fats increase your bad cholesterol and decrease your good cholesterol. To make matters worse, some people inherit genes that actually cause the body to make more bad cholesterol and less of the good kind. Unhealthy levels of cholesterol can build up quickly in people who inherit this condition of over-production.

When you consume more calories than you need, your body turns the extra calories into triglycerides that are stored in your fat cells for later use. Triglycerides are grouped in with the LDL as bad cholesterol because high levels of triglycerides increase plaque build-up in the arteries. High levels of triglycerides have been consistently linked to heart disease.

Superfoods work to keep your heart healthy and improve your ticker's longevity without the potential side effects or additional expense of cholesterol–lowering prescription medications. They can really make a difference in your heart's health. Here's how:

>> Eating superfoods means you're improving your overall diet and getting the vitamins and minerals you need every day — without extra calories. Too many extra calories cause elevations in triglycerides (see the nearby sidebar) and an increased risk for heart disease.

>> Some superfoods, such as colorful fruits and vegetables, contain natural disease-fighting substances called flavonoids. These can reduce inflammation of your arteries, decrease your cholesterol, lower your blood pressure, and stimulate antioxidant activity. Antioxidants repair damage done to the cells in your body by smoking, pollution, poisons, fried foods, and also as a byproduct of normal metabolism. Remember to eat the rainbow every day.

>> Fish, nuts, and seeds all contain healthful polyunsaturated fatty acids that keep your cholesterol in check. Fish oil (which has omega-3 fatty acids) is particularly super because it also helps regulate your heartbeat and your blood pressure.

>> Fruits, vegetables, and oatmeal all contain dietary fiber that lowers cholesterol and helps keep you feeling full, which can prevent overeating, a risk factor for heart disease.

Losing Weight

More than 70 percent of the United States' adult population is overweight, and a third of that population is obese. Overweight is defined as having a body mass index (BMI) over 25. Adults with a BMI over 30 are considered obese. (See Chapter 20 for more information on calculating BMI.) Obesity is the second most preventable health risk, just behind smoking. It's a problem worldwide and one that just keeps getting, um, bigger.

Another problem is how quickly this overweight epidemic has spread to children. The World Health Organization estimates that 20 million children under the age of five are obese. Children are being diagnosed with high cholesterol, high blood pressure, and type 2 diabetes — all previously thought to be exclusively the problems of adults — at alarming rates. Why is this happening?

As with heart disease, poor eating and physical inactivity are largely responsible for weight gain. Weight loss isn't easy, but for many people it's necessary to lose weight in order to restore and maintain good health. Superfoods, along with a healthful diet and exercise plan, can help you lose the extra weight. Some superfoods that fill this bill include omega-3 fatty acids, green tea, dark chocolate, and chia (an edible seed that absorbs water and keeps you feeling full for hours).

Protecting Against Cancer

When people are asked what health condition they fear the most, cancer is the number one answer. This fear is justifiable; cancer is the second leading cause of death in the United States, just behind heart disease. Although many people believe that cancer is an uncontrollable health condition, evidence suggests otherwise, and some of the superfoods may help prevent cancer and improve the well-being of cancer patients.

Every day, people defy their prognoses and beat cancer, and eating healthy foods often has a lot to do with it. The role of nutrition in the prevention of cancer has been studied for many years. The largest cancer research organization in the United Kingdom, World Cancer Research Fund (WCRF), supports the notion that between 35 and 70 percent of cancer is related to eating an unhealthy diet. A healthy diet rich in superfoods, on the other hand, may decrease your risk of many cancers.

Many superfoods have cancer-fighting properties. In general, you should seek those foods with the highest amounts of phytochemicals, fiber, and antioxidants. For example:

» Lycopene, a phytochemical found in tomatoes, is being studied for its reduction of risk for prostate cancer. According to the American Cancer Society, foods rich in lycopene may lower the risk of other cancers as well.

» Berries contain phytochemicals that have been shown to help fight the development of cancer. These phytochemicals trigger antioxidant reactions that neutralize damage done to your cells.

» Red wine contains two polyphenols called catechins and resveratrol, both of which provide cancer protection by inhibiting the growth of cancer cells.

» Broccoli contains a chemical that has been found to slow down the progression of cancer cells, especially hormone-sensitive cancers such as breast and ovarian cancer.

» A lot of money has been spent on research to explore the cancer-fighting properties of garlic and garlic extracts. Several studies already support the theory that garlic can reduce the risk of cancer, and more studies are underway to explore exactly how garlic functions in cancer protection.

» Several beans (legumes) are great sources of fiber, which has been proven to help reduce inflammation in the colon and has been associated with a reduction of colon cancer.

Improving Digestion

Most people suffer digestive stress at one time or another. For example, constipation is common and can lead to abdominal bloating, hemorrhoids, and unnecessary pain. Indigestion or acid reflux (heartburn) is a common cause of emergency department visits and can lead to damage in the esophagus if not treated. Regularity of the digestive system is important for the proper metabolism of the foods you eat so they can be utilized by the body. (For more on fiber, flip to the earlier section "Coping with carbohydrates.")

One way to help your digestive system is to eat foods with lots of fiber. The average American diet consists of about 10 grams of fiber a day — far less than the 25 to 40 grams per day that your body needs. Boost your fiber intake by adding superfood fruits, vegetables, nuts, grains, and legumes to your diet. A food is considered to have a high fiber content when it has more than five grams of fiber per serving. The following list contains just a few superfoods that are high in fiber:

» Almonds	» Lentils
» Apples	» Lima beans
» Avocados	» Oatmeal
» Black beans	» Quinoa
» Broccoli	» Blueberries
» Chia	» Soybeans

TIP

Water isn't a superfood, but it's an important and essential addition to your diet to help the super-fiber foods work better. Drinking half your body weight (in ounces) of water each day helps counter the fluids that fiber absorbs. If you weigh 120 pounds, for example, you should aim to drink 60 ounces of water a day (a little less than four pints).

REMEMBER

Good digestive health is very important for the body to absorb nutrients and water, so make sure you're getting your daily fiber and alert your doctor with any concerns.

Easing Inflammation

When it comes to staying healthy, your body is always in a tug-of-war with detriments like pollution, unhealthy foods, smoke, too much alcohol, excessive sunlight, and even the side effects of fighting infections and digesting high-fat meals.

Exposure to these things causes cell damage and inflammation (the body's response to this damage, such as tissue swelling, redness, and triggering of the immune system). Chronic inflammation, or inflammation that happens over and over again, can lead to problems in many areas of the body, such as the joints, the heart, the colon, and even the skin.

Your body works hard to fight inflammation and cell damage. You can give your body an edge in this tug-of-war by eating superfoods rich in antioxidants and prostaglandins, discussed in the following sections.

Addressing the role of antioxidants

Antioxidants are natural substances, such as the compounds that give fruits and vegetables their colors, and vitamins like C and E, which fight cell damage. They work to fight inflammation by neutralizing free radicals in the body. Free radicals are unstable molecules that can travel throughout the body trying to take particles from healthy cells — a process that creates more free radicals. Free radicals damage cells, causing inflammation and starting a chain reaction in tissues as more and more cells become affected.

Superfoods are packed with antioxidants that move through the body and stop the free radicals so they don't damage healthy cells. Many of the superfoods we discuss in this chapter have antioxidant properties. Here are some of the most powerful ones:

>> Acai berries

>> Blueberries

>> Broccoli

>> Cranberries

>> Green tea

>> Pomegranate

>> Spinach

Investigating fats and inflammation

Your body makes chemicals called prostaglandins that contribute to starting or stopping inflammation reactions in your body (depending on the type of prostaglandins). Have you ever taken aspirin or ibuprofen for a headache? These medicines stop inflammation by blocking the prostaglandins. That's great, but sometimes they have rather unpleasant side effects; for example, some people experience an upset stomach when they take aspirin or ibuprofen.

Some foods can increase the amount of inflammatory prostaglandins (the bad ones) and decrease the amount of anti-inflammatory prostaglandins (the good ones) in your body. Eating these foods increases inflammation in your body. Eating a diet high in saturated fat (the type of fat found in red meat; see the earlier section "What's the fuss about fats?" for more info) is a major cause of this prostaglandin imbalance and the resulting inflammation. Fortunately, superfoods combat that inflammation.

A type of polyunsaturated fat known as omega-3 fatty acids is especially good for you. Omega-3s have been researched extensively and found to reduce inflammation. So eating foods rich in omega-3 fatty acids can help prevent heart disease, cancer, and arthritis. You have to get these fats from the foods you eat; your body can't produce them. If you don't get enough from your diet, it's important to take a good-quality supplement.

Monounsaturated fat is also good for you. It's the fat found in olive oil, and it may be one big reason why people who eat Mediterranean diets tend to be very healthy.

The following superfoods are packed with good poly- and monounsaturated fats:

>> Fish and seafood contain lots of omega-3 fats.

>> Chia, walnuts, and flaxseeds are great plant sources of omega-3s.

>> Avocados and olive oil are healthy monounsaturated fats.

These are just a few of the many superfood options that can help pump up your body's anti-inflammatory defense system.

Aging Beautifully

Superfoods do a lot of things, but trying to turn a frog into a prince might be pushing it. Offering some benefits that can help you live a longer and more vigorous life, however, is definitely within their call of duty.

Eating superfoods helps you feel and look youthful, so the earlier you start with superfoods, the more benefits you can gain. Of course, these foods need to be a piece of the whole puzzle, not the sole solution for beautiful skin and a healthy body. Don't forget about smart lifestyle choices too — exercising regularly, giving up smoking, and limiting your alcohol consumption.

Keeping that youthful glow

The health and beauty sections of every store are stuffed with creams, lotions, cleansers, moisturizers, and cosmetics designed to minimize the signs of aging. But a diet that includes superfoods can do just as much — and even more — to keep your skin healthy and young-looking.

The skin deals with so many different factors — sun, pollution, extreme weather, and other irritants — that it needs a continual supply of antioxidants to help protect it. Fortunately, superfoods are chock-full of many of the main nutrients your skin needs, including the following:

>> **Vitamins A, E, and C:** These are all common additions to popular skin creams because they're helpful in protecting the skin and vital in repairing damaged skin. Common foods that contain high levels of these vitamins include carrots (vitamin A); nuts and seeds (vitamin E); spinach (vitamins A and E); and broccoli, strawberries, and oranges (vitamin C).

>> **Zinc and selenium:** Zinc, which is active in the synthesis of collagen, is another common addition to sunscreens and skin lotions. Pumpkin seeds are an excellent source of zinc, as are nuts and beans. Selenium exhibits antioxidant effects that have been found to reduce skin cancer. Selenium is found in fish and nuts (especially Brazil nuts).

>> **Bioflavonoids:** Sometimes known as "vitamin P," bioflavonoids aren't really vitamins. They're the pigments found in the skins of colorful fruits and vegetables. These pigments contain concentrated antioxidants that actually are more powerful than vitamins. They help increase vitamin C levels and reduce destruction of collagen in the skin.

>> **Alpha-lipoic acid (ALA):** This is a fatty acid made by the body and found in foods such as broccoli and spinach. Although the body produces ALA, it doesn't make nearly enough to be helpful for fighting disease and inflammation. Plus, your body produces less as you age, so making sure you get enough from your diet becomes even more important the older you get. Alpha-lipoic acid not only has antioxidant properties but also can help recycle some vitamins and other antioxidants.

Pumping up your pep

Gaining some super sensations from what you eat and drink is a common goal. How often have you told coworkers you need coffee, chocolate, or an energy drink to get you through the slumps in your day? The problem with artificial stimulants is that they often pose unwanted dangers to your body. Plus, many of these options are high in sugar and artificial additives. A better option: Go natural and use superfoods to put some pep in your step.

Getting a natural boost of energy is important not only for getting through your daily routine but also for summoning extra energy to tackle your exercise program or other activities. When you use the right foods and eat small meals throughout the day, you can really ramp up your metabolism and get that extra energy you need.

If you're on the go and can't find the time to grab a healthy meal, these superfoods can be a great option:

- » **Goji berries:** Rich in antioxidants, goji berries have been used in Chinese medicine for years. They've also been found to help boost energy and enhance your mood.

- » **Green tea:** This is another superfood that has been used for hundreds of years. The American Journal of Clinical Nutrition found that green tea's effect on energy was similar to that of caffeinated coffee.

- » **Chia seed:** The Aztecs used chia seeds to prepare for battles and long explorations. The seeds can absorb ten times their weight in liquid and are slow to digest, offering sustained energy for several hours. Chia seeds can be added to protein shakes or other meals to help give you that sustained energy throughout the day.

- » **Quinoa:** This protein-rich seed, though considered a grain, is actually a leafy plant that's related to spinach and beets, and it can give you a power punch. Much as Aztecs used chia, the Incas used quinoa as a source of energy for their battles.

SUPERFOOD SUPPLEMENTS

Superfood supplements have exploded filling shelves in every pharmacy and supermarket. Many manufacturers claim you can get more superfood benefits by taking supplements than you can by eating healthful foods. Superfood supplements give your nutrition a boost by concentrating some of the nutrients, but they shouldn't replace the healthy foods in your diet. You need to continue to eat wholesome foods that provide you with fiber, protein, and other nutrients that build your body and keep you strong. Eating a junk food diet is unhealthy no matter what supplements you take.

Superfood supplements are great for those times when you're under a lot of stress, trying to lose weight, or fighting infections, or if you're a picky eater. But your best option still is to get the energy-building properties you need from the food you eat rather than solely from a supplement bottle.

Seeing — and believing

Many bodily functions change with age, and vision is no exception. Many people develop the need for some type of visual correction as they grow older. Just like other age–related conditions that can be alleviated by superfoods, the eyes can be aided by the following superfood constituents:

>> **Beta carotene:** You've probably heard that eating carrots is supposed to help improve your vision and reduce your risk for macular degeneration, a progressive disease of the retina. That's because carrots contain a lot of beta carotene, a precursor to vitamin A. Beta carotene is virtually a staple ingredient in vision-related nutritional supplements.

>> **Acanthocyanins:** These are bioflavonoids that give color to the skin of fruits and veggies. Their antioxidant properties help protect not only your eyes but also other organ systems.

>> **Lutein:** Lutein is concentrated in your retinas. Carrots have high levels of lutein. Other good sources are broccoli, spinach, and orange and yellow fruits. Kale not only has lutein but also is a great source of vitamin A.

>> **Omega-3 fatty acids:** Omega-3s protect the light-sensing cells in your eyes. One Harvard study found that people who eat fish at least twice a week cut their risk of developing age-related macular degeneration in half. Other studies found that omega-3s also may be helpful in reducing cataracts.

5

Healthy Aging

Chapter 23

The Four Major Health Concerns as You Age

O ver the years, thousands of people have searched for the elusive Fountain of Youth, and although some have claimed to have found it, for most, it remains a hidden treasure. Great strides have been made in lengthening lifespan and uncovering the secrets to healthy aging, but there's still progress to be made. As much as you may wish otherwise, most people know there's no magic pill for good health and longevity. It takes commitment, work, and sometimes even denial of self — giving up poor eating habits, the couch potato lifestyle, and the stressful schedules so many are addicted to — to stay healthy as you get older. You may be taking care of the externals, but don't overlook the basics of good health, which are also the basics of aging well.

Balance is a big key in life, and healthy aging is no different. Skipping over essential healthcare is like ignoring routine maintenance on your car — the end result can be costly and dangerous. Healthy aging is a current hot topic. You can thank the baby boomer generation — the oldest of these people are now well into their 60s — for today's emphasis on youthful, healthy aging. This chapter discusses why people are living longer and better today than in previous generations, what impacted life expectancy a century ago, and what impacts health and longevity today.

If you were a fine wine, you could honestly say, "I'm not getting older, I'm getting better," and mean it. You may not be aging like fine wine, but you can help yourself age well, especially when it comes to avoiding the four biggest health risks of aging: cancer, diabetes, cardiovascular disease, and osteoporosis. You have the benefit of technology and research providing the tools to carry you further in life, with fewer health problems than any generation before you. Your job is to pick up the tools — the information, screening techniques, and recommendations for healthier living — and use them.

Life is full of choices and every one of them influences health in some form. Because you can't look into the future, the best thing to do is to live as if every lifestyle choice you make has health ramifications down the road. This chapter should convince you that everyday changes can add up to healthier years — for years to come.

Life Expectancy in the 21st Century

The last 100 years have seen a tremendous change in the way people live and the ailments they fall prey to. The epidemics of yesterday have been wiped out in industrialized countries, and life expectancy has increased. But even though folks are living longer today, this life expectancy brings a whole new set of problems and solutions.

Today, many folks take for granted that they'll live into adulthood, while in the past, people were well aware of the unpredictable threats on their lives. Some of the most damaging health threats in the world today can be modified by lifestyle choices. Making healthy choices is the basis of healthy aging and the recurrent theme of this book.

To examine why people live longer lives today, you must first look at why people *didn't* live as long more than a century ago. This section focuses on the differences.

That was then . . .

Malnutrition, acute illnesses, infant mortality, and war were major contributors to shorter life expectancy 100 years ago. In the period from 1918 to 1919, the influenza virus (the flu) infected more than 400 million people worldwide and killed nearly 40 million. Today people still die from the flu, but not nearly at the mortality rates common in the past.

Poor living conditions and poor sanitation were also major causes of death. Each incident people experienced had a negative cumulative effect on their health. Even diseases that didn't result in death left people more likely to develop other chronic illnesses when they grew older that led to poor life expectancy.

REMEMBER

The statistical probability of a person 100 years ago going through life unscathed to a ripe old age was extremely low. Here are a few of the problems that caused widespread disease and mortality then:

>> **Crowded and unsanitary living conditions:** These scenarios resulted in multiple outbreaks of malaria, cholera, dysentery, typhoid fever, yellow fever, and flu. Survivors often faced lifelong health consequences.

>> **War:** War caused death directly and also exposed soldiers to foreign disease. During the American Civil War between 1861 and 1865 there were twice as many deaths from disease associated with poor health, malnutrition, and unsanitary conditions than from battle wounds. More than 200 million people died in the beginning of the 20th century from a combination of combat and disease.

>> **Viral and bacterial infections with no medical treatments or vaccines:** Viral and bacterial infections caused death in high numbers of both adults and children before vaccines were available. Worldwide there have been many pandemics (affecting a large group, even the world) from the Spanish flu in 1918 to the Asian flu in 1957 that killed more than 50 million people. Polio, smallpox, diphtheria, and measles killed many adults and children before the advent of vaccines and still do in developing countries.

>> **Hazardous work environments and hard physical labor:** Starting as young as age 13, people worked 10- to 12-hour shifts exposed to dangerous fumes and bacteria and with minimal protective equipment. The number of work-related deaths peaked around 1900 and then started to improve with the formation of unions and other safety requirements.

>> **Lack of certain nutrients:** Soldiers, sailors, and the poverty stricken suffered from malnutrition, leading to lack of nutrients. These nutritional deficiencies included the following:

   • **Pellagra:** A deficiency of niacin (vitamin B3) that may include symptoms of dermatitis, diarrhea, dementia, and death.

   • **Goiter:** Goiter is caused by a lack of iodine in the diet that can lead to hyperthyroidism (elevated thyroid hormone) or hypothyroidism (low thyroid hormone). Complications include shortness of breath, heart problems, impaired mental function, and birth defects.

- **Scurvy:** Lack of vitamin C led to scurvy, a condition where the body can't properly absorb iron, causing anemia.

- **Rickets:** This affliction was due to a lack of vitamin D, which is necessary for bone mineralization. Children with rickets had bones that didn't fully develop and were deformed, often with the classic bowing of the legs.

. . . This is now

There has been a change in the major health concerns today versus 100 years ago, but globally, some similarities still exist. Worldwide, infectious disease is still a major cause of death, and the threat of newer strains of viruses and bacteria are always present. In addition, the mutation of "superbugs" that are immune to many antibiotics has been created by overuse of antibiotics. Such antibiotic-resistant bacteria are an increasing threat. More and more of these bacterial infections are difficult or impossible to treat with current antibiotics.

REMEMBER

Major medical discoveries and inventions have improved the outcomes of many conditions by earlier diagnosis and better medications and treatments, but lifestyle changes have resulted in the current prevalence of chronic and often preventable diseases, such as heart disease, cancer, respiratory illness, diabetes, and stroke, which have the highest mortality rates today.

Over the years, medical advances have fueled the changes that have overcome some major health threats to society. Here is the list of major contributors:

» **Infant vaccinations:** Today, over 90 percent of children age 3 or younger receive vaccinations. As a result, some of the deadly diseases, like smallpox and polio, are completely controlled in developed countries, while worldwide programs try to spread this success into the underdeveloped countries. Due to increased vaccination rates today, diphtheria, tetanus, pertussis, measles, mumps, and rubella rarely occur. Furthermore, new vaccines are available (like for chicken pox) that weren't available 30 years ago. People born in 1955 were the first to receive vaccinations in infancy, starting with polio. That factor alone significantly increased that generation's lifespan. In the years to follow, more childhood vaccines were added, such as measles in 1963, mumps in 1967, and rubella in 1969.

» **Antibiotics:** People have been receiving antibiotics since the 1940s for bacterial infections, such as syphilis, tuberculosis, malaria, and pneumonia. Penicillin was discovered in 1928 and first used medically in 1940. Since then, resistant bacteria have been on the rise. In the 1950s, new resistant bacteria showed the need to limit use of antibiotics to keep new resistant bacteria for emerging. Despite that knowledge, the improper use of antibiotics is much more widespread over 70 years later, leaving researchers nervous about the inevitable development of newer resistant bugs. Follow your doctor's recommendation about taking antibiotics seriously to help avoid further resistant strains from improper antibiotic use. For example, don't ask for antibiotic prescriptions every time you have a cold. Colds are caused by viruses, but antibiotics only treat bacteria.

>> **Medical technology:** Medical technology drives the improvements in modern medicine. To make better medications, vaccines, and diagnostic tests, advances in medical equipment are necessary to identify and create them. Enhanced diagnostic imaging has enabled diagnosis of diseases in their early stages, which often improves the outcome. Patients with disease that has advanced to organ failure get hope from technology advancements in prosthetics, organ transplantation, and tissue repair. Here are a few of the major breakthroughs:

- The *artificial heart* can be used to keep heart failure patients alive until they can receive a donor heart.

- *Computer-aided tomography (CAT) scan* produces three-dimensional images of the body that can show doctors whether a tumor is present and how deep it is in the body, to guide diagnosis and treatments.

- *Magnetic resonance imaging (MRI)* uses magnetic fields and radio waves that causes atoms to give off tiny radio signals, and create clear detailed images (even better that CAT scans) to allow cross-section and three-dimensional views of soft tissue and bone. This makes it possible to detect cancer and other ailments early.

REMEMBER

Despite these amazing advances, some diseases are still very much in play; for example, cardiovascular disease (CVD) is still the leading cause of death in the world. Cancer, diabetes, and osteoporosis all are major health threats as you age. Each of these health concerns is discussed further later in this chapter.

The Basics of Pro-Aging: The Best Actions You Can Take

You can't prevent the passage of time, but when you're *proactive* about your life choices, you can control some of the risk factors in your life associated with illness and disease. Being proactive doesn't automatically guarantee you won't develop a chronic disease or illness, but not doing anything or actively taking part in known risk factors that are linked to chronic disease or illness may lead to health problems.

You may not realize just how much control you have over how long you live. Seemingly casual choices you make every day have the most profound impact on your health. In fact, it's estimated that if everyone in the United States led a healthy lifestyle (outlined in the following list), more than 50 percent of the cases of cardiovascular disease and diabetes could be avoided and more than 50 percent of all cases of cancer prevented.

The earlier in life you choose to follow a lifestyle of disease prevention, the more you can lower your risks of developing chronic disease. Chronic disease and illness come from many different factors, some of which you can control — such as life-style choices — and others you can't — like your age and genetics.

TIP

The following tips show you how to avoid the most damaging and preventable threats to your health and aging:

>> **Don't smoke — and if you already do, stop.** Really. Smoking increases the risks for the top three killers: heart disease, cancer, and cardiovascular ailments, including strokes. It also damages your lungs and other parts of your respiratory system. At least 60 chemicals in cigarette smoke cause cancer, and as a cigarette burns, it produces the poisons carbon monoxide, ammonia, formaldehyde, arsenic, and cyanide.

Smoking raises your blood pressure and decreases the flow of oxygen to your brain and body. It's also a significant risk factor for other health concerns, including emphysema, chronic bronchitis, stroke, and osteoporosis. Smoking causes more than 480,000 deaths annually (including deaths from second-hand smoke).

>> **Limit alcohol consumption.** If you drink alcohol, do so in moderation. That means a maximum of two drinks a day for men and one drink a day for women. (A standard drink is one 12-ounce bottle of beer or wine cooler, one 5-ounce glass of wine, or 1.5 ounces of 80-proof distilled spirits.) Women are more likely to have liver damage from drinking two or more drinks a day than men are, so it's especially important for women to keep alcohol consumption to no more than one drink a day.

REMEMBER

Alcohol is a depressant and can exacerbate the symptoms of depression and other mental disturbances. Alcohol intoxication causes problems with coordination, speech, and decision making, leading to risky behaviors. At toxic levels of alcohol intake, vomiting, difficult breathing, seizures, and even death can occur. Alcohol has an addiction potential, with around 8 percent of adults having an alcohol use disorder. With addiction and chronic alcohol consumption, disease in the liver, pancreas, nervous system, and gastrointestinal system can occur. If you've had any history of addiction to alcohol or any other substance, you shouldn't drink at all.

However, in moderation, studies have found that consumption of alcohol can have protective measures in cardiovascular disease. Consumption of red wine may be particularly favorable because red wine contains certain polyphenol antioxidants associated with cardiovascular health.

WARNING

If you're pregnant, you should *not* drink at all because any alcohol intake by a pregnant woman can harm a fetus.

>> **Maintain a healthy, balanced diet.** The importance of a balanced and healthy diet as you age can't be overstated. A poor diet can lead to an increased risk of many health problems, including osteoporosis, heart disease, and impaired memory. Eating well, on the other hand, makes you feel and look better, keeps your body functioning optimally, wards off colds and sickness, and contributes to lowering blood pressure and cholesterol levels, which in turn helps protect you against heart disease and stroke. (Chapters 21 and 22 talk more about good nutrition.)

>> **Exercise regularly.** Over time, a sedentary lifestyle can lead to obesity, a preventable yet dangerous epidemic that poses a threat to people's longevity. And it's on the rise. As you age, regular exercise should be a cornerstone of healthy living. As your body slows down, you may be tempted to skip the exercise because it's harder to do, you feel challenged physically, or you accept that being less active is part of normal aging. Don't fall prey to this thinking!

REMEMBER

As you get older, exercise doesn't need to be strenuous; it just needs to be consistent. Regular physical activity helps your body function more effectively. (See Chapters 19 and 20 for more info on activity and exercise.)

>> **Manage stress in your life and develop healthy coping mechanisms.** Stress causes the release of the hormones cortisol, norepinephrine, and epinephrine, which under acute stress have a protective effect on the body. But *chronic* stress allows hormones to hang around longer than usual and cause the formation of free radicals. (See the chapters in Part 3 for more information on the effects of stress.) Although these little buggers don't cause death directly, they do contribute to development of problems like high blood pressure and heart disease.

>> **Get enough sleep regularly.** You need sleep, both psychologically and physiologically. The body uses this time for healing and growth and produces many hormones essential for proper functioning during the deepest sleep stages. Sleep irregularity can have a direct impact on some disorders, such as epilepsy and migraines, and has been associated with diseases such as cardiovascular disease, clinical depression, diabetes, and other serious conditions. (See Chapter 19 for more on sleep.)

>> **Visit your doctor for the recommended screening tests for your age.**
Several important tests can help protect against cancer, heart disease, stroke,
diabetes, and osteoporosis. Some of these tests (discussed later in this
chapter) find diseases early, when they're most treatable, while others can
actually help keep a disease from developing in the first place.

If Staying Young and Healthy Is So Easy, Why Isn't Everyone Doing It?

There's nothing terribly complicated about living a healthy, life-prolonging life-style. So why are more people falling prey to partially preventable diseases every year? This section explores some of the biggest reasons behind the staggering numbers of preventable deaths. Take these pointers to heart so you can recognize any that may be present in your own life and make changes to effectively enhance the quality of your life, both now and in the future, no matter what your age.

Short-sighted thinking

Here's a little secret: Everyone is mortal. Despite this common knowledge, few people think about the inevitability of their own deaths and the things they can do to prevent death from happening prematurely. If they did, there would be far fewer accidents of every type, no one would ever break a hip falling off a ladder, and cigarette sales would plummet.

The idea that death can be postponed leads to thinking that "tomorrow" is a good time to start a dietary overhaul, an ambitious new exercise regimen, and, of course, a plan to quit smoking and drinking. For many people, tomorrow is also a good time to finally call and set up the routine physical or breast exam they've been avoiding for the past five years.

REMEMBER

A little realism can go a long way toward a new way of living that can literally save lives — at least for a few more years.

TIP

How can you inject enough realism to make you want to change but not so much that you feel it's all too futile anyway? The following ideas may help:

>> **Take a quiz.** Online sites allow you to input your health information and get a prediction of how long you'll live. Seeing your projected timeline in black and white may be enough to get you motivated to make changes. One such site is www.livingto100.com.

>> **Pay attention to how you feel.** Often the little nagging symptoms that can signal something big brewing are ignored. One way to keep track of what's going on with your health is to keep a journal. Don't do this if you're already obsessed with your health — most likely you already keep track of your symptoms. Do this only if you're the type of person that ignores warning signs like shortness of breath, chest pain, or headaches. You may see a pattern that needs to be addressed.

>> **See your doctor.** Make it clear when you make the appointment that this isn't a "sick" visit but rather a consultation. Ask your doctor what you can do to improve your health, and then *do it.*

REMEMBER

Many people have joined a "managed care" system where there are limitations on treatments and a focus on cutting costs, often leaving individuals managing their own care. The plethora of health information on the Internet (not all accurate, but abundant) can lead people to self-diagnose or make their own clinical decisions based on information they find on the Internet. It's not bad to be informed, but it can be dangerous if this information is replacing doctor visits.

Confusing what feels good with what is good

Making healthy food choices can have a major impact on health and aging. Most people know some of the fundamental eating habits to avoid, such as eating fried foods and high-sugar snacks. Those same people also know that fruits and vegetables are good for you. So why are so many people unable to make the decision to eat the way they know they should?

REMEMBER

Could it be that some people's inability to stop eating poorly is an addiction, similar to addictions to tobacco and alcohol? More likely, it's the cavalier attitude many people have about their health that keeps them eating poorly until they're slapped in the face with the reality of poor health. You may have heard the saying "cancer is the cure for smoking." Well, you'd think diabetes and heart disease would be the cure for obesity . . . but sadly, they often aren't. This battle is never ending in the medical profession. Moving to healthy eating habits is difficult. Eating what's good for you just doesn't feel as good as eating what's bad for you in many cases. It's not that you can't ever eat a fast food meal again — you can. You can't, however, eat fast food or packaged food all or even most of the time and stay healthy.

The desire for a quick (and easy) fix

Given a choice, most people will take the quick fix over hard work every time. Lose 25 pounds in a week, guaranteed? Sign me up! Quit smoking overnight? Here's my money! Build a beautiful body in only two minutes a day — and you don't even have to stand up? That's for me!

It's human nature to want something for nothing, but when it comes to living longer, you have to put in the time and effort — hours in the gym, self-control in the grocery store, and discipline in your lifestyle choices. And make no mistake: It takes time and effort to eat healthier foods, exercise, and maintain a focused, balanced low-stress lifestyle. You have to give up things — horribly unhealthy foods that taste so wonderful as well as time you feel short on anyway — to get yourself in a positive aging routine.

Some of the more recent "quick fix" ideas have involved getting hormone supplements to stay young. Here's the real story on some of the most often touted anti-aging hormones:

» **Human growth hormones (HGH):** HGH is produced by your pituitary gland and is required for growth and cell repair. Levels start dropping at around age 40, and by age 70, HGH production may have dropped as much as 75 percent. HGH supplementation sounds like the perfect way to reverse the effects of aging. But does it work?

Some studies have shown an increase in muscle mass and decrease in body fat in patients with a documented deficiency who received injections several times a week. The studies didn't, however, demonstrate an increase in strength along with the increase in muscle mass in those that didn't have a deficiency in the hormone. Evidence supports that HGH use in those who have a deficiency does offer benefits, but it doesn't appear to be the simple answer for those who aren't deficient but are looking for a shortcut.

» **Dehydroepiandrosterone (DHEA):** DHEA is a hormone produced by the adrenal glands and is converted into the hormones estrogen and testosterone. Levels of DHEA drop as you get older, and it's been theorized that raising DHEA levels may increase muscle mass and bone density, boost the immune system, and delay aging symptoms, such as joint pain, decreased muscle and libido, and lower energy.

However, a study of 144 people over age 60 conducted by the Mayo Clinic over a two-year period showed no increase in muscle strength, bone mass, endurance, or quality of life. An earlier, smaller, and shorter study did show some reduction in body fat and insulin resistance in those taking DHEA. Based on the evidence, use of DHEA without diagnosed deficiency doesn't seem to offer much benefit. As with other hormones, DHEA can help those who have a deficiency.

>> **Testosterone therapy:** Like many hormones, testosterone production starts to decrease around age 30. Low testosterone levels can cause impotence in men and decreased sex drive, bone loss, muscle loss, and low energy levels in both men and women.

- **Men:** In men with low testosterone, supplementation can increase all the above, so the interest in testosterone as a way to keep older men "young" developed. However, using testosterone supplements if you have normal testosterone levels already can be risky; high levels of testosterone have been linked to breast cancer in men and can cause prostate enlargement, which can accelerate already present prostate cancer. Testosterone can also increase risk for blood clots.

- **Women:** Women with low testosterone can have improvements in weight management and libido with supplementation, but they may also develop male characteristic side effects such as increased facial hair and deepened voice. These don't occur if you're truly deficient and monitored correctly.

REMEMBER

Hormone supplementation can be valuable, but only if you have a hormone deficiency. If you're having symptoms of fatigue, erectile dysfunction, inability to lose weight, muscle wasting despite exercise, or decreased libido, supplementation with hormones may help, but you need to discuss testing with your doctor instead of grabbing a bottle off the health store shelf. People who don't have a deficiency and are using supplementation as a shortcut to improve strength, endurance, and energy may have adverse reactions.

Modifying your lifestyle is key

Wading through the mire of information, articles, products, and research on aging is enough to leave you feeling conflicted and confused. Medicine is starting to center on the behavioral modification that effectively helps people practice healthy lifestyles. So familiarize yourself with the truth and resolve to let it guide your decisions.

REMEMBER

In the end, living a healthier lifestyle is nine-tenths attitude change and one-tenth real effort. If you change your attitude about food, eating healthy will no longer seem like a punishment. Changing your exercise attitude makes exercise a pleasure rather than a pain. Getting rest is the energy for tomorrow. This type of attitude pushes you forward and educates you further about the dangers and rewards of better lifestyles and healthier aging. Here's to the first leg of your journey to healthful living and aging.

Looking at Cancer: The Four Most Common Forms

Few health diagnoses strike as much fear as the words "You have cancer." Unlike in years past, today cancer can be conquered or kept under control in many cases. Yet cancer is one of the top causes of death worldwide. Here's some of the main cancer terminology you should know:

>> **Grade:** The grade of a tumor (cancer) is based on how abnormal the cells look under a microscope. The higher the grade of a tumor, the quicker it will grow and spread.

>> **In situ:** The term *in situ* means that the cancer cells haven't spread beyond the specific site where the cancer began; it's still contained in the ducts or lobules of the organ where it started.

>> **Metastasis:** When the cancer cells in one part of the body have grown and spread by the blood stream or lymphatic system to other areas of the body, the cancer has *metastasized*. Metastasis generally occurs in later stages of cancer — hence the importance of early detection.

>> **Stage:** *Stage* describes the severity of a person's cancer. Most cancers are staged based on the extent of cancer spread in the body. Early stages generally occur when the cancer is still limited to the organ where it began, whereas late stages indicated spread beyond that organ to other sites of the body (metastasis).

The chance of developing cancer increases with age; 56 percent of all cancer diagnoses and 70 percent of all cancer deaths occur in people over the age of 65. About 5 to 10 percent of all cancer cases can be attributed to genetic factors (like ethnicity and family history) that are beyond your control, but a whopping 90 to 95 percent of cases have their roots in lifestyle choices. So think of how much you can slash your risk of getting cancer by eating a healthy diet, staying physically active, and steering clear of tobacco. Your daily lifestyle decisions have a lot more impact on your health than you may realize.

This section covers the four most commonly diagnosed cancers — lung, breast, prostate, and colon — as well as their specific risk factors and preventive measures. These are the cancers most easily diagnosed through routine examinations. Early detection can increase cure rates.

Lung cancer

About 1.3 billion people worldwide smoke, even though it's no secret that smoking can kill you. If you aren't convinced yet, what will it take to get you to stop smoking? Check out the following statistics of lung cancer:

>> Is the most common cancer worldwide

>> Is the deadliest cancer and has the highest worldwide mortality rate

>> Causes more deaths than the other three most common cancers combined (colon, breast, and prostate)

>> Has surpassed breast cancer as the most common cancer in women

The good news? Most lung cancer is preventable because 90 percent of cases are caused by smoking. Imagine how quickly new cases of lung cancer would drop if everyone just quit lighting up.

Differentiating among the different types

Lung cancer falls into two general categories, small-cell lung cancer (SCLC), also called *oat cell cancer*, and non small-cell lung cancer (NSCLC). NSCLC is much more common — around 85 percent of lung cancers are NSCLC. SCLC grows and spreads more quickly than NSCLC and is almost entirely caused by smoking.

NSCLC can be divided into three different types based on how it appears under a microscope:

>> **Adenocarcinoma:** These cancers account for about 40 percent of lung cancers and have a better prognosis than other types of lung cancer. Adenocarcinomas are often found in the outer regions of the lungs and initially develop in the mucus producing cells.

>> **Large-cell (undifferentiated) carcinoma:** Around 10 to 15 percent of lung cancers fall into this category; large-cell carcinoma has characteristically large, rounded cells, grows rapidly, and has a poor prognosis.

>> **Squamous cell carcinoma:** This cancer accounts for about 25 to 30 percent of all lung cancers and most commonly occurs near the center of the lung in one of the bronchus (one of the two main branches of the windpipe). Smoking is the main cause.

Understanding your risk

Unlike some cancers, doctors know what causes lung cancer. Take a look at the risk factors:

>> **Smoking:** Cigarette smoking is the number one cause of lung cancer. Ninety percent of lung cancer cases occur in people who smoke. Smokers have 20 times the risk of lung cancer versus those who don't smoke. The more cigarettes you smoke, the higher your risk of developing lung cancer. Cigarette smoke contains over 4,000 chemicals, many of which are proven to be cancer-causing substances called *carcinogens.* Carcinogens cause irreversible damage to your body's normal cells and greatly increase the chance they'll change into cancerous cells that can grow out of control. For information and resources on how to quit smoking, go to smokefree.gov (provided by the National Institutes of Health) or the American Lung Association website at (www.lung.org).

>> **Radon inhalation:** *Radon* is a gas that can't be detected by sight, taste, or smell and is the second most common cause of lung cancer. Radon gas causes between 15,000 and 22,000 lung cancer deaths each year in the United States. Radon gas comes up through the soil and in through cracks in your home or another building's foundation. It tends to build up in unventilated basements, pipes, drains, or walls. Home sales in many places now require radon testing. Call the National Radon Hotline at 1-800-557-2366 to talk to an information specialist or go to the National Cancer Institute's fact sheet on radon and cancer at www.cancer.gov/about-cancer/causes-prevention/risk/substances/radon/radon-fact-sheet for more info.

>> **Workplace chemicals:** Certain jobs, including mining, pipe-fitting, and ship-building, may cause exposure to carcinogenic materials in the workplace, including asbestos. Exposure to asbestos increases the risk of lung cancer because inhaled fibers and dust can become embedded in the lung cells, causing a chronic inflammatory reaction that may eventually result in the development of cancer. Workers' risks are much higher if they smoke in addition to having these exposures to carcinogenic materials or chemicals on the job.

>> **Secondhand smoke:** The Environmental Protection Agency (EPA) has classified secondhand smoke as a known cause of cancer in humans. *Secondhand smoke* (also known as *environmental tobacco smoke*) is classified as any mixture of smoke given off by the burning end of a cigarette, cigar, pipe, or smoke exhaled from a smoker's lungs that can be inhaled by another person. About 53,800 people die every year in the United States from secondhand smoke exposure. Secondhand smoke contains all the same chemicals as the smoke inhaled directly by smokers, including formaldehyde, benzene, vinyl chloride, arsenic, ammonia, and hydrogen cyanide, all of which

immediately hurt your heart and lungs. Go to www.cancer.org/cancer/cancercauses/tobaccocancer/secondhand-smoke for more information.

>> **Age:** As with many cancers, your risk for developing lung cancer increases with age. The longer you smoke and the more cigarettes you smoke, the greater your chances of developing lung cancer. Less than 2 percent of lung cancer cases occur in people under age 45. The development of lung cancer increases thereafter, with the average age at diagnosis being around 70.

>> **Family history:** People who have a *first-degree* relative (mother, father, brother, or sister) with lung cancer have a higher incidence of lung cancer because some lung cancer is linked to mutations in the genetic cells that can be passed on to blood relatives.

Realize that you can get lung cancer even if you never smoked. Of those who develop lung cancer, 19 percent never smoked.

Playing your part in prevention

If you want to reduce your risk for lung cancer, stop smoking, never start smoking, stay away from those who do, and avoid exposure to asbestos or chemicals (like radon and chromium) that can cause lung cancer. Eliminating these risks of lung cancer and lung disease and getting thorough medical evaluations for occupational exposures can greatly reduce your risk of lung cancer.

People with certain work exposures may need to have yearly X-rays or other imaging due to the time that some cancers take to develop. Some cancers may be missed with X-rays alone while computed tomography (CT) scans can be more sensitive, so see your doctor to establish the proper testing if you have a history of occupational exposure.

What if you used to smoke but you quit? By quitting, you improve your quality of life and that of those around you. Smokers who never quit smoking lose about a decade of life, but those who quit between the ages of 35 and 44 gain back nine of those years; those quitting between age 45 and 54 gain back six, and those who quit between age 55 and 64 regain four. Your risk for developing and dying from lung cancer starts to decline when you kick the habit. After ten years, your risk of a heart attack is the same as a non-smoker's; your risk of lung cancer is about 50 percent lower than a smoker's and continues to decrease with time. It takes nearly 20 years for your lungs to return to "almost" normal, but some damage always remains. For people who've quit smoking and do develop lung cancer, studies show they usually respond better to treatment and may live longer than those who continue to smoke.

Simply reducing the number of cigarettes you smoke isn't as beneficial as completely quitting. Lung cancer risk is similar in heavy smokers (16 to 18 cigarettes per day) who halve their intake compared to heavy smokers who never cut down. So do yourself a favor and really *quit.*

Recognizing the symptoms of lung cancer

In the early stages of lung cancer, you may not experience symptoms. Many cases of lung cancer are found when screening or diagnostic tests for something else incidentally identify lung cancer. By the time any symptoms develop, lung cancer is most likely in advanced stages and has metastasized. That's why the mortality rate for lung cancer is so high. The following are the most common lung cancer symptoms:

>> Cough that persists or worsens without any particular reason

>> Hoarseness

>> Fever or night sweats

>> Coughing up blood

>> Weight loss and loss of appetite

>> Shortness of breath, wheezing, or chest tightness

>> Chronic infections such as bronchitis or pneumonia

Talk to your doctor if you experience any of these cancer symptoms.

Treating lung cancer and considering the prospects

Lung cancer treatments are based on the type of lung cancer, how advanced the disease is at the time of detection, and your underlying general health. If the cancer is found to be treatable and your health supports treatment, doctors usually use some combination of chemotherapy, radiation, and surgery:

>> **Chemotherapy:** Chemotherapy is used to shrink tumors, keep tumors from spreading, or simply to help relieve pain from some of the tumors when someone is receiving *palliative care* (comfort measures only). Chemotherapy drugs damage healthy cells as well as cancerous cells and can have severe side effects that may seem worse than the cancer symptoms themselves (including nausea, vomiting, hair loss, and increased risk of infection). These types of reactions depend on the type of agents used; some chemotherapy agents cause fewer symptoms than others. An *oncologist* (a doctor specializing in cancer) can determine the best option for your specific cancer situation,

>> **Radiation:** Radiation uses X-rays to kill cancer cells. This procedure can be accomplished by directing a radiation beam through the outside of the body or directly inserting radiation "seeds" into the cancer. The delivery method depends on the type of cancer, stage, and location of the cancer. The goal of radiation therapy is to destroy cancer cells while minimizing harm to the surrounding healthy tissue. Radiation treatment for cancer is directed by a radiation oncologist.

>> **Surgery:** Lung cancer treatment may involve removing a portion, a lobe, or a whole lung. Lymph nodes surrounding the cancerous area may be removed during surgery to determine whether the cancer has spread outside the lungs, which will determine if other treatment is needed.

REMEMBER

Regardless of the treatment, lung cancer can have a poor prognosis if not found early. The following statistics apply to lung cancer:

>> Every day, 432 Americans die of lung cancer.

>> Only 18 percent of lung cancer patients are alive five years after diagnosis.

>> The five-year survival rate is 54 percent for patients with localized tumors; unfortunately, only 15 percent of cases are diagnosed that early.

>> For those diagnosed after their lung cancer has metastasized, the five-year survival rate is only 4 percent.

>> More than half of all lung cancer patients die within one year of being diagnosed.

Breast cancer

Many young women state that their biggest health fear when growing older is breast cancer. Even though lung cancer has a higher mortality rate and heart disease is a greater health risk (see these diseases' respective sections in this chapter), breast cancer is still what many women worry most about. On the flip side, many women don't worry about breast cancer because it doesn't run in their families. This false sense of security can be a costly mistake if it keeps you from having preventative testing.

Consider the following breast cancer facts:

>> Globally, breast cancer is the most commonly diagnosed cancer among women and is the second leading cause of cancer death for women.

» About 1.7 million people worldwide are diagnosed with the disease each year, with substantially more cases in developed countries (especially the United States, England, and Australia) than in developing countries.

» About 1 percent of all breast cancer occurs in men — about 2,500 cases each year.

» Less than 5 percent of breast cancer cases are diagnosed in women under age 40, but it's the leading cause of cancer death in women ages 20 to 59.

» Breast cancer is more common with age. Fifty percent of diagnosed breast cancer is in women over age 65.

» The five year survival rate of those diagnosed with early stage breast cancer is 99 percent.

You can't completely prevent breast cancer; everyone is at risk. Great strides have been made in breast cancer awareness in recent years, with more women utilizing self-exam and diagnostic techniques regularly.

Differentiating among types of breast cancer

Breast cancer is classified in different ways according to its location and whether it's metastasized. The following list describes other terms you may hear used to describe breast cancer:

» **Adenocarcinoma:** Most breast cancers start in the glandular tissue (lobes and ducts) of the breast; cancers of glandular tissue are called adenocarcinoma. There are two types of adenocarcinoma:

  ● **Ductal carcinoma in situ (DCIS):** *In situ* means "in place," so ductal carcinoma in situ means the cancer remains inside the walls of the milk ducts and hasn't spread into breast tissue or metastasized outside the breast. This is the most common type of noninvasive breast cancer, accounting for around 20 percent of newly diagnosed cases. It's also called *pre-invasive breast cancer.* Almost all women diagnosed at this stage can be cured.

  ● **Lobular carcinoma in situ (LCIS):** LCIS begins in the lobules of the breast but hasn't invaded through to surrounding breast tissue. LCIS isn't a true cancer; it may be the early stage of cancer or may simply increase a woman's risk of getting cancer later. Recent evidence shows that some LCIS may develop into invasive lobular carcinoma (that is, invasive breast cancer that begins inside the lobules). Having LCIS increases your risk, so it's important to follow the screening guidelines for breast cancer closely if you have this diagnosis.

>> **Invasive ductal carcinoma (IDC):** IDC, which starts in a milk duct and then breaks through the duct wall to the fatty part of the breast, accounts for 80 percent of all invasive breast cancers. After the cancer breaks through the milk duct wall, it can metastasize through your blood stream or lymphatics to other organs like the liver, lungs, or brain.

>> **Invasive lobular carcinoma (ILC):** Ten percent of invasive breast cancers are ILC, which begins in the lobules (milk producing glands). ILC is harder to feel on examinations and harder to detect on mammograms than IDC but can metastasize in the same way, through lymphatics and blood vessels.

>> **Inflammatory breast cancer (IBC):** This uncommon type of breast cancer accounts for only 1 to 5 percent of cases. Instead of containing a single lump or tumor, the entire breast becomes warm and red, with the skin taking on the appearance of an orange peel. This condition occurs because the cancer cells are blocking the lymph vessels in the skin. IBC is more likely to spread (metastasize) than ductal or lobular cancers. This cancer is aggressive, with about one third of patients already having metastasis when they're diagnosed.

>> **Paget disease of the nipple:** This cancer is rare and accounts for only 1 to 3 percent of all breast cancers. The upside of this cancer is that it has an excellent prognosis (meaning that there are good cure rates) in most cases. The disease starts in the breast ducts and then spreads to the skin of the nipple and then to the areola, the dark circle around the nipple. You may feel itching or burning and notice crusted, scaly, and red areas, which may ooze or bleed.

Understanding your risk

You can control some risks for developing breast cancer. Unfortunately, with breast cancer the risks you can't control outweigh the ones you can. For these reasons, early detection is important. The following are major risk factors for breast cancer:

>> **Gender:** Both men and women can develop breast cancer:

- Women are far more likely to develop breast cancer than men. The ratio of women to men with breast cancer is 100 to 1. The National Cancer Institute predicts that one in eight women born today will develop breast cancer in her lifetime.

- Risk factors for men include age (the average age for breast cancer in men is about age 67), obesity (obese men have higher levels of estrogen in their body), testicular and liver disease, and a disease called Kleinfelter's syndrome, which occurs in men who are born with two or more X chromosomes. Exposure to high levels of radiation also increases men's risk.

>> **Age:** As your age increases, so does your chance for developing breast cancer. This rise is due to exposure to estrogen over your lifetime and the fact that there has been a longer time for cells to have cancerous changes. According to the National Cancer Institute, for women age is a factor as follows:

- Age 30 to 39 — 1 in 227 probability of breast cancer

- Age 40 to 49 — 1 in 68 probability of breast cancer

- Age 50 to 59 — 1 in 42 probability of breast cancer

- Age 60 to 69 — 1 in 28 probability of breast cancer

- Age 70 and up — 1 in 26 probability of breast cancer

>> **Family history of cancer:** A woman's risk of developing breast cancer increases if she has a *first-degree* relative (mother, sister, or daughter) diagnosed with breast or ovarian cancer before the age of 40. Other combinations of family history risk factors are moderate risks, such as having two close relatives from the same side of the family diagnosed with breast cancer (one must be mom, sister, or daughter, while the other can be an aunt, grandma, or even Uncle Bob).

Scientists have found that women with genetic mutations (random structural changes) to genes *BRCA1* and *BRCA2* (short for Breast Cancer 1 and Breast Cancer 2) and others have up to an 85 percent chance of developing breast cancer in their lifetime. Less than 10 percent of breast cancer cases are related to inheritable genes, however. If you do have a strong family history, your doctor may want you to have earlier or more frequent testing done.

>> **Long-term estrogen exposure:** A strong correlation exists between breast cancer development and the hormone estrogen. Estrogen stimulates cancer cells to grow and divide rapidly. A woman's estrogen levels rise during puberty and then decrease during menopause. The longer a woman's breasts are exposed to estrogen, the greater her risk for developing breast cancer. Therefore, breast cancer risk may be higher in women who started menstruating before age 12 or in women who went through menopause after age 55. Research has also implicated hormonal birth control — whether oral, injected, or implanted — as a risk, especially if used for more than five years. Hormone replacement therapy after menopause that is used for more than five years also increases breast cancer risk.

>> **Drinking alcohol:** The bottom line is the more alcohol a woman drinks, the greater her risk for breast cancer. Around one in fifty cases of breast cancer in the United States may be attributed to alcohol consumption; in countries where alcohol consumption is higher, the risk may be as much as one in six cases. You can control this risk by watching your alcohol intake.

>> **Being overweight:** Being overweight holds a much stronger correlation to the development of breast cancer and has an adverse effect on survival in post-menopausal women. You can curb this risk by keeping a healthy weight (see Chapter 20 for more on how to lose weight).

>> **Physical inactivity:** Women who don't exercise may have an increased risk of breast cancer.

>> **Eating animal fat (meat and dairy):** Countries with a higher intake of animal fat from red meat and high-fat dairy products have a higher incidence of breast cancer. These fatty foods may boost the hormones that promote breast cancer. Meat may become a source of carcinogens and/or *mutagens* (which cause cell mutations or DNA changes) like HCAs (heterocyclic amines) when cooked at high temperatures. (Chapter 21 has info on the benefits of a meat-free, plant-based diet.)

Playing your part in prevention

"Know thy breasts" should be the defining statement for early detection of breast cancer. Breast cancer prevention starts with regular breast self-exams, beginning when you're in your 20s. Using a step-by-step approach on a specific schedule (discussed in the following section), women can be aware of how their breasts normally look and feel.

REMEMBER

Monthly self-exams provide you with a baseline; if anything changes from month to month, you're the first to know. Report any breast changes to a health professional as soon as they're discovered. Remember that a breast change doesn't mean you have cancer!

TIP

The best time for a woman to examine her breasts is one week after her period is over, when her breasts aren't tender or swollen, so she can feel any abnormalities or lumps that may be present. This examination is no small task at times; some women have very lumpy breasts, and the lumps may change from month to month.

REMEMBER

Women who are pregnant or breastfeeding should still keep examining their breasts regularly, even though the breasts may be tender. Women with breast implants should ask their surgeon to help them differentiate between breast tissue and the implant. To ensure proper technique, women should review their self breast exam (SBE) process with their healthcare professional during their clinical breast exam.

Clinical breast exams should be done at every yearly gynecologic exam. At age 50, women need to have the first of their recommended annual mammograms as well as yearly breast exams, unless they had an abnormal breast exam or there's a strong family history of breast cancer. Mammograms are currently the best and most reliable screening method, although it may take as many as six to ten years for breast cancer tumors to be detected by mammography. Your doctor may recommend an earlier screening if you have a personal or family history with breast cancer.

TIP

Sometimes ultrasound is used and is good for distinguishing whether a detected lump is a cyst (likely to be benign) or a solid mass (which could indicate a tumor). This technique is good to use in women with breast implants and dense breasts because a mammogram sometimes has difficulties "seeing" through dense tissue or implants. Ultrasound is also a great method for guiding physicians to do needle biopsies of suspicious lumps.

WARNING

The American Cancer Society recommends that women at high risk (such as a previous history of breast cancer, positive BRCA1/2 mutations, or a strong family history) for breast cancer should have an MRI scan in addition to (not in lieu of) their mammograms. MRIs are more sensitive, picking up more spots than a mammogram, and may result in more false positive results. The two tests together give better data to screen a woman at high risk for breast cancer.

Recognizing the symptoms of breast cancer

When feeling for a lump in your breast, keep in mind the following things:

>> Cancer cells are an abnormal overgrowth — meaning *irregular* in shape. A lump will generally be hard and may have a bumpy texture. However, you should get any lump, no matter what it feels like, checked out by a healthcare professional.

>> If you feel something different from what you felt before on yourself breast exams, get it checked.

>> If you see any dimpling of the skin, retraction of the skin or nipple, swelling, redness, open sores, thickening of the skin, or nipple discharge, get checked right away.

TIP

The technique recommended for self breast exams has changed. There's evidence that the woman's position (lying down), area felt, pattern of coverage of the breast, and use of different amounts of pressure increase the sensitivity of the self breast exam.

To perform a self breast exam, use these steps (see Figure 23-1):

1. **Standing in front of a mirror, look at your breasts for any changes of size, shape, contour, dimpling, pulling, redness, or flaking skin around the nipple or surrounding skin.**

2. **Lie on your back with a pillow under your right shoulder and place your right arm comfortably behind your head.**

   When you lie on your back, your breast tissue spreads more evenly and thinly over your chest. This position makes feeling for lumps or abnormalities easier.

3. **Place the three middle fingers of your left hand on your right breast.**

4. **Using the pads of your fingers, make small circular motions over your breast tissue to feel for lumps.**

   You should circle the tissue three times and use varying levels of pressure before moving on to the next area.

   - Start lightly to feel the skin's surface.

   - Use medium pressure to feel the tissue just under the skin.

   - Press more firmly to feel the tissue closest to your chest and ribs.

   Remember: The "tail" of the breast extends up into the armpit, so it's important to feel the armpit as well as the breast to be complete in your self-exam (see Figure 23-1 for the shape of the breast). Use enough pressure to feel all the breast tissue, but don't cause yourself pain.

5. **Manipulate your fingers over the entire breast area.**

   There are two main ways to make sure that you cover the whole breast. You can move your fingers flat across the breast in concentric circles starting at the nipple and moving in larger circles until you reach the outer edge of the breast, or you can use an up-and-down pattern starting from under your arm and across your breast to the middle of the breastbone (sternum) making a large square.

   Use this pattern to help:

   - Draw an imaginary square from just under your arm along your neck to your collarbone, then down your breast bone and over your rib cage and back up.

   - Walk the pads of your fingers up and down imaginary rows like you're mowing a lawn, feeling the breast tissue for any abnormalities or lumps. This up-and-down pattern is the most effective method for not missing any tissue.

6. **Now repeat Steps 2 to 5 on your left breast, using the fingers on your right hand.**

7. **When you're done examining your breasts from a reclining position, stand up.**

8. **Standing in front of the mirror, place your hands on your hips and look at your breasts for any changes of size, shape, contour, dimpling, pulling, redness, or flaking skin around the nipple or surrounding skin.**

   The act of pressing down on your hips contracts the muscles in your chest, which makes any changes in your breast more apparent.

9. **Place your arms by your sides and look; raise your hands above your head and press your palms to one another and look again.**

   This completes your monthly exam. Report any lumps or abnormalities to your doctor.

TIP

You can also examine your breasts while standing in the shower. The water makes it easier to move your fingers smoothly over the slippery wet skin of your breasts in a concentric circle pattern (see Figure 23-1). But make sure that you also examine your breasts while lying down because, as noted earlier, in the lying position you can more easily feel deeper tissue and therefore increase your likelihood of detecting deeper lumps.

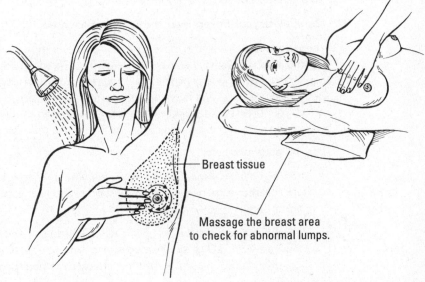

Breast tissue

Massage the breast area to check for abnormal lumps.

FIGURE 23-1: How to perform a self breast exam.

Illustration by Kathryn Born, MA

Following up on a lump

Most of the lumps you can feel are benign; most often the first sign of breast cancer is abnormalities found on a mammogram when it can't be felt on SBEs or by a medical professional. In fact, eight out of ten lumps are benign. But don't assume that a lump is benign. Make sure to have any lumps or changes evaluated by your doctor.

After you find a lump in your breast, here's what happens during a typical physician evaluation:

» You give a full health history, including any family member with breast cancer (grandmother, aunt, mother, sister, or daughter).

» You have a full breast exam, with the doctor palpating your breasts for any lumps or abnormalities.

» You schedule a mammogram, ultrasound, and/or breast MRI (one or more of these may be done depending on your situation and history).

If the physician workup reveals any suspicious lumps, you may be scheduled for one of the following procedures:

» A *fine needle aspiration biopsy* in which a needle is inserted into the lump to remove cells that are then tested for cancer

» A *core needle biopsy* with a larger-diameter needle to remove part of the lump for evaluation, usually with ultrasound guidance

» A *stereotactic biopsy* using mammograms to pinpoint the abnormal area and direct the needle into that area

» A *surgical excisional biopsy* (also called a *lumpectomy*) in which the lump is surgically cut out and removed so it can be studied under the microscope to look for cancer

If your lump is breast cancer, the earlier you can begin treatment, the better your survival rate.

Treating breast cancer and considering the prospects

Treatment options for breast cancer include surgery (lumpectomy or *mastectomy* [breast removal]), chemotherapy, hormone therapy, and radiation. The five-year survival rate for localized breast cancer is 99 percent, up from 74 percent in 1980. Unfortunately, advanced metastatic cancer has a higher mortality rate. If the cancer has spread regionally, the survival rate drops to 85 percent; those with distant metastases have a 25 percent five-year survival rate. For more on breast cancer treatment, check out the National Cancer Institute website (www.cancer.gov/types/breast/patient/breast-treatment-pdq) and the Susan G. Komen organization website (ww5.komen.org/BreastCancer/TreatingCommonBreastCancers.html).

Prostate cancer

The prostate plays a vital role in the male reproductive system. A healthy prostate is about the size and shape of a walnut. It's located underneath the bladder, in front of the rectum, and surrounds the urethra, the tube which carries urine and seminal fluid (not simultaneously) out of the body. Blood vessels and nerves also travel through the prostate tissue.

Prostate cancer occurs inside this small gland and is quite common. This cancer is treatable when caught early and is usually found during routine screening. Despite the excellent cure rate, men are particularly frightened of prostate cancer because they see it as a huge threat to their manhood. Many already feel uncomfortable with the screening procedure (a rectal exam) and are really reluctant to have biopsies and possible surgery.

Male hormones (androgens) can cause the prostate to grow, and many men develop benign enlargement of the prostate as they age. An enlarged prostate squeezes the urethra and can cause symptoms similar to the symptoms of prostate cancer. Enlargement is a very common condition, but don't assume prostate symptoms are just age-related prostate enlargement. You should definitely see your doctor to rule out cancer.

Understanding your risk

Prostate cancer is the most commonly diagnosed cancer (other than skin cancer) and the second leading cause of cancer death in American men. The good news is that 90 percent of prostate cancers are diagnosed early, while still confined to the prostate. The five-year survival rate for men with such early stage prostate cancer is nearly 100 percent.

Though the exact cause of prostate cancer isn't known, there are certain identifiable risks:

>> **Age:** The older you are, the more likely you are to be diagnosed with prostate cancer. Some clinicians feel that every male would develop prostate cancer if he lived long enough, but most men die of a different cause before this happens. Although many men are now being diagnosed as early as their 40s, the majority (about 65 percent) of diagnoses are made in men over age 65. Here's the age breakdown:

- Under age 40: You have a 1 in 10,000 chance.

- Ages 40 to 59: You have a 1 in 38 chance.

- Ages 60 to 69: You have a 1 in 14 chance.

>> **Ethnicity:** African American men are nearly 60 percent more likely to develop prostate cancer than Caucasian men. They're also twice as likely to die from the disease and are ranked with the highest percentage of prostate cancer cases in the world. Researchers haven't been able to explain these racial differences.

>> **Family history:** Men with a single first-degree relative (think father, brother, or son) diagnosed with prostate cancer have a greater risk of developing prostate cancer. A man with a family history of two or more relatives with prostate cancer is four times more likely to develop the disease himself. The risk is highest in men whose family members were diagnosed before age 65.

>> **Western-hemisphere lifestyle:** A diet high in calories from unhealthy fat, refined carbohydrates, and animal protein (both meat and high-fat dairy products), coupled with low physical activity and obesity, contributes to a variety of diseases, including cancer. The World Health Organization specifically attributes the development of prostate cancer to this Western lifestyle. (See Part 4 for more on healthier lifestyles.)

Playing your part in prevention

In order to diagnose prostate cancer early, you need to take an active part in your healthcare. Just as women should perform monthly self breast exams and receive mammograms starting at age 40, men need to start having these annual screening exams at age 40:

>> **Digital rectal exam (DRE):** This rectal exam is administered by a doctor. The doctor inserts a lubricated, gloved finger into the rectum to check the prostate for irregularities like lumps, nodules, or masses. The prostate should be smooth, uniform in shape, and symmetrical.

>> **Prostate-specific antigen (PSA) test:** This test measures the level of PSA in the blood. *PSA* is an enzyme produced mostly by the prostate to liquefy semen and normally enters the bloodstream in small amounts, but it can occur in high levels in prostate cancer. The value of the PSA test as a screening tool has recently been questioned. There is no evidence of its value in men over the age of 80.

Recognizing the symptoms of prostate cancer

The symptoms of prostate cancer are easily misinterpreted as other problems, so here are some of the most common signs and symptoms of prostate cancer:

>> Rectal pressure or pain in the space between the anus and the scrotum

>> Frequent or painful urination

» Frequent urination at night (nocturia)

» Difficulty getting the urine stream started

» Blood in the urine or ejaculate

» Painful ejaculation

» Loss of appetite and weight

» Bone pain caused from local cancer spread into the bones

Treating prostate cancer and considering the prospects

Your prostate cancer treatment options may involve surgery, radiation therapy, or hormone therapy. Discuss your best course of action with your doctor, who will monitor your health closely for any changes in your prostate exam and PSA level if you develop new or worsened symptoms. For more information on prostate cancer treatment options, head to the American Cancer Society website (www. cancer.org/cancer/prostatecancer/detailedguide/prostate-cancer-treating-general-info).

The survival stats for men with the cancer without having metastasized to other organs or tissues are as follows:

» 99 percent survive at least 5 years (up from 92 percent in 1990)

» 98 percent survive at least 10 years

» 94 percent survive at least 15 years

Colorectal cancer

Colorectal cancer occurs in the colon or in the rectum but is more commonly referred to as simply colon cancer. The colon is the first 4 to 5 feet of the large intestine, while the rectum, the connector between the colon and the anus, is the last 5 to 6 inches. Cancers in these areas are handled similarly. Colorectal cancer is the third most-common type of cancer in the world with over 1.4 million new cases diagnosed annually. In the United States, colon cancer has the third leading cause of all cancer deaths, but many deaths can be prevented with proper screening and risk reduction. In fact, screening is making a big impact; the death rate from colon cancer has been falling for over 20 years.

Understanding your risk

There's no single known risk factor for developing colon cancer but rather a group of risk factors:

WARNING

» **Polyps:** *Polyps* are small bumps or nodules that grow out of the wall of the colon or rectum, and they're the biggest risk factor of colorectal cancer. Almost all cases of colorectal cancer develop from polyps. Polyps that aren't removed may grow and eventually become malignant.

The process of changing from a benign (noncancerous) polyp to a malignant tumor can take several years. Many colon polyps are benign, but all polyps have the potential to become cancerous, some more aggressively than others. When cancer grows within a polyp, over time it can grow into (*infiltrate*) the wall of the colon and spread into blood vessels or lymph nodes, which allows it to spread by metastasis to other organs. When colon cancer has metastasized, the cure rate drops significantly. That's why detection and removal of polyps before they become cancerous or in their early stages of cancer growth is so important.

» **Age:** Over 90 percent of cases are diagnosed in people over the age of 50, with the average age at diagnosis being around 70. Your chance of being diagnosed with colorectal cancer is 50 times higher if you're age 60 to 79 than if you're younger than age 40. That is why recommendations say screening should start at age 50. But younger people *can* also get colorectal cancer, so pay attention to warning signs (see the later section "Recognizing the symptoms of colorectal cancer").

» **Family history:** Colorectal cancer is more likely to occur among people with a first-degree relative (mother, father, sibling, or child) diagnosed with colorectal cancer, especially if the cancer was diagnosed at a young age. Between 2 and 5 percent of people with colorectal cancer have inherited one of two genetic disorders. One is called *familial adenomatous polyposis* (FAP); cancer with FAP usually develops as early as age 20. The other is *hereditary nonpolyposis colorectal cancer* (HNPCC); cancer develops in 80 percent of these folks over their lifetimes, but not quite as early as in FAP. If you have one or more relatives diagnosed with colorectal cancer before the age of 50, consider having a blood test to determine whether you have the gene mutation and then take the appropriate preventative measures.

» **Gender:** Men are at slightly greater risk for colon cancer than women.

» **Meat intake:** A diet high in red meat and processed meats (such as hot dogs and lunch meats) can increase colorectal cancer risk. Eating lots of vegetables, fruits, and whole grains has been shown to decrease risk of colorectal cancer. Flip to Chapter 21 for suggestions on plant-based eating.

>> **Obesity:** Obesity increases your chances of dying from colorectal cancer. The link between obesity and colon cancer is stronger in men but also applies to women.

>> **Physical inactivity:** Not being physically active ups your chance of developing colon cancer. Chapter 20 has tips for increasing your activity, which can help decrease your risk.

>> **Smoking and alcohol use:** Your odds of developing and dying from colorectal cancer increase if you're a long-term smoker. Additionally, high alcohol intake and colon cancer have been linked. Check out the earlier section "The Basics of Pro-Aging: The Best Actions You Can Take" for details on moderate alcohol use.

>> **Chronic inflammatory bowel disease:** People who suffer from *Crohn's disease* (an inflammatory condition of the gastrointestinal tract) or *ulcerative colitis* (inflammatory bowel disease) for at least eight to ten years have a higher risk of colorectal cancer. Constant inflammation of the colon causes increased cell turnover and can speed up the growth of polyps. Your doctor may suggest doing more frequent colonoscopies starting at an earlier age in this situation.

Playing your part in prevention

The incidence of colon cancer has gone down in the last few decades because in many cases, colorectal cancer can be prevented by removing precancerous polyps found on colonoscopy screening. Early detection with regular screening exams after age 50 is the biggest factor in early detection and treatment of colorectal disease, but less than 50 percent of eligible people have been screened for colorectal cancer.

There are several types of screenings you can have done to test for colorectal cancer:

>> **Digital rectal examination (DRE):** This exam begins at age 40 (some doctors start at age 50) and continues annually. During a rectal exam, your doctor may be able to detect polyps in the rectum. If older than 50, at no time does this test replace the need for a colonoscopy.

>> **Fecal occult blood test (FOBT):** This screening starts at age 50 and continues annually. FOBT tests for hidden blood in three consecutive stool samples. Some doctors like to start testing for blood in the stool at age 40 because the test is simple, noninvasive, and helpful. This test is also useful for people who think they have blood in their stool but aren't sure.

>> **Colonoscopy:** A colonoscopy is an internal examination of the colon using a flexible lighted instrument called a *colonoscope;* it occurs after you're sedated, so you're unaware of the procedure. The purpose of the colonoscopy is to find polyps, remove them, and then study them under a microscope for signs of

cancer. Then proper follow-up monitoring will be arranged based on the type of polyps found (if any). Colonoscopies can be used as screening tests or as follow-up diagnostic tools when the results of another screening test are positive. Colonoscopy screenings start at age 50 and increase in frequency if anything is found. If nothing's found, doctors may wait up to ten years for your next scope (depending on the doctor).

>> **CT colonography or virtual colonoscopy:** This CT scan combines multiple cross-sectional images to create a detailed picture of the inside of your colon. If you're unable to have a regular direct colonoscopy, this is a good option. This test has pretty much replaced the use of the *barium enema,* in which barium coats the wall of the colon. X-rays then examine to look for irregularities that may indicate a polyp or tumor.

Recognizing the symptoms of colorectal cancer

Early colorectal cancer may not cause many symptoms. The most common symptoms are associated with changes in bowel habits, which includes one or more of the following:

>> **Rectal bleeding:** This bleeding occurs with visible blood in the stools, on toilet paper, in the toilet water, or on underpants.

>> **Microscopic blood:** This blood isn't visible to the naked eye. It's why fecal occult blood testing is important (see the preceding section).

>> **A change in usual bowel patterns:** Having constipation or diarrhea for more than seven to ten days can indicate a problem.

>> **Nausea or vomiting:** These symptoms are common complaints from people with certain cancers of the gastrointestinal tract due to the location of the cancer. Some other cancers can also effect appetite and indirectly induce some nausea.

>> **Lower abdominal pain:** Pain from either gas, cramping, or bloating that lasts longer than a week or a feeling that your stomach is distended or full should be discussed with your doctor.

>> **Shape of the stool:** Thinning of your stool into thin pencil shapes could indicate an obstruction in the intestine that is pressing on the stool, creating the thinner form.

>> **Unexplained weight loss:** Cancer can use up much of the body's energy and sometimes can release substances that can alter metabolism. Furthermore, people with cancer often develop loss of appetite that develops so slowly that it may not recognized as a problem.

WARNING

Never ignore rectal bleeding, because early detection of colon cancer can save your life. Get a second opinion if a doctor doesn't appear to be taking your case seriously. Take the case of Luke, a 30-year-old construction worker. Over a five-year period, he was evaluated by several doctors who told him his rectal bleeding was most likely from hemorrhoids, although no one sent him for a colonoscopy. By the time he found a doctor who sent him for a colonoscopy, he had advanced colon cancer and died from it within four years. If your doctor isn't taking continuing rectal bleeding seriously, get another opinion!

Treating colorectal cancer and considering the prospects

Surgery is the most common form of treatment for colorectal cancer in earlier-stage colon cancer that hasn't yet spread. However, chemotherapy and/or radiation therapy are sometimes utilized as well, especially in more advanced stages or with metastatic colorectal cancer. Surgical removal of the portion of the bowel where the colorectal cancer is found can increase a person's survival rate by 75 percent.

Some small, malignant polyps can be removed with the colonoscope, but many patients with larger colorectal cancer tumors need to undergo *bowel resection* — the removal of the portion of bowel that contains the cancerous cells. In most cases, each side of the colon can be reattached after the cancerous section is removed, but sometimes the patients have to have a *colostomy* (the bowel is attached to an opening in the abdominal wall, a *stoma*, for excretion of stool). Most of the time this solution is temporary to allow the bowel to heal and then the bowel is surgically reconnected to allow for normal bowel movements through the anus.

Colon cancer has decent cure rates, depending on the stage:

>> The five-year survival is greater than 90 percent for localized stage (confined to the inner colon wall).

>> The five-year survival rate is 65 percent for regional stage (spread to nearby tissue only).

>> The five-year survival rate is only 10 percent for metastasized colon cancer (spread to distant organs like liver, bone, lung, or brain via the blood stream or lymphatic system).

Check out the National Cancer Institute (www.cancer.gov/types/colorectal/patient/colon-treatment-pdq) or the American Cancer Society (www.cancer.org/cancer/colonandrectumcancer/detailedguide/colorectal-cancer-treating-by-stage-colon) for more on colorectal cancer treatment.

Being Informed about Diabetes

Diabetes is a chronic illness that if not diagnosed or treated properly can cause serious complications. Diabetics have problems managing the amount of glucose (sugar) in the blood. When glucose levels build up in your blood instead of being delivered to your cells as fuel, your cells become starved for energy. Over a long period of time, high blood sugar levels can lead to kidney failure, cardiovascular disease, nerve damage, arteriosclerosis, blindness, amputation, and difficulty treating infections. Diabetics also have a higher risk certain cancers, like pancreatic and uterine cancer. Unfortunately, diabetes isn't curable, but you can (and should) manage diabetes properly to control blood sugar levels and decrease the risk of these complications.

TECHNICAL STUFF

Diabetes is one of the top ten causes of death worldwide, with approximately 1.5 million deaths directly due to diabetes annually. The majority of these deaths are due to cardiovascular disease complications of diabetes. Between 1980 and 2008, the number of diabetics worldwide doubled, and it's expected to double again by 2030 because of the increase in obesity, poor diet, and sedentary lifestyle.

The following sections review the basics of diabetes to help you understand the disease and decrease your risk for getting it or improve your blood sugar control if you already have it. For the complete rundown on diabetes, read *Diabetes For Dummies* (Wiley) by Alan L. Rubin, MD.

Differentiating among the types of diabetes

Diabetes can show up in different forms:

>> **Type 1 diabetes:** *Type 1 diabetes,* the unpreventable form, is typically diagnosed in childhood or young adulthood and is formerly known as *juvenile diabetes.* In people with type 1 diabetes, the insulin-producing cells in the pancreas stop functioning. Type 1 diabetes requires insulin administration for survival and can't be controlled with diet and exercise. Possible causes of type 1 diabetes include autoimmune disease, genetic disease, and environmental agents.

>> **Type 2 diabetes:** *Type 2 diabetes* is the most common form, accounting for over 90 percent of all people with diabetes. People with type 2 diabetes make some insulin inside their bodies, but either it's not enough or their cells become resistant to it and it doesn't handle the glucose that comes in through their diet. Many people with type 2 diabetes can control their blood sugar with diet, exercise, and oral medication, but some people require insulin injections.

On average, people with type 2 diabetes die five to ten years before people without diabetes, mostly due to cardiovascular disease. However, and this is a big *however,* many of these cases are preventable.

>> **Gestational diabetes:** This form of diabetes causes high blood sugar (*glucose intolerance*) in approximately 3 to 5 percent of pregnant women and causes an increased risk of complications during pregnancy and at delivery. Women should be tested for gestational diabetes during the 24th to 28th week of pregnancy so they can be treated. Risk increases if the pregnant woman is obese or has a strong family history of diabetes. Women who have gestational diabetes have increased risk of type 2 diabetes later in life.

Understanding your risk

You can't prevent type 1 diabetes, and gestational diabetes has limited preventable causes, but you can control the risk factors for type 2 diabetes:

>> **Obesity:** This is the single greatest risk factor for developing type 2 diabetes because being overweight can prevent the body from making or using insulin efficiently. People with a body mass index (BMI) of 30 or higher have an 80 to 90 percent greater incidence of developing type 2 diabetes than people who maintain a healthy weight.

>> **Age:** Most people who develop diabetes are over age 40, with the risk increasing as a person ages; however, the obesity epidemic in children is resulting in more type 2 diabetes being diagnosed in children.

>> **Family history of diabetes:** If you have a first-degree relative with type 2 diabetes, you're at a higher risk.

>> **Gestational diabetes:** If you had gestational diabetes, you are at increased risk for type 2 diabetes. According to the National Diabetes Education Program (NDEP), between 5 to 10 percent of women with gestational diabetes develop type 2 diabetes.

>> **Physical inactivity:** You can prevent up to 80 percent of type 2 diabetes cases by adopting a healthy diet and increasing physical activity — that is, 30 minutes of moderate intensity physical activity on most days. Head to Chapter 20 for more on how to exercise to stay sharp!

Check with your doctor about a healthy diet and exercise plan to decrease your sugar levels and get back on track to a healthy weight.

Playing your part in prevention

By taking an active role in modifying your lifestyle choices, you can significantly reduce your risk for developing diabetes. Check out the following changes:

>> **Maintain a healthy weight.** If you're overweight and you lose an average of 7 percent of your body weight through diet and exercise, you can reduce your risk of developing diabetes by nearly 60 percent (70 percent if you're over 65 years old). Losing as little as 10 pounds can greatly decrease your risk. The healthy combination of weight management and exercise not only reduces your risk of developing diabetes but can also improve management of your blood glucose levels and decrease risks for serious diabetes complications if you've already been diagnosed with diabetes.

>> **Get regular exercise.** It's no secret that regular physical activity is good for you. By exercising for 30 minutes five or more days a week, you significantly reduce the risk of developing type 2 diabetes.

>> **Eat a healthy diet.** Because diabetes is an illness affecting blood sugar levels, what you eat and how often you eat it can help control and moderate those levels.

>> **Have your fasting blood sugar tested.** The American Diabetes Association recommends that you have your healthcare provider check your fasting blood sugar (a simple blood test) at least once every three years if you're age 40 or older.

WARNING

If you experience any of the symptoms listed in the following section and you're under age 40, notify your doctor immediately to schedule a blood sugar test — these symptoms can be serious no matter your age.

Recognizing the symptoms

Over 6 million Americans have diabetes and don't know it. Diabetes can be effectively managed, but it has to be diagnosed first. Many people with diabetes don't have recognizable symptoms, while others have symptoms but don't know they're indicative of diabetes. Here are some of the most major symptoms associated with diabetes:

>> **Excessive thirst and frequent urination:** When glucose builds up in your bloodstream, fluid gets pulled into the blood from your tissues to dilute it. You may feel very thirsty as well because your body needs more fluids to dilute the high blood sugar levels. As you drink fluids to quench your thirst, you also urinate more frequently.

>> **Extreme hunger even though you've already eaten:** If insulin is unable to move the glucose from your blood into your body cells, you feel hungry, even

if you just ate. Think of this as your cells asking you to take in more food for energy because they aren't getting what they need despite the high blood sugar levels.

>> **Unexplained weight loss:** Even if you eat more because you're hungry, you may keep losing weight because the energy from glucose isn't getting to your muscle tissues and fat stores, which thus diminish over time (this happens in type 1 diabetes).

>> **Tiredness and fatigue:** Without energy from food entering your cells, you get tired, weak, and irritable.

>> **Blurred vision:** When blood sugar levels are too high, your body takes fluid from body tissue, including your eyes, which makes it hard to focus.

>> **Tingling, pain, or numbness in hands or feet:** This indicates diabetic nerve damage, which often develops in type 2 diabetes.

>> **Cuts or bruises that are slow to heal:** Diabetics take longer to heal from traumatic injuries and are more prone to infection.

If you experience one or more of these symptoms and think you may have diabetes, check with your doctor for an accurate diagnosis.

Managing diabetes and considering the prospects

REMEMBER

If you have diabetes, keeping your blood sugar under control is imperative. Whether you take insulin, oral medications, or just control your diet, the key to minimizing complications from diabetes is to keep your blood sugars within the parameters your doctor sets for you. Taking insulin or oral medication doesn't mean you can eat whatever you want. Although medications help control blood sugar levels, you still have to do your part by watching what you eat.

TIP

Here are a few pointers to keep in mind:

>> Control your diet by eliminating refined sugars and empty calories (sugary juices or soft drinks, alcoholic beverages, candy, cookies, cake, ice cream, and so on) as much as possible.

>> Choose the right types of carbohydrates (like vegetables and beans, which contain fiber) to stabilize blood sugar.

>> Use the *glycemic index* (which rates carbohydrates by how much they raise blood glucose levels) to better understand what foods or food combinations you can eat to keep your blood sugar levels steady. For more information on

how to utilize the glycemic index, check out *Glycemic Index Diet For Dummies* by Meri Reffetto (Wiley).

» Incorporate a weight management and exercise program (as described in Chapter 20).

If you're diabetic, you need to check your blood sugar at least daily but sometimes more often. Your doctor can give you a prescription for a *glucometer* (a blood sugar monitor), *lancets* to prick your finger, and a log book to keep track of your blood sugars. A nurse can show you how to use your glucometer and record the readings and then have you demonstrate to make sure you're doing it correctly. Your doctor has you check your blood sugar a certain number of times per day based on your blood sugar readings and other health concerns to determine whether you need medication or whether your medication needs to be adjusted to keep your blood sugar controlled.

Cardiovascular Disease

Cardiovascular disease (CVD) is the leading cause of death in both the United States and the world at large. The deadly combination of heart disease and stroke kills over 17 million people worldwide every year, particularly those in poor countries. Cardiovascular disease is increasing worldwide due to upward trends in obesity, poor diets, smoking, and physical inactivity, particularly in the younger population.

REMEMBER

Cardiovascular disease is *not* a normal part of healthy aging. The lifestyle choices you make directly impact the health of your heart and vascular system and whether you develop CVD.

Understanding the components of the cardiovascular system is a good start to understanding the problems that occur when abnormalities arise in different areas. The cardiovascular system consists of the pump (heart), hoses (vessels), fluid (blood), and the nozzle (valves); if any one isn't working properly, you can have problems.

Differentiating among the various heart diseases and illnesses

Cardiovascular disease is a broad term to describe a mix of many problems that affect heart and blood vessel health. Having more than one of these problems simultaneously is common, which further increases your chance of dying from cardiovascular disease. The following sections explain the major problems that arise.

There's really no cure for cardiovascular disease, but prevention and screening are the best tools for delaying the onset or minimizing the damaging effects.

Coronary artery disease (CAD)

Coronary artery disease (CAD) is also known as *coronary heart disease* or *ischemic heart disease*; it kills more than 7 million people in the world each year. CAD results from *atherosclerosis* (narrowing of the arteries). In atherosclerosis, *plaque* deposits buildup in the arteries (as shown in Figure 23-2). Plaque is made up of fat, cholesterol, calcium, and other substances from the blood.

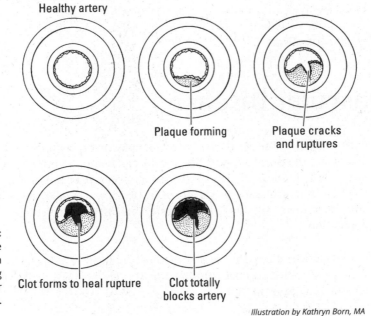

Healthy artery

Plaque forming

Plaque cracks and ruptures

Clot forms to heal rupture

Clot totally blocks artery

Illustration by Kathryn Born, MA

FIGURE 23-2: How plaque builds up in arteries causing cardiovascular disease.

According to the American Heart Association (www.heart.org), CAD's damage is caused by elevated levels of blood cholesterol and triglycerides, high blood pressure, and tobacco smoke.

High blood pressure

High blood pressure occurs when your heart has to work harder than normal to pump blood out into your arteries because they're constricted by hardened walls or partially filled with atherosclerotic plaque. The blood pressure is at the highest when the heart pumps blood out (systolic pressure) and the lowest in between pumps (diastolic pressure). The higher a person's blood pressure, the greater that person's risk of heart attack, stroke, heart failure, kidney disease, and eye damage (*retinopathy*).

Stroke

A person suffers a stroke when blood flow to part of the brain is blocked or if a blood vessel breaks and you bleed into the brain. The brain cells in that area have no longer function because the blocked or broken arteries deprive them of oxygen. Over 15 percent of people who have a stroke die within 30 days. Of the people who survive a stroke, 15 to 30 percent suffer from some type of permanent disability. The major risk factors for stroke are high blood pressure and tobacco use. Chapter 25 has more details on stroke and how to prevent it.

Understanding your risk

Cardiovascular disease is a major problem whose development is related to many choices you make every day (and a few factors out of your control, such as family history and gender). Here are some of the most common risk factors:

>> **Smoking:** Smoking has been linked to plaque buildup and high blood pressure. Smoking also causes your blood to be thicker, which increases the risk of a stroke. Even if you've smoked for years, stroke is one condition you can still reduce your risk of if you quit.

>> **Poor diet:** Reducing the intake of saturated fats, trans fats, and cholesterol decreases plaque buildup and the risk of ischemic strokes. A diet high in vegetables and fruit can reduce your risks, too (see Part 4 for more info on nutrition).

>> **Inactive lifestyle:** Overall, Americans of all ages are less physically active than ever before. Physical activity is decreasing in all age groups. This lack of movement increases risk for diabetes, high blood pressure, and elevated cholesterol, and therefore strokes.

>> **Obesity:** Being overweight is associated with elevated cholesterol levels, high blood pressure, and an increased risk of coronary artery disease. Excess fat increases the heart's work, which over time can lead to heart disease.

>> **Gender and age:** Men have a higher risk of heart attack than women. Even though the gender difference narrows after women reach menopause, men still have a higher risk. Most heart disease related deaths occur after the age of 65, although the disease starts developing years before.

>> **Heredity:** Heart disease does tend to run in families. Children of parents with heart disease are more likely to develop it also. Certain ethnic groups, such as African Americans and Hispanics, also tend to have a higher prevalence of cardiovascular disease.

WARNING

Risk factors are starting to develop at younger ages, which is setting the stage for a surge in cardiovascular disease. Childhood obesity rates and the rates of diabetes and high cholesterol are skyrocketing. These latter two diseases were once thought of as diseases of middle age but are now being diagnosed in younger populations. Some autopsies have even found plaque in the aorta and coronary arteries of children who have died in accidents.

Playing your part in prevention and managing cardiovascular disease

Cardiovascular disease isn't an inevitable part of aging; you can do things to greatly reduce your risk of becoming a heart attack or stroke statistic. If you already have CVD, take immediate steps to reduce the chances of your disease worsening. The key to preventing as well as managing CVD is modifying your lifestyle choices. Here's how:

>> Don't use any tobacco products; if you already do, stop.

>> Maintain healthy cholesterol levels and have your physician check your cholesterol levels at each routine checkup visit.

>> Reduce your blood pressure. Stop in to your doctor for a quick blood pressure check, or take advantage of the free machines at your local pharmacy or grocery store.

>> Eat a healthy diet.

>> Maintain a healthy weight.

>> If you have diabetes, control your condition. Make sure you keep your blood glucose under tight control. Poorly controlled diabetes is a major risk factor for heart disease.

>> Increase your physical activity. You should get a minimum of 150 minutes of aerobic exercise a week.

>> Figure out how to manage stress. There are many ways to reduce stress, and some of them, such as exercise, involve activities that help reduce other risks. (Head to Chapters 15, 16, and 17 for more on stress management and relaxation techniques.)

Recognizing the symptoms of coronary artery disease

You may look right past the first warning signs of coronary artery disease, and for many people, there are no warning signs at all. Their first sign that something's wrong is a full-blown heart attack. That's scary! Although not all cases of CAD are preventable — heredity plays a part in who gets it — you *can* modify or eliminate many risk factors by visiting your doctor regularly, following a healthy lifestyle, and being aware of potential early warning signs. The main symptoms of CAD are as follows:

>> **Angina (chest pain):** *Angina* refers to chest pain and/or discomfort, with or without pain in one or both arms or in the left shoulder, neck, jaw, or back.

>> **Shortness of breath:** This may occur when the coronary arteries become narrower due to the buildup of plaque (atherosclerosis).

>> **Irregular heartbeats or palpitations:** Your heart starts to skip beats, or you feel it beating irregularly (also known as *palpitations*).

If your doctor finds you have CAD, you may be able to control the disease with medications while monitoring for any changes in symptoms. In some instances, you may also need invasive tests and procedures to open up blocked arteries. Make sure you're following proper dietary and exercise recommendations as well and not just relying on medication or procedures for treatment.

Identifying and responding to a heart attack

Not all heart attacks look like they do on TV or in the movies. You may have multiple symptoms at the same time that increase in intensity, or just one symptom that doesn't seem very intense. Here are some symptoms:

>> Feeling pressure, pain, or discomfort through the chest or back that lasts more than a few minutes or that goes away and comes back. It may feel like pressure, squeezing, fullness, or sharp or dull pain.

>> Feeling discomfort, numbness, tingling, and/or pain in your jaw, upper back, shoulders, neck, or arms (usually on the left side of your body).

>> Experiencing terrible heartburn, possibly with nausea and vomiting.

>> Feeling winded (with or without chest discomfort) when exerting very little effort. The feeling subsides when you rest.

>> Feeling anxious along with shortness of breath that doesn't let up.

>> Breaking out in a cold sweat and/or having clammy skin.

WARNING

In general, any new, changing, or worsening symptoms of coronary artery disease are reasons to call 911 for immediate help. Time is critical in the treatment of a heart attack, so if you think you may be having one, call 911 for help right away.

REMEMBER

If you think you're experiencing a heart attack, call 911 and then immediately go to your medicine cabinet for a lifesaver everyone should have on hand: plain aspirin (if you're not allergic to it). Aspirin helps reduce platelet formation around the ruptured plaque. Platelets are sticky blood cells that can create a larger clot, which further decreases blood flow. Chew a 325-milligram tablet of plain aspirin; chewing aspirin speeds its absorption (you'll get over the taste later).

Osteoporosis

Osteoporosis is a progressive disease in which the bones become weak and thin — that is, lose *bone density* — which leads to an increased risk of fractures. Any bone can be affected by osteoporosis, but the most common bones that break are in the hip, wrist, and back (spine). Often people don't know that they have osteoporosis until a bone actually breaks and further evaluation reveals poor bone density. Osteoporosis affects more than 200 million people worldwide. Osteoporosis causes more than 9 million fractures worldwide every year — that's a broken bone occurring somewhere in the world about every three seconds. Worldwide, 1 in 3 women and 1 in 5 men over age 50 will experience such fractures in the future.

Understanding your risk

Women have an increased risk of osteoporosis because of hormonal influences. There are several other risk factors:

>> **Age:** In both men and women, the risk of osteoporosis increases with age, with bone loss usually starting around age 30. Women can experience up to a 20 percent loss of bone mass in the five to seven years following menopause (average age is 51), due to estrogen loss. Women usually show signs of osteoporosis around age 65. Men's bone loss tends to occur gradually, and they don't usually show signs until age 75.

>> **Gender:** Women are four times more likely to have osteoporosis than men. Women's bones are thinner and less dense than men's, and men tend to have more muscle, which serves to protect the bone.

>> **Smoking:** Smokers have increased risk of fractures over nonsmokers. Smoking is thought to decrease the amount of calcium absorbed from food as well as reduce the formation of new bone cells (*osteoblasts*).

>> **Alcohol:** People with excessive alcohol intake (more than two drinks daily for men or one drink daily for women) have a 40 percent higher risk of fracture

compared to people with moderate or no alcohol intake. Alcohol adversely affects the bone-forming cells (*osteoblasts*) and the hormones that regulate calcium metabolism.

>> **Nutrition:** People with a very low calcium and vitamin D intake have a higher risk of developing osteoporosis because calcium and vitamin D play such vital roles in bone development.

>> **Physical activity:** Bone remodeling (new bone formation) occurs in response to activity. Weight bearing exercises are the best form of activity to improve lean muscle mass and strengthen your bones (Chapter 19 has exercise tips).

Playing your part in prevention

Many cases of osteoporosis are preventable, and the earlier you start making healthy lifestyle choices the better. The best way to prevent breaking a bone due to osteoporosis is to stop osteoporosis before it starts! Take the following steps to reduce your risk:

>> **Get regular weight-bearing exercise.** Getting started at an early age helps prevent osteoporosis or at least slow the progression. By engaging in aerobic weight-bearing exercise (walking, jogging, running) and by strengthening your muscles, you're also strengthening your bones. When you lift weights, the stress on the bone causes the body to increase the calcium into your bones for added strength.

>> **Make sure you get enough calcium, vitamin D, and vitamin K.** All these vitamins and minerals make your bones strong. A diet rich in calcium is essential for bone strength. Because you need vitamin D to absorb calcium, it also plays a vital role in maintaining bone density.

>> **Talk to your doctor about available treatments if you're at high risk of osteoporosis or already experiencing bone loss.** Medications are now available to slow the rate of bone loss and even help rebuild bone. Talk to your doctor to see what type of treatment option is best for you.

Recognizing the symptoms

Osteoporosis has been called the silent thief because it can take decades to slowly thin your bones, weakening them enough to break. Unfortunately, the first sign that a person has osteoporosis is often when a fracture occurs. Other symptoms may be severe back pain, loss of height, or spinal deformities such as *kyphosis* (hump back) that occur as a result of collapsed vertebrae.

Managing osteoporosis

Osteoporosis doesn't have a cure, but current treatments and newer treatments exist that can slow the rate of bone loss and increase bone density.

REMEMBER

Hormone therapy used to be the main treatment, but after a large study showed that the benefits of hormones on the bones didn't outweigh the cardiovascular risks, doctors started using alternative therapies.

Medications such as bisphosphonates are helpful in certain cases. These therapies can help people keep living their daily lives with less worry that every little bump, twist, or turn will result in a fracture.

The quality of life for people with osteoporosis is improving. Other strategies such as fall-prevention techniques should be incorporated into a fracture-prevention program. You can find more on osteoporosis prevention, diagnosis and treatment at the International Osteoporosis Foundation website (www.iofbonehealth.org).

Chapter 24

Evaluating Your Health and History and Setting Goals for Wellness

People used to go to the doctor only when they were sick or had broken a bone. And plenty of people still avoid visiting the doctor when they're ill, let alone get a checkup if they're feeling just dandy — you know, the "if it ain't broke, don't fix it!" rule.

Well, it turns out that philosophy isn't a recipe for longevity or even good health. To keep sharp, it's important to keep healthy and take any necessary preventative measures. Today more than ever before, you have the power of early detection and healthy living to help prevent debilitating — and possibly fatal — illnesses and diseases.

This chapter discusses the general measures you can implement to prevent the most threatening illnesses and diseases today: what to look for, what age to start looking, and what tests or screenings to schedule with your doctor or healthcare provider. It also gives you some gender-specific disease-related information and looks at ways to have fun while you're getting healthy.

Investigating and Writing Down Your Medical and Family History

Staying healthy as you age actually consists of two parts: knowing what your general health risks are now and knowing what inherited tendencies can lead to disease in the future. Although your physician or healthcare provider can give you the most accurate depiction of your overall health (more on that topic later in "Visiting the Doc"), this section helps you take the first steps in assessing your present health so that you can provide the information your doctor needs. That info plus an understanding of potential inherited health problems puts you in a much better position to create personal health goals and to devise a plan (with your doctor, if appropriate) for reaching them.

Taking stock of yourself

Standing back and taking an objective look at yourself from a healthy living perspective isn't always easy. Self-evaluation is, however, one of the first, easiest, and most effective steps you can take toward eliminating behaviors that may keep you from living your best as you age.

Although seeing your doctor is important, she can go by only what you tell her when it comes to diet, exercise, and other important health factors in your life. You may be a perfect size four, but if you stay that way by eating two candy bars a day and nothing else, by skipping dinner in lieu of three glasses of wine a night, or by smoking rather than eating, your health is going to suffer. You may look okay on the outside (at least for a while), but the one person you really can't fool when it comes to your lifestyle is yourself.

Is it really necessary to let your doctor know that you've decided to give up ice cream bars and start walking two miles a day? Possibly not, if you're perfectly healthy with no family risk factors at all. But if there's anything at all concerning in your history or in your physical exam that would preclude major changes in lifestyle, you may save yourself a lot of health complications by discussing your plan with your doctor first. Besides, she may have suggestions to help ease your transition into a healthier you.

The depth of information you need to gather varies from doctor to doctor; however, many of the basics are fairly standard, including family history, allergies to medications, past medical and surgical history and medications.

Looking down the family line

Do you have a family? Yes, you do, even if you don't always like to claim them. With your family comes a family health history. Although having a sibling with cancer or a grandparent who died of heart disease doesn't mean that you're going to suffer the same fate, many disease tendencies can be inherited. Knowing your family history can give you a blueprint of potential health landmines in your genetic makeup.

Your doctor needs to know about any family history of illness, such as cardiovascular disease, cancer, and dementia because it can change prevention, testing, and treatments due to certain familial links. Research your family history and bring pertinent info to your doctor's appointment.

When compiling a family health history, start with your immediate family — brothers, sisters, mom, and dad. You can start by asking questions of your parents, such as:

>> **How long did your parents live and what did they die of (if they're dead)?** You may not get a straight answer on the cause of your grandparents' deaths because often cause of death wasn't accurately recorded a generation or so ago. Even deaths recorded as accidents may not be accurate; a "car accident" may have been caused by a sudden heart attack that caused the driver to lose control.

>> **Did they have any health problems?** Try to get specifics; "bad blood" can be anything from anemia to syphilis. Some of the more common conditions with genetic links are heart disease, cancer, addiction, and diabetes.

>> **What do you remember about them?** They may remember that grandma was blind and had only one leg without making the connection that these conditions may have been caused by diabetes.

>> **Do you have any pictures of relatives?** One look at a series of pictures of great-grandma and grandma at different ages can make it evident that osteoporosis runs in the family — they kept getting shorter.

>> **Did any diseases or defects "run in the family?"** Expect some waffling on the answer if mental conditions or birth defects were common in the family. Explain your need to know as a desire to understand your family medical history rather than pure nosiness.

>> **What about your brothers and sisters and their families?** Make sure you're recording health issues only from blood relatives, not their spouses or their in-laws.

After picking mom and dad's brain, talking to your aunts and uncles may yield new information or a different slant on things. Always start with your most talkative/nosy family members first, but remember that they may also be the most likely to embellish the family history. If your immediate ancestors have passed on or don't have the info you need, dig a little deeper by trying to access death certificates, obituaries, and family medical records from extended family members or library newspaper files. If anyone in your family is a pack rat or a genealogy buff, he may have already done much of the legwork for you and would probably be flattered if you asked for a copy of his research findings.

After you gather enough data to make up a cohesive family history, write it all down. You can get fancy, drawing an elaborate tree with actual branches, or you can write it down in simple linear fashion. The U.S. Surgeon General considers your family history recording important enough to have devised a personalized form that you can use to record pertinent info; you can find it at www.family history.hhs.gov.

TIP

If you're adopted, you may not be able to delve into your family history to any great degree. Then again, adoption agencies often do have *some* family medical history on file. Your adoptive parents may or may not have this information available for you, but the agency they used may. It's worth a phone call or visit to get any bits of information the agency has.

Even if you aren't adopted, you may not be able to come up with any concrete past family medical information. If that's the case, don't worry about it. Doctors use this info as a tool to help in some situations, but apply their expertise effectively regardless of having any pertinent family history.

Visiting the Doc

Some people would rather have a tax audit than go to the doctor. The main reason? Fear. Fear of the unknown only perpetuates the problem. The scenario of what-ifs may run through your head like a freight train on rocket fuel as you scare yourself into staying away from the doctor. You end up trying to convince yourself that nothing can be done about your less-than-healthy condition.

Note: This line of thinking may become a self-fulfilling prophecy. If you avoid the doctor for years and suffer with an ache or pain long enough, it just may turn into something serious. When that happens and you finally can't take it anymore and go to the doctor, the news is bad. "Well, Mr. Jones, if you had come to me 12 years ago, we could've caught this thing in time. With the right medication, lifestyle changes, diet, and exercise, you could've lived another 20 years." Then you say, "Gee, Doc, isn't there anything you can do with all the access to medical technology, and expertise you have?" In a case like this, nothing works better than prevention.

Taking your body to the doctor for regular checkups is an important part of a living long and well. To make sure that you cover your bases, the following sections are devoted to those appointments.

Having regular checkups: What should happen

Remembering to schedule regular maintenance visits for your car is usually easier than remembering to do it for your body. At least your car gets a sticker that reminds you when to get an oil change or a warning light that indicates a need for service. But as long as you're feeling okay, you probably don't think about getting a regular physical exam — not good, for two reasons:

>> Prevention is the key to reducing your risks of developing disease and illness, so if you don't take advantage of your doctor's insight regarding your risks, you're missing out on a key component of aging healthfully.

>> When you do visit the doctor regularly, you can immediately address any health concerns the doctor may find. If you don't visit regularly, you may not know about those health concerns soon enough to combat them before they take their toll on your body. For example, if your bad cholesterol levels are too high, your doctor may first suggest modifications to your diet and lifestyle before possibly starting you on a medication to lower cholesterol. (So follow-up appointments are also important!)

REMEMBER

For folks ages 40 and older, health examinations every one to two years are highly recommended. Younger adults don't need an exam that often — every three to five years is good unless they're having problems.

During the annual exam, your doctor performs the assessments outlined in the following sections.

Discussing current medical complaints

The first part of the exam is an opportunity to discuss your current medical situation so the doctor can further evaluate it throughout the rest of the examination. You should discuss your medical complaints one at a time, mentioning all the symptoms that you're having. Your medical practitioner will ask some directed questions, but this is your time to speak. Clinicians can obtain a lot of valuable information in the history, which helps them formulate a strong differential diagnosis.

This review of your body systems is a way for the doctor to assess your overall health quickly (and sufficiently). You'll be asked a number of questions to gather information to direct the diagnosis, treatment, and prevention, such as the following:

>> **Overall well-being:** Have you had unintentional weight loss or weight gain? Do you generally feel well? Are you able to complete activities of daily living?

>> **Skin:** Do you have any rashes, itching, dryness, changes in hair or nails, or redness?

>> **Eyes, ears, nose, mouth, and throat:** Do you have any blurred, loss of, or double vision? Do you have any eye pain, dizziness, loss of hearing, ringing in the ears, bloody nose, bleeding gums, tooth pain, sore throat, hoarseness, lumps in the neck, or neck stiffness?

>> **Cardiovascular system:** Have you had any chest pain, irregular heartbeat, shortness of breath on exertion or during the night, or pain in the lower legs with exertion?

>> **Respiratory:** Do you have shortness of breath, cough, wheezing, or recurrent bronchial infections? Have you coughed up any blood?

>> **Gastrointestinal:** Any changes in appetite, pain with swallowing, heartburn, nausea, vomiting, bloody vomit, diarrhea or constipation, blood in stool, increased gas, or pain with bowel movements?

>> **Genitourinary:** Any increased frequency of urination, pain with urination, blood in urine, difficulty urinating, history of kidney stones, recurrent infections, erectile dysfunction (male), or sexually transmitted diseases? For females, what was the age of onset of menses? Are your periods regular? What was the date of your last period? Do you have any pain with menstruation, heavy or light bleeding, or pain with intercourse?

>> **Musculoskeletal:** Do you have any pain in the joints, muscles cramping, muscle pain, weakness, or decreased range of motion?

>> **Neurologic:** Any seizures, tremors, numbness, tingling, paralysis, memory loss, problems with coordination, or difficulty speaking?

>> **Psychiatric:** Have you had any anxiety, depression, hallucinations, or delusions?

Although routine medical examinations are supposed to be just that — routine — they're also the opportunity for patients to divulge all concerning symptoms they've experienced since their last medical exam. You may come to routine examinations with multiple items to discuss, with the doctor. Likewise, the doctor may have concerns to discuss with you if you gave affirmative answers to any of her questions.

WARNING

If you have significant concerns to be addressed, don't wait until your routine examination to address them. If the steering on your car is off, you don't wait until your 12-month inspection to have it evaluated and fixed. Likewise, you shouldn't ignore symptoms affecting your most expensive possession — your body — without having them checked out and treated.

Reviewing past medical information

At this stage of the examination your doctor will want to go over past medical history. This information may pertain to your current medical complaints. She'll also see whether any past medical issues need to be reevaluated or treated further. Your doctor will revisit these same question each year to make sure that nothing has changed. Many past occurrences affect current medical ailments and future preventative examinations. Here are a few of the main categories covered in this section of the examination:

>> **Medications:** Tell your doctor about all the medications you're taking and about any recent changes in medications. In addition to prescription medication, include over-the-counter meds, herbal supplements, and anything you take for allergies. Bring in the bottles or copy their info onto a piece of paper if you can't remember all your medications off the top of your head. Remember to tell your primary physician about any medications prescribed to you by other specialist physicians.

>> **Past medical conditions or current ongoing conditions:** These conditions may include high blood pressure, diabetes, or glaucoma. List all significant problems back to childhood.

>> **Hospitalizations:** Tell your doctor about any past hospitalizations. Have all the details handy if you've been hospitalized in the last six months. Better yet, go back to the hospital's medical record department and ask them to send a copy of your hospital admission record directly to your doctor (which is typically a free service).

>> **Surgical history:** This category includes all surgeries in your life. Your doctor won't want to send you to the hospital to have your appendix evaluated if it was surgically removed a year ago.

>> **Immunizations:** See the "Immunization" section later in this chapter.

>> **For women, menstrual cycle and reproductive history:** This info includes all live births, the age of the children, and any miscarriages.

>> **Occupational history:** This one helps the doctor evaluate any potential hazardous exposures, such as asbestos or other chemicals, or hearing loss if you work with loud machinery or guns. Jobs with intense physical labor may explain back pain, joint pain, or past head injuries.

>> **Relationship status:** Talking about your family and partner relationships can help your doctor understand your home environment. This can be particularly useful if you're experiencing stress or any potential abuse situations. Knowing what kind of support network is at home is also helpful for some ailments and treatment modalities.

>> **Alcohol, tobacco, and illicit drug use:** Let your doctor know about past or present use. If you drink or smoke, be honest about how much. Be open about any abuse of prescription medications or illegal drugs. Remember, your doctor is there to help, but she has to have the truth about what you're doing.

At this point, you can also whip out your comprehensive family history (see the section "Looking down the family line" earlier in this chapter) to help your doctor assess for possible inherited problems and tendencies.

Checking your vitals

Vital signs are a group of measured tests that help give a quick assessment of a patient's basic bodily function. These functions include blood pressure, pulse, respirations, and temperature. A few other measurements can be thrown into this mix, including height, weight, *pulse oximetry* (a noninvasive measure of the oxygenation in your blood), and pain. Your doctor may check your vitals herself; most of the time, other medical personnel do it at the beginning of your appointment before the doctor even sets foot in the room. That way, she already has current vital signs details when she first looks at your chart. Scan this list for additional info:

>> **Blood pressure measurement:** Blood pressure is a measurement of the force that the blood applies to the walls of the blood vessels as the heart pumps it throughout the body. In a blood pressure measurement, the top number *(systolic)* is the pressure of the blood as it flows through your arteries during the contraction of the large chambers of the heart *(ventricles)*. The lower number *(diastolic)* is the pressure of the blood on the artery walls measured when the ventricles are filling between contractions. For example, a typical blood pressure reading is 120/80 mmHg (millimeters of mercury), commonly read as "120 over 80."

By checking blood pressure regularly and following your doctors' advice regarding diet, exercise, risk-factor reduction, and medication, you can help control your blood pressure and stave off heart disease.

>> **Temperature:** You may think that everyone's "normal" temperature when taken by mouth is 98.6 degrees Fahrenheit or 37 degrees Celsius. Some

research suggests that "normal" oral temp actually falls in a range between 98 to 99 degrees Fahrenheit. Elevated body temperature of over 100 is called a *fever*. Fever can be caused by a number of things, such as infection, some medical diseases, or heat stroke. Low body temperatures occur with metabolic disease, such as underactive thyroid, or severe cold exposure. Abnormally low temperature is called *hypothermia*. Most of the time, symptoms or pertinent medical history explains abnormal temperatures. If not, the doctor does testing that may include an examination, blood testing, urinalysis, and possibly X-rays.

>> **Pulse rate:** Your *pulse* is the number of times your heart beats in one minute. It's measured most commonly in the neck or wrist by feeling the pressure in the arteries as a result of the heart pumping. The normal pulse rate is between 60 and 100 for adults and is higher in young children. The pulse rate increases with exercise and can reach rates of greater than 200. In addition to pulse rate, you can check for the strength of the pulse and its rhythm — is it regular or irregular? A simple pulse check helps assess for potential problems with the cardiovascular system.

>> **Respiratory rate:** This measure is the number of breaths a person takes per minute. The rate is usually assessed when the person is at rest and can be measured easily by observing the chest's rise and fall while breathing. The normal adult rate is between 12 and 20 breaths per minute and is higher in children. Abnormal respiratory rates can be a result of fever, respiratory infections, diseases such as congestive heart failure, or other heart or lung problems.

>> **Height and weight:** These measurements are important. Changes in height as you age may signify changes in your spine or posture that may indicate osteoporosis or back arthritis. Weight loss that's unintentional can be related to numerous diseases. Weight gain is becoming a norm and has numerous risks involved. Try to pick up on changes in height and weight so that you can take action early.

Undergoing the physical exam

Sooner or later, you have to put on that skimpy gown and sit on the crinkly-paper–covered exam table to get checked out. Your doctor examines you from head to toe, checking most of your orifices, squeezing muscles, and pointing out any abnormalities to discuss and possibly test further:

>> **General appearance:** You'd be surprised what your doctor can determine just by looking at someone. Mobility, mood, skin color, and hygiene can all be evaluated within a minute or two of observation and general conversation.

>> **Skin:** Doctors check the skin for any suspicious rashes or moles.

>> **Head, ears, eyes, neck, throat (HEENT):** Examination of the head basically consists of checking the ears, mouth, and nose and evaluating the visual fields and pupils' reaction to light. Testing with an eye chart can evaluate your vision. While examining your neck, a doctor checks for neck stiffness, thyroid enlargement, and lymph node swelling. The throat check occurs when the doctor asks you to open your mouth and say "ahhh."

>> **Cardiovascular:** The doctor listens to the heart for any abnormal rhythm or sounds, checks for any swelling of the extremities or varicose veins, and listens to the carotid arteries of the neck for any signs of blockage.

>> **Respiratory:** After checking the respiratory rate, your doctor listens to the lungs for any wheezing, decreased breath sounds, or other sounds suggestive of disease.

>> **Gastrointestinal:** Your doctor listens for bowel sounds and presses on the abdomen looking for pain, masses, hernias, or abdominal distention. By palpating (feeling), your doctor evaluates the size of your liver and spleen.

>> **Genitourinary and rectal:** For men, this exam includes a check of the penis and scrotum and of, including evaluating the testicles for any masses. The female exam is discussed in the next list (see the Pap smear bullet). Patients start getting rectal exams at age 40 unless otherwise needed; doctors use this exam to check for blood in the stool or hemorrhoid development. In men, the rectal exam also evaluates the prostate gland for any enlargement or masses.

>> **Musculoskeletal:** Your doctor evaluates range of motion and muscle strength and checks the spine for straightness and any tenderness. Your doctor also feels for *crepitus,* a creaking sensation that may be felt when your joints are moved if you developing arthritis.

>> **Extremities:** Your doctor evaluates your extremities for swelling and any abnormalities in the muscles. She feels the pulses behind the knee and on the foot and feels for any enlarged lymph nodes in the groin.

>> **Neurological:** The doc checks reflexes of the knees, feet, and elbow by tapping them with a small hammer. Your doctor may check your gait by watching you walk and/or check your feet and hands for sensory defects.

Other tests can be done at the time of routine examinations, but not all these tests are done at every annual examination. A few of these important tests are done periodically at set times or when other circumstances arise. Here are a few tests to expect at some point, whether annually or not:

>> **Pap smear:** Women 21 to 29 years old should get a Pap smear every three years. From age 30 to 65, Pap smears should be done in conjunction with HPV (human papillomavirus) screening every three years. Sexually active women

ages 18 to 25 should also be screened for sexually transmitted diseases (STDs), including HIV (human immunodeficiency virus). The vaccine for HPV can reduce the risk of cervical cancer and genital warts (see the nearby sidebar on immunizations). Pap smears may be discontinued after age 65 if previous screenings (a minimum of three negative Pap tests in the last ten years) are normal and documented unless you're at a high risk for cervical cancer.

REMEMBER

Multiple sexual partners, early onset of sexual activity, current use of oral contraceptives, and smoking are increased risk factors for cervical cancer. However, even without these factors, you should get pap tests to help detect cervical cancer. Early diagnosis and treatment greatly increases the success rate of treatment

>> **Clinical breast exams and mammograms:** Because breast care is one of the most important aspects of women's healthcare, clinical breast exams should begin at age 20. Women age 50 and older should have a mammogram every year. Women under 50 should consider having a mammogram based on family history and genetic risk factors. Detecting changes in the breast through clinical exams and regular mammograms is the key to early diagnosis, effective treatment, and high success rates against breast cancer. Mammograms are generally not necessary after the age of 80, except in the most robust individuals with a life expectancy over ten years.

A clinical breast exam involves palpating for lumps or bumps in each breast. A *mammogram* is an X-ray of your breast that shows tissue changes; your breast is flattened and compressed for the exam because breast tissue is normally dense. This brief test can be mildly uncomfortable.

>> **Prostate cancer screening:** Prostate cancer is a leading cause of cancer deaths among men. Each year, men aged 50 to 70 and older should discuss the value of the following tests with their doctor:

- **A prostate specific antigen (PSA) screening test:** The PSA is a simple blood test that in some cases can detect cancer in the prostate before signs and symptoms are present. The only problem is that it isn't always accurate, and the evidence is mixed on whether using a PSA as a screening tool impacts the long term outcomes in men with prostate cancer. A man can have prostate cancer and still have a normal PSA. The PSA can also be abnormal when cancer isn't present thanks to certain infections, inflammation, and benign enlargement of the prostate. Therefore, the PSA shouldn't be used as a diagnostic tool; however, it can be helpful to monitor the treatment of prostate cancer.

- **A digital rectal exam:** The prostate gland is best felt with a rectal exam. This test is done to assess the size of the prostate and palpate for any other abnormalities, such as pain or masses.

The value of the PSA test has recently been called into question. The main reason is the lack of good evidence that its use as a screening tool successfully impacts clinical outcomes. At the present time, a PSA test has its greatest utility in men under the age of 70. There is little evidence that there is any benefit of a PSA test in men over the age of 80. Furthermore, prostate cancers diagnosed after the age of 80 tend to be more indolent. There is an old adage, albeit unproven, that if a man lives to the age of 100, he will have prostate cancer, but will not die from it. One thing is certain: Very few men die of prostate cancer that is first diagnosed after the age of 80.

Less frequent exams

Some tests need to be done only when you reach a certain age, have certain risk factors, or are having problems in a particular area. The following list describes some of the tests that fall into this category:

REMEMBER

>> **Cholesterol screening:** Every five years, all adults under the age of 75 should have a *lipid profile,* a cholesterol test done after you've had nothing to eat or drink for at least12 hours (called a *fasting* test) that assesses all the components of cholesterol: total, HDL(good cholesterol) LDL (bad cholesterol), and triglycerides.

The link between high cholesterol and increased risk of heart disease is well established, so these tests can help determine your risk.

>> **Eye exam:** Even if you don't wear glasses, plan to have an eye examination at least once from age 18 to 29, at least twice from age 30 to 39, every two to four years from age 40 to 64, and every one to two years thereafter.

Many significant eye problems — like *glaucoma* (increased pressure in the eye) and *macular degeneration* (deterioration of the *macula,* the central part of the retina) — go undetected in adults until serious damage is done. Certain health conditions like diabetes and high blood pressure increase your risk of eye problems and require more frequent evaluations.

>> **Fasting blood sugar screening:** Fasting blood sugar should be measured every three years, starting at age 45, to screen for *diabetes mellitus,* one of the most common chronic diseases.

Certain risk factors such as family history, excess weight, and inactivity raise your chances of developing diabetes. Untreated, the complications can be serious; diabetes can cause severe kidney, nerve, eye, heart, and blood vessel damage. But early diagnosis and treatment can greatly reduce risks of complications, improve your health, and control elevated blood sugar.

>> **Colorectal cancer screening:** A complete colonoscopy is an examination of the large intestine, using a flexible lighted scope inserted into your rectum

while you're under mild sedation. People age 50 and older should have this test done every ten years — more frequently if you have a family history of colon cancer or a previous abnormal colonoscopy. Invasive colorectal cancer screening is generally not necessary after the age of 80.

Colorectal cancer is the third-leading cause of cancer deaths among all adults. A colonoscopy offers the best opportunity to detect cancer at an early stage, when successful treatment is likely. Some cancers may be prevented by detection and removal of polyps.

>> **Bone-mineral density exam:** Women age 65 and older should have a bone mineral density measurement at least once to check for *osteoporosis,* a disease in which bones become fragile and more likely to break. If the results are abnormal, this test should be repeated every two to three years to look for further changes that may warrant treatment.

REMEMBER

Osteoporosis takes its toll quietly, often without symptoms. But the information from a bone density test enables your healthcare provider to identify osteoporosis (and therefore your risk of fractures) and treat it if present.

>> **Hearing test:** Adults over the age of 64 should have at least one hearing assessment. Your healthcare provider will ask about your hearing; if you're having difficulty or noticing small changes, she will probably recommend a hearing test. Proper treatment, including cleaning of your ears or treating infections, can greatly improve your ability to hear.

IMMUNIZATIONS

You may think immunizations are just for kids, but some immunizations are as important for adults as they are for children, especially if you have certain risk factors. According to the Center for Disease Control (CDC), the following vaccinations should be on your to-do list if you fall into any of the categories described here:

● **Influenza:** If you're age 50 or older or you have a weakened immune system, you should have yearly flu shots. The influenza vaccine is also good protection for healthcare workers and caregivers, school children, and working adults. The Center for Disease Control (CDC) recommends that everyone over 6 months of age get annual flu shots starting when the vaccine is available and at least by October. Influenza can lead to pneumonia, dehydration, and death in people who are debilitated and can worsen heart disease, diabetes, and asthma. Around 36,000 Americans alone die from the flu and its complications each year.

● **Tetanus diphtheria pertussis (Tdap):** You need this Tdap series of combined vaccinations if you're an adult who didn't receive the primary series as a child. In

(continued)

(continued)

addition, all adults should receive a *booster* (an injection given to make sure the levels of protection in the blood stay high) of Td (tetanus and diphtheria only) at least every ten years thereafter. *Tetanus* is a preventable disease caused by a bacteria introduced into a wound, and it's fatal in around 30 percent of cases. *Diphtheria,* fatal in 5 to 20 percent of cases, is a highly infectious preventable disease seen only rarely today in developed countries due to high vaccine rates. *Pertussis,* also known as whooping cough, is a highly contagious serious disease seen most recently in those aged 11 to 19 when their immunity wears off.

- **Shingles (herpes zoster):** If you had chickenpox as a child, you're at risk for *shingles,* which is a reactivation of the chickenpox (varicella) virus that causes a blistering, often painful skin rash. If you have had chickenpox, you should have one dose of the zoster vaccine at age 60 or older. Even if you have previously had shingles, you should have the vaccine to protect you from getting it again.

- **Pneumonia:** If you're at least 65 or have medical conditions that increase the risk of pneumonia — such as chronic lung diseases (asthma, bronchitis, emphysema), chronic heart conditions, diabetes, kidney disease, or liver disease — you should get vaccinated for pneumonia. You need a vaccination called PCV13, followed by a second type of pneumonia vaccine called PPSV23 vaccine 6 to 12 months later if you have a normal immune system. In people with compromised immune systems, the second vaccine should be given eight or more weeks after the PCV13. The PCV13 covers 13 different types of pneumococcal bacteria, and the PPSV23 covers 23 types. Although neither vaccine prevents *all* types of pneumococcal infections, they do provide protective benefit against the most common types.

- **Human Papillomavirus (HPV):** This vaccine is recommended for young females (starting at age 9 and up until age 26) to decrease the risk of cervical cancer and genital warts due to HPV. Young men (age 9 to 26) should also be vaccinated. Ideally, you should receive this vaccine before becoming sexually active, but women who are already sexually active should still be vaccinated. A complete series of this vaccine consists of three doses. Presently, no booster is required.

- **Meningitis:** Although meningitis is rare, outbreaks on college campuses or other areas where large numbers of people live in close contact, such as military bases and institutions, can occur. Therefore, the following people should receive the meningitis vaccine (called the meningococcal vaccine): college students, military recruits, people with immune problems, people with damaged or removed spleens, people traveling to countries where meningitis is common, and anyone who has been exposed to someone with meningitis.

- **Hepatitis B:** Hepatitis B is a virus that can cause serious damage to the liver. Vaccination consists of a series of three vaccines. The following people, among others, should receive the hepatitis vaccine: medical personnel; people with HIV, kidney disease, or liver disease; and people who receive blood products on a regular basis, such as hemophiliacs.

Determining Your Goals and Putting Them on Paper

To achieve goals, you need plans. No architect creates a building and no engineer creates a computer without a written plan. You're the architect and engineer of your lifestyle, and you need a plan when building for healthy aging. Your plan of action acts as a set of blueprints for the changes you want to create for your health and well-being. The plan turns your major goals into a multitasked project with clear milestones, deadlines, and specific tasks in a specific order.

REMEMBER

The simpler the plan, and the less disruption it causes to your daily life, the more likely you are to stick to it. Think of your body as a machine that needs certain maintenance. Plan on the regular, routine maintenance, and if any signs of break-down appear, get to the doctor sooner rather than later to prevent any worsening of the situation. The body is complex and therefore somewhat unpredictable, so accept that you have to adapt to changes and make adjustments to keep your body aging well. Have you ever seen a set of blueprints that didn't have to have changes made before the final construction was complete? Your plan will likely also have modifications along the way.

Developing your goals

When determining and implementing your goals, follow a few guidelines to make them effective:

>> **Develop your goals as clearly as possible.** Your goals should be deliberate and well thought out. Each goal should be defined as a specific task that's action oriented. If the task is clearly action oriented, you can actually do something to accomplish it. Having a goal of "losing weight" isn't as clear as "losing five pounds a month by cutting out afternoon and after dinner snacks and walking two miles a day." The second goal has specific, action oriented tasks for you to work on.

>> **Make sure that your goals are measurable.** This factor is critical. If you can measure your goals, you can manage them. Just like in a game of sports, if you don't assign a point value to a score, how do you know who's winning? With goals, if you can't measure them, how do you know whether you've accomplished them? The difference between a goal and a wish is as simple as these two statements:

- I want to lose weight.

- I want to lose 25 pounds.

The second statement is actually a goal.

>> **Set firm but realistic deadlines.** There isn't much point of having a goal if you never set a time frame to reach it. But be realistic so you can succeed and feel accomplished. Don't write "I want to lose 10 pounds in the next week"; this impossible benchmark will just add to your frustration.

>> **Own your goals.** Many people don't stick to their goals because they don't really take ownership of them. Your goals must be a burning desire for *you* — not for someone else. If you're a smoker, and the loved ones in your life want you to give it up, and you know that you should (but you're really trying to do it for their sake), you aren't really owning this goal. Feeling the conviction and desire for your goal is essential because you'll encounter obstacles, challenges, and temptations that try to sabotage your attempts to reach it. Whether your goal is going to the gym four days a week, eating healthy food to lose weight and maintain it, choosing a positive attitude over a negative one, or protecting your skin from sun damage — every goal has obstacles. Choose goals that you're passionate about. You're much more likely to achieve them.

Keep these guidelines in mind and start fine-tuning your goals by letting the following questions and considerations guide you:

1. **What's your current state of health?**

   - Weight

   - Medical conditions

   - Exercise and physical activity

   - Nutrition and diet

   - Mental, emotional, and spiritual

2. **Where do you want to be in regards to your health and well-being?**

3. **How did you get where you are today regarding your current state of health?**

   - What did you do right?

   - What would you do differently?

4. **What do you do next to get from where you are to where you want to be?**

5. **What should you be doing more or less of?**

6. **What should you start doing that you aren't?**

7. **What should you stop doing altogether?**

8. **Can you set realistic timeframes for each of your goals?**

9. **Where do you want to be in one year in relation to your goals?**

REMEMBER

Change is good, although for many people it can be uncomfortable. Discomfort often comes from fear of the unknown or fear of failure. If you notice a gap between where you want to be and where you are now, see it as an opportunity for improvement rather than an insurmountable obstacle or a failure; don't let fear keep you rooted in the same old spot. Be positive.

Recording your goals

Plenty of research supports the effective correlation between writing down your goals and achieving them:

» Writing down your goals forces you to organize your thinking.

» Thinking about what you must do to accomplish your goals helps you plan your tasks more thoughtfully.

» A well-written plan provides the ability to review it for flaws as well as to identify strengths and weaknesses.

» A written plan allows you to focus on just a few key objectives.

» Writing your plan ahead of time instead of flying by the seat of your pants saves time, energy, confusion, and mistakes.

You may want to keep your plan in a notebook or a three-ring binder that's easy to refer to on a daily basis. As you write your plan, do the following:

» **List every task and activity.** For example, if you want to start exercising, list the activity you want to begin, the time you want to allot, the time of day you're going to exercise, and where you're going to exercise. You also need a schedule for starting slow and increasing your exercise time and intensity.

» **Prioritize your goals.** What's the most important thing you hope to accomplish? If you're losing weight because you're diabetic, changing your diet to decrease your blood sugar may be more important than how many pounds you lose.

» **List your goals sequentially.** You may want to increase your aerobic exercise to a certain point first, and then start using weights. Or you may want to start with one weight, and then increase to another level.

>> **Identify your limitations.** Limitations aren't failures and should be built into any plan. For example, you may have a chronic foot injury. If you know that the injury flares up from time to time, have an alternate plan for those times, such as switching from walking to swimming for exercise.

>> **Expect setbacks and remain flexible, keeping your focus on the solution.** Don't let bumps in the road throw you off track.

>> **Have measures and standards for tracking your progress and deadlines.** For example, "I will be walking three miles daily at a speed of four miles an hour on the treadmill."

All successful people work from written plans. Action without planning is the number one reason for failure.

Pushing for Persistence to Successfully Reach Your Goals

Making plans and setting goals is fun; carrying them out can be less enjoyable, especially over the long run. Yet few things are as rewarding as completing goals, so the effort is well worth it.

You may not always feel like keepin' on, but by starting small and gradually increasing your efforts and goals, you can achieve great changes that can impact the way you age for years to come. The road to the top seems much easier if you take your goals one step at a time, stay realistic about what you can do, and find support along the way.

This section focuses on the mental side of carrying out your goals — especially when the ruts and bumps start to rattle your confidence.

Staying focused — and optimistic

Few things in life are more motivating than a realistic positive attitude. Referring to your plan and rechecking it to make sure that your goals are realistic and attainable can keep you from giving up because your goals aren't being met. (Flip to the earlier section "Determining Your Goals and Putting Them on Paper" for more on forming your plan.) Being both realistic and positive is essential: Being overly positive may tell you that you're going to be 30 pounds thinner in a month, but being realistic tells you that's not likely and that 4 to 8 pounds (1 to 2 pounds a week) is a better, more attainable goal.

Sometimes, despite your most upbeat efforts, pessimism starts to worm its way into your daily routine. "What's the use? I'll never get there" becomes your new mantra, and it can become a self-fulfilling prophecy.

TIP

To be successful at goal-setting and attainment, many successful people use a powerful tool called *visualization*. Imagine yourself as your ideal self and keep that focus. For example:

>> See the action-oriented goals you need to accomplish in order to become that healthy person you want to be.

>> See the obstacles in your way and visualize removing them from your path.

>> See yourself where you want to be and who you want to be and lock in on those images.

The more often you visualize your ideal, the closer you come to attaining it. You can even write down a detailed description in your notebook of what you see to help reinforce the images. As you review your goals every day, visualize yourself acting them out and accomplishing them. Be sure you refer to this list when you're stuck or off track.

REMEMBER

As mentioned earlier, the process of goal-setting takes practice. The most successful people in the world fail more times than unsuccessful people do. And successful people have failed at meeting a goal on time. You're the boss of your own body, and it's counting on you not to quit. If you don't meet a goal or deadline, set a new one. If you have a big goal, break it down into smaller, more manageable tasks. Just don't give up!

How often should you review your goals? It depends on how quickly you want to achieve them. Some people review their goals daily, and that's usually a good plan. The more often you use your goals *and* act on them, the better you get at creating goals, solving problems, and achieving the results you want.

Measuring your progress

Almost nothing is more satisfying than a written record of success. Forgetting how far you've come is easy when you don't have a tangible record of it. By setting specific measures on your goals and accurately tracking your performance each day, you reinforce the changes to your health and well-being (like incorporating healthy choices and maintaining a positive mental attitude) and make it easy to refer to when you need to revise goals.

TIP

Jotting down notes related to your activity is also helpful. For example, did you feel especially hungry on a given day? Tired? Angry? Were certain exercises extremely difficult to do, or was a certain activity impossible to continue because of fatigue? Knowing what worked for you and what didn't can help you plan a more realistic and successful plan.

Tracking your diet is the first step to taking control of it. Counting calories and recording them in a notebook is one way. But now you can also easily keep track of your diet and exercise digitally with nutrition tracking apps for your smartphone or tablet. Most of these have websites that interface with the app so your account is updated whether you input data on your phone or on your computer. Many also work with fitness trackers to record exercise minutes and calories expended and also allow you to add friends to provide support (and healthy competition) to keep you on track. Find the one that works best for you and your needs. Here's a list of apps and sites to consider:

>> **MyFitnessPal (www.MyFitnessPal.com):** This free calorie counter and diet plan has a very comprehensive food database and allows you to input new items by scanning the bar codes on packages or adding your own personal recipes to the database. It tells you how many calories you have used and how many you have left for the day based on your weight loss goals. You can also track exercise here. The free version is highly useful, but a paid premium version offers some additional tracking options.

>> **My Food Diary (www.myfooddiary.com):** This flexible food and exercise diary generates reports and enables community through social connections. It offers a risk-free seven day trial and is $9 per month after that.

>> **Lose it! (www.loseit.com):** This easy-to-use program helps you stay in your calorie budget and offers an option that allows health professionals to interface with you and follow your progress as they coach you. The basic plan is free, but a paid premium plan is also available that offers more features.

>> **SparkPeople (www.sparkpeople.com):** This completely free network of sites provides a detailed nutrition and activity tracker aimed at helping you live healthier. You can watch videos and access a social media community to provide support and encouragement.

>> **Weight Watchers online (www.weightwatchers.com):** Like all Weight Watchers programs, this system requires a paid subscription, but it provides support and encouragement through videos, 24/7 expert chat access, recipes, diet recording, seamless activity tracking, and a food budget.

If you are less tech-oriented and want something you can hold in your hand that's already laid out for you, a company called BodyMinder sells journals for recording anything related to exercise and diet. Look in the fitness section in any bookstore for different choices to see what fits your needs best.

Removing obstacles and getting back on track

On your course to a healthier lifestyle, you're going to experience detours, potholes, bottlenecks, and of course, the occasional flat tire. All the more reason to set goals; they can't prevent obstacles, but when they're written clearly, action-oriented, and measurable, they can help you get up and going again. To minimize the obstacles that may block your path, try a three-step approach:

1. **Identify your obstacles.**

Don't take it personally — goals aren't about perfection but reality. Building failure into your plan just makes sense.

For example, maybe your goal is to improve your lean muscle mass by 20 percent in six months with strength training. You plan to work out with weights four days a week, one hour each session. Three months into your goal, you're in a car accident and in the hospital for a week. Your recovery period puts you behind schedule, and you can't make it back to the gym for three months. You failed to meet your goal. What do you do? Set a new goal.

Your roadblocks can come from work, family, or financial obligations, or they can be less tangible factors like motivation. When you can identify them, you can prepare for and overcome them when they occur. You can have a plan B.

2. **Prioritize the obstacles in the order you need to overcome them.**

By prioritizing and writing them down on paper in your planning notebook, you can see what's standing between you and your goals. No matter how challenging the obstacle, write it down. For example, if your biggest obstacle to exercising is that your fitness center's hours no longer fit your schedule, list "Look for ways to change schedule to get to gym" as a priority, with "Look for a new gym" as a second priority if the first fix isn't possible.

REMEMBER

The more you practice problem-solving skills, the better you become at resolving these roadblocks and the more quickly you achieve your goals. You also realize just how often obstacles come across your path and you become more confident at setting larger or more challenging goals.

3. **Rewrite a new goal to address each obstacle.**

In Step 2, a person who can't find time for exercise may need a new, more specific goal. He may have to write "find 30 minutes three times a week to exercise by cutting out XYZ" (replacing XYZ with a real event). This suggestion may sound simple, but change isn't always easy. He may have to eliminate 90 minutes of something he enjoys, like watching TV or spending time on the computer.

To overcome obstacles, your goals must be desirable and you must be committed to them.

Finding support

Unless you're a Lone Ranger type, you're likely to find lifestyle changes like dieting, quitting smoking, and starting an exercise program much easier if you have company along the way. A good friend or a whole support group of people can encourage you, help you get back on track when you waver, and cheer you on when you succeed. Plus, a little healthy competition may spur you all on to success. The beauty is that you can find people who specialize in helping you achieve your goals if you find it hard to go it alone. Most digital diet and activity trackers (including those mentioned in the earlier section "Measuring your progress") provide optional mechanisms for social community connections that enable you to follow a friend's progress and share your own.

Finding support for specific goals can be simple. Want to quit smoking? Find a friend or relative to team up with, or join a group like Nicotine Anonymous, a spinoff organization of Alcoholics Anonymous. Diet plans? You can find dozens, both online and live, to choose from. Not interested in baring your problems in public? Look for the hundreds, if not thousands, of online support groups for every type of issue under the sun, including support for specific diet plans and forums that discuss exercise videos made by different groups or individuals.

Just making your goal known to someone else — even if it's just your mom or best friend — increases the likelihood that you'll stick with it. Want to make the stakes higher? Organize a group where each person contributes a monetary amount and the person closest to his or her goal after a set time wins the pot. Or make your own personal reward system; put money toward something you really want and then hand the money to someone else to "keep" for you until you reach your goal.

TIP

Going it alone can be successful, but it can be a lonely road. Team up with friends or make some new ones, and the journey toward your goals will seem much shorter — and a lot more fun, too. Even the Lone Ranger had a sidekick.

Chapter 25

Stroke Risk Factors and Prevention

I f you really want to stay sharp, you need to keep the blood supply to your brain flowing smoothly to feed your brain cells. In other words, you must minimize your risk of having a stroke. In a stroke, the blood supply to a certain area of the brain is blocked either because of a clot or because the blood vessel has broken open. In either case, without the oxygen it requires from the blood supply, that area no longer functions; it dies.

This chapter gets you up to speed on what leads to stroke, what the symptoms of stroke are, and how to prevent stroke.

Noting the Types of Stroke

There are three main types of strokes:

>> **Ischemic stroke:** This type is the most common, accounting for almost 90 percent of all strokes. During an ischemic stroke, a blood flow is blocked in a blood vessel that's supplying blood to an area of the brain.

There are two types of ischemic stroke: *thrombotic* and *embolic.* A *thrombotic* stroke occurs when a clot resulting from atherosclerosis buildup finally blocks the inside of the blood vessel (like debris buildup ultimately clogging a pipe).

An *embolic* stroke occurs when a clot forms elsewhere in the body (often from the heart) and travels up into the brain arteries until it can't go any further and blocks blood flow (like a rock lodging in a pipe and blocking flow).

>> **Hemorrhagic stroke:** This type of stroke occurs when a weakened blood vessel wall breaks open, causing bleeding into the brain and lack of blood flow to the brain area that blood vessel supplied. It's usually much more damaging and has a higher mortality rate than ischemic stroke. The most common cause of hemorrhagic stroke is uncontrolled high blood pressure that affects an *aneurysm* (a weak spot on the artery wall that balloons out and may eventually burst from pressure), or an *arteriovenous malformation* (an abnormal tangle of weakened blood vessels that are prone to rupture).

>> **Transient ischemic attack (TIA):** *Transient ischemic attack* is often referred to as a "mini stroke" because it causes a short interruption of blood flow to the brain. Like an ischemic stroke, it's caused by a clot; however, with a TIA, the blockage is temporary (transient), so the symptoms are also temporary. A better name might be "warning stroke" because about one-third of people experiencing a TIA go on to have a stroke within the year. Most TIAs last less than five minutes (the average is less than one minute), but you should call 911 right away if you suspect a TIA.

Stroke is a big and growing concern in the United States. Here are some facts:

>> Stroke is the fifth leading cause of death in the United States and a major cause of serious long-term disability.

>> About 800,000 Americans have a stroke each year; 610,000 of these are first or new strokes and 190,000 are in people who have had prior strokes.

>> One American dies of a stroke every 4 minutes on average.

>> Stroke kills 130,000 Americans each year — that's 1 out of every 20 deaths.

>> 87 percent of all strokes are ischemic strokes.

>> Stroke costs the United States an estimated $34 billion each year. This amount includes the cost of healthcare services, medications to treat strokes, and missed days of work due to stroke.

>> 49 percent of all Americans have at least one of the three major risk factors for stroke (high blood pressure, high cholesterol, or smoking).

Paying Attention to the Warning Signs of Stroke

These days, the damage caused by a blocked artery can potentially be prevented (or lessened), provided you get medical treatment in time. Powerful clot-dissolving medications and even direct removal of a clot can lessen disability or even save your life if you have a stroke or heart attack. Patients who arrive at the emergency room within three hours of their first symptoms tend to have less disability at three months after a stroke than those who received delayed care. Every minute counts.

REMEMBER

Here are the most common stroke symptoms. File this list away; it may save your life or the life of someone you love:

>> Sudden numbness or weakness of the face, arm, or leg — especially on one side of the body

>> Sudden confusion or trouble speaking or understanding

>> Sudden trouble seeing in one or both eyes

>> Sudden dizziness, trouble walking, or loss of balance or coordination

>> Sudden severe headache with no known cause

TIP

The American Stroke Association (www.strokeassociation.org) offers the word *FAST* to help you remember these sudden signs and symptoms of stroke:

>> F: Face drooping

>> A: Arm weakness

>> S: Speech difficulty

>> T: Time to call 911

Underscoring the Importance of Stroke Prevention

Preventing stroke is working. Since 1972, the chances of dying from stroke have declined by 50 percent. A lot of people have benefitted by making an effort to prevent stroke. The result has been longer and healthier lives. Between 1970, the treatment of heart disease and stroke has added almost seven years to the length of an average American's life. People have realized that stroke prevention strategies have real and worthwhile benefits. That's why you now see blood pressure cuffs in every pharmacy and healthier options on fast food menus.

Historically, prevention is something the U.S. healthcare system has *not* embraced. The approach to health has been to wait until something bad happens and then act. But this strategy is a poor way to deal with stroke because by the time something bad happens, damage to your blood vessels — and brain — has already occurred. More and more insurance companies are seeing the payback provided by prevention. Although their motives may be more financial than altruistic, patients are certainly benefitting from their increased emphasis on screening, fitness, and health promotion.

The moral of the story is that you have to take an active role in taking care of yourself. Noting how to deal with contributing factors such as high blood pressure, unhealthy diet, heart disease, and diabetes increases your chances of preventing stroke. No one else is going to do it. The opportunities are there, but they aren't going to force themselves into your life.

Accepting what you can't change

Some risk factors you can't control. Factors such as family history, age, sex, and race — and whether you've had a previous stroke — are situations you simply must accept. In terms of genetics, lightning does strike twice in the same family. You can't change the fact that your parents, grandparents, aunts, and uncles all have or had high cholesterol and that you're more likely to be predisposed to the same fate. But you *can* take steps to watch your diet and treat high cholesterol with medication if needed.

>> **Family history:** A family history of stroke increases the likelihood of stroke for an individual. The fact that many of the risk factors for stroke, such as hypertension and atherosclerosis, can be inherited makes family history an increased concern.

>> **Age:** Your risk of stroke increases with age. Almost 75 percent of strokes occur in people age 65 and older.

>> **Gender:** Men are more likely to suffer from stroke than women. But women increase their stroke risk if they smoke and take estrogen or birth control pills. More women die from stroke than men, but this is partly due to the longer life span of women. They're usually older (and therefore are more likely to die) when they have their first stroke.

>> **Race:** African Americans and Latino Americans have strokes at double the rate (or more) of whites of the same age and sex. This difference isn't entirely explained by higher incidence of high blood pressure and diabetes. Good evidence indicates the other risk factors are the same for individuals of different races. This means that blacks and Hispanics have even more to gain from the effort to prevent stroke.

>> **Previous stroke:** If you've had one stroke, your chances of experiencing another are about ten times higher (about 5 percent per year — the first year may be higher) than if you've never had a stroke (about 0.5 percent per year, depending on your age).

Zeroing in on what you can change

Other risks *are* treatable or preventable. Here's a quick overview of these factors:

>> **Hypertension:** As the first part of this chapter discusses, high blood pressure is the most important factor determining the likelihood that you'll have a stroke.

>> **High blood lipids and cholesterol:** How to combat the devastating effect of blood fat and cholesterol on the blood vessels is covered earlier in this chapter.

>> **Heart and vascular disease:** The numbers tell the story. Individuals who have heart disease are twice as likely to suffer a stroke as those who don't. Diet and lifestyle changes can decrease heart disease risk as well.

>> **Smoking tobacco:** Smokers have four times the number of strokes that nonsmokers do. Smoking increases your chances of heart attack and emphysema as well. Smoking is one of the most controllable stroke risk factors. Stop doing it or, better yet, never start. Quitting may not be easy, but it's certainly worth it. A year after you have stopped smoking, you return to the same stroke risk as a nonsmoker your own age.

>> **Diabetes:** Unfortunately, you can't eliminate diabetes, but you can control it with diet and medication. You can also control the accompanying conditions of high blood pressure and obesity to reduce stroke risk.

>> **Obesity:** Individuals who are obese are more likely to have hypertension, diabetes, high cholesterol, and heart disease, all of which increase the risk for stroke. Weight control is best achieved through diet and exercise.

>> **Oral contraceptives and estrogen replacement:** Both these common drugs increase the tendency of blood to clot, hence the increased risk of stroke caused by blood clots in women taking these pills. Birth-control pills, especially when combined with cigarette smoking, significantly increase a woman's chance of stroke.

>> **Alcohol and drug abuse:** Heavy drinking increases your risk of both heart disease and stroke. Light or moderate drinking is associated with a decreased rate of both stroke and heart disease. These facts have been known for years. Certain drugs like cocaine cause severe spikes in blood pressure that can result in stroke or heart attack.

High Blood Pressure: Stalking the Silent Killer

High blood pressure is sometimes called the *silent killer.* You can have high blood pressure for years before you have any sign of a problem. As the heart strains to push the blood at high pressure through arteries, it enlarges, and the arteries start to show signs of wear and tear. Although you can have *atherosclerosis* (a buildup of plaque on the blood vessel lining) without having high blood pressure, atherosclerosis is usually much worse and gets worse more quickly when accompanied by high blood pressure. High blood pressure is the number-one risk factor for stroke. It not only damages artery walls but also promotes the development of atherosclerosis that can cause stroke by formation of blood clots.

After several years of untreated high blood pressure, you may notice some changes: You may suffer from headaches and dizzy spells or have more frequent nosebleeds. As the atherosclerosis worsens, you may develop poor circulation in your feet.

The condition of your brain generally reflects the poor condition of your heart and blood vessels. As your vessels are repeatedly injured and continue collecting cholesterol and calcium in atherosclerotic plaques, clots form at these sites — clots that may be breaking free and traveling downstream to the brain to cause a stroke. You may begin to have trouble thinking and remembering as small brain arteries battered by high blood pressure are damaged. These arteries, weakened over the years, may even burst, causing a stroke.

Understanding blood pressure

Young blood vessels are quite rubbery, flexible, and pliable. When the heart beats, the blood is forced into the blood vessels under pressure. Your blood vessels stretch out and expand a little as blood pumps through them. When your heart beats, blood is forced through the vessels at the maximum pressure, called *systolic blood pressure*. Between heartbeats, the tight, rubbery girdle of the blood vessels squeezes back down on your blood and keeps it moving through your arteries. Your blood pressure never drops to zero between heartbeats because of your elastic blood vessels. The lowest blood pressure that occurs between heart beats is called the *diastolic blood pressure*.

REMEMBER

Pumping blood through a more rigid blood vessel system requires higher pressure. As you get older, your blood vessels become more rigid. Any atherosclerosis makes them even less elastic. The result? Your heart has to beat much harder, creating a higher systolic pressure and a lower diastolic pressure. What's interesting is that older people with high blood pressure tend to have a high *systolic* pressure, whereas younger individuals with high blood pressure often have a high *diastolic* pressure.

Defining high blood pressure

Blood pressure is recorded as two numbers: the higher (systolic) pressure during a heartbeat *over* the lower (diastolic) pressure between beats. For instance, your doctor may tell you that your blood pressure is 120 over 80 and write it down as 120/80. (That, by the way, would be good news for you; this number is a normal blood pressure reading.)

If your blood pressure is consistently high after several measurements, you have high blood pressure. But what is considered high blood pressure? Well, various levels of blood-pressure readings set off different alarms:

>> **Pre-hypertensive:** If your blood pressure is higher than 120/80 but lower than 140/90, you're *pre-hypertensive* and likely to develop hypertension if you don't take measures to stave it off. National guidelines recommend that you walk more, lose weight, and reduce sodium in your diet.

>> **Bad and really bad:** If your blood pressure is higher than 140/90 but lower than 160/100, you have Stage 1 high blood pressure (bad). If your blood pressure is higher than 160/100, you have Stage 2 high blood pressure (really bad).

Getting your blood pressure checked

TIP

These days, you have no excuse for not knowing your blood pressure. It's easier than ever before. You don't even have to wait till your next doctor appointment to check your blood pressure; just walk into your local drugstore, sit down at the blood pressure booth near the pharmacy counter, and take your blood pressure yourself. Don't cross your legs when you're taking your blood pressure, which can sometimes raise your blood pressure a few points. If you're taking care of someone who can't make it to the drugstore, you can buy your own machine. These do-it-yourself blood pressure machines are excellent for monitoring your blood pressure at home. Such monitoring is important, especially when you're starting a new blood pressure medication.

Battling a lifelong threat

Most cases of hypertension are never cured. Blood pressure is controlled, not fixed. Many people take one bottle of blood-pressure pills, find out their blood pressure is better, and then stop, thinking the job is done. This isn't the way it works. You need to take blood-pressure medication every day for the rest of your life — unless you have an unusual, treatable cause of high blood pressure, a miraculous new treatment is found, or your blood pressure normalizes with *significant* lifestyle modifications (stopping smoking, eating a salt-free diet, or losing lots of your excess weight).

Your efforts in treating your blood pressure will be well worth it in preventing not just stroke but also lots of other life-threatening health conditions (Table 25-1).

TABLE 25-1 **The Effects of High Blood Pressure**

Effect	Risk
Hardening of arteries (atherosclerosis)	Stroke, heart attack
Bulges in blood vessels (aneurysms)	Bleeding ruptured aneurysms
Enlarged heart	Heart failure, heart transplant
Injury to kidney blood vessels	Kidney failure and dialysis
Burst arteries in retina of eye	Blindness, vision loss

Who's at Risk for High Blood Pressure

High blood pressure isn't the result of a single cause but a combination of factors. Some contributing factors you can't control, like your age or your family history. Other factors stem from lifestyle issues that you can influence, including smoking, a high-salt diet, and obesity. The following sections introduce the range of conditions that may lead to high blood pressure.

Heredity

If you have high blood pressure, chances are pretty good that someone else in your family does as well. If you *don't* have high blood pressure, and a family member does, you should check your blood pressure *now*, regardless of your age, and keep a close watch on it through the years. Start exercising and keeping your weight under control now; doing so can help delay the onset of high blood pressure and all its problems.

TIP

Whether you're hypertensive or are trying to prevent high blood pressure, you can benefit from the experiences of your family members. The drugs and diets that they find work best for them may also work best for you because of their genetic relationship to you.

African American ethnicity

African Americans as a group have a very high rate of high blood pressure. It starts at a younger age and results in very high rates of heart attack and stroke — higher than other groups with the same blood pressure. An estimated 36 percent of African Americans have high blood pressure compared to 25 percent of white Americans. African Americans have approximately 50 percent more strokes than white Americans. The reasons for these differences are unknown.

African Americans have a higher prevalence of certain risk factors, including diabetes and obesity. Cultural and dietary factors play a major role, but less access to prevention and treatment may also contribute. These factors explain part of the increased stroke rate in African Americans, but not all of it. Underlying genetic predisposition remains a primary factor. Fortunately, with persistence, African Americans can be successfully treated for high blood pressure, especially with certain classes of medications.

Diet and lifestyle

If you're overweight, your heart has to work harder because it has to pump blood to a larger area of body mass. Time and again, studies support that losing weight reduces blood pressure. Unfortunately, many people who are overweight have difficulty losing weight despite trying. If they've developed high blood pressure, they may postpone starting blood pressure medication too long, thinking they'll eventually get their weight under control. In the meantime, the high blood pressure is injuring their arteries.

Carrying extra weight also increases the likelihood that you'll develop diabetes and high cholesterol. Treating your high blood pressure is critical even *before* you reach your ideal weight. But realize that people within normal weight ranges also can have high blood pressure. There is no guarantee that losing weight *will* get your pressure under control, though it will still help your body in many other ways.

Adding unhealthy sodium through table salt

Fast food fries are the worst of all foods. Not only are they high in calories and the worst of all kinds of fats — *trans fats* — but they also contain massive amounts of table salt, which can raise blood pressure. Salt that you eat goes into your bloodstream and is excreted by your kidneys. When the concentration of salt increases in your blood, the body draws water into the blood from other tissues to dilute the salt until your kidneys have time to excrete it. The extra blood volume and extra work for the kidneys increases your blood pressure.

TIP

Try restricting salt to see whether your blood pressure comes down. If you're living with someone on a low-salt diet, join in. You get used to the change of taste in just a few weeks. Throw away your salt shaker and substitute healthy herbs and spices to enhance the flavors of your food. Your taste for salt will sharpen as you reduce the amount you add to your food at the table.

Neglecting potassium and calcium in the diet

Diets high in potassium promote better health and may result in lower blood pressure.

TIP

Good sources of potassium are fruits such as cantaloupe, bananas, apricots, and oranges, as well as dairy products, lean meats, and dried legumes. Interestingly, salt substitutes often include potassium. So you can kill two birds with one stone by switching out table salt (see the preceding section).

TIP

Just like potassium, calcium can help reduce your blood pressure. Key sources of calcium are dairy products — use low-fat dairy products such as skim milk or yogurt. You can also find calcium in sardines, certain grains and legumes, and even vegetables such as broccoli. Calcium helps maintain bone and muscle tissue — particularly important as you recover from stroke.

Considering caffeine

Caffeine, found in coffee, tea, soda, chocolate, and energy drinks, has many metabolic effects, including raising blood pressure. If you're overweight or have underlying high blood pressure, this effect is even more prominent. Caffeine-induced spikes in blood pressure usually last about three hours but depend on the amount of caffeine consumed. Such spikes can damage blood vessel walls even in people without high blood pressure. If you like caffeinated drinks, limit your intake to one to two a day rather than drinking them constantly. Or consider switching to decaf.

Alcohol: Handling a double-edged sword

According to the National Stroke Association (www.stroke.org), alcohol has been linked to stroke in many studies. Drinking too much can increase blood pressure and the risk of stroke. People who drink more than two alcoholic drinks on average a day have a 34 percent higher risk of stroke and have strokes up to five years earlier in life than those who drink less or don't drink at all.

Drugs that may lead to high blood pressure

Many medications contain chemicals that can raise blood pressure. Here a few of the most common offenders:

>> High doses of aspirin

>> Nonsteroidal anti-inflammatory drugs (NSAIDS) such as ibuprofen or naproxen

>> Stimulants such as caffeine pills or amphetamines

>> Decongestants/cough syrups containing phenylephrine

>> Diet aids

>> Steroids

REMEMBER

You're wise to consider and list all medications — including diet supplements, diet aids, and vitamins — you take. Even the medicated salve that you rub on your sore muscles should go on the list. Birth-control pills, Viagra — the whole medicine cabinet. Then show the list to your doctor who is working with you to manage your stroke risk and every doctor who prescribes medication for you. A complete list is important not only in relation to your high blood pressure but also because such supplements may interact in an undesirable way with other medications you may be prescribed.

Lowering Blood Pressure to Reduce Stroke

TIP

For people who have never had a stroke, treating blood pressure cuts the risk of stroke nearly in half. In older patients, treating people with high systolic blood pressure reduces the chances of dementia by half. If you've had a stroke, the chances you'll have a second one are reduced by 30 percent if you treat your high blood pressure. Regular and frequent monitoring of your blood pressure helps ensure that your treatment program is working. If you're taking medicine for blood pressure, you should still exercise and eat a healthy diet.

Control through diet and exercise

If you're currently overweight, consume an unhealthy menu of high-sodium and high-fat foods, *and* you avoid regular exercise, you may be able to lower your blood pressure by making some positive lifestyle changes. Even if you're recovering from a stroke, you can follow these recommendations:

» Exert enough to make you breathe faster while exercising.

» Get your weight under control (see Chapter 20 for practical weight-loss approaches).

» Eat more fruits high in potassium (such as cantaloupe, bananas, apricots, and oranges).

» Restrict your sodium intake by cutting back on table salt, processed meats, and packaged convenience foods.

» Consume low-fat dairy products or dark green leafy vegetables to increase your calcium.

» If desired, enjoy alcohol in moderation. Limit yourself to a maximum of one drink a day for women and two drinks a day for men.

» Reduce your caffeine intake. Switch to decaffeinated drinks like decaf coffee or herbal teas.

» Avoid cold tablets, decongestants, cough syrups, and diet drugs that have warnings about high blood pressure.

Control with medication

Too many who suffer from high blood pressure are too slow to start treating it in the most successful manner possible. Although diet and exercise *may* help lower blood pressure, they alone are often not as effective as medication. This may be because people can't keep up the improvement effort, or their lives don't really allow for them to — or because the underlying cause isn't related to their diet.

WARNING

But taking medication does require you to be responsible. You must take the prescription as directed and get needed blood testing on time to make sure the drug is not causing dangerous side effects. You need to monitor your blood pressure while on medication to see if the drug is working. If your blood pressure is difficult to control — not uncommon — you may need to take two or more drugs to get your pressure to recommended levels. In that case, you have to be aware of all the possible ways the two drugs can interact (cause problems when used together that each wouldn't cause by itself).

Lowering blood pressure too much

Drugs can reduce your blood pressure too far. If your blood pressure is too low, you feel light-headed, dizzy, or weak. In this situation your blood pressure may drop so low when you stand up suddenly that you faint or almost faint. If you're having these symptoms, call your doctor. You'll probably be told to stop taking the medicine until your doctor can evaluate whether you need a lower dose of the medication or a completely different medication.

WARNING

Don't stop taking blood-pressure medicine suddenly without checking with your doctor. Doing so can cause your blood pressure to rebound or shoot up higher than ever as the blood pressure lowering effect of the drug is removed, which can be dangerous.

For men only

A possible side effect with almost all blood-pressure medications is impotence. If you're an older man, especially if you have just had a stroke, problems getting and keeping an erection can already be an issue. Any preexisting erectile problems may potentially get worse when you start blood-pressure medication. Usually, problems can be resolved by either adjusting the dose or changing the drug; bring up the issue with your doctor.

Drugs for Lowering Blood Pressure

When your high blood pressure needs to be treated with medication, you need to meet with your doctor to determine what medication is right for you. Several classes of blood pressure lowering drugs are commonly used:

» **Angiotensin-converting enzyme (ACE) inhibitors:** These drugs lower your blood pressure by blocking the effect of angiotensin II, a hormone in your blood that narrows your arteries and causes the release of another blood pressure raising hormone.

>> **Angiotensin II receptor blockers (ARBs):** Like ACE inhibitors, these drugs block the effect of angiotensin II but by a different mechanism. They prevent it from attaching to a receptor so it can't function.

>> **Beta blockers:** These drugs block the effect of blood-vessel constricting effects of epinephrine (adrenalin) and slow the heart rate.

>> **Calcium channel blockers:** These drugs relax blood vessels and increase the supply of blood to the heart while decreasing the heart's workload.

>> **Diuretics:** Also known as water pills, these drugs help your body get rid of unneeded water and salt, which decreases blood volume and therefore blood pressure.

TIP

For more information on high blood pressure and blood pressure medications, the American Heart Association at www.heart.org.

Checking Out How Fat Works

Researchers have shown a clear relationship between fat and atherosclerosis, heart disease, and stroke. This section explains the role fat plays in your body and how it can impact your health.

Fat: Slow-burning fuel

The way fat in your diet is turned into fuel for your daily energy needs is pretty interesting. And complicated. Basically, a carefully controlled, slow-burning fire from within combines oxygen with fuel to produce heat, water, and carbon dioxide. This process is called *metabolism*.

You breathe in oxygen and breathe out carbon dioxide. You consume food and excrete the unusable "ashes" of your internal fire. The more complex sugars and starches in your diet are rapidly converted to glucose and similar simple sugars. These act as quick-burning, readily converted fuel throughout your system — sort of like gasoline. Proteins burn more slowly, perhaps like coal, with many complex reactions.

The fats are the slowest-burning form of fuel. They're akin to petroleum oil, perhaps — highly concentrated, complex stores of energy. Pound for pound, fat contains twice the energy of sugar or protein. Fat's form of energy, however, isn't immediately available. Fats have to be refined and processed in your cells before their energy can be recovered and used.

Breaking down fat in the digestive system

So what happened to that salted butter that drenched your large popcorn at the movies last night? Or the egg-and-sausage biscuits you packed away for breakfast this morning? Or the pizza with extra cheese you grabbed for dinner? Here are the gruesome details.

Converting the fat to a usable form requires special digestive enzymes that are made in the liver and pancreas. The liver is essentially a large chemical processing unit that handles most of the complex reactions involved with the digestion of food and the removal of many toxins from the blood. The pancreas is also a digestive organ but is more specialized. It makes insulin to control blood glucose levels and powerful digestive enzymes to dissolve and break down the fats you eat.

The fat in your food doesn't dissolve very easily. Ever try to clean up grease spilled on the floor? As you attempt to wipe, it smears around. Water alone doesn't help. You have to add soap. The soap dissolves some of the fat and forms little globules with grease in the middle and soap around the outside in a protective shell that will dissolve in water. What you get is a slurry of water made cloudy with tiny spherical globules of soap-ringed grease.

Something similar happens in the lower part of the stomach as food leaves to enter the small intestine. The soap used by the body is called *bile*. The liver produces bile, which breaks the fat into small globules and works with the *lipase* from the pancreas to reduce the fat molecules to their constituent parts so that they can be absorbed by the small intestine. The small intestine churns the fat together with the bile and slowly absorbs the fat.

WARNING

Fat begets fat. Special fat receptors in the stomach slow down the release of fatty food into the intestine so that the intestines don't overload the bloodstream with large amounts of fat. Slowing digestion of food in the stomach brings its own problems. Food remaining in the stomach for hours ferments and irritates the stomach. Your grumbling stomach wants solace. You feel hungry (ever crave a few scoops of ice cream hours after you eat pizza?). Fat in your system is unique in that it encourages you to eat more.

The stomach churns the fat into small globules that can also be readily attacked by *lipases*, enzymes produced by the small intestines and the pancreas. Lipases take the large fat molecules in your bacon burgers and omelets and break them down into simpler fat molecules that are small enough to pass through the membranes of cells lining the intestines and then into the bloodstream to pass through the liver or directly to the heart. Along the way, tiny fat molecules are coated with special proteins that work a little like soap to keep the fat dissolved in the blood. This system is highly efficient — about 95 percent of the fat you take in makes it into your bloodstream. But if you take in a high-fat diet, this streamlined system lets the fat from pepperoni pizza and bologna sandwiches get into your blood and create atherosclerosis over time.

Getting to Know the Two Types of Fat: Cholesterol and Triglycerides

There are two major forms of fat found in the body and in food:

>> Cholesterol

>> Triglycerides

Cholesterol is manufactured in the body — almost four-fifths of the cholesterol in your blood is homemade right in your liver. You also take in cholesterol when you eat meat, cheese, dairy products, and eggs.

Triglycerides are the most common type of fat in the American diet and body. They're in the vegetable oil, olive oil, and shortening you dress your salads with and fry your potatoes in.

The following sections give you the skinny on these two fats.

Cholesterol is waxy

Cholesterol is a waxy form of fat, quite firm and water-repellent. It's present in all cells as part of the outer cell membrane, with the highest concentration in the sheath that wraps around nerve fibers. This fat called cholesterol has some special functions: It forms the molecular backbone of several hormones, including estrogen and testosterone. And it's a fundamental component of the bile your liver makes to emulsify fats when they're digested.

The processing of fats varies from person to person, depending on diet and genetics. Some individuals have unusually high levels of cholesterol in their blood despite consuming a cholesterol-free diet. This can usually be traced to an inherited abnormal enzyme or molecular abnormality.

TIP

The USDA recommends limiting your cholesterol in your diet each day to a scant 300 milligrams (200 if you have diabetes, high cholesterol, or heart disease), one-third of a gram. A boiled egg, for example, contains about 225 milligrams of cholesterol; a chicken breast, around 60 milligrams. As vital as it is to your cells, you can eat only a small amount of cholesterol before it becomes a threat to the health of your blood vessels.

Triglycerides are greasy or oily

There are three classes of triglycerides:

>> **Saturated:** Solids, such as shortening and butter

>> **Unsaturated:** Liquids, such as vegetable and fish oils

>> **Trans:** Begin as unsaturated but have hydrogen added for processing and longer shelf life (such as hydrogenated vegetable oil in peanut butter)

Unsaturated fats are the most benign of the triglycerides. In fact, these fats can be downright good for you (more about that in the next section). *But watch out for saturated and trans fats.* These forms of fat cause the body to produce more cholesterol, increasing the risk of atherosclerosis and, subsequently, heart disease and stroke.

TIP

Dieticians recommend that all the fats combined provide only 20 to 30 percent of the calories in your diet. This generally means you should eat no more than 44 to 66 grams, depending on body size and how much food you consume. (Four grams equals one teaspoon, so that's 11 to 16.5 teaspoons of fat a day.) Candy bars, donuts, cookies, and hotdogs can, by themselves, each contain a teaspoon or two of fat, which starts to add up.

Fat Transporters: HDL, LDL, and Others

The bloodstream is a highway-transport system that carries fats to their destination. But it's a water-based system, and water and fats just don't mix well when they get together. So to help, special transport proteins serve as bodyguards, accompanying fats on their journey. Without these bodyguards, the fats and the water in the bloodstream would stay separate and cause all sorts of traffic jams and congestion in your blood vessels.

To prevent that, here's what happens: After they're processed in the intestine and absorbed into the intestinal cells, fats are packaged in small droplets protected by the transport proteins. These fat-protein packages are called *lipoproteins.* There are four types of lipoproteins. Their long names are real tongue-twisters, but you may already be familiar with their nicknames.

HDL: The good

HDL, which stands for *high-density lipoprotein*, is recognized as the *good* fat trans-porter. HDL's smooth surfaces don't stick to the blood vessels — thus, no clog-ging of the throughways or risk of blood clots. Another favorable attribute is that HDL collects cholesterol from other tissues and brings it back to the liver for pro-cessing and excretion. This lipoprotein, then, not only reliably carries its passen-gers to their destinations but also finds the bad guys and turns them in for deportation.

REMEMBER

The functions of lipoproteins circulating in the blood are very complex. The rela-tionship of blood vessel health, heart disease, and stroke isn't completely under-stood. However, study after study supports the finding that people who have more HDL in their blood have less heart disease and stroke.

LDL: The bad

LDL — *low-density lipoprotein* — is recognized as the *bad* fat transporter. LDL has earned its reputation for a few reasons. It's the major carrier of cholesterol through the blood vessels. LDL doesn't hold tightly to the cholesterol or triglycer-ides it carries but instead deposits them throughout the body's tissues. LDL's outer surfaces are coated with proteins that stick to blood vessels and attract a lot of mean friends, including white blood cells and platelets that get into the fray and invite their own friends. The result is a waxy plaque of atherosclerosis that begins to enlarge as more LDL collects at the site clogging the arteries.

VLDL: The ugly

These *very-low-density lipoproteins* are fat trucks that contain little protein but are loaded with triglycerides to be delivered to fat and muscle cells for storage. VLDL particles are formed in the liver from excess fat or sugar in the diet. They have a triglyceride core with a thin layer of protein. The VLDL protein layer breaks open easily, exposing blood vessels and other tissues to the toxic effects of their hard, fat cores.

Chylomicrons

Chylomicrons are fat and protein particles that transport both cholesterol and tri-glycerides from the intestine directly to the rest of the body. The source of HDL, LDL, and VLDL particles is the liver. The small intestine is the source of chylomi-crons. Unlike most food you eat, fat carried by chylomicrons bypasses the liver and goes directly to the rest of your body where the oils and hard fats are removed for storage in fat or muscle cells.

Chylomicrons are largely triglyceride fats and, as such, not healthy. They increase your risk for heart disease, although the relationship to stroke isn't as clear. They're controlled the same ways that LDL is. When LDL is elevated, the triglycerides are often elevated, too. The focus among doctors now is generally to focus on lowering the bad LDL cholesterol, but they want to lower the chylomicrons/triglycerides to be sure they come down as well.

The stroke connection

So what does all this have to do with stroke? These fats and their bodyguard lipoproteins can irritate the sensitive lining of your blood vessels, leading to atherosclerosis. When irritated, the blood vessels can become increasingly inflamed, scarred, and overlaid with potholes and patches. Eventually, the atherosclerotic plaque ruptures and blocks the vessel entirely or becomes so rough that stroke-causing clots form there. Either way, stroke can result.

Testing for Fat Trouble in Your Body

How do you know if you're at risk for stroke because of high cholesterol? Not necessarily from the numbers on your bathroom scale — though if you're carrying a substantial spare tire around your waist, that is a bad sign. But to get a sense of your current risk, you need a blood test called a lipid panel that measures your levels of cholesterol and its components.

Your weight isn't always an accurate indicator of your cholesterol level. Thin people can have high cholesterol, and overweight individuals may have healthy cholesterol readings. However, being overweight *is* often an indicator for heart disease and a suggestion that cholesterol may need to be investigated.

TIP

See Chapter 20 for information calculating your body mass index (BMI). If your BMI is greater than 24, you're officially at higher risk of stroke, heart disease, and diabetes.

Testing your blood for cholesterol

The most accurate way for determining your blood lipid levels is to have your blood tested under fasting conditions (see next section for more). Typically, a single blood sample can be used to measure cholesterol, triglycerides, and the three lipoproteins in your cholesterol. The results of this fasting lipid panel help you and your doctor estimate your cardiovascular risk.

Although not related to lipid levels, two other tests for determining stroke risk are often done from the same blood sample: *homocysteine* and *C-reactive protein* tests. At certain elevated levels, these two tests can predict increased risk of stroke. When blood vessels are injured or irritated, white blood cells, platelets, and other components of the blood signal the problem to the rest of the body. When the liver receives the signal, it produces C-reactive protein. You want your test results to show ten or fewer *micromoles* per liter for homocysteine — and you don't want to see *any* measure of C-reactive protein in your blood.

Fasting before your blood test

All the interpretations of the blood lipid test results are based on the assumption that you have eaten nothing for 12 hours prior to the test (though you can drink all the water you want). The goal is to estimate the load of fat you carry in your blood between meals, not the fat content of your food.

Almost every bit of fat in the diet gets into the bloodstream one way or another. When you eat fat and it enters your stomach, it slows down the digestive process. It takes up to ten hours to clear all the fat from your last meal out of your blood so if you forget you're supposed to be fasting and eat something, you should reschedule the test — only the HDL and total cholesterol levels will be close to accurate if you have the test now. You need the LDL values. But don't fast more than 14 hours, or your body's response to the prolonged fasting may skew the results. The easiest thing to do is stop eating after 7 p.m. and then go to the laboratory when it opens at 7 or 8 a.m. to have your fasting blood drawn.

Get instructions from your doctor about which of your morning pills you should take on an empty stomach. This is especially important if you're on diabetic medication.

Interpreting blood test results

After reviewing your lipid profile blood test results, your doctor will take into account your unique set of circumstances and offer an action plan. Your treatment plan will depend on a great many factors including your age, your prior history of heart disease and stroke, whether you have diabetes, and other risk factors. Treatment guidelines are updated as new information is gained from ongoing clinical trials.

Desirable values for cholesterol, triglycerides, and the lipoprotein breakdown are as follows:

Test	Desirable Value
Cholesterol, total	100–199 mg/dL (milligrams per deciliter)
Triglycerides	0–149 mg/dL
HDL	40–59 mg/dL
LDL	0–99 mg/dL
VLDL	5–40 mg/dL

Total cholesterol

When talking about blood lipids, people are no doubt most familiar with the target for total cholesterol, which is the sum of all the lipoprotein components. The desirable range is below 200 milligrams per deciliter (mg/dL). Levels greater than 240 predict a very high risk of stroke and heart disease. Until menopause, women tend to have lower levels of cholesterol than men the same age. Pregnancy, when cholesterol levels tend to be high, is an exception. However, values for both men and women tend to increase with age.

Triglyceride levels

Normal levels are less than 150 mg/dL. Higher values mean higher risk for stroke and heart disease. Very high levels of triglycerides require treatment similar to that for high LDL.

HDL levels

Remember, HDL is the *good* fat transporter, so a higher range of this lipoprotein is positive news. An HDL reading above 40 is desirable; at 60 or above is even better. At this level, some think the HDL will start carrying excess cholesterol out of the body, reducing the likelihood of atherosclerosis inside your blood vessels. Some recommend that for women 45 and older, the target HDL should be 60.

LDL levels

A desirable level of LDL — the *bad* fat transporter — is 99 mg/dL or lower (70 if you have heart disease). Whether this or another level of LDL is your treatment goal depends on the plan you work out with your doctor. In general, the higher your LDL level, the higher your risk for stroke and heart disease. An LDL level above 190 is a red-light condition for your heart and brain, but you need to pay attention to any level over 100 to minimize risk.

Cholesterol-to-HDL ratio

Some research indicates that the ratio of total cholesterol to HDL also predicts the occurrence of stroke and heart disease. Divide the cholesterol level by the HDL level. According to the American Heart Association, the optimal ratio is 3.5-to-1; a higher ratio means a higher risk of heart disease and stroke. You definitely want this ratio to be less than 5-to-1.

Monitoring your efforts with blood tests

REMEMBER

When you make changes to your diet with the goal of reducing cholesterol, periodic blood tests on a regular basis are an important measure of your success over time. You wouldn't diet to lose weight without getting on the scale at regular intervals, would you? Following your lipid panel is no different.

Keeping Fats in Check with Statin Drugs

As mentioned earlier in the chapter, deciding whether you should take cholesterol-lowering statin drugs involves a detailed knowledge of your risk factors and the levels of the different lipids in your blood. Some doctors are conservative, and others very eager, in prescribing statins. These drugs have saved thousands of lives, but there are serious side effects in some individuals. You don't want to take statins if you don't need to. See your doctor.

Despite your best efforts, diet and exercise may only do so much to lower your cholesterol. If, after three months, you aren't making headway toward reducing cholesterol, and your body mass index isn't coming down, then don't delay seeking medical treatment to reduce cholesterol.

The skinny on statins

Drugs called *statins* can reduce your chances of having a stroke. Research studies have shown that the use of statin medications over the course of ten years can reduce your risk of stroke by one third. If you've had a stroke, the reduction would probably be greater. Statins have been found to decrease the risk of premature death and heart attack as well. There is also good clinical trial evidence that statins actually reduce the thickness of some atherosclerotic plaques — that is, partially reverse atherosclerosis — which is pretty amazing. Here are some common statin drugs:

Commercial Name	Generic Name
Lipitor	Atorvastatin
Zocor	Simvastatin
Pravachol	Pravastatin
Lescol	Fluvastatin
Mevacor	Lovastatin
Crestor	Rosuvastn
Livato	Pitavastin

How statins work

Statins stop your liver from making cholesterol. They don't stop you from *eating* cholesterol, though. Diet and taking statins have to work together to benefit you. Don't assume you can go back to bacon and eggs for breakfast the day you take your first pill. Continue to avoid trans and saturated fats while taking a statin drug; otherwise, you defeat the purpose of taking it.

Statins, as with any major drug, stimulate a bit of controversy. Although their long-term effects aren't really known yet, the benefits seen in the trials are pretty hard to dispute.

Side effects of statins

Nausea, diarrhea, constipation, and muscle ache and muscle cramps (especially in the legs) are some of the more common side effects of statin drugs. There are two serious side effects, however.

Liver damage

Liver damage from statins is usually seen in an elevation of liver function tests in the blood that indicate liver injury. See why it's important to get your blood tested regularly? Six to twelve weeks after you start the drug and then every four to six months is recommended as an appropriate interval to check liver function. A mild increase in these liver function tests doesn't necessarily mean you have to stop taking the drug; however, you may need to lower the dose and check your blood more every couple of weeks for a while. Your doctor will determine what is best for you. If a serious liver problem does develop, or the liver tests remain elevated, stopping the statins usually reverses the problem.

REMEMBER

If you're going to take statins, you need to follow your doctor's instructions and get blood tests done when recommended. Otherwise, warnings of serious side effects may be missed.

Other drugs that reduce cholesterol can make liver problems worse. One of these drugs is gemfibrozil (Lopid). In high doses, the B vitamin niacin does a pretty good job of lowering cholesterol, but beware of adding it to statins. Consuming daily or B-complex vitamins isn't known to cause this effect.

Do's and don'ts for taking statins

Here's a handy list of things to keep in mind about statins:

>> **Eliminate grapefruit juice from your diet.** Grapefruit and grapefruit juice prevent the metabolism of several drugs, including all statins. Don't eat or drink it.

>> **Take statin drugs daily.** Your liver makes cholesterol at night. For maximum effect, take statin drugs late in the day. Morning dosing of statins is totally fine. It's much more important to get it in daily than to forget to take it at night (especially if you usually only take pills in the morning).

>> **Get your blood tested regularly.** You need to monitor the results of the statin drugs. Check blood lipids, liver function, and, if needed, muscle-breakdown products.

>> **Avoid certain medications.** If you're on statins, you shouldn't be taking certain medications, including drugs that kill fungal infections, the antibiotic erythromycin, gemfibrazol (Lopid), the antidepressant Serzone, or high doses of the B vitamin niacin.

>> **Be alert to certain side effects.** If you notice unusual muscle aches and pains or muscle cramps, report these to your physician at once; because these symptoms can signal serious side effects of statins.

Reviewing the major risks

Many of the risks for stroke are linked — one condition aggravates or causes another, like a chain reaction in your vascular system. High blood pressure puts more wear and tear on blood vessels and worsens atherosclerosis because the plaque formation results from the body's attempt to patch and heal an artery lining injured by high blood pressure. Atherosclerosis is further aggravated by diabetes because high blood glucose levels lead to blood vessel injuries and more plaque formation. Ultimately, this cycle results in more clots that can break loose and cause strokes.

Heart and Vascular Disease

The heart and the brain are interrelated. If you've had heart disease, you're more likely to have a stroke in the future. If you have had a stroke, you're more likely to have a heart attack in the future. The reasons and level of risk vary based on the type of heart disease. Several heart diseases are connected to stroke because heart disease produces conditions that increase blood clotting, which results in stroke. Treatment almost always includes some medication to slow blood clotting.

Atrial fibrillation

This is a condition in which the contractions of the upper chambers of the heart (the *atria*) are irregular, which results in inefficient pumping of blood. This leads to pooling of the blood in the atrial heart chambers. This pooled blood is more likely to clot, and those clots are more likely to be pumped out of the heart and travel in the liquid blood like boats on a river. These clots (the boats) flow up to the brain where they lodge in the brain's arteries and block blood flow to the brain cells served by those arteries. The result is an *embolic* stroke. Embolic strokes are caused by *emboli* or traveling blood clots. If you have atrial fibrillation, you should be treated for it. The risk of stroke from atrial fibrillation adds up at about 5 per-cent per year. You can't let this go on very long before you're more likely to have a stroke than you are to win a coin toss. Medications to treat atrial fibrillation are blood thinners that help prevent this "standing blood" from clotting. They include warfarin (commonly known by the trade name Coumadin), as well as newer class of drugs called *oral factor Xa inhibitors.* (See the section "Treating to slow blood clotting" for more details.)

Heart attack

TIP

If you have a stroke and you've had a heart attack in the past, it's a good idea to get a good look at the heart to see whether it contains any blood clots that may break loose and cause further strokes. This can usually be done with ultrasound imaging called an *echocardiogram.* No invasive procedures are needed in most cases.

Having a stroke means you may also have a heart attack. A cardiologist (heart specialist) or other doctor can look for conditions you should treat to prevent a heart attack. For example, a stress test may show that one of the arteries to your heart is almost completely blocked. This condition may be treated with a stent to hold the artery open. Drugs such as aspirin that prevent stroke by slowing down clotting also helps prevent heart attacks, as does reducing cholesterol.

Heart valve disease

If you have a mechanical (artificial) heart valve, your risk for stroke is significantly increased. If you do have a stroke, communicating and coordinating your care between your heart specialist (cardiologist) and your stroke specialist is critical. One reason is that you're undoubtedly on an anticlotting medication. Your clotting control will have to be reevaluated after the stroke, and your medication may need adjustment. Additionally, the valve itself must be checked, usually with an echocardiogram.

Treating to slow blood clotting

The main course of action is treatment to prevent clotting that can cause either heart attack or stroke. Physicians choose specific drugs based on your individual needs according to both your past medical history and current clinical situation. If you need to have slowing of blood clotting, your doctor has to choose from two main categories of oral blood-thinning drugs: antiplatelets and anticoagulants.

Antiplatelet drugs include aspirin, clopidogrel (Plavix), dipyridamole (Persantine), and prasugrel (Effient), which thin blood by deactivating blood cells called *platelets* that stick together and plug leaks in blood vessels, a process that can lead to atherosclerotic plaque formation. *Anticoagulant drugs* thin blood by blocking the clot-forming factors in your blood. There are two main types of anticoagulants in use today: warfarin (Coumadin/Jantoven) and the oral thrombin and factor Xa inhibitors.

Warfarin stops clotting by depleting your body of a key ingredient needed to make the glue that sticks a clot together — the vitamin K dependent clotting factors. Warfarin is used for treatment of blood clots in the leg (*deep venous thrombosis* or DVT) and the lung (*pulmonary embolism*) and to prevent clot development with atrial fibrillation and artificial heart valves. Warfarin requires a regular blood test called an *international normalized ratio* (INR) to monitor how thin it has made the blood so it can be kept at the proper level. Warfarin interacts with many other medications as well as some foods, so you need to work closely with your doctor to avoid these. The main risk of warfarin use is bleeding, although if you're in an accident that causes traumatic bleeding (or you're bleeding for any reason), its effect can be reversed by giving you vitamin K intravenously as an antidote. This is especially important when emergency surgery is needed for prompt treatment of traumatic bleeding.

The oral thrombin inhibitor is dabigantran (Pradaxa) and the oral factor Xa inhibitors include apixaban (Eliquis), rivarozaban (Xarelto), and edoxaban (Savaysa). All these drugs are approved to use in atrial fibrillation and the treatment of DVT, but they can't be used to prevent clotting from artificial heart valves. They have set doses and don't require blood test monitoring like warfarin does. They do interact with other drugs (although less than warfarin), so make sure your doctor knows what other drugs you're taking. The biggest problem with this class of medications is that there is currently no antidote for use in people who are bleeding or who require emergency surgery.

Controlling Diabetes

In a nutshell, diabetes (discussed in Chapter 23) is a condition in which the body doesn't produce or use insulin properly. Diabetes can lead to stroke as well as decreased vision, kidney disease, nerve damage, and heart disease.

Insulin lets your body cells use the sugar (carbohydrates) you take in through your diet. When it's available and functioning properly, insulin keeps your blood sugar (glucose) level controlled by making the sugar available to body cells for energy. If more glucose is taken in than your body needs for energy, it's converted to fat stores for later use. Too much insulin, and your blood glucose can drop so low that your brain stops working and you can lose consciousness and die. Too little insulin, and your blood can be so filled with glucose that it injures cells. In diabetes, either your pancreas stops making enough insulin or your body stops responding to insulin. Either way, the result is higher levels of glucose in your blood that are the hallmark of diabetes.

What does diabetes have to do with stroke? High blood sugar levels make blood vessels more prone to injury. As a result, diabetic arteries don't endure the wear and tear of life as well as nondiabetic arteries. The effects of major risk factors for stroke — atherosclerosis and high blood pressure — are increased in diabetics. See the domino effect here? It's a case of multiple-risk factors conspiring to set you on the path to stroke.

TIP

Doctors have a large number of tools in their medical bags to find the perfect combination of diabetes treatments that work for you. Work closely with your doctor. The more you know about diabetes management, the better the two of you can work together to keep your blood glucose under control.

WARNING

As with many drugs, diabetic medications cause interactions with other drugs. Simply changing medicines may resolve any problems if a drug interaction occurs. However, communicate any and all of your prescriptions, over-the-counter medications, and supplements to the physician treating your diabetes. Drugs that may interact with diabetic medications include aspirin, acetaminophen, ibuprofen, sulfa drugs, some antibiotics, warfarin and its cousins, a drug called probenecid given for gout, and beta blockers used to treat blood pressure and many heart conditions.

Diabetes increases your risk of stroke. However, the closer you keep your blood glucose to normal levels, the healthier your arteries are. The more tightly you control your blood glucose, the more careful you have to be with your diet and medication management. Follow your doctor's instructions precisely.

REMEMBER

And don't get so focused on your diabetes that you forget other important risk factors. When you have diabetes, you also have a lot to gain by treating high blood pressure, stopping smoking, and getting your blood lipids in good shape. Diabetes makes virtually all other risk factors for stroke worse.

Fighting Obesity with Diet and Exercise

America is in the middle of a national obesity epidemic that is threatening recent progress in combating high blood pressure and atherosclerosis. Obesity ultimately leads to more strokes and heart attacks as the population ages.

The principle of weight gain

REMEMBER

One basic principle explains all the extra fat tissue you have on board. Here it is: The amount of weight you gain is equal to the difference between the amount of energy you *consume* and the amount of energy you *expend*.

You lose weight by a combination of two strategies: First, you exercise more to build muscle mass and burn energy from fat reserves. The greater muscle mass is always burning glucose, even when you're resting. Just like your brain. Second, you consume less energy. Energy is measured in calories. Calories come from food. It's really that simple.

Changing your eating habits

If you're overweight, it's likely a state that took years to achieve. You have developed eating habits that help you sustain — and perhaps continue to add to — your extra pounds.

TIP

If you need or want to lose weight, consider it a long-term commitment. Research the topic, give it some soul-searching, evaluate your current lifestyle, explore various eating plans, talk to your doctor or a nutritionist, and find an eating plan that you feel you can stick with and incorporate into your life. Eating is a lifelong activity, and *how* you eat is a habit you can change to achieve a healthy weight.

While you're losing weight, remember to pay attention to other risk factors. Losing weight doesn't mean you can ignore high blood cholesterol, smoke cigarettes, and elevate your blood pressure with diet pills and loads of salt. Measure your weight, check your blood pressure frequently, toss the cigarettes, and work with your doctor to get the cholesterol in your blood tested.

Seeing through the advertising hype

TIP

Turn off the TV and take a walk! In a culture like America's, the average person confronts immense adversarial forces when he or she decides to eat less. Billions of dollars are spent to sell you food. These advertisers are smart. They don't just sell food. They also sell convenience, warm family gatherings, popularity, cost-savings, and even romance through food. Who wouldn't be persuaded to drive to the nearest chain restaurant after viewing happy, fit, attractive people downing huge quantities of fat-soaked food — at a special price? Obesity is promoted every day by a huge gamut of corporations who want you to buy their products.

It's a lot easier to sell fat, sugar, and salt than carrots, lettuce, and pinto beans. There have been relatively successful government campaigns to get folks to stop smoking. More recently, campaigns to reduce obesity are educating Americans about the perils of being overweight. But restaurant and junk food advertisers still hold great power in America. Consequently, you have to rely on your own discriminating skills to overcome the advertisers' power over your purchases and eating habits.

Exercising as a lifelong habit

The other strategy for weight loss is to expend more energy. In a word, exercise. And for most people, exercise *is* an effort. Generally, people's jobs and lives don't require much physical exertion, so they have to find ways to incorporate such activity into our routines. And for many, it's not easy or exciting.

Explore exercise seriously. Read up on it, talk to your doctor, or meet with a personal trainer. Consider the spectrum of physical activities available to you — from pilates to power-walking, from handball to horseback riding — and find something you can incorporate into your routine as a lifelong habit. Make it something you enjoy so you'll actually do it regularly.

TIP

Exercise doesn't have to be complicated; you don't have to buy expensive machinery, join a pricey fitness center, or take classes to learn a new sport. Your route to weight loss can be as simple as walking for 45 minutes a day in your neighborhood or at a community park. The great benefit of walking is that you can take it anywhere. If you're traveling, you don't have to worry about packing extra equipment. If it's raining, you can find a mall to walk in. And it's as easy to do alone as it is in the company of a friend.

Making a Plan for Reducing Stroke Risk

First, take steps to address risk factors that offer the greatest threat — with the result that the treatment offers the greatest benefit:

- » Stop smoking.
- » Get treatment for high blood pressure.
- » If you have atrial fibrillation, take medication to prevent blood clots.
- » Control your blood cholesterol.
- » Exercise regularly.
- » Achieve and then maintain a healthy weight.

Next, act *before* things get bad. If you wait to treat your blood pressure until you have a heart attack or a stroke, that's too late. Blood-pressure tests and cholesterol screenings are routine parts of medical exams. Even if you're a young adult who is concerned for a parent or grandparent who has suffered a stroke, you can also personally benefit from putting the information in this chapter to good use *now*.

At your last check-up, you may have learned that your blood pressure or your cholesterol levels were on the high side of normal. Your doctor may have said something like, "Well, it's a little high, but we don't need to consider medication at this point. Just watch out for it."

TIP

Actually, if you hear things like that from your doctor, you need to get busy with lifestyle changes. You don't have to allow your arteries to harden until you have blood pressure so high it requires medication. If you eat greasy food today, expect to take blood-pressure pills and spend hours in doctors' offices tomorrow. Work with your doctor now to learn everything you can to prevent high blood pressure, atherosclerosis, diabetes, and other risk factors from ever getting out of control. It's up to you. This is an opportunity for you to do something now that is guaranteed to pay off for you in the future.

Collecting the evidence

It's a great idea to establish a relationship with a physician that will work with you to anticipate health problems and start treating them early. Certain data is important — whether or not you've had a stroke — in order for you to effectively monitor your condition. But you also need to educate yourself. You need to know the basics of medical tests used to evaluate and monitor your cardiovascular health. To be a more informed patient, know the following:

>> **Blood-pressure tracking:** Know your blood pressure and keep track of your readings. You don't have to visit the doctor every day to keep tabs on this critical bit of information. This detective work can be done at a free machine in a drug store. Or buy your own machine that you can use conveniently at home.

   Blood pressure is usually measured once a day, but it does vary over the course of the day. It's usually higher in the morning and lower during sleep. You may want to track it several times a day for a period of time; having our own blood pressure machine makes this approach affordable and practical.

>> **EKG reading:** EKG stands for *electrocardiogram*. This test indicates irregular heart rhythm or damage from heart disease. It also tells whether you've had a (silent) heart attack or if your heart is enlarged.

>> **Cholesterol level:** This one requires drawing a bit of blood. A fasting *lipid panel* will tell you about the different types of cholesterol and whether yours are normal or high. A lot of emphasis is placed on LDL and HDL cholesterol, the bad and the good, respectively. Let your doctor tell you the best levels for you depending on your medical condition. Be sure you know the numbers and have agreed on a target level to reach with your doctor.

>> **Diabetes testing:** A fasting blood sugar test screens for diabetes. (See the earlier section "Fasting before your blood test" for info on this procedure.)

>> **Other blood tests:** These include a comprehensive metabolic panel, which looks at your blood chemistry including sodium and potassium levels as well as kidney and liver function tests.

>> **Carotid ultrasound for atherosclerosis:** Atherosclerosis of the carotid artery is an important risk for stroke. Carotid ultrasound tests the carotid arteries in your neck for signs of plaque buildup that can cause critical blockages that can lead to stroke.

>> **Chest X-ray:** This test can give more evidence about your heart.

>> **CT or MRI scan:** If you've already had a CT or MRI scan of your brain, collect the reports so that you have a record of your brain's condition.

Setting your prevention goals

Talk with your physician, about where you stand on modifiable risk factors. Then get started on lessening your stroke risk. Here are some tips for mapping out a successful plan:

>> **Write it down:** Commit your goals to paper. Seeing them in print helps you see what you're aiming for.

>> **Establish a timeline:** If you list "Lose 30 pounds" as one of your goals, determine a deadline goal for achieving that goal. Be realistic.

>> **Break it down into steps:** If you jot down "Stop smoking in six weeks" but stop there, chances are you'll still be stubbing out cigarettes two months from now. Breaking it down into manageable steps, such as "Week One: Get a nicotine patch and substitute a walk for a cigarette break at work immediately," "Week Two: Reduce per-day cigarette consumption by half," and so forth, makes it easier to accomplish.

>> **Keep your list close at hand:** Tape it to the refrigerator. Post it on your bulletin board. Put it on your smartphone and calendar. The point is to keep your goals in front of you.

IN THIS CHAPTER

Realizing the power of positive thinking

Balancing your life with healthy approaches

Staying connected with family and friends

Knowing the benefits of having a spiritual life

Enjoying sex for years to come

Chapter 26

Don't Worry, Be Happy: The Keys to Maintaining Health and Vitality

The power of positive thinking is more than just a cliché; it's supported by medical facts. Positive people live longer, healthier, happier lives than negative people. Flexible people who handle change with grace are less stressed as a result. They resolve conflicts and overcome health challenges better than those who resist change. A positive outlook is the octane booster that can power you through each day, giving your body the extra edge it needs to survive. Negativity pulls you down and makes you reluctant to move forward. People who are positive and go with the flow maintain better balance in their lives. And those who are emotionally and spiritually connected to a higher power have a stronger will to live, thereby increasing their longevity.

This chapter examines the role a positive attitude plays in keeping you healthy, happy, and serene no matter what your age or circumstances.

Factoring In the Importance of a Positive Attitude

Aging can bring major life changes. Staying positive and happy isn't always easy in your older years, when you may lose people near and dear to you, have unexpected health issues, have children move away, retire from a job that meant the world to you, or need to move out of the family home.

Yet, contrary to popular opinion, getting older doesn't mean you become more negative. Aging and negativity don't go hand in hand. One large study reported in the *Journal of Personality and Social Psychology* indicated that as people age, they become happier rather than sadder and are able to regulate emotions more effectively than younger or middle-aged adults. Even if you're not Mary Sunshine by nature, you can learn to develop a positive overall outlook.

Why bother? Although being optimistic isn't a surefire ticket to living into your 100s, several studies have shown that pessimism can increase your risk of dying at a younger age. Consider the following studies:

>> A study done in the Netherlands involving nearly 1,000 participants age 65 to 85 showed that people who described themselves as being highly optimistic had a 55 percent lower risk of dying than pessimists did during the ten-year study period. The risks of dying from heart disease were 23 percent lower for optimists during the same period.

>> The Ohio Longitudinal Study of Aging and Retirement began in the 1970s with over 1,100 people and concluded more than 20 years later with over 600 people over age 50. The study showed that people with a healthy attitude toward aging lived more than seven years longer than those with a negative attitude.

>> The Mayo Clinic reported that when psychological tests given to over 800 people were reviewed, pessimistic people were 19 percent more likely to have died in any given year than optimists.

WARNING

Like everything else, you can carry optimism too far so it ends up being more harmful than beneficial. Being too optimistic can lead to a carefree attitude that results in unfortunate, but often avoidable, problems resulting from taking risks rather than precautions. Excessive optimism can also lead to an overly trusting attitude, which can allow others to take advantage of you. You've probably heard stories of overly trusting seniors who have been conned out of large sums of money by individuals or organizations. Again, balance is the key, and you have to have the right amount of positive thinking but maintain common sense when it comes to your health, money, and other important life issues.

The bottom line? Being optimistic can help you live longer — but don't leave common sense at the door. In some situations, skepticism or a touch of pessimism is the best approach.

Embracing a Healthy, Balanced Approach to Life

If you feel that life is a balancing act, you're in good company. Most people spend time trying to keep their lives in balance because keeping life in balance, or a state of equilibrium, leads to a happier, less stressful life.

Everyone's life brings unfortunate obstacles and difficult challenges, but also rewards, opportunity, and satisfaction. When your scale starts to weigh down due to negative life events, the challenge is figuring out how to regain balance. You don't want to fall into patterns of negativity and pessimism, which increase stress and make bad situations worse. Finding balance may be very difficult at times, but it's worth the effort. Look for ways to maintain balance so you can keep from getting overwhelmed and lead a healthier life even when you're under stress.

Turning around negativity

You may already be convinced that a positive attitude can benefit your life, but how do you become a positive person if it doesn't come naturally? It's not as hard you think — being aware of your negativity is half the battle. Figuring out how to turn negativity around is the other half.

Although a little negativity is normal in daily life, constant negativity can make you stressed, anxious, depressed, or bitter. It can wear away your self-esteem and perpetuate a pattern of self-destructive behaviors. Some negative thoughts that can negate a positive attitude include the following:

>> **Worrying about what other people think about you:** Studies show that most of the time, other people aren't thinking about you at all, except to wonder what you think of *them*. Ironic, isn't it?

GETTING INTO THE BLUE ZONE

A *blue zone* is a demographic/geographic area of the world where people live significantly healthier and longer lives. In his book *The Blue Zones: Lessons for Living Longer from the People Who've Lived the Longest*, Dan Buettner identifies five world regions that produce super high rates of healthy and functional centenarians: Sardinia, Italy; Loma Linda, California; Nicoya Peninsula, Costa Rica; Okinawa, Japan; and Icaria, Greece. What makes these people age so successfully? Buettner identifies nine lessons:

- **Move naturally.** Incorporate regular physical activity as a part of daily life.

- **Have a life purpose (a reason to get out of bed in the morning) at all ages.**

- **Build time to relax into daily life.**

- **Moderate calorie intake.** Stop eating when you're 80 percent full.

- **Eat a plant-based diet and lots of legumes.** Head to Chapter 21 for more on plant-based eating.

- **Moderate alcohol intake.** Enjoy a glass of wine, and not more.

- **Belong to a faith-based community, no matter the denomination.**

- **Put family first in the priority list — all generations.**

- **Have a strong social circle of friends to act as a support network.**

To maintain health and vitality as you age, you can learn a lot from those folks who have already travelled that path successfully. For more information on how to get into the blue zone, check out www.bluezones.com/live-longer.

>> **Preoccupation or obsession with stressors:** Although thinking through problems can be beneficial, constantly brooding about stressors produces only one thing — more stress. (See the chapters in Part 3 for a load of specific stress-reducing strategies.)

>> **Dwelling on the past and things you can't change:** You can learn lessons from the past, but constantly thinking about "what might've been" is unhealthy, unproductive, and weighs you down.

>> **Self-criticism:** Self-improvement is fine; putting yourself down isn't. After all, the world has enough people who feel the need to criticize, so why would you do that to yourself? Instead, be your own best cheerleader. You deserve the same respect and compassion from yourself that you give to others.

TIP

Turning yourself from a negative perspective to a positive attitude takes conscious effort and a lot of practice. The following suggestions can get you started:

>> **Figure out how to recognize negative thoughts.** Stop entertaining them. As soon as you notice them, push them out of your mind (and keep them out).

>> **Replace the negative thoughts with positive ones by turning concerns on their head.** Instead of thinking that you'll never be as productive at work as your friend, try to determine what it is that makes your friend productive. Positive attitude, the ability to say no when necessary, the ability to delegate? Which of those things can you modify in yourself to make yourself into a more productive person?

>> **Put the negative thought into perspective.** If you find yourself using terms like *always* and *never* to describe situations — as in, "I'll never be promoted" or "She always gets the best assignments" — you may need to adjust your perspective on life. Very few things are black and white, and honestly examining your feelings, or writing them down, may help you see where you've fallen into negative thought patterns. Feelings are just that — feelings. They're not facts, and very often your feelings don't match the facts in a given situation. If you can find the discrepancies, you can begin to adjust your thinking.

REMEMBER

Bring out a mental stop sign whenever you find yourself drifting into negative thoughts. Replacing those negative thoughts with positive ones may be awkward at first, but within a few weeks, you may well find that negativity is no longer a habit. And like many bad habits, negativity breeds health risks. Make being positive your new habit for a longer, more enjoyable life.

Being less confrontational

As you get older, you may feel like you spend much of your life fighting with people — your younger boss, your kids, your spouse, the girl at the supermarket, your best friend. On one hand, you don't want your middle name to be Doormat, but on the other hand, being in constant conflict with other people is exhausting. It upsets your stomach, and it demolishes your hard-earned optimistic view of life. Some people — hopefully you're not one of them — feel that everything in life is worth fighting about, and they spend most of their life in emotional turmoil. Learn to choose your battles; some things really aren't worth fighting about. Ask yourself, "Will this matter in a month?" If the answer is no, why get yourself tied up in knots over it?

However, conflict *is* a part of life. Some people never figure out how to handle it well. Handling conflict means taking the high road sometimes and searching for the win-win solution in every situation. This resolution isn't the same as giving in. If everybody wins, everybody's happy, including you. Facing conflict and traveling the paths to overcoming it builds character and confidence.

Defuse conflict by using some of these techniques:

>> **Know what you believe and stick to it.** Have a core set of values — a balanced mix of self-awareness and confidence — while still being open-minded and accepting of other viewpoints. These values allow you to take a stand when moral or ethical issues arise and feel confident every time. Having a firm foundation of beliefs lets others see you as committed rather than defensive and antagonistic.

>> **Look for common ground.** Keep focused on a positive, solution-based outcome. You may only agree to disagree, but you can do it without killing each other.

>> **Realize that other people are human too.** Other people often may not live up to your expectation of them. Don't be surprised, disappointed, or upset to the point of argument when this happens. Being human, however, is a two-way street; you may not always live up to others' expectations — or your own! Cut yourself the same break that you'd give someone else when you're not living up to your expectations. And if you're not living up to someone else's expectations, look at yourself with a clear eye instead of assuming that you're in the right every time. Maybe you really can do better.

>> **Think carefully before setting yourself up for confrontational situations.** Do certain topics push your hot buttons with certain people? Then don't talk about them with that person unless you're in the mood for a good argument. Does driving 12 hours in the car with your spouse turn you into someone who would argue that the sky isn't blue? Make alternate plans. (Maybe one of you could fly and the other could drive, or you could stop halfway and stay overnight.) Recognize your conflict triggers and avoid them.

>> **Figure out why something is upsetting you.** Every argument has a root cause, and often the thing you're actually arguing about isn't really the source of aggravation at all. Ask yourself, "What's really causing this conflict, and why am I reacting the way I am?"

>> **Always think win-win.** There's almost always a way for both parties to feel they've won. Put away your swords. Look for a way that each side can walk away with a benefit. Resolving a conflict can be a great lesson in seeing an issue from another person's perspective, whether you agree with it or not. After you arrive at a win-win solution, accept it and implement it. Make sure that each person takes responsibility for agreeing with the decision.

>> **Check your emotions at the door.** Conflict resolution is about problem solving, which is a logical process. Emotions color your perceptions and your

logic and cloud the rational thinking that's essential to arriving at a mutually acceptable solution.

>> **Put your heads together.** Two heads are better than one, and three may be better yet. The more people who are focused on the solution, the better the odds of a successful outcome.

Staying Active and In Touch with the World

Staying active as you get older means far more than riding your bicycle around the block every evening. It involves both physically being involved in activities in your community and mentally being involved with the world around you. Being connected to your world is good for your health and mental attitude, and it can also benefit those around you.

TIP

Not sure where to start? Here are some suggestions.

>> **Know what's going on in the world.** Read the newspaper. Watch the evening news. Subscribe to a weekly news magazine or read one at your local library. Being in touch with what's going on locally, nationally, and internationally decreases feelings of isolation. Being in tune gives you something more interesting to talk about with others than the state of your bowels.

>> **Get a job.** Many seniors work part time not only to earn a little extra spending money but also to stay active. Love antiques? How about a part-time job in an antique store? Love books? Would working at a bookstore or library interest you? Love to do woodwork? How about hitting the weekend craft shows and hawking your wares? Job opportunities are limited only by your imagination and, contrary to what you may think, many businesses love to hire seniors because of their positive work ethic and maturity.

>> **Help others out.** Volunteer opportunities are unlimited, and many organizations are desperate for help. Hospitals are always in need of volunteers, and so are groups that help new citizens learn English. Many libraries have volunteer programs, and Meals on Wheels is always in need of drivers.

Want something more exotic? How about a mission trip (not all are religiously based) to a foreign country? You're never too old to hold babies or talk to teens in an orphanage. Many organizations offer yearly mission trips to the same area so that volunteers can make lasting connections there. Check out www.mmex.org or www.missionfinder.org for any number of organizations looking for volunteers for a week, a month, or a year, all over the world.

>> **Get out and travel.** Going to a new place not only gives you something to talk about but also sharpens your mind, stretches your map-reading skills, and is fun. Go on your own or with an organized group; you have no excuse for staying home when an organized tour does all the legwork for you.

>> **Find a new hobby or expand an old one.** Do you love to sing? How about joining the local theater group (roles exist for all ages) or a barbershop quartet, or just singing in the church choir? Do you fiddle around on guitar? How about finding some local musicians and holding a jam session, or even form a band? Build model airplanes and join a local flying group. Crochet blankets or quilt. Join a book club — or start one in your neighborhood. There may be a dozen people on your street just looking for something new to do; ask around and you may find two or three folks with interests similar to yours.

>> **Be civic minded.** Volunteer to man voting booths. Stump for your favorite candidate — or become a candidate yourself! Neighborhood associations are often crying for help. Don't stay away because you don't know anyone; most times you'll be greeted with open arms if you offer help.

>> **Use your computer.** The age group that's 55 and older has had the highest increase in computer usage. Yes, a lot of trash is on the Internet, but you can also find interesting chat rooms and instruction of all kinds; you can even take college courses online. There's more to the computer than playing solitaire, so check out the home and garden forums, the classic car boards, or the health chat rooms and talk to interesting people without ever leaving home. Listen to TED talks on whatever subject interests you at www.ted.com.

>> **Exercise:** You need to stay in shape to accomplish any of the other suggestions in this list. You can enjoy many activities with friends while getting some exercise. Grab your golf clubs and walk nine holes of golf. It's a great way to socialize and exercise at the same time. Get a foursome and play tennis. If you want some alone time, head to the gym and get some quality personal time while you work out. People over age 55 who exercise regularly are on a fraction of the medications that sedentary patients require. With the cost of medications today, using exercise to reduce some of your medication load is a great incentive.

Connecting with Your Spiritual Side

Some type of spiritual belief system is found in virtually every society on earth. People want and need to believe in something greater than themselves. Some studies have shown that spiritual beliefs and religiosity (participation in an organized religion) increase with age, leading to considerable research into the effects of religion and spirituality on health issues and aging since the 1990s.

You may concede that being spiritual or religious makes people feel healthier, but there are also measurable results to support their belief. Here are just a few:

>> A 1992 study reported in the *American Journal of Psychiatry* stated that religious faith increased the ability of older adults to cope with illness, loss, disability, and mortality issues.

>> A study reported in the *Southern Medical Journal* in 1998 reported that subjects who attended church once a week were 43 percent less likely to have been admitted to the hospital for any reason, and those who were hospitalized had markedly shorter stays.

>> An article in *The Journal of Pain* reported that daily spiritual experiences were associated with more positive attitudes and resulted in a decrease in reported pain.

>> A Duke University Medical Center in Durham study of over 4,000 participants over the age of 65 found that those who pray and attend religious services on a weekly basis, especially those between the ages of 65 and 74, had lower blood pressure than their counterparts.

The commonality in these studies is the presence of spirituality and faith in people's lives on a regular basis. Whether it takes the form of a formal religion or a more personal spiritual discipline doesn't matter. The point is that being connected to a power greater than yourself provides you with meaning, hope, and peace and lessens stress. So what is there to lose? Find what works for you and make it part of your daily life.

Connecting with Others: The Significance of Support

According to a social survey, family relationships and good health are the two highest-rated variables when measuring happiness. Why? The ability to form deep, lasting bonds with other people in which you can share life experiences, learn, grow, trust, and support one another fulfills a fundamental human need. The absence of such relationships and bonds leads to isolation and depression.

How do the relationships with the people in your life affect your attitude and how you spend your days? The following sections look at how staying in touch with your nearest and dearest can be a blessing, positively contributing to both your mental and physical well-being.

Family and friends: Life preservers of the human kind

As you get older, your family and friends can be your most critical lifeline. Numerous studies have shown that having a strong social network results in a longer, healthier, and happier life. Although keeping in touch with friends and family far away or making new friends may be difficult, the long-term results are worth it.

Keeping in touch with those nearby

When you live around the corner from family and friends, you may need to walk a fine line between being in touch and being in touch *too much*. Gauging the proper balance between closeness and too much togetherness isn't always easy, but, by using common sense, you can maintain close relationships without overstepping boundaries.

TIP

If you have close family and/or friends nearby, it may be beneficial for both of you to have definite times to get together instead of just dropping in and being dropped in on. Making "dates" to get together once a week, once a month, or once a day — whatever suits your particular lifestyle — gives both of you the freedom to plan your day and to know that you'll be seeing each other regularly.

Staying connected when miles separate you

Maintaining connections to loved ones who are hundreds of miles away has never been easier. With the advent of cellphones that transmit pictures instantly through text messaging, emails, and social media like Facebook and Twitter, you need never be far out of touch with the ones you love. Of course you can always pick up the telephone to let your fingers do the walking.

And if you need to see people in person to feel connected, airlines offer dozens of flights a day to wherever you want to go. Airfares vary considerably, so get familiar with websites like www.travelocity.com or www.expedia.com, just to name two of many that offer discounted flights, hotels, and car rentals. Some airlines offer the best deals on their own individual websites.

REMEMBER

Although all the modern methods of connection are wonderful, don't forget one of the old fashioned — and certainly more permanent — ways of staying in touch: letter writing. Although it's becoming a forgotten art, letter writing not only is a way to stay in touch but also leaves a permanent legacy of your thoughts and day-to-day life behind.

Being a grandparent

If your children have children, being a grandparent can be really fun. Grandchildren bring all the joy of children with none (or at least fewer) of the hassles.

Being a good grandparent takes practice but brings great rewards. If you don't have any grandchildren, you can always volunteer at school functions or get involved with organizations such as Big Brothers Big Sisters to develop meaningful relationships with younger people. Some hospitals also have an "Adopted Grandparent" program for hospitalized children.

What makes a wonderful grandparent?

>> **Love your grandchildren unconditionally.** This one comes naturally to most grandparents!

>> **Respect their parents.** This is often a tough one; respecting their parents means following their rules for child rearing, supporting them in their decisions, and not sneaking forbidden goodies to your grandchildren behind their parents' backs.

>> **Know your boundaries.** Holding back on visiting or being involved with grandchildren's lives can be hard, but their parents' wishes must be paramount. Visit as often as you're invited — not as often as you want — and your relationship will be much happier.

Making new friends

It can be harder, and a little scary, to forge new relationships as you get older. When you're younger, work relationships and parenting relationships lead naturally to friendships, but when you're older, meeting new people can be more difficult.

However if you put your mind to it, you can certainly find new friends. Here are some tips:

>> Take classes at the YMCA.

>> Join a gym.

>> Find an organized sports league, such as bowling or softball.

>> Join church or town social groups.

>> Volunteer.

Adjusting when friends and family become caregivers

There's a very good chance that you may need the help of family and/or friends for daily care as you get older. Statistics show that one in four families provide care for older family or friends. In fact, 85 percent of all long-term care is provided by unpaid caregivers.

As hard as being a caregiver can be, being the person receiving the care can be just as hard. Being dependent on others can lead to depression, anger with the person providing your care, and frustration at losing your independence.

TIP

Even if you need help with daily care, you can maintain some independence. For example, you can

>> **Make some of your own decisions.** What do you want to eat? Wear? Where do you want to sit? What time do you want to go to bed? There's no reason to give up all your decision-making, unless your choices are inconvenient for the person doing your care. Making decisions helps keep you sharp and gives you some feeling of control over your life.

>> **Keep in touch with the world.** Needing assistance doesn't mean you can't stay in touch with your world. Read the newspaper or check out the nightly news. Knowing what's happening in the world not only helps you feel connected but also gives you something to talk about at the dinner table.

>> **Do as much as possible for yourself.** The trouble with needing assistance is that it's easy to let your helper do more for you than necessary, which can escalate into an unnecessary increase in dependence. Yes, it's much easier to have someone else do your hair or pick out your clothes, but allowing others to take over leads to becoming passive and disinterested in your world. Using your hands and fingers less results in stiffness and loss of agility, so don't give up physical tasks just because others can do them faster or neater. Remember, use it or lose it.

Love relationships: With or without them, how you age

You may have had the same partner for the last 40 years, or you may have a new love interest. You may be newly single, or still single after all these years and very happy. You can't argue with happiness, but some research suggests that having a partner may have its benefits.

According to a study done by the Center for Disease Control, which surveyed over 127,000 adults, married adults are healthier, smoke and drink alcohol less, are physically more active, and are less likely to be limited in activities of daily living. Many studies have come to similar conclusions, including the following:

>> Married people are less likely to be admitted to a nursing home and much less likely to die in hospitals.

>> Married women at age 48 have an 8 percent risk of dying before age 65, versus a divorced woman's risk of 18 percent. A married man at age 48 has a 12 percent risk of dying before age 65, versus a divorced man's risk of 35 percent.

>> Married people may be healthier because they have increased social support from their spouse, improving psychological well-being and immune function.

On the other hand, staying single doesn't mean that a person has to be alone or unhappy, nor does it mean that a person's health has to suffer as a result. Singlehood may be a choice, and a very happy one at that.

Is being single less beneficial from a health and happiness perspective? Consider these points:

>> Marriage seems to benefit men from a health and emotional perspective more than women, possibly because single men have traditionally engaged in more risky behaviors, such as smoking and drinking too much.

>> People who've always been single fare just as well as people who've been married, and both do better than those who've been divorced or widowed.

>> Differences between married and single people are decreasing over time. This in part is due to the fact that some choose to be committed to someone in a relationship without getting married. Living together without tying the knot is more common now than ever before.

>> With the divorce rate increasing, many of the stats on health are changing due to the health effects of divorce.

>> The degree to which marriage matters differs across cultures.

S-E-X: Why Getting It On May Help You Live Longer

Getting older and being sexually active aren't mutually exclusive. Sexual satisfaction is still possible at any age. Although age-related changes may necessitate some adjustments, where there's a will there's a way. For both men and women, physiological changes to the body make having sex a different experience as you age, but different doesn't mean worse; it just means adapting. After you understand what to expect sexually of yourself and your partner as you both get older, you see that sexual pleasure and intimacy don't have to fade over time.

Sexual activity is good for . . . everything

Sex certainly does have benefits. Regular and enthusiastic sex offers a host of measurable physiological advantages, probably more than anyone even knows. Sexual activity has positive effects on hormones, immune function, endorphins, and muscle strengthening; even if the effect is just a big smile on your face, sex does the body good.

Take a look at these examples of what sex can do for the body:

>> **You live longer.** Men who reported the highest frequency of orgasm lived longer than men who had less-frequent orgasms.

>> **You have a reduced risk of heart disease.** Research shows that men who had sex three or more times a week reduced their risk of heart attack or stroke by half.

>> **You can get some exercise.** A regular bout of sex burns around 50 calories — about the same as walking 15 minutes on a treadmill. The pulse rate in a person who's aroused rises from about 70 beats per minute to 150. However, don't substitute sex for other forms of exercise. You'd have to engage in sexual activity for many hours to achieve the same aerobic benefits as other options.

>> **You experience a sense of well-being.** Levels of the hormone oxytocin increase during intercourse and in turn releases endorphins. Endorphins give you a sense of well-being and can even reduce pain because of their action on pain receptors.

>> **You get sick less.** People who have sex weekly have higher levels of an antibody called immunoglobulin A, which can be important for the immune system when fighting infections.

Recognizing the effects of aging on sex

Normal aging isn't responsible for diminished sexual desire. Older people can still feel the need for sex. As long as a partner is available, regular sexual activity is as normal as it is during any other time during your life. Just because people get older doesn't mean that they don't believe that sex still contributes to their physical and psychological health and well-being.

REMEMBER

In most instances when people refrain from sex, it's not because of lack of desire but rather a functional problem that may be wrongly assumed to be uncorrectable. Many men feel that it's just inevitable that they'll have to jump in line to get erectile medication, while women assume that after menopause they'll need a firecracker under their derriere to get them interested in sex.

Studies show that the physical capacity for male erection and male and female orgasm continue almost indefinitely, even if achieving orgasm is desired but not always achieved. Research reveals that people over the age of 55 still engage in the same varied sexual practices they did when they were younger, such as masturbation and oral sex, in addition to intercourse. However, age does bring physical changes that need to be taken into account and adapted to if you want your sex life to remain lively as you get older.

Age-associated changes in men

Biological and physiological changes in men can impact their sexual function. These changes include the following:

>> **A decline in levels of the hormone testosterone:** *Testosterone* is the male sex hormone responsible for creating and releasing sperm, initiating sex drive, and providing muscular strength. Between the ages of 15 and 18, testosterone levels peak. By the time men reach their mid- to late-20s, testosterone levels start a slow decline. By the age of 40, some men notice a significant drop. At age 50, half of all men experience a significant reduction in testosterone levels, resulting in sexual side effects. For the majority of men with low testosterone levels, the major complaint is a diminished sex drive. Eighty percent of men who complain of a low libido also report the inability to maintain a strong erection.

>> **The duration of the refractory period:** The *refractory period* is the length of time between ejaculations. As men age, this period of time increases. The refractory period varies widely among individuals over a lifetime, ranging from minutes to hours to days. When a man is in his youth, he may be able to ejaculate multiple times within the period of a few hours. As he ages, he may not be able to sustain an erection, let alone ejaculate, for as many as 24 hours after his previous orgasm.

TECHNICAL STUFF

There are several reasons for this change. An increased infusion of the hormone oxytocin during ejaculation is believed to be chiefly responsible for the refractory period. The amount that oxytocin increases may determine the length of each refractory period. Another reason may be a decrease in the amount of blood flow to the penis from vascular disease, which is more common with age. Another chemical that could be responsible for the increase in the refractory period is prolactin. Prolactin suppresses dopamine, which is responsible for sexual arousal.

ANDROPAUSE

There's new interest in treating age-related hormone deficiencies in men, often referred to as *andropause*. In the past doctors often wrote off male hormone-related issues as depression, early diabetes, or just old age. New testing of hormone levels and the subsequent treatments have shown promising results for people with low testosterone and human growth hormone (a hormone released from the pituitary that can decline with age). If you're deficient, treatment can improve libido, erections, energy, and weight and muscle management. If you think you may have hormone deficiencies, talk to your doctor about the available testing and potential treatment.

WARNING

>> **Erectile dysfunction:** One of the greatest fears for men as they age is erectile dysfunction. Fortunately for many, changes in lifestyle choices can eradicate the problem. Nearly half of men between the ages of 45 and 65 may have difficulty getting an erection or maintaining an erection sufficient for intercourse. The most common cause of erectile dysfunction are hormone deficiencies, poor dietary habits, lack of exercise, weight problems, uncontrolled or untreated high blood pressure, vascular disease, and diabetes.

If you experience erectile dysfunction, talk with your doctor. It may indicate coronary heart disease or diabetes. Erectile dysfunction doesn't cause heart disease, but it may be evidence that the process of arterial blockage is occurring in other areas of the body.

Being aware of the sexual changes your body can go through as you age can help you be better prepared. Here are some additional age–associated changes men may experience and should address with their doctors:

>> Decrease in the number and frequency of morning erections

>> Reduced sexual arousal, both mentally (visual, psychological) and physically with respect to erectile and orgasm potential

>> Reduced duration and strength of orgasm

WARNING

If you experience a loss of sexual desire and other related sexual side effects, speak with your healthcare provider. Treatment options may be available.

Age-associated changes in women

Besides puberty, *menopause* (the termination of menstrual periods) is the most dramatic change that affects women sexually as they age. Menopause usually occurs between 42 and 56 years of age with the average age being 50. During menopause hormonal production diminishes, and the lining of the vaginal wall becomes thinner and more rigid. The production of vaginal lubrication drops, which can make intercourse uncomfortable and is a big reason that women lose interest in sex. However, many over-the-counter products aid in lubrication. If extra lubrication isn't effective, see your healthcare provider to consider prescription treatments.

REMEMBER

A woman's capacity to achieve orgasm can remain at near peak levels well into her senior years, even though it may take quite a bit longer to achieve. Menopause doesn't negatively impact a woman's desire or interest for sex. In fact, the freedom from worrying about unwanted pregnancy can be very liberating for post-menopausal women.

Solving sexual problems together

Both partners in a sexual relationship can experience sexual issues. The key to maintaining a positive relationship is to work together on challenges that arise. The following may help keep things hot as you get older:

>> **Lubrication:** To help with vaginal dryness, decreased erection, or atrophied vaginal tissues, use a little lube, such as K-Y jelly. A little goes a long way to solve these problems.

>> **Patience:** It's probably going to take a little longer to get things going — for both of you. Take the time to enjoy what you're doing — enjoy longer foreplay. Sex isn't a race, anyway.

>> **New underwear:** Liven things up a bit. Ditch the granny panties and the tighty whiteys for something more visually stimulating and fun. You can always pretend that you're buying those thongs for a friend. Or shop online — no one will ever know.

>> **Sex toys:** Don't be embarrassed; they sell these toys online now, and they may help by stimulating areas you didn't even know you had.

REMEMBER

Above all sex is supposed to be fun — let it be.

6

The Part of Tens

Find out ways to make your home safer. From improving your lighting to bathing safely, gain tips to prevent injuries at home.

Get the scoop on ten (plus) almost-superfoods that will help to keep you healthy and active.

Chapter 27

Ten Ways to Make Your Home Safer as You Age

Home may be the place you feel safest, but statistically, it's the place you're most likely to be injured. People age 65 and older consistently experience the highest numbers of home-injury-related deaths. Preventing injuries at home is common sense, but most people don't think about dangerous situations until they get injured. In this chapter, we offer some hints to stay sharp about being safe at home at *any* age.

Take Precautions to Prevent Falls

Falls are the leading cause of injury deaths and the most common cause of nonfatal injuries and hospital admissions for trauma. Each year in the U.S. nearly one-third of older adults experience a fall. Check out these suggestions to keep yourself from becoming a statistic:

>> Install a hand rail — that extends the full length of the stairs — on each side of all stairs in your house.

- » Keep all stairways, pathways, and walkways well lit and free of clutter.

- » Get rid of all throw rugs and carpets with corners that can flip up or have them taped down tight to the floor.

- » Install grab bars along the toilets and showers, and use a non-slip mat or adhesive safety strips inside the bath or shower.

- » Wear sturdy shoes with thin, non-slip soles.

- » Stay off ladders and don't climb on chairs, because poor vision and balance contribute to falls.

TIP

You also want to do your part to keep your sense of balance and flexibility. Maintain an active lifestyle that includes exercise as part of your daily routine with a focus on balance, strength, and flexibility. And if you experience dizziness, consult your doctor to see what's at fault.

In Case of Fire . . . Plan Ahead

A home fire is dangerous at any age, but the odds of injury increase when you get older. To prevent injury from fire, do the following:

- » Install smoke alarms on every level of your home and test them monthly. Change smoke alarm batteries at least once a year. New systems available can be wired so if one alarm goes off it sets off all the alarms.

- » Develop and practice a fire escape plan with your family that identifies two exits out of every room with a place to meet outside.

- » Buy a hanging escape ladder for rooms on the second story.

- » Install alarms on the stove or an automatic shut-off for the times when the stove is accidentally left on. Never leave food cooking on the stove while you leave the room.

- » Don't smoke in bed. If possible, don't smoke in the house at all — a cigarette left burning outside is much less likely to cause a house fire.

Be Sure Your Meds are Safe

With every year, the number of prescription and non prescription medications you take is likely to grow. Keeping the pills you take straight can be a real challenge, even if you aren't suffering from memory loss. Taking the wrong medication is more common than you may think and depending on the med and how much you took, can be very dangerous.

WARNING

If you suspect you have taken the wrong medication or took a dose twice by mistake, call your doctor first. If your doctor isn't available, call the Poison Control Hotline at 800-222-1222 or 911.

Other safety precautions include the following:

>> **Use a medications tracker.** This tool indicates which medication to take when and what dose with instructions, such as taking pills with food. This tracker helps minimize error. You can register for some services to call and remind you to take your meds.

>> **Get a pill box.** This method is one of the cheapest and easiest ways to keep your meds straight. There's a covered compartment for each day of the week, so you have your medication for a week organized, and you can see if you remembered to take your pills because, if you didn't, they're still in the compartment.

>> **Ask your doctor if there's a way to simplify your schedule.** Can you take any of your meds just once a day, in a higher dose, rather than twice a day? Never change your medication schedule on your own.

>> **Get rid of old medication.** Call your local hospital or doctor to find out how to dispose of unwanted or expired medications to eliminate the possibility of taking the wrong medications or expired medications that may be harmful rather than helpful.

>> **Post emergency numbers.** Next to every phone in the home, list the numbers of Poison Control and other numbers you or someone else assisting you may need in an emergency.

Stock Your Emergency Supply Kit

No matter what your age, a first aid kit in a convenient and memorable location (next to your kitchen fire extinguisher, for example) is a must. Refresh and restock your first aid kit twice a year, replacing any expired or missing supplies. Have enough supplies to survive for three days. Include the following:

>> Sterile adhesive bandages in assorted sizes

>> Hypoallergenic adhesive tape and sterile roller bandages (2- and 3-inch)

- » Acetaminophen, Ibuprofen
- » Benadryl
- » Calamine lotion
- » Antibiotic ointment
- » Hydrocortisone cream
- » Antiseptic wipes
- » Hot/cold packs
- » Thermometer
- » Tweezers
- » Small scissors or other cutting tool
- » Light source (flashlight) with extra batteries
- » CPR mouthpiece
- » Disposable rubber gloves
- » Phone numbers for poison control and emergency contacts

Update Your Life-Saving Skills

Do you know what to do if someone is having a heart attack? Acting quickly can save a life. One way is through cardio-pulmonary resuscitation (CPR). When you're able to perform CPR on someone during a heart attack, you can help save her life until emergency help arrives. Look for a CPR class near you through the American Heart Association, your local fire department, or a hospital.

TIP

Consider purchasing your own automated external defibrillator (AED), an instrument specifically designed for home use to help save a life. The FDA may require someone who purchases an AED to present a physician's prescription for the device. They cost between $1,500 to $2,000.

While you're at it, learn the Heimlich maneuver. According to the U.S. Department for Housing and Urban Development (HUD), the death rate due to choking is highest among people over age 75.

Let Lighting Lead Your Way

Too often people overlook the importance of good lighting; it's one of the best and least-expensive insurances against home injuries. As age progresses, vision changes. In general, after age 40, your eyes function best for distant viewing, so exceptionally good light is important in all areas of the home, especially the kitchen, laundry, other work areas, and over steps.

TIP

The following suggestions can get you started toward a safer environment:

>> Install a night light in your bathroom.

>> Install overhead lights to illuminate all areas of a room.

>> Install task lighting under counters in the kitchen.

>> Install overhead lights over the entryway so visitors can be seen.

>> Consider outside motion sensors that automatically turn on when visitors (expected or unexpected) make an appearance.

Reach Easily

As you age, your body has a harder time maintaining balance and finding its equilibrium, so reaching for objects becomes more of a challenge, increasing the likelihood of an injury in the process. These suggestions may help:

>> Incorporate adjustable upper shelves, pull-out lower shelves, and Lazy Susans into your cabinets and closets.

>> Replace cabinet knobs or pulls and sink faucets with levers for easier handling.

>> Keep the items you use often low and within reach to avoid climbing on ladders and stools.

>> Enlist the help of family or neighbors to move items so they're within your reach.

Bathe Safely

The bathroom seems one of the most popular places for home accidents. To minimize the possibilities there, follow these guidelines:

>> Install grab bars and rails to reduce falls around the tub and toilet.

>> Consider a stall shower with a low threshold and shower seat instead of a tub if you're planning to remodel.

>> Remove bath mats or double-tape them down and place non-slip surfaces in the tub or shower.

>> Clean up water spills immediately.

>> Wear an in-home personal emergency response system that automatically calls for help in case you injure yourself and can't get to the phone.

REMEMBER

Older people are in the top 90 percent risk group for being burned by hot water. The thermostat on the hot water heater should be set below 120 degrees Fahrenheit.

Prevent Poisoning

Poisoning is the third-leading cause of unintentional injury-related death in the home among older adults, and certainly one of the most preventable. Take a look at these three poison sources:

>> **Carbon monoxide (CO):** Carbon monoxide poisoning is the leading cause of accidental poisoning deaths in America. Install at least one carbon monoxide detector near your sleeping areas. A CO detector sounds an alarm if too much CO is present. Major sources of CO come from tobacco smoke, an idling car in the garage, combustion appliances (gas or kerosene heaters), and fireplaces.

>> **Food poisoning:** Many older people have the inability to do everyday tasks, such as preparing meals and grocery shopping. As a result, many may eat food that's past its expiration date, resulting in food poisoning. In some cases, this can lead to dehydration from gastrointestinal distress.

>> **Chemical poisoning:** Keep all chemicals (including common household cleaners) away from food and stored in different containers than non-food items. Choose non-toxic products when you can. Avoid mixing chemicals

because some chemical reactions can cause watery eyes, nausea, and vomiting. Only use chemicals in well-ventilated areas. Older people are more prone to accidental spillage due to loss of muscle strength and can't tolerate or escape the fumes as quickly.

Make Sure that You Can See Clearly Now

Vision loss is very common as you age. An entire industry is devoted to making things easier to see to prevent problems as you get older. Some of the visual aides that can help include

>> Talking blood pressure cuffs, blood glucose monitors, and thermometers

>> Marked stove dials so you can tell the temperature setting by feel

>> Large magnifying glasses to enlarge instructions on pill bottles

>> Boil alert gadgets that fit on a pan and rattle when the water is boiling

>> Liquid level indicators that fit on your cup and buzz when the liquid is an inch from the top

TIP

One good source of low-vision aids is www.1hb.org, the website for Lighthouse for the Blind. The toll free number is 888-792-0163.

Chapter 28

Ten (Plus) Almost-Superfoods that Can Help Round Out Your Diet

S everal foods fall short of the truly "super" standard, but they're still good for you. These are called almost-superfoods. Using the best preparation and cooking methods is the best way to keep these foods almost-super.

This chapter covers almost-superfoods that are delicious, are usually easy to find in grocery stores, and add variety to your diet while keeping your body healthy and your mind sharp.

Whole Grains

Most of the bread, buns, cereals, and pasta you see lining the shelves in your local grocery store are made from refined white wheat flour. When flour is refined, the fiber- and nutrient-rich bran and covering are removed, leaving flour that yields a softer texture for baked goods and a milder flavor for pasta. Most flour is enriched with iron and B vitamins, which is good, but you're still missing a good bit of fiber.

Whole-grain products retain the fiber and natural nutrients found in grains, such as wheat, barley, and spelt (similar to wheat but with a sweeter, nuttier flavor). Eating 100 percent whole-grain cereal, baked goods, and pasta adds fiber to your diet and helps slow down the digestion and absorption of the starches in the grain. Most people consume grains on a daily basis; it's recommended to incorporate at least three servings of whole grains every day.

Look for "100 percent whole wheat" or "100 percent whole grain" on the ingredients list to be sure the product you're buying is really made from the whole grain.

Increase your intake of whole grains by substituting whole-wheat flour for part of the refined flour in your favorite recipes.

Poultry

Chicken and turkey are lower in saturated fats than beef and are often used in place of red meat in low-fat diets to reduce the cholesterol-raising and inflammatory effects of eating saturated fat. Much of the fat in poultry is contained in the skin, so you can keep your chicken or turkey low-fat by removing the skin.

One cup of cooked chicken breast meat without the skin has only 1 gram of saturated fat and slightly more than 200 calories (dark meat from the legs and thighs has a little more fat and calories). Turkey has even less saturated fat than chicken.

Buy a whole chicken or turkey and roast the bird in the oven, and then remove the skin before serving (roasting with the skin on makes the meat more flavorful). You'll have enough for dinner and lots of leftovers that you can use for other meals. Add cooked, chopped turkey or chicken to a regular garden salad to turn it into a full meal. Or make healthful sandwiches on 100 percent whole-grain bread, with a slice of cheese, tomatoes, and lettuce.

You can also find organic, free-range poultry, which means the birds were raised in healthier conditions and were not exposed to hormones or antibiotics. Organic and free-range poultry is more expensive, but it's becoming more popular every year.

Bison

The meat from American bison (and game meat such as venison and elk) is much lower in fat than other red meat, and can serve as a delicious substitute for beef. Bison tastes very similar to beef but is actually a bit richer.

TIP

Bison can be used in most dishes that call for beef; however, since bison is lower in fat, you'll have better results if you use lower temperatures for cooking, especially for ground bison. Bison steaks can be prepared just like beef. They're best if not cooked past medium doneness (about 145 degrees Fahrenheit measured with a meat thermometer), meaning the steak is still pink in the middle.

Depending on where you live, bison may be available in your local grocery store, or you may have to travel to a larger store or purchase it online. You can also use venison (deer meat) or elk to replace beef in your diet. They have similar nutritional profiles, but a slightly gamier (but still delicious!) flavor.

Yogurt

Eating yogurt is a great way to get calcium into your diet, plus yogurt contains friendly bacteria that happily populate your digestive system. The bacteria help to keep your digestive system healthy by keeping the bad bacteria and yeast at bay, while the good bacteria make short-chain fatty acids that help to maintain and repair the walls of your digestive tract.

Some brands of yogurt contain added live bacterial cultures called *probiotics* that increase the amount and type of friendly bacteria in the yogurt. Eating these brands of yogurt may improve regularity and may even reduce the symptoms of other digestive disorders.

Yogurt is available in a wide variety of flavors. You need to read the label to be sure you're not ruining the nutritional value of your yogurt by adding too many calories. One cup of nonfat yogurt has less than 90 calories, but sugar and high-fructose corn syrup can ratchet the count up to over 200 calories.

TIP

To save calories, choose brands that are sweetened with Splenda, or buy plain yogurt and add just a touch of sweetness with a little honey and plenty of freshly sliced fruit.

Snap Beans

The nutritional content of green and yellow snap beans makes them a great addition to any superfoods diet. The mild flavor and versatility means that fussy eaters can enjoy these vegetables. Snap beans are low in calories and are a good source of vitamin C, potassium, and folate. Green snap beans are also rich in vitamin A, lutein, and beta-carotene, which trigger antioxidant activity to help prevent damage to the cells in your body.

Green and yellow snap beans are easy to find in the grocery store. Fresh or frozen are best; however, they're available in cans, too — just watch out for added sodium. Snap beans are frequently cooked and served as a side dish (top them with some almonds and olive oil — two popular superfoods). Green beans are also a favorite ingredient in many casseroles (just beware of added fat and calories).

TIP

Raw snap beans taste great and have a wonderful crunch. Try serving them with your favorite vegetable dip or as a healthful ingredient in your salads.

Cabbage

Cabbage is a good source of vitamin C, vitamin K, and *sulphorophane,* a phytochemical that may help to fight cancer. According to the journal *Cancer Letter* in 2008, diets rich in cruciferous vegetables, including cabbage, reduce the risk of colon and prostate cancer.

You can find fresh cabbage (and possibly red cabbage) in the produce section of every grocery store; look in the deli for premade slaws and salads. Store-bought cole slaw is usually fattened up with creamy dressings, but you can make a healthier slaw at home by using a vinegar-based dressing instead.

Add cabbage pieces to soups and stews, or sauté some cabbage in a little olive oil with onions. You can eat a lot of cabbage without harming your diet: One cup of raw shredded cabbage has only 18 calories.

Winter Squash

You can find fresh squash in the produce section of your grocery store. Winter squash comes in several varieties, including butternut, acorn, and turban squash, plus pumpkins. The bright orange flesh contains lots of vitamin A and *carotenoids* (phytochemicals related to vitamin A) such as beta-carotene and lutein, which help to keep your vision normal.

Winter squash is also a good source of calcium, potassium, and vitamin C, while remaining low in calories. One cup of cooked, cubed squash has fewer than 100 calories.

To cook a squash, slice it in half, scoop out the seeds and pulp, and place both halves, cut side down, in a baking dish. Then add one inch of water. Bake at 350 degrees Fahrenheit until the flesh is soft when you pierce the rind with a sharp knife. Serve the orange flesh with a little olive oil or walnut oil, salt, and pepper.

TIP

Save the seeds and toast them for a healthy snack. Pumpkin seeds are rich in omega-3 fatty acids.

Cauliflower

Like other cruciferous vegetables (kale, broccoli, and cabbage), cauliflower contains sulphorophanes that help reduce your risk of some cancers. Cauliflower is rich in vitamin C and potassium, contains substantial amounts of folate (a B vitamin), and is very low in calories.

In addition to finding cauliflower in the produce section of the grocery store, you can find it in the frozen foods section. It's available as a single vegetable or in a variety of blends with other vegetables like broccoli. Just watch out for high-calorie sauces and sodium.

Add raw cauliflower florets to salads or use them to scoop up a tasty vegetable dip. Or serve steamed cauliflower as a side dish. Simply remove the outer green leaves, break the florets into bite-sized pieces, and steam for about eight minutes.

Canola Oil

Canola oil is good for you because it's rich in both monounsaturated fats (like olive oil) and omega-3 fatty acids (like flax oil). The healthful fats in canola oil are good for your cardiovascular system and help reduce inflammation. Canola oil is also low in omega-6 fatty acids. These kinds of fatty acids are good for you in small amounts, but they may increase inflammation in your body when consumed in large amounts.

Canola oil is good for cooking because it has a very light flavor compared to the stronger taste of olive oil, and canola oil stands up to heat much better than flax oil, which breaks down quickly when exposed to the high temperatures of cooking.

You can avoid saturated fats when you use canola oil in place of butter because canola is very low in saturated fat. There are also several products made with canola oil, such as mayonnaise and margarine (look for foods marked "trans-fat free").

Grapes

Grapes contain polyphenols such as resveratrol, anthocyanins, and other flavonoids that help reduce inflammation. According to an article published in 2001 in the journal *Circulation*, subjects who drank grape juice every day for two weeks had better blood flow. Red wine remains a superfood because the fermentation improves the absorption of the polyphenols. However, grapes are close behind, and grape juice is a good choice for those who don't drink alcohol.

Grapes contain B vitamins, vitamin C, and potassium. One cup of grapes has only 62 calories, so eating a cup of grapes may help tame your sweet tooth without adding a lot of calories.

Choose grapes with dark purple colors because they have the highest concentrations of phytochemicals. You should store your grapes in the refrigerator; you also can freeze grapes, which turns them into a cool summertime treat. Enjoy grapes as a snack or drink grape juice as a beverage.

Raisins are dehydrated grapes. They're very sweet because the natural sugars are more concentrated. However, a study published in 2008 in the journal *Nutrition Research* found that raisins don't have the same negative impact on your blood sugar as other sweets, which may be important for people who have diabetes.

Raisins don't have the same nutritional content as grapes because some nutrients are lost during dehydration. Raisins do, however, retain some of the phytochemicals like oleanolic acid, which may fight tooth decay by reducing the bacteria in your mouth.

Mangos

Mangos are sometimes considered to be an exotic fruit, but they're becoming more popular and therefore easier to find in grocery stores. Their golden yellow flesh tastes something like a cross between a peach and a pineapple.

Mangos are rich in vitamin A and vitamin C, plus a phytochemical called *lupeol* that, according to a 2008 article in the journal *Nutrition and Cancer,* combats prostate cancer cells in the lab. Mangos also contain another phytochemical called *mangiferin* that may help to prevent cancer and immune system diseases, according to research published in the journal *Biochemical Pharmacology* in 2003.

Mangos can be eaten alone or used in salads, fruit smoothies, and salsas. Ignore the color of the mango when you're picking one out. Instead, gently squeeze the fruit; it should be slightly soft when it's ripe. Firm mangos can ripen at home at room temperature. Once they're ripe, they can be stored in the refrigerator for up to five days.

Index

almost-superfoods *(continued)*
  grapes, 564
  mangos, 565
  overview, 559
  poultry, 560
  snap beans, 562
  whole grains, 560
  winter squash, 562–563
  yogurt, 561
alpha waves, 161, 325
alphabet pegs, 149–150
alpha-lipoic acid (ALA), 428
Alzheimer's disease, 20, 33, 50–51, 406
ambition, in flow, 219
American Academy of Dermatology, 414
American Bison meat, 561
American Cancer Society, 424, 454, 460, 464
American Demographics magazine, 320
American Diabetes Association, 467
American dream, 316–317
American Heart Association, 361, 420, 421, 470, 520
American Journal of Clinical Nutrition, 429
American Journal of Psychiatry, 539
American Lung Association, 446
American Medical Association, 360
American Psychological Association, 158, 225, 226, 227
American Stroke Association, 501
amino acids, 411
amnesia, 16
amygdala, 18, 130–132
anaerobic exercise, 369–370, 371
analytical thinkers, brain of, 38–39
andropause, 546
aneurysm, 500
angina, 473
angiotensin II receptor blockers (ARBs), 512
angiotensin-converting enzyme (ACE) inhibitors, 511
animal products, 411, 412, 453. *See also* dairy; meat
anterograde amnesia, 16
anti-aging hormones, 442–443
antibiotic-resistant bacteria, 436–437
antibiotics, and life expectancy, 436–437
anticoagulant drugs, 524–525
anti-inflammatory superfoods, 425–427
antioxidants, 52, 161, 423, 424, 426
antiplatelet drugs, 524

anxiety, 320. *See also* stress; stress management
aphasia, 131, 134
apixaban, 525
apostrophes, in cryptograms, 56
appearance, evaluation of by doctor, 485
appreciation, meditation as increasing, 330
apps, diet and exercise, 496
arteriovenous malformation, 500
arthritis, 353, 361
artificial heart, 437
arts, involvement in, 169
asbestos, 446
asparagus, 401
aspirin, 474
associations
  within long-term memory, 139
  for memory blocks, 117
  as memory technique, 123, 190–193
  for recalling words, 115
  for remembering faces, 204
  visual images and memories, 144–145
  visual-spatial memory skills, 45–46
  when studying, 179
AT, 271–272
atherosclerosis
  carotid ultrasound for, 529
  coronary artery disease, link to, 470
  high blood pressure with, 504
  low-density lipoprotein, relation to, 516
  overview, 422
  overweight, link to, 361
  shortness of breath from, 473
  statin drugs as partially reversing, 520
  stroke, link to, 517, 522
  thrombotic stroke due to, 500
atrial fibrillation, 523
attention. *See also* meditation
  improving, 217–218
  listening to music, as distraction, 36
  memory, effect on, 125, 181, 216–217
  memory, foundation of, 120
  mental roadblocks due to excessive, 32
  mindfulness, 217–218
  monotasking, 217
  multitasking, 117
  overstimulation, avoiding, 215

fructose, 410

fruit. *See also specific fruits*

fighting cancer with, 397

heart-friendly, 402

in-the-moment exercise for eating, 315–316

juices, 411

as low-stress food, 335

in plant-based diet, 383–384, 394

fruitarians, 382

fullness, 390, 391

fundamentalism, 322

Future Shock (Toffler), 226

G

GABA, 135

Gage, Phineas, 12–13

galactose, 410

game meat, 561

games. *See also* puzzles

brain, effect on, 11

combating TOT with, 25

video, and visual-spatial skills, 207

gamma waves, 32, 325

gardening, 344

garlic, 398, 421, 424

gastric bypass, 378

gastrointestinal system. *See also* colorectal cancer

discussing complaints with doctor, 482

examination of by doctor, 486

fat breakdown in, 513–514

plant-based diet, effects of, 404

stress, effect of, 233–234

superfoods improving, 425

Geller, Uri, 19

gender. *See* men; women

genetic conditions, combating, 389

genetic risk factors, 452. *See also* family history

genitourinary system, 482, 486

gestational diabetes, 466

glaucoma, 488

glial cells, 406

glucometer, 469

glucose, 398, 410, 465, 525

glucose intolerance, 466

glutamate, 52

glycemic index, 468–469

goals

fitness, setting, 363

health, carrying out, 494–498

health, setting, 491–494

measuring progress, 495–497

obstacles, overcoming, 497–498

realistic positive attitude toward, 494–495

recording, importance of, 493–494

regaining memory of, 215–216

reviewing, 495

stroke prevention, 530

support for, finding, 498

goiter, 435

goji berries, 429

Goldman, Daniel, Dr., 219

gout, 405

grade, cancer, 444

grains

almost-superfoods, 560

fighting cancer with, 397

good carbohydrates, 410

heart-friendly, 400

in plant-based diet, 384, 394

grandparents, 540–541

grapefruit, 522

grapes, 564

graphic novel, drawing, 38

graphs, visualization through, 203

gratitude, meditation as increasing, 330

Graves' disease, 405

green tea, 429

greens, 387–389, 397

Greger, Michael, Dr., 387

groundedness, meditation as providing, 329

guidance, inner, 330

guided relaxation exercise, 256

gyms, 345–346, 371

H

H. M. (neurosurgery patient), 133

habits, 330, 375–376

hand clapping, 35

hand weights, 374

hands, massage for, 275

happiness, 328–329. *See also* positive attitude

happy memories, 187–188

high fructose corn syrup (HFCS), 410

high-density lipoprotein (HDL), 422, 516, 519, 520

higher self, 330

highlighting, 180, 183

hippocampus

    development of, 187

    emotional context of memories, 130–132

    foundation of memory, 120

    overview, 14, 16–17

    shrinkage of, 164

    stress, effects on, 20

    visual-spatial memory, 46

hoarders, 287

hobbies, 8, 538

home. *See also* clutter

    organizing, 290–291

    stress at, 227–229

home safety

    bathroom, 556

    falls, preventing, 551–552

    fires, planning for, 552

    first aid kit, 553–554

    life-saving skills, updating, 554

    lighting, 555

    medication, 552–553

    overview, 551

    poisoning, preventing, 556–557

    reaching for objects, 555

    visual aids, 557

homocysteine tests, 518

honey, 385

hormonal birth control, 452, 504

hormone therapy, 442–443, 452, 476

hormones

    age-related changes to, 545, 546

    stress, 239, 240

hospitalizations, 483

hot towels, for relaxation, 277

hot tub, using for relaxation, 277

house. *See* clutter; home; home safety

HPV (human papillomavirus), 486, 487, 490

HUD, 554

human growth hormone (HGH), 442, 546

humors, ancient notion of, 11

hunger, as diabetes symptom, 467–468

hydration, 339, 350, 425

hydrogenation, partial, 412

hydrostatic (underwater) weighing, 368

hygiene, and life expectancy, 435

hypertension. *See* high blood pressure

hyperthyroidism, 435

hypoglycemia, 398

hypothalamus, 239

hypothermia, 485

hypothyroidism, 435

I

IBS, 404

iconic memory, 204

icons, explained, 2–3

ideal body weight, 358–360, 378–379

idealized images of life, 316–317

illicit drug use, 484, 504

illness. *See also* diseases; *specific illnesses*

    affecting life expectancy in past, 434–436

    due to extra weight, 360–362

    effect of sex on, 544

    stress-related, 322

imagery. *See* visual imagery; visualization

immersion. *See* flow state

immune system, 234, 420–421, 544

immunizations, 436, 483, 489–490

immunoglobulin A, 544

impermanence, appreciating, 318

implicit memory, 140

impotence, 511

impulse buying, 283

in situ cancer, 444, 450

inactivity, 453, 462, 466, 471

inches, calculating BMI based on, 359

incomplete proteins, 411

independence, maintaining, 542

indigestion. *See* acid reflux

individuality, islands of, 216

infants

    response to motherese, 33

    vaccination of, and life expectancy, 436

infectious disease, 435, 436

infertility, stress-related, 236

inflammation, 233, 425–427

inflammatory bowel disease (IBD), 404, 462

inflammatory breast cancer (IBC), 451

influenza vaccine, 489

influenza virus (flu), 434–435

information processing, by brain, 13–14

injuries, preventing. *See* home safety

in-line skating, 345

inner guidance, 330

insight, through meditation, 312–313

insoluble fiber, 410

insomnia. *See* sleep

Institute of Medicine, 339

instruments, playing, 33, 34

insulin, 398, 525

intellectual activity. *See* mental stimulation

interest, role in remembering, 179

interests, regaining memory of, 215–216

interference, with memory, 192

international normalized ratio (INR), 524

International Osteoporosis Foundation, 476

in-the-moment exercise, 315–316

invasive ductal carcinoma (IDC), 451

invasive lobular carcinoma (ILC), 450, 451

iodine, 415

IQ (intelligence quotient) tests, 28–30, 48

iron, 392, 415

irregular heartbeats, 473

irritable bowel syndrome (IBS), 404

ischemic heart disease, 470

ischemic stroke, 361, 500

islands of individuality, 216

isolation, in postmodern era, 321

ItunesU, 162

J

Jewish story of Simon, 307

jigsaw puzzles, 47

jobs. *See* work

Johns Hopkins University Medical Center, 166

journal, stress, 250–254

The Journal of Pain, 539

Journal of Personality and Social Psychology, 532

journey system of mnemonics, 150–151, 155

juices, 411

junk mail, 292

juvenile diabetes, 398, 465. *See also* diabetes

K

Kabat-Zinn, Jon, 308

kilocalories. *See* calories

kilograms, calculating BMI based on, 359

Kleinfelter's syndrome, 451–452

knowledge, 179. *See also* semantic memory

kyphosis, 475

L

labels, organizing with, 290

lactose, 410

lancets, 469

language

    expressive aphasia, 134

    infant responses to, 33

    temporal lobe, relation to, 14, 130, 131

    Wernicke's aphasia, 131

language skills

    finding right word, 23–26

    IQ tests, measuring with, 28–30

    memory strategies, 26–28

    overview, 23

    tip-of-the-tongue phenomenon, 24–26

    using variety of words, 25–26

lap-band surgeries, 378

large-cell (undifferentiated) carcinoma, 445

L-arginine, 402

late meals, effect on sleep, 350

late-night cramming, 174

law of effect, 194–195

LCIS, 450

LDL, 422, 516, 519

lean body mass, 365

learning. *See also* study techniques

    brain shrinkage, protecting against, 20–21

    deeply, 175–176

    law of effect, 194–195

    music training, effects on, 35

    during old age, 165–169

    relearning, 176–178

    rote, 178–179

    sectioning, 175

    stages in, 189

    teaching as, 183–184

M

macronutrients, 409–413

macular degeneration, 430, 488

magazines, as clutter, 283

magnesium, 402, 414–415

magnetic resonance imaging (MRI), 437, 454, 529

mail, handling, 292–293

main points, reviewing after reading, 184

major minerals, 414–415

mammograms, 453–454, 487

"managed care" systems, 441

mangiferin, 565

mangos, 565

mantras, 304

maple syrup, 385

maps, mental, 208

marbles, effect of moving, 208

margarines, 412

marijuana, 122

marriage, benefits of, 542–543

masking noise, for better sleep, 351

masks, sleep, 351

massage, 274–276

mastectomy, 457

master password, 295

mats, exercise, 375

mattress, choosing, 349

Mayo Clinic, 233, 442, 532

maze, drawing, 37

meals. *See also* diet; plant-based diet; superfoods
  effect on blood-sugar level, 399
  planning, 417, 418–419
  spreading out, 338–339

meaning
  foundation of learning, 190
  foundation of memory, 120
  meditation and sense of, 330

measurable goals, 491–492, 495–497

meat
  alternatives to, 393
  American Bison, 561
  autoimmune diseases, effect on, 405
  breast cancer, relation to, 453
  colorectal cancer, relation to, 461
  complete proteins in, 411

  environmental impact of industry, 406
  poultry, 560
  saturated fats in, 412

media, breaking away from, 215–219

medical advances, 436–437

medical examinations. *See* doctor, consulting with; regular checkups

medical history, 478–479, 483–484

medical problems. *See also specific medical problems*
  affecting sleep, 353
  discussing with doctor, 481–483
  due to extra weight, 360–362

medication. *See also specific medication*
  blood thinners, 523, 524–525
  for diabetes, 526
  for lowering blood pressure, 510–512
  to promote sleep, 351
  raising blood pressure, 509
  reviewing with doctor, 483
  safety, 552–553

medications tracker, 553

medicine, lifestyle, 387

meditation
  awareness, 309–313
  benefits of, 305–308, 323–326
  breaking habits with, 330
  challenges, overcoming, 314, 316
  concentration, developing, 310, 311–312
  contemplation, 311, 312–313
  cultivation, 311, 313
  as inner technology, 324–325
  Jewish story of Simon, 307
  mindfulness, 315–316
  mountain metaphor, 303–308
  overview, 301, 303
  path to just being, 308–310
  personal practice, creating, 313–314, 316
  versus popular "solutions", 322–323
  problems addressed by, 316–323
  quick instructions for, 302
  reasons to practice, 327–330
  receptive awareness, 311, 312
  spiritual roots of, 306
  techniques for, 303–304
  tuning in to body with, 326–327

retrograde amnesia, 16

reviewing, 174, 184

rewards, 194–195, 377

rheumatoid arthritis, 405

rhyming mnemonics, 27, 149

rickets, 436

riddles, 54–55, 65–66, 95–96

right hemisphere, 8, 34–35, 39, 128–129, 325

risk factors, controlling, 437–440. *See also specific medical conditions*

ritual, sleep, 350

rivarozaban, 525

road map, clutter, 285

rote learning, 178–179

routine checkups. *See regular checkups*

routines
    branching out of, 166–168
    exercise as, 375–376
    maintaining organization through, 300
    mindfulness during, 217–218
    sleep, developing, 349–353

S

safety. *See* home safety

salad bars, 342

salt, effect on blood pressure, 508

samadhi, in meditation, 311

sanitation, and life expectancy, 435

saturated fats, 412, 427, 515

scanning body for tension, 259

scanning documents, 298

Schor, Juliet B., 226

SCLC, 445

scores, IQ test, 30

scrapbooking, 37, 188

screening tests, 440. *See also specific health conditions; specific tests*

scrunch exercise, 270

scurvy, 436

secondhand smoke, 446–447

sectioning learning, 175

"see one, do one, teach one" adage, 184

seeds, 385, 397, 400, 563

selenium, 415, 428

self
    friendship with, 327–328
    higher, 330

self breast exam (SBE), 453, 454–456

self-awareness, 215–216

self-criticism, 534

self-evaluation of health, 478–479

Selye, Hans, 224, 236

semantic information, 27

semantic linking, 190

semantic memory
    age-related changes in, 158
    associations, making, 190–193
    defined, 16, 143
    Dominic O'Brien's tips for, 191
    encoding new information, 189–190
    overview, 188–189

Seneca, 116

sensory aphasia, 131

sensory motor strip, 134

sentimental clutter, 282, 289–290

serial recall tasks, 178

serotonin, 135, 334, 396–397

set point, emotional, 329

sex drive, 545

sex life, 235, 278, 543–547

sex toys, 547

sexually transmitted diseases (STDs), 487

shaking off tension, 277

shallow breathing, 260

sheep-counting, 356

shingles (herpes zoster) vaccinations, 490

shoes, for exercise, 375

shopping lists, 26–28

shortness of breath, 473

short-term (working) memory
    defined, 139
    doodling, effect on, 36–37
    H. M.'s loss of, 133
    hippocampus, role in, 131–132
    versus long-term memory, 138–141
    music as enhancing, 34, 35
    myths regarding decline in, 10
    overview, 185, 197
    problems with, 193

About the Authors

Timothy E. Parker is the "World's Most Syndicated Puzzle Compiler," according to Guinness World Records. He is also the creator and senior editor of the Internet's Universal Crossword, the author of the annual bestselling *USA Today Crossword Calendar*, and the Puzzle Producer for *Merv Griffin's Crosswords*. He is the author of *Brain Games For Dummies* (Wiley).

Brent J. Agin, MD, is recognized by the community as the go-to medical advisor in the field of healthy aging. He sees patients of all ages and maintains a diverse array of clientele, including professional athletes and celebrities. He's board certified in family medicine, receiving both his undergraduate degree and his MD at Michigan State University. He completed his internship and residency at the University of South Florida.

He is the coauthor of *Healthy Aging For Dummies* (Wiley) and *Superfoods For Dummies* (Wiley).

Sharon Perkins is an RN with over 20 years of experience and an author of six *For Dummies* books, including coauthoring *Healthy Aging For Dummies* (Wiley).

John Boghosian Arden, Ph.D., is the director of training for Psychology in the Kaiser Permanente Medical Centers in Northern California. In this capacity, he oversees 20 training programs in as many medical centers. He is also the local director of training at Kaiser Permanente in Vallejo, California, where he served in the past as chief psychologist.

Dr. Arden is the author of *Improving Your Memory For Dummies* (Wiley) and four other books: *Consciousness, Dreams, and Self* (winner of the 1997 Outstanding Academic Book of the Year Award by Choice — a publication of the American Library Association); *Science, Theology, and Consciousness* (nominated by an international panel of jurists for the Templeton Prize and published by Praeger); *Surviving Job Stress* (Career Press); and *America's Meltdown: The Lowest-Common-Denominator Society* (Praeger).

Stephan Bodian has been practicing and teaching meditation for more than 40 years. As the founder and director of the School for Awakening, he offers workshops, intensives, retreats, and classes devoted to meditation, self-inquiry, and spiritual realization. He is the author of *Meditation For Dummies* (Wiley). His most recent book is *Wake Up Now: A Guide to the Journey of Spiritual Awakening* (McGraw-Hill Education).

For more information on Stephan's workshops, retreats, classes, and phone counseling and mentoring sessions, visit his website (www.stephanbodian.org).

Marni Wasserman's life is rooted in healthy eating. As a culinary nutritionist, health strategist, and owner of Toronto's first plant-based food studio, Marni uses passion and experience to educate individuals on how to adopt a realistic plant-based diet that is both simple and delicious. She is dedicated to providing individuals with balanced, nutritious choices through organic, fresh, whole, and natural plant-based foods and other natural lifestyle modalities.

Marni is a graduate of the Institute of Holistic Nutrition in Toronto (where she is now on the faculty) and the Natural Gourmet Culinary School in New York, and she is the founder of Marni Wasserman's Food Studio & Lifestyle Shop in Midtown Toronto. This is where she teaches her signature cooking classes and offers collaborative workshops and urban retreats. Her food studio is also a place where people can purchase sustainable superfoods and lifestyle products. It was recognized as one of Toronto's top ten cooking schools in 2008.

Marni is the author of *Plant-Based Diet For Dummies* (Wiley). She is also the co-author of *Fermenting For Dummies* and several well-received e-books.

You can learn more about Marni by visiting her on Facebook (www.facebook.com/marnisfoodstudio), following her on Twitter (@marniwasserman), checking out her Pinterest page (www.pinterest.com/fullynourished), or visiting her website (www.marniwasserman.com).

Allen Elkin, PhD, is a clinical psychologist, a certified sex therapist, and the director of the Stress Management & Counseling Center in New York City. He is the author of *Stress Management For Dummies*, 2nd Edition (Wiley). Nationally known for his expertise in the field of stress and emotional disorders, he has appeared frequently on *Today, Good Morning America,* and *Good Day New York,* as well as programs on PBS, CNN, FNN, Fox 5, and National Public Radio. He has been quoted in *The New York Times, The Wall Street Journal, The Washington Post, Newsweek, Men's Health, Fitness, Cosmopolitan, Glamour, Redbook, Woman's Day, Self, Mademoiselle, McCall's, Parents,* and other publications. Dr. Elkin holds workshops and presentations for professional organizations and corporations, including the American Society of Contemporary Medicine, Surgery, and Ophthalmology; the U.S. Drug Enforcement Administration; Morgan Stanley; IBM; PepsiCo; and the New York Stock Exchange. He is the author of two other books on stress, *Urban Ease: Stress-Free Living in the Big City* (Penguin Books) and *Relax in the City Week by Week,* (Duncan Baird).

John R. Marler, MD, a board-certified neurologist and stroke researcher, is Associate Director for Clinical Trials at the National Institute of Neurological Disorders and Stroke. He is a fellow of the American Stroke Association and recipient of the association's Feinberg Award for Excellence in Clinical research. He has been administering clinical research in stroke since 1984. He completed his neurology residency training at Mayo Clinic in Rochester, Minnesota, and graduated from West Virginia University Medical School in Morgantown, West Virginia. He is the author of *Stroke For Dummies* (Wiley).

Shereen Jegtvig began her first career as a chiropractor in 1990. She then began her second career as a health and nutrition writer. She returned to college and earned a master of science degree in human nutrition with special interest in the effects of omega-3 fats on cognitive function. Today, at nutrition.about.com, she focuses on teaching readers why they need to eat superfoods as well as presenting helpful dietary tips and how-to info. Shereen knows that a pomegranate or a carton of blueberries won't help anyone's health if they never leave the refrigerator. She is the coauthor of *Superfoods For Dummies* (Wiley).

Tracy Packiam Alloway, PhD, is the director of the Center for Memory and Learning in the Lifespan at the University of Stirling, UK. She was the 2009 winner of the prestigious Joseph Lister Award by the British Science Association for bringing her scientific discoveries to a wide audience. She is the author of over 75 scientific articles and books on working memory and learning, and has developed the world's first standardized working-memory tests for educators, published by Pearson Assessment. Her research has received widespread international coverage, appearing in outlets such as the *Scientific American, Forbes, US News,* ABC News, BC, BBC, *Guardian,* and *Daily Mail.* She is a much-in-demand international speaker in North America, Europe, Asia, and Australia and provides advice to the World Bank on the importance of working memory. She is the author of *Training Your Brain For Dummies* (Wiley).

Publisher's Acknowledgments

Acquisitions Editor: Tracy Boggier
Project Manager: Linda Brandon
Development Editor: Linda Brandon
Copy Editor: Megan Knoll
Technical Editor: Allison Batchelor
Project Consultant: Michael Wasserman
Art Coordinator: Alicia B. South

Production Editor: Vasanth Koilraj
Illustrator: Kathryn Born, Pam Tanzey
Cover Photos: DrAfter123/iStockphoto

Apple & Mac

iPad For Dummies,
6th Edition
978-1-118-72306-7

iPhone For Dummies,
7th Edition
978-1-118-69083-3

Macs All-in-One
For Dummies, 4th Edition
978-1-118-82210-4

OS X Mavericks
For Dummies
978-1-118-69188-5

Blogging & Social Media

Facebook For Dummies,
5th Edition
978-1-118-63312-0

Social Media Engagement
For Dummies
978-1-118-53019-1

WordPress For Dummies,
6th Edition
978-1-118-79161-5

Business

Stock Investing
For Dummies, 4th Edition
978-1-118-37678-2

Investing For Dummies,
6th Edition
978-0-470-90545-6

Personal Finance
For Dummies, 7th Edition
978-1-118-11785-9

QuickBooks 2014
For Dummies
978-1-118-72005-9

Small Business Marketing
Kit For Dummies,
3rd Edition
978-1-118-31183-7

Careers

Job Interviews
For Dummies, 4th Edition
978-1-118-11290-8

Job Searching with Social
Media For Dummies,
2nd Edition
978-1-118-67856-5

Personal Branding
For Dummies
978-1-118-11792-7

Resumes For Dummies,
6th Edition
978-0-470-87361-8

Starting an Etsy Business
For Dummies, 2nd Edition
978-1-118-59024-9

Diet & Nutrition

Belly Fat Diet For Dummies
978-1-118-34585-6

Mediterranean Diet
For Dummies
978-1-118-71525-3

Nutrition For Dummies,
5th Edition
978-0-470-93231-5

Digital Photography

Digital SLR Photography
All-in-One For Dummies,
2nd Edition
978-1-118-59082-9

Digital SLR Video &
Filmmaking For Dummies
978-1-118-36598-4

Photoshop Elements 12
For Dummies
978-1-118-72714-0

Gardening

Herb Gardening
For Dummies, 2nd Edition
978-0-470-61778-6

Gardening with Free-Range
Chickens For Dummies
978-1-118-54754-0

Health

Boosting Your Immunity
For Dummies
978-1-118-40200-9

Diabetes For Dummies,
4th Edition
978-1-118-29447-5

Living Paleo For Dummies
978-1-118-29405-5

Big Data

Big Data For Dummies
978-1-118-50422-2

Data Visualization
For Dummies
978-1-118-50289-1

Hadoop For Dummies
978-1-118-60755-8

Language & Foreign Language

500 Spanish Verbs
For Dummies
978-1-118-02382-2

English Grammar
For Dummies, 2nd Edition
978-0-470-54664-2

French All-in-One
For Dummies
978-1-118-22815-9

German Essentials
For Dummies
978-1-118-18422-6

Italian For Dummies,
2nd Edition
978-1-118-00465-4

Available in print and e-book formats.

Available wherever books are sold. **For more information or to order direct visit www.dummies.com**

Math & Science

Algebra I For Dummies,
2nd Edition
978-0-470-55964-2

Anatomy and Physiology
For Dummies, 2nd Edition
978-0-470-92326-9

Astronomy For Dummies,
3rd Edition
978-1-118-37697-3

Biology For Dummies,
2nd Edition
978-0-470-59875-7

Chemistry For Dummies,
2nd Edition
978-1-118-00730-3

1001 Algebra II Practice
Problems For Dummies
978-1-118-44662-1

Microsoft Office

Excel 2013 For Dummies
978-1-118-51012-4

Office 2013 All-in-One
For Dummies
978-1-118-51636-2

PowerPoint 2013
For Dummies
978-1-118-50253-2

Word 2013 For Dummies
978-1-118-49123-2

Music

Blues Harmonica
For Dummies
978-1-118-25269-7

Guitar For Dummies,
3rd Edition
978-1-118-11554-1

iPod & iTunes
For Dummies, 10th Edition
978-1-118-50864-0

Programming

Beginning Programming
with C For Dummies
978-1-118-73763-7

Excel VBA Programming
For Dummies, 3rd Edition
978-1-118-49037-2

Java For Dummies,
6th Edition
978-1-118-40780-6

Religion & Inspiration

The Bible For Dummies
978-0-7645-5296-0

Buddhism For Dummies,
2nd Edition
978-1-118-02379-2

Catholicism For Dummies,
2nd Edition
978-1-118-07778-8

Self-Help & Relationships

Beating Sugar Addiction
For Dummies
978-1-118-54645-1

Meditation For Dummies,
3rd Edition
978-1-118-29144-3

Seniors

Laptops For Seniors
For Dummies, 3rd Edition
978-1-118-71105-7

Computers For Seniors
For Dummies, 3rd Edition
978-1-118-11553-4

iPad For Seniors
For Dummies, 6th Edition
978-1-118-72826-0

Social Security
For Dummies
978-1-118-20573-0

Smartphones & Tablets

Android Phones
For Dummies, 2nd Edition
978-1-118-72030-1

Nexus Tablets
For Dummies
978-1-118-77243-0

Samsung Galaxy S 4
For Dummies
978-1-118-64222-1

Samsung Galaxy Tabs
For Dummies
978-1-118-77294-2

Test Prep

ACT For Dummies,
5th Edition
978-1-118-01259-8

ASVAB For Dummies,
3rd Edition
978-0-470-63760-9

GRE For Dummies,
7th Edition
978-0-470-88921-3

Officer Candidate Tests
For Dummies
978-0-470-59876-4

Physician's Assistant Exam
For Dummies
978-1-118-11556-5

Series 7 Exam For Dummies
978-0-470-09932-2

Windows 8

Windows 8.1 All-in-One
For Dummies
978-1-118-82087-2

Windows 8.1 For Dummies
978-1-118-82121-3

Windows 8.1 For Dummies,
Book + DVD Bundle
978-1-118-82107-7

Available in print and e-book formats.

Available wherever books are sold. **For more information or to order direct visit www.dummies.com**

Take Dummies with you everywhere you go!

Whether you are excited about e-books, want more from the web, must have your mobile apps, or are swept up in social media, Dummies makes everything easier.

Leverage the Power

For Dummies is the global leader in the reference category and one of the most trusted and highly regarded brands in the world. No longer just focused on books, customers now have access to the For Dummies content they need in the format they want. Let us help you develop a solution that will fit your brand and help you connect with your customers.

Advertising & Sponsorships

Connect with an engaged audience on a powerful multimedia site, and position your message alongside expert how-to content.

Targeted ads • Video • Email marketing • Microsites • Sweepstakes sponsorship

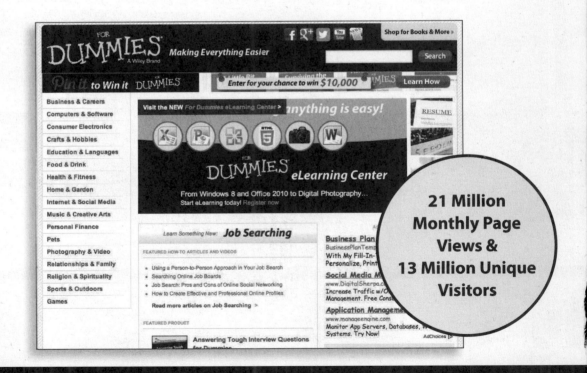

21 Million Monthly Page Views & 13 Million Unique Visitors